THE FIFTY-YEAR WAR

THE FIFTY-YEAR WAR

CONFLICT AND STRATEGY IN THE COLD WAR

NORMAN FRIEDMAN

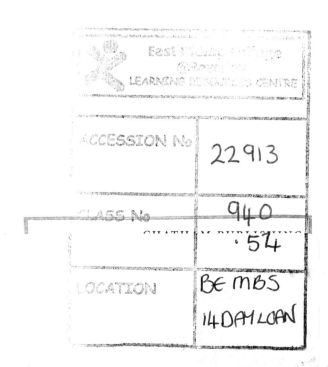

First published in Great Britain in 2000 by Chatham Publishing,
61 Frith Street, London W1V 5TA

Chatham Publishing is an imprint of Gerald Duckworth & Co Ltd

British Cataloguing in Publication Data
A catalogue record for this book is available from the
British Library

ISBN 1 86176 140 6

Printed in the United States of America on acid-free paper.

In memory of my parents,
Leo and Marion Friedman

CONTENTS

ACKNOWLEDGMENTS

This book can be traced back to my own Cold War experience at Herman Kahn's Hudson Institute and to several colleagues there who recalled their own experiences, particularly Frank Armbruster, the late Dr. Don Brennan, Andrew Caranfil, and William Pfaff. Several friends read early versions of this book, and made extremely valuable suggestions: A. D. Baker III, Dan David, David Isby, Stuart Slade, David Steigman, Dr. Thomas Hone, and Steve Zaloga. They caught some important errors; I am responsible for any that remain. A colleague at the old Hudson Institute, B. Bruce-Briggs, provided some very important insights into U.S. decision making in the 1950s and 1960s. Charles Haberlein of the U.S. Naval Historical Center was very helpful. Dr. E. R. Lewis, former librarian of the House of Representatives, supplied details of the "second Tonkin Gulf resolution" of May 1965. I am also grateful to my very patient editor, Patricia J. Kennedy.

As in past projects, my wife Rhea made this one possible by her loving support. In this case she contributed much more. She read and critiqued several early versions, making invaluable editorial and substantive suggestions that helped shape this book.

INTRODUCTION

The Cold War ended quietly. A little after 7:30 P.M. on 25 December 1991 the Soviet flag was hauled down for the last time in the Kremlin in Moscow. The country it represented ceased to exist. The Communist Party, which had led it in half a century of war against the West, had already been outlawed. The massive armies and fleets that had so menaced the West were beginning to rot. Their industrial base, broken up as the Soviet Union dissolved, was failing. Even the names of Soviet cities were changing to reflect the new reality: Communist Leningrad once more became the czar's St. Petersburg.

There was never a victory parade, nor had there ever been a declaration of war. Yet the Cold War was a real war, as real as the two world wars. It was not, as some imagine, an accident of misunderstanding. Conflicts such as those in Korea, Malaysia, Vietnam, and Afghanistan were all campaigns in the larger war. Throughout, the Cold War was shadowed by the hot war that might have been fought, the expected shape of which determined governments' reactions to unfolding situations.

For about half a century the war shaped our lives and, indeed, our world. Moreover, the aftermath of the Cold War is likely to shape the world for many decades to come. The unpleasant surprises of the past few years, particularly in the areas around the old Soviet border, are all consequences of the way the Cold War was fought and of the way it ended. Lessons drawn by surviving Communist governments, in China, Cuba, North Korea, and Vietnam, are also likely to help shape the next few decades.

How well did the West understand what was happening in the Soviet Union? How well should it have understood? If the West could not understand the Soviet Union and other Communist powers, then what hope has it of understanding more alien phenomena such as Islamic fundamentalism? Did the West defeat the Soviets, or did the Soviet system carry with it such damning flaws that the outcome was inevitable? The answers matter for our future.

The course of the Cold War roughly followed that of World War I, though it ran at a much slower pace. In each case, war began with a massive direct assault. The war then bogged down into a costly and wearying struggle without much shape and without any discernible end. The Cold War stalemate was enforced largely by fear of nuclear war. A major Cold War campaign—Korea—and many minor ones can be seen as Soviet attempts to break out via peripheral operations, as the British had in the Dardanelles in World War I. One might see the Soviet buildup of the 1970s as equivalent to the German "Michael" offensive of 1918; both turned out to be last bursts of energy by the losing side. Reagan's military buildup and simultaneous economic attack on the Soviet state were the equivalent of the Allied counteroffensive. The most interesting parallel may be the suddenness of the Communist collapse, which seems to have been as unexpected in the Cold War as the German defeat had been in 1918.

Another parallel was in war aims. Germany struck in 1914 to stave off the imagined threat of growing Russian power. She attacked France mainly for fear that the French would support her allies, the Russians. Because the kaiser thought his war was defensive, he could not be deterred from attacking. The Allies also fought a defensive war. Both sides eventually developed a variety of war aims, but they were always somewhat vague.

The Communists believed that, by their very existence in power, they would inspire revolution in the capitalist world. It followed that the capitalists would inevitably attack them in self-defense. Thus their own attacks on the capitalist world were preemptive (i.e., fundamentally defensive). Western intervention in the Russian Civil War seemed to prove the point. Internal opposition ("counterrevolution") could be ascribed to foreign influence.

There was, moreover, an unstated suspicion that the example set by the capitalist world might ultimately undermine Soviet authority. The mere existence of a capitalist world thus became a form of aggression. No capitalist government could be considered truly legitimate. These ideas, which were never really questioned during the lifetime of the Soviet regime—and rarely understood in the West—explain why the Cold War could not end short of the collapse of either the West or of the Soviet state. Like World War I, it was a fight to the finish.

For the West, as in World War I, the goal at first was merely to fend off the Soviet attack. By the early 1950s, the hope was generally that the Soviet Union could be tamed to the point that it would become a conventional nation-state, accepting the legitimacy of other governments. Many believed that the Cold War ended about 1963, with Khrushchev's retreat after the Cuban Missile Crisis. Some saw the Cold War that ended with the Soviet breakup as a second conflict, perhaps ignited by the United States. In fact, given the ideology that underpinned the Soviet state, the Cold War could not end as long as that state endured. A particular leader, such as Mikhail Gorbachev, might order a truce, but the system was the problem.

To Westerners, the Soviet Union was a paradox: seemingly a country like other countries, but at the same time primarily an exporter of revolution, to which all non-Communist governments were illegitimate. The same contradiction complicated Soviet foreign policy. As a state, the Soviet Union sought conventional relationships with other states. State-to-state contact was handled by the Foreign Ministry (a Commissariat before World War II), which concentrated on the West after 1945. The revolutionary side of foreign policy was run by the Soviet Communist Party's International Department, in charge of party-to-party relationships. Thus, during the October War of 1973 in the Middle East, the Foreign Ministry counseled restraint, to preserve the valuable détente developed with the United States. The International Department counseled support for the Egyptians and the Syrians. The result was near paralysis in the Kremlin.

The Soviets' revolutionary pretensions magnified the effect of the Chinese schism. In their attempt to maintain their leadership of the world Communist movement, the Soviets found that they had to court foreign parties. The terms of rule in Eastern Europe changed dramatically, ultimately with disastrous consequences. The Soviets could not compel the Vietnamese to sacrifice their desire for revolution in order to protect Soviet relations with the United States. The Vietnam War resulted. By way of contrast, such sacrifices had been quite common under Stalin.

Another important Cold War theme was the relationship between the Communists and the Western left. The Communists' rhetoric, with its demands for social justice, seemed to make them part of the left. However, the rhetoric was essentially camouflage. The Communists cared only about seizing and maintaining power. They were unconstrained by tradition or law. Moreover, their policy would not be tempered by reliance on mass appeal. In this they were much more like the Fascists or the Nazis than like any Western liberal-left party.

The main difference between the Communists and, say, the Nazis was in the coating applied to the same hard core of arbitrary rule by force. However, because the Communist Party's language was that of the liberal left, it was very difficult for more democratic parties to disown. The party's professed ideals attracted many Western supporters during the 1920s and 1930s, particularly after the onset of the Depression seemed to show that capitalism had failed. Many on the left imagined that the Communists were evolving towards something like Western democratic Socialism. They willingly ignored the unpleasant facts of dictatorship and organized terror. Soviet intelligence arms and their Western allies were also very successful (at least before World War II) in destroying the reputations of émigrés and defectors testifying to the facts of Soviet life. Even after Khrushchev's "secret speech" of 1956, many preferred to imagine that Stalin had perverted an essentially liberal state, which over time might evolve into something like a Western European Socialist democracy. Such hopes explain much of the reluctance to recognize sustained Soviet aggressiveness.

Conversely, those who opposed the Communists sometimes found it difficult to distinguish them from the Western liberal left, which attacked non-Communists. The non-Communist victims in turn came to see anti-Communism as an attack on legitimate Western liberalism. That is how McCarthyism in effect destroyed American anti-Communism for a generation.

Matters were further complicated by the Communists' use of terms like democracy and Socialism. To them, democracy meant a system in which they could gain and maintain power; many Communist regimes called themselves People's Democracies. By Socialism they meant the system in force in these countries. Thus, to a Communist, a program to democratize Western Europe so that it could develop into Socialism was not a benign political campaign, but rather a plan to overthrow Western social systems. The Communists thought of Communism as a future stage of development, attainable only once Socialism had been perfected. For Khrushchev and Brezhnev "building Communism" was thus the goal: the happy situation in which goods would be so plentiful that everyone would have whatever he needed. Socialism was the prior stage in which workers were no longer exploited (as under capitalism), but goods were still scarce, so that wages had to be based on what workers produced. None of this had much to do with reality; a standard Soviet-era joke was that capitalism was the exploitation of man by man, whereas Communism was the reverse.

The Soviet vocabulary seems to have shaped the rulers' perceptions of what was happening inside the Soviet Union. Ex-Soviet and ex-satellite commentators on the Cold War period talk about "the Lie," the distortion of reality through the lens of ideology. The special vocabulary makes it difficult to see in Soviet pronouncements what Westerners rightly saw and feared. It also made it difficult for Western leaders to communicate with men like Stalin.

The lie blinded Soviet leaders, for example, to what might seem an obvious difference between foreign Communist parties near power, and entirely impotent ones; all had to be treated as the likely heirs to current non-Communist governments. In the 1950s, the FBI penetrated the U.S. Communist Party, turning one of its most senior men, Morris Childs. Because of his Party position, he was treated on almost equal terms by such giants of the Communist world as Khrushchev and Mao. The FBI gained a uniquely privileged view, for example, of the developing Sino-Soviet split.

Many centuries ago Sun Tzu said that the general who knows himself and his enemy wins; the general who knows himself survives; the general who only knows his enemy loses. The West's central strategy, which, both at the outset of the Cold War and in the 1980s, was containment, was based on a combination of self-knowledge and understanding of the basic character of the Soviet system. Stalin knew his own system, but not his enemy's; he survived. Mikhail Gorbachev lost the Cold War because he had lost sight of the essentially coercive or terrorist character of his own system. He believed the propaganda and missed the reality. To those inside the system, unaware of its character, the collapse must have seemed as mysterious as the collapse of 1918 looked to the Germans. How many Russians already believe a German-style stab-in-the-back theory?

Because the war was fought in slow motion, domestic politics was enormously important. Much of what happened on the Soviet side can be traced to changes in leadership. For example, the Soviet buildup of the 1970s seems to have been an inevitable consequence of Khrushchev's replacement by rulers sympathetic to the demands of the Soviet military and military industry. Mikhail Gorbachev lost the Soviet Union and the Cold War largely because of his inept attempt to meet a new challenge: large-scale Western adoption of military computers. Computers played a double role in the Soviet Union's political demise: to produce enough of them Gorbachev had to relax control, and once that happened the new information technology told too many Soviet citizens far too much.

Curiously, although we have come to think of the Cold War as two-sided, most of the time it was at least triangular. We are familiar with the "China card" and, by extension, with Chinese use of the "American card," but it is surprising how much Stalin hoped to rely on a "British card" in dealing with the United States after 1945. There are many other examples. Stalin supported Mao's Chinese revolution to expel the West from Asia—but feared that he might demand back the lands he and his czarist predecessors had acquired from China over the past three centuries. The U.S. government of the time supported the Western Europeans against Stalin—but also helped dismember their colonial empires. In Korea, the British fought the Chinese alongside the Americans—but feared that, thus provoked, the Chinese would seize their Hong Kong colony and eject them from important trade.

The Cold War supplied a vocabulary and a worldview to both the Soviets and the Western powers at a time when events were often driven by other forces, such as nationalism. For that matter the new Third World governments often found that they could gain vital support only by appealing to Cold War considerations. With the war over, the support dried up—and several regimes, like that of Joseph Mobutu in the Congo, collapsed.

During the Cold War, few envisaged an end to it. Predicting the future is a very risky business, subject perhaps more than any other to Murphy's Law. For about a decade during the Cold War I was in that business, at Herman Kahn's Hudson Institute in Croton-on-Hudson, New York. Sometimes the Soviets called us the General Staff of the U.S. government prosecuting the Cold War. We appreciated the compliment. Although it rather overstated our importance, we were probably as aware as any of the situation, at least as it was perceived in Washington. Members of our staff had been involved in most Cold War strategy since the early 1950s.

In the fall of 1973, when I joined the institute, the future seemed decidedly bleak. No end to the Cold War (except, perhaps, the collapse of the West) seemed to be in sight. The Soviets seemed quite vigorous. They were beginning to take very successful risks in the Third World. Traumatized by Vietnam and Watergate, the

U.S. government seemed entirely unable to cope. Nor did it seem likely that the U.S. economy could generate the sort of military power that the Soviets were deploying in Europe. It was already apparently intimidating many of our allies into a stance uncomfortably close to neutralism.

About a decade later, the Soviets were clearly in trouble, but few imagined that their problems could be fatal. As in the past, the Soviet leadership would surely survive by bearing down a bit harder on a generally compliant population. The question for the future still seemed to be whether the United States and its Cold War–weary allies could manage to survive in the face of a single-minded Soviet threat. No one that I recall from the mid-1980s suggested that the Soviet Union might collapse altogether, ending the war.

We knew that, even as Mikhail Gorbachev was speaking of reducing tensions, weapons continued to pour out of his factories. We might have been forgiven for thinking that he was interested mainly in gaining breathing space in an ongoing contest. No one, as late as 1990, seems to have imagined that the Soviet Union itself had only a year to go, and that the mighty Communist Party of the Soviet Union would soon be fighting to remain in existence, having been nominally outlawed. Presumably, past Soviet rulers had known instinctively that abandoning the world revolution would destroy them. Gorbachev inadvertently proved that they were right: to abandon the struggle was to question the legitimacy of the Communist Party itself.

Was the Cold War, then, about Communism versus capitalism? Or was it about old-fashioned Russian imperialism, cloaked in a largely irrelevant ideology? If the issue was really Communism, then no similar Cold War is likely to return very soon. If it was Russian imperialism, then a resurgent Russian nationalism may eventually bring a second round. Remember that the rivalry leading up to World War I was one of competing national interests, not ideologies.

With the collapse of the Soviet Union much information on the Soviet side of the Cold War is now available. Only now can we integrate what the Soviets were actually doing (in weapons production, for example) with their internal policy decisions. Similarly, many key Western documents, such as the National Intelligence Estimates (NIEs) reflecting current ideas on the Soviet threat, have now been declassified. We can, then, understand a great deal of Cold War strategy, technology, and tactics on both sides. This history is probably the first to integrate what we now know of the military technology used during the Cold War with what we now know of the diplomatic and economic record. The results, as in the case of the Cuban Missile Crisis, can be surprising.

Could the war have been avoided? Could the mountain of money have been left unspent, the hydrogen bombs not built, soldiers and civilians not killed in places like Vietnam and Korea and Cambodia and the Congo? As I explain in the book's first chapter, Lenin and Stalin thought the death of the capitalist West was both inevitable and necessary for survival. The basic struggle could not end, as Lenin once said, until one side or the other collapsed.

This book is divided roughly chronologically into six parts. Part One opens with Stalin's early moves against the West, beginning with the Spanish Civil War. It describes both sides' positions at the end of World War II. It ends with the appearance of the weapon that kept the Cold War cold: the atomic bomb.

Part Two opens with a description of the deepening hostility between the wartime allies—the Americans, the British, and the Soviets—caused by Stalin's offensive into Europe. It ends with Stalin's postwar military buildup—and with desperate U.S. attempts to counter it without risking bankruptcy. It depicts the rise of postwar nationalism, which afflicted both the West and the Soviets (in the form of Tito and Mao).

Part Three is the story of how both sides handled the stalemate that emerged when both had the atomic bomb. It includes the Korean War, in which U.S. nuclear supremacy bought surprisingly little, and the French debacle in Indochina. It also describes the different conclusions Eisenhower and Khrushchev drew from the new situation, with consequences such as the Western disaster in the Middle East and the schism between Khrushchev and Mao, which split the Communist world.

Part Four opens with the missile race between the two superpowers, probably the only true arms race to occur during the Cold War. It includes the Cuban Missile Crisis and the beginnings of the U.S. intervention in Vietnam.

Part Five describes the Vietnam War and its consequences, as Western military power declined while the Soviets built up under Brezhnev.

Part Six describes the West's counterattack, which finally brought down the Soviet Union and ended the Cold War. It explains how the computer revolution, which the West exploited, turned the tables on the Soviets and then brought them down.

Above all, this book is about connections: between, for example, Stalin's view of Tito and his view of Mao Tse-tung (with implications for the way the Korean War began); or between his goals in Europe and his willingness to support revolution in East Asia. Similarly, there is an important connection between President Kennedy's reaction to unrest in Latin America and his reaction to revolution in Southeast Asia. There is a connection between Soviet perceptions of the U.S. role in Vietnam and the outbreak of the 1967 Mideast War. There are connections in technology, too. For example, the strength of the U.S. consumer plastics industry translated almost directly into a powerful military rocket program—which the Soviets, without much of a consumer industry of any kind, could not match. There are also important analogies: in the face of perceived military inferiority, Mikhail Gorbachev had to behave towards President Ronald Reagan in the 1980s much as President Richard Nixon had had to behave towards Leonid Brezhnev in the 1970s. These connections and analogies may well point to the post–Cold War future.

PART ONE

SETTING THE STAGE

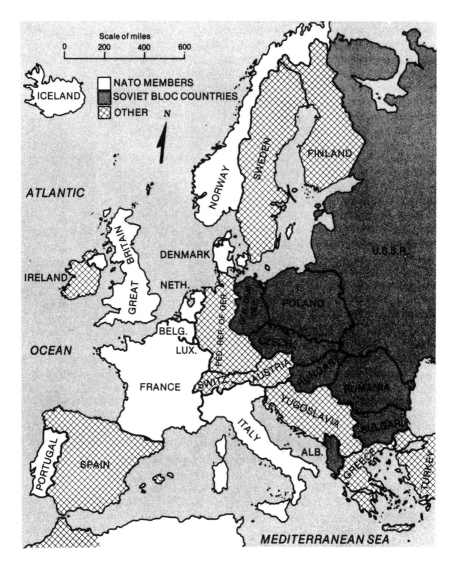

Western Europe

The greatest Cold War prize was Western Europe, shown here after the formation of NATO in 1949. At this stage Austria was still divided into Western and Soviet zones of occupation. Greece and Turkey were not yet NATO members, and West Germany (the Federal Republic) had not yet been rearmed. This map does not show the drastic change in the Polish borders, which gave Poland a considerable seacoast at the expense of pre–World War II Germany (and which gave the Soviet Union a substantial part of pre–World War II Poland, farther east). Note the white area at the bottom of the map, comprising Algeria—which, under NATO rules, was part of metropolitan France and thus had to be defended as such.

Reprinted from Alfred Goldberg, general editor, *History of the Office of the Secretary of Defense,* volume 1, *The Formative Years 1947–1950* (Washington, D.C.: Historical Office, Office of the Secretary of Defense, 1984), page 476.

1 WAR AND COMMUNISM

The Cold War began in Spain, in 1937, when Stalin tried to hijack the ongoing civil war. It was the first Soviet attempt after the Russian civil war to gain control of another country.[1] Because it failed, and because a Russian wartime alliance with the West soon followed, the Spanish gamble was not widely understood. Many in Western Europe saw it as a first, badly needed attempt to resist Hitler and Mussolini. Stalin's attempted hijacking seemed connected to his heavy-handedness in the Soviet Union, where he was conducting an ongoing purge. After all, Stalin had long been identified with a policy of "building socialism in one country," proclaimed as long ago as 1924.[2]

In fact Stalin had never abandoned expansionism.[3] He was merely reviving an abortive campaign begun during the Russian civil war. According to the Communist ideology, which he had inherited from Lenin, people everywhere followed their class interests: workers everywhere, then, should follow the Communist Party, which professed to represent their interests. National boundaries were little more than an illusion: the Bolshevik Revolution in Russia was inevitably the beginning of a world revolution. That it had begun in Russia, a primitive country with only a small working class, was an accident, even an unfortunate one. The revolution could not really triumph until it took over a country with a much larger working class, such as Germany. Otherwise the mass of inherently conservative peasants might overwhelm the workers.

World War I had taught Lenin and Stalin that it took war or comparable disaster to break societies open so that revolution could triumph.[4] Neither admitted that the war had also demonstrated that workers thought in national rather than in class terms. For all the prewar Socialist agitation, in 1914 workers in each country thought of foreign workers as potential enemies, not brothers. The war did not break them of that habit; quite the contrary. Many of them flocked to nationalist movements, first Fascism and then Nazism. Even the Russians' internationalism was never altogether sincere. Those who joined their movement eventually discovered that it was about supporting Russia—and Russian nationalism.

Lenin tried to spread the revolution to Germany, because he doubted that it could survive in Russia alone.[5] In 1919 he ordered the German Communists to try their own coup. The German workers refused to follow, and the German Communist Party was badly damaged. Lenin tried again when his forces invaded Poland in 1920. Just as the Soviets seemed to be winning, they fatally split their forces. We now know that Lenin had ordered forces diverted to link up with an imagined insurrection in eastern Germany.[6] The world supposed that Stalin, who commanded the split-off force, had done so out of egotism, and that he never forgave the main force commander, Marshal Tukhachevskiy, who had made him look foolish. The Soviets failed again in another attempted coup, the "March Action" of 1921.

The Austro-Hungarian Empire, disintegrating under the stress of defeat, also offered possibilities. In 1919 Bela Kun briefly ran a Communist regime in Budapest. He foolishly attacked Romania and Czechoslovakia, both of which had Allied backing. The Hungarians proclaimed a Soviet republic in Slovakia, but it collapsed when they withdrew. Soviet troops attacked the Czechs and the Romanians. However, with the Russian civil war raging, Lenin could not keep them there for long; when they were withdrawn, the Hungarian offensives collapsed. Nor was Kun able to overthrow the Austrian government. Communist coups in Bulgaria (1923) and Estonia (1924) also failed.

Meanwhile, in March 1919 Lenin formed the Communist International (Comintern), a general staff to direct world Communist parties in the world revolution—if it ever came. Lenin had already singled out the German Communist Party (KPD) for its potential for spreading the revolution to the West. He used the secret apparatus built up for this purpose to control the KPD, so that by 1923 it was effectively an auxiliary of the Soviet party. The Comintern in Moscow also placed its own secret agents in the foreign parties, to insure that they followed its line.[7] No one outside the new Soviet Union knew just how seriously Lenin or any other Soviet took the revolution. Was the Soviet Union a new kind of subversive threat, or was it no more than a reincarnated Russia, with similar national interests?

Lenin's German experience in 1919 showed that a coup would fail unless the local Communist party either dominated the local Left or could somehow neutralize other worker movements. His failures in Bulgaria and Estonia showed that coups often needed immediate armed support to prevent or overcome foreign intervention. Thus, building up the Red Army might be a prerequisite for success. Lenin proclaimed a new policy of "peaceful coexistence," which actually meant continuation of the struggle by nonmilitary means. To Westerners, this was hypocrisy. Surely peace required that each government accept the legitimacy of all others.

More fundamentally, Westerners misunderstood that the Communist Party was unlike any Western political party. Its central rule, beginning with Lenin, was disciplined acceptance of whatever line the Party took. Communists said that only the end, Communism, mattered. The means—the Party's current line—was nothing more than tactics. Lenin had won in Russia because his Party had avoided the endless debates over means (and scruples) that had sapped its rivals. Even at its most open, in the mid-1920s, the Party was ruled by a very small circle. To make a radical change in the Party line therefore required the support of only a few key men.

Westerners did not understand that the line was infinitely flexible. By way of contrast, a Western politician needed the support of a mass power base. No matter how cynical, he had to convince those followers—who had real alternatives—to remain loyal. Thus any Western politician had to act with a certain consistency. The prerevolutionary Communist leadership had to carry only a small, compact mass of revolutionaries with it. After the revolution, they made sure there were no legitimate alternative parties. Given his prestige as the Party's effective founder, Lenin decided virtually all questions. When he fell ill, the Party's inner circle took over. Stalin won his battle to dominate that circle partly by winning arguments over the appropriate line, i.e., the appropriate tactics, the Party should follow. His main rival for power, Leon Trotsky, who had created the Red Army, advocated a continued world revolution.

Stalin sold the other members of the inner circle an alternative: Socialism would first be built up in one country. All efforts would go into repairing the terrible damage created by world war followed by civil war. The Soviet Union had to be built into a great military power—which, to Stalin, meant a great industrial power. By risking war before the Soviet Union was stronger, Trotsky was endangering the revolution, i.e., the Soviet Union itself. Partly (but by no means entirely) on the basis of this argument, Trotsky was ejected first from the Party, then from the country itself in 1927.

In 1929 Stalin improved his own position by selling a "revolution from above." His series of Five Year Plans built the industrial base for strong military forces. In line with his doctrine of building Socialism in one country, Stalin used the Comintern to further Soviet national ends, for example to steal key Western industrial and military secrets. Revolutionary action was deferred. As the center of the world revolution, the Soviet Union had to be defended by all revolutionaries: if it fell, they would not survive. Since most Westerners regarded Communist revolution as a fantasy, they misread Stalin's doctrine as admission that the Soviet Union was settling down as a conventional great power that was giving only lip service to the continuing revolution.

Westerners particularly misunderstood the significance of the powerful forces Stalin was building to defend the revolution. The failures of the early 1920s had convinced him that, once revolution broke out abroad, he had to have powerful military forces to support it. Thus there was no contradiction between building up Russia and building a world revolution. Revolution would bring countries under Stalin's control, since he headed both the world Communist movement and the Soviet Union. Thus the world revolution would automatically further Soviet

national interests. Moreover, Stalin expected another major war among the capitalists, which would break open Western societies and give Communism another
chance to expand. Lenin had already predicted that stresses in capitalist societies
made such a war inevitable. The issue was how to prepare to exploit the opportunity that war would bring.

Early Soviet military development depended heavily on assistance by another
pariah state: Germany. Under the Versailles Treaty, the Germans were not permitted to experiment with vital new military technologies such as tanks and aircraft. Lenin and Stalin offered them secret factories and test fields. The Germans
helped the Soviets learn to use the new weapons—and built prototypes of their
own, from which they developed many of the weapons they used against the Soviet
Union in 1941.

By about 1932 Stalin was supreme.[8] Like Lenin before him, he now defined the
Party line. Although he had risen largely by attacking Trotsky's policies, he felt no
qualms about adopting them a few years later—while ordering his secret police to
hunt down and kill Trotskyites. The logic of power was simple: Trotsky and his followers were nothing more than obstacles to be removed, or potential threats to be
eliminated. Words, particularly public words, meant nothing at all. Thus, when he
made his deal with Hitler, Stalin said that, unlike "bourgeois politicians," he and
Hitler could maneuver entirely freely.[9]

There was one exception. To some extent Stalin relied on assistance by Communist parties (and their sympathizers) outside the Soviet Union. Many had
joined because of beliefs in professed Communist ideals. Where membership in
the Soviet party generally brought material rewards, the opposite was the case outside. Sudden radical shifts in the Party line could be profoundly disconcerting.
Some members might come to see in the Soviet Communist Party and its hacks
something quite foreign to the ideals for which they had fought and suffered. They
might switch to parties, like the Social Democrats, which better reflected their
beliefs. They might even question whether, once Communism had triumphed, the
Soviet Union—or, for that matter, Stalin—should continue to dominate the world
movement. That was one reason he distrusted Communists who had spent World
War II in the West; he preferred men who had spent the war under his control in
Moscow and who could, therefore, be trusted to follow blindly.

In 1932, as Hitler sought power in Germany, the German Communist Party was
powerful, but its left-wing rivals, the Social Democrats, were even stronger. Both
competed for workers' votes against Hitler's Nazi Party, which also claimed Socialist roots. Hitler was, in theory, Stalin's deadly enemy, having vowed to block Bol-
shevism (Communism) from taking over Western Europe. To Stalin, however, Hitler was a way of destroying the real enemy, the non-Communist Left.

The German Communists knew how to obey the Party line, however that
twisted. Stalin ordered them to cooperate with the Nazis. Above all they were not
to make common cause with the Social Democrats. Past failed Communist coups

had demonstrated that the German Communists were unlikely to prevail against the Nazis; a Soviet attaché vetoing a proposed 1932 alliance with the Social Democrats said that for Moscow "the road to Soviet Germany lies through Hitler."[10] As proof that Communism and Nazism were very close relatives, once Hitler was in power in 1933, most German Communists became ardent Nazis: they were interested mainly in power and in following an all-powerful leader. Some Nazis said that the only difference between the two was that the Nazis were concerned with national origins.[11] German Social Democrats (Socialists) were a different proposition: the Nazis had to destroy them.

Later the Communists would twist events to say that Hitler had come to power because the German Socialists had been unwilling to bury their differences with the German Communists. Stalin still valued the earlier ties to German industry, particularly military industry. Hitler seemed to be much like Stalin, capable of a totally cynical separation between what he said and what he did. His public anti-Communism (including purges) in Germany did not mean that he could not befriend the Soviet Union, at least privately. By the fall of 1933 the Soviets were making overtures, and the Germans were not rejecting them.

From Stalin's point of view, Hitler's rise offered real advantages. Hitler would surely bring the desired European war. Moreover, Stalin could exploit the threat Hitler so clearly presented. Having helped Hitler into power, he presented himself as the greatest bulwark against Hitler. Comintern documents which have recently come to light show exactly how cynical this policy was.[12]

Stalin soon authorized Communist parties in Europe to join left-center coalitions known as popular fronts. The idea was not altogether new; Stalin had tried it unsuccessfully in China in the 1920s. Given the threat of Hitler, the Social Democratic parties that, in the past, had feared the Communists would now accept them as coalition partners. Such participation would legitimize the Communists in the minds of many previously hostile left-wing voters. The first popular front was formed in France in July 1934. Still dominated by non-Communists, it later governed France for about two years. Once war broke the European states open, the Communists brought into coalitions would have their opportunity. The popular front would become very important in postwar Europe.

Admitting that the non-Communist Left was legitimate and should even be courted could be read as an admission that the Party at home did not hold an ideological monopoly. To a thinking man, alternatives might be possible. Members of the Party's inner circle, the Old Bolsheviks who had fought alongside Lenin, might use Stalin's tactical shift as a lever to dislodge him. Stalin had gained his power by playing them off against each other, but in 1934 they were still in positions of nominal power. Hitler showed Stalin how this problem could be solved.[13]

He, too, had an inner circle, which in theory limited his absolute power. He faced a potential internal opposition built around the "storm troopers" (SA) who had fought the street battles of the 1920s and 1930s. Many believed that Hitler would have to come to terms with their leader, Ernst Roehm, who represented the left wing of the Party. In June 1934 Hitler had the SA decapitated in a massacre, the "night of the long knives." Stalin was fascinated. He ordered his secret services to provide full details.[14] He acted about six months later.

Sergei Kirov, the Party boss of Leningrad, was often described as the second most powerful man in the Soviet Union, probably Stalin's heir apparent. He was murdered on 1 December 1934. Many historians believe that Stalin was responsible.[15] He used the murder to justify the destruction of most of the Leningrad party apparatus (a potential rival to his own men in Moscow) and then waves of arrests. The terror began in earnest with a series of show trials in Moscow in 1936, in which the Old Bolsheviks, the men who had stood with Lenin in 1917, were made to confess treason of the most grotesque sort.[16]

The murder justified removal of the Party's statutory protection of its members. To bring them and the country at large to heel, Stalin enforced random terror over the next two years on the model provided by Ivan the Terrible.[17] Early in 1937 the secret police were given quotas for arrests and executions; it was clearly unimportant (to them and ultimately to Stalin) just whom they seized and shot. Often victims were denounced simply to settle old scores. Data compiled for the Politburo during Khrushchev's thaw showed that in 1938, sixteen million people were in prison, compared to 122,000 in 1927. Between 1935 and 1940, 18,840,000 people passed through the hands of the secret police; seven million were shot in prison. Many others died in camps.[18] The acts of betrayal which brought victims to their fates tended to bind the betrayers to Stalin.

This terror was fundamentally different from what had gone before, both in sheer scale and in the range of victims. Loyalty did not matter, because persecution was random. In the new lunatic system a man granted enormous honors one week could often be arrested and shot within a month, with no rational explanation. Some later described Stalin's system as a social elevator, in which men changed status (up and down) with astonishing speed.[19] The elevator left very few older men in positions of any power by 1939. Survivors came to relish security above anything else, hence to be even more fawningly loyal than their predecessors. Survivors learned that the Party was whatever Stalin said it was; contradictions with past policy and practice were of no significance.

As for the foreign Communist parties, as was his custom, Stalin decided to solve this problem before it could become evident: in 1937–38 he ordered numerous senior foreign Communists to Moscow and had them shot. Members of foreign parties were made to denounce their colleagues as "Trotskyites." Their consequent sense of guilt often bound them even more tightly to Stalin. Trotsky himself, who might have inspired resistance to Stalin, was killed by a Soviet agent in Mexico City in 1940.

The Spanish civil war was Stalin's first real opportunity to try a takeover by popular front tactics. In July 1936 Spanish officers led by Gen. Francisco Franco revolted against the recently elected Spanish Republican Popular Front government, claiming that they were fighting communism and atheism. It was soon clear that Stalin would be the Republic's only reliable arms supplier. He agreed to send arms only after the Republic, in October 1936, agreed to pay for them by sending its entire gold reserve to the Soviet Union.[20] There has been some speculation that Stalin had to intervene in Spain because if he did not help defend a popular front government, he would have lost credibility in the world movement and particularly in the ongoing campaign against Hitler.[21] Of the major Western powers, the British were quite hostile to Stalin, regarding Franco as a lesser evil. They espoused neutrality and arms embargo. The friendly French popular front government could provide very little, partly due to internal opposition by the French Right but also because so little weaponry was being produced in France (partly due to the Left's resistance to rearmament).[22]

Stalin ordered his men to take over the Spanish popular front. For him, the war had to be fought simultaneously on two fronts: against Franco's Nationalists and against potential rivals within the Spanish government and its army. Many would come to see the second war as paranoid sabotage of the first, whole units being betrayed to Franco. Stalin more likely saw the external war as his main opportunity to win an internal one; once the external war was over, the Republic was unlikely to offer his men nearly as much freedom of action. He largely won the internal war but lost the larger one against Franco.

Stalin learned that limited wars could not promote the revolutionary expansion he wanted. German and Italian intervention in Spain, which went far beyond what could be done from Russia, crushed the Republic and Stalin's expectations. On the other hand, the popular front tactic had clearly been effective. If Stalin could deter the major powers from attacking him, then a general European war would be a great opportunity.

With the completion of the Second Five Year Plan (1937) Stalin probably felt well enough armed to deter any attack upon him. His apparent attempts to stiffen French and Czech resistance to Hitler in 1938 seem to have been designed to precipitate the desired war in the West.[23] In August 1939 Stalin shocked the world by signing a nonaggression pact with his arch-rival, Hitler. The main bulwark against the Nazis had, it seemed, given way. By signing, Stalin was rejecting an attempt by the British and French to form an anti-German coalition. The pact has often been read as the key event precipitating World War II—Stalin's great blunder.

That is to look at events in retrospect. To Stalin, there was every likelihood that a war would resemble World War I, grinding down both the Germans and their Western enemies. Faced with serious opposition in the West, the Germans would hardly chance attacking a Soviet Union whose armed forces had been built up so heavily. After war broke out, senior Comintern officials were told that by 1942, perhaps, all the combatants would have been exhausted. It would then be time to strike west to support the revolutions the Party could foment.[24]

The pact had to be explained to millions of Communist sympathizers who had been attracted by Stalin's anti-Nazi stance: Stalin needed time to build the military strength to face Hitler. That surely seemed reasonable enough to citizens of democracies that were woefully ill prepared for another world war, and it is still the usual explanation. However, it made little sense. Stalin had been arming for years. He was anything but ill-prepared (except for having shot so much of his officer corps, which he did not see as a problem). Overall, the pact demonstrated just how nimbly Stalin could change his Party line, and just how slavishly his followers were expected to follow. British Communist trade unionists struck against British defense industries, even though Britain was then at war against Hitler.[25]

Under secret protocols, Hitler agreed to split Poland with Stalin, moving the Soviet border hundreds of miles west. Stalin attacked the Polish rear as the Germans advanced, just as Mussolini attacked France just before the Germans won. President Roosevelt accused Mussolini of stabbing the French in the back, yet Stalin was able to sell the claim that he was rescuing White Russians and Ukrainians who had been isolated from their brethren across the Polish border. (Mussolini could claim that he was gaining back territory the French had taken less than a century before.)

Hitler placed the Baltic States (Latvia, Lithuania, and Estonia) and Finland within a Soviet sphere of influence. He also agreed to provide crucial military technology. In return, Stalin provided Hitler with supplies he needed to keep the war going.

For Westerners, the land-grab aspect of the pact—the clear departure from Stalin's old policy of "socialism in one country"—was obscured because in return for Lithuania (territory uncomfortably close to Leningrad) the Soviet zone of Poland was reduced from more than half of the country (including a zone in Warsaw).[26] Stalin's public explanation of the pact justified the advance into Poland as providing greater defensive depth against Hitler. However, in 1939–40 it was quite clear that Stalin not only considered his Polish zone permanent, but that he planned to acquire the rest of Poland as well.[27]

He had to eliminate any potential opposition. This, in 1939, was concentrated in the Polish army officer corps. Stalin had his secret police massacre captured Polish officers and other notables at Katyn Forest (and other places) in 1940.[28] In April 1943 the Germans found the mass graves. From London the Polish government in exile demanded an explanation. Stalin took the opportunity to break with the "London Poles." He had already formed the nucleus of a future Polish government from among Polish Communists in Moscow, who were loyal to him. (Denying Soviet involvement in Katyn became a test of loyalty for postwar Communist Polish governments.)[29]

Stalin clearly revealed his motive for the massacres at the Tehran Conference in 1943. He said that to control Germany after the war he would destroy the core of the German army, fifty thousand officers. Churchill saw the remark as a ghastly reference to Katyn, which had just been discovered. The Katyn revelations soured many Britons who previously had enthusiastically supported the Soviets.

Stalin also obscured his ambitions by taking his time about seizing other territory in his new sphere of influence. He demanded base rights from all four countries, in theory to improve his own defenses. The Baltic states, defenseless without German guarantees, soon agreed, but that did not end Soviet pressure. Each soon found itself electing a pro-Communist government. By the fall of 1940 these states, which had broken away from the Russian Empire in 1918, were applying to join the Soviet Union. The West never accepted the result—but it also never saw the 1939–40 land grabs as part of a march to the west—a cold war.

The Finns rejected Stalin's initial demands. A border incident was manufactured, and the Finns fought against the Soviet invasion that followed. In the end, Stalin settled for the bases and border adjustments he had originally requested. It seemed that the Finns had sacrificed heavily for very little. Soviet documents show, however, that Stalin and his foreign minister, Molotov, planned to annex the whole country. Almost as soon as the Red Army crossed the border, they set up a puppet Finnish Communist government. The Finnish sacrifice (and possibly Western talk of direct military aid) apparently convinced Stalin to settle for what he could easily get.[30] His own army's poor performance in Finland encouraged Hitler to believe that, despite the Red Army's great paper strength, it could easily be defeated. In 1940 the Germans outdid Stalin's expectations. France, the greatest military power in Europe in 1935, quickly collapsed, leaving a relatively undamaged Germany free for further adventures.[31]

Stalin must have wondered whether he could buy Hitler's continued friendship with supplies. By October 1940 he realized that Hitler might well strike, and he cancelled production of any weapons which would not be ready to fight the massive land war that was probably coming. He was not sure, because, through the fall of 1940, as he planned for war, Hitler offered Stalin a new treaty (an extension of the Tripartite Treaty binding Germany to Italy and Japan) and even pressed for a summit conference with Stalin.[32] He also spread misinformation: Germany would concentrate on completing the defeat of Britain. Stalin seems to have hoped that Hitler did not yet want war, and that the war party in Berlin might lose if he continued to provide the materials the Germans so badly needed. He rejected numerous reports that the Germans had already decided to attack.

Stalin's own army, built at enormous cost under the Five Year Plans, did poorly when Hitler tested it in 1941. The West never saw Stalin's plans for Western Europe demonstrated. However, as his armies fought the Germans, Stalin again looked to the future. Poland was still a problem. Despite the 1940 massacres and the Nazis' efforts, much of the nucleus of a postwar government had survived to work in the underground Home Army loyal to the London Poles. When the Red Army swept into Poland in 1944, Stalin encouraged the Home Army to rise against the Germans in Warsaw. They expected the advancing Red Army to link up with them. Instead, it halted. Soviet antiaircraft gunners even fired at British and American planes trying to drop supplies to the Home Army. Stalin was allowing Hitler to complete the job he had begun in Katyn in 1940. As in the case of Katyn, denial of Stalin's abandonment of the Home Army became a test of postwar Polish loyalty.

Thus it seemed by mid-1944 that Stalin was abandoning his prewar popular front tactics, on the theory that possession of territory by the Red Army was all that mattered. Then Stalin's tactics changed once again.

His new tactics were laid out with startling clarity in an 11 January 1944 memorandum written by his ambassador to Britain (1932–43), Ivan Maisky.[33] Stalin probably valued Maisky most for his insights into Western thinking. He was brought home from London to become deputy foreign minister and to head a wartime Commission on Reparations. Maisky told him that the West would not interfere with popular front tactics. Only actual revolutions would cause problems. Thus Stalin could use popular front tactics to advance Communism beyond what the Red Army could seize. Restraint could pay enormous dividends.

There were already strong Communist parties in France and Italy. Their prestige was based on, respectively, strong resistance and partisan records. Stalin had a long meeting with the Italian party chief, Pietro Togliatti, on 4 March 1944.[34] He was ordered to join the broad-left coalition government being formed by Marshal Badoglio. Similarly, in November the French Communist leader, Maurice Thorez, was ordered to create a broad-left bloc drawing in the Socialists and Radicals.[35] Thorez was to disarm his Party members, on the ground that maintaining a private army (once the legitimate French army had been restored) undermined his credibility. Better to join a popular front and thus gradually build Socialism.

Maisky also built on Stalin's expectation, based on Marxist theory, that ultimately the United States and Britain would come to blows over trade.[36] The British might be encouraged to act as a counterweight against the Americans. In London Maisky probably became well aware of growing antagonism between the United States and Britain due to U.S. pressure to decolonize the British Empire. As a sea power, Britain might be inclined to accept the Soviet Union as the leading land power in Europe. Although Maisky rated the British as more cunning than the Americans, he also thought them readier to accept the realities of power. Stalin knew that British Socialists (of the Labour Party) filled important posts in Churchill's War Cabinet. In 1944 he mused to Labour Party visitors that world revolution might no longer be needed, since Socialists could gain power in England without overthrowing the monarchy.[37]

Stalin and Maisky were not alone in expecting that Britain and the United States would form a triangular relationship with the postwar Soviet Union.[38] For example, just after the war George Orwell built *1984* partly around just such a relationship. No one in Britain or the United States knew how badly the war had crippled Britain, and thus of how predominant the United States was.

Both to conciliate the British and to avoid the reaction Maisky feared, Stalin vetoed late-1944 plans by the Greek Communists to revolt against the Greek government and its British supporters. They rose anyway, and the grief they caused Stalin was just the embarrassment Maisky had predicted. Stalin's interest in a postwar accommodation with the British probably explains his October 1944 agreement with Churchill to divide control of the Balkans, giving Britain Greece and a fifty-fifty role in Yugoslavia and Hungary.

For Maisky, the postwar settlement was to guarantee Soviet security both in Europe and in Asia for long enough to build such strength "that no power or combination of powers . . . could even think of aggression" there. It would be necessary for Europe, or at least continental Europe, to become Socialist, "thereby excluding the possibility of wars occurring in this part of the world." The military buildup would take about ten years after the war and full Socialization thirty to fifty years. With Germany defeated, France was potentially the only rival military power on the Continent. Maisky advised that any French revival be blocked.[39] Thus at Yalta, Stalin opposed giving the French an occupation zone in Germany; he joked that France should be nothing more than a holiday resort. Roosevelt argued that French troops would be needed when U.S. troops were withdrawn.

Blissfully unaware of the ultimate goal of a popular front, the two Western powers would help open up ("democratize") the former Axis countries. For example, the United States accepted the participation of the Italian Communists in the new government formed for Italy in 1944. The Czech government in exile was so friendly that it had already signed a mutual security treaty providing Soviet bases on its territory. Maisky expected the Czechs to spread Socialism through Eastern and Southern Europe. Tito, a Communist, was likely to govern postwar Yugoslavia. Bulgaria had been a czarist satellite and its population was so friendly that, even though the government joined the Axis, it had not declared war against the Soviet Union.

Maisky also took account of Stalin's obsession with Soviet naval power. To maintain access to the Atlantic and Pacific, the Soviet Union needed Petsamo in northern Finland and the Kuriles north of Japan. For better access to the Mediterranean, it should revive the old czarist demand for control over the Turkish Straits leading from the Black Sea to the Mediterranean. The Soviet Union must have "free and convenient" use of transit routes across Iran to the Persian Gulf.

Stalin's naval ambitions showed in late-war attempts to gain bases in both northern Norway (lying on the route from his naval bases to the Atlantic) and on the Danish island of Bornholm, which blocked the exits from the Baltic. In 1944–45 Soviet troops advancing to occupy Petsamo went on to occupy the northern tip of Norway. In November 1944 the Soviets asked the Norwegian government for base rights on Bear Island and on Svalbard (Spitzbergen), an archipelago off the northern Norwegian coast where they already operated mines. The next April the Norwegians offered to agree that the defense of Svalbard was a joint Soviet-Norwegian responsibility. The Soviet Foreign Ministry thought they were accepting the idea that Soviet bases would balance a British attempt to gain bases and thus to "Portugalize" Norway. By July 1945, the Soviet General Staff was urging at the least a twenty-five- to thirty-year lease on the Varanger area of Norway.

In March 1945 the deputy Soviet ambassador to Sweden suggested seizing Bornholm. After considerable discussion, on 4 May the Baltic Fleet was ordered to seize it. As ordered, the local Soviet commander told the Danes that his presence was temporary, pending settlement of military questions relating to Germany.

Stalin was not yet at war with Japan. Maisky thought it best to let the British and Americans exhaust themselves to defeat Japan; "the USA's imperialist ardor in the postwar epoch would be somewhat dampened. . . . This would also be our revenge for the Anglo-Americans' [not opening] the second front [in Europe soon enough]. . . ." Soviet influence in China should be strengthened "by every means."

This was the only part of Maisky's advice Stalin did not follow completely. By early 1945 the U.S. government badly wanted Stalin to join the war against Japan because it feared the very large undamaged Japanese army forces apparently in Manchuria. At Yalta in February, Stalin agreed to attack within three months of the end of the war in Europe—for a price. Under the terms of a secret protocol specifically intended to reverse the results of the Russo-Japanese War, he would receive the Kuriles and the southern half of Sakhalin, as well as a lease on Port Arthur and a protectorate over the port of Dairen. He and the Chinese would jointly control the Chinese Eastern and Manchurian Railway, built by the czars and used by the Japanese as a pretext for their 1931 invasion of Manchuria.[40] Stalin asked for but was not given an occupation zone in Japan.[41]

The Maisky memorandum seems to settle a major historical question. For many years historians have wrestled with the question of just why the Cold War broke out after World War II. Did Stalin act out of classic Soviet (and Russian) insecurity? Did his wartime partners refuse to accept legitimate Soviet claims? Many historians have focused on a contemporary document written by Maxim M. Litvinov, the wartime ambassador to Washington—and Stalin's Jewish foreign minister during popular front days, who was replaced by Molotov just in time for Stalin to sign the pact with Hitler. In November 1944 Litvinov, now deputy foreign minister, suggested carving Europe into spheres of influence. To postwar apologists for Stalin, Litvinov was proposing a policy of mutual restraint. In fact by that time Stalin was clearly following Maisky's advice. Moreover, Litvinov's advice can be read as more aggressive than Maisky's. Where Maisky wanted a gradual advance to power throughout Europe, Litvinov wanted the Westerners to surrender entirely in Eastern Europe. Clearly the rest would have been open to later subversion.

Neither advisor envisaged a Soviet armed advance into Western Europe. For each, the question was how much of an advance Stalin could achieve without risking war. War among the capitalists was an opportunity that Stalin might exploit. Stalin was fond of saying that World War I had liberated one country from imperialism; World War II had liberated more; a World War III might well destroy imperialism (capitalism) altogether.[42] After dinner one evening in 1945, Stalin said that he expected the war to end soon. The Soviet Union would recover in fifteen or twenty years "and then we shall have another go at it."[43]

Themes in Soviet behavior can be traced from the revolution of 1917 to the end of the regime more than eighty years later. The core of the regime was the Party. Because it had no interest in gaining power by democratic means, the Party limited its numbers: membership was an important privilege, not to be extended freely. With the Party in power, membership meant, among other things, access to attractive jobs. To enjoy that privilege, members accepted Party discipline: they would follow whatever line the Party decided to take, however suddenly it might change. Conversely, because virtually all decisions, including quite trivial ones, had to be made at the top, only a few issues could be handled at any one time. For example, policy could not easily be adapted to the many very different situations to be found across the vastness of the Soviet Union. Ultimately that would cause serious problems. For example, the same nationality policy that might barely appease a Ukrainian might awake dormant national feeling in an Uzbek.

Once in power, Lenin argued that Russia's conservative society would accept radical change only if everyone knew from the start (and was constantly reminded) that no alternative would be tolerated. Police terror was therefore imposed before real opposition manifested itself. Many years ago a British historian of the Soviet Union, Edward Crankshaw, pointed out that the secret police, who enforced government policy, became the real government.

This was much the system the czars had used. Unlike Western European monarchs, they concentrated all power in their own hands, having wiped out the only competition, the mass of nobles whose power was independent because it was based on land ownership. All rewards (i.e., offices) were based on service and loyalty to the czar. The structure was rigid but brittle; it collapsed quite suddenly when the last czar (Nicholas II) abdicated.[1] With the Revolution, the head of the Party took over the czar's absolute power: all positions in the country were now his to give.

The effect was feudal. Each highly placed individual had a circle of followers, whose fortunes depended on his own. Favoritism was the rule, not the exception. For example, senior weapon designers who had done badly under Stalin often prospered under Khrushchev, and vice versa. Misfortune under Stalin helps account for the rise, under Khrushchev, of Pavel Sukhoi (whose design bureau Stalin closed) as a fighter designer and of V. N. Chelomey as a missile developer (it helped that Chelomey hired Khrushchev's son Sergei as an engineer). It explains why Khruschev tried to throw Andrei N. Tupolev, who had a close relationship with Stalin, out of the military aircraft program. Once Khrushchev was gone, many of his favorites suffered. Such political-personal conflicts had major impacts on which weapons the Soviet Union bought.

The Party needed some way to convince the country to obey. It tried to take over the role the czars had assigned the Russian Orthodox Church, in which the czar was God's vicar on earth (in effect, both pope and secular ruler). Obedience to the czar had been the road to personal salvation. The Communist Party could not offer immortality, but it did offer spiritual values. It promised the individual that his sacrifices would help build a truly just society: the Socialist Soviet Union was "building [towards] Communism." As in czarist times, police terror supplemented (and sometimes nearly replaced) this sort of faith. The U.S. State Department's senior Soviet expert, George F. Kennan, made just this analogy between czarism and Soviet Communism in 1946.[2] Like its forebear, the Soviet state was both rigid and weak, compared to its Western equivalents. Both were always afraid that their subjects would learn too much about the superior Western political systems—which were much stronger because they incorporated a social contract between government and citizenry. Thus the first major plot to overthrow a czar (Nicholas I) was mounted by officers ("Decembrists") who had seen Western Europe during the fight against Napoleon. In 1945, fearing his own version of the Decembrists, Stalin imprisoned all Soviet troops who had surrendered to the Germans, and who therefore had been tainted by prolonged exposure to the West.[3] As Winston Churchill put it early in 1952, the central factor in Soviet policy was fear and the Soviets feared Western friendship more than enmity.[4]

Once in power the Party attracted two kinds of adherents. Some, like Khrushchev, were idealists who wanted to help build a new society to replace the czarist system which had so clearly failed in World War I. Many younger educated Russians were probably willing to sacrifice a great deal in the name of modernization. Lenin knew, however, that the idealists might not unquestioningly obey his Party line. There would inevitably be lines that some of them would not willingly cross.

Lenin therefore needed and depended on hacks, attracted to power and rewards. Men with little talent could not rise without Party connections, so their loyalty could be assured. Often the mass of bureaucrats resented (and held down) those with real talent. The hacks had little use for idealists or for the sort of ideological issues the Party veterans liked to debate. As the general secretary of the Party (appointed by Lenin in 1922), responsible mainly for organizational work, Stalin controlled Lenin's hacks. The hacks controlled the country. Lenin's death in 1924 opened the way to full power.[5]

The key to Party control was exclusive control of rewards. Just as the czar had formed a "service nobility," in the 1930s Stalin created a *nomenklatura,* literally a list of individuals whom the Party would reward. In effect it was the Soviet ruling class.[6] Different levels received different privileges. Members included prominent scientists, technologists, and artists. The key difference from a Western aristocracy was that no one held privilege by right of birth; the privileges all went with particular jobs, which the Party could take away. That was one reason Soviet generals sacked by Khrushchev were so bitter: they suddenly lost their perquisites. Khrushchev himself suffered as a pensioner, because so much of what he had enjoyed had been bound up with his job. Quite naturally those in the *nomenklatura* used their power to insure that their children got plum jobs and thus had entrée into the *nomenklatura.* That insured a degree of nepotism and corruption, which would embitter those outside the *nomenklatura.*

At the management level, jobs were awarded primarily for political loyalty rather than for competence. Yet the country seemed to need trained officers and engineers, whom Stalin called specialists—men whose rewards came from their talents rather than from their loyalty. All were clearly potential threats. They could show up the nonentities the Party placed in responsible positions. Lenin and Stalin tried to break the talented middle class which had served the czars and which had survived the revolution.[7] In the 1920s and 1930s candidates for higher education or officer training were screened on the basis of their class backgrounds, those of proletarian or peasant background being preferred.[8] Descendants of former officers, aristocrats, and the bourgeois were almost all excluded.

A similar problem applied at the factory floor or collective farm level. The Party rejected any kind of incentive pay as un-Socialist. Workers were supposed to work harder out of Party spirit, not in order to gain better wages. Even senior officials supposedly received little more than average workers. In fact there was a very elaborate but more or less secret incentive system based on Party position, using secret wage packets and special stores. The Party took pains to conceal the special privileges and advantages its senior members enjoyed.

Certainly by the late 1940s it was clear that the Party was no longer inspiring anyone to work particularly hard. Periodically reformers suggested the obvious solutions. The best workers should be paid more, and the better industrial enterprises should be systematically rewarded. That was exactly how capitalism worked. In the Soviet Union no such solution was possible, because it would have eroded the basis of the Party's control of the system. Thus economics became, by the 1950s, a way of obliquely discussing the Party's proper role in the country. Even though most economic reformers did not understand it, they were all potential subversives.

Stalin solved the problem of the specialists. Once his purge gained momentum, specialists in industry discovered that they had little value; they could be arrested and shot or imprisoned as easily as the mediocrities they scorned. At the very least, the terror imposed on some of them could cow the rest, keeping them under control. Production suffered, but by 1937 Stalin probably thought that he had enough military hardware stockpiled to frighten his foreign enemies. He could afford to solve his political problems.

Much the same thinking applied to the Soviet military. For Stalin, material factors dominated war; individuals were interchangeable. If he had enough tanks, he could dispense with potentially disloyal officers. Thus the success of the Second Five Year Plan probably made an army purge inevitable.[9] To the outside world, by 1937 Soviet military thinking was probably the most advanced in Europe.[10] The commander of the Red Army, Marshal Tukhachevsky, was considered a military genius. He and his colleagues had created the mechanized forces Stalin now deployed. But to Stalin, he was a potential rival, to be stamped out. Much the same thinking can be seen in modern Third World dictatorships, in Khrushchev's purge of the Soviet officer corps in the 1950s, and in the timing of Mao's Great Cultural Revolution in the 1960s. Hitler did not share Stalin's materialism; he assumed that the Red Army did poorly in Finland because too many of its officers had been killed, and thus that it would do even worse when his army attacked it the following year.

There was a delicious irony. The army purge was devastating, but it was not quite as brutal as contemporary observers imagined. Many middle-level officers were not, as has been assumed, shot. Demoted or imprisoned or even thrown out of the army, they reappeared after war broke out to defeat Hitler. For example, Marshal Rokossovsky emerged from prison to command an army front.[11] Hitler should have realized as much, because well after the purge, in August 1939, the Red Army in the Far East trounced the very experienced Japanese at Nomanhan in Manchuria. Probably the forces that fought in Finland, which is much closer to Moscow, were infected by Stalin's and the Party's tendency to interfere in tactical decisions.

Apologists claimed that the purge was needed to unite the country before the great stress of World War II.

To Stalin, the purge was a gratifying success, one worth repeating. He would later say that the country needed periodic purges to keep the Party in a state of tension, which probably meant obedience. Soviet citizens concluded that survival required demonstrated Party loyalty of a particularly dull sort. Initiative, even if it were apparently supportive of the Party's stated goals, was dangerous. Sometimes the Party seemed to prefer apathy to active mass support. Apathy probably explains the failure to meet production goals after World War II, when Soviet workers discovered that Stalin did not intend to reward them for the sacrifices they had just made.

In the late 1940s Stalin purged the "Leningrad group" of industrial planners and managers. He seems to have feared that they might have developed some independence of thought during the long siege which cut them off from the rest of the

Soviet Union, and which required independent action on their part. He used "Titoism" (rather than the prewar "Trotskyism") as a charge in a massive purge of the new Communist governments of Central Europe.[12] The foundation for a major new purge in the Soviet Union was laid with the 1952 "doctors' plot." It would have included a major attack on all Jews in the Soviet Union, presumably as a way of rallying other Russians.[13] It is not clear whether the new purge was connected with an expected war. Its timing may have been set by Stalin's acquisition of the atomic bomb. Stalin's ferociously anti-Western remarks of the early 1950s can be read as defiance in the face of a feared Western reaction to a planned super-pogrom rather than as a movement towards war.[14]

The postwar purge might have included the senior Soviet officers who had won World War II—whom Stalin saw as potential rivals. He sent some of them, such as Marshal Zhukov, his wartime ground commander, into what amounted to exile, in secondary positions far from Moscow, for example, in the Far East. Khrushchev would capitalize on Zhukov's combination of prestige and resentment in his later fight against surviving Stalinists, such as Molotov.

From the point of view of the Cold War that would follow World War II, the great purge blunted some important instruments of Soviet power, such as Stalin's superb intelligence service. As in the Soviet Union generally, competence was not enough to save anyone. A few skilled agents disappeared instead of answering the summons home, but most went and were soon shot.[15] Moreover, Stalin often disregarded or misused the material he received. His reluctance to believe 1941 war warnings is well known, though recent accounts suggest that the problem was too many warnings predicting invasion on too many different dates. A paranoid Stalin would not form any center which might have sorted out the mass of information he received (an Information Service was formed after the war).

Survivors of the prewar intelligence disaster concluded that they had better tell Stalin only what he wanted to hear.[16] Stalin certainly still had spies in very important positions in the West, mainly agents recruited prewar by the Comintern. They had joined for ideological reasons, and they were relatively unaffected by the purges. The best known were the "Cambridge Five" in England and Richard Sorge in Japan.[17] Comintern-recruited spies provided Stalin with details of the Anglo-American atomic bomb program and of Allied code breaking. They obtained details of British and American policy through at least the Berlin Blockade and the early phases of the Korean War. Molotov, for example, got Western negotiating documents during the 1947 Paris Conference called to start the Marshall Plan. Stalin's spies probably told him just how small the U.S. nuclear stockpile was in 1948–49.

However, Soviet policy seems rarely to have benefited from the flood of excellent material. For example, Stalin would have tried to wreck the Marshall Plan whatever he knew of the details of U.S. thinking; it was enough that the Plan required intrusion into the economies of states which accepted aid—and that was public knowledge. There is much evidence that Soviet perceptions of Western forces and developments were badly distorted, despite enormous efforts mounted to gather information. Triumphs of technical espionage were sometimes quite valuable, but Stalin's general paranoia demanded that access be very limited. Even unclassified Western publications often did not circulate. The mania for internal secrecy had the ironic effect that Soviet intelligence officers tended to distrust the mass of open information freely available in the West; they apparently valued nothing they did not have to pay or steal to get.

Stalin generally tried to be his own intelligence officer, interpreting himself the material he was given. That was not too different from the way that the prewar Roosevelt administration handled its vital Japanese communications intercepts. The consequences were the same: both Stalin and Roosevelt were surprised in 1941 attacks. Both the United States and the Soviet Union eventually reacted similarly, forming intelligence assessment staffs. However, Soviet paranoia drastically limited the effect of the "Committee of Information" formed in the 1950s, whereas the CIA became quite powerful. Its main purpose was to draw conclusions from the information it gathered. By way of contrast, the KGB seems to have tended to provide its masters with nearly raw intelligence. It showed no interest in shifting their distorted perceptions of the West.

Soviet espionage did pay some very real dividends in Western responses. In 1951, with the defection of Burgess and McLean, it became clear that the Soviets had penetrated the British Foreign Office; it soon seemed likely that the Secret Intelligence Service had also been compromised. The fear of further penetration, and that moles had recruited successors, echoed through the next three decades. One effect was to discourage potential Soviet defectors, who rightly feared that they would be betrayed by Soviet moles. Given the British experience, fear of moles almost destroyed the CIA in the sixties.[18]

Above all, terror cemented Stalin's control of Soviet life. Local Party bosses existed to implement the commands from the center; pluralism was inconceivable. The most dramatic manifestation of central control was the planned economy. It was argued at the time that only by planning could primitive postrevolutionary Russia create the modern industrial economy, which in turn would generate military muscle. Plans necessarily set goals for every factory. Managers often imagined that simple political enthusiasm (or loyalty) could make up for stodgy competence. Goals were often unrealistic. The managers' incentives were tied to fulfillment (or, even better, overfulfillment) of those goals. Particularly under Stalin, propaganda emphasized heroic feats of overproduction (by "Stakhanovites"). Once Stalin's terror deepened in the 1930s, moreover, many managers knew that they could be shot (for "sabotage") if they failed to meet their assigned goals.

The goals, moreover, had to be stated in bald quantitative terms: so many tons of steel produced, so many rivets manufactured, so many miles of track laid, so many new prototype aircraft built. Only in a very few cases could quality be enforced. Stalin built the system primarily to arm the Soviet Union. Managers who produced more guns got the butter, so for them there was never any real choice between guns and butter. Workers who might have wanted more butter had no say in the matter. Managers benefited enormously from any acceleration of production; there was no incentive for self-control. Thus, left to its own devices, the system would gobble up Soviet resources without any limit. Only Stalin could shut it off, for example, to provide capital for something new.

This planning system applied throughout the Soviet Union, and it survived World War II. Those within it had every incentive to demand more and more resources, and military demands were the best justification. One great lesson of World War II was that the stockpiles (for example, of ammunition) so laboriously built up prewar had proven inadequate. The postwar conclusion was that production would have to accelerate at the outbreak of any future war.[19] Factories should therefore be designed with increased capacity (e.g., extra machine tools) and extra floor space, and materials should be stockpiled. Given the emphasis already placed on military production, it is not clear where the extra workers would have been found; stockpiling added considerably to the cost of every program from the early 1960s on. But stockpiled materials and parts provided defense plants with a valuable buffer against the pressures brought by the transition to a cash economy in the 1990s.

Planning implied an ability to predict future needs. For example, to build tanks a plant had to receive enough engines, guns, and armor steel, among other things. The plant producing the engines needed its own supplies of steel, and the plan had to anticipate the transportation of tanks from one plant to the other, and from the tank plant to the consumer, the army. As anywhere else, different programs in effect competed for the same resources. For example, World War II tanks and military aircraft often used the same engines. However, to set priorities required many decisions—almost all of which had to be referred to the top. That was not too difficult for Stalin, whose army (at least in 1940) used a limited number of different weapons and vehicles. After World War II, however, the variety of Soviet weaponry increased enormously. With a few exceptions, such as ballistic missiles, priorities became almost impossible to establish.

Planning goals had never been altogether realistic. They were generally set in terms of what the Soviet services might want, rather than in terms of what the Soviet economy was likely to produce. Perhaps most importantly, Stalin's system of plans, rewards, and horrific penalties encouraged lying, not only to the outside world but also within the system. It was far better for a manager to claim that the planned goals had been met than to admit that the plan was unrealistic. Widespread theft and corruption also badly distorted Soviet economics. Petty bureaucrats had enormous and arbitrary power, so they could easily extort bribes. The government often paid for nonexistent plants and other enterprises.[20]

The planning process produced reams of statistics, which were published to prove that the system was succeeding. They were largely accepted by a credulous world. Thus it was commonly agreed that by 1950 (the end of the first postwar Five Year Plan) the Soviet economy had recovered to pre-1941 levels of production.[21] At the Twenty-first Communist Party Congress (1957), Khrushchev claimed, undoubtedly on the basis of Soviet statistics, that the Soviet Union might catch up with the West by 1970.[22] Many in the West believed him; at the December 1957 NATO meeting the Italians claimed that the Soviets had the economic initiative.[23] The Soviet system never produced accurate figures of its own, so these lies were used internally as well as externally.

The most famous case of fraud was Brezhnev's cotton scandal. To test a new reconnaissance satellite, the Uzhbek Republic (which produced most Soviet cotton) was ordered to lay its entire cotton crop out in view. The satellite saw far less than what had been reported, on which large bonuses had been paid. The Uzhbek Party leadership was shaken up and some members were shot. The incident made the surviving Uzhbek chiefs more nationalistic, and less willing to back Moscow when the crisis came in 1989–91.[24]

Planners could never estimate what the production machine could accomplish. Besides, it was always easier to build new plants than to maintain or improve existing ones (the Soviets called this "extensive" rather than "intensive" development), so the cost of new programs could be very high—and the programs themselves became much more complex. By the 1960s typical practice was for the (nominally) governing Council of Ministers to issue a decree approving a new weapon, such as a missile. The decree might be the size of a telephone book, because it would list the contribution each of hundreds of industrial enterprises was expected to make to the program, and the dates on which it would have to deliver its products. None of the enterprises involved could demand that any of the others produce as ordered; that was all up to the Council of Ministers. Most enterprises had several such documents, each stamped to show that it had the highest priority. This system of production was Stalin's legacy: the center was supreme, and the center could never make enough decisions.

The planners always demanded more than the system could possibly produce; the managers often lied to make up the difference. Also, planning was inflexible; it could not take inevitable problems—bad weather, for example—into account. The demand for complete Five Year Plans made matters even worse. Stalin limited the problem by not taking rigid planning too seriously. Everyone knew that he said that all problems were due to men—who could be eliminated. His successors inherited the rigid system, but also an overwhelming desire to protect themselves by taking the rules much more seriously. They were doomed to sclerosis.

The industrial workers who executed the plans had to be fed. If the government simply bought food, it would have to provide the peasants who grew it with consumer goods; forced industrialization would have been impossible. Stalin solved that problem by seizing the peasants' land, food, and animals, turning them into landless agricultural industrial workers. The result was horrific. Peasants resisted by destroying animals and crops. Stalin let them starve, and he killed many of those who did not starve. As many as ten million people may have died in the process, mainly in the Ukraine.[25] Stalin's actions left bitterness which the Germans exploited during World War II, which caused continued rebellion postwar, and which probably contributed to the breakup of the Soviet Union after 1991. For the moment, Stalin readily accepted that Soviet agriculture was never as productive as its czarist predecessor. Not until at least the mid-1950s did the number of farm animals in the Soviet Union reach 1914 levels.[26]

The United States entered the Cold War to keep Stalin from taking over Western Europe. Despite wartime devastation, Western Europe was still (at least potentially) one of the most productive centers of the world. If Stalin could add its capability to his own, he could overpower the United States. To survive at all, America would have to become an unacceptably militarized garrison state.[1] This was much the same reason for which the United States had recently resisted Hitler and the Japanese. They, too, had threatened to unite too much of the world against the United States and its allies.

In Stalin's case, conquest might be by subversion rather than by invasion. As Stalin's post-1945 offensive developed, both the British and the Americans began to fear a kind of bandwagon effect.[2] Successes on the Continent might encourage Stalin's sympathizers in Britain. Success in Britain might affect Americans. Thus it seemed entirely possible that Stalin might do what a military invader could not: he might be able to leap the Channel in Europe (to England) and even the Atlantic.

Hitler's pattern of successes and failures had important implications for Stalin. Where Hitler had won—on the far side of the Channel—he had, in effect, discredited the conservative governments that he had defeated militarily. In Western Europe, such governments were restored by the victorious Allies, but they were still somewhat shaky. Communist parties had gained enormous prestige for their contributions to the resistance against Hitler (at least for resistance after June 1941). In many cases they seemed to have formed the hard core of resistance. Thus it seemed that Stalin had a real chance of taking over even countries his army had not occupied. Where Hitler had failed—in Britain—the victorious political system had the prestige that mattered. It would be much more difficult to unseat.

Even after the devastation visited on it, Germany remained the key European industrial power. At the end of World War II much of her industrial base was still intact, or at least repairable. More importantly, most of the highly trained work force had survived the war.

German industrial potential could be seen as either a threat or as a promise. At first Stalin could not decide which aspect was more important; his troops concentrated on shipping the industrial plant east, out of Germany. Without the German work force, it bought him less than he might have expected. The French wanted to detach the key industrial area of the Ruhr. They would profit from it, and in its absence Germany was less likely to revive as a threat. Within a few years opinions had changed drastically. The British and the Americans were the first to see Germany as the key prize in Europe, the powerhouse of revival. One sign of their understanding was that they resisted the French attempt on the Ruhr. Stalin came to a similar conclusion, although in his case he was more interested in strengthening Eastern Europe. He also saw the possibility of denying recovery to Western Europe, and thus maintaining exactly those conditions of collapse in which his Communists might prosper. These considerations explain why so much of the Cold War was fought in and around Germany. In the Far East, Japan offered a similar, but much smaller, economic potential.

Late in World War II, these potential problems were still largely unrecognized. President Roosevelt was concerned mainly with building a stable postwar world based on principles he thought were universal.[3] Those principles shaped the way the United States fought the Cold War. First among them was the belief, largely unstated, that only democratic governments were truly legitimate. Many Americans then believed—as they do today—that free countries would automatically be both friendly and peaceful. Conversely, it seemed that dictatorships, being inherently aggressive, had caused World War II. This ideology carried a Cold War cost. In Western Europe, Americans were clearly fighting to save democracies. However, in the Far East, Latin America, and Africa the United States often found itself supporting dictators—an embarrassment the Soviets and their friends often took pains to point out. That embarrassment was unavoidable, since dictators sympathetic to the United States ruled some very strategic places. Indeed, the problem was not new. During both world wars, the United States fought alongside Russia, which at both times—at least before 1917, in the case of World War I—was ruled by a tyranny of obscene proportions.

After 1941, the U.S. government finessed its dilemma by portraying the totalitarian Soviet Union as a quasidemocracy. For example, according to the 29 March 1943 issue of *Life* magazine, then probably the most widely read in the country, Russians "look like Americans, dress like Americans, and think like Americans." The secret police (the NKVD) were "a national police similar to the FBI." According to *Collier's*, the Soviet Union was neither Socialist nor Communist, but "a modified capitalist set-up [moving] towards something resembling our own and Great Britain's democracy."[4] Professionals at the Moscow Embassy called former Ambassador Joseph E. Davies' wartime bestseller, *Mission to Moscow*, "Submission to Moscow."[5]

This wartime propaganda was intended largely to overcome widespread prewar antagonism to the Soviet Union and domestic American Communists, its allies. By the late 1930s the basic character of Stalin's regime was fairly well known, even if the sheer scale of his killings was not. Many Americans had considered Stalin a dangerous tyrant, bent on spreading his power beyond his borders. American anti-Communists who equated Hitler and Stalin had found proof of their views in the 1939 Hitler-Stalin Pact. By this time many on the American Left, including the labor movement, had concluded that it was dangerous to accept Communist aid; quite soon their organizations became subject to Party discipline, following the line as it was set in Moscow. For example, the leadership of the largest American union, the AFL, consciously excluded Communists wherever possible. On the other hand, many on the Left accepted Communist help, particularly after Stalin had approved the popular fronts. For example, in the 1930s the CIO, an important labor federation, was heavily penetrated. Given the enormity of the threat presented by Hitler, many on the Left were more than willing to overlook Stalin's flaws. However, many more conservative Americans still disliked the Soviets for their policies, perhaps particularly for their attempts to suppress organized religion.

During the 1930s the Roosevelt administration's New Deal placed the government in alliance with the American Left. Many on the extreme Right took this alliance as evidence of Communist penetration of the administration; they went further to smear the Left as Communist-oriented. Once war broke out and the Soviets became allies, the situation reversed. These same extreme right-wingers, who often also opposed aid to Britain and U.S. involvement in the war, could be attacked by the administration as unpatriotic. By extension, their much more respectable anti-Communist allies (who often opposed administration policies) could be smeared as pro-German. The administration's efforts came very close to equating any disagreement with its policies as treason. These efforts culminated in a series of July 1942 indictments of extremist opponents of the war on the ground that they were conspiring to destroy morale in the armed forces; a trial that followed ended inconclusively.[6] In it, the prosecution came very close to dividing the world into Fascists and anti-Fascists; and anti-Fascism had to include friendship for the Soviets. This was not too different from the classic Communist practice of dividing the world into Communists and anti-Communists (i.e., Fascists). The net effect of U.S. government pro-Soviet propaganda was to leave many on the Right, including many Republicans who could not be classified as far-right fanatics, suspicious that the Roosevelt administration itself had been penetrated by (and was even partly controlled by) Soviet agents. When exactly such penetration was revealed after the war, they would feel vindicated.

The American belief in free governments clearly extended to the European colonial empires. As a firm anticolonialist, Roosevelt had included the right of self-determination in the Atlantic Charter of 1941, despite British objections. As late as the end of 1944, he clearly hoped that the Soviet Union and a revived China would help keep the Europeans from reoccupying the colonies the Japanese had overrun in Asia. This hope was unrealistic: the Soviet Union was itself an empire (its nature hidden by the fact that its colonies had been officially amalgamated into its government).[7] Moreover, Stalin showed no interest in breaking up the British Empire. China was weak, and would likely remain so. However, Roosevelt often showed that he could disregard facts. He seems to have relented, in the case of Vietnam, only as his health—and with it, his will—collapsed in the spring of 1945.

Many Americans thought that decolonization was inevitable. If they supported it, the resulting independent governments would become friends—and trading partners. Many Europeans considered the U.S. policy self-serving. In effect the Americans hoped to exploit the European investments which had made those countries prosperous enough to be worthwhile markets. For their part, many Americans bitterly remembered prewar British attempts to exclude them from trade with their colonies. After the war, the British badly needed a massive recovery loan. The American negotiators used their leverage to open up trading rights.[8] More than any other issue, in 1945 the colonial question divided the United States from potential European allies.

In 1945 most Americans agreed with George Washington: the country should avoid entangling alliances. It had taken enormous political effort to make the public see World War II as America's war, not merely one foisted on it by corrupt Europeans. Close wartime cooperation with the British came after a long history of confrontation. Despite the strong cultural affinity between the two democracies, the Special Relationship built up during the war might easily have languished. Even the personal relationship between Churchill and Roosevelt was clearly declining by 1944, and the two postwar leaders, Attlee and Truman, had not met before the Potsdam Conference in July 1945, at the end of the war in Europe.

Americans also agreed that world prosperity would guarantee world peace. It seemed that World War II had resulted mainly from the stresses of the Great Depression. Countries had been unable to recover from the Depression due to a crash in world trade. That had not been accidental. As different countries' economies declined, the prices they charged for their exports fell. It should have become easier for them to export what could no longer be sold at home. World trade should have pulled them all out of recession. However, to protect their home industries from foreign competition, governments imposed higher and higher tariffs, which choked off trade by raising the prices of imports. Many economists knew this was suicidal, but the movement was too popular to resist. For example, in the United States President Hoover vetoed the Smoot-Hawley Tariff, but Congress overrode him.

Now there was a second chance. By 1944 the U.S. economy was larger than any other. As late as 1949 it accounted for almost half of everything the world produced. Americans could force other governments to lower tariffs in return for the loans they needed to recover from wartime devastation. A World Bank would finance recovery and trade. Naturally it would work in dollars, which became the world's reserve currency, backed by gold. Hopefully, free trade would finance most reconstruction, supported by relatively modest loans. These ideas were ratified by a world monetary conference, held at Bretton Woods in 1944, which the Soviets attended.[9] The resulting agreements came into force on 1 January 1946.

Assistant Secretary of the Treasury Harry Dexter White, a Soviet agent, had drawn up the terms of the agreement.[10] As late as December 1945 the Soviet trade and foreign ministries recommended ratification, since the Soviets would then obtain reconstruction credits. Stalin personally vetoed Soviet membership.[11]

As it happened, the war had been far more devastating than anyone had imagined. The United States aided recovery both through the United Nations Relief and Rehabilitation Agency (UNRRA: $530 million) and by providing long-term low-interest loans. The largest, to the British, amounted to $3.75 billion (the British wanted $5 billion). Signed on 6 December 1945, it was approved by Congress in July 1946, with repayment to begin in 1951.[12] About $1 billion went to France. Within two years it was clear that these measures had failed. UNRRA proved extremely inefficient. Money provided to governments on a one-time basis melted away without restoring economic health; it was used mainly to pay short-term debts. The failure of the two postwar loans suggested that the problem lay deeper than simple indebtedness due to the war. If Western Europe were to be restored, the U.S. government had to involve itself in its economic structure. From that thinking the Marshall Plan emerged.

The Bretton Woods agreement had important Cold War effects. To encourage trade, it demanded that each currency be freely convertible into every other. At first that was impossible: money in shaky currencies would swiftly have been converted into safe dollars and sent to the United States, drying up foreign economies. Then the United States began spending its dollars heavily abroad, both for aid and to support troops stationed there. Stationing large numbers of troops in foreign countries was equivalent, in monetary terms, to importing too much from those countries. In 1958 the European economies were finally stable enough that the free convertibility imagined in 1944 could be allowed. The Europeans could—and did—demand gold from the United States in exchange for the dollars they held. As gold began to flow out of the U.S. treasury, intense domestic pressure built either to bring U.S. troops home or to convince foreign governments to pay the costs of U.S. troops helping to defend their countries.[13]

Foreign governments proved less than anxious to turn their dollars into gold, because dollars were inherently valuable: Bretton Woods had made them the central Western currency. U.S. military deployments abroad were less of a problem than the U.S. government thought. Through the 1960s, the Europeans were willing to shore up the Bretton Woods system despite apparently adverse effects on their own economies.[14] The system survived until the early 1970s, when President Richard Nixon was forced to abandon the gold standard and float the dollar.[15]

In 1945 few could have imagined that the United States could sustain a fifty-year war. World War II strategy had been shaped by the perception that the American public demanded the quickest possible solutions. The regular election cycle made it difficult for the country to set and maintain long-term policy. Real differences of approach characterized the eight Cold War administrations: Truman, Eisenhower, Kennedy-Johnson, Nixon, Ford, Carter, Reagan, and Bush. Congressional continuity helped offset changes of administration, since every president needed congressional assent to press ahead with his policies. Leadership of key congressional committees was determined by seniority: long-serving chairmen such as Fred Vinson had enormous power. They were largely discredited in the wake of Vietnam; from 1974 on, chairmen were elected by their committees. By the 1980s the situation had stabilized, but now the chairmen always had to fear revolts within their committees.

The U.S. government of 1945 could not avoid foreign entanglements altogether, because it shared occupation duty in Germany and Austria with Britain, France, and the Soviet Union. At Yalta in February 1945, President Roosevelt told a surprised Stalin that he doubted the American public would tolerate more than two years of occupation after the war. To preclude German revival, Stalin suggested a much longer occupation, twenty years at least.[16] Austria was a special case because, although part of wartime Germany due to the Anschluss of 1938, she was treated as the first victim of Nazi aggression. The Soviets installed a coalition provisional government for the entire country when they liberated Vienna in 1945. Its chief was an elderly Socialist, Dr. Karl Renner, whom the Soviets presumably expected to be malleable.[17] Renner proved wily. The Allies accepted his coalition in their occupation zones, so there was no prospect of permanently splitting up the country. A peace treaty neutralizing it was nearly reached in 1947, before the Cold War froze altogether.

In the Far East, the United States occupied Japan with four under-strength divisions. Allied countries (but not the Soviet Union) contributed token units.

Like Austria, Korea was a special case, a victim of aggression. As it had no recent experience of self-rule, at Yalta Stalin suggested a joint trusteeship governed by an American, a Soviet, and a Chinese representative, possibly joined by a Briton. Soon that suggestion was reduced to an agreement that U.S. forces would disarm the Japanese in the south, and the Soviets in the north, the country later to be united under its own government. The demarcation line between the two countries' forces, the 38th parallel, was roughly that across which Russian and Japanese forces had faced each other in 1904.[18]

For the United States, another important fact of life in 1945 was that U.S. ground power was likely to decline very quickly as soldiers were demobilized. Politically it would be very difficult to rebuild a mass army. On the other hand, the U.S. Navy was likely to remain dominant in the world, even after many of its new ships were laid up. Then, too, for the moment, the U.S. had the dominant air striking power, because it alone had the atomic bomb. U.S. strategists, then, thought in terms not of maintaining garrisons abroad, but rather of reacting to overseas crises. Ships could steam from the United States; aircraft could fly abroad as needed (with the important caveat that they could not be effective without foreign bases). There was no concept of large-scale permanent forward naval deployment, and there was no forward air deployment.

Americans assumed that peacekeeping would be done under the auspices of the new United Nations. The post–World War I League of Nations had failed, it was said, because the United States had stayed out. This time the United States would be a prime mover; it would help stabilize the world by offering its dominant armed forces as part of the necessary international police. Surely all the wartime Allies had similar interests in stability, which would help them rebuild.

Most Americans still imagined that Britain, their wartime partner, was a super-power. Indeed, during the war Roosevelt often said that he feared postwar British hostility. Surely the British could be relied upon to keep the peace in Europe and throughout her world empire. Thus in 1945 Americans increasingly saw their country as primarily a Pacific power. The negotiations for the British loan brought home reality: Britain was virtually bankrupt. World War II had cost Britain about a quarter of her prewar wealth, and left her the world's largest debtor. Only the war-time Lend-Lease Act had saved the country from fiscal disaster in 1941, and with the end of that aid she was virtually back to her 1941 position. Few in pre-victory Britain seem to have realized just how bad their country's situation was. They soon found out; postwar rationing, for example, was more stringent than wartime rationing. For the first time, bread was controlled.

Like the Americans, the British lacked any tradition of long-term peacetime alliances. However, merely to survive, they had to concentrate on rebuilding their international trading position.[19] For example, for years after the war work on new warships was suspended because the same electrical engineers and installers needed for the ships were also needed to design and make export goods. Within a few years the British would conclude that they could not guarantee their own security without help from the United States.

British income came not only from exports but also from the financial services provided by the City of London. The stronger the pound, the more attractive those services.[20] To keep the pound strong, Britain had to limit any borrowing (internally or externally) to pay for defense. She badly needed a period of peace during which to recover. The Korean War was a horrifying surprise: an attempt to rearm, in 1951, caused economic crisis. In a larger sense, British attempts to maintain great-power armed forces through the 1950s badly slowed economic recovery; inevitably the British had to change their strategy (in 1957, after Suez). Even then there was not enough money for recovery. Thus through the 1970s Britain suffered a fiscal crisis (a run on the pound) about every other year.

Britain (and several other countries) did have one other source of recovery funds: their colonial empires. The desperate need for postwar aid helped make them particularly reluctant to give up their empires—and caused them to spend heavily to resist the nationalists the war (and the Americans) had encouraged. To Americans fighting the Cold War, this sort of expense drained vital capability to resist Stalin's push into Europe. Many Europeans felt they were safeguarding valuable investments, for which they had paid heavily in the past. They argued that, without their efforts, their colonies would never have been able to extract and sell the natural resources that made them so valuable.

One other factor had to be kept in mind. Europeans were strongly affected by their recent direct and extremely sobering experience of combat on their own soil. They had gone into World War II, in most cases, already sobered by the horrible human cost of World War I; and that had been suffered largely on the battlefield. World War II extended into their towns and cities. For the United States, war was still something that happened far away, to its soldiers. Even after long-range nuclear weapons blurred that distinction, Western Europeans tended to see the United States as far too willing to fight another war. Through the Cold War, they would support resistance to Soviet pressure, but at the same time they would try to restrain U.S. initiatives which seemed to risk war.

The atomic bomb kept the Cold War cold. To a far greater extent than any previous weapon, it seemed capable of destroying a whole country with a few strokes. Although both Cold War sides maintained large nuclear arsenals, the sheer threat of these weapons seems to have restrained leaders on both sides. In 1945 the United States had a nuclear monopoly, and the attacks on Hiroshima and Nagasaki seemed to show just how devastating the new weapon could be.

The bomb also came at a crucial moment in military development. It promised enormous military effectiveness at a very low cost, since one bomb could, in theory, do the work of hundreds or thousands of heavy bombers. Similarly, one bomb could wipe out an army formation. In the past, it would have taken another army, supplemented by numerous aircraft, to face down that sort of force. This new and relatively inexpensive capability could be contrasted to conventional (i.e., non-nuclear) forces, whose cost was skyrocketing. For example, the new jet aircraft entirely outclassed the propeller-driven types that had fought World War II. They were far more expensive on an airplane-by-airplane basis. To deal with them demanded heavy investments in new kinds of electronics, such as improved radars.

Mass armies also were suddenly far more costly. The main lesson of World War II had been that to be effective they had to be extremely mobile and supple. All the troops now needed motorized transportation. Tanks had to be far more widely distributed throughout an army. In effect every division had to be more than equivalent to a wartime armored division—and during World War II no army had been able to make more than a minority of its divisions armored. Even the U.S. Army, the richest army of all, had been able to provide only enough trucks to move about a third of the troops in each division at any one time. Now truck strength had roughly to be tripled. Artillery had to be made far more mobile, too. The cost of a U.S. Army division more than tripled. Other armies, which had not been nearly as motorized as the U.S. force, found it even more expensive to modernize their units. For the U.S. Army, as with all Western armies, the number of divisions inevitably would fall.

This was not immediately obvious. Until late in World War II, the key factor in army size was sheer manpower. It was relatively inexpensive to arm most soldiers. The effect of the shift in army organization was to make each armed soldier far more expensive. That applied even to reservists, because the cost of armies was no longer mainly the cost of the men themselves. It was much more the cost of their trucks and tanks and mobile artillery—and of the logistical "tail" needed to keep that machine running. To make matters worse, equipment soon became obsolete. The tanks which dominated 1945 battlefields, for example, could hardly face the tanks the Soviets had developed by 1950. From a U.S. perspective, perhaps the worst development was that wartime troop-carrying trucks, which had been similar to civilian models, were replaced in the 1950s by specialized armored personnel carriers. They could not be made on civilian production lines. That drastically reduced the advantage offered by the vast Western automotive industry.

The problem was difficult because, unlike his Western enemies, Stalin managed to maintain—and modernize—a large army after 1945. Because his economy was so heavily militarized, it could produce the necessary flood of special vehicles at what Stalin and his successors considered a reasonable price. Thus the great question for the West, through the Cold War, was how to face a massive Soviet ground force with the relatively small army the West could afford, without itself becoming and remaining militarized.

The bomb seemed the ideal equalizer, particularly while the United States retained a nuclear monopoly. Moreover, it seemed to be the only available equalizer. During World War II the U.S. Army had used large numbers of tactical aircraft to make up for its limited numbers of troops and tanks. Loitering over a battlefield, those aircraft had been, in effect, mobile artillery. They were slow enough that their pilots could easily pick out targets. The new jets were a very different proposition. Their pilots could not easily distinguish ground targets in time to hit them. Nor did they have the endurance to linger above a battlefield, waiting for troops to call for fire. This problem would not be solved until the advent of "smart" bombs and missiles in the late 1960s.

For the moment, that made the bomb much more important to a West that would be badly outnumbered by the Soviets.

Naval forces presented similarly terrifying problems. Very expensive new types of ships would be needed to deal with the new kind of submarines the Germans had introduced at the end of the war—whose technology the Soviets had captured. Again, it was by no means clear that the West could or would buy them in the necessary numbers. Again, the bomb could be an equalizer. Attacks on enemy submarine bases could eliminate the problem "at source," and thus preclude a vast investment in new antisubmarine ships.

Ironically, the atomic bomb did not quite live up to its 1945 image. Hiroshima and Nagasaki had been particularly vulnerable because most of their buildings were so flimsy and so flammable. Cities in northern countries, such as the Soviet

Union, were far sturdier. The key consideration was probably the blast power of the bomb. At ground zero, an A-bomb was far more devastating than any nonnuclear weapon. However, targets could not withstand even a fraction of that destructive power. What counted was how far from the center of the explosion the bomb was still able to destroy, say, a modern building: its blast radius. That was proportional, not to the bomb's explosive power, but only to its cube root.[1] Moreover, of the bomb's power (yield), only about half went into blast. The rest went into heat and into other radiation (such as neutrons and X-rays). Much of the material devastated by the bomb became radioactive and was sucked up into the mushroom cloud created by the bomb, to return to earth as dangerous fallout.

On this basis, the bomb which destroyed Nagasaki (14,000 tons TNT equivalent, or 14 kilotons) had the blast (explosive) power of about 7,000 tons. Its blast radius was somewhat less than twenty times that of a one-ton bomb: hundreds of yards rather than miles. An A-bomb could wipe out a factory or a neighborhood, but hardly an entire city. A target might escape altogether if the bomber missed by as much as half a mile, about a thousand yards. For example, the more powerful bomb dropped on Nagasaki killed fewer people than the one at Hiroshima because it badly missed its aim point. Conversely, to double the radius of devastation caused by the Nagasaki bomb its yield would have to be multiplied *eight* times, to 112 kilotons.

Obviously, radiation and fallout could kill people whose buildings had not fallen on them, so a bomb could be deadly well outside its blast zone. However, it eventually emerged that people could be sheltered from such dangers relatively easily. It was far more difficult to protect them from the immensely powerful blast of the bomb itself. That is why evacuation from blast centers—from the places where bombs would actually go off—was later an important theme in U.S. thinking.

There was another way to look at the sheer power of an atomic bomb. Each bomb could cover only a limited area. Evenly distributed, four hundred one-ton bombs (eighty wartime bomb loads) could probably destroy buildings as well as a single Nagasaki bomb. Several German cities survived multiple *thousand* plane raids. On the other hand, the heat wave and radiation (including fallout) could kill unprotected people at a distance, and the high wind created by the bomb could destroy structures outside the blast zone.

In July 1946 the British estimated that five or ten bombs on a city—the equivalent of a massive wartime air raid against Germany—with the prospect of more to follow, would probably cause it to be evacuated altogether. On this basis thirty to 120 bombs would cause the UK to collapse without invasion, by knocking out the key British cities. Because it had fewer main centers, the Soviet Union might be disabled by slightly fewer bombs (about one hundred).[2]

Thanks to his spies, Stalin apparently was well aware of these figures: he had nothing to fear from U.S. bombs until there were enough (several hundred) to be sure of imposing decisive damage. He also knew that for the moment the United

States had only a very few atomic bombs. It had taken an enormous effort to manufacture the fuel for the first few. Also thanks to his spies, Stalin was convinced it would take years for the United States to make its first few hundred bombs.

Ironically, Stalin probably knew more facts about the U.S. atomic stockpile than President Truman did. Truman did not realize that although U.S. scientists knew how to build bombs, they had few if any ready for use, and the jerrybuilt wartime production machine was not geared to rapid production. The Joint Chiefs, who knew how thin the stockpile was, initially did not make the bomb a central factor in their war plans against the Soviets. As tension between the West and the Soviets mounted, and as atomic bombs became more important to U.S. strategists, the gap between what civilian policymakers saw as U.S. dominance and the reality of the country's very weak nuclear force became more and more significant. Only in the late 1940s was the productive machine geared up.

Stalin shocked U.S. policymakers: he was unawed by the U.S. nuclear monopoly. He maintained that the bomb did not frighten him at all. Americans found his confidence inconceivable; surely Stalin was simply bluffing. Because the size of the U.S. bomb stockpile was so secret, they were unaware of the central fact, that there were far too few U.S. bombs to destroy the Soviet Union. American analysts thought instead that Stalin's reaction was rooted in Soviet politics.[3] The war between Germany and the Soviet Union had begun with a German surprise attack. Stalin told Russians that the Soviet Union had won because "permanently operating factors" such as the country's sheer mass precluded any quick defeat. Those factors included the political strength that Stalin claimed the Party provided. He could hardly have admitted that a future Hitler armed with atomic weapons would have overcome all of that ideological and moral strength.

Stalin privately admitted that a sufficient number of bombs could destroy the Soviet Union.[4] He doubted that the United States could threaten him seriously until about 1955—which ironically, was about the date U.S. analysts thought the Soviets would have enough bombs (after their 1949 test) to threaten the United States.

The number of bombs was not the only barrier to a U.S. attack against the Soviets. The bombs that ended World War II—the only type available for the first few postwar years—were massive, weighing nearly five tons each. It was well known that they could be delivered only by the heaviest U.S. bomber, the B-29 Superfortress, thousands of which had survived World War II.

It was much less well known that only a very few such aircraft could actually deliver atomic bombs. By the end of World War II only forty-six B-29s had been "silver plated" to carry atomic bombs, with an H-frame, a special hook, special sway bracing for the bomb, and special wiring for fuzing and to monitor the bomb. In November 1946, only twenty-four "silver plates" remained in service, all with the 509th Composite Group, which had dropped both bombs on Japan and then one on the ships in the 1946 Bikini tests. Not all of the "silver plates" survived postwar demobilization. Of thirty-four in existence in the summer of 1947, only eighteen were operational that fall.[5]

Thus, through 1947 any U.S. ability to mount a nuclear attack against the Soviet Union was extremely limited, both as to the number of weapons available and to the number (one per airplane) which could be delivered.

Even so, there was a general perception in the years immediately after World War II that the atomic bomb was the decisive weapon of the future. The great question for Americans was how long their monopoly would last—and what to do with it while it did. For example, in 1946–47 there was considerable interest within the U.S. government in the Baruch Plan, under which nuclear weapons would be handed over to the United Nations—and no country would be permitted to develop such weapons for itself.

The U.S. government hoped that its monopoly would last because it possessed the two vital secrets of bomb production and design, one crucial to each of the two kinds of atomic bombs used at the end of World War II. The bomb dropped on Hiroshima used U-235 fuel ("oralloy," Oak Ridge alloy, after the location of the main production plant). Critical details of the process for extracting oralloy from the much larger bulk of mined uranium were highly secret. Given oralloy, the bomb could use a simple gun design. The alternative (used against Nagasaki) was to fuel the bomb with plutonium, an artificial element made in a reactor. In that case extraction was a relatively straightforward chemical process. However, the design of the bomb was not. The core of plutonium had to be crushed (imploded) by an explosive "lens" assembly—whose design was the bomb's secret.

By mid-1945, unknown to the U.S. government, Soviet spies had stolen both secrets. Having been given the information he needed, Stalin ordered a crash program. He knew that the U.S. government expected him to try to build a bomb of his own. If it knew how close he was, it might accelerate its own production program, building enough bombs to threaten him before he had enough of his own. Stalin therefore ordered a deception program. From their spies, the Soviets knew that the U.S. government would estimate the potential of the Soviet bomb program on the basis of the uranium ore available to them. Based on their own geological information, the Americans thought that the Soviets would depend on mines in Eastern Europe. The Soviets managed to downplay the quality of their ores, and particularly the critical fact that they had found a substantial supply of high-grade ore in their own territory.

The British were the other threat to the U.S. monopoly. They had shared in the wartime nuclear project; British scientists had served at Los Alamos, where the bombs had been conceived. The British had arranged uranium supply from the main source, the Belgian Congo. Under the Quebec Agreement (19 August 1943) the British formally agreed to submerge their program into the U.S. Manhattan Project. They and the Canadians sat with Americans on a Combined Policy Committee (CPC), which allocated uranium to the United States and Britain. Under the

Hyde Park Memorandum (19 September 1944), the British were promised postwar collaboration in bomb development as well as a veto over the bomb's use.

As with several other wartime agreements, these were not widely disclosed within the U.S. government, with very unfortunate consequences. For example, when he became vice president in March 1945, Truman was not informed of the atomic agreements, nor did he learn of them when he became president in April. Even after the war, Congress was not informed of either the British contribution or of the agreements. The Hyde Park Memorandum itself was reportedly misfiled under "torpedo tubes" because of its reference to Tube Alloys, the British cover name for the bomb project.[6]

Congress quite naturally wanted to protect the atomic monopoly. On 26 July 1946 it passed the Atomic Energy Act, prohibiting transfer of information about its nuclear program to any foreign country. The new law also transferred the U.S. bomb program to a civilian Atomic Energy Commission (AEC), advised by a Military Liaison Committee. Congress's Joint Committee on Atomic Energy (JCAE), which was not controlled by the administration, could veto any change in the law.

By this time the U.S. government had developed the Baruch Plan. Any transfer of key information to the British would have aborted it.[7] That objection disappeared when the Soviets rejected the Baruch Plan on 18 February 1947. A few, such as General Eisenhower, then army chief of staff, probably suspected that Stalin had acted because he was well on his way to getting his own bomb.[8] Once that happened, the United States would badly need to rebuild its wartime alliance.

The British had already decided that they had to have their own bombs if they were to retain their position as a great power. The British scientists who had served at Los Alamos had taken home with them much of the necessary knowledge. On 1 January 1946, before the AEC Act passed, the British Chiefs of Staff advised the Attlee government to develop a British bomb. To Americans, it seemed likely that the British would get the bomb well before Stalin could (they were wrong). That would place a nuclear stockpile within reach of the powerful Red Army. The U.S. government tried unsuccessfully to convince the British to place their plutonium-making reactor and any bombs they made in North America.

The CPC survived the war. As equal partners in it, the British could demand half of the Congo ore, all of which had previously gone to the Americans. Until late 1947, the Americans did not need much uranium, because they were not producing very many bombs. Late in 1947, however, the U.S. Joint Chiefs decided to emphasize nuclear weapons in their war plans; suddenly the United States needed many more bombs—and a lot more uranium.

CPC membership was suddenly a valuable bargaining chip for the British, who hoped to accelerate their program with the help of U.S. nuclear secrets. However, as Stalin's threats mounted, the British found U.S. bombs a valuable deterrent against Stalin. They were therefore willing to sign over the entire Congo production (amounting to 90 percent of what the United States needed) for 1948–49.

They even agreed to provide the United States with surplus uranium already on hand. Further, they agreed that the 1944 agreement giving them a veto on using the bomb was null and void (in 1951 President Truman verbally reaffirmed the veto, in hopes of gaining British support for initiatives in Korea).[9] By this time the nuclear relationship with Britain was becoming increasingly important because it seemed that future supplies (once the Congo was exhausted) would come mainly from two British Commonwealth members, South Africa and Canada.

The British considered the 1948 agreement part of a growing security relationship that included the beginnings of NATO. For its part the Truman administration thought that it could bypass the AEC Act to provide the British with the nuclear design information they wanted. However, the JCAE did not relent even after Stalin tested his own bomb in August 1949. A series of British nuclear spy scandals, beginning with the January 1950 arrest of Dr. Klaus Fuchs (who had been at Los Alamos), suggested that any secrets shared with Britain might soon be available in Moscow. Even after the AEC Act was amended on 30 October 1951 to allow limited exchange of nuclear information, the AEC bureaucracy successfully blocked it.[10]

For the moment, the administration proposed to provide complete U.S. bombs to the British in exchange for British-produced plutonium. That plan was abandoned when two more spies, Guy Burgess and Donald McLean, fled to Moscow in June 1951 to avoid being arrested.[11] McLean was head of the American Department of the British Foreign Office and had been a member of the CPC between January 1947 and August 1948. The British did not yet have an atomic bomber. In 1950, while the plan to provide bombs was being considered, they were given eighty-seven B-29s (which the British called Washingtons). They were not "silver-plated" and thus could not have delivered nuclear weapons. However, this transfer may have been tied to the abortive plan to supply Britain with U.S. bombs.

Despite the AEC's efforts, the British tested their bomb on 3 October 1952. AEC intransigence probably had cost the British a year's delay. On the other hand, the new U.S. design ideas developed since 1945 would have allowed the British to get considerably more out of the material they had, and thus to build up the stockpile they wanted (which would help the United States) much more quickly. They could also have produced much more powerful bombs.

Through the 1940s, then, the most important facts about nuclear bombs were their size and their scarcity. Scarcity bred interservice rivalry in the United States. The nascent U.S. Air Force argued that bombs could be decisive in any future war, if they were used in sufficient numbers. This idea, which was central to its doctrines, colored the air force's interpretation of intelligence. It stressed the Soviet ability to deliver a massive surprise attack. Lt. Gen. Curtis LeMay, who later commanded the air force's Strategic Air Command (SAC), argued that it might be necessary to define Soviet *preparations* for an air attack as an aggressive act. In that case U.S. bombers could attack the Soviet bomber bases preemptively. Otherwise the Soviets might be able to execute a nuclear equivalent of the Pearl Harbor surprise attack, from which the United States might be unable to recover.[12] The air force was confident that it could penetrate Soviet air defenses at will. That in turn made it doubt the value of any U.S. air defense system.

To the air force, then, all the scarce nuclear weapons were best concentrated in its hands, to be used for the knockout blow. The U.S. Navy saw things very differently. It doubted that atomic bombs could quickly end a war. As in the past, war would undoubtedly be protracted. Nuclear weapons were best used to solve the problems of such a war—for example, to eliminate the Soviet submarine threat—that would make it difficult for a Western army to maintain itself in Europe, or for the air force to maintain its air bases in England.

The navy therefore argued that it needed nuclear weapons of its own. The aircraft it had in 1945 were far too small to deliver the huge new atomic bombs. However, the navy designed a new class of heavy carrier-based bombers, which were large enough. It also argued that it might usefully attack the Soviet land targets the air force planned to strike. Its aircraft carriers had demonstrated dramatic mobility during World War II. Given a new generation of aircraft they could do so again.

In a key decision, President Truman refused to grant the air force the nuclear monopoly it wanted. Eventually he allowed the navy to carry nuclear bombs on board its carriers. Truman's decision was significant because it opened the vital possibility, to be realized in the 1950s, that atomic bombs might be used not only against Soviet cities but also to solve the pressing military problems presented by Stalin's massed army and his massed submarine force. Later the great question would be whether a Western defense dependent on the tactical use of nuclear weapons was really tenable.

These bombs became much more important to the U.S. government as its vast stock of arms and equipment left over from World War II aged. At first the equipment was still modern. Men demobilized in 1945–46 could be mobilized again to use it, to form the sort of modern mass forces needed to deal with the massive forces Stalin was building up. The men and the stockpiled equipment made it possible for the United States to fight in Korea.

By the end of the Korean War, not only had much of the reserve been expended, but also most of the wartime equipment was clearly obsolete. The United States would incur massive costs if it had to replace its stockpile. Atomic bombs became a very important cost-saving alternative. By that time they were so central to U.S. strategy that the productive machine had been built up. Once the necessary investment had been made, the bombs themselves were relatively inexpensive—and plentiful. Certainly they were an inexpensive alternative to massive nonnuclear forces. By this time new technology had made it possible to build bombs small enough to be delivered by fighters and by small missiles.

PART TWO

OUTBREAK

Middle East

Cold War and Nationalist tensions collided in the Middle East. Boundaries are shown at the end of the Israeli War of Independence (1948–49). In 1950 Jordan and Iraq were both close British allies; Egypt was more restive. Aden was a British colony, and neighboring Oman was, in effect, a protectorate. Iran was on the point of expelling British influence, in the form of the Anglo-Iranian Oil Company. Syria and Lebanon were both ex-French colonies. An Egyptian blockade of Sharm al Shaikh (written here as Sharm ash Shaykh), the gateway to the key Israeli port of Aqaba, would help provoke war with Israel in 1956, in tandem with an Anglo-French attack to secure the Suez Canal.

Reprinted from Alfred Goldberg, general editor, *History of the Office of the Secretary of Defense*, volume 1, *The Formative Years 1947–1950* (Washington, D.C.: Historical Office, Office of the Secretary of Defense, 1984), page 476.

At the end of World War II neither the Americans nor the British were quite sure what to make of Stalin. Both governments had spent the war years extolling him and the sacrifices the Russian people had made in the fight against Hitler. Through most of the war Roosevelt had followed his hunch that he could trust Stalin to help forge a peaceful postwar world. He thought that he could moderate Stalin's behavior.[1] Only in the last few weeks of his life had he begun to change his mind; by mid-March he acknowledged that Stalin had broken every agreement made at Yalta.[2] Even then the pragmatic, nonideological Roosevelt did not understand Stalin.

During the war, Roosevelt had had to present Stalin as a popular, almost democratically chosen leader, not least to counter a darker feeling in much of the United States that Stalin and Hitler were very nearly equivalents—neither of whom deserved any sort of support. For example, as a senator, Harry Truman (who would succeed Roosevelt) had once said that ideally the United States should allow Stalin and Hitler to destroy each other (but that Hitler should never be allowed to win). In 1943 former ambassador William Bullitt warned Roosevelt that Stalin planned to extend the Soviet system into Europe as far as possible. Stalin was a Caucasian bandit "whose only thought when he got something for nothing was that the other fellow was an ass." Roosevelt rejected Bullitt's advice. In May 1944, Secretary of the Navy James V. Forrestal told George Earle, the former governor of Pennsylvania, that "you and I and Bill Bullitt are the only ones around the President who know the Russian leaders for what they are."[3]

Like Roosevelt, Churchill sometimes also described Stalin in very favorable terms; he also thought he could deal with the Soviet dictator. To at least some extent Stalin charmed both Western leaders. He was a consummate actor and cynic. Neither wartime Western leader had ever encountered anyone like him. Both badly needed Stalin to tie down and then destroy the large German armies in the East.

The American public was unaware of doubts expressed within the government. For that reason, and given wartime warmth, Americans took what they saw as

Stalin's postwar betrayal very hard. American public opinion turned from mildly pro-Soviet to implacably anti-Communist.

Roosevelt's death on 12 April 1945 confused American policymaking. Truman, his successor, had not been involved in foreign policy. He had to struggle to find out exactly what agreements had been made in wartime. Roosevelt had been, in effect, his own secretary of state. He had relied on James F. Byrnes for domestic affairs. Truman appointed Byrnes secretary of state mainly because, under the constitution as it was then in force, the person holding that position would be his statutory successor (he had no vice president, having been Roosevelt's vice president); he considered Byrnes "eminently qualified to be President."[4] Truman had little interest in foreign policy, so he planned to leave that area to Byrnes—who himself had very little foreign policy experience. Byrnes's first real immersion into wartime policymaking had been at Yalta. It was soon clear that Byrnes had not been privy to secret protocols agreed to there, such as those trading Chinese and Japanese territory in return for Stalin's agreement to enter the war.[5] Unlike Roosevelt, Byrnes was not disposed to favor Stalin. He and Truman were much influenced by Forrestal.

The British were more aware of Stalin's character and of his ambitions. Before World War II, they had fought his agents in the empire, most notably in India. At home, Stalin's men fought home-grown trade unionists in the Labour Party. The new Labour government that defeated Winston Churchill in the 1945 elections hoped that Stalin would revert to his prewar pattern of developing his own country without seeking expansion by conquest. The Labour government also hoped to mediate between Stalin and the Americans, "the Left talking to the Left" while the legacy of wartime transatlantic cooperation remained.[6] Because the British (and other Europeans) had entertained fewer illusions about Stalin before 1939, they were less surprised than Americans by the outbreak of the Cold War. They often found American outrage against Stalin extreme.

Neither the U.S. nor Britain had anything comparable to the plan Maisky had drawn up for Stalin in 1944. A British Post-Hostilities Planning Staff, formed in August 1943, predicted that although the Soviets would dominate Eastern Europe they would not extend their influence over Western Europe.[7] The British Foreign Office disagreed, predicting the Soviets could not forego the temptation to fill the likely power vacuum in Western Europe. The head of the Foreign Office Northern Department, Christopher Warner, who later wrote the key paper on British policy against the Soviets, did not want to plant the idea of an anti-Soviet bloc in British military minds, but liked the idea of British armaments "ostensibly directed against Germany." A Western (European) Bloc would preclude Soviet domination of Europe.[8] In July 1945 the Post-Hostilities Planning Staff presented a digest of a series of regional studies in which it predicted that the Soviets would be ready to launch a premeditated general war in 1956.[9]

Until France had been rebuilt, Britain would need a large army—an unprecedented effort—to face down a new kind of threat. In 1944, the Germans bombarded London with V-2 missiles, against which there was no defense. The V-2 threat had ended only when the launching areas had been overrun by Allied troops. The Soviets might use similar missiles in a future war. It followed that, to keep Britain herself secure, a Soviet advance across Europe had to be halted outside V-2 range. In the past, the British had concentrated on the direct naval threats (invasion and blockade) and on the bomber threat. They had therefore maintained strong naval and air forces; to afford them, they had drastically limited their peacetime army. They had also benefited heavily from the French policy of maintaining a large army to block Germany. Now, with France in ruins, that army was gone. Until it could be rebuilt, the British, themselves badly damaged by the war, would have to add a big peacetime army to their other defense costs.

As Maisky had predicted, anything beyond popular front tactics would alarm the Western powers. At Yalta in February 1945 Churchill and Roosevelt had protested strong-arm tactics in Poland, where Stalin's Red Army had installed a pro-Soviet provisional government built around the men Stalin had chosen in 1943. The two Western Allies demanded free elections throughout Eastern Europe. Stalin agreed.[10]

Plans for a similar takeover of Romania were frustrated when on 23 August 1944 King Michael ousted the pro-Axis Antonescu government and joined the Allies. The Communists who entered the new government were, to Stalin's frustration, local men the previous regime had imprisoned. Stalin wanted his own Moscow loyalists; he had hoped that Antonescu would execute the local men. The Romanian Armistice Convention (12 September 1944) gave the Red Army control of the Romanian armed forces. All regional and local officials (including police) not considered acceptable were removed as "fascists." In December, at the Soviets' behest, a new "popular front" government took office. The Red Army supported a coup, which installed a Communist regime on 6 March 1945. Elections held in 1946 were rigged in the Communists' favor.[11]

To the Americans and the British, the March 1945 coup clearly violated the Yalta promise of free elections, made a few weeks before. Still, President Roosevelt accepted Stalin's arguments that the coup was necessary to maintain military strength and security: Romania lay across Soviet lines of communications. In addition, Churchill chose to abide by the October 1944 agreement leaving Stalin control of Romania; after all, Stalin was scrupulously accepting British control of Greece.[12]

Churchill also had accepted that Bulgaria was in Stalin's Balkan sphere of control. Although the country had never declared war on the Soviet Union, the Red Army occupied it beginning in September 1944. On 8–9 September a coup brought Soviet protégés (the "Fatherland Front") into power. Afterwards, the presence of a powerful Soviet army precluded any reversal.[13] The West did not protest: Bulgaria had, after all, once been a czarist satellite.

Stalin did, however, follow his revived popular front policy in Hungary. The invading Red Army installed a provisional anti-Nazi government, including former senior officials of the ousted Horthy (pro-Nazi) government, as well as non-Communist liberals. The Horthy officials were to be replaced with Communists in key positions. That did not happen. The occupying Red Army did not overturn the free general election, which in the fall of 1945 surprised the Communists by bringing the conservative Smallholders 57 percent of the vote; the United Front of Communists and Social Democrats won 34 percent.[14]

Similarly, Czechoslovakia would be permitted free elections in 1946. Stalin was being patient.

Germany was a much greater prize. The postwar settlement gave Stalin only part of it. He planned to set up a popular front both in his zone and in those the Western Allies might occupy. After taking full control of his own occupation zone, he would undermine British influence in the rest of Germany, which would not be difficult if the Americans withdrew.[15] Walter Ulbricht, who had spent the war in Moscow, returned to Germany in 1945 carrying Stalin's tactical plan of gradualism and camouflage. Local activists found it difficult to accept. As in Hungary, to the Soviets, the results of the first elections were less than satisfactory.

In all of these places, Stalin could determine what would happen because his armies were in control. Further south, he had much less control because Josip Broz Tito had not only largely liberated Yugoslavia, but also controlled subsidiary Communist parties in Albania and Greece. Tito insisted on showing his revolutionary enthusiasm. Stalin criticized him for revealing his Communist orientation too blatantly, for example by having his troops wear red stars on their uniforms. He even ordered Tito to allow King Peter to return until Communist rule had been consolidated.[16]

Tito was too impatient to agree. The British, U.S., and Czech ambassadors reported that Tito terrorized the population so as in effect to rig the November 1945 Yugoslav elections; the population would have voted anti-Communist if it could have.[17] Tito also clearly resented Stalin's orders.[18] He had already angered Stalin by declaring in a 27 May 1945 speech at Ljubljana that his country would never again be dependent on anyone. He particularly resented Soviet attempts to recruit Yugoslavs as their agents (to work against the Yugoslav Communist Party); he bitterly recalled that Stalin's prewar purges had included the head of the Yugoslav party. Tito tried unsuccessfully to approach the U.S. government in 1946.

When the Germans left Greece in October 1944 the Tito-controlled ELAS movement was the major force in the country. The British then entered the country. Stalin ordered the Greek Communists to cooperate with the Government of National Unity the British were forming.[19] Tito disagreed. He ordered the Greek Communists to try an armed uprising, which began in December. It failed due to serious tactical errors. Enough Greek Communists survived to start a prolonged civil war in which the British supported the Greek royal government. Stalin's men, ironically without Stalin's blessing, were now at war with a major Western power, Britain.

As a Yugoslav nationalist, Tito also caused friction further north. Yugoslavia claimed the major Italian-held seaport of Trieste, which served much of Central Europe. At the end of the war Tito's troops advanced towards it, but the British got there first, accepting the German surrender. Tito occupied much of the hinterland. The overt British rationale was that Trieste was needed to support occupation forces in Austria. However, Britain was already fighting Communists in Greece. Italy might be taken over by its strong Communist Party. Churchill told Truman that a strong stand in Trieste might split or neutralize the Communist movement in Italy. Truman initially refused to allow U.S. troops to be used for Balkan political purposes, but he soon reversed himself. Tito's troops also occupied parts of southern Austria, up to the city of Klagenfurt (which had been allocated to the British zone of Austria), on the ground that ethnic Slovenes (Yugoslavs) had occupied parts of southern Austria before 1919. Tito's troops withdrew from this area in May 1945.[20]

It was assumed that Communism was indivisible, hence that Tito was taking his orders from Stalin. Whatever Stalin's preference, he could not disown Tito without admitting that he was not in full control of the world revolution. Truman considered Tito's tactics "reminiscent of those of Hitler and Japan." Churchill made probably his first mention of an iron curtain "drawn down upon their [Soviet] front. We do not know what is going on behind." As it happened, Tito was angry because Stalin refused to back him on Trieste and Austria, but no one in the West knew that. Although the citizens of Trieste voted in 1949 to join Italy, Yugoslavia's occupation ended only in 1954; the city was ceded to Italy and its hinterland largely to Yugoslavia—which by then was no longer a Soviet satellite.[21]

The Polish takeover in 1944–45 was the first clear indication to naive Western governments that Stalin wanted permanent control of Central Europe. After Western protests, a few non-Communists were admitted to subsidiary positions. It was soon obvious that the elections in Poland were anything but free. On 5 July 1945 the United States and Britain officially recognized the new regime, which was essentially Stalin's. They knew that they had little or no leverage over whatever happened so far to the east. Allied recognition of Stalin's regime was later called the "crime of Yalta."[22]

Truman, newly in power in April 1945, when Soviet intentions became clear, commented privately that so far all agreements with the Soviets had been "a one-way street." Secretary of the Navy Forrestal told him that Poland was not an isolated case, that American acquiescence would convince Stalin that the United States would not object if he took over all of Eastern Europe.[23] For the moment Truman backed off, partly because he badly wanted Stalin to enter the Pacific war to force a quick decision and thus to save American lives. He did not yet have the atomic bomb to ensure a rapid Japanese surrender. Then too, like Roosevelt, he saw Stalin as a necessary pillar of postwar peace.

In July 1945 the three Allied heads of state met at Potsdam to decide the future of Europe. They agreed on general points, such as that the German economy would not be broken up. Despite Soviet wishes, France would have a share of the occupation of Germany and would be treated as a Great Power. Details, such as treaties with the Axis powers, would be settled by a Council of Foreign Ministers, meeting on a rotating basis in their capitals. Until treaties had been negotiated, the Axis countries would be occupied by Allied troops. As the Cold War ground on, the Soviets periodically would demand a peace treaty as a way of forcing the Western Allies out of their occupation zones in Germany, including Berlin.

Truman consciously avoided any hint of a postwar alliance with Great Britain, which Stalin might read as directed against him.[24] He still hoped to bind the Soviet Union into postwar mutual security and trade arrangements. However, Truman also felt that he had to show Stalin that he could not be pushed around. For example, during the conference, the U.S. government learned that the Soviets had been pressing for bases in Norway since November 1944. To Secretary of State Byrnes, who was close to Truman, "Russia is like a greedy kid—never satisfied. When it gets one concession it always has a couple more to request."[25]

Truman remembered how quickly U.S. influence waned after 1918 as its big World War I army was demobilized. This time, in the atomic bomb, he had a weapon that would remain effective even after demobilization. It might help convince Stalin to control his appetites. Truman may have thought that, having the bomb, he no longer needed the close wartime alliance with Britain and so could be freer to treat the Soviets on a more or less equal footing.

He also had an economic weapon. The war left the Soviet Union badly damaged. Only the United States, it seemed, could provide the necessary assistance for reconstruction. As early as late 1943, Ambassador Averell Harriman had told President Roosevelt that a $5 billion reconstruction loan would provide both valuable leverage and a market for U.S. industry. Although there had been very little trade between the two countries before the war, Harriman (and many others in the United States) believed that the Soviets could pay for U.S. goods with their vast natural resources. In January 1945 Foreign Minister Molotov asked for $6 billion. The U.S. Treasury suggested a thirty-two-year, $10 billion loan to buy American goods (Harry Dexter White, who is now known to have been a Soviet agent, wrote the proposal).[26] In Moscow, Ambassador Harriman was enthusiastic: it was very much in U.S. interests to improve the Soviets' standard of living, since that would make the Soviets much friendlier. However, it was essential to make sure that the money was spent on purposes the U.S. government approved.[27]

In the fall of 1944 both the OSS (the wartime U.S. intelligence agency) and the U.S. embassy staff in Moscow had already warned that Stalin would use any loan for arms, not for civilian reconstruction.[28] By March, the U.S. government was becoming far less enthusiastic; Ambassador Harriman soon warned that although the United States should show that it favored Soviet reconstruction, it would also have to use its economic leverage to moderate increasingly hostile Soviet behavior.[29] Roosevelt urged patience.

Soon after he succeeded Roosevelt as president, Truman was made aware of the Soviet request for loans. By this time Congress had banned the use of Lend-Lease money for postwar reconstruction. Any requests, like the Soviets', would be subject to specific congressional approval. The Truman administration considered granting a $1 billion credit.[30] When he met Molotov at the White House in April 1945, Truman warned the Soviet foreign minister that Congress could deny foreign aid; he hoped Molotov would keep that in mind in considering Anglo-American proposals regarding Poland.[31] There was some doubt that the Soviets really needed aid so badly that the U.S. had much leverage.

In June the situation seemed to favor the Soviet loan. At the end of July Truman signed into law a bill expanding the lending authority of the Export-Import Bank to $3.5 billion, which would include enough for a $1 billion loan for the Soviets. The American embassy in Moscow again warned that the money would probably be used for rearmament. Secretary of State Byrnes was quite impressed with the embassy's report, but there was considerable pressure in Washington to lend the money, much of which would pay for material still in the Lend-Lease pipeline. The loan was approved in principle. Truman consented to negotiations.[32]

The State Department began to list issues to be negotiated in connection with the loan. These included ensuring that the liberated people of Europe could solve their pressing economic problems "by democratic means," as well as outstanding U.S. claims against the Soviet Union (including a Lend-Lease settlement). Meanwhile the embassy in Moscow told Byrnes that Stalin was clearly sacrificing individual needs for economic-military power. Some in the State Department suggested that withholding the $1 billion credit might be keeping Stalin from increasing his military potential, already seen as a threat. The discussion within the U.S. government had delayed any response to the Soviets. To cover its embarrassment, in March 1946 the State Department said that the relevant files had been misplaced, apparently when the files of the Foreign Economic Administration were transferred to the State Department.[33]

By this time Stalin had made his speech (described in the next chapter), which many thought of as a declaration of cold war. The Soviets were still interested in aid, but they would not discuss the issues that most interested the U.S. government. Although maintaining control in Eastern Europe was paramount, the Soviets let it be known that the chief obstacle to their cooperation was U.S. insistence on repayment for wartime Lend-Lease aid.[34] In fact nothing approaching full repayment had ever been envisaged; repayment for the first six months of material shipped was to have begun five years after the end of the war, without interest. Payment for the rest was indefinitely deferred. By early 1946 the Soviets were irritating the Americans by saying that they already had repaid Lend-Lease with their blood.

In March 1946 French Premier Leon Blum and his financial advisor, Jean Monnet, arrived in Washington. Without financial support, their government would probably fall and the Communists might take power. Their Lend-Lease debt was written off and they were lent $1.3 billion. Secretary of State Byrnes rejected loan applications from Czechoslovakia, Hungary, and Poland on the ground that "we must help our friends in every way and refrain from assisting those who either through helplessness or for other reasons are opposing the principles for which we stand."[35]

The French loan and another large loan to China exhausted available Export-Import Bank funds. Until Congress provided it with more money, it would have no money to lend to the Soviet Union. Before that could happen, Congress took up the question of a very large loan to Britain. The loan was clearly unpopular in Congress; it was an exceptional measure, which passed only because of increasing awareness of Soviet hostility, and a sense that Britain had to be supported as a bulwark against Stalin.[36] At this point Congress would hardly lend the Soviets $1 billion. By the end of May 1946 the Truman administration clearly understood that the Soviet loan had no chance of passing. The Soviets did not know as much, however, and the possibility of a loan might still provide the U.S. some leverage. Thus as late as July President Truman told the Soviets that they still had a slim chance of receiving the money. But by September 1946 the loan was dead.

The loan died in the context of increasing Soviet aggressiveness. At Potsdam, Stalin had reopened the czars' old dream of an outlet to the Mediterranean. He connected a demand for sole trusteeship of the former Italian colony of Tripolitania (Libya) with a demand for joint control of the Turkish Straits (the Dardanelles), through which his ships would have to pass to get to Libya. In August he demanded revision of the Montreux Convention (under which Turkey controlled the Dardanelles), bases in the straits, and the return of the border provinces of Kars and Ardahan in eastern Turkey. The straits and Libyan demands were repeated at the September 1945 Foreign Ministers Conference. The Americans and the British resisted; Byrnes saw Libya as a gateway to the uranium in the Belgian Congo. To British Foreign Secretary Ernest Bevin, the Soviets clearly intended to use Libya as a military base, which could threaten the sea route through the Mediterranean. Withdrawn under Western pressure, Stalin's demands concerning the straits and Turkey's border provinces were revived early in 1946. At the same time, Soviet troops massed near the Turkish border.

Stalin also wanted free passage to the Persian Gulf through oil-rich Iran. His troops already occupied northern Iran under a 1941 agreement with the British. Both countries had occupied the country in order to provide supplies to the Soviet Union via a safer alternative to the sea route around northern Norway and Finland. Under a January 1942 treaty, they agreed to try not to disturb the country's economy and to withdraw all troops six months after the end of the war. The Soviets, however, closed off their five northern provinces—a major food-producing area—not only to visitors but also to trade. That caused famine elsewhere in Iran, for example in Teheran. Late in 1945 Communists seized power in parts of the northern province, Azerbaijan, and Soviet-leaning Kurds rebelled elsewhere in the province. When Iran appealed to the UN Security Council in January 1946, the Soviets vetoed intervention. When the British withdrew in March 1946 as agreed, the Soviets did not. Soviet tanks moved south, as close as twenty-five miles from Teheran. Then the Soviets suddenly pulled out, possibly to avoid ruining Stalin's efforts in Europe.[37] The Iranians agreed to form an Iranian-Soviet oil company (with the Soviets holding 51 percent of the stock) subject to parliamentary approval (which was not given).

In August 1945 U.S. Army–Air Force proposals for bases in Norway and Denmark were killed to avoid justifying Soviet demands for bases in those countries.[38] Stalin still did not want to alarm the West. He began to realize that pressure on Spitzbergen would help justify U.S. efforts to gain permanent bases in Iceland and Greenland. Stalin relaxed the pressure, and in February 1947 the Norwegian parliament rejected the Soviet base. Much the same thing happened with the Danish island of Bornholm, from which the last Soviet troops left on 4 April 1946.[39]

Through the fall of 1945, it gradually became clear that Soviet occupation would eventually mean Soviet domination. Soviet authorities in Hungary and Romania obstructed U.S. companies trying to trade there. As in the past, the U.S. government strongly supported free trade as the basis for a peaceful and prosperous postwar world. U.S. access to markets was hardly the same as U.S. political control of foreign countries. To Stalin, trade access and political control were very nearly the same thing. Late in 1945, Byrnes tried to settle outstanding problems in Bulgaria and Romania. Truman, hardening towards his former protégé, rejected his attempt as grossly inadequate. He would replace Byrnes with Gen. George C. Marshall as soon as possible.[40]

Truman later wrote that on 5 January 1946 he read Byrnes the draft of a proposed letter (which he never sent); it said that the deals reached at Potsdam had been outrageous. He had no doubt that Stalin planned to invade Turkey to gain access to the Mediterranean. "I do not think that we should play compromise any longer . . . we should let our position on Iran be known in no uncertain terms . . . and we should maintain complete control of Japan and the Pacific. We should rehabilitate China and create a strong central government there. We should do the same for Korea. . . . I'm tired of babying the Soviets."

Meanwhile, Communists gained considerable power well beyond the zone controlled by the Red Army. The Communist Party dominated the wartime French resistance. Had the Allies not landed in France in 1944, the Soviets would have been welcomed there; a Soviet defector later said that the Red Army had planned to march across Germany to overrun France.[41]

As it was, the French Communist armed militia could threaten civil war once the Free French army took over France in 1944. General de Gaulle felt compelled to pardon the Communist chief, Maurice Thorez, who had been sentenced to death as a deserter when he fled France for the Soviet Union. Apparently in return, Stalin ordered Thorez (much to the latter's disgust) to disarm the militias. It was far too early to contemplate an armed uprising; Thorez might well win as part of a popular front.

De Gaulle understood the Communists' power well enough that his first foreign policy initiative (10 December 1944) was to sign a treaty with Stalin.[42] For the moment, the Soviets would be a counterweight to the British and the Americans, whom the French lumped together as the "Anglo-Saxons." Once France recovered, and was backed by other Western countries, she would be able to resist Soviet pressure. The treaty applied both in case of German aggression and in the event one of the signatories launched a preventive war against Germany. Similar clauses were in the Soviet-Czech treaty of 12 December 1943 and in treaties signed in 1945 with Yugoslavia and Poland, but *not* in the 26 May 1942 Anglo-Soviet treaty. Thus the treaty Stalin offered de Gaulle was like the ones he signed with future satellites, not with a wartime ally he could not expect to control in future. De Gaulle had to exchange representatives with the new satellite Polish regime as the price of the treaty. He was the first Western head of state to do so. At about the same time he signed the Soviet treaty, de Gaulle rejected Churchill's offer of an Anglo-French treaty. But by April 1945 de Gaulle was becoming wary of Stalin. Privately he said that the United States had to remain linked with Europe to maintain the balance of power. Visiting Washington in August, he encouraged Truman's alertness to the emerging Soviet threat. That October, the French general staff, which de Gaulle closely supervised, was developing the concept of a strong Western defense organization, with American and even German participation. Nothing could yet be made public.[43]

In the first postwar elections (for a Constituent Assembly to form the Fourth Republic) in October 1945, the Communists had the largest share of the vote, 26 percent, followed by the Socialists and the Mouvement Républicaine Populaire (MRP).[44] The three parties formed a government. On 20 January 1946, disgusted, he said, by political squabbles, de Gaulle resigned as president. He did not want to be in office when the vital American loan, then being negotiated, was signed, because he knew that its terms would be unpopular. He had no party base, and the Communists and Socialists were reducing the presidency to a ceremonial post.

A Communist, Charles Tillon, was minister of armaments (as minister of aviation, he had spread Communists through the French aviation industry). Other Communists held such important portfolios as Industrial Production, Reconstruction, and Veterans. Many Communists served in the police, including, potentially very significantly, the new riot police, the CRS (Compagnies Républicaines de Sécurité). The French press seemed to be Communist-controlled.[45] Maurice Thorez, head of the French Communist Party, told Stalin that France was ripe to go Communist.[46]

Moreover, the Soviets benefited from the widespread French dislike of the Americans and the British. They could neutralize the power of the "Anglo-Saxons," yet were not close enough to invade the country. The French were bitter that the

British had held back key fighter squadrons during the disastrous Battle of France in 1940, and they resented wartime attacks on French forces in places like Oran in June 1940 (where the British destroyed a French fleet), Lebanon and Syria in 1941, and North Africa in 1942. Above all they probably resented those who had managed to fight on after the disaster of 1940. Few of the French seem to have realized that they had been included in the German occupation and in the UN Security Council mainly by the British, against Stalin's wishes. French Socialists spoke of France as a "third force" which might mediate between East and West.[47]

Some in the French cabinet already wanted a much closer relationship with the United States. At the September 1945 London foreign ministers' conference, Georges Bidault, de Gaulle's foreign minister, dropped the Ruhr scheme after the Americans and the British told him it might help the Soviets extend their influence into Germany.

However, overall the French tripartite government refused to take sides as the rift between the United States and the Soviet Union widened. They offered Thorez the largely ceremonial role of president (he accepted the vice presidency).

Thorez thought he could move. As a first step, he proposed to eject the MRP from the governing coalition. The Socialists demurred. They knew that the French army had told the MRP that it would be hostile to a Communist government. On the other hand, the Socialist premier, Felix Gouin, vetoed a February 1946 MRP proposal to send the French deputy chief of staff to Washington to discuss common defense against the Soviets. That spring he did follow the Americans in dropping the idea of detaching the Ruhr and the Rhineland from Germany, but the Communists and the MRP killed the idea.[48] Moreover, the trade terms included in the May 1946 French loan placed France clearly in the capitalist West (no political conditions had been attached).

The Communists' popularity began to fade. In June 1946 the MRP won the largest number of votes, and it chose the prime minister, Georges Bidault. Although through 1946 it seemed possible that the Communists would win enough seats in the next election to form a government, that never happened. For the moment, Thorez chose to continue as part of the French governing coalition.

No formal alliance linked the United States to Britain, but to the Joint Chiefs, the British Empire was the last bulwark between the United States and Soviet domination of Eurasia. If Stalin won there, the United States and her potential allies might not be strong enough to stand up to him. The Joint Chiefs remembered 1940, when the United States had supported Britain in hopes of keeping Hitler down. Now as then, the U.S. position as a world power depended on that of the British.[49] The U.S. Joint Chiefs of Staff predicted that Britain would fight if the Soviets penetrated Turkey.[50] Soviet success there would open the Middle East to infiltration. Once the Soviets gained control of the Dardanelles and the Persian Gulf (classic czarist objectives), they would close the Aegean by winning in Greece. That would cut off the entire eastern Mediterranean. In January 1946 Bevin told two important American Republicans, Sen. Arthur Vandenberg (who was later a vital supporter of the Marshall Plan) and John Foster Dulles, that Soviet moves in Turkey and Iran were part of a larger attempt to control the vital Middle East.[51]

Bevin's governing Labour Party was ambivalent, with a strongly pro-Stalin left wing. Prime Minister Attlee saw no inconsistency in defending against the Communists vital interests, such as those in Greece, while trying to conciliate Stalin. Knowing the cabinet's feelings, in January 1946 Bevin approved only limited actions in Iran. On the other hand, during the first UN Security Council session (in London) in February 1946, Bevin's principal private secretary remarked that there was "hardly any doubt any longer that Russia is intent on the destruction of the British Empire."[52]

Both the British and the Americans would pull back several times from such hard-line positions. Through much of 1946 they hoped that Stalin was more moderate than he appeared, that they could still somehow deal with him. Toughness was more a bargaining position than a declaration of war. Yet again and again the Soviets seemed implacable. Stalin's hostility had two complementary effects. First, it alienated both the Americans and the British. Second, and at least as important, it forced them into an alliance that neither had really wanted at the end of World War II. Their reluctance became particularly evident in Germany.

Meanwhile U.S. and British public opinion was soured, not by Soviet aggressiveness, but by what the public saw as Stalin's betrayal of their wartime trust. In September 1945 Igor Gouzenko, a code clerk at the Soviet Ottawa embassy, defected. During World War II, both Churchill and Roosevelt had ordered their own intelligence agencies to cease operations against the Soviet Union.[53] They had even discouraged attempts to detect Soviet spies. Because Stalin still believed in the larger anticapitalist war, he had seen no point in suspending espionage aimed against his wartime Western allies. Gouzenko's treatment illustrates the transition in Western attitudes. At first the Canadian government refused to look at his material, on the theory that it belonged to a friendly government. Once it looked, it was clear that that government was not at all friendly.[54] Gouzenko told the Canadians that there was considerable talk in the Office of the Soviet Military Attaché in Ottawa regarding the "next war" the Soviet Union would fight against the Anglo-Saxon countries.[55] The Canadians found that Soviet espionage, begun in 1924, had continued through World War II.

Canadian Prime Minister Mackenzie King discussed Gouzenko with President Truman on 30 September 1945; this discussion made up Truman's mind about ongoing Soviet espionage.[56] For the first time Truman heard that an assistant secretary of state (who turned out to be Alger Hiss) was a Soviet agent. King was so shocked by wartime Soviet espionage that he reversed his earlier stand that the atomic secret should be shared with the Soviets.

The publicity accorded Gouzenko contrasted with a case in the United States earlier in the year, while the Soviet Union was still a valued ally. The FBI had arrested several Soviet agents operating from the offices of *Amerasia* magazine. The case was suppressed partly because the wiretaps involved were illegal. It would later be charged that the administration wanted to avoid embarrassment by any exposure of Soviet espionage.[57]

By this time many Americans were becoming disillusioned with Stalin. For example, his tactics in occupying Poland were causing considerable distress among Polish Americans. As early as April 1945 they were charging the Truman administration with appeasement and with having made a "tragic historical blunder" by refusing to oppose Stalin. At about the same time the FBI began to send President Truman reports that some of his senior advisors were Soviet agents. Much of its information came from a single former Communist, Whittaker Chambers, who had left the Party in 1938 and whose reports the bureau essentially had ignored until he was re-interviewed on 10 May 1945.[58] The Gouzenko revelations, some of which were soon made public, supported Chambers' revelations. He and Chambers both named Assistant Secretary of the Treasury Harry Dexter White, as did Elizabeth Bentley, from 1938 through 1945 the key courier in the Soviet spy ring in Washington.

Those who did not want to believe that anyone as senior as White (or Hiss, who was also named) could be a spy—that the Soviets had not penetrated the Roosevelt administration—could say that all of the ex-Soviet spies were unreliable at best. Many in the Truman administration had suffered for years from right-wing charges of Communist penetration; they did not realize that the new charges were accurate. White, for example, was actually promoted. Frustrated by the administration, Hoover began to leak the names of Communists he claimed were employed in high places in the administration. The Republicans gained control of Congress in the 1946 elections, for the first time in more than a decade, partly on the strength of their charge that the Truman administration had failed to deal with internal subversion. This victory encouraged further Republican use of the subversion theme, and probably ultimately led to the McCarthy fiasco—which in turn largely discredited American anti-Communism.

The great irony was that by 1949 the U.S. government had direct evidence, obtained by breaking Soviet codes, revealing who many of the Soviet spies in the United States had been. Due to wartime Soviet coding errors, U.S. code-breakers were able to break many World War II messages to and from Soviet spymasters in the United States. Yet President Truman was never informed of either the code-breaking program (Venona) or of its product; he continued to the end to think that the evidence against luminaries such as White and Alger Hiss was little more than hearsay. We now know that he was blocked from access at the personal behest of Gen. Omar Bradley, the U.S. Army chief of staff, on security grounds.[59] As it happened, the Soviets already were well aware of Venona through British spies and also through their own spy in the U.S. code-breaking organization.[60] Because the Venona material was not released until after the end of the Cold War, cases like that of Alger Hiss caused enormous strains in U.S. society. In the 1950s, in the wake of McCarthyism, a U.S. academic who believed Hiss guilty was likely to be considered a right-wing extremist.[61]

We now know that the Gouzenko affair had another consequence. After it and the defection of Elizabeth Bentley, Stalin's intelligence chiefs decided that his American spy network was vulnerable; he ordered it shut down for fear of endangering their most valuable agents, such as Kim Philby.[62] For several years immediately after the war, it appears that Stalin had little intelligence about his new primary enemy. Perhaps the main sources he retained were British spies, such as Kim Philby and Donald McLean, who were attached to the Washington embassy.

On 9 February 1946 Stalin declared cold war. Speaking during the Soviet election campaign, he abandoned the conciliatory tone he had adopted as a wartime ally. No peaceful international order could be constructed in a world with a capitalist economy. Soviet steel production would be tripled to help prepare the country for "any eventuality."[1]

This was not an entirely new theme. As early as March 1945 Party spokesmen (agitators) in the Soviet provinces were saying that after the war the alliance with the West would have to give way to a Soviet challenge.[2] There were also some visible signs that the wartime alliance was being discarded. During the war, Earl Browder, chief of the American Communist Party, thought Stalin's conciliation with the West was permanent. He went so far as to abandon the disciplined Party structure, telling American Communists to cooperate within the American political system. In April 1945, with the war in Europe not yet over, Browder was publicly attacked by Jacques Duclos, a French Communist acting at Stalin's behest. Within about a year he would be purged altogether from the American party. Stalin clearly was reverting to his earlier policies, well before any real conflict had begun between the Soviet Union and the West.

George F. Kennan, the State Department's chargé in Moscow (and one of its leading Soviet experts) sent his famous "long telegram" to answer a shocked State Department's request for an explanation both of Stalin's rejection of the Bretton Woods agreement and of his election address. According to Kennan, Stalin was reviving the classical Communist theory of permanent warfare. Stalin believed that conflict within the capitalist system, most likely between Britain and the United States, was inevitable and would be the engine of further Communist expansion. Although he would prefer to avoid war, Stalin warned that "smart capitalists, seeking escape from inner conflicts" might attack him, as Hitler had.[3] Kennan wrote that the Soviets were "committed fanatically to the belief that with US there can be no permanent modus vivendi. . . . [The] problem of how to cope with this force is undoubtedly greatest task our diplomacy has ever faced and probably greatest it will ever have to face." It was futile for the West to hope that the Soviet Union might make concessions in order to be accepted into the emerging world organizations. Stalin had no interest in a stable world society, unless it was one he dominated. Nor was he particularly interested in world trade. The Soviets might accept trade credits, but they would not be affected by their denial. On the other hand, Stalin had no fixed plan for world dominion. His system would generally avoid unnecessary risks; "it can easily withdraw—and usually does—when strong resistance is encountered. . . . Gauged against the Western world as a whole, Soviets are still by far the weaker force. Thus, their success will really depend on degree of cohesion, firmness, and vigor which Western World can muster."

Kennan predicted that Stalin initially would try to seize areas he considered particularly strategic, such as northern Iran, Turkey, and possibly Bornholm. Later he would take what he could as the opportunity was offered. The Soviets would try to drive Western powers out of the colonies and underdeveloped countries. However, Kennan believed that Stalin wanted the Libyan trusteeship more to stir up conflict in the West than for strategic advantages. Similarly, Stalin probably would seek ties to countries already somewhat antagonistic to the West, such as Germany, Argentina, and the Middle Eastern countries.

Many years later, Molotov, Stalin's right-hand man on foreign policy, confirmed that Kennan had been right. In retirement (and in disgrace for his Stalinism), Molotov told a friend that the essence of Communism was the offensive against capitalism, just as he had said in a 1926 speech: "The policy of our party is and remains the final triumph of socialism on a world scale."[4] He also emphasized that "there is no alternative to class struggle," which in Soviet-speak meant the continuing war between the Soviet and Western systems.[5] Yet there was no timetable (as Kennan had pointed out); in connection with the postwar Soviet expansion through Eastern Europe, Molotov remarked that the goal had been "to squeeze out the capitalist order. . . . Of course, you had to know when and where to stop."[6] For example, he recalled rejecting a Bulgarian attempt to annex a maritime province of Greece after the war because the time was not yet ripe to court trouble with the British and the French; the idea was desirable but premature.[7] The ultimate goal was far larger. Molotov recalled projects to reclaim Alaska and to Communize the United States, which he called the country most suited to Socialism.[8]

According to Kennan, Stalin's war was not an assault by the Left on the Right. Stalin particularly hated the non-Communist left because it could attract workers who might otherwise support the Communists. Whereas European workers might well refuse to support right-wing parties that had opposed them before the war, they would support Socialist parties—which would quite likely oppose the Communists in an election. Indeed, it was sometimes said that only the democratic Left really cared about (and abhorred) Communism, as a direct perversion of its ideals (many on the Left, however, refused to see the difference between Communism and their own beliefs).

Through the early 1960s, the U.S. government would help European unions and left-liberal parties face down Communist efforts to control them. Aid had to be covert, since the parties would have rejected (or would have been compromised had they openly accepted) American money offered during the Cold War. In addition, the CIA underwrote a variety of anti-Communist publications and forums, most prominently the Congress for Cultural Freedom, which was intended to encourage the Western anti-Communist Left.[9] The CIA was particularly careful not to influence it. Frank Wisner, the CIA's director of policy coordination, later said that "in much of the Europe of the 1950s, socialist people who called themselves 'left' were the only people who gave a damn about fighting Communism," hence were the ones to help.[10]

At this time the Soviets seemed to be winning the political battles of the Cold War by building and using a network of fronts similar to the propaganda system they had built before World War II. For example, most French intellectuals seemed almost reflexively pro-Soviet, willing to accept any explanation of Soviet behavior. Without U.S. subsidies, Western liberal and left-wing anti-Communists simply could not have competed. This program largely ceased in the early 1960s. Then, during the Vietnam War, CIA funding for the Congress and for liberal anti-Communist newspapers and magazines (such as the Congress's magazine, *Encounter*) was exposed.[11] Many of those involved, such as John Kenneth Galbraith, George Kennan, and J. Robert Oppenheimer, were not even remotely tools of the U.S. government, and they were badly embarrassed. CIA funding was dropped (the Ford Foundation kept the Congress in business), but other groups which had benefited from CIA financing were exposed. As might have been expected, the reaction among unwitting foreign recipients of CIA support was particularly unfortunate. In the United States, given the anti-Vietnam mood, the fact that CIA money had financed publications tarred them with the brush of corruption, much as the Right had always charged that pro-Soviet left-wing parties were supported mainly by Soviet money. One conclusion popular at the time was that liberal anti-Communists could best be treated as government dupes.

Kennan offered an important element of hope. The Soviet system placed itself under continuous stress. Like Hitler's, that system could overcome some of its problems by seizing territory and resources. The West could block a Soviet expansion. This policy of resisting Soviet expansion would soon be called containment. In a marvelous irony, it mirrored the Soviet concept of the way capitalism would succumb to its own "internal contradictions"—and to revolutionary parties which fostered them. Kennan proposed containment in a July 1947 *Foreign Affairs* article, "The Sources of Soviet Conduct." The British chargé in Moscow, Frank Roberts, echoed Kennan's analysis.

There was also a very public call to action by a far more important Western figure. On 5 March 1946 Winston Churchill made his famous speech at Westminster College in Fulton, Missouri, announcing that an Iron Curtain had fallen over Central Europe, from Stettin on the Baltic to Trieste on the Adriatic. (This was some-what exaggerated, since Communists had not yet taken over Hungary and Czech-oslovakia, though they would do so within the next two years.)

Although Truman sat alongside Churchill at Fulton, he still hoped for some kind of settlement with Stalin. For its part, the audience at Fulton sat silently during the "Iron Curtain" part of the speech and applauded strongly when Churchill said, "I do not believe that Soviet Russia wants war" (he then said it wanted the *fruits* of war without fighting for them). Apparently most U.S. newspapers of the time agreed with the audience's antiwar sentiment; they treated Churchill's speech unenthusiastically.[12]

Meanwhile, on 1 March 1946 the British Joint Intelligence Committee concluded that Stalin planned to consolidate a belt of satellite countries extending into Turkey and Iran.[13] In April, Christopher Warner, the superintending under secretary of the Northern and Southern Departments of the Foreign Office (dealing with the Soviet Union and the Mediterranean) wrote a memo entitled, "The Soviet campaign against this country and our response to it." He recommended a "defensive-offensive" strategy in which the British government would expose and attack Communist penetration wherever it was attempted.[14] Bevin, the British foreign secretary, rejected the idea. He had just opposed strong American pressure on the Soviets over Iran (having, in effect, lobbied for exactly such pressure not too much earlier). Presumably he had been made to realize that the British cabinet was not yet convinced that Stalin was the enemy.

At the same time Prime Minister Attlee decided that Britain could no longer afford to hold the Middle East or the route to it, which ran through the eastern Mediterranean.[15] The lifeline to India and the East, running through Suez, no longer seemed as important in an era of air-atomic power. Egypt and Greece were valuable only to protect the line through the Mediterranean. Perhaps an agreement could be reached with Stalin to neutralize the whole area. British forces could withdraw to a line across central Africa, to protect remaining prizes such as South Africa and Rhodesia. The whole British defense and foreign policy community argued Attlee down. In a war against Stalin—the only likely scenario—the Middle East would provide not only oil, but also one of the few areas from which an aerial counterattack (against Soviet oil and industry) could be mounted. To remain a world power Britain must hold the Mediterranean and the Middle East. She could no longer afford to do so alone.

In February 1946 the British Joint Staff Mission in Washington had reported that the American service chiefs wanted to continue full collaboration under cover of other activities. The chiefs apparently were acting without formal political guidance. They were, however, increasingly aware that Stalin might want war. They also knew what sort of war he might be able to fight. Planning studies had been under way since late in 1945. At that time they were a speculative exercise of the sort all staffs pursue in peacetime; the Soviets were the projected enemy because no other country was strong enough to attack the United States or Western Europe. By the time plans had been drawn clearly enough to be reviewed by higher authority, in March 1946, war seemed far more possible. On 27 July 1946 the Joint Chiefs advised that U.S. military policy be directed specifically against the Soviet Union.[16] Although Stalin was considered too canny to welcome a major war, he might miscalculate. Given current events in Turkey and in Iran, the planners suggested that war, if it came, would most likely begin in the Middle East.

By this time the U.S. forces were shrinking rapidly as the country demobilized. Men were discharged under a point system which favored those with the longest service, hence the greatest expertise. The decrease in troop strength was so swift, and the rise of a new Soviet threat so rapid, that in January 1946 the War Department decided to retain through June many men who had expected to be discharged by March. A wave of protests showed that it would be difficult to maintain credible forces overseas.

In March 1946, with crises beginning in the Near East, the Joint Chiefs advised President Truman that even if he suspended demobilization before 1 April, the U.S. Army in Europe would amount to only six infantry divisions, four independent regiments, four tank battalions, and the thirty-eight-thousand-man constabulary designed to occupy Germany. All were under strength. A seventh under-strength infantry division might sail from the United States within thirty days. The rest of the army's general reserve amounted to three divisions in the United States. If demobilization continued (as it did), by May two of the European infantry divisions and about half of the general reserve would be gone. In June, President Truman discussed remobilizing and sending thirty divisions to Europe if Stalin tried to expand his power there. That was politically impossible. Soon the U.S. Army in Germany was reduced to an under-strength infantry division and a division-sized constabulary. Neither unit could face serious combat against Soviet forces.

The army could be brought back to full strength only by drafting men. In his January 1946 State of the Union address President Truman asked Congress to extend the wartime draft beyond its planned expiration on 15 May. The army pushed for Universal Military Training (UMT). All acceptable males would undergo brief military training. They would form the large pool of trained manpower needed for wartime expansion. Truman considered the draft sufficient; only enough men would be taken into service to fill out the authorized force. However, in 1947 Congress cut the proposed budget for fiscal year 1948 by 10 percent. There was little point in a draft if the extra men it brought in could not be paid. Truman allowed the draft to expire, with the caveat that it might be reintroduced if needed. By early 1948 all the services were well below their authorized strengths. After the shock of the Czech crisis in February 1948, Truman proposed UMT, but had to settle for a selective draft, the first in peacetime.[17] This draft law was set to expire on 24 June 1950, coincidentally the day before the outbreak of war in Korea. On 27–28 January 1950 Congress overwhelmingly agreed to a three-year extension, adding a provision allowing the president to mobilize reservists. The draft continued through the Vietnam War.[18]

For the time being, with at least three times the combined British, French, and U.S. forces, Stalin's armies could probably overrun Europe west of the Rhine and instantly seize the channel ports of the Low Countries. Occupation forces in Germany and Austria would have to withdraw as quickly as possible either from the entire Continent or into Italy or Spain (the JCS favored retaining a foothold on the Continent). While invading Germany, the Soviets could also could attack U.S. and British forces in northern Italy and also strike the Middle East. In the Far East, the U.S. had only enough troops to defend Japan. South Korea, China, and the Philippines would have to be evacuated.

Probably the Middle East could be held. The roads leading there from the southern Soviet Union were so primitive that any Soviet offensive in that region would be badly delayed. There might well be time to evacuate occupation troops from southern Europe and reestablish them in places like Egypt. And, given the poor roads, the strength of any Soviet offensive might be so limited that even U.S. forces too weak to hold Germany might suffice for the Middle East.

If the Allies could hold the British base at Cairo-Suez, they could block any of the Soviet troops pouring south from crossing the desert to take the southern shore of the Mediterranean. That in turn might keep the Soviets from setting up air bases to block Allied shipping. For the later phase of the war, successful defense of the Middle and Near East (including Turkey) would keep open an important land route for a counterattack against the Soviets.

This plan would be World War II repeated. The West would have to go on the defensive for at least three years while strength for a decisive ground offensive was built up. The lessons of 1940–44 seemed quite relevant. Occupying Soviet forces could be harassed by local resistance forces, but they could not be ejected without a major buildup, which could not be managed under peacetime conditions. For example, later in the 1940s the United States and Britain sponsored special clandestine national groups intended as the nuclei of future guerilla forces. At the end of the Cold War, these same groups would provide some embarrassment due to their far right-wing connections.[19]

For the first years of the war, aircraft might be the only available striking force. The situation recalled British strategy in 1940–43, when Bomber Command was the only weapon at hand that could reach Germany. The range of the B-29 was limited. Only by using forward bases could the bombers reach Soviet targets. Thus by the spring of 1946 the JCS was pressing for alliances that would provide the bases needed for the bomber offensive. Britain offered by far the best possibility; B-29s from the United Kingdom could reach well beyond Moscow, to the Donbas.

However, B-29s based in Britain could not fly beyond the Urals, nor could they hit the Soviet oil center at Baku. To do that they needed Middle Eastern or, possibly, North African, bases.[20] Fortunately, the British controlled much of the Middle East. Thus the proposed air offensive dovetailed with the defense of the most valuable British imperial possession remaining after the loss of India: the Middle East. For a wide variety of reasons the British planned to retain garrisons there in peacetime. It was not yet obvious that Middle Eastern nationalism would soon endanger the British position.

In July 1946 the U.S. chiefs of staff (Generals Eisenhower and Spaatz and Admiral Nimitz) agreed that U.S. planners should consult informally with the British on U.S. war planning concepts (PINCHER) and on the possible use of British bases. No notes would be taken, and any arrangements would be disavowed if leaks occurred.[21] (Presumably the confidential Anglo-American staff talks of 1940–41 were the precedent.)

The British informally agreed that in an emergency the U.S. Air Force (then known as the Army Air Force) could use five bomber bases in East Anglia, and nuclear bomb loading pits were ready by mid-1947.[22] These agreements did not amount to a formal invitation to the Americans by the British government, which would come only in 1948.[23] At about the same time, Adm. Richard L. Conolly, commander of U.S. naval forces in the Mediterranean and the Near East, asked the British to provide bomber bases at Cairo-Suez should war break out.[24]

Although at first blush the U.S. strategy might seem inevitable, in fact it reflected the U.S. Army's own concept of war: facing enemy strength with strength. During World War II, that concept had resulted in the Allies' direct attack against Germany through France. At that time American generals had fought down British attempts to use an "indirect approach" through the "soft underbelly" of Europe via the Mediterranean. In the army's view, the U.S. stand in the Middle East was acceptable only because it would take several years to build up the requisite strength—which could not be assembled in peacetime. Given the far greater numbers of Soviet troops, any dilution of American strength to fight on the flanks of the Central Front had to be fought down, as in World War II. Strategic air attack was a fallback to be used while sufficient ground forces were raised.[25]

The navy's view was fundamentally different. It emphasized mobility, including the ability to land armies as and when desired. Stalin had a long perimeter. If all of it were threatened, Stalin might find it difficult to concentrate his forces on any one front. The navy argued that it should be kept strong enough to support a major landing on the strategic flank of any Soviet Army advance into Western Europe (for example, the Black Sea). To defend against this possibility, the Soviets would have to divert such large forces that they would be unable to keep up their main attack. Once landed, U.S. troops could tear up the lines of communication supporting advancing Soviet troops. The navy therefore demanded enough strength to secure the eastern Mediterranean.[26]

To the navy, U.S. ground forces were too valuable to waste in fixed positions. They ought to be used to stiffen coalition troops, who would provide much of the weight on land. Highly mobile naval strike forces were also the best way of assuring free use of the sea lanes to Europe by destroying Stalin's submarines and naval air-craft at the source: in their bases. At worst, navy task forces had a far better chance of destroying these predators than would poorly protected convoys.

The navy's preferred strategy caused it to concentrate on carrier strike forces. From the other services' point of view, the carriers were a potential drain of scarce resources better devoted to buying enough army (and strategic air) strength to execute the war plan. The navy never was able to explain, let alone sell, its alterna-tive national strategy. Possibly it did not yet take the JCS planning process seriously enough. In any case, the navy did not give up. Through the 1950s early air strikes from the Norwegian Sea were a fixed part of its thinking, and its strategic ideas were revived in the 1980s as the U.S. Maritime Strategy. The combination of peripheral attacks and coalition land attacks proposed by the navy long predated the nuclear age; it can be discerned in the Crimean War and in Mahan's writings on the problems the British would have to solve in a late nineteenth-century war against Russia.

Given limited U.S. resources, it was no surprise that the JCS studies emphasized a bomber offensive against urban/industrial targets, in hopes of destroying the Soviet ability and will to fight. First estimates suggested that would be difficult. The first air war plan, MAKEFAST (October 1946), concentrated on Soviet trans-portation, since wartime experience showed that only attacks on specific target sets had much effect. Unfortunately, it would take over a million tons of bombs to deal with even a fraction of the dense East European rail net. It would take a long time for attacks on industry to have much effect. That left petroleum, a prime World War II target. At this stage the air planners excluded nuclear weapons because it was not yet clear that they would be available; the United States was still trying to bring them under international control in the UN. Joint Staff planners were not cleared for nuclear information until the winter of 1947.

In fact, through 1947 the U.S. nuclear threat was largely a bluff. The stockpile was so embarrassingly small that the number of bombs was not even committed to paper. In September 1946 there were only six or seven bombs (in component rather than in assembled form). Worse, by early 1947 the three U.S. plutonium-making reactors, hastily assembled in wartime, were nearly out of action. As of January 1947 one bomb was probably operable and one had a good chance of being operable. Neither was in assembled form. When the AEC commissioners reported to Truman on 3 April, the number whispered in his ear was zero, because there were no assembled weapons. Having imagined that there were substantial numbers of weapons backing him up, President Truman seems to have been pro-foundly shocked.[27] A few months later there were no more than nine usable bombs, and only one production reactor was still working. Not until October would the JCS even estimate the number of bombs the United States needed.

The U.S. and Britain were brought into cooperation as Stalin turned Germany into a battleground. To Stalin, Germany was the greatest prize of all. It was both a potentially valuable future resource and an immediate source of reparations to rebuild the Soviet Union. His mainly rural occupation zone produced much of the food the entire country consumed. The industrial resources he wanted lay mostly in the western zones occupied by the other powers. Under agreements reached at Yalta and at Potsdam, the Soviets and the Poles would take war reparations from the Soviet sector in the east. The western sector would provide reparations for the western countries. Because the western zones were more industrialized, the Soviets were granted 10 percent of the industrial capital there that exceeded German peacetime needs. They could take another 15 percent of excess capital in return for food, raw materials, and commodities from the Soviet zone.

Early in 1946 Stalin sealed off his own zone in Germany and created a popular front by forcibly merging Communist and Social Democratic parties there. He feared electoral defeat in the three western zones as long as the Western allies controlled them. His solution was to press for German unification in the belief that he could win the entire country.

He hoped to cause chaos in the U.S. and British zones on the theory that discontented Germans would welcome a popular front. Then Stalin might unify Germany on his terms by uniting popular fronts in all the occupation zones. For example, his agent, Assistant Secretary of the Treasury Harry Dexter White, provided the Soviets with the plates the United States used to print German occupation currency. Large quantities of Soviet-issued currency helped undermine the early postwar German economy.[28]

With the border sealed, the British had to import food for their zone, paying scarce hard currency to keep their occupied population alive. The alternative was to abandon any pretense that the German economy was unified. The British zone would have to be built up as a separate economy. At a Foreign Office meeting in April 1946, the separatist policy in Germany was equated to the formation of a Western bloc opposed to the Soviets "and that meant war."[29]

But a British policy directed against Stalin was by no means a foregone conclusion; the Labour Party's left wing despised Bevin and his ideas. For example, in May 1946 some Labour ministers warned against treating Stalin as an enemy. The British seemed to go much further. In September 1946, much to Stalin's surprise, the British sold the Russians a crucial batch of modern Nene and Derwent jet engines.[30] Copied and placed in mass production, these engines powered the first generation of modern Soviet jet fighters, the MiG-15s, which went into combat in Korea. The declassified British record of the sale shows that it was made in the face of strong U.S. protests, supported by the British chiefs of staff. It was never subject to formal cabinet approval; instead, it was slipped past on the ground that the engines, which had already been sold to France, were not on the secret list. It seems significant in retrospect that the sale was pushed through by the Board of Trade, whose president, Sir Stafford Cripps, was a decidedly left-wing Labourite.

Yet the British could not afford to maintain their German zone in the face of

Soviet financial pressure. They had to move towards the Americans. The issue was so delicate that in the summer of 1946 Attlee forbade his commander in Germany from jointly planning with his U.S. counterpart.[31] In July 1946 U.S. Secretary of State James F. Byrnes suggested that occupation zones willing to work together should do so. However, Bevin feared that by excluding the Soviets (as Byrnes wanted) he would commit his country to irrevocably dividing Germany. His officials argued that otherwise he could not stem the financial flow; they also assured him that the decision to divide the German economy could be reversed. To reduce the burdens on their economies (particularly the British economy), the United States and Britain had to suspend war reparations shipments to the Soviet Union. The U.S. and British zones were merged into "Bizonia," effective 1 January 1947. One mark of the new arrangement was a common currency, which replaced the occupation currency the Soviets had counterfeited.

Bevin seems to have relented under cabinet pressure. After a successful December 1946 meeting of the Council of Foreign Ministers in New York, he said that the Russians had finally learned to cooperate, that their toughness and bitterness could be attributed mainly to inexperience.[32] The Soviets may have gone out of their way to charm Bevin, seeing him as a key to the sort of Anglo-Soviet relationship they had in mind.

For the time being Bevin pursued an objective his party could wholeheartedly support: regional security. Bevin's pursuit of a formal Anglo-French alliance might be described as a way of insuring against a renascent Germany—but it would also allow the British to assemble the strength to face the Soviets.[33] The alliance also would help to prop up the French government. The treaty would be the first formal British guarantee of the security of any continental country; earlier arrangements with France had been quite informal, which was why there had been some question as to whether Britain would go to war in 1914. Progress on the treaty was initially blocked by French insistence that the Ruhr be separated from Germany, and then by British fears that France might collapse into civil war within a year. An Anglo-French treaty was finally signed at Dunkirk in March 1947.

For Americans, the process of disillusionment continued. In a remarkable 18 June 1946 interview, Maxim Litvinov, still deputy foreign minister, told a CBS reporter, Richard C. Hottelet, that if the West met Stalin's demands, he would ask for more and more. The best that could be hoped for, he said, was an "armed truce." Differences between the Soviet Union and the United States probably could not be reconciled.[34] Since Hottelet's office was bugged, Stalin soon knew of Litvinov's seditious remarks. Molotov later said that Litvinov was spared "by chance." Stalin decided that executing Litvinov would cause a scandal that would complicate relations with the West. At the least, it would have proven Litvinov right.[35]

In July 1946 President Truman had his counsel, Clark Clifford, prepare a long report on Soviet conduct, as preparation for the forthcoming Paris Peace Conference. Clifford and an associate, George Elsey, reached much the same political conclusions Kennan had: the Soviets were expansionist, and they had to be resisted. The report also showed that the president's senior policy advisors for the first time had reached a consensus on this point. Truman still hoped to be able to deal with the Soviets. He suppressed the report: "If [it] leaked it would blow the roof off the White House, it would blow the roof off the Kremlin." Nonetheless, the report deeply affected his views of the Soviets.[36]

Truman's own party still included a left wing that favored some sort of accord with Stalin. It was led by former Vice President Henry Wallace, in 1946 Truman's secretary of commerce (and a supporter of the big, and recently killed, Soviet loan). At a rally in New York on 12 September 1946, Wallace said that "the tougher we get, the tougher the Russians will get. . . . We have no more business in the political affairs of Eastern Europe than Russia has in the political affairs of Latin America, Western Europe, and the United States. . . . To make Britain the key to our foreign policy would . . . be the height of folly." Truman had approved the speech without carefully reading it. Wallace claimed that he was speaking for the president. Truman realized that his carelessness had trapped him; to make his views clear, he fired Wallace. Wallace would go on to run for president on the Communist-backed Progressive Party ticket in 1948. By that time he was backing Stalin's policies so strongly that he described the February 1948 pro-Soviet coup in Czechoslovakia—a defining event in the Cold War—as a necessary step to counter a planned U.S.-backed coup.[37]

Stalin's hopes for Germany began to go awry. He tried to break up Bizonia at the 10 March–24 April 1947 meeting of the Council of Foreign Ministers in Moscow. The new U.S. secretary of state, George C. Marshall, concluded that no settlement with the Soviets could be reached.[38] Only the United States had the financial power to back resistance to Stalin.

The French and Italian Communists were expelled from their governments in May 1947, though not for trying to take them over. The French Communists had voted, on their own initiative, against the economic program of Prime Minister Ramadier, in hopes of sinking his government. When he survived, he expelled them. A year earlier Stalin had rejected an attempted Communist takeover of France, for fear of alarming the Western powers. The Italian Communists had rejected crucial American aid because Stalin wanted reparations and would not offer his own aid. They had supported Tito on Trieste. They had also rejected any attempt to soften the peace terms Stalin offered.

Although they never again entered Cold War governments, the French and Italian Communist parties retained very large numbers of adherents. For example, through the 1950s and the early 1960s, NATO planners expected to receive most of their battlefield supplies through France. Through the 1960s, U.S. military planning documents raised the question of whether strongly Communist French trade unions would or could have disrupted lines of communication through France in the event of war.

Stalin was appalled by the May 1947 expulsions in France and Italy. Popular front politics, which might have worked in the Soviets' favor, had been abandoned without his sanction. He was also upset by Tito's continued shows of independence, which might make the West too suspicious. He created a coordinating body, the Cominform (Communist Information Bureau), to bring the European Communists into line. By the time the Cominform met for the first time in September 1947, Stalin had decided that the popular fronts were unlikely to succeed. He had the new organization's head, his heir apparent, Andrei A. Zhdanov (who would die the next August, apparently of a massive heart attack), condemn the French and Italian parties for "right deviationism" (i.e., for forming popular fronts). Stalinist plans, which were not carried out, called for Tito to be charged with "left deviationism."[39] The West wrongly saw the Cominform as a revival of the prewar Comintern rather than as a means of controlling both the new satellite states and the Communist parties which did not yet control their governments.

By this time the Turkish and Iranian crises in the Near East had run their course. In August 1946 Stalin demanded that Turkey accept Soviet partnership in defense of the Turkish Straits. The U.S. ambassador warned that acceptance would end Turkish independence and remove the last barrier between the Soviets and the Persian Gulf.[40] The battleship *Missouri* was sent to Turkey, ostensibly to return the body of the deceased Turkish ambassador, but actually to announce U.S. support for Turkey. This mission led to the creation of the Sixth Fleet. Two days after the United States formally rejected Stalin's demands on Turkey, the Yugoslavs shot down two American aircraft. Some in Washington feared war. Stalin also rejected the demilitarization of the Greek Dodecanese Islands, which had been held during the war by the Germans and Italians. He seemed to expect to use them as bases when Greece went Communist.

In U.S. eyes, the Turkish crisis was linked with a continuing Soviet attempt to gain control of all or part of Iran. Departing Soviet troops left behind a revolutionary government in Azerbaijan. Control of Iran would give Stalin direct access to the Persian Gulf. The British might find it impossible to defend the oil fields of Iraq. The Soviets would gain access to Saudi Arabia, a developing source of oil. The Soviets also supported a Kurdish independence movement, which attracted adherents not only in Iran but also in neighboring Iraq. The establishment of a Kurdish state would, the U.S. government believed, probably collapse the Iraqi government and possibly make Iraq a Soviet satellite. To encourage the Iranian government, the United States extended military aid in the fall of 1946. The Azerbaijan crisis collapsed after the Iranian army marched into the rebellious province late in November, in the face of Soviet protests.[41]

The other Near Eastern crisis, in Greece, continued. To Americans, it seemed to be part of a larger scheme to gain access to the Mediterranean and the Middle East. In the fall of 1946, the U.S. government decided to extend U.S. military aid to all three threatened Mediterranean/Near Eastern governments: Greece, Iran, and Turkey. The British were already supplying Greece and Turkey. The United States would encourage them to continue. However, because the British economy was still declining—due in part to the load imposed by the Soviets in Germany—on 21 February 1947 the British told the Americans that they would have to withdraw their troops and support from Greece and Turkey.[42] Under his existing policy, President Truman had to replace British aid. On 12 March 1947 he asked Congress for $250 million for Greece and $150 million for Turkey.

Because the Greek civil war seemed a result of Stalin's expansionism, Truman's decision had wide significance. Under the new Truman Doctrine, the United States would assist countries under Soviet attack. Aid to Greece and Turkey prepared the U.S. government for the much wider assistance effort mounted a few years later as the Marshall Plan and as the Mutual Defense Assistance Program (MDAP) under NATO.[43] Maisky had been right: a proletarian revolution would galvanize the West. The U.S. government rejected traditional isolationism in favor of sustained intervention in postwar Europe. The war Stalin had not wanted had brought the United States into Europe.

To the French, the Truman Doctrine meant that the United States was serious about taking on the Soviets. As a consequence, Foreign Minister Bidault took a firm position at the spring 1947 Foreign Ministers Conference in Moscow.[44] In July 1947 the general staff warned Prime Minister Ramadier that neutrality was no longer possible; France must have U.S. military aid. By this time (early 1947) a fuel crisis had forced the French to cooperate with the British and the Americans in the Ruhr, and thus to abandon any hopes of taking over the Saar and the Rhineland. French politics began to polarize: the Communist ministers left the government, but over a social issue rather than due to any U.S. pressure.[45] Major Communist-fomented strikes in November–December 1947 were the last straw for the French government. On 14 November 1947, to signal its resolve to resist Soviet pressure, its police raided Beauregard Camp near Paris, which belonged to the Soviet embassy. In December 1947 the French cabinet formally authorized talks with the British, the Americans, and the Benelux countries to form an alliance.[46]

THE MARSHALL PLAN AND NATO

As the events in France and Italy showed, the nature of Stalin's threat to Western Europe was at least as much political as it was military. Through his control of popular fronts, Stalin hoped to subvert existing governments. He hoped that continuing and deepening economic hardship would demonstrate to the people of Western Europe that capitalism had failed. Early in 1947 it seemed that he might be right; the Western European economies were faltering. On top of an anemic postwar recovery, Europe had a very hard winter in 1946–47. The economic recovery stalled. The situation seemed hopeless. Very large U.S. loans to Britain and to France had done little good.

Secretary of State George C. Marshall thought the situation could be reversed, and his optimism proved decisive. Having been disillusioned at Moscow the previous month, he announced at Harvard on 5 June 1947 that the United States would provide European recovery funds. This time the Europeans would have to accept a degree of national planning (with U.S. review) and membership in a pan-European economic organization, the OEEC (Organization for European Economic Cooperation, later the OECD, Organization for Economic Cooperation and Development). The program, which became popularly known as the Marshall Plan, was formally termed the European Recovery Program (ERP). Representatives of all the European governments, including the Soviet Union, were invited to a conference convened in Paris.[1] The Soviets were not expected to join; the Marshall Plan was a direct attack on Stalin's hopes that economic chaos would bring him victory in Europe.

Until this time, Stalin had toyed with schemes to attract American financing for reconstruction. He continued to seek a postwar loan as late as 1947. One scheme was to attract U.S. money to pay for the settlement of displaced European and Russian Jews in the Crimea (Stalin called it "California in the Crimea").[2] Stalin initially opposed independence for Palestine, partly because he considered it a competitor for his resettlement scheme, but probably also because in 1945–47 he still hoped that favoring Britain would help split that country from the United States. Once

Stalin could no longer hope for U.S. money, he felt free to use anti-Semitism, always popular in Russia, as the basis for his next purge.[3]

Stalin briefly thought that he could get Marshall Plan aid without accepting the program's conditions. A Soviet economist, Evgeniy Varga, told him that the plan was no more than a desperate U.S. attempt to head off that country's inevitable postwar domestic economic crisis. U.S. manufacturers desperately needed European markets in which to unload their goods.[4] While it is true that the Marshall Plan helped end the U.S. recession of 1948, Varga's interpretation of American motives was pure fantasy. When Molotov arrived in Paris, he discovered as much. Soviet intelligence told him that the Americans and the British had secretly agreed that the Marshall Plan would help defend Western Europe against a Soviet threat.[5]

Molotov wired Stalin that joining in the plan would amount to accepting American economic domination. Given Stalin's usual techniques, Molotov was presumably echoing his master's views. To receive aid the Soviet government would have had to reveal how it planned to spend the money. How would Stalin explain the vast military projects his starving country was being forced to support? He said simply that the plan was the beginning of the creation of an American-led coalition. Stalin apparently initially ordered the Eastern Europeans to attend the conference in order to disrupt it; they were then to withdraw after three days, taking as many other delegations with them as they could. He seems to have reversed himself because he was afraid that the delegates might not follow through.[6] The Czechs and the Poles had announced their intention to attend before the reversal was ordered.[7]

In Western Europe, the plan presented Stalin with a dilemma. If it succeeded, Europe's economic crisis would pass and the popular front would lose an important opportunity. Yet, if Western Communist parties opposed the plan, they would lose support, since to most Europeans the plan offered hope. By the time the Cominform met in September 1947, the popular fronts were finished and the Italian Communists were being attacked for their tardiness in rejecting the Marshall Plan. Stalin demanded that the Italians and the French proclaim their loyalty to the Soviet Union and their fierce opposition to the United States.[8] They were told to prepare for armed uprisings. Stalin's order to oppose the Marshall Plan damaged both the French and the Italian Communists in 1948 elections.

Stalin apparently feared that the plan had the potential to roll back his power in Eastern Europe. The Czech and Polish governments wanted to participate (knowing this, Stalin announced that the Poles had rejected the plan before they even voted on it).[9]

It was time to end the fiction of independent Central European governments. Hungary came first. There, the Communists gained control of the political police. Using them, their leader, Matyas Rakosi, destroyed the non-Communist parties bit by bit with what he called "salami tactics." In the fall 1947 election, Rakosi's men stole votes on a large scale. Two Marxist parties triumphed. Hungary was the first Eastern European government to proclaim Communist status, in 1949.

The Hungarian election of 1947 shocked many Europeans: it showed just how far Stalin's men could and would go. Fear of Stalinist expansionism in France helped defeat the French Communist Party in the 1948 election.[10]

Bevin was more interested in security treaties than ever, but in the summer of 1947 he deferred attempts to negotiate them with the Benelux countries because the advent of the Marshall Plan made economic cooperation more urgent.[11] When the Soviets withdrew from the Paris conference in July, Bevin renewed his call for a Western alliance. On 17 December 1947, in the aftermath of yet another failed Foreign Ministers Conference, he told the French foreign minister that it was time to create some sort of federation in Western Europe and that American backing would be needed. That day, he proposed to Marshall that a treaty group (Britain, France, and Benelux) be loosely but formally linked with the United States and Canada. Bevin formally proposed a Western European Union (now including Greece, Scandinavia, and possibly Portugal) in a major speech to the House of Commons on 22 January 1948.[12] He thought that, until a European alliance was in place, the U.S. Senate would reject wider American participation. In Washington there was a real fear that talks on a security treaty would jeopardize passage of the Marshall Plan.

By this time the military situation in Europe seemed so bleak that U.S. and British commanders in Germany feared that Stalin might run them out of the country and off the Continent. In January 1948 Adm. Richard L. Conolly, commander of U.S. naval forces in the Mediterranean and the Near East, arrived in London to discuss Dunkirk-style plans to save occupation forces in the event of a Soviet attack on Germany. By this time efforts to deal with Stalin's political threat seemed to be working. The British Joint Planners feared that disclosure of the talks, which had been directed at a military threat, would demoralize the Europeans and thus hand Stalin victory without war.[13]

Meanwhile, as another consequence of the Marshall Plan, Stalin ordered the Czech government rolled up. Czechoslovakia was unique in that the Communists had won a plurality (38 percent) in a free election in 1946 and thus had a reasonable chance of gaining power legitimately. However, in 1948 it seemed likely that the Communists would do poorly in the next election because they now opposed the Marshall Plan. Czechoslovakia's continuing independence had seemed to demonstrate that Stalin was willing to tolerate friendly though non-Communist regimes in Central Europe. But Stalin found that independence (demonstrated by the Czechs' attempt to attend the Paris meeting) unacceptable. In February 1948, the Communists staged a coup and seized power. No Soviet troops were present, although the local Communist party had formed an armed militia that helped the Communist-dominated police. No one doubted that Stalin was responsible. According to Pavel Sudoplatov, then a senior Soviet operative, Prime Minister Edvard Benes had been compromised by the Soviets during the prewar Czech crisis. When Stalin decided to take over the country, Sudoplatov was sent to demand Benes's help.[14]

To many in the West, the Czech coup demonstrated that Stalin would not brook any opposition, no matter how mild. Western governments were particularly wary because their failure to defend Czechoslovakia in 1938 had given Hitler a green light to continue his aggression. Ironically, the coup, triggered by the Marshall Plan, may have been crucial in convincing Congress to enact the program without crippling amendment.

In 1948 Stalin apparently did show some restraint: he did not seize power in Finland. When the Soviets defeated the Finns in 1944, they formed a Communist-dominated popular front, but despite Stalin's wish to punish the Finns for their resistance in 1939–40, they did not occupy the country. Soviet troops were badly needed elsewhere. In 1945, the Communists won a quarter of the seats in the Finnish parliament. In 1948 they and their allies controlled both the state and mobile police. However, the Social Democratic Party had not been broken up. A. A. Zhdanov, the senior Soviet official on the spot, had helped plan the 1939–40 Winter War against Finland and had helped Sovietize Estonia. He seems to have realized that a Czech-style coup would not have succeeded; to give the Communists power the Soviets would have to invade. Zhdanov personally refused such requests at least twice during the first half of 1948. An invasion would have been too blatant.

On 22 February 1948, Stalin offered Finland a friendship treaty. Similar treaties had just been concluded with Hungary and Romania. The Czech coup was underway. The Finnish president stalled for a month. A delegation of Finns went to Moscow to negotiate the treaty. Stalin suddenly changed course and dramatically weakened the treaty; unlike Hungary and Romania, Finland did not have to enter a military alliance with the Soviet Union. A planned coup had apparently just been abandoned. A snap mobilization of the Finnish army, which greatly outnumbered the two Communist-controlled police forces, may explain what happened. It has been suggested that Stalin knew that the Finnish army could fight, and he may have feared the cost of maintaining order in the face of an unfriendly population.[15]

In the newly Communist countries of Eastern Europe, the new ruling parties prospered. They were the essential means of control. However, the Soviets knew that most of the new Party members were opportunists. They were right: many would defect under stress, as in Poland and Hungary in 1956, or they would simply lie low, as in East Germany in 1953. To exert control over foreign Communist parties, the Soviets created secret police in the image of their own NKVD (later the KGB). These new organizations answered, not only to their own governments, but also to the Soviet secret police.[16] In the event the governing Communist party collapsed, they would preserve Soviet control. The KGB connection would become particularly important in 1989.

By this time Truman could point to many examples of Stalin's aggression. The European Recovery Program and a revived U.S. military were, he said, "two halves of the same walnut."[17] Truman's phrase reflected both his personal judgement and one important implication of the Marshall Plan. Truman linked Marshall Plan funding with national defense, and he had to include both the plan and rearmament in the same balanced budget.[18] The cost of rebuilding Germany and Japan, while not included in the Marshall Plan funds, served much the same purpose of giving their populations a viable alternative to communism. It would soon be obvious that Truman could not afford rearmament and maintain any sort of balanced budget. One or more of the services would have to be cut deeply if anything was to survive. On the other hand, Truman considered Stalin's subversive threat far more urgent than his military threat—as long as Stalin did not have the atomic bomb. Thus to the president it seemed quite sensible to concentrate on economics and politics.

On 25 March 1948 the new secretary of defense, James Forrestal, asked Congress to add a $3 billion supplemental to the $9.8 billion budget for fiscal year 1949. Half of it would increase uniformed personnel, from 1,374,000 to 1,734,000. That was rearmament, done the old-fashioned way. The men would be armed with weapons left over from World War II. Unfortunately, some of those weapons, particularly aircraft, were now obsolete. The other half of the supplemental would buy production versions of the new weapons the services had been developing since the war. Some early production had been paid for out of money left over from World War II, but anything not spent by the end of FY48 (30 June 1948) had to go back to the Treasury.[19] The supplemental paid for the bombers the air force needed to execute its new atomic war plans.[20]

The huge wartime U.S. military production machine had been demobilized. It was estimated in 1947 that it would take at least a year to reconvert U.S. industry.[21] When the United States had mobilized for World War II, companies had pressed for arms contracts because they were still suffering from the Great Depression. They could, moreover, expect increasing orders as the world political situation continued to deteriorate. This time the U.S. economy was healthy. Moreover, it seemed that defense orders would be held to a trickle, because no one in Washington was very willing to balloon the defense budget.

An exception to reconversion was made for the aircraft industry. In 1945, aircraft makers expected lucrative civilian contracts for airliners and even for personal aircraft (far-sighted developers talked of building homes with their own hangars opening onto communal runways). By 1947, however, aircraft companies still depended on military contracts for 80 to 90 percent of their business. As wartime contracts ran out, companies began to starve. The new U.S. Air Force argued that it should be sized to require enough orders to maintain a healthy industry. It would also need equipment to train the million and a half men the air force would need for a five-year war, and personnel to man the bases essential for the mobilized force. The desired 70-group (three squadrons each) force level was set by Lt. Gen. Ira C. Eaker, deputy commander of the army air forces, on 29 August 1945, when he was told that a previous goal, 78-groups, was not affordable.[22] On the other hand, specific companies would not be protected. For example, Curtiss, one of the largest U.S. wartime aircraft manufacturers, was allowed to go out of the aircraft-making business in 1948.

The aircraft industry had to be kept healthy because technology was changing so fast. A jet fighter that was state-of-the-art one year might be obsolete three years later. For example, in 1946 the hottest U.S. Air Force fighter was the new F-84 Thunderjet. Two years later the air force was buying the swept-wing Sabrejet (F-86), which totally outclassed the F-84. Three years after that the air force was buying the F-100 Super Sabre, its first supersonic fighter—which outclassed the F-86.[23] By the late 1940s, there were also prototype medium-range (about 1,500 to 2,500 miles) jet nuclear bombers, such as the U.S. B-47 and the Soviet Tu-16; each was capable of carrying ten-thousand-pound weapons. Their existence would further accelerate new aircraft development, because they were so difficult to intercept. Fighters were generally coached into a tail chase, during which they could hope to stay with a bomber long enough to shoot it down. To win, the fighter needed a speed advantage, perhaps as much as 50 percent. It would take supersonic fighters to deal with the subsonic jet bombers available in the early 1950s. These aircraft would take some years to develop. That is why reconnaissance B-47s were so successful in eluding subsonic Soviet fighters when they flew over the Soviet Union in the 1950s.

Existing subsonic fighters could be coached into position to intercept fast bombers, but they needed much more powerful weapons: first rockets and then guided missiles directed by radar and computer. They became much more complex than their World War II predecessors. Not only did the unit price of aircraft rise dramatically, but also the cost of the associated maintenance organization. By the early 1950s the U.S. Air Force would think in terms of systems in which the radar and computer aboard the fighter were as important as the airframe and engine. At the same time, work began on surface-based antiaircraft missiles to replace the existing guns. German wartime work on antiaircraft missiles provided inspiration. By the mid-1950s the United States, the Soviet Union, and Great Britain were all developing and deploying such weapons. Unlike guns, they were most effective against high-flying aircraft, since the further away the target (within limits), the more time the missile had to adjust its course.

Atomic weapons, too, had transformed the air defense problem. During World War II, no air force could sustain a loss rate of about 5 percent for very long, since it would be wiped out within a few weeks or months. Now a few successful bomber attacks might cripple a country. Even if 95 percent of the bombers were shot down, the rest might destroy a country. For the U.S. government of 1948, matters were not entirely bleak. As long as the Soviets had no atomic bombs, the United States did not have to pay the very high prospective cost of air defense. However, once the Soviets developed bombs of their own, the situation would be transformed. Suddenly the cost merely of defending the United States would rise disastrously, adding a new dimension to the budget.

For Stalin, Germany was still the key target in Europe. Given the presence of Allied armies of occupation, popular front victories throughout the country still offered him the only chance of victory short of war. To win, he had to defeat the Western effort at economic revival. The November–December 1947 Council of Foreign Ministers meeting broke up without making any progress on a German peace treaty. Given Soviet obstructionism, the three Western powers occupying Germany (Britain, France, and the United States) met in London on 23 February 1948, as the Czech crisis worsened. Three days later they invited the Benelux countries to join the conference. It was time to set up a German state; the French decided to join their zone to the bizone to form a "trizone." Stalin concluded that, once the Western Allies merged their zones, they would not allow any Communist-oriented popular front to gain power. He decided to take action.

In March 1948 Gen. Lucius D. Clay, commanding the U.S. occupation force in Germany, wired Lt. Gen. Stephen J. Chamberlin, the director of army intelligence, that he feared imminent Soviet attack.[24] The cable was particularly impressive because Clay had been almost alone among senior administration figures in scoffing at the possibility of war with the Soviets. Clay later said that he had considered war unlikely, and that he had been trying to alarm the U.S. public to a slowly developing crisis. Privately he said that when visiting him in Berlin in February 1948 Chamberlin had asked him for a strong message that could be used to sell Universal Military Training (i.e., preparedness against the Soviet threat) to Congress. Clay apparently thought the cable would be used only in closed session, and was shocked that it was made public.[25] However, Clay's willingness to send a message suggests that he saw both in Prague and in Berlin alarming signs of Soviet aggressiveness. The CIA discounted the immediate threat of war, but it admitted that Stalin might strike any time after the next two months. Soon the Soviets began to interfere with ground traffic between the Western zones of occupation and Berlin.

On 3 April 1948 President Truman signed the Marshall Plan into law. Under the four-year program about $13 billion was spent. Marshall Plan spending and the Korean War mobilization put enough cash back into European economies to get them working again. The key to success was probably that the U.S. government insisted on helping decide how cash was to be spent: as seed money, and often to change the way the European economies worked. For this reason, amounts smaller than the loans made in 1945–46 to Britain and France bought much better results. Overall, European weakness made it possible for the U.S. government to press ideas which otherwise might not have been acceptable. For example, a 30 March 1949 draft NSC report on "Measures Required to Achieve U.S. Objectives With Respect to the USSR" includes, as a primary political/economic objective, encouraging "in all appropriate ways the political and economic unification of Europe."[26] The European Recovery Program was the beginning of the European Union. The habit of cooperation born under ERP made it easier for European governments to work together for common defense.

The new German trizone was offered Marshall Plan aid. Stalin had little access to the trizone, but the three Western Allies occupied zones in Berlin, 110 miles inside the Soviet zone of Germany. The temporary settlement reached in 1945 included a formal agreement to allow the Western powers air access to their zones in Berlin, but no formal agreement had been reached on surface access. Yet the western part of the city lived on supplies moved across Soviet-occupied territory.

In March 1948 the head of Stalin's German party (the SED), Wilhelm Pieck, had warned that the October 1948 elections in Berlin were likely to be disastrous unless "one could remove the Allies from Berlin."[27] Stalin decided to demonstrate to the Germans that the Western powers could not protect them. Ground access to West Berlin was cut off in stages, culminating on 24 June 1948 with suspension of all rail and barge traffic into West Berlin and prohibition of any supply from the Soviet zone. The city's western citizens were offered ration tickets redeemable in its Soviet-occupied eastern zone.

The Allied response, the Berlin airlift, was dramatic. Berlin was supplied entirely by air. The operation was all the more remarkable in that a January 1948 U.S. Army study had concluded that it would be impossible. The initial force of seventy C-47s could lift about 225 tons per day. Using more of its aircraft, the U.S. Air Force offered two thousand tons a day, and the British added another 750. A new airfield, Tegel, was built, largely by the Berliners. Daily tonnage capacity rose to 4,500 and then to 5,600 tons. Rations in Berlin were still quite short, but tolerable.

By instigating the crisis over Berlin, Stalin converted a nascent American-British entente into an effective military alliance. Bevin proposed reviving the wartime combined (U.S.-UK) planning staff to consider both the logistics of the airlift and further military steps (such as moving heavy bombers into Europe). Thus from 12 to 21 April 1948 U.S., British, and Canadian planners met in Washington to prepare an outline emergency war plan based on the earlier U.S. plans. The British would defend both the United Kingdom and the Cairo-Suez area; most U.S. troops would have to be concentrated in the United States, for local defense. The weak U.S. and British ground forces in Western Europe would have to fall back, initially to the Rhine and then, in a fighting retreat, to evacuation ports in France and Italy.[28] The U.S. Navy's carriers would operate mainly in the Mediterranean, to gain air superiority and to attack Soviet forces moving south to the Middle East.

As yet there were no other Allies on the Continent. The British had seen little point in expending their own scarce resources there. Like the Americans, they remembered World War II. As in 1940, at the outset they would probably be chased off the Continent. Their main threat against the Soviets would be, as in 1940–44, air attack, which would be mounted mainly from the United Kingdom itself. Again, as in World War II, securing the sea routes between North America and the Commonwealth would be vital. The Middle East was also clearly vital. All of this made defense of the Continent distinctly secondary, which meant that Britain did not have to maintain a large army in Germany. However, by 1948 there was for many a growing fear that if the Soviets could conquer enough of Western Europe, they could place their air and, in the future, missile forces in position to bombard the United Kingdom. Thus ultimately it was impossible to separate defense of the UK from the defense of Western Europe.[29] To get resources for that purpose, the British began to retreat from their initial preoccupation with defending the Middle East.[30]

During March and April 1948, the British chiefs of staff drew a "stopline," beyond which a Soviet advance would be a direct threat to the United Kingdom.[31] In September they set it at the Rhine, to keep the Soviets out of France and the traditional invasion coast of Europe (the Benelux countries); Britain had gone to war in 1914 to deny the Germans control of this coastline. So much would be needed merely to defend this line that resources could not readily be spared to protect any country outside it. Conversely, it would be important to bring any country inside the "stopline" into an alliance, and to secure American pledges to help protect it. Attractive allies were Iberia (Spain and Portugal), which controlled important naval bases, and western Germany (for its industrial potential). On the other hand, Scandinavia would not be included unless Sweden, which supposedly was well-armed, joined. This choice seems odd in maritime terms. Scandinavia blocked Soviet access to the sea approaches to Britain and to the Atlantic.

The French were vital partners, because potentially only they offered a large enough army to stop Stalin's hordes. The British and the Americans were likely to contribute mainly air and sea power. The French were reluctant suitors, still afraid to offend Stalin unless the Americans signed a treaty with them. On the other hand, they were greatly affected by the Czech coup. When Bevin proposed a collective treaty (France and Benelux with Britain) on 13 February 1948, the French offered only bilateral treaties, all directed against Germany, like the one they had signed at Dunkirk. The Benelux countries demanded a collective treaty.

Bevin had already warned the United States and Canada that time was running out if the Soviet thrust to the Atlantic was to be stopped. There was a real fear in Washington that premature emphasis on a collective treaty might preclude passage of the Marshall Plan or inspire isolationists looking towards the 1948 presidential election. Bevin argued that a treaty was needed to assure Europeans of American support, to stop the spread of a gnawing insecurity. The State Department answered on 3 March 1948 that the United States could not get directly involved until the Europeans themselves united to protect the Continent; a series of bilateral treaties would not do. The French cabinet accepted the collective treaty the same day, specifically to satisfy the United States. Britain and France signed the Brussels Pact (Western Union), a treaty with the Benelux countries, on 17 March 1948.[32] The French knew that they had considerable leverage: in August they almost killed the evolving transatlantic treaty (which became NATO) by demanding that the United States immediately promise troops and military supplies to France as well as an integrated command structure including France.[33]

With U.S. rearmament only beginning, the only immediate leverage the United States had was its powerful air and naval forces. In Berlin, General Clay recommended that the squadron of B-29s in Germany be reinforced to a group (this buildup was completed on 2 July 1948), that a fighter group move up its planned arrival in Germany from August, and that B-29s deploy to Britain and perhaps to France. Two B-29 groups were earmarked for Britain and the necessary invitation was issued on 14 July 1948. Given his intelligence sources in the West, Stalin probably knew that the bombers brought to England were not nuclear-capable.[34]

The new de facto allies had plenty of military-age manpower, but they lacked enough modern weapons. For Truman, badly strapped for money, military assistance was a less costly way of building U.S. security, because the United States did not have to pay for manpower. Then, too, as before 1941, orders for military equipment could help revive the U.S. defense industry. In August 1948 Truman approved an NSC recommendation that he seek legislation to broaden his authority to provide military assistance. The new Mutual Defense Assistance Program (MDAP) included transfers of U.S. equipment (including ships and aircraft) and arms purchases abroad (the offshore program, OSP) to revive local defense industries.

Despite the air of desperation implied by the stopline strategy, the British doubted that war was imminent. Surely Stalin would need a few years to recover from World War II. The British approached this question in several ways. One was to estimate that it would take two five-year plans to rebuild his country to the point at which he could risk war: that put the "year of maximum danger" at about 1956. A "five plus five" rule (no war for five years, the probability of war gradually increasing over the following five years, and then sharply after that) was enunciated at least as early as October 1946 and possibly about a year earlier. It became the formal basis for British planning by August 1947. Another approach was to imagine that Stalin would not move until he had enough atomic bombs (about one hundred) to devastate the United States. That would take about five years after Stalin's first test, the date for which was estimated as 1952. Thus, 1957 became the likely date for war (in December 1945 the British Joint Chiefs estimated that only the U.S. could initiate atomic warfare before 1955). The British recalled how in 1934 they had begun to rearm against Hitler after making the very lucky guess that Germany would probably be ready to fight in five years, so that 1939 would be "the year of maximum danger."[35] In 1949, the "year of maximum danger," 1957, became the target date for planning British military modernization. In March 1950 (that is, after the Soviet nuclear test) the British Joint Intelligence Committee brought forward the date by which war was likely, based on Soviet progress in "atomic research," but national planners could not change their goals to match; 1957 remained the target year for British rearmament.

To the British, the Americans seemed to lack any comparable long-range perspective. Early in 1949, with the crisis in Berlin winding down, the U.S. government apparently accepted the British concept that 1957 would be the "year of maximum danger."[36] But U.S. planners were certainly looking well ahead as they opposed the British stopline idea. To them it was politically disastrous: countries outside the stopline might easily fall to the Communists. Italy was a case in point. The U.S. government valued it for its strategic location; its loss would demoralize Western Europe, the Mediterranean, and the Middle East. In northern Italy, World War II had ended as a civil war, with partisans fighting Fascists still loyal to Mussolini. That war ended because the British and the Americans occupied the country. No one knew whether the Communists would simply dig up their weapons and resume guerilla warfare once Allied troops were withdrawn after a peace treaty was signed. Early in 1948 the CIA estimated that in an armed uprising the Communists could probably gain temporary control of northern Italy. If Yugoslavia and/or a Communist France supplied serious assistance, the Italian government might be unable to regain control without foreign help. Probably it could not beat off a determined Yugoslav attack.[37]

The 1948 Italian election seemed crucial. The CIA backed the Christian Democrats, who won 48.5 percent of the vote. In this context it would have been disastrous to accept the British view that since Italy would not be able to defend itself for a long time, it had best be left outside the stopline. Thus British commanders in Austria and in Trieste were instructed not to help defend Italy in the event of war. The U.S. wanted these troops withdrawn into Italy in the event of war to support Italian resistance. Soon the U.S. government would argue that Italy should be invited to join NATO because otherwise she might accede to Soviet demands early in a war, or might even go Communist.

By January 1949 Stalin was hinting at compromise on Berlin. The blockade was finally lifted on 12 May 1949, just short of eleven months after it had been imposed. The citizens of Berlin—and of the "trizone"—were provided with a vivid demonstration of Western resolve at a crucial time. Within a few months, a West German state would be proclaimed. Many in the United States apparently saw Stalin's retreat as a hopeful indication that the Cold War had passed its peak. In effect the Berlin Blockade was the last of the series of Soviet offensive actions which marked the onset of the Cold War in Western Europe.

We now know that Stalin considered blocking air access to Berlin. He seems to have abandoned this idea when his air force pointed to superior Allied air strength. According to a recent Russian account, "it was no accident" that in July 1948 Stalin's Politburo passed a resolution calling for better national air defense.[38]

Stalin probably saw the blockade as a continuation of his efforts to gain control of Germany through politics and strong-arm tactics. He probably knew that standing U.S. and other Western forces in Europe were weak, and that the United States could not yet destroy the Soviet Union through nuclear attack. On the other hand, any open fight would lead to a drawn-out war against the United States, and thus probably to a World War II–style U.S. mobilization.

In November 1948, the Austrian Communists secretly planned their own coup, assuming, remarkably, that while the Social Democrats might resist them, the occupying Western military forces would not. Stalin soon quashed them. They were showing too much initiative and too little judgement. One crisis at a time—in Berlin—was enough.[39]

Bevin's brainchild, the NATO treaty, was signed in Washington on 4 April 1949. The five core countries (Britain, France, Benelux) were joined at the foundation of NATO by the flanking states vital to sustained defense of sea lanes in the Atlantic (Norway, Denmark, Iceland, and Portugal) and the Mediterranean (Italy). Denmark not only controlled the straits leading out of the Baltic, but she also owned Greenland and the Faeroes. The French initially rejected the inclusion of Italy, as that would extend the alliance to the Mediterranean; but they changed their minds after the United States pressed the issue. For a time, there was talk of a separate Mediterranean pact, since some of the North Atlantic countries were reluctant to become involved in that area. On the other hand, Spain, which the British wanted to include, was not allowed to join.[40] Memories of Franco's close relationship with Hitler from the Spanish civil war onwards were still too painful. As recently as the Potsdam Conference Stalin had tried to enlist his wartime allies in displacing Franco in favor of a "democratic" regime. He apparently badly wanted to avenge his 1936–39 defeat. In 1945 the Spanish Left was still quite powerful, only barely contained by Franco's tough dictatorship. George Kennan emphasized these points in an early 1946 telegram to the U.S. State Department.

Spain offered several benefits. As the early war plans showed, it might be essential for a badly damaged NATO army to be able to retreat into Spain. In addition, Spain (and Spanish Morocco) controlled the mouth of the Mediterranean. There were also less tangible benefits: Spain had strong connections to both the Latin American and, to a lesser extent, the Arab worlds. For example, in 1948 Franco extended a large credit to Perón of Argentina (at that time quite anti-American). If the Soviets took Spain, this connection might well open Latin America to them.

Unfortunately, the United States still had no diplomatic link with Franco, who was even then being treated as a pariah (Congress, for example, had vetoed Spanish participation in the Marshall Plan). The U.S. government asked the Vatican to pressure Franco to moderate the more unacceptable features of his regime, such as the excesses of the Falange (the Spanish Fascists) and of the Spanish church.[41] By 1948 both the British and the Americans were trying to end Franco's isolation and include him in the emerging Western defense system, and gradually to turn public opinion in that direction. President Truman was a major opponent: as a Protestant and a Freemason he was infuriated by Franco's persecution of both groups.[42] To him, Franco was a totalitarian, indistinguishable from Stalin or Hitler. Apparently the outbreak of war in Korea and McCarthy's pressure to get tough against Communists but to stop attacking their enemies wore Truman down, so that a U.S. ambassador took up residence in Madrid in February 1951. Formal military talks soon began, the result being the 1953 bilateral defense treaty granting base rights. Reintegration into Europe (and membership in NATO) would not be possible for many more years.

Ireland, which would have been valuable for bases on the Atlantic, also did not join NATO. As in World War II, no Irish government could ally itself with the British, no matter how sympathetic it might be.

Because the U.S. government could not support its European partners' fight to hold on to their colonies, it tried to limit the NATO treaty, which made an attack on one partner an attack on all, to Europe proper. The French disagreed; in March 1949 they had made inclusion of French North Africa (Algeria was legally part of metropolitan France) a precondition for their acceptance of the NATO treaty.[43] France regarded these territories as a vital link to the French Union and as a possible national redoubt in the event of invasion (the Free French had used North Africa precisely for this purpose after 1942). To the Americans, however, any inclusion of the French colonies in North Africa would invite other countries to demand inclusion of their own colonies (the British in the Middle East were a particular concern). In the end the Americans had to accept some of the French departments in Algeria. In return the United States eventually obtained bases in French North Africa.[44] American willingness to include Algeria probably reflected a shift in U.S. strategy at home, under fiscal pressure, in which air bases in the western Mediterranean were considered more useful (because they were more defensible) than those at Cairo-Suez.

The situation in the Mediterranean shifted again later, when Greece and Turkey were admitted to NATO. Once Italy had been admitted to NATO, both governments considered a separate Mediterranean treaty a second-rate security arrangement. The British wanted a more comprehensive arrangement that would safeguard their interests in the Middle East. They had fought in Greece to safeguard those interests. The U.S. government, however, would not agree to any such arrangement. Once war broke out in Korea, and NATO began its transformation into a military pact, the Greek and Turkish governments fought harder for admission. Without membership in NATO, all they had were vague guarantees from the British and the Americans. The British argued that the whole point of NATO was that it extended the concept of an Atlantic community. Moreover, accession would provide the Turks access to NATO plans—which would reveal just how little help they could expect in wartime.[45] In May 1951, however, the U.S. State Department informed the British and the French that the United States would support the Turks and the Greeks for NATO membership. In effect this was the price the British had to pay for the desired extension of U.S. military commitments to the eastern Mediterranean—which was suddenly practicable because of U.S. rearmament due to the Korean War. The French were less enthusiastic, possibly because they were much less interested in the eastern Mediterranean. Accession was, however, approved at a September 1951 NATO conference. Both countries were formally admitted in February 1952.

None of this solved a major British problem. Although the fleet base at Malta was included as a NATO base in the Mediterranean, the very important colony of

Cyprus was not. Nor was the vital informal empire in the Middle East. The British complained bitterly that, to the Americans, the Mediterranean was important only as a flank for forces in Europe (the Sixth Fleet could make flanking attacks on advancing Soviet forces) and as a valuable area for basing heavy bombers. After 1952 Cyprus became the main British land and air base in the Mediterranean, but Malta was still the naval base.[46] Within a few years the British would be embroiled with both new NATO neighbors. Terrorists on Cyprus were demanding union with Greece (*enosis*), and the Turks demanded protection for ethnic Turks on the island. Nor, as it turned out, could the French rely on NATO in Algeria, despite that area's inclusion as NATO territory. From about 1955 on, then, unresolved Mediterranean issues would threaten to tear NATO apart. In 1949–52 that still seemed far in the future.

For the time being, Stalin's dual subversive-military threat to the West had been contained. The U.S. government needed a formal long-range strategy for the future. It was already strongly influenced by Kennan's ideas of containment. On 24 November 1949 President Truman formally adopted containment as U.S. strategy by approving a National Security Council paper, NSC 20/4, which had been requested to form the basis for the FY51 budget (in fact it was completed too late for that purpose). Kennan's State Department policy planning staff wrote the first draft of the paper.

Containment was not merely an attractive strategy; it was inescapable.[47] The United States could not afford to build up the sort of armed force needed to win World War III. Even if it could build up that sort of force by, say, 1957, technology was moving so quickly that it would soon be obsolete. Stalin could afford to wait out the U.S. force; as Kennan had pointed out, he had no fixed plan to follow. The United States could not afford to maintain a modern force capable of meeting Stalin whenever he chose to act. On the other hand, the United States could affordably build and maintain enough forces to make a war risky for Stalin. It could also provide enough to its new allies to encourage them to resist. To back up its standing forces, the U.S. could build up the ability to mobilize in an emergency to fight a big war, when and if that broke out.[48] If Stalin could be held off for five or ten years, "by that time something [might] have happened to reduce the intensity of the Communist threat."[49]

Containment initially applied to Europe, the perimeter consisting of the NATO and associated countries (such as Greece and Turkey, which were not yet members in 1949). By the fall of 1950 Greece and Turkey had been invited to coordinate their own plans with those of the new alliance. They joined formally in 1952. West Germany joined in 1955, when she began to rearm.[50]

The Truman administration did not count entirely on passive containment. By 1948 it had secretly decided to help whatever resistance movements existed or could be raised in Eastern Europe and in the Soviet Union, albeit not to the extent of risking outright war. The British government agreed.[51] This was much the strategy Winston Churchill had followed after being forced from the Continent in 1940. The Allies tried at least four areas: the Baltic States, Poland, the Ukraine, and Albania. It was known that the Balts resented forcible incorporation into the Soviet Union. The remnants of the Polish Home Army were fighting the Communist government. After the Germans were driven out, the Ukrainians began a rebellion, presumably because of their unhappy memories of Stalin's vicious collectivization and massacre in the 1930s. It may have continued as late as 1956. Albania was probably a test case for satellite-state dissatisfaction. After the split with Tito, it had no land border with any Soviet satellite and hence was safe from direct armed intervention. In September 1949 Bevin and Acheson agreed to try to bring it down.[52]

Having penetrated the British secret service, the Soviets were well aware of Allied plans; they seized virtually all the émigrés who were delivered into the target areas. Remarkably, a string of failures in the Baltic (using ex-German torpedo boats to deliver agents) failed to alert the British to the possibility that they had been compromised.[53] Later, a British historian would point out that there was apparently no critical mass of potential resisters in Central Europe; the war, with its terrible suffering, was too recent a memory.[54]

The administration also set up radio stations which offered, among other things, a message of resistance: the Voice of America and the European-based Radio Free Europe.[55] The Soviets began jamming these stations in 1948.[56]

Although resistance movements did not form, expectations grew. They were to be dashed in Hungary in 1956.

Ironically, in 1952 the Republicans would claim that the Democrats' containment policy had been far too passive, that they would work to roll back the Soviet conquest of Central Europe. The Democrats could not reply; the attempts to overthrow Soviet power were secret.

Initially, the combination of containment and support for internal resistance seemed to have a fair chance of winning within a relatively short time. In 1948, Air Marshal Tedder, the RAF chief of staff, toasted the beginnings of the resistance efforts with the hope that the war might be won within five years.[57] Stalin's terror held together the Soviet empire while he was alive. However, Tedder had a point. Within five years, the empire was apparently in such poor condition that Stalin's heir, Beria, was willing to entertain radical reforms. Had Stalin lived a few years longer, presumably the problems Beria perceived would have become far less tractable. The system really might have begun to crash. On the other hand, Tedder and his colleagues did not realize that, absent Stalin, the Soviet system could gain considerable time by internal reform. Ultimately, however, as Kennan had foreseen, the system generated internal pressures it could not sustain.

Containment was paradoxical. In long-range terms it was an offensive strategy. However, any direct military attack on the Soviets might bind citizens to their government, as when Hitler invaded in 1941. That the West had to hold back was bad for U.S. morale. The Soviets seemed to be able to extract concessions from the United States because they could take greater risks. The United States had just won the greatest war in history. Why was it impossible simply to defeat the Soviets? Why was it necessary to avoid fighting them?

Popular discontent with the evolving containment policy played into the Republicans' hands. Containment looked like inactivity in the face of Stalin's aggression. As they approached the 1948 election, the Republicans charged that the United States was losing the Cold War because the Truman administration was too "pink" to want to win. The administration was unable to trumpet many of its own triumphs, such as the CIA's successful support of the Christian Democrats in the 1948 Italian election. In 1952 the Republicans would castigate the Democrats for "twenty years of treason," including the concessions at Yalta and the loss of China. There was even talk that in 1945 the U.S. Army could (and should) have driven east to liberate Eastern Europe as soon as the Germans collapsed. To compound the administration's problems, there were real cases of subversion. As in Britain, Stalin's recruiters had enjoyed some signal successes in the 1930s. The administration badly wanted to avoid any publicity connecting it to Soviet spies.

It did not help that some prominent members of the Roosevelt administration, such as Alger Hiss, were accused of having been either Communist sympathizers or secret Communist agents. How much had they contributed to that administration's sympathetic view of Stalin? To the disastrous U.S. policy in China? Hiss's case was particularly corrosive. Richard Nixon made his name largely by attacking him. Many liberals believed that his case had been fabricated. Belief in Hiss's innocence became a litmus test for post-McCarthy U.S. liberalism (conversely, belief in his guilt became a litmus test for conservatives). Not until 1996 did released decoded Soviet spy cables from the 1940s finally prove that Hiss had been a spy.[58]

Some of the Soviet cables had already been decoded in 1949, but they were never shown to Truman. Although the Soviets had stopped using the codes involved (later it would emerge that they had been informed about the decoding project), the U.S. and British governments were very reluctant to admit what they knew. The messages used code names, not the actual names of spies, so investigators had to deduce whom the spies were, from details that only gradually emerged as the codes were slowly broken. Thus the Soviets could never be sure of just how badly their operation had been compromised. Unfortunately, out of ignorance, Truman tended to support prominent men like Hiss when they seemed to be under fire from irresponsible accusers. It might have been much better (if more painful) had the Truman administration let the truth come out in 1948–50. Since that did not happen, the administration's many Republican enemies in Congress were handed an issue which became more deadly as U.S. armies entered combat against other Communists in Korea.

Americans were not entirely sure whether the enemy was Stalin himself, with his Nazi-style political system, or something more diffuse: Communist ideology.

Before World War II public anti-Communism had been largely the province of the far right, which tended to lump communism with left-liberal politics. Now it seemed that the Right's arguments had some merit after all. Stalin's use of broad fronts in Europe, and the emergence of their Communist cores, seemed to show that Communist subversion was at least as potent a force as Stalin's Soviet Army.

The Communists were secretive; how could anyone know just how powerful they really were? How much of the liberal establishment concealed Communists or their treasonable sympathizers? Republican politicians naturally mounted a crusade against the Truman administration, conducted mainly through the House Un-American Activities Committee (HUAC). HUAC actually predated World War II, having been established originally to investigate Nazi sympathizers. By 1938 it had begun to concentrate on Communists, its research director, J. B. Mathews, recently having defected from the Party. It attacked popular fronts—and the New Deal agencies, many of which were clearly left-wing. At times its charges became so wild that it discredited itself. In 1947, it was revitalized, partly after J. Edgar Hoover, director of the FBI, appeared before the committee to support its policy of attacking subversives (i.e., domestic Communists) by publicizing their connections with the Party. In doing this he was indirectly attacking the Truman administration, which had failed to act on his own recommendations, including accusations that high administration members were Soviet spies (Hoover also displayed an undue appetite for quashing the civil liberties of Party members, on the ground that they were subversives).[59] The net effect of HUAC's policy was to expose supposed Communists, thus destroying their careers—since, given the growing Cold War mood, it was difficult to imagine that they were not traitors. Moreover, given the Communists' own claims that sympathizers fed their power, HUAC could attack not only formal (card-carrying) Party members, but also "Communist sympathizers" and "fellow travelers," sinister categories which could not possibly be defined.

Some of HUAC's earliest investigations focused on Hollywood. Clearly the committee sought the greatest possible publicity; but it could also argue that in Hollywood Communists had an unusually good opportunity to influence American opinion. The great question was whether secret Communists could further Soviet policies effectively simply because their allegiances were undisclosed.[60] In each case, witnesses were asked to "name names" of friends who were Party members. The leading Hollywood producers announced that they would blacklist all known Communists, presumably as a defense against potential attacks.[61] Later, when anti-Communism was no longer fashionable, those who had been blacklisted would sometimes be described as victims of an American purge—which, ludicrously, was compared to Stalin's purge, in which people actually died in their millions, not merely having been denied open employment. Those who "named names" were often excoriated. They often were ex-Communists disgusted with the degree of control the Party (and through it, Moscow) tried to impose on its members; some argued that although they had named their friends, in fact true Communists could not have real friendships. The tensions generated by blacklisting and "naming names" continue to haunt the U.S. film industry.

The next step clearly was to arrest Communists as Soviet agents. Under the Smith Act, which prohibited organizing or belonging to an organization plotting the overthrow of the government, the leaders of the American Communist Party were indicted on 29 June 1948. Earl Browder, who had led the Party before the war (and who had actually helped run its espionage activities) must have been glad that he had been purged, since he was not placed on trial. Apparently the prosecution arose out of J. Edgar Hoover's perception (which was hardly unique) that there was a good chance of war between the United States and the Soviet Union. In the event of a crisis, he wanted a legal basis to round up Communists, who might otherwise act as Soviet agents. He saw the 1948 prosecution as a useful test case. Perhaps the biggest surprise of the trial was that the Party had been so deeply penetrated for so long by the FBI; one mid-level official, Herbert Philbrick, had been working for the FBI since 1940. The jury convicted the Communist leadership, and the Supreme Court upheld the conviction; Hoover had the precedent he needed. Ultimately, however, there had to be some question as to whether outlawing a political party, no matter how obnoxious, fit a U.S. policy of fighting Stalin's totalitarian regime in the name of freedom. This issue split HUAC's brand of countersubversives from classic liberals who saw the Cold War as a fight between freedom and slavery, in which the very idea of freedom would ultimately destroy Stalin's slave system.

Sen. Joe McCarthy of Wisconsin saw in anti-Communism a heaven-sent opportunity. His success was almost accidental. He had been elected in 1946 on a Republican platform charging the Truman administration with having been too soft on the Soviets. He tacked a reference to "205 Communists" in the State Department onto a February 1950 speech to the Republican Women's Club of Wheeling, West Virginia—hardly a prime speaking opportunity—and was surprised that it attracted enormous attention. The Communists in question of course were never named and the number changed repeatedly. However, McCarthy's charges seemed to explain why the United States had just "lost" China and the outbreak of the Korean War in June 1950 seemed to make subversives in government a more urgent issue.

There is no evidence that McCarthy took his crusade terribly seriously; it was a lever to gain fame. He would accuse almost anyone of being a Communist, merely for the boost it would give his career. Although he conducted only a few hearings, he greatly increased the effect of HUAC and other "Red-hunters." McCarthy was terrifying simply because his charges were so outrageous. He began simply by using numbers to dress up quite conventional attacks on Communists, who were portrayed in much contemporary right-wing literature as a vast subterranean conspiracy. Many people simply could not believe that a senator could be so irresponsible, so they took the charges seriously. Since none of them could be proven, McCarthy had to keep making more and more outrageous charges, simply to keep going. Moreover, McCarthy attracted important supporters, such as J. Edgar Hoover and Richard Nixon, and then the Hearst newspaper chain. By the spring of 1951, McCarthy had become a partisan issue, and the Democrats happily disproved many of his charges. However, he had no shame; he hit back with an even more outrageous charge, in June 1951, that Gen. George C. Marshall, the World War II army chief of staff, probably the most admired man in the administration, who was then secretary of defense, was a Communist. The charge was particularly explosive because Marshall's forces were fighting for their lives in Korea. Although the Republicans now knew that McCarthy was totally irresponsible, they backed him because otherwise they would have had to support the Truman administration, and they hoped to win the 1952 election on a platform blaming the administration for having failed to fight the Communists effectively enough. President Truman detested McCarthy but could not destroy him, for fear that his administration could too easily be painted as pro-Communist. He and others tried to dismiss McCarthyism as a manifestation of a classic paranoid streak in American politics. This psychological explanation had an unfortunate consequence, in that it became too easy to dismiss the reality, that there really were some Communist subversives.[62]

Given McCarthy's irresponsibility, it was inevitable that he and his followers would seek to brand liberals, who certainly had nothing to do with Communists, with the Communist label. One unintended consequence was that the anti-Communist liberals in the CIA-funded Congress for Cultural Freedom could, in effect, prove that they were not simply American tools by attacking McCarthy. Indeed, opposition to McCarthy came to be a test of good faith within the organization.

In 1952 the Republicans won not only the presidency but also control of the Senate. McCarthy gained power, becoming chairman of the Investigations Committee of the Committee on Government Operations—which he used to conduct his own equivalent of HUAC hearings. He could now attack all branches of the government; he could do much more than simply give speeches. With a much greater capacity for damage, McCarthy was now a major problem for the new president, Dwight Eisenhower. Eisenhower's instinct was not to attack McCarthy directly, because that would only play into his fantasies about subversion and the administration's protection of Communists. Instead, he waited, knowing that McCarthy would soon overreach himself. People, even those on the Right, were beginning to admit that McCarthy was difficult to support. McCarthy finally eventually overreached himself, accusing the U.S. Army of harboring Communists, and was crushed in 1954.[63] However, the apparatus of loyalty oaths, investigators, and blacklists created out of McCarthy's crusade survived for many years.

The ultimate effect of McCarthy and his ilk was to discredit the idea that the Communists were an aggressive danger, at least within the United States; they looked much more like the pathetic (or heroic) victims of a powerful government running amok. In fact there really was a Communist subversive threat within the

United States, but it was small-scale; the worst of it was probably penetration by small numbers of people within the government who actually were working as Soviet agents. They were subject to normal security measures; there was no need for an elaborate mechanism of loyalty oaths and investigations to root them out. Too many sincere left-wingers or liberals were being attacked as targets of opportunity; conservatives too often used anti-Communism to enforce their own views. Moreover, by 1954, when McCarthy fell, some of the heat had gone out of the Cold War. Stalin, the Communist Hitler, was dead. With the end of the Korean War, Communists were no longer fighting Americans. In the wake of McCarthyism, anti-Communism itself was linked in many American minds to a sort of wild reaction to liberal ideas; the epithet "Communist" was often used to attack anyone trying to change the existing social order. That applied, for example, to the growing civil rights movement. Because irresponsible charges of Communism had had such terrible consequences, by the end of the 1950s it had become almost impossible to label anyone as a Communist. One consequence was that pro-Soviet propaganda often could not be discredited. Those who persisted in attacks on domestic Communists and their sympathizers were increasingly labeled as extremists; the Communists and their friends were often lumped with others on the Left as activists.

All of this was much more than domestic politics. The gradual change in perceptions eventually undermined the moral basis for the Cold War. If domestic Communists were not a real threat, it became difficult to believe that the foreign variety was any more menacing. For that matter, if many American Communists could be portrayed as virtuous unfortunates victimized by McCarthy, then it was more difficult to believe that foreign Communists were particularly evil. That mattered because, traditionally, Americans have sought a moral basis for their wars; they have been uncomfortable with the simple but brutal logic of national interest, which so often governs Great-Power behavior. In this decade, for example, Saddam Hussein was demonized (as a new Hitler) to justify American participation in the Gulf War. Clearly Saddam is a bloodthirsty tyrant—but so are several of our Middle Eastern allies. Americans were uncomfortable with the other justification for war: allowing Saddam to retain control of Kuwait would eventually give him control over the oil of the gulf, and thus the ability (which he would surely use) to blackmail the West. Resistance to blackmail would probably have entailed an economic disaster for the West, including the United States.

Stalin's thrust into Europe did threaten American national existence, but it was at least as important that many Americans perceived him—and, by extension, Communism—as an unalloyed evil, worth staving off. Without direct experience of life in Communist countries, Americans could not easily credit the reality that Communism in power ran an obscene slave system and, moreover, that Communism, not Stalin, was the problem. Although few said as much, many began to make a moral equation between Communism and the Western system.

That did not end the Cold War, but it left Americans with the feeling that the war was mainly about national security, rather than about a larger moral issue. The rhetoric of slavery versus freedom did survive, at least into the 1960s, but the effect of McCarthyism was to make it seem quite hollow, little more than a cloak for much more conventional Great-Power thinking. When the war in Vietnam began to go bad, that feeling of hollowness strengthened dramatically. Opponents of the war pointed to anti-Communism as the bankrupt policy that was killing young Americans for vague imperial purposes. Fewer and fewer Americans understood that in fact the Soviets and their associates were still mortal enemies, answering to a fundamentally aggressive ideology, because with the demise of active anti-Communism the sense of an American ideology (which was hardly merely anti-Communism) had largely disappeared.

Through the 1940s, Stalin had to deal with two potential rivals, each of whom had fought his own revolution: Tito in Yugoslavia and Mao in China. After the war, Tito's revolutionary enthusiasm, and particularly his support for the civil war in Greece, helped sabotage Stalin's program to win quietly in Western Europe. It cannot have helped that Tito was seen (and greeted) throughout Eastern Europe as a major hero due to his wartime exploits. After the war he began to form a Balkan federation of newly Communist states—without Stalin's permission. Tito was pushing much too hard, and he was far too popular. Moreover, he kept talking about the Yugoslav road to Socialism, which might inspire others in Central Europe to follow their own paths. He had to go.[1]

In February 1948 Stalin approved a Bulgarian-Yugoslav union, which Albania might eventually join. The Bulgarians were Stalin's men. Tito feared that the union was merely a popular front on a grand scale; he would be squeezed out. He got his own politburo to reject the union. Stalin publicly attacked Tito and on 28 June 1948 he expelled the Yugoslavs from the Cominform.[2] Stalin told intimates that he would destroy Tito with "his little finger."[3]

During the summit conference on the abortive Balkan Union in February 1948 Stalin told the Yugoslavs to end the Greek war. At about the same time he told the unwitting Greek Communists that they were helping the world revolution by keeping the Americans out of China at a crucial stage. Once Stalin had broken with Tito, he apparently feared that the Greek Communists might side with the Yugoslavs. To prevent that, he told them that he supported their struggle. In the fall of 1948, for example, the Soviets and the satellite governments even formed a commission to coordinate aid to the Greeks' Democratic Army. The commission was a sham. In April 1949, Stalin told the Greeks to abandon the war.[4] For his part, Tito had lost interest. Having lost their main sources of supply in Yugoslavia, the surviving rebels fled to Albania. The Greek government won.

Beginning in the fall of 1948, the Soviets built the Bulgarian, Hungarian, and Romanian armed forces up to well beyond the levels allowed under their Soviet-sponsored peace treaties. The balance of power tipped. Before the break, Yugo-slavia had been the greatest military power in the Balkans. By 1950 the Yugoslav military, particularly its air arm, was deteriorating badly because its supply of spare parts had been cut off. Stalin's war plan, completed in 1950, called for an initial assault limited to satellite armies (including the Albanians), with Soviet troops involved only in the follow-up. The plan was tested in an elaborate January 1951 war game in Budapest. U.S. intelligence estimated that a Soviet invasion of Yugoslavia would have been successful.[5] it now appears that Stalin did not order a war because the U.S. intervention in Korea convinced him that the Americans might also intervene in Yugoslavia. Even so, as late as 1955 Molotov argued against a Soviet withdrawal from Austria on the ground that the forces there would be use-ful in the event of war against Yugoslavia.

Denied the option of invasion, Stalin ordered Tito assassinated.[6] This plan died only with Stalin himself.

From a Western perspective, a Yugoslavia hostile to the Soviets was quite val-uable. It would threaten the flank of any Soviet attack against Greece or Turkey.[7] Tito was therefore given Western aid in 1951. He refused any direct association with NATO. U.S. analysts considered Trieste the barrier. An entente (culminating in 1954 in the Balkan Pact—also known as the Bled Agreement—when the Trieste problem was resolved) developed between Greece, Turkey, and Yugoslavia.[8] By that time a new Soviet ruler, Nikita Khrushchev, was courting Tito, and any hope of incorporating Yugoslavia into NATO was dead.

In China, Mao Tse-tung began much as Tito had, fighting a civil war on his own initiative. As he had with Tito, Stalin actively tried to restrain Mao, partly to gain prizes for the Soviet Union, and partly to avoid inciting the West during his strug-gle for control of Germany. China was probably the first Soviet attempt to gain power via a popular front. In the 1920s the country was split between a variety of warlords and a Nationalist (Kuomintang, or KMT) government led by Sun Yat-sen, who had overseen the 1911 rebellion that overthrew the Manchu dynasty in favor of a republic. The Soviets supported both Sun's successor, Chiang Kai-shek, and the Chinese Communist Party they had created in 1921. Under Soviet pressure, Chiang admitted the Communists to the KMT. They tried to take it over in 1926–27. In September 1927, Chiang killed numerous Communists in their main base, Shanghai. Stalin ordered an abortive Communist uprising, which caused Chiang to break relations and eject Soviet advisors. Probably as a result of Chiang's victory, the Sixth Congress of the Comintern (1928) denounced "bourgeois nationalist" forces in colonial countries (such as China) as reactionary and untrustworthy.[9] Moscow's experts tried and failed to rebuild the Communist Party in several Chinese cities during 1927–31.

Mao then built his own Party in rural guerilla bases in south China, to which survivors of the urban debacles fled. Mao's rural Communists outnumbered Sta-lin's urban men. He rejected their arguments favoring conventional over guerilla tactics. The rural-urban distinction mattered to Stalin because the Soviet Communist Party had triumphed in the cities. A Communist Party based in the countryside was a dangerous heresy, no matter how warmly its leader praised the genius enthroned in Moscow. By 1945, after a series of disasters and triumphs, Mao and his followers controlled a substantial part of northern China. In 1945 they governed 95.5 million people rather than the four million of 1937. The Communist army grew from about 100,000 to 900,000 (plus a 2.2-million-man armed militia).

At the end of the war, Stalin's army occupied Manchuria, an industrialized northern part of China which had been under Japanese occupation since 1931 and under Japanese domination since the Russo-Japanese War of 1904–5. In 1945 the region was virtually untouched by war. Its industries were four times as large as those of the rest of China, representing 70 percent of all Japanese-controlled industry in China.[10] The Soviets considered Manchurian industry legitimate war booty, and in September 1945 they began dismantling it. They seized $3 billion in gold as well as half a billion yuan (Chinese currency). Much food was confiscated (Manchuria ran an agricultural surplus). The Soviet troops worked very quickly, because they had tentatively agreed to begin withdrawing from the region as early as 3 December. U.S. objections that Manchurian industry and its output ought to go to China as war reparations were dismissed.

Manchuria was adjacent to the main Communist Chinese base areas in north China. Stalin might have seen an opportunity to support Mao in the conquest of China. He seems, however, to have preferred to deal with a weak Nationalist government from which territory could be extracted (he had tried to take over the Chinese province of Sinkiang in 1944). In return for major concessions, such as recognition of the independence of Outer Mongolia (at the time, Stalin's only satellite) and joint operation of the Manchurian railway and of the naval base at Port Arthur, Stalin recognized Chiang as the sole legitimate ruler of China. A Sino-Soviet treaty to this effect was signed in August 1945 in Moscow.

Despite the treaty, the Soviets in Manchuria helped Mao. They armed Mao's Manchurian army with matériel captured from the Japanese during the Soviet assault. They also hindered the Nationalists from occupying Mukden (Shenyang), the region's main city.

U.S. troops entered China to take over from the occupying Japanese, and then to hand over power to the recognized Chinese government headed by Chiang Kai-shek. To the U.S. government, a strong China would help guarantee peace in Asia. The civil war erupting in the wake of the Japanese defeat had to be quelled. The U.S. government sent Gen. George C. Marshall, the wartime army chief of staff, to China to broker a coalition between Chiang and Mao, partly in the belief that Mao was an agrarian reformer amenable to compromise rather than a hard-line Communist. At that time Mao was leading a popular front. He had once been interested in U.S. aid, in 1944. He envisaged a postwar neutrality between the two great powers. To make himself more attractive to the Americans, he had even softened his ideology. Chou En-lai told Marshall that "we will certainly lean to one side [i.e., towards Stalin]. However, the extent depends on your policy towards us." Marshall arranged a truce in January 1946. The Communists agreed that the KMT government could move its forces north to reestablish Chinese sovereignty in Manchuria; the Soviets were persuaded to stay long enough to maintain order until they arrived. Chiang's U.S. advisor, Gen. Alfred C. Wedemeyer, advised him to consolidate his position in the south before sending much of his army north, into Communist country. Chiang refused, probably for fear that Mao might use any delay to set up a new Communist state in the north.[11]

When the Soviets evacuated Manchuria, fighting broke out there. Chiang had about three times as many troops as the Communists, and his army was far better equipped. Initially a KMT offensive was successful. However, in June 1946, just as Chiang's troops were about to occupy the important Manchurian city of Harbin, the U.S. government pressed for a new cease-fire. Chiang told General Marshall, the U.S. representative, that he was on the point of winning the war. His army had just inflicted twenty thousand casualties on the Communists at the cost of seventy-six hundred to itself—but it had not destroyed the Communist army, and Marshall warned that the Chinese were overextended.

Given a respite, Communist troops regrouped and fought back. The Republican charge that the Truman administration "lost" China is probably traceable to the imposed cease-fire at Harbin.[12] Talks failed, and full-scale civil war broke out in January 1947.

By that time, many in the U.S. government doubted that Chiang could win, whatever assistance he was given. In June 1947, the U.S. ambassador reported that the Nationalists were likely to lose drastically in northeast China. The JCS believed that Stalin was behind Mao; the only difference between China and the Near East was the absence of a strong government, like Turkey's, around which effective resistance could be built. It seemed to the JCS that the Soviets planned to integrate Manchuria into the Siberian economy, thus denying its considerable industry and resources to China. Surely the new Truman Doctrine should be extended to the Far East.

For his part, Stalin did not want Mao to destroy Chiang altogether. He told Mao to reach an accommodation in which he would control north China while Chiang retained the south. He pressed for this "two China" arrangement as early as the fall of 1945 and continued to do so through 1947. One rationale was that a Communist offensive into south China would invite U.S. intervention. Where the Japanese had failed the United States and Chiang might succeed in uniting all of China under hostile control. Stalin was already finding it difficult to control the European Communists, and he knew that Mao was far more independent than they were. He may well have feared the creation of a powerful independent Communist state on his border. Perhaps he feared Chinese reactions to his wartime attempt to annex Sinkiang; he may also have feared a later Chinese attempt to take back the many regions czarist Russia had seized and that the Soviet Union had retained.[13]

Mao's troops were able to conduct major offensives both in Manchuria and in southern China late in 1947. A large Nationalist army was encircled in Manchuria; Chiang's order to hold fast precluded evacuation. When the army surrendered on 19 October 1948, Chiang lost four hundred thousand troops, and the Communists gained virtual parity with the Nationalist army. Not long afterwards, most of the remaining Nationalist army was destroyed in a battle in central China. Beijing (Peking) fell on 31 January 1949.

When Mao's army reached the Yangtse in late March 1949, Stalin suggested that it halt, to stop the war.[14] He considered his warning to Mao not to cross the river so important that it was delivered by the first very senior Soviet official to visit Mao, Mikoyan. Stalin had previously told Djilas that he was afraid the United States might intervene in the Chinese war and drag in the Soviet Union. He repeatedly tried to plant fear of U.S. intervention in Mao's mind, warning that the Soviet Union would be unable to intervene if that happened.

Mao refused to halt. Chiang tried to gain U.S. help by claiming that the civil war in China was the first stage in a third world war already underway, but the U.S. government refused his plea to help stabilize a line of defense on the Yangtse. Wedemeyer reported that the Yangtse, patrolled by Chiang's navy, would certainly stop the Communists. In fact defense was compromised by profound divisions on the Nationalist side, and by disastrous KMT losses in north and central China (135 divisions, 1.1 million men in all). The Nationalists tried to stall a Communist offensive by negotiating. Their hope was that an intensifying Cold War might bring active U.S. support. Chiang, who was not formally head of state but who still controlled the government, apparently thought the mainland would be lost before the Americans decided to intervene, and therefore emphasized strengthening Formosa (Taiwan). Nationalist hopes that the navy would block the river declined when the cruiser *Chungking* (formerly HMS *Aurora*) defected to the Communists on 2 March. The first Communist crossing, on 20–21 April, was simplified by the defection of the Changyin fortress covering the southern side of the mouth of the river. There was also a key defection upstream.[15]

Mao proclaimed his republic on 1 October 1949. Victory had come with stunning speed; in 1947 Mao had expected the war to last five years or more. The last isolated resistance on the mainland ended in the middle of 1950.[16]

To Mao, this was not yet quite victory. His KMT enemy still occupied Formosa and several offshore islands, including Matsu and Quemoy of later fame.[17] While the United States certainly would not have helped Mao eject Chiang from Formosa, there was little interest in actively supporting him there, and none in helping him return to the mainland. On 19 October 1949, the CIA predicted that without full-scale U.S. intervention Formosa would probably fall before the end of 1950. Chiang's supporters in Congress added $75 million for "the general area of China" to the 1949 military assistance program. Secretary of State Acheson warned that Chiang's government was morally bankrupt, and therefore incapable of using the money effectively. For the moment, the United States would continue to recognize

Chiang's government and would try to deny Formosa to Mao by diplomatic and economic means. Chiang's American partisans tried but failed to reverse this decision.[18]

Britain and most of the European countries soon recognized Mao's government, the British because they wanted to preserve their valuable coastal trade. Although conservatives in Congress quickly denounced British recognition, many in the State Department wanted the United States to follow suit.[19] The French refused to recognize the People's Republic after it recognized Ho Chi Minh's Vietnamese government on 18 January 1950. Mao deliberately pressed Stalin to recognize Ho so as to split him from France, which he considered a potentially hostile Western power.[20] Stalin was placed in the uncomfortable position of having to choose between France, still potentially neutral in the Cold War (and hostile to German rearmament), and Mao. He took until 31 January 1950 to recognize Ho's government, and the communiqué was quite lukewarm. In February 1950 Stalin avoided signing a Chinese-type mutual security treaty with Ho. After the end of the French Indochina War, the French continued to recognize Taiwan as the legitimate Chinese government in order to maintain friendly relations with the United States, partly as leverage to gain support in Algeria. Free of Algeria and much less interested in the American alliance, de Gaulle recognized the People's Republic in 1964.

Chiang lost for several reasons. Americans concentrated on his overcentralized, weak, unstable, and corrupt government. Necessary reforms would have been too damaging to his supporters. Corruption worsened as rapid inflation destroyed the value of officials' salaries. There is some evidence that Communists in Chiang's wartime government helped destroy its economy.

Chiang's overextension into north China and Manchuria had been deadly. Leadership was poor, due partly to the loss of over one hundred thousand officers during the Sino-Japanese War. More than two-thirds of those lost were graduates of the Central Military Academy. Only 27 percent of regimental or divisional commanders had had formal military training; below that level, tactical ability was not expected (officers were simply expected to show a good example). Poorly led troops were reluctant to engage in hand-to-hand combat, were terrified of operating at night, were road-bound, and had poor fire discipline. They tended to stay behind city walls, waiting for relief that never came; to save face they tended not to retreat when they should have done so. On the other hand, units fought willingly; it was their leaders who surrendered or defected.[21]

Before and during World War II, Chiang had been presented as the heroic defender of China against the Japanese invader. Now it seemed that he was being denied the matériel he needed to fight his battle. The reality, that Chiang lacked popular support and was unable to defeat the Communists whatever he was given, seemed little more than Communist propaganda. Americans found Mao's victory shocking. It seemed to give Stalin even more of the one resource the West so clearly lacked, manpower to be expended in war. It also seemed to demonstrate that the

West was clearly on the losing side of the Cold War. The Republicans charged that Communists in the U.S. government had insured Mao's success; the State Department China specialists had spread defeatism. Some of them were among the first victims of McCarthyism.

After Stalin's split with Tito, the U.S. government sought a similar split between Mao and Stalin. Stalin seems to have been aware of this shift in American policy.[22] In 1956 Mao told the Soviet ambassador that in 1949 there had been "many rumors" to the effect that Stalin feared he would be another Tito.[23.] In 1957 Mao said that during the Moscow talks Stalin said that the nationalism of the Chinese (i.e., their unwillingness to follow his wishes) would have dangerous consequences.[24]

In fact Stalin had little to fear, as most of Mao's colleagues on the Chinese Central Committee favored Moscow. Moreover, during the civil war, probably stung by the Americans' unwillingness to favor him, Mao had constructed a theory of U.S. hostility and fear of U.S. intervention.[25] For example, in August 1949 he construed several U.S. actions as evidence of U.S. intervention: the maintenance of U.S. naval bases in Tsingtao, Shanghai, and Taiwan; the stationing of U.S. troops in various cities; minor clashes between U.S. troops and Chinese Communist troops; the use of American pilots (under contract) to ferry KMT troops; and the bombing of the cruiser *Chunking* by the U.S. Air Force (actually, by the KMT air force).

For Mao, China was the center of the world. He believed that the Americans could not possibly abide a Communist victory there. China was the most important pro-Soviet state in an "intermediate zone" in Europe and Asia that the United States had to subjugate before attacking the Soviet Union. The Truman Doctrine, the Marshall Plan, the rehabilitation of Germany and Japan, the American occupation of Korea, U.S. assistance to the KMT, and the stationing of U.S. Marines on the Chinese coast were all operations in the "intermediate zone." A year later the war in Korea would fit neatly into this picture.

Stalin knew that he could neither eliminate Mao nor invade China. His experience with Tito had had such unpleasant consequences that he could not afford a similar breach with Mao. For his part, Mao badly needed aid. In breaking with Tito, Stalin had shown that he would not tolerate anything short of complete submission. Mao seems to have believed he had become more valuable to Stalin after the conclusion of the NATO treaty in April 1949, which increased Stalin's obsession with buffer zones along his border, for example, in Sinkiang and in Manchuria.

Some of Mao's non-Communist supporters saw the Americans as a viable alternative to Stalin, despite Mao's pessimism. Because it was richer than the Soviet Union, the West could be much more helpful in rebuilding China. It might be best to adopt neutrality and maintain close relations with both sides, rather than joining in the Cold War. One of Mao's long-time friends, Zhang Zhizhong, pointed out that Chiang's ties with the United States had been an underlying cause for the defeat of the KMT.

Rejecting his friend's advice, Mao decided to take his chances with Stalin.[26] He went to Moscow in mid-December 1949 to meet and embrace Stalin, who greeted him coldly. Mao wanted to replace the "unequal" treaty Stalin had negotiated in 1945 with Chiang, and to obtain Soviet aid for reconstruction. But the two leaders did not get along well, not least because of a deep cultural difference. Stalin was uncomfortable with Mao's elliptical and poetic language and with his classical Chinese historical allusions.[27] Even so, in February 1950 the two exchanged conciliatory words and signed a thirty-year friendship treaty. Against a request for $3 billion in aid, Mao got a $300 million loan, on which interest had to be paid. China was initially barred from using the loan for military purposes, but in 1950 Stalin secretly agreed that half of it could be used to buy Soviet naval equipment to seize Taiwan.[28]

The secret clauses of the friendship treaty were quite embarrassing for Mao. His revolution had been fought, in part, to eliminate foreign control over parts of China. Now he had to cede to Stalin what the Western powers had given up. A secret protocol excluded nationals of any third country from Sinkiang and Manchuria. Stalin particularly wanted to keep Americans out. In 1957 Mao told Gromyko that "only imperialists" would have imposed such conditions; and in 1958 he called the northeast and Sinkiang Soviet "colonies." Stalin had wanted a broader agreement limiting nationals of third countries elsewhere in China. The Chinese must have been particularly incensed because they were forced into a preliminary discussion of this agreement the day after they had loyally denounced Secretary of State Acheson's claim that the Soviets were trying to annex exactly the territory the agreement covered. Another secret protocol required China to sell a specific quota of strategic materials to the Soviet Union and gave the Soviets a veto on sales to third countries. A particularly humiliating protocol gave the Soviets in China the right to try Soviet nationals in their own courts, just as the hated Westerners had done before the revolution.[29]

Mao was anxious to secure Stalin's protection against possible American attack—the possibility of which Stalin discounted. He did not want to be maneuvered into war against the United States; thus he rejected out of hand Mao's request for direct Soviet help in attacking Taiwan.[30] Earlier Stalin had used Mao's fears to justify continued occupation of Port Arthur; Soviet troops there would deter American or KMT attack. Mao had wanted immediate withdrawal; he rejected foreign occupation of any kind. In this, and in Mao's attempts to eject the Soviets from Dairen and from the Manchurian railroad, Stalin saw signs of just the sort of Chinese nationalism he feared.[31] Under the agreement, Stalin was able to occupy the old czarist (pre-1905) naval bases at Port Arthur (Lushun) and Dairen (Luda) until the Americans withdrew from Japan under a peace treaty, but (only in the case of Port Arthur) not later than 1952.[32] From a Chinese point of view, this was a considerable improvement on the thirty-year leases in the 1945 treaty. On the other hand, Mao had to repeat Chiang's recognition of the independence of

Outer Mongolia, a Soviet satellite (but territory traditionally part of China). For the moment, Stalin was even able to extract a secret agreement that Soviet troops could move to Port Arthur across Manchuria at any time, without warning the Chinese. Mao also agreed to set up a joint espionage system among Chinese nationals living overseas.

In a bizarre incident during the negotiations, one of the Chinese delegates, politburo member Gao Gang, asked Stalin to station more troops at Port Arthur and to use Tsingtao as a naval base. He apparently even offered Stalin Manchuria as the seventeenth Soviet republic. Most of the Soviet Politburo applauded, but Stalin refused; he seems to have considered the proposal a provocation. Gao was apparently hoping to unseat Mao by showing the Communist leader's slavish support for Stalin. The head of the Chinese delegation, Liu Shaoqui, denounced Gao as a traitor.[33] Mao now saw himself as the leader of a pan-Asian rebellion against the Western colonial powers. Stalin tacitly conceded this role to him.

On 30 December 1949, President Truman approved containment for Asia, but in modified form. Given Tito's recent defection from Stalin's camp, Mao was seen more as a successful nationalist (hence as part of a wider trend sweeping Asia) than as the overseer of a Soviet satellite. The United States distanced itself from Chiang. The JCS advised that "the strategic importance of Formosa [Taiwan] does not justify overt military action." At a 5 January 1950 press conference Truman announced that "the United States government will not provide military aid or advice to Chinese forces on Formosa."[34] Truman's statement could be read as an invitation to seize Taiwan and then to normalize relations.

Stalin apparently valued continued KMT occupation of Taiwan as the main barrier to a rapprochement between Mao and the United States. With the disappearance of KMT forces on Taiwan, Mao would no longer need Soviet forces to protect him. There is indirect evidence that Stalin sought a continued struggle over Taiwan as an essential way of maintaining Mao's friendship and subservience. Mao was provided with combat aircraft—but not with the amphibious vessels needed for an invasion.[35] In another attempt to preclude rapprochement, Stalin pressed Mao to seize Hong Kong shortly *after* the British recognized his regime. The United States could not have accepted such an attack.

Stalin's other act supporting Mao, a walkout in the UN, seems also to have been intended to preclude rapprochement.[36] The Soviet representatives protested continued seating of the Nationalists. At the time some Western journalists deduced that the Soviets wanted the walkout to fail, to keep the Nationalists in the UN and so to prevent U.S. recognition of Mao's People's Republic.

Under the new containment policy, the United States sought to create a defensive line running from the Aleutians to Japan south through the Ryukyus to the Philippines, based on a Pacific pact modeled on NATO and built around Japan, rather than Germany, as its powerhouse. As in the case of Germany, national sovereignty must be restored before any alliance could be formed. The pact was closely associated with the projected Japanese peace treaty—which would end the U.S. occupation. The State Department wanted the treaty to overcome rising Japanese resentment of the occupation. The U.S. Joint Chiefs were not so sure. As long as Japan was occupied, it was safe from Communism. Keeping Japan under U.S. control would help deter Stalin from attacking anywhere. Early in January 1950, Stalin ordered the Japanese Communists to resist the peace treaty, which he saw as a prelude to rearmament.[37]

In April 1950, the State Department made John Foster Dulles its advisor on Far East policy, partly in hopes of defusing Republican attacks on administration policy.[38] Visiting Australia, New Zealand, and the Philippines, he discovered that all three governments saw the United States as a vital protector against a resurgence of *Japanese* militarism, not Chinese or Soviet aggression. The situation was not too different from the one in Europe in about 1946. All three governments rejected any partnership with Japan. The new Sino-Soviet threat was not particularly convincing because quite obviously it could not project its power over the sea.

The British feared an attempt to exclude them from the area. If the planned pact were limited to the offshore islands running south to the Philippines, the Communists might feel free to invade Hong Kong; Malaya was already under guerilla attack. However, if the pact included the British colonies, it could be criticized as little more than disguised colonialism. The pact was abandoned in favor of a series of mutual defense treaties, initially between the United States, Australia, and New Zealand, "ANZUS," signed at San Francisco on 1 September 1951. A parallel mutual defense treaty was signed between the United States and Japan immediately after conclusion of the peace treaty, on 8 September 1951. An existing agreement between the United States and the Philippines was expanded into an additional treaty.

The pact failed because the Japanese and German situations were quite different. After 1945 Germany was still a vital part of the overall European economy, and the other Europeans themselves tried hard to integrate her with her neighbors, particularly France and the Low Countries. Thus political and economic ties predated any military ones, and there was some chance at reconciliation. To achieve that, the Germans were forced to confront the unpleasantness of their own history, which was much more widely known in the United States. Perhaps most importantly, West Germany badly needed her Western defenders. Every West German understood that the country's vitals were nearly under the guns of powerful Soviet and satellite armed forces in East Germany.

In the Far East, Mao's triumph and U.S. containment cut Japan off from her major natural trading partner (and wartime victim), China. The postwar Japanese industrial recovery was based on trade with the United States and the West, not with the Far Eastern countries she had tried to colonize. Nor was there an obvious strategic connection between the countries around the Asian rim, which in the 1950s were uniformly poor and undeveloped. U.S. occupation policy under General MacArthur failed to force the Japanese to confront their recent history. Japanese society was ill prepared to accept blame for wartime aggression; in Japan the Pacific war was almost invariably portrayed as an act of *Western* aggression.

Finally, wide straits separate Japan from Asia. She did have to fear aerial attack, but self-defense was a far more remote problem than in West Germany. One consequence was that, unlike the Germans, the Japanese did not perceive a vital need for outside defensive forces. The U.S. government needed Japanese bases, it seemed, more than the Japanese needed the U.S. forces occupying them. In such a climate the Japanese saw little need to explain their past. Perhaps more importantly, their defense did not depend at all on assistance by their recent victims (except for the United States, which did not demand any sort of moral reckoning).

9 RISING NATIONALISM

Both in the Middle East and in Asia, the Western powers confronted a new force: nationalism. It was a potential wedge between the Americans and the Europeans, given American insistence that decolonization was inevitable—hence American support for nationalists who hated their imperial masters. During the war President Roosevelt often said that personally he hoped to see the British Empire dissolved (to which Churchill replied that he had not become the king's prime minister to do so).[1] As long ago as the 1920s Lenin and then Stalin had hoped that colonial nationalists would turn to them for support. They had taught themselves that capitalism could not survive without colonial markets, so any attack on the European empires would ultimately bring down the home countries. In 1946 a more realistic view would have been that the home countries expected income from their largely undamaged empires to support reconstruction; they also were relying on supplies of relatively inexpensive raw materials. In the case of France, the mere existence of an empire seemed to make up for the ignominy of defeat in 1940.

For the time being, the Communist threat to empire was limited, because Stalin was far more interested in Europe. Thus he tried to discourage the Communist/nationalist leader in Indochina, Ho Chi Minh, because he feared tainting the Communists in France, a much greater prize.[2] Once he had decided to abandon the popular fronts in Europe, he was too eager to encourage his minions to strike, against both local nationalists and the colonists. In Indonesia, for example, a failed Czech-style Communist coup (August 1948) caused many years of resentment against the Party.[3] Stalin was also obsessed with Party loyalty. Thus in 1948 he chose the Indians rather than the Chinese to lead the revolution in Asia, even though they were by far the weaker Party.[4]

However, the empires still had a direct Cold War significance. In the wake of World War II, the debilitated colonial powers, Britain, France, and the Netherlands, all had to spend scarce treasure to face down threats to imperial rule. Given U.S. attitudes towards empire, none of these powers could expect U.S. support.

The fighting drained military resources that were already far too thin to deal with Stalin's Red Army.

Access to several of the colonies was crucial to Western survival in the Cold War, in a parallel with the situation in 1940–41. At that time, as in 1948–49, the U.S. focus was on Europe. To fight a modern war, the United States needed raw materials produced in Southeast Asia, in European colonies such as Malaya and Burma. A Japanese threat to seize that area, and thus to deny access to the United States, might have precluded U.S. participation in the European war. Thus the needs of a European war, like the later needs of a Cold War, made very remote Southeast Asia important.[5] The significance of the oil regions of the Middle East was of course obvious.

Colonial rule depended on the prestige of the mother country. For example, the British ruled an informal empire in the Middle East through local kings, pashas, and sheiks. To the extent these leaders could identify with a greater external power, they could claim legitimacy. Conversely, the mother country's disasters weakened them. Thus British defeats in North Africa in 1942 encouraged nationalist Egyptian officers to rise against the local British client, King Farouk. They hoped that a German victory would bring Egypt full independence—which it nominally had achieved under a 1936 mutual defense treaty. Much the same stress could be seen in formal colonies. In East Asia, the Japanese had conquered under the banner of "Asia for the Asians."[6] They withdrew in 1945 leaving both collaborators who believed the slogan and Western-sponsored anti-Japanese guerillas who felt that they deserved to rule the countries they had helped liberate.

The British, moreover, said that they were fighting freedom's battle. Many of their colonial subjects could not understand why that goal did not apply to them. Partly under American pressure, and partly to secure needed wartime help and resist Japanese blandishments, the Britain had promised India postwar independence. Prewar, the Indian army had maintained order all the way from the Persian Gulf to Malaya. Once that army was gone, much more expensive British troops would have to be substituted.[7] When Burma, an important prewar source of oil and rubber, demanded independence, the British had no choice but to provide it. However, Malaya, including Singapore, remained British. So did Hong Kong.

After the British lost India, they retained a very valuable informal empire in the Middle East, much of it secured with the fall of the Ottoman Turkish Empire in 1918. They had installed kings of the Hashemite family in both Iraq and Jordan. Under League of Nations mandates, the British promised to guide their new possessions to independence. When they granted independence to Iraq in 1930, they extracted a mutual defense treaty providing British base rights there. Egypt, a British protectorate, signed a similar treaty in 1936; Jordan followed in 1946. The British retained their influence mainly through the royal governments they had installed. They believed that by withdrawing from domestic control they had assuaged nationalist feelings and thus that the royal governments could accept

British guidance in foreign affairs (as symbolized by the treaties). The royal Arab governments did, however, have to bow to strong popular feelings—at the least, to protect them against the nationalists' charges that they had sold out to the British.

The other mandated territory, Palestine, was a problem. The British had never been able to install a government that could take over upon independence. Growing numbers of Jews, who claimed the country as their Biblical heritage, competed with Arabs. After World War II the situation sharpened because survivors of the Holocaust in Europe demanded a homeland (which the British had already promised during World War I). For their part, the British feared infuriating the Arabs, who controlled oil. Yet they could not long afford to continue to garrison the increasingly rebellious country. They turned to the UN, successor to the League of Nations, which had provided the original mandate.

In 1947 the UN decided to partition Palestine between Jews and Arabs. Stalin supported the new Jewish State of Israel, on the reasonable theory that its very existence would undermine the British position in the Middle East. With Stalin's backing, the Czechs supplied vital weapons, including aircraft. Stalin may also have hoped, wrongly, that the Jewish Socialists who had founded the state would eventually shift in his direction. Not surprisingly, Arab nationalists throughout the Middle East demanded that the Jews be ejected. None of the British-sponsored kings could have resisted this call. The Arab armies attacking the Jews included those of the three British allies, Egypt, Iraq, and Jordan. The only one even partly successful was the British-led Arab Legion (Jordan). In the end, the Jews won, forming the new State of Israel.

The 1948–49 war ended in a series of truces on the new state's three borders. In 1950 the two interested imperial powers, the British and the French, agreed with the United States to limit arms sales to the combatants. They also guaranteed the 1948–49 settlement. Moreover, under standing mutual defense treaties, the British in theory would have to defend Egypt, Iraq, and Jordan in the event Israel attacked them. However, the British were under no obligation to help the Arabs attack Israel in some future war.

By this time British and American strategists were intensely interested in defending the entire Middle East against a possible Soviet attack. Egypt was the key military position. Yet the Egyptians were uninterested in any Soviet threat. Their recent humiliation at Israeli hands mattered far more. Nationalists in all the Arab countries blamed the defeat on the incompetence of the Arab potentates through whom the British ruled. By failing to secure the victory for the Arab kings, the British had not lived up to their end of the protectorate arrangements. Worse, the postwar British Labour government was quite willing to drop the old rulers in favor of the new middle-class nationalists. It found that when traditional rulers like Egypt's King Farouk were needed, the respect and dignity taken away a few years earlier could not be restored.

Unfortunately Egypt, which the British had occupied since 1882, was probably also the most hostile part of the informal empire. Not surprisingly, in November 1950, in his annual speech from the throne, King Farouk denounced the 1936 treaty under which Britain maintained a large force in the Suez Canal Zone (as well as the 1899 treaty under which the Sudan, the source of the Nile, was controlled partly by the British). To limit Egyptian ambitions to dominate the entire Nile valley, the British had supported Sudanese self-determination in the face of Egyptian royal demands. Farouk was echoing the long-held views of his premier.[8] In response the Iraqi premier, Nuri as-Said, denounced his own country's mutual defense treaty.

The British badly needed Egypt, but the Egyptians hated them. In 1951 they devised what they thought was a way out: they could form a multinational Middle East Command (MEC), under a British officer. If the Egyptians joined MEC, they would cede them the Suez base—which would then become a MEC base. British troops would remain, but they would no longer be an army of occupation. For their part, the Egyptians pressed an alternative to MEC in the Arab League's Arab Collective Security Pact (ASCP), which had been created in April 1950. Ostensibly directed against Israel, it was actually intended to cement Egyptian influence against Iraq—a theme that was far more important to the Egyptians than regional defense against a distant Soviet threat.[9]

The British also had to reckon with the American presence in Saudi Arabia. The Hashemites favored by Britain had been driven from the country. In contrast to the British in Iraq and Iran, a U.S. oil company, Aramco, developed the vast fields discovered in Saudi Arabia, mainly after World War II. The Saudis also provided the United States with base rights, at Dhahran—which was seen, in the late 1940s, as an alternative to Cairo-Suez. To the British, the U.S. presence in Saudi Arabia was a threat because Aramco might offer the Saudis a better deal than that the British were providing in their own dependencies.

In 1951 Aramco agreed to a fifty-fifty profit-sharing agreement with the Saudi government because American oil companies in Venezuela had already made a similar agreement.[10] The British-owned Anglo-Iranian Oil Company was paying the Iranian government only 25–30 percent of its profits. Iranians resentful of the arrangement ignored the fact that they were receiving a percentage of the company's worldwide profits, not merely those accruing from its Iranian operations.[11] Anglo-Iranian was a valuable prize: in 1951 Anglo-Iranian was the third-largest crude oil producer in the world, producing 40 percent of Middle Eastern oil. Its huge refinery at Abadan, the largest in the world, accounted for most of the aviation fuel in the Eastern Hemisphere.[12] The Iranian economy had declined so badly that the U.S. State Department feared a Communist takeover.[13] In the Iranian parliament, Dr. Mohammed Mossadegh's National Front demanded nationalization of the oil industry. Mossadegh became premier in March, when his predecessor was assassinated; on 2 May he nationalized the oil company.

The British feared that if they dealt with Mossadegh they would be encouraging nationalists who wanted to sweep them from their informal but vital Middle Eastern empire. That would ruin Britain. It would be better to let the Soviets get Iran's oil than to deal with Mossadegh.[14] It was unlikely that he would be replaced by the Communists. Their American allies saw Mossadegh as a bulwark against Communism, who had to be a nationalist to survive. Moreover, he typified the new breed of nationalists who would soon rule the Middle East, and who had to be befriended.[15] The U.S. government pressed the British to grant now what it would later have to concede. It refused to support an attack on Mossadegh.

As Mossadegh pressed them, the British reinforced garrisons and sent war ships to Abadan. However, privately Prime Minister Attlee rejected military intervention.[16] Under a 1921 treaty, Mossadegh could have requested Soviet assistance in the event of a British invasion. When Mossadegh seized the Abadan refinery and ejected the British technicians there, the British did nothing. Unable to operate the refinery themselves, the Iranians lost their chief source of income—and the West lost a vital source of oil.

Mossadegh inspired the Egyptians. The British feared that they would abrogate the 1936 mutual defense treaty and seize the base. Both it and the canal were vital Cold War assets. Surely the U.S. government would help defend them. From an American point of view, however, the obvious military value of such assets (as affirmed by the Joint Chiefs) conflicted with a basic policy of befriending the emerging post-colonial Third World.[17] British departure was inevitable. Overt U.S. support of the hated British would not help in a postcolonial era. The U.S. government hedged. Without careful preparation in the UN, it could not openly support any British defensive action.

In October 1951 the Egyptian parliament voted unanimously to abrogate not only the British treaty but also the much older Sudan agreement. Egyptian nationalists wanted Farouk to crown himself king of Egypt and the Sudan. Prime Minister Nahhas Pasha rejected partnership in MEC.[18] By this time Attlee's government had been replaced by Winston Churchill's Conservatives. Churchill felt that Attlee's irresolution on Iran had emboldened the Egyptians. He told his foreign minister, Anthony Eden, that if the Egyptians kicked the British out, those in Britain who had placed the Conservatives in power would be furious that Britain had abandoned a key to the survival of the British Empire.[19] In Suez, the British were trustees of vital free world assets.

As Egyptian guerilla incidents multiplied, the U.S. government suggested that Egyptians' sovereignty over the Sudan be recognized in return for agreement on MEC. Instead, on 19 January 1952 Egyptian auxiliary police attacked the British in Ismailia, and sixty-four of them were killed before they could be turned back. Sheppard's Hotel, a symbol of British power, was burned down amidst severe riots in Cairo.

U.S. logic dictated against providing the British with military support.[20] With the Korean War buildup under way, it was no longer likely that the Soviets would try to seize the Middle East by force. Thus a U.S. policy paper approved by President Truman on 29 April 1952 (NSC 129/4) emphasized the danger that a combination of instability, anti-Western nationalism, and the Arab-Israeli conflict would bring Soviet-oriented regimes into power. The United States might have to support local nationalists against the British.

In July 1952, Egyptian nationalists (antimonarchist officers allied with Islamic nationalists of the Moslem Brotherhood) overthrew King Farouk. Their leader, General Naguib, gave up on the Sudan (he was half-Sudanese) and secretly offered to join a proposed revised version of MEC, MEDO (the Middle East Defence Organization), if granted sufficient assistance, particularly arms.[21] However, like his predecessors, he was determined to eject the British from Suez.

This was an attractive offer, and the necessary U.S. funds were earmarked. Naguib seemed a key member of a new generation of Arab rulers, the successors to the pashas and kings of the colonial era. The British had a veto over any U.S. arms supplies because they, the Americans, and the French were all part of NEACC, the Near East Coordinating Committee set up in Washington in 1950 to regulate Western arms sales to the Middle East. The British balked; they feared that arms sales would encourage the Egyptians to stall on the vital Canal Zone negotiations. When the Eisenhower administration finally managed to make an offer, the Egyptians were disappointed by its small scale and by the fact that it did not include jets; and the U.S. made the deal conditional on the Egyptians' joining MEDO and resolving the Suez Canal and Sudanese issues. The Egyptians found the situation particularly embarrassing because for months their press had been reporting the imminent arrival of U.S. weapons.

Egypt no longer seemed nearly as secure as it had when early war plans included bombers flying from Cairo-Suez. The U.S. government became interested in a Middle Eastern defense based on the "northern tier," Turkey and Iran. Both countries considered the Soviets serious enemies; both had been involved directly in the Cold War since 1946. Neither was directly involved in the Arab-Israeli confrontation (neither was ethnically Arab). The British would connect the "northern tier" to Iraq, their regional ally, which linked the northern states to the Middle East proper. Ultimately the "northern tier" became the Baghdad Pact.[22]

Iran was now more vital than before in Cold War strategy; but the chaos Mossadegh had unleashed might provide the Communist Tudeh Party with an opening. A satellite Iran would be a great step towards controlling the whole Middle East— and its oil. To the U.S. Joint Chiefs, it was more important that Iran be oriented towards the United States than that British oil interests be supported.[23] Direct financial assistance might avert economic collapse. The British argued that the Iranian economy was, in effect, too primitive to collapse, even without oil revenue.[24] Despite a U.S. offer of economic aid in return for a compromise solution, on 22 October 1952 Mossadegh cut diplomatic relations with the British. The U.S. government then offered to advance up to $100 million against future oil revenue and to have U.S. oil companies buy and market Iranian oil.[25]

Then U.S. policy changed: President Eisenhower entered office early in 1953. Conditions in Iran were still worsening. Churchill's Conservative government was pressing for action. Eisenhower's secretary of state, John Foster Dulles, seems to have considered his relationship with the British more important than had his counterpart under Truman. Kermit Roosevelt, who was responsible for the CIA's part in the coup, withheld word of the plan from the Democrats, who were considered too sympathetic to Mossadegh. Allen Dulles of the CIA—John Foster's brother—wanted any coup delayed until the Republicans and the new secretary of state got into office[26] Eisenhower abandoned the loan offer, as in effect it would have been directed against the British. In June 1953, Mossadegh asked the Soviets for a $20 million loan, which they reportedly approved.[27] On 8 August the Soviets announced they were beginning financial aid negotiations. The new Soviet ambassador to Iran was the same man who had been in Prague during the 1948 coup; Eisenhower concluded that Iran was headed towards Communist control. He ordered a coup set in motion. The CIA and the British overthrew Mossadegh.[28]

In financial terms, the British were forced to accept a defeat worse than the one Mossadegh had threatened. Under an August 1954 agreement, they kept only 40 percent of Iranian oil production (the United States got 40 percent, the Dutch and the French 20 percent). In addition, they had to give the Iranians 50 percent of the profits, so Britain's share of those profits was only 20 percent of the total.[29] The Iranian parliament was dissolved in favor of direct rule by the shah.

For the moment, the Iranian coup was probably most significant because it convinced the CIA that coups were a practical way to solve foreign policy problems. The Egyptian crisis continued unabated. As in Iran, American and British views were opposed. The British wanted to retain their base, to tame the local nationalists. To the Americans, the Egyptian nationalists were the men of the future. The problem was how to gain their confidence without sacrificing too much of America's special relationship with the British.

While all this was happening in the Middle East, in the Far East, the British fought a hot war to retain control of Malaya. The British colony had a very large indigenous Chinese population. As Mao began to win his civil war in 1948, some of them began their own uprising against the British. Between 1948 and 1952 the British managed to isolate the guerillas from the Chinese population. Crucially, there was no border with China across which guerillas could flee or get arms. That held down the size and firepower of the guerilla force. The main British weapons were excellent relations with the Chinese citizens and, consequently, very good intelligence. After 1952, the British went on the offensive, hunting down guerillas using small patrols (usually ten soldiers and two trackers). The guerilla leadership fled the country in 1954. The British success in Malaya was often contrasted with the contemporary French failure in nearby Indochina (Vietnam).

The French had worse problems. Although antagonistic to all the European empires, President Roosevelt had been particularly opposed to the French—some said, because he personally detested Charles de Gaulle, the Free French leader.[30] for example, until March 1945 he personally barred the French from the U.S.-dominated Pacific theater, with the intent of keeping them from reclaiming Indochina after the war. With the defeat of France in 1940, the French Empire had, moreover, become a battleground between the Vichy regime, which collaborated with the Germans, and the Free French, who opposed them.

The Free French found it difficult to admit that their passion for freedom was limited to France itself. In 1946 they transformed the French Empire into the French Union, in theory a voluntary association of territories, all of whose inhabitants would eventually become French citizens. Even before the war, the French had claimed that their empire was gradually being integrated into metropolitan France, and the French parliament included colonial members. But those members were elected by French settlers; few of the colonial subjects were citizens. Even so, the ideal of full participation by French colonies persisted. Algeria, the most important colony, had been considered part of metropolitan France since 1848, and in Indochina the richest province, Cochin China, also sent representatives to Paris. The reality was much less impressive; colonists of French descent still ruled. Moreover, the French had no intention of allowing the voluntary association to dissolve.

Yet serious problems were already evident. When they had helped to conquer French North Africa in 1942–43, U.S. troops had been welcomed by local nationalists.[31] The U.S. government needed French support much too badly to set North Africa free, but its calls for freedom and equality echoed. In the Middle East, the British occupied the two French mandates, Syria and Lebanon, in 1941. In 1946 they and the Americans forced the French to grant both the independence promised prewar.[32] De Gaulle read this pressure as part of an Anglo-Saxon assault on the grandeur of France. That did not make him any friendlier during negotiations on the future of Europe.

In the Far East, the French managed to hold on to at least nominal authority in Indochina through most of the war, but in March 1945 the Japanese took over. They declared Vietnam, one of the three countries of Indochina (the others were Laos and Cambodia) independent, under Emperor Bao Dai. In 1925 he had ascended the throne of Annam, one of the three Associated States of Vietnam, as a French figurehead. To broaden his base of support, Bao Dai tried several times to recruit Ngo Dinh Diem, a well-known Vietnamese nationalist connected to the conservative Catholics, as prime minister. Diem refused on the ground that Bao Dai's independence was a farce. He became the post-1954 president of South Vietnam.[33]

There were already many nationalist groups in Vietnam. One of them, formed in 1941, was the Viet Minh League, led by a Communist, Ho Chi Minh. By 1945 he had elbowed aside (or co-opted) the other nationalist groups, some of which were tied to the Chinese Nationalists across the northern border.

With the French out of the way, in May the Viet Minh organized a "liberated" zone in Tonkin as the nucleus of a Vietnamese republic. Japanese efforts to destroy the Viet Minh failed, partly because by the summer of 1945 they needed all their forces to control the cities and key villages and lines of communication. In July 1945 the Viet Minh contacted the French and asked for independence in a minimum of five and a maximum of ten years. The French governor would act as president until independence. The French refused, as Ho had expected. When the war ended, as in other Asian colonies, the Japanese turned over many weapons and important positions to Asian nationalists. Thus on 19 August 1945 the Viet Minh entered Hanoi, capital of the northern province of Tonkin. Soon they controlled the whole province. Bao Dai asked the Viet Minh to form a Vietnamese government; they asked him to abdicate. He did so on 25 August.[34] On 2 September 1945 Ho proclaimed the Democratic Republic of Vietnam. It controlled Tonkin and neighboring Annam. However, in the third Associated State, Cochin China in the south, the Viet Minh found themselves competing with many other organizations, including Trotskyites who argued against cooperation with any foreign power, including the Allies.

As an anti-Japanese guerilla, Ho had sought U.S. support. He received some, and he thought he could gain U.S. recognition. Until early 1945, President Roosevelt had favored some sort of trusteeship status, probably under Chinese control, for postwar Indochina.[35] This idea had been part of Roosevelt's larger expectations for a postcolonial world in which a strong China would help preclude the return of the European empires to Asia. As Roosevelt sickened dramatically early in 1945, he apparently found it much more difficult to maintain this sort of plan in the face of realities such as the weakness of China and the antagonism of the Soviets. He decided to allow the French to retake the colony, if they could. The Truman administration continued this policy.[36]

Southern Vietnam was part of the British-run Southeast Asian theater of war, so the British took the Japanese surrender there. The Viet Minh cooperated with the British. When the Trotskyites and other revolutionary parties resisted, the British destroyed them. That left Ho as the sole legitimate nationalist in the south. However, Cochin China had always been the center of French rule, the only part of the country that had sent representatives to the French parliament. Cochin China had enormous economic value. Looking to the fate of their empire, the British decided to help the French retake their colony beginning in October 1945. Within a few months the French had largely taken over.[37]

Northern Vietnam (Tonkin) was a Chinese responsibility.[38] Vietnam was a traditional Chinese sphere of influence, torn from the Chinese Empire by the French in 1884–85. The Chinese thus had little interest in welcoming back the French. Moreover, during the war they had supported Ho as a way of attacking the Japanese in Vietnam. They charged a high price for the restoration of French power: France had to give up all her concessions and extraterritorial rights in China. Chinese living in Vietnam received special privileges, and there were also important trade concessions involving the Yunnan-Haiphong Railroad, which the French owned.[39]

Like Tito, Ho consolidated his position in 1945–46 using his own resources. The results of a countrywide election he held on 6 January 1946 (open in Tonkin and Annam, covert in Cochin China) seemed to confirm his popularity, although there is some question as to whether he used strong-arm methods to, in effect, rig the results.[40] In March the French acknowledged Ho's DRV as the legitimate Vietnamese government within the French Union. However, they refused to give up Cochin China; Ho considered it integral to his Vietnam. The March agreement with Ho envisaged a referendum to decide whether Cochin China should be part of an independent Vietnam, but the French managed to defer it on the excuse that conditions in the south remained unsettled. Finally on 1 June 1946 the French announced the creation of an Autonomous Republic of Cochin China.[41] War began with two chance incidents on 20 November 1946.

By early May 1947 the French no longer thought they could reach a settlement with Ho. They asked Bao Dai to form a rival (anti–Viet Minh) government. Like Ho, he demanded that the French include Cochin China in his country. Unlike Ho, he accepted membership in the French Union; France would control his foreign policy.[42] While Bao Dai hesitated, the French tried and failed to wipe out the Viet Minh in a major offensive (between October 1947 and early 1948).

The French felt that they could not give in because defeat in Indochina would encourage rebels elsewhere in their empire. They already faced nationalist movements in North Africa (Algeria, Morocco, Tunisia) and in Madagascar.[43] Yet they had only sixty thousand troops, against a required five hundred thousand. The French army had the numbers, but French law prohibited the use of draftees outside metropolitan France. Ho controlled much of Tonkin; the French were limited to the two main cities, Hanoi and Haiphong, and to a string of small forts.

U.S. intelligence doubted that the French would prevail. They lacked the necessary forces, and they were deluding themselves that the Vietnamese could not fight, that the Viet Minh were effective only because they had Japanese in their ranks. They also did not yet realize that Ho Chi Minh himself was a Communist; they thought merely that he had opened hostilities in 1946 because he had come under the control of extremists. The French also had what the CIA considered the naive view that the people of Annam and Tonkin, where the war was being fought, resented Viet Minh terrorism, and thus would welcome a moderate pro-French government. As of January 1947 the French claimed that it would take large French forces six months to "restore order" in northern Vietnam; the U.S. analysts thought it would take two years or more. Once order was restored, the French hoped to establish a separate South Vietnamese state, which they would control—and which the U.S. analysts were sure would be unable to control northern Indochina, and would excite popular contempt. Surely instability would spread from northern

Indochina into the other French possessions, Laos and Cambodia.[44] When the French mounted a major offensive in the fall of 1947, the U.S. analysts predicted that it would fail; it would not force the Vietnam Republic (Ho's government) to negotiate with the French, and the resulting decline in French prestige would be felt elsewhere in the French Empire. The French were deliberately minimizing the scope of their rather large operation to avoid UN intervention in the war. It seemed unlikely to the U.S. analysts that the French would be particularly successful. Moreover, "the French expectation that the Vietnam Government would be willing to negotiate on French terms ignores the intensity of the hatred and contempt felt for the French by most of the population of northern Indochina. These feelings are not associated solely with the Vietnam Republic, but would continue even if the Vietnam Republic should suffer severe defeat. None of the political figures advanced by the French or by native groups in French-held area as alternatives to President Ho can command enough popular support to weaken the Vietnam Republic by inspiring important defections from it."[45]

By 1948 Vietnam was clearly consuming French energies, which the Truman administration would have preferred to focus on Europe. The French asked for Cold War support. In July 1948 they were told that if they reunited Cochin China with the rest of Vietnam and granted that country a real measure of independence, the United States would reconsider providing material support to continue the war. Otherwise the French would surely lose. Only an authentically Vietnamese national movement could resist Ho. The French seemed to understand; on 8 March 1949, they gave Bao Dai independence within the French Union. The next February they warned that without long-term U.S. aid, they might have to withdraw from Indochina.

By mid-1949 the French were planning to move forces from Germany and North Africa to Vietnam. Unfortunately, at least in the U.S. view, exactly those forces were crucial to the continuing defense of Western Europe, which in U.S. eyes was far more important. U.S. analysts feared, too, that because the French would necessarily be using U.S.-supplied arms and equipment in Vietnam, U.S. prestige in the Far East would suffer. That was entirely apart from the fear that French resources wasted in Indochina would hardly contribute to French economic recovery, and thus would leave France vulnerable to Communist political attack. The French strategy, moreover, depended on continuing U.S. aid and even on public support for their position in Indochina—which, Americans feared, would merely give the Communists an opportunity to charge that the United States was a colonial power.[46]

Unfortunately for the French, Mao's 1949 victory provided Ho with a source of supplies and a refuge to the north, across the border in China. For Stalin, Ho's successes were bittersweet, since they threatened the popularity of the French Communists.[47] Mao obviously had no such inhibitions. U.S. intelligence estimated that France was already exerting very nearly the maximum force she could in Indochina; if the Chinese supplied any appreciable support, the French would be unable to go on containing Ho without outside assistance. French pressure on the United States and Britain for direct aid surely would increase.[48]

Vietnam had not been included in the Asian containment perimeter defined in December 1949, but soon the NSC warned that if Indochina fell, so might Thailand and Burma (the secretaries of state and defense added Malaya and warned of losses further west). CIA analysts warned that a Communist-dominated Vietnam, working with the Soviets and the Chinese, would probably force Malaya and Indonesia into Communist hands.[49] In March 1950 President Truman approved the immediate use of $15 million of a $75 million 1949 appropriation of military aid to the general area of China (intended by its supporters to help Chiang Kai-shek). In April 1950 President Truman approved a NSC policy statement describing Indochina as the key area of Southeast Asia for U.S. security interests. It was still agreed that only full Vietnamese independence would solve the problem. However, conditions were deteriorating so fast that immediate aid might have some psychological value.[50] Only later would it become clear that Bao Dai's independence was only a façade. The French retained control; in many cases French administrators simply remained in place.

The Dutch had also had a colonial empire. In 1942 the Japanese ejected them from their most valuable colony, the Netherlands East Indies. It was a major Cold War prize: its territory lay across the vital shipping lane from the Middle East to Japan, and it had massive natural resources, including oil. The U.S. government refused to allocate the amphibious shipping they needed to re-conquer the colony. The Dutch saw a solution: they made sure that the former colony was included in the British area of responsibility, Southeast Asia. However, when the war ended, Sukarno and Hatta, two of the chief nationalists, declared independence. The Japanese turned many of their weapons over to the nationalists.

British, Indian, and Australian occupation forces began to land on 30 September 1945. Indonesian resistance, particularly in Surabaya, convinced the British that they did not want to occupy the country, although they did keep enough troops to offer the Dutch the option of trying to reoccupy. They pressed the Indonesians and the Dutch to negotiate, but talks broke down. It took two years for the Dutch to rebuild their own army, ruined by defeat in 1940, to the point where their troops could arrive in any numbers. In July 1947 the Dutch landed substantial forces to fight what they called a police action. They secured half of Java and the richest areas of Sumatra, but the nationalists did not surrender. A seventeen-month cease-fire ended in another Dutch attack in December 1948. This time the provisional capital, Jogjakarta, was taken, together with Sukarno, Hatta, and the cabinet. Again, guerilla warfare precluded any early decisive victory. That gave time for diplomatic pressure, particularly by the United States, to force the Dutch to cede sovereignty at the end of 1949. They retained West New Guinea, previously part of the Netherlands East Indies—which the Indonesians later seized.

The Dutch had hoped, vainly, that their involvement in an evolving Atlantic defense would gain them U.S. support in the East Indies. Instead, they encountered Senate pressure to end Marshall Plan aid to them. In March 1949 the United States threatened to deny arms deliveries contemplated under NATO. As might be imagined, Dutch resentment festered. The Dutch opposed the United States (and supported the British and French) over Suez in 1956.[51]

The one major U.S. colony in Asia, the Philippines, was granted independence in 1946, as scheduled under a prewar act of Congress. As elsewhere in Asia, the wartime resistance movement included a Communist component, the Huks (Hukbalahaps). The Philippines became a test of the U.S. belief that Communist insurgencies could be overcome by enlightened policy. By 1950, the corrupt and repressive Quirino government faced an expanding Huk rebellion. The United States provided support for new troops while applying pressure for local reforms. A Filipino leader, Ramón Magsaysay, revived his army's morale. It helped that, unlike the 1949 elections, those conducted in 1951 were seen as honest. The lesson seemed to be that vigorous and popular native leadership, which had been absent in Nationalist China, was the key to success. However, it was also extremely important that the Huks lacked any external source of support, although they did enjoy what amounted to sanctuaries in remote areas of the Philippines.

Magsaysay's very successful U.S. advisors later went to South Vietnam, after the French had been ejected. There they tried to apply the same combination of a dynamic nationalist (but pro-American) leader and economic development. This time, however, the Communist insurgents would enjoy external support and a sanctuary.

10 STALIN'S MILITARY BUILDUP

Stalin had never completely demobilized. In the 1970s the CIA estimated that the ten-million-man Red Army had been cut, by 1947, to about 2.6 million. This was about five times the size of its U.S. counterpart, which had fallen from a similar wartime peak. Security troops added something over a million more to the Soviet total.[1] After 1947, Soviet forces began to rebuild. Between the winter of 1948–49 and mid-1950 Stalin added about a million men. According to U.S. estimates, ground force manpower peaked (with a total of about six million under arms) in mid-1952. By 1950 Stalin was credited with 175 Soviet divisions, plus satellite units. This was the horde NATO would have to face, should war break out.

For Westerners, the compelling military image of 1945 was a massive but somewhat ill-equipped Red Army (renamed the Soviet Army in 1946) overwhelming a qualitatively superior and far better led German army. How could the West face down a future Soviet horde if the Germans—the military magicians—had failed? Could it ever mobilize enough troops? What could it do if Stalin managed to supply his troops with weapons on a Western scale of sophistication and numbers?

The reality was worse; we now know that the Soviets often won by out-generaling the Germans. Overall, they did not outnumber the Germans by nearly as much as many imagined. To achieve crushing strength, the Soviets had to uncover parts of their front. Deception by the Red Army kept the Germans from realizing where the Soviets had thinned their lines.[2] As for the Red Army's superior numbers, recent accounts suggest that after about 1943 human losses were difficult to make up, so that late-war tactics were far from profligate.[3] The late-war Red Army relied heavily on firepower, just like its U.S. counterpart.

The myth of the horde was comforting in a perverse way. The Germans, who had lost their war, provided the West's picture of how the Soviets had won. To preserve their pride, the Germans badly wanted to believe that the Red Army had won through force of numbers rather than through superior skill, and through the quantity rather than the quality of their equipment. A cynic might suggest that the British also found it comforting to consider the Germans supercompetent. That belief helped excuse poor Allied performance on the Western Front in 1940, and poor British performance in the Western Desert in 1941–42.

By 1948, moreover, the horde was being modernized, probably in accord with Maisky's 1944 recommendation that a postwar Ten Year Plan (1946–55) be instituted. Each service worked out its own plan, which Stalin apparently reviewed personally. A select group of Politburo members integrated the plans.[4] It seems unlikely that the end date for the Ten Year Plan (1 January 1956) implied the Soviets would be ready for war by 1957. Nor is it clear whether British intelligence was ever aware of Stalin's planning horizon; Stalin chose his date before the British chose theirs. The first five years (1946–50) coincided with a national Five Year Plan to rebuild the badly damaged Soviet Union. The necessary manpower came from demobilized troops. Later in this period forces were built back up, to be equipped with new types of weapons, mainly during the second half of the ten-year period (1951–55). Among other things, the Soviet force facing Europe was converted from a horse-drawn, marching army to a motorized one.

Much of the new technology came from the Allies (via both Lend-Lease and espionage) and from the Germans. The advancing Red Army seized important technology and overran German experts who found themselves in the Soviet sector at the end of the war. In 1946 many of those experts were deported to the Soviet Union, where special scientific institutes (NIIs) were set up. The Soviets usually ran their own programs parallel to the Germans'. Returning to Germany in the 1950s, the deportees brought the best information they had about the general state of Soviet technology. Interviews to glean this information were conducted under an Anglo-American program, Dragon Returns/Wringer.[5] The program exemplified a belief that the primitive Soviets could not develop advanced technology on their own.

Many Soviet weapons developed during this era certainly were direct copies of foreign prototypes, important examples being the B-29 bomber, U.S. and British radars provided under Lend-Lease, and the German passive homing torpedo. Each program developed not merely a current system but, much more importantly, the knowledge to build subsystems that could later be used in other weapons. For example, the structures of Soviet jet bombers of the 1950s, such as the Tu-16 Badger and the Tu-95 Bear, were based on that of the B-29, as were their defensive (gun) fire control systems. German torpedo homing mechanisms were adapted to Soviet torpedoes.

Jet fighters were a case in point. Even before the end of the war, the Soviets had captured German jet engines, which they soon copied. Stalin ordered designs of fighters powered by these engines in February 1945. The Soviet aircraft entered production in 1946–47. In March 1946 the Soviet fighter designers were ordered to develop a second generation of transonic (Mach 0.9) day fighters. The German engines could not yet be scaled up to provide enough power. British engines did offer enough power, but Stalin objected that Britain would not possibly be foolish enough to sell the engines. Anastas Mikoyan, his commissar for foreign trade, assured him (accurately) that it would. By April negotiations were under way to buy British engines to be copied and improved for large-scale production. The sale was made in September and the first engines were shipped in March 1947. Their descendants powered the MiG-15 used extensively in Korea. Later, German-type engines were developed.

Stalin had already ordered an urgent program to duplicate the U.S. atomic bomb—and to provide him with an airplane to deliver it. During the war the U.S. government had consistently refused Stalin's frequent requests for such aircraft. In 1944 three B-29s force-landed in Siberia after bombing Japan. Stalin ordered them copied as the Tu-4 (NATO Bull); he ordered a thousand made.

Stalin saw the ballistic missile, pioneered by the Germans in the form of the V-2, as a way of end-running the West's superior aircraft. British and U.S. studies late in the war suggested that it would take decades to produce a weapon to defend against the V-2. On the other hand, each V-2 was so expensive that production absorbed an absurdly large fraction of German technical resources. All those expensive V-2s did was drop a few thousand tons of explosives on London and Antwerp—the equivalent to a thousand-plane raid carried out over several months. However, with lightweight nuclear warheads a prospect after the war, the V-2 became far more attractive.

Like his wartime allies, Stalin obtained examples of the V-2 at the end of the war. Because Stalin purged the aircraft production ministry in 1946, ballistic missile development was assigned to the Ministry of Arms Production (under Dmitriy F. Ustinov), which previously had been responsible for artillery.[6] On 14 April 1947 the Politburo approved development of an improved V-2, the first Soviet ballistic missile (R-1).[7] V-2s assembled from German components were test-fired from a new range at Kapustin Yar, the first launched on 18 October 1947. The first eighteen R-1s were delivered in 1950. By that time an improved R-2 (with better than twice the range) had been developed by a special rocket design bureau headed by Sergei Korolev.

Production was a different matter. Soviet artillery designers and builders had had no experience with lightweight aircraft-type structures. In August 1950 the Soviet Army asked for thousands of R-1s and R-2s, but General Yakovlev, head of artillery development, balked.[8] He rejected rockets as too awkward, inaccurate, and ineffective—which they were until the Soviets had a nuclear warhead. Given the structure of the Ten Year Plan, the years 1950–51 were crucial, since that was when choices were made for the 1951–55 plan period. Yakovlev's 1951 successor, Marshal M. I. Nedelin, ordered production. He probably knew that warheads suited to rockets would soon be available. Ironically, although nuclear warheads were developed for the first two Soviet ballistic missiles, R-1 and R-2, it seems unlikely that they were ever fitted.

Stalin's production machine emphasized numbers of completed units rather than the mix of units and spares common in the West (where many manufacturers find the after-market, for spares and maintenance, more profitable than the basic market for all-up units). Each tank, for example, was considered expendable, backed up by other tanks—but not by much in the way of spare parts. The backup tanks might be considered combat spares. In peacetime, only a small fraction of the force would be active, since each active unit would be running down its expected lifetime. For example, in the 1980s Soviet units in Germany had special tanks on which they trained (and which they expected to wear out). The tanks they were to use in war were kept in special warehouses. In war a tank probably would be destroyed long before it had a chance to wear out. There was no point in wasting effort on spares or on facilities to rebuild damaged units. Instead, fresh tanks would be thrown into battle. Thus the Soviets tended to build many tanks (or airplanes, or ships) for each one in service. Since maintenance was relatively unimportant, Soviet units tended to devote much less manpower and resources to support, compared to Western practice.

That shaped tactics in a way foreign to Westerners. A division equipped with short-life weapons (and without extensive repair facilities or maintenance workers) could not sustain combat for very long. It therefore had little need for an extensive logistical tail. In war, divisions would be expended quickly and replaced with fresh ones. The remnants of the expended division would be withdrawn from combat and replenished with fresh troops and equipment before moving back. This contrasted with Western practice, in which the division was sustained in combat for a protracted period. Its losses were made up piecemeal. In the Western system replacement personnel learned from the larger number of combat veterans still manning the division. In protracted combat, the Soviets would use several divisions to deal (in rotation) with each Western division. Thus to understand the combat potential of the Soviet Army simply by counting its divisions was misleading.

A new program of submarines, inspired by the German Type XXI, was the naval equivalent to the land horde that threatened Western Europe directly. In a future war, the United States, the arsenal of the West, would have to keep a Western army supplied. To do that, it would have to maintain sea lanes across the Atlantic. Moreover, at the far end of those lanes, it would have to keep European ports clear of mines. The Soviets had captured not only the new German submarine technology, but also new mine technology.

Westerners have tended to associate the post-1945 Soviet buildup with external events, such as the creation of NATO or the outbreak of war in Korea. In fact, however, the Soviet services were reporting their postwar needs before the end of the war in Europe. At least in the case of the navy (which was probably typical), the ten-year plan was approved before the end of 1945, well before anyone had thought of NATO. A dramatic rise in the Soviet budget was probably an inevitable reaction to the advent of new types of weapons, such as jet aircraft. Truman faced much the same phenomenon, but had to worry about balancing his budget. He therefore sharply cut his standing forces. Had he not done so, the U.S. budget would have grown enormously in the late 1940s—as Stalin's did.

Probably the reason Stalin's rearmament has been associated with NATO is that Stalin managed to keep it secret until he cared to announce it. Thus for the West, the first whiff of Soviet rearmament was probably a March 1949 press announcement that the defense budget would grow from 18 percent of the 1948–49 national budget to 19 percent in 1949–50 (i.e., by about 6 percent), at a stated added cost of over ten billion rubles. The figures appeared only in Russian-language publications; the announcement may have been intended to stiffen East European Communists in the face of the new NATO. It may also have been part of an internal propaganda campaign to explain that the country had not been rebuilt after World War II due to necessary increases in defense spending.

According to declassified Soviet figures, in 1950 defense accounted for 20 percent of the national budget. The 1952 figure, 112.6 billion rubles, was an increase of about 37.5 percent. The 1953 budget, 124.2 billion rubles, was over 32.1 percent of a national budget drastically reduced (on paper) by realigning prices. The 1954 budget was 100.3 billion; the 1955 budget, 107.4 billion. The budget fell to 97.8 billion in 1956; 96.7 in 1957; and about 96 billion in each of the years from 1958 to 1960. In about 1955 the national budget began to rise sharply. The portion devoted to defense fell from 19.9 percent that year to 11.1 percent in 1960.[9]

The continuing increases after 1952 tell an interesting story. Western observers thought the budget was leveling off and then falling because the Soviets were producing fewer weapons. The falloff in weapons production was probably due partly to a loss of productivity; it can also be attributed to the greater sophistication of the weaponry now in production. For example, plans to build large numbers of destroyers (originally Project 41, NATO "Tallinn," then Project 56, NATO "Kotlin") failed because these later ships took much more effort to produce. The drop in military spending after 1955, however, probably can be attributed partly to a shift to consumer production (the 1954 drop was presumably a price realignment). All of the numbers, moreover, were deceptive.

Probably neither Stalin (nor his successors) nor his Western enemies ever really understood the Soviet economy. Although cash was almost irrelevant, they all acted as though amounts in rubles had real meaning. Khrushchev was particularly proud of budget cuts that now seem meaningless. Each Soviet enterprise had to show a profit, in terms not of what it sold but rather of what it produced. Military customers could often force down prices to get what they wanted within an apparently limited budget. To make up for the discounts their customers enjoyed, virtually every military plant also made civilian goods, at prices high enough to absorb the military discounts. Mixed production probably was justified originally as a way of adding capacity for use in an emergency, but it turned out to be a vital way of balancing books. Thanks to this system, in the 1980s Soviet tanks all "cost" one hundred thousand rubles each, a ludicrous figure at the nominal exchange rate of about one ruble to the dollar. At a Paris air show, the head of the Sukhoi design bureau said that a Su-27 cost no more than a MiG-29, even though it was far larger and far more sophisticated. He was both right and wrong: the Soviet state "paid" the same for each fighter, but the resources going into each were quite different.

Gorbachev's economists discovered just how meaningless the budget figures were when they met in the summer of 1987 to design an economic reform package.[10] Yegor Gaidar, later Yeltsin's prime minister, said that a proposed one-hundred-billion-ruble (12 percent of GNP) deficit would collapse the economy. Then the chief planner said that since the 1987 deficit was 127 billion rubles, a deficit of only one hundred billion would be an improvement. In 1989 Gorbachev admitted the first budget deficit in Soviet history, thirty-six billion rubles. But all these figures were fantasies because the State Bank, controlled directly by the Ministry of Finance, printed money as needed.

Defense plants produced quality products by picking out the best from very large lots; the rest was either scrapped or imposed on the civilian economy. Hundreds of vacuum tubes, for example, might be made to provide the military with one or two.[11] In addition, parts of the nominally civilian economy, such as Aeroflot and the merchant fleet, had military roles. For example, special aircraft used to test military lasers wore Aeroflot colors.[12] Thus the Aeroflot budget included part of the military burden.

Probably because the Soviets devoted so much of their economy to military purposes, they grossly overestimated Western capacity, knowing the huge size of the Western economies. Their bizarre estimates became known only after the fall of the Soviet Union.[13] Descriptions of overwhelmingly powerful Western ground forces (and the mobilization capacity backing them) made hilarious reading to Westerners who found it difficult to pry very small amounts of money out of their reluctant governments—and who themselves had often overestimated what the Soviets extracted from an economy whose size was far smaller than the Westerners imagined.

Without a real internal market, the price of any one good or service bore little relationship to the real cost (including the opportunity cost) of producing it. Without the discipline of cost, waste was rampant. Alternatives could not be compared in any realistic way. On the other hand, whatever the planners did not demand could not be bought, no matter how many rubles there were. Many defense plants found themselves running secondary enterprises to provide for their employees—and to produce the goods they needed to barter (with other defense plants) for essential items.[14]

After the collapse of the Soviet Union, Westerners began to hear about different kinds of rubles used in budgeting: normal ones for the civilian economy, special "defense" rubles, other special rubles to be used for foreign exchange.[15] Goods needed for military purposes were priced artificially low, that is, rubles bought much more for the military than for civilians. The situation was aggravated because military producers received benefits, such as additional housing for their workers, as routine rewards for winning major production orders. Nonmilitary producers had to make do with much less. Partly for these reasons, but largely because of massive internal deception, plans generally seem to have been wildly over-optimistic. Economic limits seem to have been entirely unknown to military and many industrial planners.

U.S. intelligence agencies tried to estimate what defense cost the Russians (the CIA's model carried the unfortunate name SCAM, for Soviet Cost Analysis Model). In the late 1970s, the usual figure was about 11 to 13 percent of GNP. That rose to about 15 to 17 percent when the CIA was forced to accept that Soviet military production was no more efficient than civilian production.[16] In the late 1970s, Leonid Brezhnev reportedly told an associate that one ruble in three was going to defense, a figure he believed his citizens would not tolerate. After the Soviet Union collapsed, shocked Westerners estimated that the Soviet GNP was no more than a third the estimated size. If both the GNP figure and the intelligence guess are correct, the actual defense spending burden was probably something more like 55 percent, the sort of figure the United States supported, briefly, during World War II—and never since. Russians now estimate that fully 62 percent of all machine-building and metalworking output went to directly to the military, with another 32 percent going for investment, leaving consumers with only 5 to 6 percent of the goods produced.[17]

Westerners, who ought to have known better, were often mesmerized by Stalin's ability to command his economy. Surely, given the slavish attitudes of most Soviet citizens, whatever Stalin ordered would be done. A generally rosy Western view of the Soviet command economy persisted virtually unchanged from 1945 until the collapse in 1989–91. For example, in the late 1970s many in the U.S. defense establishment envied the Soviet forces' absence of critics like the ones they had in Congress and in the media. Those dismayed by the military's envy had a favorite question: would senior officers prefer to command U.S. or Soviet forces? The answer, for anyone who wanted to stay in uniform, was preordained; but for many a more honest answer would have favored the Soviets.

It was not so much that Westerners overestimated gross Soviet military production (it was sometimes underestimated), but that they grossly overestimated the flexibility of the Soviet system to meet new military requirements. Soviet planners preferred a stable situation in which they could easily predict just what each enterprise had to supply to the other in order to produce the desired results. For them, it was preferable to keep a weapon in production rather than to phase it out in favor of some other product. Similarly, it was far easier to maintain a design office dedicated to a technology than to eliminate it in favor of some radically different one. Capitalism is often described as "creative destruction." The Soviet system was far more conservative.

By the late 1970s some Soviet military economists were saying that warfare was changing so rapidly that it was becoming impossible to forecast what would be needed should war break out; it was more important that the economy be agile than that it be able to produce vast numbers of the weapons already in production.[18]

Throughout the Cold War, many within the U.S. defense establishment often bemoaned the fact that the United States was spending a far smaller fraction of its gross output on defense than the Soviet Union. However, the fraction *not* spent on defense sometimes produced the technological basis for later defense programs without having cost the defense program anything. The proliferation of micro-computer chips in the 1980s is a prime example. In this case, an industry created largely by defense spending grew well beyond its roots and then returned enormous and unintended dividends to the defense program. That could not happen in the apparently defense-oriented Soviet Union, where the civilian economy got only the scraps of military research. There was no separate civilian research base. Western misperceptions of the limitations built into the Soviet economic and military system are a major irony of the Cold War.

We have very limited descriptions of plans against which to measure Soviet industrial performance. We know that the naval program failed very badly. We can therefore guess that the Soviet economy stalled in the late 1940s and early 1950s. (The navy may have been a special case due to greater emphasis in other areas.) We do know that Soviet workers who expected some reward for helping to win World War II were badly disappointed. Many became bitter when the Party continued to promote men who were politically sound rather than those who had proven themselves qualified during the war. As it became obvious that military reconstruction was the main priority, sullen workers apparently found it more and more difficult to meet the very high production goals announced by the government.

Truman's need to control spending while paying for the Marshall Plan (and its equivalents in Germany and Japan) drove the United States inexorably towards reliance on nuclear weapons. This shift was not undertaken either lightly or very willingly; it was inevitable. It was colored to a considerable extent by the emergence of a separate U.S. Air Force in 1947 due to Truman's attempt to unify the services. Largely on General Marshall's advice, he had hoped that unification would bring real efficiencies—which were badly needed after rearmament and the Marshall Plan converged in 1948.

The reality was that the services had very different, though complementary, points of view. These differences helped save the United States from pursuing a strategy so narrow that it could not adapt to the surprises of the Cold War. For the moment, however, unification was driven mostly by advocates of independent—which largely meant strategic—air power. They argued that German successes in 1940 could be traced to a lack of air-mindedness on the parts of the British and French governments, and that only the heroic efforts of the Royal Air Force had saved Britain from defeat in 1940. Few realized that wartime air power had been most successful when integrated with ground and sea forces. Most of the attempts to achieve decisive results by air attack alone (such as the strategic bombing of Germany) had failed. Even in 1940 the Germans were unable to invade England largely because they had not built anything resembling a viable invasion fleet to operate in the teeth of a Royal Navy that was still for the most part intact.

Similarly, the U.S. Army saw little point (in 1948 or thirty years later) in anything other than a frontal defense of West Germany. To it, anything spent on the periphery of Europe was wasted. The navy saw a peripheral strategy as a way of weakening the Soviet force facing the army. Throughout the struggle for unification, the air force argued that naval aviation, which provided the striking power the navy would use on the Soviet flanks, was redundant. In return for the army's support, it offered to support squelching its old rival, the marine corps.

Even the services' basic outlooks were radically different. In the navy, operational (line) officers predominated over the staff. In the two ground-oriented services the staff predominated. A naval line officer was expected to execute his mission while avoiding obstacles (rules) the staff might impose. In the army or air force, the staff specified how the mission was to be executed. The organizational differences between the services were quite natural. Naval units are widely dispersed, so rigid control is difficult or impossible. Army units and aircraft often operate in close proximity. Unless they follow detailed standard operating procedures, they may interfere with each other. The navy feared that its old rival, the army, was merely cloning itself to form the new air force. The two ground services would surely always outvote it. (Matters turned out to be more complicated.)

After a bitter struggle, the 1947 National Security Act created a new, independent U.S. Air Force (but preserved naval aviation) and a few transservice institutions, such as the Central Intelligence Agency (CIA) and the National Security Council (NSC). The act created the office of the secretary of defense, with a small staff. The Joint Chiefs of Staff (JCS)—the service chiefs and their staffs—including war planners—became far more important as a corporate entity, because beginning in 1949 they had to draw up a single budget for all the services. As it became obvious that money would be very tight, they had to decide which programs to kill—in effect, what U.S. national strategy would be. Truman appointed James V. Forrestal the first secretary of defense. As secretary of the navy, he had fought bitterly to undermine unification, which he and top naval officers considered an army plot. Surely he would make life miserable for anyone else appointed secretary of defense; if given that job, he might make unification work.[1]

The key issue, which the 1947 act did not resolve, was which services would have which roles and missions. In March 1948 the Joint Chiefs met at Key West. In return for the air force's agreement to stop trying to kill off its aircraft carriers, the navy agreed not to form a strategic bomber force of its own. However, the navy remained responsible for performing "collateral" functions under which it had to hit targets deep inland—for example, attacks on land-based aircraft (threatening sea communications or amphibious landings) and on enemy land communications. Secretary of Defense Forrestal approved the agreement on 1 July.[2]

The air force had second thoughts. Its chief of staff, Gen. Carl Spaatz, told Forrestal that he still wanted to kill off naval aviation. Forrestal told him that Congress itself had recognized the navy's need for an air arm in the 1947 act.[3] Moreover, although at Key West the chiefs agreed orally that the navy should not be denied use of atomic weapons, Spaatz continued to try to gain exclusive control. Army Chief of Staff Omar Bradley agreed. Eventually the air force gained a temporary but incomplete victory.[4]

The FY49 budget (enacted in 1948) was the first under rearmament, and the last under which the services could independently submit their requests. The navy got permission to build a supercarrier capable of launching bombers large enough to carry atomic bombs. That would have broken the monopoly Spaatz wanted for his new service. The rest of the budget made it clear that the United States could not build the sort of groundforce needed to face Stalin down. At this time the U.S. Army had only ten under-strength divisions. So much of its force was already deployed overseas that its general reserve—its insurance against surprises— amounted to only two and one-half divisions. It is a measure of the army's pessimism that it asked only for twelve full-strength active divisions. Those divisions would, however, have been backed by a large reserve force: thirteen national guard units and twenty-five reserve divisions.

U.S. war planners still expected to fight a long war against the Soviets, culminating in a massive ground offensive. However, preparation for such a war was becoming manifestly unaffordable. The forces needed to fight the war being planned in 1948–49 (were it to break out in 1952) would cost $19.3 billion in FY49, rising to $22.78 billion in FY52 as the full force came into service. President Truman thought the limit for future years would be $15 billion; for the present, Congress added nearly a billion dollars for additional aircraft procurement, the FY49 total coming to $13.94 billion, some of which could be spent in FY48. The situation in FY50 (a budget to be written during 1948) would be worse, because a recession had just begun. Tax receipts fell and money had to be allocated for relief, all without running much of a deficit. Defense was pegged at $14.5 billion; the Marshall Plan cost about a third as much, $4.2 billion. It now appears that initial Marshall Plan investments unexpectedly helped limit the effects of the recession.[5]

Air force nuclear bombers offered a less expensive form of defense. During the winter of 1947–48 air force planners suggested that destroying Soviet cities would create such shock that the Soviet government might be paralyzed. Their "nation-killing" concept was by no means universally approved within their service.[6] The air force did adopt the idea that for maximum shock value the atomic air offensive should be mounted as quickly as possible, rather than being spread out over the first few months of the war, as previously imagined. In 1948 the Strategic Air Command (SAC) proposed to drop two hundred bombs within forty-eight hours of the outbreak of war.

On the theory that four bombs could destroy any city, and that one hundred Soviet cities were worth attacking, on 29 October 1947 the JCS had asked for four hundred bombs by 1 January 1953. In reality, there were very few bombs available. They were stored unassembled, because radiation would damage the glue holding them together, and because their polonium initiators had a very short half-life. Including time for glue to dry, it took between twenty-four and thirty-six hours for a thirty-nine-man team to assemble a Mk 3, the first U.S. mass-produced bomb. By the spring of 1947 no new permanent teams had been trained. The SAC commander, General Kenney, pointed out that he could not strike quickly, since it would take so much time merely to assemble bombs at his bases.[7]

Because it had lost many of its best personnel as the United States demobilized, SAC could not easily mount large operations. For example, of 180 SAC B-29s available in May 1947, only 101 were able to mount a dummy attack against New York City.[8] When the Czech crisis came in February 1948, there was no effective U.S. nuclear attack force. Of 567 B-29s in service (plus forty-five B-50s), only thirty-two were "silver plates" capable of delivering atomic bombs. The planned conversion of nineteen bombers had been slowed by the requirement that all personnel involved in the over six thousand man-hours of modification be specially cleared (this requirement was relaxed in October 1947). There were only two bomb assembly teams (by the end of 1948, however, SAC could assemble ten bombs a day, and the rate was due to double by the end of 1949). Nor was much known about the targets to be attacked in war, or about Soviet air defenses.[9]

As a measure of what SAC was expected to do, the January 1949 emergency war plan (for a war to be fought before the Soviets got bombs of their own) listed strategic targets: industrial facilities in seventy Soviet cities, twenty of which (including Moscow and Leningrad) were given first priority. Attacks would be mounted from the United Kingdom, Cairo-Suez, and Okinawa.

In 1948 each service chief drew up his program as the first step in a $30 billion buildup (to be completed by 1952) deemed necessary to face Stalin down. Merely to maintain existing forces would cost $18.6 billion, $4.6 billion more than in FY49. Costs were rising partly because the military's industrial base had been badly eroded since 1945. Major new orders triggered severe inflation in the price of military goods. Because the services were so short of personnel, they economized on apparently minor items such as maintaining the equipment left over from World War II. As a consequence, when war broke out in Korea in 1950, only about 23 percent of the 3,457 M24 light tanks and only about 57 percent of the 3,202 M4 medium tanks in the United States would be serviceable.[10]

The JCS had limited room within which to maneuver. It could not abandon the services' peacetime roles—which helped fight the emerging Cold War. Troops on occupation duty made it impossible for Stalin to seize more territory without triggering a war he might not want. Ships on foreign stations encouraged U.S. allies by their presence. Then, too, enough forces had to be provided to execute their most vital roles under the emergency war plan: the strategic air offensive, protection of essential sea lanes, and defense of the continental United States. The list concealed the deep division between the navy and the other services. The navy argued that sea control could not be divided from other naval operations. A naval offensive pinning down Soviet antishipping forces surely contributed to the safety of sea lanes throughout the world, yet it might not be described as a pro-shipping operation. Ground-based air and army forces were far more closely tailored to particular roles or particular areas.

Cairo-Suez was a case in point. Army Chief of Staff Omar Bradley thought abandoning it would save money by eliminating a carrier task force (and six to eight divisions by D-plus-3). But to the navy, the task force in the eastern Mediterranean was much more than support for a particular kind of operation. It was needed to evacuate U.S. troops from Europe so that they could fight elsewhere. The task force also would mount air attacks on southern Russia. To deal with it, the Soviets would have to divide their forces, precluding a knockout blow against the British bases SAC badly needed.

As the budget squeeze worsened, the army had to give up any hope of mounting early offensive operations. The air force cut its force to SAC units based in Britain and Iceland. That left it its new core capability, the atomic air offensive. The navy tried to retain as many strike carriers as possible in the face of army and air force opposition. Chief of Naval Operations (CNO) Adm. Louis Denfeld charged that under the army–air force proposals the United States would be deserting the Europeans with whom it was negotiating the NATO treaty. He doubted that the nuclear air offensive would do much good. Targets had not been located accurately enough to hit, and bombers might be unable to penetrate heavy Soviet air defenses. Navy carriers in the Mediterranean might well be more successful in attacking the lines of communication supporting Soviet forces invading Western Europe.

Even the very austere army–air force plan would have broken President Truman's $14.4 billion ceiling for the FY50 budget. Secretary Forrestal concluded that, under the ceiling, U.S. forces would be limited to mounting a strategic air offensive from England. It would take $4.1 billion more to hold lines of communication through the Mediterranean.

Truman seems to have assumed that, as long as the United States held a nuclear monopoly, war was very unlikely. The international situation was very delicate: the Berlin blockade had just begun. To ask Congress for a massive increase in military spending would inflame the situation: it would look (to both the U.S. public and to Stalin) like preparation for war. Truman would submit the $14.4 billion budget on the understanding that a supplemental could be requested if and when needed. The joint chiefs refused to certify that they could safeguard the country with $14.4 billion.

To meet the chiefs' demands, Truman would have had to gut the Marshall Plan. In Truman's view, the plan was far more important to security than raw military power. Without economic stability and European recovery, security would be an illusion. Congress cut the army and navy budgets while adding almost a billion dollars to the air force. Truman refused to spend the entire amount, keeping $735.7 million "in reserve."[11]

As the budget process ground on, Forrestal recalled Gen. Dwight D. Eisenhower to active service as a special advisor to the president and secretary of defense (11 February 1949): he would manage a budget compromise. Since strategy and budget had to be considered together, Eisenhower would also be responsible for U.S. strategy. During World War II, he had been supreme Allied commander, with responsibility for naval and air as well as ground forces. Postwar, he had served as army chief of staff until retiring in February 1948.

Unlike past U.S. strategists, Eisenhower had to take the new allies into account.

While it mobilized, the United States would help hold a line in Western Europe, preferably at least on the Rhine. In effect the United Kingdom could be considered the left flank and air bases in northwest (i.e., French) Africa (to support the air offensive) the right flank of this line. If the line did not hold, at the least a substantial bridgehead should be maintained on the Continent. Failing that, an invasion would have to be mounted to retake Western Europe. That might be possible about D-plus-24 months, when the necessary forty-one U.S. divisions and sixty-three tactical air groups would be ready. Detailed calculations made it clear that the United States and the Allies could barely retain a toehold in Europe. Europe was clearly the first priority. Very little could be spared for the Far East; the U.S. government drew an Asian defensive line that excluded Korea.

The Middle East could not be written off. As in World War II, it would be supplied via the sea route around the Cape of Good Hope and the Suez Canal. The navy continued to argue for a carrier force powerful enough to dominate the whole Mediterranean—and to attack the southern Soviet Union and the advancing Soviet forces. The air force and the navy continued to fight over carrier strength and roles.

In March 1949 President Truman appointed a new secretary of defense, Louis Johnson, who was more attuned to budget requirements than his predecessor. Budget agreements would be enforced. The president had already set a $15 billion ceiling for FY51. As an approach to consensus, the navy, the army, and the air force each was asked to prepare budget estimates for all three services. The air force proposed that the navy's fleet carriers—its potential strategic competitors—be cut altogether. As a starting point in calculating a budget, Eisenhower allocated to each service the smallest force any of the services proposed for it. That would reduce the air force but would give it a major victory by eliminating the service's main rival, the navy's fleet carrier force.

Cuts in standing forces saved relatively little. Much of the budget was paying for the purchase of expensive new weapons. Johnson had to kill at least one major new project. The navy's new atomic strike carrier *United States,* which had been authorized under the expansionary FY49 budget, was an obvious candidate. Army Chief of Staff Omar Bradley backed the air force. The carrier would perform a role already assigned to the air force. Clearly it was not needed to control vital sea areas. General Eisenhower seems to have agreed with the army and air force views. Having seen draft copies of the services' comments, in April 1949 Johnson cancelled the ship. That so outraged the navy that Secretary Sullivan resigned.

Through the summer of 1949 the naval aviators seethed. It seemed to many in the navy that the air force had won not by logical argument but rather by good public relations. The navy attacked not only the air force's "atomic blitz" concept but also the efficacy of its new B-36 bomber. It seemed, for example, that the air force had been counting on funds released by the cancellation of the carrier to finance continued B-36 production. A campaign of leaks, the "Revolt of the Admirals," brought these questions before Congress. For good measure, it was suggested that Johnson favored the bomber because of political connections with its manufacturers dating back to World War II. A naval officer volunteered publicly to fly a modern naval fighter to shoot down a B-36; he hoped to prove that the air force bomber could not penetrate modern air defenses.

The administration was furious. To Truman, the issue was not whether the United States could effectively fight a hot war. It was whether the United States could survive a drawn-out cold war, during which it would have to preserve credible military forces without exhausting the country. Public debate of defense issues could be extremely dangerous, because it could inflame the public to demand a much higher defense budget. Those pressing for higher spending were unlikely to associate an increased budget either with higher taxes or with the economic disaster of sustained deficit spending. Truman was well aware that his budgets were tight; he was responsible for the consequences of overspending. He did not want to be end-run by any of the services. The U.S. nuclear weapons monopoly simplified Truman's problem, because it made war unlikely. The task of the U.S. services, then, was to deny Stalin a cheap victory—and to be ready to expand should the unexpected happen. Given the U.S. nuclear monopoly, the main threat was Stalin's political weapon, which would become more effective as Western economies weakened.

In the aftermath of his unsuccessful revolt, Denfeld, who had led the fight against the air force, had to resign. The navy's defeat was symbolized by the abolition of Navy Day, celebrated in October on Theodore Roosevelt's birthday, in favor of Armed Forces Day. On the other hand, Adm. Arthur W. Radford, Denfeld's vice chief, became CinC Pacific and then chairman of the Joint Chiefs. Capt. Arleigh Burke, who ran the navy staff cell opposing the air force, was promoted, becoming chief of naval operations in 1957.

Moreover, despite opposition by the army and air force, Johnson approved Denfeld's proposal that the $130 million released by cancellation of the supercarrier be spent instead on modernizing two existing fleet carriers—which, incidentally, would then be able to handle bombers only slightly smaller than those planned for the supercarrier. The navy's heavy bomber program survived. Possibly the strength the navy had shown had convinced Johnson not to push too far.

Overall, though, it was now clear that money would go mainly into U.S. nuclear capability; nothing else was really affordable. Thus through 1949 demands for nuclear bombs continued to grow. Clearly Stalin would eventually have a bomb of his own. Once that happened, some U.S. nuclear weapons would have to be used against Soviet nuclear forces. In June 1949 the JCS decided to double the national stockpile by 1 January 1956.[12] This larger stockpile would provide a small general reserve and a post-hostility reserve to guarantee the peace after a war.

There was also another possibility. Atomic bombing might somehow slow down a Soviet advance through Europe, a new mission called "retardation."[13] It might, then, make up for the disastrous cuts in U.S. ground forces. The JCS ordered a quarter of the U.S. atomic effort devoted to retardation, since success would make possible Eisenhower's new bridgehead strategy. The British, who had previously seen ground forces in Europe as a screen behind which to mount a strategic air offensive, were shocked. To them the new strategy explained why the Americans now considered Europe more important than the Middle East (they were apparently unaware of the fight over the carrier force which would have been needed to defend the eastern Mediterranean).[14]

Retardation would be difficult. Because the Soviets had stockpiled a great deal of what they would need to keep fighting, destroying supplies in the Soviet Union might buy very little. However, destruction of their oil industry might prevent the Soviets from fighting a prolonged campaign.

Suddenly much more had to be done very quickly with the limited supply of bomb fuel (oralloy and plutonium). Fortunately there were some new design ideas. A new levitated-core design required much less fuel; 63 percent more bombs could be made from a fixed amount of material, with 75 percent more total yield.[15] Now the AEC could provide all four hundred bombs by 1 January 1951; by 1 July 1949 there were at least the 133 bombs required by the current war plan. The new design was tested in 1948, in the first atomic tests since Bikini (1946). One test in this series led to production of a bomb less than half as heavy (but just as powerful) as earlier types, hence light enough to place aboard guided missiles.[16] A further improvement, boosting, made it possible to use even less material, and to build far more powerful bombs.[17]

Now much lighter bombs could be made. In May 1950 the AEC was ordered to build one that a fighter-bomber could carry. Once this Mk 7 was available in 1952, SAC's monopoly was broken altogether, because it no longer took a massive bomber to deliver a nuclear weapon; now carrier-based fighters could deliver atomic weapons more powerful than those that had destroyed Hiroshima and Nagasaki.

Probably the most important consequence of the AEC research was that nuclear scarcity soon gave way to nuclear plenty: within a few years, bombs had become much less expensive, and they could be made in staggering numbers. Nuclear weapons became by far the *least* expensive way of attacking an enemy. In 1949 (probably at the end of the year) the U.S, stockpile amounted to 169 atomic bombs. Five years later there were 1,630, about ten times as many; ten years later there were 12,305, almost ten times again as many.[18]

Significantly, it soon became possible to set the way in which the bomb's energy was distributed between blast, heat, and radiation. From the 1950s on, there was considerable interest, at least in the United States, in "clean" bombs designed to release most of their energy as radiation rather than blast. That would kill troops in the open. Radiation, particularly neutrons, would also penetrate armored vehicles to kill their crews. Behind a layer of earth, defending troops and sheltered civilians would be safe. Without much blast, little or nothing would be thrown up to create fallout to contaminate an area. Structures would be left intact. Existing weapons of this type were discussed in connection with the Quemoy crisis in 1958. Later, as "neutron bombs" or Enhanced Radiation Weapons (ERWs), they aroused considerable political controversy.

The mathematics of bomb design was extremely complex. Far beyond the 1950s no one could guarantee that a specific design would work, or what its yield would be. The United States sought a test ban in 1958 because by then it appeared that all variations on known themes had been tried. Later that belief proved premature. In addition, during the 1960s, several U.S. warheads suffered corrosion due to the interaction between their high explosives, their fuel, and even the glue holding the assembly together. It turned out that spots of corrosion were enough to ruin the symmetry of the bomb and thus cause it to fizzle.[19] After 1963 many U.S. tests were run simply to determine whether such problems were fatal, and to check cures.

Although the air force now finally decided that SAC was its core, others remembered that wartime strategic bombing had largely failed. On 23 October 1948 an uneasy Forrestal asked the JCS to evaluate the air war plan. A 12 May 1949 report by an interservice committee under air force general H. R. Harmon was depressing. SAC attacks might cut Soviet industrial production by 30 to 40 percent (and might kill 2.7 million of twenty-eight million Russians in the target area).[20] They would probably unify the Soviet people around their government. Moreover, attacks on Soviet industry would not stop the Soviet Army, although they might make an advance difficult to sustain. The British would need thirty days to set up the limited defenses they had around the key bomber bases. Both air transport capacity (for atomic bombs, which were stored in the United States) and aviation fuel were limited.[21] The Joint Intelligence Committee agreed with Admiral Denfeld that much of the plan depended upon grossly inadequate intelligence. However, a February 1950 report by the JCS's new Weapons Systems Evaluation Group (WSEG) concluded that if the deficiencies were corrected, 70 to 85 percent of the bombs would be dropped in the target areas, and each bomb could destroy half to two-thirds of an industrial target. A proposed companion nonnuclear air offensive was abandoned as prohibitively expensive.[22]

Through 1949 the U.S. budget problem worsened. The budget deficit continued to rise, because nondefense security programs such as the Marshall Plan and MDAP continued to grow. In the fall of 1949 it seemed that, even if the recession ended, it would reach $5 billion in FY51 (the FY48 deficit had been $1.8 billion). Truman's economists doubted that the United States could sustain the deficit for long. Yet Stalin could marshal "almost any predetermined amount of military power or politico-economic pressure by squeezing it out of a lowered standard of living for the masses."[23]

Free societies seemed unable to match Stalin; free men would not elect governments promising them perpetual poverty in order to maintain those governments;

they would vote Communist. What Truman's economists did not realize was that free men were also far more productive; they could match a large part of Stalin's machine without bankrupting themselves. That was not evident in 1949 mainly because Western Europe had been so badly damaged by World War II. Once the West recovered fully, the situation would improve drastically—although, given Soviet lies, Westerners tended not to realize just how drastically.

The budgetary frustrations did have one positive outcome. Forced to frame a new strategy to defend Europe, General Eisenhower became the key U.S. expert on the issue. He was the natural choice, having commanded the victorious Western allies in Europe in 1944–45. In 1950 he was the natural choice to become the first Supreme Commander, Europe (SACEUR), responsible for combined NATO forces. In that job, he could try to turn his 1949 ideas into some sort of reality.

PART THREE

CRISES IN A NUCLEAR WORLD

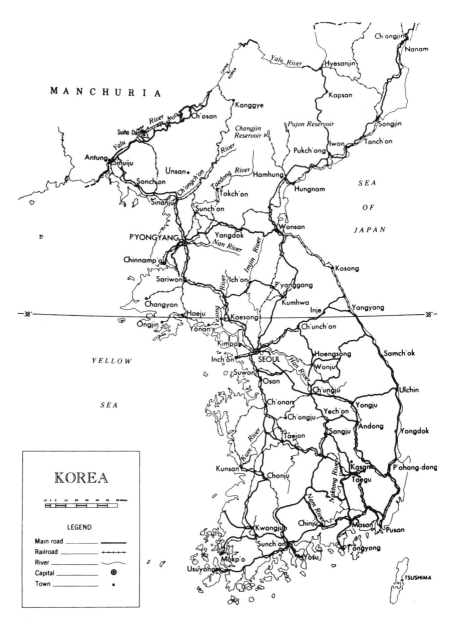

Korea

Note how close the South Korean capital, Seoul, is to the 38th Parallel dividing the two Koreas, and also how far south the North Koreans pushed (to Pusan). The map does not show the industrial complex, built by the Japanese, which straddled the Korean-Manchurian (Chinese) border (Japan occupied Korea before she controlled Manchuria). In 1950 South Korea was largely agricultural. Since the Korean War the status of the two Koreas has essentially reversed.

Courtesy Army Map Service. Reprinted from G. G. O'Rourke with E. T. Wooldridge, *Night Fighters over Korea* (Annapolis, Md.: Naval Institute Press, 1998), page 75.

On 29 August 1949 the Soviets exploded their first atomic bomb. Suddenly Stalin had the one weapon with which he might usefully attack the United States. A joint estimate, based on the capabilities of known or deducible plants, placed the Soviet nuclear stockpile at 10 to 20 bombs in mid-1950, 25 to 45 in mid-1951, 45 to 90 in mid-1952, 70 to 135 in mid-1953, and 200 by mid-1954.[1] It was assumed that in an attack about half the Soviet bombs would get through and that one hundred successfully placed on target would seriously damage the United States. The "year of maximum danger," when Stalin would be able to contemplate world war, moved forward from 1957 to 1954 (the British still timed their modernization for 1957).[2]

Stalin had learned about the Anglo-American bomb project as early as 1941 from his spies in Britain and in the United States. Once the bomb had been demonstrated, he badly wanted it. In 1945 he assigned Lavrenti Beria, the chief of his secret police, to develop a Soviet bomb by 1948. A special design bureau was established. As in the United States, secret cities were built to house the bomb developers and producers. Stalin's designers chose the plutonium route. Their first reactor went critical on 25 December 1946. Beria missed Stalin's 1948 deadline, but the first Soviet bomb was successfully detonated in August 1949. It was virtually a replica of the one exploded over Nagasaki. (Stalin specifically rejected a proposal to use an improved Soviet design.)[3]

In 1945 the JCS estimated that Stalin would have a bomb within five years, probably because it had taken the United States about three (Secretary of War Stimson thought it would take Stalin four years). In 1947 the CIA estimated that the Soviets would get the bomb about 1953, and not before 1951. It appeared that the Soviets were about where the Americans had been about 1943, and it was assumed that they were progressing at one third the U.S. rate (presumably they had one production reactor rather than three). The air force dissented; it expected a Soviet bomb in 1949–52. In March 1948 the Joint (U.S.-British) Intelligence Committee thought 1950 the earliest possible year, mid-1953 the most likely date.[4] This date was still received wisdom as of mid-1949.[5]

As yet no one realized how much Stalin had gained by espionage. It seemed that he had no source of uranium ore comparable to the Congo; he would have to make do with mines in Eastern Europe, particularly in Bulgaria (a Czech mine, from which much had been expected, turned out to produce very poor ore). We now know that the Soviets made particular efforts to conceal their own discovery of richer sources of ore.[6]

Because everyone expected the Soviets to build a bomb, as early as 1945 there was considerable interest in ways to detect an explosion at a great distance.[7] The U.S. Air Force proposed sampling the upper atmosphere for radioactive debris. After many false starts, regular investigative flights began in mid-1949, just in time to detect Stalin's first bomb. There is no evidence that the explosion was expected just then; the radioactive samples were greeted with incredulity.[8]

President Truman waited three weeks (to 23 September) to announce the test results, partly to gain further confirmation. He hoped for a Soviet announcement, which would have saved him from disclosing the secret U.S. capacity for nuclear monitoring. Truman also wanted to avoid any implication that the British were devaluing the pound (already set for 18 September) as a panicky reaction to the Soviet test.

The bomb debris picked up by aircraft provided considerable information on the composition and even the design of the bombs it detected. This type of monitoring continued into the 1990s. As British intelligence liaison in Washington, Kim Philby, a Soviet mole, was briefed on the secret U.S. nuclear monitoring technique, which he presumably reported to his masters.

The Soviet bomb program followed much the same pattern as that of the Americans.[9] In 1954 the Soviets tested their first production strategic bomb, RDS-3I. Since the earlier RDS-2 was made in very small numbers (only six in the first series), and since the tactical RDS-4, the first series-produced bomb, did not enter production until 1954, the Soviet inventory was probably no more than ten or twenty bombs until about 1955. That contrasts sharply with contemporary U.S. estimates; in mid-1953, for example, the Soviets were credited with 120 bombs (80 kilotons) each, growing to three hundred by mid-1955.[10] U.S. intelligence presumably overestimated the pace of the Soviet production program. Most likely Stalin was intensely interested in demonstrating a single bomb to break the U.S. monopoly, but was less interested in costly mass production.

Stalin's bomb exploded as the FY51 defense budget was being considered. Truman almost certainly still believed that the Soviet threat was economic and political, not military. It was not yet time to mobilize. In a new budget submitted on 9 January 1950, Truman added another army division (bringing the total to ten) and another fleet carrier (bringing the total to seven).[11] Secretary of Defense Johnson ordered cuts for FY52 so severe that in mid-April 1950 the army chief of staff decided to deactivate one of the four occupation divisions in Japan.

There were, however, signs that war might be imminent. The Berlin blockade seemed to show a new degree of militancy and a new boldness bordering on reck-lessness. Stalin seemed to be changing the Party line to favor war over the earlier strategy of waiting for capitalism to crumble. Thus the Soviet Army was now described as the precursor, rather than the exploiter, of revolution. Stalin seemed to make no real distinction between measures short of war and war itself. Stalin's buildup was quite apparent, so that as of early 1950 the JCS said the Soviets could now attack Europe from a standing start, offering the West no time to mobilize.[12]

In view of the Soviet bomb test, President Truman had already ordered a State–Defense Department team to reassess U.S. national security policy. The team was headed by Paul H. Nitze, who had succeeded George Kennan, the architect of containment, as head of the State Department Policy Planning Staff. As a member of the postwar U.S. Strategic Bombing Survey, Nitze had his own ideas of just how effective strategic weapons were likely to be. At an 11 October 1949 con-ference he pointed out that soon it would be impossible to use nuclear weapons to deal cheaply with a Soviet conventional attack.[13] The Soviets might hit back with their own nuclear weapons. The United States would have to buy the sort of expen-sive conventional forces the Truman administration thought it could not afford. Without superior overall military power, containment would be no more than bluff.

Nitze thought that the United States could afford to do more to defend itself. The Soviets already spent nearly 40 percent of their GNP on defense and industrial investment, but the United States spent only 22 percent (including 6 percent for defense and 2 percent for foreign assistance). The United States economy was believed to be at least four times the size of the Soviets' (actually the gap was far greater). Assuming the ratio believed at the time, in absolute terms, the 22 percent spent by the United States was at least 88 percent of the Soviet GNP. However, because the Soviet standard of living was so low, the "fighting value" of each dollar the Soviets spent on defense was much greater than that of each U.S. dollar. For example, $40 billion (three times the U.S defense budget) would only buy sixty U.S. divisions, compared to Stalin's two hundred. To match the Soviets, the United States would have to spend far more. Nitze argued that World War II showed that the country could do just that. During the war, the country had spent as much as half its national income on defense. Nitze's comparisons were, if anything, under-stated, because there was evidence that the Soviets were not meeting their announced economic targets.

Some argued that any jump in U.S. defense spending would touch off an arms race. To Nitze, the Soviets were already at full stretch. Their economy had very lit-tle potential for further investment either in armaments or in additional plants to make more of them later on. The U.S. economy, by contrast, seemed to have enor-mous potential. The Bureau of the Budget was skeptical. The country had attained its very high wartime output partly by allowing its industrial plant to deteriorate. That could not have been maintained for very long. Nor was it clear just how much further the U.S. economy could stretch. Even though it was in recession in 1949, with 3.5 million unemployed, some sectors, such as heavy industry, were working at full capacity. Money spent on new orders would be eaten by inflation unless prices were controlled or new taxes imposed.

The NATO countries might also do more. They outproduced the Soviet Union by over a third and had four times the GNP of the satellite states. Nitze suggested that their governments could spend a great deal more by accepting a lower standard of living. Secretary of State Dean Acheson rejected that as unrealistic.[14] Cutting the Europeans' standard of living would play into Stalin's hands. The whole point of the Marshall Plan was to show that the American alliance equated to prosperity, not a new form of wartime misery.

Nitze feared that the usually careful Stalin might be taking greater risks in order to hold on to his world revolution. Stalin had felt threatened by Tito, whose revolutionary enthusiasm had become too attractive to the various European Communist parties. Mao might offer similar attractions to Asians such as Ho and the Malayans. A more militant Stalin might try more Czech-style coups, for example in France. The French certainly were nervous; a few months later, Dr. James B. Conant, president of Harvard and a government consultant, remarked that French intellectuals were not writing anything that would be held against them if the Communists took over.[15]

Nitze submitted his report, NSC 68, on 7 April 1950.[16] A buildup would neutralize the Soviet nuclear threat by providing the United States and Canada with an adequate air defense. It would create standing forces sufficient to hold off an initial Soviet attack in Europe and the Middle East while the immense military potential of the United States and the Allies could be brought to bear. Without a buildup, the only protection available to Americans would be Stalin's presumed fear that the Soviet Union would suffer atomic attack if he attacked the United States.[17]

Nitze argued that a strong defense posture would make the Europeans more confident and thus better able to resist Soviet threats and blandishments. The existing situation was not encouraging. At the beginning of 1949 the five Western European Union countries (UK, France, Benelux) had between them ten divisions in Europe (two British and three French in Germany, five more divisions in France and Belgium) and thirty-two independent brigades (equivalent to major portions of another ten divisions). Within ninety days they could add only three light infantry battalions and twenty-five light infantry companies. These units lacked much of their statutory equipment. Manpower was not the problem. Had sufficient equipment been available, there were enough men already in uniform to form eight more divisions, five infantry brigades, four armored regiments, ten artillery regiments, seven antitank regiments, and three infantry battalions.[18]

The United States therefore supplied equipment. Its first (1949) Military Assistance Plan was designed to equip a fourteen-division ground force: nine French, one Belgian, two Norwegian, and two Danish.[19] With the two British divisions and two U.S. divisions (or their equivalents) in Germany, NATO would have about fourteen divisions on or near the Central Front. In an emergency it could call on additional units from Britain (one and two-thirds divisions) and the United States (six divisions, as of October 1950). It took time to raise the new units; as of October 1950 the French were contributing only six divisions (four infantry, two armored).

In 1950 the Soviets had twenty-two divisions in East Germany and two each in Austria, Poland, and Hungary. Leaving at least a division in each country to maintain control, the Soviets might strike the NATO Central Front with twenty-two to twenty-five divisions. According to a military rule of thumb, an attacker needs at least a three-to-one margin over the defense at the point of contact. Thus the Soviets had nothing like a strong enough force in place in Central Europe to be sure of overrunning NATO. To build it, they would need reinforcements from their westernmost military districts.[20] A military crisis would become a logistical race between NATO and the Soviets. To match the Soviets, NATO would mobilize reserves.

The JCS soon completed a parallel study of just what it would take to provide sufficient forces by 1954, the crucial "year of maximum danger." The target force proposed late in May 1950 amounted to twelve army divisions, 370 major warships, and seventy-seven air force wings. To get there, by FY52 the country would need ten divisions, 311 major combatants (up from 237), and fifty-six wings (up from forty-eight). This was not an enormous force, but Truman would have none of it. Early in June he told a reporter that he planned to cut defense spending, thanks to economies his administration was realizing.[21] To accept Nitze's reasoning would mean abandoning any hope of holding U.S. military expenditure to a sustainable level. A hot debate within the government ended only with the outbreak of war in Korea. The subsequent mobilization proved that Nitze had been right: the United States really could do a great deal more without prohibitive pain. Truman would be remembered more for his Korean War buildup than for his earlier stance against military spending.

Given the perceived size of Stalin's army and NATO's weakness, early in 1950 the JCS thought that in the event of attack the NATO army would have to retreat from position to position in France. The French government refused to contemplate any retreat from the Rhine. Its demand was written into the March 1950 NATO Medium Term Defense Plan (for a 1954 war).[22] In September, the Danish and Dutch governments opposed plans to stand on the Rhine and Ijssel Rivers, which would have left their countries exposed.

Any attempt to make a stand would require very strong forces, far beyond what the NATO countries could supply. Early in 1950 the British made their first commitment to supply troops to Germany in an emergency. That reversed earlier thinking, in which the British expected an air offensive, mounted mainly from Britain, to stop the advancing Soviets. Now the British government accepted the argument that if the Soviets got close enough they could bomb out British bases (not to mention London itself) before aircraft based there could have much impact. Moreover, the Europeans (particularly the French) could not be expected to provide large ground forces unless the British showed that they were serious by adding to the two divisions already in Germany. The 1950 plan called for doubling this force. The British could do no more on the ground, because they were also maintaining large air and naval forces.[23]

France was the main potential reservoir of ground strength, but she was not nearly powerful enough. NATO planners wanted thirty-two ready divisions on the Central Front, plus another eighteen to fight a delaying action east of the Rhine. In 1949 only seven non-French divisions were in place in Europe. In 1950 a nervous French government told Acheson that its citizens would not make major sacrifices unless they believed the NATO program could succeed—that Allied countries would join them in supplying the divisions needed to make up the fifty-four-division force that NATO said it needed. If U.S. aid were forthcoming, the French offered to modernize their five NATO divisions and raise fifteen more.

Germany was the only remaining reservoir of manpower in Western Europe. In November 1949 the U.S. Army proposed forming German divisions although U.S. official policy was to demilitarize the country. Although the JCS approved the idea in May 1950, President Truman rejected it as "militaristic." At best the Germans might pay the costs of Allied forces in Germany.

Money was the rub. Every man added to a NATO army meant buying more equipment and more vehicles. In 1950 the U.S. government felt that it was spending as much as it could. Any growth had to come from the Europeans. Yet when Secretary of State Acheson pressed the British and the French to rearm, they could only offer $3.5 billion over three years, against the hoped-for $10 to $12 billion.[24]

The outbreak of war in Korea reversed the U.S. position on Germany, but it did not quell French nervousness. The French were still worried by the possibility that a resurgent Germany might attack. Using nuclear weapons, NATO might resist the Soviets without needing the German troops.

The French already equated the atomic bomb with Great Power status. They had formed their own atomic energy organization in 1945. In 1951, expecting that France would soon have the bomb, the French army began to consider its tactical uses, which might make up for NATO's weakness. A secret program to build a bomb was formally approved by the French cabinet on 26 December 1954, presumably inspired in large part by a desire to reverse the humiliation of the defeat at Dien Bien Phu that May.[25] Much preparatory work had already been done. The official order to build a bomb (and to test it by 1960) was signed on 11 April 1958. The French bomb was first tested on 13 February 1960, in Algeria.[26]

By that time the British had already developed their own bomb. Because they could not afford numerous tests, they could not field anything like the variety of weapons developed by the United States or the Soviet Union. They therefore badly wanted to revive close wartime cooperation with the United States. Several times the U.S. government considered providing physical data so that the British could use American-supplied weapons in wartime. It generally drew back for fear of disclosing design information.[27] Early bombs required considerable assembly before use. Much could be deduced even from information such as the location of the bomb's center of gravity, moments of inertia (about various axes), its yield, safety features, vulnerabilities, fusing and firing features, and in-flight procedures.

NSC 68 amounted to a more militarized version of containment. The obvious alternative was preventive war. After the first Soviet nuclear test, it was discussed so widely that in April 1950 Secretary of the Air Force Finletter specifically rejected it in a speech at the Air War College. However, in August 1950, after the Korean War had broken out, Secretary of the Navy Francis Matthews advocated a U.S. buildup to the point of invincibility, to be followed by a preventive attack, which would guarantee future peace. Apparently this was a trial balloon floated by the secretary of defense, Louis Johnson. Although Secretary of State Dean Acheson disavowed Matthews' remarks, President Truman did not fire him. The preventive war idea was echoed by Gen. Orvil Anderson, commandant of the Air War College. Truman fired Anderson and publicly rejected preventive war. However, the air force tried to revive the idea in 1952 (a State Department summary survives).[28]

Once Stalin had the bomb, the U.S. targeters naturally added a third strategic task, to blunt any atomic attack he might mount. The JCS now established three target categories, which would survive to the end of the Cold War: the *destruction* of Soviet industry and urban areas (Delta), the *blunting* of the Soviet nuclear offensive (Bravo), and the *retardation* of a Soviet advance (Romeo).[29]

The U.S. Strategic Bombing Survey, recently completed, had concluded that the key German targets during World War II should have been the petroleum and electric power industries (the destruction of the latter, which was not achieved, would have collapsed German industry). Most of the three hundred targets on the first national list of targets (completed in August 1950) were in the Soviet electric power and petroleum industries.[30]

As it turned out, the JCS' priorities ran counter to those SAC was developing for itself. Late in 1950 Lt. Gen. Curtis LeMay, the SAC commander, rejected the list. His pilots might well miss many of the targets. For example, many electric power stations were so isolated that they would be difficult for navigators to find. Attacking them would offer no "bonus damage" (i.e., misses would be entirely wasted). LeMay offered instead to attack (1) liquid fuels; (2) military, governmental, and economic control points; and (3) industrial capital. A new target plan submitted in October 1951 was never approved.[31]

A SAC Emergency War Plan approved by the JCS on 22 October 1951 gives some idea of what could be done at that time. It would take about six days to set up the initial attack. The heavy bomber force (B-36s) would fly from Maine to drop twenty bombs in the Moscow-Gorky area, landing at British bases. Medium bombers (B-29s and B-50s) flying from Labrador would drop twelve bombs in the Leningrad area, also landing in England. Medium bombers from England would fly along the Mediterranean coast to attack the Volga and Donets Basin with fifty-two bombs, landing in Libya and Egypt. Bombers from the Azores would attack the Caucasus with fifteen weapons, landing at Dhahran. Bombers from Guam would drop fifteen bombs on Vladivostok and Irkutsk.[32]

The JCS naturally considered Bravo (blunting the Soviet weapon) the most important task. Even if some Soviet bombers struck first, SAC could hit many others still preparing to attack. After the Korean War broke out, the Joint Chiefs decided that although Bravo was primary, retardation would be done first. SAC resisted; in an informal agreement reached in mid-1951 the army agreed that SAC's campaign against Soviet cities would contribute to retardation by paralyzing the Soviet government. That December SAC was forced to agree to a list of retardation targets nominated by Lt. Gen. Lauris Norstad, the NATO air commander.[33] Plans for Romeo attacks provided for eventual navy participation.

For SAC, Bravo was heaven sent. The list of Delta targets, essentially the important Soviet cities, was not likely to grow very much. However, as the Soviet strategic force grew, the targets it represented multiplied. To deal with them, the air force needed more bombers. For example, in 1953 SAC identified 409 potential Soviet bomber fields. In 1952 the air force unilaterally abolished the interservice Air Intelligence Production Division, merging it into Air Force Intelligence. The other services were permitted to assign representatives to the Estimates and Targets Division of the Air Intelligence Directorate. However, they had little influence on the very large air force organization.[34] Because the air force almost completely controlled air intelligence, it defined the threat against which its bomber force was being built. It seems not to have occurred to SAC that at some point the Soviet bomber force might seem so impressive that SAC's own vulnerability would become a major issue. SAC's emphasis on Bravo targeting did not imply a preemptive war plan. The full Soviet strike might take as long as thirty days to develop. A reasonably agile SAC, then, might well reduce its impact. Because, as it happened, the SAC war plan received no review by any other command or organization until 1956–57, no one asked the natural question: Exactly how did SAC expect to know that the Soviets were about to attack? No satisfactory answer was ever given. In the early 1950s the CIA and other agencies tried hard to place agents near Soviet airfields simply to provide timely warning that a strike was being set up. Overflights were too infrequent to provide systematic warning.

SAC's practices can be explained more charitably. It was caught in a dilemma of its own making. On the one hand, it claimed extreme efficiency, so a limited target set (pre-Bravo) would have justified only a relatively small force. On the other hand, many of its officers had to suspect that in wartime Murphy's Law would apply very forcefully, so that the small force justified by optimistic peacetime calculations would hardly suffice. To get the large force SAC really needed, it could either have embraced Murphy's Law (calling into question whether it could do its job at all) or found a rationale for a much larger force still based on optimistic calculations. The other services must have envied SAC's ability to get the forces it needed without admitting its weaknesses. Once SAC had taken this course, it could not easily retreat.

Overall, SAC was by far the least expensive part of the U.S. military force to expand. The central question of NSC 68 was whether any strategic attack force, however powerful, could deter a nuclear-armed Soviet Union from attacking in Europe or Asia, since the Soviets might well calculate that their own strategic forces would be able to deter the United States. The budget-breaking part of NSC 68 was the call to expand nonnuclear, nonstrategic forces to the point where they might really be able to stand off a Soviet ground attack. Shortly after NSC 68 was completed, the outbreak of war in Korea seemed to demonstrate that nuclear deterrence was indeed quite limited, and thus that very powerful nonnuclear forces were needed. Thus NSC 68 became the plan for U.S. rearmament.

13 THE "SUPER"

The Soviet atomic test roughly coincided with proposals that the United States develop a "super" (hydrogen) bomb. The idea had been raised even before the atomic attacks on Japan. Up to a thousand times as powerful as an atomic bomb, a "super" would match the early expectations for the atomic bomb. In 1949 it was said that, both practically and psychologically, the "super" would be as powerful, compared to the atomic bomb, as the atomic bomb had been to its conventional predecessor. With the advent of H-bombs, U.S. strategists distinguished between serious and decisive attacks. A seriously damaged country could keep fighting. Decisive damage would eliminate the other side's ability to strike back, or reduce its civil, political, and cultural life to chaos, or both. It took H-bombs to do decisive damage.

The fusion bomb (H-bomb) concept was well known: it would use the same nuclear reaction that powers stars (an A-bomb uses nuclear forces in a very different and far less efficient way). To ignite the fusion reaction required extremely high temperature and pressure. The technical problem was that only an atomic bomb could produce those conditions, but the pressure it produced was directed outward instead of inward. Somehow the outward-directed violence of an atomic explosion had to be made to heat and compress hydrogen sufficiently to ignite it before it blew the bomb apart. Solving this problem took considerable ingenuity. Advocates thought they had a solution in 1949, so that production of a bomb would be no more than a matter of development, but they were wrong.

Advocates of the project pointed out that the possibility of an H-bomb was already well known, and that the Soviets could probably develop one as quickly as the Americans. They might already be doing so. We now know that the Soviets had been working on a "super" since 1946, and that they began specific design calculations on one in the summer of 1949.[1]

At the end of September 1949, a special AEC committee headed by the wartime chief of the atomic bomb project, Dr. Robert Oppenheimer, recommended against development. The H-bomb would be so powerful as to threaten the future of the human race itself. Should the Russians develop one, surely the large U.S. atomic bomb stockpile would be a sufficient deterrent. The AEC's General Advisory Committee also recommended against the "super."[2] That did not kill it. The AEC commissioners refused to take a position. Because the issue extended beyond the usual questions of cost, feasibility, and the most efficient use of expensive fissionable material, they laid the question before President Truman. The commissioners thought there was at least a fifty-fifty chance a "super" could be built, and that it could be completed within three years.

Knowledge of the idea was already so widespread that a decision *not* to go ahead could hardly be kept secret. Conversely, to engage the scientific community sufficiently to produce the H-bomb the president would have to make his policy clear and public. At first the AEC feared that a few H-bomb bursts (perhaps as few as ten) would dangerously pollute the atmosphere, but by late November calculations had shown that the number was at least many hundreds, so this consideration was no longer important.[3]

Of the five AEC commissioners, Gordon Dean and Chairman Lewis L. Strauss supported development. Dean argued that foregoing the weapon would be demoralizing. Moreover, until it had been developed, no one could know just what it would do. The H-bomb would be a powerful deterrent: a single bomb could destroy Moscow. Another commissioner, H. D. Smyth, thought that the mere threat to develop the "super" might be used to convince Stalin to accept an agreement to control nuclear weapons.[4]

The chairman of the JCAE, Senator McMahon, considered the "super" a matter of common sense. With fissionable material still very expensive, the United States had too few A-bombs to knock out the Soviets. Using fusion bombs against Soviet cities would free lower-yield fission bombs to destroy Soviet air and naval bases, and thus to reduce the Soviets' ability to retaliate. If the Soviets used "supers" to wipe out American cities, surely the United States would want to be able to retaliate. "Modern warfare, even if waged with pre-atomic weapons only, is the real instrument of genocide—not a single agent like the super. The havoc which Germany visited upon Russia and Western Europe and which the Allies visited upon Germany and Japan during World War II probably surpasses the destructiveness of a dozen supers."[5] To the Joint Chiefs, "possession of a thermonuclear weapon by the USSR without such possession by the United States would be intolerable."[6] According to Paul Nitze, the United States could not afford inferiority. He did fear that emphasizing the possible use of weapons of mass destruction would hurt the U.S. position. The H-bomb would add less to U.S. than to Soviet power, since the United States was already building a large atomic stockpile. Nitze therefore recommended that the bomb be developed and tested, but that production be held up pending further analysis.[7]

On 31 January 1950 President Truman ordered development of the hydrogen bomb. He considered this decision a formality, since work on the H-bomb had been under way since increased bomb research had been approved the previous October. He did not realize that the "super" might not be possible to build. In 1949 some U.S. physicists thought they knew how to build it, at least in principle, but they were wrong. The very inventive solution, developed by Teller and Ulam in 1952, was to use the bomb's radiation, which moved much faster than the blast, to compress the hydrogen, or "secondary," element. The U.S. government seems to have kept this secret until the late 1970s.[8]

A test device, incorporating a huge refrigerator to keep the hydrogen liquid, was soon built and exploded, with spectacular results, on 1 November 1952.[9] The United States tested the first deliverable H-bombs early in 1954, in a series of tests code-named Castle.[10] Initially the emphasis was on building the most powerful "super," the city-buster. However, the same technology also led to extremely light lower-yield bombs, a fact of great significance to later missile builders.

Just how inventive Teller and Ulam were is suggested by the fact that it took the Soviets some years to stumble onto it. Andrei Sakharov, the Soviet designer, did not initially guess the Teller-Ulam idea. Instead, he went ahead with a "layer cake," an idea which the U.S. designers already had discarded. As the name suggests, the outward-directed blast compressed and heated a layer of fusion material wrapped around the primary (fission) element and surrounded by a heavy shell which would keep it from bursting apart instantly. The Soviets touted this bomb, which they tested on 12 August 1953, as the world's first deliverable H-bomb, but it was nothing of the sort. Fusion contributed some, but not very much, of its explosive power. Sakharov and his two main collaborators, Zeldovich and Khariton (who had led the Soviet atomic program) developed their own version of the Teller-Ulam principle early in 1954. A bomb embodying it was tested on 22 November 1955.

Sole U.S. possession of the secret of the H-bomb made the AEC and JCAE very reluctant to provide the British with nuclear weapons design information. After the British exploded their first atomic bomb in October 1952, U.S. scientists agreed with their British counterparts that it would be best to pool design information. With the U.S. explosion of the first H-bomb (1 November 1952) it seemed to the AEC and JCAE that the United States was, if anything, drawing further ahead of the British; their contribution would be less and less valuable.

However, the new president, Dwight D. Eisenhower, placed increased emphasis on NATO and on nuclear weapons to balance massed Soviet ground forces. He began to talk about sharing nuclear weapons with the NATO allies. To do that, they needed basic information, such as the size, weight, and shape of U.S. weapons they might use in wartime, as well as weapons effects and plans to use weapons in European defense. This was not weapon design information, but the AEC feared that its shape would give away the H-bomb secret. The British were particularly interested in weapon dimensions and weights because they expected that in wartime their new jet bombers would be armed mainly with U.S.-supplied weapons. Otherwise they would have far too few weapons; in 1954 the RAF planned to buy only about twenty bombs, against a capacity to deliver about two hundred. Congress approved the required changes to the AEC act on 30 August 1954.

The British cabinet formally decided to develop an H-bomb on 26 July 1954, discussions having begun earlier that year (previously the British had believed the H-bomb was beyond their means).[11] As an interim step, in January 1956 Defence Minister Duncan Sandys formally proposed that the RAF use U.S. bombs in wartime. A detailed agreement was reached that August. Under this "Project E," bombs were held under USAF custody at RAF bases; they could be released by presidential order. Project E was developed in concert with the plan to provide Thor IRBMs (with U.S. warheads) to Britain. Eisenhower pressed both projects forward after Suez, because he badly wanted to rebuild the Special Relationship with Britain.[12] AEC and JCAE opposition to both new projects was not fully overcome until the shock of Sputnik was felt in the fall of 1957.

The British cared mainly that their "H-bomb" should have a yield of about a megaton, rather than the kilotons of conventional atomic bombs. The bomb's designer, John C. Ward, later said that he understood the Teller-Ulam configuration within six months of seeing the shape of an American H-bomb, which was long and slender rather than very fat as in a layer cake. Those concerned with U.S. nuclear security had been right. On the other hand, designing a two-stage bomb was tricky. The British developed a boosted atomic bomb as a backup, to insure that they exploded some sort of megaton bomb in 1957.[13] On 8 November 1957 one of their bombs yielded a greater-than-expected 1.8 megatons. On 28 April 1958 another bomb yielded 3 megatons.[14] Britain now had the H-bomb. The United States no longer had a monopoly in the West.

On 2 July 1958 President Eisenhower signed a revised AEC act allowing transfer of nonnuclear weapons parts to countries (i.e., Britain) which had already made substantial progress in developing nuclear weapons, "provided such transfer would not contribute significantly to that nation's atomic weapons design, development, or fabrication capability." Since the British had demonstrated a true H-bomb, they could receive U.S. H-bomb components. A new U.S.-British agreement on nuclear cooperation was concluded on 3 July 1958. As amended on 7 May 1959, this agreement allowed for the supply of both nonnuclear materials and bomb designs. The British showed the Americans their bomb designs. U.S. designers concluded that they had tested weapons equivalent to those the U.S. had tested in 1954–55, and their designs approximated those the U.S. had developed by 1956. However, the British had enough new ideas to make the exchange worthwhile.[15] By about 1961 the British were making their own version of the U.S. B-28 bomb. All later British bombs were reportedly based on U.S. designs. Project E became "technically effective" on 1 October 1958 when seventy-two aircraft armed with Mk 5 bombs were operational at three RAF bases. It ended in 1969 when British bombs replaced U.S. weapons in Germany. Due to U.S. legal requirements for custody, it was impossible to disperse a bombed-up force of British bombers preloaded with the U.S. weapons.[16]

Coincident with the opening of American atomic secrets to Britain was the gradual transfer of U.S. bombs, both atomic and hydrogen, from AEC (civilian) to military custody, and from storage in the United States to overseas bases. Initially plans called for the president to authorize transfer to the military in an emergency. SAC's bombs would have been carried to its overseas bases on board its own cargo aircraft, for example. In 1950, when he considered using nuclear weapons in Korea, President Truman agreed that nine bombs should be moved to the SAC base on Okinawa.

Everywhere else, nonnuclear bomb components were stored on U.S. bases and on board ships, but the crucial nuclear components had to be flown out from the AEC storage sites in the United States. That was one reason any atomic war would have been fought in fairly slow motion. To President Eisenhower, that was impractical. In 1954 he decided to deploy nuclear components overseas, but only to places where the United States would have sole control over them (which then meant Guam and the carriers). Storage of complete weapons was approved for Britain and Morocco in April 1954 and for West Germany that June. Even so, at the end of the year the Defense Department had custody of only 167 of the 1,630 U.S. atomic weapons. Only in 1958 did its stockpile exceed that of the AEC (4,017 vs. 3,385 weapons). The next year, however, the Defense Department had 8,337 of the 12,305 U.S. weapons. That was partly due to the proliferation of missile warheads, which could not possibly have been held back in AEC custody.

Through 1949–50 U.S. strategists were forced to make some very unpleasant calculations. If Stalin struck, they could not possibly hold everywhere; they had to choose. Their problem, as it turned out, was that once Stalin struck anywhere, they had to resist; and this resistance cost much more than the place they defended was worth. Resistance mattered because the effort and determination they showed would, perhaps illogically, demonstrate just how serious they were about the primary theater of Cold War, Europe, where a Western defeat would have been mortal.

In 1950 northeast Asia was anything but stable. Mao had just won his war in China. U.S. occupation forces had just pulled out of South Korea, into which they had come under wartime agreements. Most unsettling of all, on 12 January 1950 Secretary of State Dean Acheson said publicly what the JCS well knew: given the weakness of its forces, the United States had had to make choices. Asia was far less important than Europe. There, the United States would defend only an offshore "island chain" consisting of Japan—the region's only real industrial power—the Ryukyus, and the Philippines. The chain included neither Formosa nor South Korea.

Stalin almost certainly considered Korea much more important than Acheson did. Czarist Russia had valued the country to such an extent that it had gone to war against Japan in 1904 to retain it. Then, Korea had been described throughout the world as the "dagger pointing at the heart of Japan." Conversely, the Chinese thought of it as a dagger pointing from Japan to them.[1] In 1950, it seemed unlikely to Stalin that anyone in Japan would ignore a Communist victory in Korea. As soon as American occupation forces left, the Japanese would welcome a Communist government of their own. Far from being an unimportant part of a peripheral area, Korea was at least central in the Far East. The U.S. view, in which purely military considerations made island chains defensible, was laughable.

Stalin had his own problems. Mao might well prove to be an Asian Tito; it was essential to bind him closely and irrevocably to the Soviet Union. From this point of view China was far more important than Korea; Stalin would certainly have been willing to let Korea be devastated if that would keep Mao in check. For the moment, he had to demonstrate his own loyalty to Mao. In January 1950 the Soviet delegation to the United Nations walked out, arguing that no Security Council meeting could be valid without the Chinese Communists. That would have unexpected consequences six months later.

In 1950 North Korea already had a Communist government, installed in 1945 (in popular front form) by the occupying Red Army. Stalin had apparently long had plans for Korea: in 1942 he formed the 88th Infantry Brigade, one of whose four units consisted of Koreans, to train cadres for a future Korean People's Army. Its commander, Kim Il Sung, became ruler, earlier Korean Communist leaders being ousted in his favor.[2] South Korea had a government, under Syngman Rhee, installed by U.S. occupation forces. Both Kim and Syngman Rhee espoused reunification. In 1948 Kim apparently resolved to unify Korea by force.[3]

Once in power, Kim organized the North, the industrial heart of Korea, on Soviet political and economic lines. Two one-year plans (1946 and 1947) were pronounced successes, with statistics published; but the 1948–49 two-year plan failed disastrously. He visited Moscow in March 1949 to ask for help. No mutual defense treaty was signed; instead, Kim got a ten-year economic and cultural treaty. By early 1950 some of Kim's advisors argued that it was folly to rebuild with only a third of the country's labor force when the much more populous South could easily be conquered. The North Koreans drafted a land reform law for the South as early as May 1949, so clearly quite early they had conquest in mind.[4]

Kim also faced a challenge. The Communist leader in the South, Pak Hong-yong, hoped for a revolution that would install him in power (and, given the larger Southern population, make him supreme). In 1949 Syngman Rhee's army was effectively suppressing his guerillas. He was therefore anxious for Kim to come to the rescue. Much the same argument would surface in Vietnam in 1959, when Communists in the South felt hard-pressed by an effective South Vietnamese government. Pak encouraged Kim by promising him that two hundred thousand guerillas would rise once an invasion began. Kim apparently blamed Pak for his own failure; on 8 February 1963, celebrating his army's fifteenth anniversary, he told army officers that Pak was a liar who did not have even one thousand members, let alone two hundred thousand; no one had ever revolted as promised.[5]

Stalin chided Kim for not being more aggressive: "You must strike the southerners in the teeth." However, he was chary of attacking the U.S. forces, which were about to withdraw. In 1949 he said that Kim should attack only if U.S. and South Korean forces came north. Yet there is also evidence that Stalin was interested in a direct attack south. For example, decisions about Korea reportedly were made at a strategic planning session in Moscow in 1948; at a follow-up meeting in Harbin in January 1949 the Chinese agreed that by the following September they would return to the Koreans twenty-eight thousand troops of Korean descent who were then fighting in the Chinese Civil War.[6] At this time Kim, who had been an anti-

Japanese guerilla in China in the 1930s, hoped that Pak's guerillas could overthrow the South by the fall of 1949.[7] In that case his army would be playing Stalin's preferred role of supporting an ongoing revolution, rather than assaulting entrenched enemy troops.

As early as 1947 the U.S. government pondered ways of withdrawing its expensive troops from South Korea without surrendering the country to the Communists. A local army was formed, initially as the South Korean Constabulary. U.S. troops were to have left beginning on 15 August 1948, but their departure was delayed to 15 January 1949, partly because some units of the South Korean Constabulary (Army) mutinied at Communist instigation in October and November 1948. Early in 1949 the CIA warned that Kim would probably invade soon after any U.S. withdrawal. Even a weak U.S. force deterred attack by its mere presence, but large forces would be needed once an attack began. Moreover, a Korean collapse would convince many Japanese that the United States would not protect them. The U.S. Army disagreed; if the Soviets wanted South Korea, they would more likely infiltrate guerillas.[8] A nervous Syngman Rhee tried to convince the U.S. government not to withdraw its troops, but occupation was too expensive to sustain. He also failed to extract a U.S. commitment to defend Korea. Americans may well have feared that Rhee was only another Chiang. Yet arming and training a South Korean army could be risky: Rhee might well try, as he had threatened, to go north.[9] To prevent that, the United States denied him combat aircraft. In mid-1950 Rhee's five best divisions (four on the border and one covering the capital, Seoul) had only one artillery battalion each, rather than four, as in U.S. divisions. Their 105mm howitzers were outranged by the guns supplied by the Soviets to the North Koreans. The other three South Korean divisions were intended mainly to deal with the expected threat of subversion or guerilla warfare. They were under strength and poorly armed. Throughout the army, large-unit (regimental-level) training had just been completed.

There was considerable wishful thinking. By January 1950 the U.S. Army believed that the "increasingly efficient" South Korean army was an effective deterrent against a North Korean invasion. Thus the CIA discounted the southward movement of North Korean troops that month as no more than a defensive maneuver "to offset the growing strength of the offensively-minded South Korean Army." It was aware that the Chinese were releasing troops from Manchuria to the North Koreans (which would solve what it called a North Korean manpower problem) and was also aware that tanks and heavy field guns were being assigned to North Korean units near the border. War was still six months away.[10] On 19 June, with war less than a week away, the CIA reported that, although the North Koreans had gained increased offensive capability, they were still unlikely to overrun South Korea, due in part to the anti-Communist attitude of the South Koreans and the morale of their troops. At this time the agency rated the two armies equivalent in combat effectives (manpower), training, and leadership, the North leading in armor, heavy artillery, and aircraft. Thus the North Koreans were credited with the ability to attain limited objectives in South Korea, including the capture of the capital, Seoul, which was so close to the border. Anything more would depend on Soviet aid.[11] There was no question but that the North Koreans wanted to take over the South, but the agency's assessment was that they would be limited to propaganda, infiltration, sabotage, subversion, and guerilla warfare, none of which was likely to be very successful.

Kim's own army had been equipped, first, with the weapons left by the Soviet force that withdrew in 1948. His Soviet military advisors praised his army's performance in a July 1949 border battle at Kaesong.[12] In September, Kim asked Stalin for permission to attack the South. He argued that Rhee was already unpopular, and that his economy was collapsing. Stalin was skeptical: by December 1949 Rhee's army had neutralized the guerilas. After one of Kim's patrols crossed the border with South Korea, Stalin forbade any further crossings without his express approval.[13] He did not consider Kim ready for war. Although his army was far more powerful than Rhee's, Stalin was impressed by Rhee's rhetoric and by his army's willingness to attack. In 1949 he apparently doubted that Kim's regime would survive.[14]

Stalin supplied tanks, which had served the Red Army so well during World War II. They were part of the standard model army that every Soviet client state built after World War II. They were also the offensive arm Kim needed for the strike south.[15] Rhee's U.S. advisors had made what turned out to be a devastating error of judgement. They had decided that mountainous Korea was poor tank country. Not only had Rhee been given no tanks (which might have been considered dangerously offensive), but he had also received no antitank weapons beyond bazookas, which were ineffective against the heavy frontal armor of the North Korean T-34 tanks. Few South Koreans had even seen tanks before the invasion. As in many other wars, once in action their mere appearance helped cause panic.[16]

Events began to move in the wake of Acheson's January 1950 speech. In Moscow, Molotov read Mao a translation of Acheson's speech.[17] Soviet spies had probably already told Stalin that the United States did not plan to defend Korea. Kim renewed his plea to liberate South Korea. Now that Mao had won in China, surely it was his turn. Stalin gave him the go-ahead on 17 January 1950.[18]

Whose war would this be? The written record makes it very much Kim Il Sung's. He asked again and again, until Stalin consented. However, Stalin was expert at inducing his creatures to ask for what he wanted, approving when they fit his desired pattern. He left no written record of his own initiative, yet there seems to be no question that Stalin made sure that he alone made key decisions. Surely a choice to fight fell into this category.

At this time Mao was so anxious to invade Taiwan that, while still in Moscow in February 1950, he ordered formation of the necessary paratroop units. At the end of March 1950 he approved a series of amphibious operations, beginning with the

Zhoushan Islands, followed by Quemoy and then by Taiwan itself. On 21 April he ordered demobilization, probably to concentrate what equipment he had in the units assaulting Taiwan. He asked the Soviets to speed delivery of naval matériel needed for the Taiwan operation (and for coast defense). Mao found that his buildup for the Taiwan operation was taking longer than expected, and early in June 1950 the date of the invasion was set back to the summer of 1951.[19]

Mao doubted that Kim could successfully invade the South.[20] He and his army feared that the United States would react to Kim's invasion, and that the resulting war might endanger their state.[21] Mao therefore tried and failed to dissuade Kim. During the two months leading up to the war both Kim and Stalin deliberately kept all details of the operation from Mao. For example, nearly all Soviet weapons were sent by sea rather than by rail through China. In the mid-1950s senior Chinese military men were still furious at having been excluded from Kim's decision-making, particularly given the high price China was later forced to pay for participation in the war.[22] Mao presented Stalin with an interesting opportunity. He had only enough force either to attack Taiwan or to support a Korean War. Engaged in Korea, he could not invade Taiwan—which Stalin saw as the outstanding issue between Mao and the United States. Mao could not turn Titoist and embrace the West as long as Chiang survived on the island.[23] Moreover, once he entered the war, Mao would become entirely dependent on Soviet-supplied munitions. If the United States did not intervene, or lost, Japan would soon fall into Communist hands. Yet Mao could not refuse Stalin, the chief of the world revolutionary movement, and his only viable source of assistance.

On 9 February Stalin ordered the preparation of a "Preemptive Strike Operations Plan."[24] Having failed to dissuade Kim, Mao offered him the two divisions of Koreans who had served in the Chinese army—as well as Chinese soldiers, which he would have needed to conquer Taiwan.[25] He put back his plan to seize the island to 1951, after the Koreans should have won.[26] Kim began probes into South Korea in the spring of 1950. Prisoner interrogations convinced his high command that the South Korean army would present few problems.[27] Kim planned for victory in twenty-two to twenty-seven days. He expected Pak's guerillas and Communists to help decisively.[28] Amateurishly, the North Koreans made no allowance for any possible failure of their plan.[29]

Stalin gave Kim the final go-ahead after he was briefed by his own and Chinese experts on 10 June. To mask his responsibility, he used Gromyko's signature on the final telegram.[30] To avoid embarrassment, Stalin withdrew Soviet advisors from the border.[31] He also demanded a cover story: the war would be presented as a counterattack (though it was planned as a pure offensive). Thus Stalin had the authors of the Soviet military encyclopedia describe a fictitious U.S. attack plan developed in May 1949, to be executed in the summer of 1950 by over one hundred thousand South Korean troops armed by the United States.[32]

While Stalin and Kim secretly plotted, Chiang's stock rose in American eyes. To the Joint Chiefs, Mao was Stalin's chief ally, and the United States was "to all intents and purposes" at war with the Soviets. Chiang's continued resistance helped dissipate Communist energies. In the spring, following Mao's conquest of Hainan (a large island off the Chinese coast), the Truman administration agreed to expedite shipment of weapons already sold to Chiang (except for tanks and jet aircraft).

Chiang had an important friend in the Far East. General Douglas MacArthur, commander in chief of U.S. forces there, argued that in hostile hands Formosa (Taiwan) would become an "unsinkable aircraft carrier" from which enemy aircraft could neutralize Okinawa and northern Luzon and thus isolate Japan from supporting bases in the island chain. Japanese aircraft on Formosa had been used successfully against MacArthur in the Philippines in 1941.

The attack had to begin before the July rains, which would muddy the ground, making the North Korean tanks useless. Its exact timing was left to Kim. He attacked on 25 June 1950, achieving complete tactical surprise, despite numerous warnings.[33] The key was the U.S. expectation that Stalin was too cautious to take such a chance. Moreover, he seemed much more interested in Europe. Thus the effect of the invasion was stunning: for the first time Stalin seemed willing to risk—however remotely—general war. The attack might even be a distraction to conceal preparations to strike Western Europe. Only as this fear receded (by the end of June 1950) could American forces be spared to defend Korea.[34] Conversely, Acheson argued forcefully that Korea had to be defended precisely in order to keep Stalin from trying for anything more.[35] Later it would seem that in Korea Stalin had found a way to fight without direct involvement or, therefore, direct risk. For example, the Soviets might use East German irregulars to attack West Germany. The Western Allies would be unable to attack the supporting Soviets, just as, during the Korean War, they were unable to strike at China.

The U.S. delegation to the UN asked that force be authorized to punish the North Korean aggressors. Having walked out, the Soviets could not veto the motion, which was adopted by the Security Council. Given a UN mandate, President Truman felt no need for a formal declaration of what he characterized as a "police action." Later the Republican Congress would snipe at him. Not having voted for war, they did not feel responsible for its prosecution. Fourteen years later, Lyndon Johnson said that the great lesson of Korea had been that Congress had to be brought on board before the United States could be committed to war. Hence his Tonkin Gulf Resolution.

The United States contributed the UN commander, General MacArthur, who was both CinC Far East and U.S. occupation chief in Japan. Indeed, quick U.S. intervention was practical only because a large U.S. occupation force, the four under-strength divisions of the Eighth Army, was in Japan.[36]

Other countries made substantial contributions; Korea was a coalition war.[37] The British in particular hoped that their effort would give them a say in U.S. decisions. They and other Europeans feared, not that Stalin planned a wider war, but that U.S. actions in Korea might cause escalation. For example, open war with China might activate clauses of the Sino-Soviet treaty, which would bring the Soviets into the war—and they might strike in Europe rather than in the Far East.

For his part, Stalin may not have considered the UN a factor in the U.S. reaction to Kim's invasion. He was probably far more concerned to keep Mao in line.[38] The walkout was never repeated: Soviet vetoes paralyzed the United Nations for nearly four decades.

For Mao, already convinced that the United States would eventually attack China to topple his revolution, the firm U.S. reaction to the North Korean attack was worrying. It seemed impossible that the United States would go to much effort merely to defend South Korea, particularly since Acheson had said as recently as January that the country was not a vital U.S. interest.[39] Since Mao believed that the conflict might well spread to China, early in July he ordered preparations for war, beginning with the reinforcement of the force on the Korean border.[40]

Once war broke out, the United States tried to force the Pacific Pact and Peace Treaty issues in hopes of binding Japan to the West. Soon all four U.S. divisions in Japan—which helped hold down the local Communists—might be committed to Korea. Early North Korean successes might well encourage anti-American sentiment. The occupation itself clearly grated on the Japanese. The sooner it was over, the more likely the resulting Japanese government would be friendly, and the treaty it signed favorable.[41]

Kim's forces won early victories against both South Korean and extemporized U.S. resistance. North Korean success was ominous. It seemed to demonstrate that the Soviets could develop armies very quickly, where little real military expertise had previously existed. The growing strength of the European satellite armies became far more significant.

The U.S. units rushed from Japan had been badly run down. The army as a whole had its units within divisions cut by a third. That was much worse than it appeared: a division with two rather than three regiments would have two rather than three battalions per regiment and two rather than three rifle companies per battalion: twelve rather than twenty-seven rifle companies in all. The divisions in Japan in 1950 had three rifle companies per battalion (eighteen companies per division, 62 percent of authorized infantry firepower). However, because the U.S. Army had judged that Japan was unsuitable for tanks, the divisions had only 14 percent of their planned tank firepower.

President Truman quickly approved manpower increases to bring the Far East force to war strength. Unfortunately, the only reservoir of trained manpower was the general reserve divisions in the United States, the insurance against emergencies elsewhere. Korea was, after all, a peripheral theater of operations. Everyone in Washington agreed that Western Europe was the key to Cold War survival. There, a few under-strength NATO divisions faced massive Soviet forces, which had not been drawn down to support the war in the East.

Truman had seen little point in maintaining large and expensive standing forces. Clearly the United States would need substantial forces *if* it had to fight. The affordable solution was large well-equipped reserves; as it happened, the Army Annual Report issued in June 1950, at the outbreak of war, reported the completion of equipment for the last of the twenty-five authorized reserve divisions. On 19 July President Truman announced that he was calling up reservists.[42] Unfortunately reservists, even those who had so recently fought World War II, needed time-consuming training before they could be considered combat-ready. That was even truer of full reserve units. The army called back selected reservists to fill out the five divisions in the United States. To replace the four earmarked for Korea, four Army National Guard infantry divisions and two regimental combat teams were activated, with the understanding that they would not be combat-ready until 1951. The two marine divisions were brought to full strength.

Korea thus demonstrated flaws in the reserve concept. Past U.S. wars had always allowed the time to bring reservists up to combat standard, but this war came as a surprise. Then, too, the men themselves were now the least of the cost. Due to the revolution in ground force composition, each of those fully equipped reserve units consumed a large quantity of weapons and other equipment. That left less to be distributed among the active units—and even less in stockpiles, which might be raided in an emergency. Fortunately the defense industrial base built during World War II had been preserved—and could be reactivated. There were still substantial stocks of World War II ammunition.

From the point of view of the Cold War, perhaps the most significant U.S. decision made at this time was to rearm on a global scale, not merely to fight the war in Korea. Korea seemed to prove that Nitze's NSC 68 had been correct: Stalin was now ready for war. President Truman approved rearmament (to be complete in FY54) on 30 September 1950. The defense budget was more than quadrupled. President Truman now discovered that the choice was often not guns *or* butter but rather more butter due to more money flowing through an economy making more guns. Probably because the economy was in recession when the buildup began, Keynesian pump priming generated growth rather than ruinous inflation.

Much of the new money went into weapons (and into research) tied to the larger Cold War. SAC was pumped up to execute its new Bravo (blunting mission); the Korean War coincided with the advent of Stalin's atomic bomb. There was finally production money for the B-47 jet medium bomber, SAC's mainstay through the 1950s. It required air-to-air refueling, which in turn made it necessary to develop the KC-135 jet tanker—which became the parent of Boeing's jet airliners. Money was also available for a larger subsonic jet bomber with intercontinental range, the B-52, and for work on long-range missiles. Overall, the air force strategic component had to grow simply to add Bravo capability. When in September 1951 the JCS approved (over other service objections) an air force proposal to grow to 126 combat wings rather than the eighty planned in 1950, with fifty-seven rather than thirty-four SAC wings, it marked a historic change in U.S. strategy: the air force now had priority.[43]

The other two services were not suffering too badly. The anemic ten-division army was fleshed out, well beyond the needs of the Korean War. The army soon more than doubled its prewar force to a total of twenty-one divisions: thirteen ready divisions abroad (six in Korea, two in Japan, five plus a division equivalent in Germany) plus the existing five-division general reserve in the United States plus three special training divisions for draftees. Moreover, all these units were at full strength, fully equipped. On the other hand, the JCS rejected a 1952 army proposal to increase further, to twenty-seven divisions. This force was too small to fight a general war but too expensive to sustain; the army would still depend on reserves for a big war.

The navy finally got its large carriers, beginning with USS *Forrestal* in the FY52 budget. Carriers had already proven extremely valuable when the North Koreans overran airfields in South Korea; they were clearly a vital way of responding to the emergencies the Cold War was likely to breed. The six-carrier force considered barely affordable in 1950 was suddenly doubled to twelve. The two under-strength marine divisions were fleshed out and a third added.

To Nitze and his colleagues, the buildup was intended to raise the *sustained* level of defense spending. The Cold War would last long after the Korean conflict had ended; there would be no peace dividend. Not everyone agreed that the public would tolerate even $20 billion per year, let alone what Nitze had in mind. As a young army officer, Secretary of Defense Marshall had lived through very lean times between the two World Wars, when the U.S. public lost interest in defense. To him, the U.S. defense industrial base rather than its standing forces was the key deterrent. He saw the buildup as a one-time $108 billion gift, to be spent slowly to keep the production base alive, so that in the next emergency it could equip reserves who could be called up as needed. Nitze disagreed: there would not be time to mobilize next time. U.S. armed strength could deter Stalin. Nitze won.[44]

The U.S. economy performed remarkably well. Inflation was held down (it rose from 2 percent in 1950 to 8 percent in 1952) partly by price controls and by higher taxes, but much more by the fact that the economy grew about as fast as the defense budget: GNP grew from $278.5 billion in 1948 to about $325 billion in 1951.[45] Consumers were able to continue spending at earlier levels while companies invested in the economy to fuel further growth. The economy seemed set to continue to grow about 5 percent per year for the next several years, leaving room for further defense growth.[46]

To Nitze, all this was possible because so much less was being demanded than in World War II. As planned in November 1950, peak spending, at an annual rate of about $70 billion in the second half of FY52, would amount to about 25 percent of U.S. GNP, compared to 42 percent in World War II (which would have been $130 billion in 1952). The military manpower target for June 1952, 3.2 million, was only

4.5 percent of the labor force, compared to over 17 percent in World War II. The military would absorb 15–20 percent of the U.S. steel supply, compared to over 50 percent in World War II. Civilians might find it difficult to obtain everything they wanted, but they could probably spend within 10 percent of their 1950 budgets, which had broken previous records. They would be nearly a quarter better off than in 1944, over half again as well off as in 1939.[47]

The Republicans argued that expensive conventional forces (apart from those needed for Korea) actually bought little. A nuclear stalemate was developing; without effective defense against Soviet nuclear attack (which seemed to be impossible), the United States would do better (at much lower cost) to base its defense mainly on the threat of nuclear retaliation. Most notable among the Republican critics were Sen. Robert H. Taft and John Foster Dulles. Taft was a potential 1952 presidential candidate. Dulles had been chief foreign policy advisor to Gov. Thomas E. Dewey, the Republican candidate in 1944 and 1948, was advisor to the State Department in 1950–52, and would be Eisenhower's secretary of state.

Nitze argued that deterrence might be an illusion. Where a U.S. government might fear the destruction of its citizenry, the far more ruthless Soviets might feel much less inhibited. Conventional forces were needed because without them advances by Stalin would offer the United States a choice only between surrender and nuclear war. Moreover, new air defense technology might dramatically tip the nuclear balance by making it possible for the United States to fend off a Soviet bomber attack. Surely, as overall Western strength increased there would be real opportunities to roll back the Iron Curtain, short of overt military action. Within a decade, the West might hold the balance of power.

For the moment, it was painfully clear that Secretary of Defense Johnson had cut too much muscle in his pursuit of defense fat. President Truman fired him on 11 September. Later he said that Johnson had let him down so badly, and in so many ways, that he had been meaning to fire him since May—well before the outbreak of war. Johnson's intrigues against Secretary of State Acheson (and, incidentally, against support for Western Europe) may have been part of the problem.

As the North Koreans advanced, MacArthur became more and more pessimistic. He asked for up to two of the four divisions in Japan; he was offered all four. He was already planning to land behind the North Korean's front, and he asked for a Marine Regimental Combat Team (about a third of a division) to lead the operation. On 9 July he sent a panicky message asking for four *more* divisions, since his troops, fighting against "overwhelming odds of more than ten to one" could barely hope to hold the southern tip of Korea. The next day he asked that the marine unit be built up to a full division. Since he had not yet received the troops already in the pipeline, it was not clear that he needed so much more.[48]

He was already displaying those unsettling traits of grandiosity and instability that would soon prove disastrous. To Washington, Korea was clearly a secondary theater; the key to the Cold War was in Europe. To satisfy his ego, MacArthur had to make Korea something much more important. His UN mandate was simply to repel the North Koreans, preferably without crossing the 38th Parallel, the prewar border between the Koreas. He was to continue north only if that was necessary to eliminate a "serious risk" to South Korea.[49] He told visiting Army Chief of Staff Lawton Collins that he would destroy the North Korean Army rather than merely push it back over the border. He might have to occupy North Korea to do so. The war had become a crusade, in which MacArthur was the hero. To execute it he wanted more men than the JCS or the nervous allies could provide. To get them, he kept asking for more troops before those already in the pipeline arrived. Collins reminded his staff that resources were limited; they should not get "too grandiose."[50]

MacArthur already saw Chiang Kai-shek as a reliable and vital ally. He held the only large local reservoir of manpower. A panicky MacArthur strongly urged the use of KMT troops. In return, Chiang had to be "unleashed" against Mao. Chiang had already made exactly these calculations. The U.S. government thought otherwise. It did not know that Mao had already decided that any U.S. operation in Korea was an indirect attack on China, hence that he would probably intervene if Kim faltered. Rather, it hoped to keep the vast Chinese army out of the war. Any sort of military arrangement with Chiang would be suicidal.

The United States therefore rejected Chiang's offer as early as 30 June. President Truman ordered the Seventh Fleet to the Formosa (Taiwan) Straits. It protected Chiang against any Communist attack—but it was also ordered to stop Chiang's own air and sea attacks against the mainland. With his preconceptions, Mao saw this not as neutrality but rather as the expected open U.S. intervention in the Chinese civil war. He seems not to have believed that until late June 1950 the U.S. government had wanted no part of the Chinese civil war. It still hoped to conciliate Mao. The U.S. government refused to bomb the bases Chiang claimed were being developed to invade Formosa.[51]

Moreover, the UN allies fighting in Korea were less than enthusiastic about Chiang. The British and their Commonwealth partners in particular badly wanted to maintain relations with Mao, to safeguard both Hong Kong and valuable trade relations.[52] They refused to have their forces employed alongside the Nationalists.

Ultimately the U.S. Army retreated into a strong defensive perimeter around the southern port of Pusan. By the time they had definitely been stopped, on 1 September, the North Koreans had suffered badly: their initial combat strength of eighty-nine thousand may have been reduced to only fifty-eight thousand. Conscripted peasants, who were hardly effective, filled out the North Korean army. Much of the work of stopping the North Korean advance was done by mid-July, i.e., by troops already in the Far East.[53] By this time the Joint Chiefs were badly frightened. MacArthur had convinced them to earmark for him virtually all the trained reserves in the United States, except for one airborne division (the 82d). His projected amphibious attack seemed risky, and it would use up all of the reserves MacArthur already had. If anything went very wrong, the United States would have nothing to fall back on; the newly called-up National Guard divisions would not be ready for at least four months.

On 28 August Stalin sent Kim a congratulatory telegram (without his signature).[54] He probably already suspected that the Americans would redress the balance. Given how well his spies were placed, he may well have been aware of MacArthur's plans for an amphibious landing. It was time to lever Mao into the war. He urged Mao to position nine divisions on the border with Korea, ready to intervene if the situation deteriorated. Mao already feared that U.S. forces would continue on to attack China once they defeated the North Koreans.[55] The Chinese deployment, completed by late August, precluded any invasion of Taiwan until 1952. This delay turned out to be permanent.[56]

Stalin told the East Europeans that the United States might attack them to compensate for its failure in Asia. He seems to have placed special emphasis on Czechoslovakia.[57] It is not clear to what extent this war scare was much more than a justification for the ongoing purge in Eastern Europe. To Americans, however, it suggested that Stalin was preparing to fight. President Truman warned publicly against Soviet intervention. U.S. nuclear bombers were transferred to the Far East. It is not clear to what extent Stalin knew about them.[58] Mao considered Korea was one of two threatening border regions. The other was Indochina, into which some KMT troops had retreated at the end of the Chinese civil war. The outbreak of war in Korea coincided roughly with Ho Chi Minh's border offensive designed to clear the Sino-Vietnamese border of French troops—and of the KMT survivors.[59] Mao told the Vietnamese that they were part of a two-pronged attack against the U.S. When the situation in Korea reversed in September 1950, he became far more cautious. For example, he withdrew Chinese troops from the Indochinese border.[60]

On 15 September MacArthur counterattacked. His marines, backed up by the 7th Division to form X Corps, landed in the enemy's rear at Inchon, near Seoul, the hub of the South Korean road and rail net. The landing was difficult because huge mudflats obstructed the harbor (except at high tide) and because a small fortified island, Wolmi-Do, dominated the narrow channel. Although MacArthur was obsessed with secrecy, in August 1950 Chinese intelligence predicted the Inchon landing, although it incorrectly assumed that the Eighth Army, which had made numerous amphibious assaults during World War II, would carry it out. Late in August, Mao warned Kim's personal representative in Beijing, naming three potential invasion targets, including Inchon. The North Koreans apparently did not react; perhaps they could not have redeployed their army in any case.[61]

The effect was devastating; the North Koreans were taken in their rear. A reinforced Eighth Army broke out of Pusan and drove north, linking up with X Corps on 27 September. Seoul, near the prewar border, fell on the twenty-eighth. The North Korean army disintegrated, 130,000 prisoners being taken. It was not rebuilt until mid-1951, and even then was used mainly as a general reserve. Shortly after the Inchon landing, the North Koreans informally asked for Chinese troops. Chou En-lai quickly sent five senior officers to Korea to observe conditions and frame plans for a Chinese intervention force.[62]

Now Korea could be reunited on U.S. terms. When JCS members visited Mac-Arthur in August, they agreed that he should be authorized to pursue the North Koreans beyond the prewar border.[63] On 1 September the NSC approved this hot pursuit, but it also cautioned MacArthur, because it feared escalation.[64] If either the Soviets or the Chinese moved troops into North Korea, or even announced their intentions to do so, he was to stop, take the defensive, and await further UN instructions. North Korea should be occupied only in consultation with the UN. The JCS objected that the order was too rigid; some operations might naturally extend into North Korea. As rewritten, a prohibition on extending operations near the Chinese and Soviet borders became a prohibition on operations *across* those borders. Similarly, where the NSC order originally barred any but South Korean forces from the border areas, now it was merely overall policy not to do so.[65]

By late September the war seemed won, and the State Department was drafting terms: surrender of all North Korean forces, occupation of key points, and UN-supervised elections.[66] MacArthur planned to advance to a line in North Korea, across the country's narrowest neck. Beyond that line he would use only South Korean troops.[67]

Stalin pronounced the war lost. On 29 September Kim pleaded for Soviet troops. Stalin put his Far Eastern ground forces on alert, but he was in no hurry for war with the United States. He sent supplies but no troops. On 1 October Kim asked Mao to intervene. That day Beijing received an intelligence report that UN troops were crossing the 38th parallel. The next day Mao told Stalin that he would enter the war. He ordered his twelve-division intervention force, which was already in Manchuria, to get ready to move into Korea. That could begin on 15 October. Another twenty-four divisions deployed along railways could be sent the following spring or summer. Mao complained to Stalin that due to his force's grossly inferior firepower, it would take the manpower of four Chinese armies (three infantry divisions each) heavily reinforced with new artillery to deal with a U.S. army (two infantry and one motorized divisions), several of which were deployed in Korea.[68]

On the other hand, meeting late in September, Mao's generals told him they would win because (1) U.S. troops were politically unmotivated; (2) they were inept in night attacks, close combat, mountain assault, and bayonet charges; (3) U.S. forces were tactically inflexible, limited by their fixed doctrine; (4) U.S. troops were afraid of dying and relied too heavily on firepower; and (5) the U.S. suffered from a long supply line across the Pacific. The first argument in particular must have appealed to Mao's belief that political fervor trumped all other factors in war—as he had apparently proved in the Chinese civil war.

On 2 October Chou publicly warned the United States that China would intervene if UN forces pursued Kim into North Korea, but the decision for war had already been taken, at least by Mao, in September. He had held back because he considered it far better to appear to be defending North Korea from invasion. Two weeks prior to the Inchon landing Mao's generals suggested that the best time to intervene would be after the allied army crossed into North Korea.[69]

Mao was more militant than his politburo, which wavered. China was in no condition to fight another big war. Lin Biao, who had been chosen to lead the force into Korea, objected that it would suffer badly given the lack of air and naval support; he preferred to defend the border while supporting Korean guerilas. He was relieved. Mao argued that the U.S. attack in Korea was part of an encirclement: further attacks could be expected in the Taiwan Straits and from the Philippines and Indochina. The industrial heartland of northeast China would be threatened by an American occupation of North Korea.[70] Stalin offered to join Mao in the war: the Soviet Union and China together were stronger than the United States and her main ally, Britain. If a third World War was inevitable, it would be better to fight before Germany and Japan had rearmed.[71] Meanwhile he probed for a cease-fire, offering terms much like those the U.S. government was then secretly drafting.[72]

For Mao, war would consolidate his victory in China. Too many of his citizens had long been friendly to Americans and to other Westerners. War would break such ties. Conversely, U.S. success could destabilize the regime; there were already rumors that U.S. troops would land on the mainland, or that Chiang would soon fight his way back, or that the Third World War was at hand. Encouraged by U.S. successes, opponents were already staging armed uprisings, wrecking communications lines, and attacking government supporters.[73] On 8 October Mao told Kim that he would soon intervene in the war. Chou En-lai went to Moscow to settle details of military cooperation.

As the Americans advanced, Stalin told Chou that he might not be able to provide much help at all, and that he would provide air cover only for China itself, not for the advancing Chinese army. In 1970 Mao claimed that Stalin vetoed Molotov's agreement to provide the desired air support, presumably for fear of directly engaging U.S. forces and thus risking war. The Chinese viewed Stalin's decision as a betrayal of the promise of support in the treaty they had so recently signed.[74] Bargaining with Stalin, Chou told him that the Chinese would not intervene.[75] Mao pointedly suspended war preparations. Without Chinese troops, the North Koreans would soon collapse. Stalin called Mao's bluff: on 12 October he told Kim to retreat across the Chinese border to set up a government in exile. That would leave U.S. forces on the Chinese border.

Mao caved in, and he carried his politburo with him.[76] He later attributed the horrific casualties his army suffered to Stalin's failure to provide the promised air support.[77]

On 7 October the UN passed a U.S.-drafted resolution calling for Korean reunification.[78] MacArthur read it as authorization to liberate all of North Korea from the Communists. He sent patrols over the border on the seventh, and his army followed beginning on the ninth. By mid-October organized North Korean resistance had virtually ended.

President Truman feared that MacArthur would push the Chinese into the war. He apparently was not convinced otherwise by a 12 October CIA paper, which argued, despite considerable evidence to the contrary, that the Chinese were unlikely to intervene.[79] If they did, they could be effective but not decisive, since they lacked air and naval support. China still had such severe domestic problems that the strain might destroy the regime altogether. The agency reached this conclusion despite known Chinese troop movements in Manchuria, despite statements by Chou En-lai (that the Chinese would intervene if UN forces went beyond the 38th Parallel), and despite propaganda charges of border violations and atrocities—which were surely designed to justify intervention. The only argument for intervention was the one that had convinced Mao: the Communist world would suffer badly if the UN completely destroyed the North Koreans.

On 15 October Truman met his Far East commander at Wake Island. MacArthur said that the war had been won. The Chinese had missed their chance; they might have been decisive had they intervened in the first or second month, but now they could probably put no more than fifty or sixty thousand troops across the Yalu, and they lacked air cover. The Soviets' aircraft were "no match for our Air Force" and no Soviet troops were readily available.[80] MacArthur was probably denigrating the Chinese to make a much greater goal seem within reach: the destruction of Mao's regime itself.

By late October it was clear that MacArthur planned to advance all the way to the North Korean border with China, the Yalu River, much farther north than the JCS or Truman had contemplated. He explained that the South Korean forces were not strong enough to secure North Korea by themselves.[81] The prize of decisive victory seemed far too attractive to throw away.

However, this was a special kind of war. It had limited objectives, because it was part of a larger Cold War, in which the really valuable prizes might not be affected by what happened in MacArthur's war. This could cheer neither MacArthur nor the troops he led. As in Vietnam, more than a decade later, the U.S. government limited its war because the consequences of escalation were actually worse than the consequences of losing. MacArthur too closely identified personal glory (in victory) with the objective he had been sent to achieve. His plaintive cry was that "there is no substitute for victory."

The four armies of Chinese "People's Volunteers" (twelve infantry divisions plus supporting artillery) began crossing the Yalu into Korea on 19 October 1950. A few days later, the first of them attacked U.S. and Korean units. They had some successes. Early in November, for example, they trapped a U.S. Cavalry Regiment when nearby South Korean units gave way. MacArthur's advance stalled. Then the Chinese suddenly withdrew, ending their "first phase offensive." The Chinese considered these attacks probes needed to develop the tactics for their major ("second-phase") offensive.

Heady with the successes he had already achieved, MacArthur concluded that the incompetent Chinese had been beaten. He would cut the Chinese off within North Korea by destroying the bridges that had carried them across the Yalu, as well as all installations on the Korean side of that border river. That was far beyond his instructions to stay well clear of the border. The JCS would not have known as much (until he attacked), had not MacArthur's air force commander passed news of the plan to his service's chief of staff. The U.S. government had just promised the British to consult them before taking any steps involving Manchuria. MacArthur told the JCS that the Chinese were "pouring across" the bridges; if they kept coming, his force might be destroyed. The attacks were approved, despite the promise to the British.[82]

MacArthur demanded more troops, but none would be available until the called-up National Guard divisions had completed their training. To fill out his force, the South Korean (ROK) army could be built up. Five of its divisions had survived the initial North Korean attack. Now the army in Korea proposed (and Truman approved) doubling that force, creating a new division each month with U.S. equipment. The first three new divisions appeared in October 1950, although as yet they were not nearly battle-ready.[83]

To the Joint Chiefs, MacArthur's orders had been straightforward. The Chinese had entered the war; he was to fall back on the defensive and await new orders. MacArthur quoted a JCS message to the effect that, should the Chinese enter the war, he was to continue action as long as he had "a reasonable chance of success," but not to attack any targets inside China without direct approval.[84] In justifying the attacks at the Yalu, MacArthur already promised that his air power could keep further Chinese troops out of North Korea. His army would destroy those already in place. One more major attack would end the war.

MacArthur presented a darker side to his political advisor. Should the final attack fail, he would escalate, to destroy the sources of enemy power in Manchuria. The Soviets might well enter the war. However, MacArthur had the great equalizer, grossly superior air power, virtually unchallenged in Korean skies. There was one worrying detail: his pilots had not seen the Chinese streaming into North Korea, hence had not attacked them. MacArthur convinced himself that had been only because so few had come: perhaps only thirty thousand.[85] In fact the Chinese had moved more than ten times as many men. MacArthur's air power could not have kept them out.

The JCS was less apocalyptic. Surely MacArthur could find a defensible line short of the Yalu. Given a buffer zone between his forces and the border, the Chinese might be able "to withdraw into Manchuria without loss of face." MacArthur denied that there was any such line; he had to occupy all of North Korea. To do less would be to "betray" the Koreans and to show fatal weakness throughout Asia.[86]

The Chinese felt they had taken the measure of their sophisticated enemy: they could and would win. They poured more troops into Korea. Four days after MacArthur launched his "final offensive," the Chinese attacked with twenty-six divisions. They destroyed South Korean units and then attacked the U.S. units whose flanks had thus been opened.

The result was probably the worst U.S. military defeat in this century. The U.S. units losing ground this time were not the hastily assembled task forces of the previous summer. They were well equipped and they had been seasoned by almost half a year of fighting. On 6 December the Chinese captured Pyongyang. Their "second phase" campaign had cost them 30,700 dead and missing.[87] China was now a major military power.

As in June and July 1950, MacArthur painted the grimmest possible picture in order to gain more forces—and permission for escalation, to protect them. His army could not deal with overwhelming Chinese numbers; and surely the Chinese would pour in even more troops, now that the Yalu had frozen over. Worse, two hundred bombers had just been discovered on air fields in China near the Korean border. They could destroy MacArthur's only remaining edge, his air power, by hitting U.S. air bases in Korea and Japan. Yet to strike the Chinese bases would be a major escalation.[88]

MacArthur seemed to be maneuvering the United States into a war against China itself. Perhaps he was unconsciously playing into Stalin's hands; surely Stalin had been behind Chinese intervention. In January 1951 President Truman called that "a gigantic booby trap." Shortly afterwards Gen. Omar Bradley, the chairman of the JCS, made the famous remark that, since Western Europe was the main prize and the Soviets the main enemy, a full-scale war against China would be "the wrong war at the wrong place at the wrong time and with the wrong enemy." His remark is often misapplied to the war in Korea itself.[89]

The situation seemed so bad that on 30 November 1950 President Truman announced that he was considering using the atomic bomb to win the war. The British were terrified. The Soviets would surely intervene—not necessarily in Asia. They might, for example, attack U.S. nuclear bomber bases in Britain. Prime Minister Attlee told Parliament that he expected to be consulted before so grave a decision was taken. He convinced Truman (against all advice) to revive the wartime British veto. Probably Truman feared that without this concession the British might well have ejected SAC from their country.[90]

The Chinese, having pushed MacArthur out of North Korea, initially wanted to rest and refit. Kim urged Mao on; it was time to seek a decisive battle. Mao's commanders urged caution; they were willing to advance on Seoul only if they could destroy the divisions blocking access to the capital. They feared that, if the divisions could withdraw in good order, they would counterattack later, when the Chinese were at the end of their supply lines. Despite limited casualties, many Chinese troops were severely frostbitten and could not keep fighting. Troops were tired and unwilling to keep advancing. On 22 December Mao ordered a third-phase offensive. The UN forces were indeed pushed out of Seoul on 4 January 1951. It seemed they were being routed. The situation seemed so bad (partly due to MacArthur's hysteria) that the JCS decided to evacuate U.S. forces altogether "as soon as it became apparent that the Chinese Communists intended to drive the UN from Korea." Mao seems to have been aware of the U.S. mood, and to have been encouraged by a truce proposal presented by thirteen neutral countries, which he interpreted as a U.S. attempt to stop the war before it was completely lost. His commanders noted that the UN force was withdrawing in good order. They might be luring the Chinese army into South Korea for a repeat of the Inchon landing and encirclement. The offensive ended on 8 January, UN forces having retreated eighty miles. The North Koreans protested that the Chinese had stopped "on the crest of victory." The success, albeit limited, intoxicated the leadership in Beijing; public rallies demanded that the Americans be "driven into the sea."[91]

MacArthur complained publicly that the European allies were making China a sanctuary.[92] In effect, he was challenging the primacy of Europe over Asia in U.S. cold war calculations. Otherwise quibbling by the Europeans could hardly have mattered. Surely the theater in which he commanded had to be paramount. MacArthur's resorting to the press was unacceptable; Truman ordered him to clear any statements before issuing them. MacArthur clearly had no use for constitutional limits; by February he was back in full cry.

Mao was as irrationally optimistic as MacArthur was irrationally pessimistic. He offered terms he had agreed with Stalin: the United States must evacuate Korea and recognize his regime.[93] They were unacceptable. The stakes had become far too high. Korea might not be in Europe, but to Europeans it measured U.S. resolve. In Germany, for example, advocates of appeasement were saying that the United States had proven weak.[94]

MacArthur's alternating panic and overoptimism had drawn far too many resources into his command. The Joint Chiefs could be blamed for going along with MacArthur through 1950, but on the other hand he was far too famous, as the hero of the Pacific in World War II, to be blocked. The peripheral war had sucked in the bulk of the trained U.S. officer corps and NCOs. Their loss in some Korean catastrophe would cripple the army for decades. It would preclude an effective future defense of Europe. In this sense the war was no longer so peripheral.

MacArthur told the Joint Chiefs that Mao was vulnerable; surely, with all his army fighting in Korea, little could be left to secure China itself. It might be time to "unleash" Chiang Kai-shek's army. At the least, it might so damage the Chinese as to eliminate them as a threat to any other country in Asia. The U.S. contribution to such a war might be limited to blockade and to air and naval attacks.[95] After all, Mao's China was clearly at war with the United States. The U.S. government was less enthusiastic. Bringing Chiang into the war might carry a high cost with the British, who were extremely important allies in the larger Cold War. Friendly Asian governments considered Chiang's government "reactionary, politically incompetent, and already repudiated by [his] own people." Moreover, the United States was fighting as part of a UN-sponsored coalition—a condition which both justified the operation and limited American options. Most UN members would probably reject any direct alliance with the KMT for fear of making a general war more likely.[96] The following year MacArthur had to admit that Chiang could do little without direct U.S. support; even then he might well fail.

On the other hand, the U.S. Joint Intelligence Committee estimated that there were still 600,000 to 650,000 active dissidents in China, of whom perhaps 300,000 professed association with the Nationalists, but lacked any sort of control or direction as guerillas. The CIA found 165,000 guerillas, almost none of them under Chiang's control. Officers controlling them seemed unwilling to risk them in combat. However, the effort begun in mid-1951 continued through the end of the war.[97]

In Korea, Lt. Gen. Matthew B. Ridgway rallied the Eighth Army (of which he had just taken command) as it retreated, unbroken, under Chinese pressure. He began a slow advance on 17–25 January. By March 1951 Seoul had been retaken and the UN army was back at the 38th Parallel. Now the Far East Command (i.e., MacArthur) reported that Stalin had approved large-scale intervention towards the end of April; that he would risk general war. President Truman authorized retaliation against Manchuria in the event of a major Communist air attack. But there was considerable suspicion that MacArthur was too interested in widening the war. The order was not sent for fear that MacArthur would execute it prematurely.[98]

MacArthur had been increasingly insubordinate since February. However, President Truman had been reluctant to discipline him. He was securing congressional approval to dispatch strong U.S. forces to Europe. Anything that dramatized MacArthur's demand that all effort be concentrated in Asia might sabotage that infinitely more important project. Thus MacArthur managed, in February, to tell the press that he could not advance beyond the 38th Parallel unless he was allowed to reduce Chinese superiority—which meant attacking China directly.[99] In mid-March, he personally wrecked a U.S. armistice initiative (of which he had been officially informed) by threatening that if the Chinese they did not withdraw at once, they would be "forced to their knees."[100]

Truman would have liked to fire MacArthur as soon as the end of 1950, but could not do so as long as the Senate debated sending further U.S. troops to Europe. Then his hands were freed: on 4 April Congress approved the NATO force. On 11 April Truman finally fired MacArthur for gross insubordination.[101] MacArthur provided the ammunition, in the form of a letter he sent to Congressman Joseph W. Martin Jr., the House Minority Leader. In it he made his usual charge that the Truman administration had failed in Korea because it favored Europe over Asia, and that it did not realize that "there is no substitute for victory." On 5 April

Martin read the letter on the floor of the House. The JCS unanimously supported Truman. It had lost confidence in MacArthur's judgement. Early in 1951 he wrote that the army in Korea was demoralized and broken, but visits by members of the JCS revealed the opposite. By April 1951 the JCS wanted urgently to relieve Mac-Arthur because they thought he would act unwisely in the event of the predicted major enemy offensive.

The offensive, when it came, was limited to Chinese and Korean troops. They were repulsed with heavy losses to the attackers.[102] The Eighth Army dug in slightly north of the 38th Parallel. The Chinese had lost their edge; now the UN force had so much firepower that their human-wave attacks could be defeated. The Chinese commander, Gen. Peng Dehuai, reported to Mao that his own army's morale was declining, whereas U.S. morale was rising sharply.[103] However, Ridgway was no MacArthur. In May he told the U.S. government that it was time to negotiate. Mao had much the same reaction. He no longer expected U.S. recognition. The Americans did not realize how poor Mao's position was.[104]

Truce talks began at Kaesong on 10 July 1951. They were fruitless. Both Stalin and Mao smelled U.S. weakness; otherwise why did the Americans not exploit their military advantage? With Stalin's approval, Mao revived demands for a U.S. with-drawal. Negotiations deadlocked over the issue of repatriating prisoners: many of the Chinese and North Koreans refused to go home. Americans hoped this dem-onstration of poor morale would help deter Stalin from any other adventures.

Ultimately, however, it was Stalin who kept the war going. In August 1952 Mao sent Chou En-lai to Moscow to discuss some way of ending the war. North Korea was being ground down systematically; Kim wanted out. Stalin told his allies to continue to bleed (and thus to pin down) the United States. He told the Chinese that war in Korea was providing them a valuable education in modern forms of warfare at no cost except in men, who were expendable.[105] Stalin's leverage was that he supplied the arms the Chinese were using. If he cut them off, they would soon be vulnerable to invasion. Chou asked Stalin to guarantee aid if the Americans widened the war. Stalin agreed to keep his forces in Port Arthur as a deterrent.[106]

Meanwhile, MacArthur had returned home to an enthusiastic reception. Many Republicans reverted to the old themes of isolationism. The wily Europeans were once more demanding U.S. blood to defend them. The future lay not in a tired Europe but in populous Asia; it was more important to keep Asia from going Communist. This line of reasoning fit well with the charge that Truman had "lost" China; an unleashed MacArthur could somehow have regained it. He told a con-gressional committee that "we practically give up the Pacific Ocean if we give up or lose Formosa" (i.e., Chiang). MacArthur tried (and failed) to win the 1952 Repub-lican presidential nomination.

Since it was the Republicans who attacked the U.S. policy of restraining Chiang, once they were in office in 1953 the Seventh Fleet was ordered to cease shielding Mao from his attacks. Chiang had to promise to avoid mounting any significant attacks without consulting the United States. U.S. patrol aircraft were moved to Taiwan, and bases for further forces were prepared.

In Korea, by the end of the winter of 1951–52 lines on both sides had been fortified in depth, and the war was coming to resemble World War I. As long as the mass of Chinese troops was still in the sanctuary beyond the Yalu, no battle in Korea could be decisive. This stage of the war seemed so pointless that President Truman's popularity collapsed. He decided not to seek reelection in 1952. Dwight D. Eisenhower would win that year's election partly on a pledge to go to Korea and find a solution.

Americans were unaware that the peace talks were stalled mainly due to Stalin's insistence that the war continue. Military pressure was difficult to apply, partly because U.S. casualties would be unacceptable while any sort of peace talks continued. That made air attacks an attractive alternative; but by mid-1952 most potential targets in North Korea had already been destroyed. The main exception was the string of hydroelectric plants along the Yalu River, spared because they were so close to the Chinese border. The situation was so desperate that in June an attack was approved. It knocked out power in North Korea for two weeks.[107] The British were furious that they had not been notified in advance of this major escalation.

Nor were they happy that the stalemate in this peripheral theater was tying down the forces the United States might need in the event of an emergency in Europe. By mid-1952 the U.S. Army could not expand any further. It had already taken what seemed at the time a desperate step, integrating African-Americans into its combat formations.[108]

Once Stalin was dead, his heirs allowed the truce talks to succeed, as part of a larger policy of disengagement. At the same time relations with Israel and with Yugoslavia were restored. Territorial claims to Turkey were abandoned.[109]

The war left a permanent American garrison on the inter-Korean border, guaranteeing the safety of South Korea but hostage to any sudden North Korean attack. South Korea had to build up substantial military power of its own. Despite that cost, the country was able to match other Asian "tigers" in economic growth during the 1970s and beyond. The North Korean problem outlasted the Cold War.

Americans who fought in Korea long remembered the mass Chinese attacks, the apparently inexhaustible human waves surging forward as they were mown down. It seemed that the Chinese accepted as routine horrific losses on a scale no European or American army could sustain. A few years earlier the Japanese had apparently showed much the same attitude towards life. Human life seemed to be a matter of indifference to Asians. The Soviets seemed to think more like Asians than like Westerners. We now know that the Chinese were very much aware of their losses.[110] On the other hand, we also know that Korean and Chinese manpower, used to repair roads and bridges, drastically limited the effects of the U.S. aerial interdiction campaign. It seemed that future wars might be unwinnable unless firepower, preferably nuclear, could be applied freely.

Chinese officers who had served in Korea were impressed by U.S. firepower; their army had to be modernized. The way to the West having been blocked, they had to turn to the Soviets for help. Stalin had, it seemed, won his battle to bind Mao to himself. Mao proclaimed victory. The United States and allied forces had, he said, been so badly bloodied that general war between China and the U.S. had been significantly delayed.[111] Highly motivated troops could overcome their material disadvantages.[112] The disastrous Great Leap Forward extended just such ideas to industrial development.[113]

Mao argued that his victory had encouraged other Asians, particularly the Vietnamese, to press forward with their own revolutions. Its end certainly released Chinese advisors for service with Ho Chi Minh. In 1964 Gen. Vo Nguyen Giap, who commanded at Dien Bien Phu and then during the Vietnam War, credited these advisors with the successful growth of his army in 1953–54. His remarks may have been colored by his need for renewed Chinese assistance.[114]

The Korean War dramatically effected the weak Japanese economy. The United States made the purchase of Japanese goods (to support the war) a policy, in hopes of building up the Japanese economy. The postwar Japanese industrial revival began.[115] The war also began Japanese rearmament, as General MacArthur pressed Japan to create a National Police Reserve and to expand its existing Maritime Safety Agency (coast guard) towards naval capability. Japanese minesweepers, which had been engaged in clearing U.S.- and Japanese-laid mines around the home islands, were pressed into service in Korea.[116]

Similarly, simultaneous NATO rearmament, initially paid for largely by the United States, greatly helped the German economy, which in 1950 was still quite weak. It increased enormously demand for German steel and other products. Until then, Germany had been a valuable prize because of its industrial and human potential. Within a few years, that potential would be realized.

When war in Korea broke out in June 1950, NATO had made little progress in raising enough forces to resist a Soviet attack—which, for the first time, seemed really possible. Germany was still the only available reserve of manpower, and the previously unthinkable—German rearmanent—suddenly seemed not only conceivable, but also desirable. By starting a war in Korea, Stalin made his own worst nightmare come true: Truman dropped his opposition to rearming Germany.

The Europeans were certainly aware of the potential dangers. They needed some way to enlist German troops without reviving the old German general staff, the directing brain that had planned two world wars. The French proposed a solution: German divisions would be integrated into a European Army fielded by a European Defense Community (EDC); a European Minister of Defense would be responsible to a European parliament voting a common defense budget. The Germans would not form their own unified independent army, but they would help defend Europe. It was not immediately clear, however, that any of the European governments would adopt EDC.[1]

To the Truman administration, EDC—or at least German participation in NATO forces—was a prerequisite for any sort of successful European defense. To encourage the Europeans, in the fall of 1950 it offered to station more troops in Germany and to form a unified European defense force under a U.S. commander. The Korean War buildup provided not only these troops but also a larger strategic reserve from which Europe might be reinforced in an emergency. The NATO governments liked the idea. In December 1950 their ministers approved creation of a unified command (SHAPE, Supreme HQ for Allied Powers in Europe) and asked that a U.S. officer (they recommended General Eisenhower) be appointed as its chief, SACEUR (Supreme Allied Commander Europe). SHAPE became operational under General Eisenhower in April 1951.

An expanded peacetime U.S. military presence in Europe was intended to make it clear that the United States planned to protect Western Europe from the Soviets, rather than liberate it after a Soviet invasion. In December, the new SACEUR, General Eisenhower, asked for twenty U.S. divisions. In January he scaled that down to ten or twelve, which would form the core of a fifty- or sixty-division NATO Army large enough to defend Europe but too small to attack the Soviets. In mid-February 1951 General Marshall, the secretary of defense, told a Senate committee that the administration was sending four divisions. Marshall said that it would be a real struggle to create even four, given the demands of the war in Korea. On 2 April the Senate voted forty-nine to forty-three to demand congressional approval for any troops beyond four (the four-division force was approved on 4 April). Truman rejected the limitation, but later administrations did not challenge it. The new divisions joined the one already in existence and the division equivalent already in place to form the Seventh Army.[2] The Senate limit on further deployments made quick reinforcement of Europe a perennial theme in U.S. military planning.

If EDC did come into force, NATO strategy would have to change. A NATO relying mainly on French and British troops could plan a fighting retreat across a devastated Germany, towards a line of resistance on the Rhine. Space would help dissipate the expected Soviet armored thrust. However, the Germans clearly would be reluctant to accept national destruction as a way of saving other NATO territory. Inevitably they moved towards a forward defense, an unrealistic concept in the world of armored warfare ushered in by World War II (ironically, by the Germans themselves). To carry out its new strategy (adopted mainly because it needed more troops in the first place) the alliance would probably need more troops.

By the outbreak of war the Germans might contribute ten divisions, and after the Korean buildup the United States might provide another fourteen. In its first estimates (1951), Eisenhower's SHAPE staff wanted the alliance to field thirty-one divisions on the Central Front at the outbreak of war, adding another thirty-four within the first thirty days.[3] It was rather optimistically imagined that the French might build up to nineteen divisions by 1954, and the British to eleven, for a total of fifty-four after thirty days of combat. That met an earlier requirement.[4]

In fact the Europeans could not possibly have met SHAPE's goals; they were still prostrate. In January 1951 U.S. experts estimated that to buy sufficient forces, the Europeans would have to double their pre-Korea budgets. The gap worsened as the estimated cost of the required force rose. Moreover, the Europeans did not share the Americans' sense of crisis. Their governments found it difficult to convince their populations to sacrifice at wartime levels. Their economies had not yet fully recovered from World War II. For example, in 1951 average per capita income in Western Europe was $597, compared to $2,143 for the United States.[5] Thus the Europeans could not afford additional taxation. The sudden stockpiling associated with the Korean War triggered inflation of about 9 to 10 percent in the United States, Britain, Italy, and Germany. Because of the additional strain of the war in Indochina, France suffered a 20 percent inflation rate, and French living standards fell.[6]

The British showed how serious the problem was. In 1951 they sharply increased defense production. The draft was extended from eighteen to twenty-four months and the standing force in Germany, the British Army on the Rhine (BAOR), was doubled, to four armored divisions. To pay for defense, the Labour government had to scale back cherished social programs; as a result, the party lost the election that year to Winston Churchill's Tories. His government had to abandon rearmament as unaffordable.[7]

Stalin's threat seemed to loom larger. In the late fall of 1950, perhaps encouraged by the UN disaster in Korea, he alerted the Eastern Europeans to be prepared for war in 1952.[8] Truman thought that Stalin wanted simply to bleed the United States without risk. His ambassador to Moscow, retired Adm. Alan G. Kirk, agreed. In December 1950 Kirk put the chances for war as three to two against but emphasized that, as canny as he might be, Stalin, flattered by his advisors, might (like Hitler) want to win world domination before he died. Others pointed out that Stalin might find it irresistible to move if the U.S. Army lost most of its trained officer corps and NCOs in some Korean catastrophe.

In November 1950 Stalin tried to head off German rearmament with a request that the other three powers occupying Germany meet to discuss withdrawing their forces and implementing the Potsdam agreement on demilitarization. Despite having joined NATO, the French had little faith in the U.S. deterrent, and said that they felt too weak to defend themselves; they feared antagonizing Stalin. That was probably a diplomatic reference to the continued power of the French Communist Party. Premier René Pleven said that he would be unable to rouse his country to rearm until he had demonstrated to his own electorate that he had made every effort to reconcile the Soviets. Since France was NATO's largest reservoir of military manpower after Germany, that was a double blow. Truman, determined to gain the German contribution, got Pleven to agree to reject any Soviet proposal which would prevent either western Germany or a unified Germany from assisting in the defense of the West.[9] At a preliminary conference, Stalin's diplomat, Andrei Gromyko, was surprisingly effective. Then Stalin sabotaged him. In April 1951 he ordered Gromyko to introduce a new item to the agenda: the Atlantic Treaty and U.S. bases in England, Norway, Iceland, and in other countries of Europe and the Near East. The conference broke up.[10]

True to his word, Pleven ordered his army expanded. The draft was extended from twelve to eighteen months; twenty divisions would be provided by 1953 for European defense. Unfortunately there were men (provided by the longer draft) but no equipment: the French hoped the United States would pay for most of that. Soon it was clear that American funds were limited; surplus equipment from World War II was largely gone, and the Korean War buildup was consuming French military spending. The French Assembly rejected a plea for added taxes for defense. The government soon cut its goal to twelve divisions in 1953 and fifteen by 1955. As Congress, frustrated by slow progress in Europe, cut military aid, the French abandoned any hope of providing even fifteen divisions by 1955.[11] German troops were absolutely vital.

Meanwhile, in January 1951 Stalin had held three days of secret meetings with top Eastern European party and military officials. In a climactic speech he claimed that the Korean War had demonstrated the weakness of the West; it was time to attack. Soviet military superiority over the United States would last only three or four more years (i.e., through 1954, the NSC 68 "year of maximum danger"). The Socialist world had to mobilize not only economically but also politically.

The 1954–55 date recalls Stalin's earlier view that the Americans would not have enough atomic bombs until 1955. The Korean attack had been a probe; the Eastern Europeans should prepare for the Soviet-led invasion of Western Europe.[12] In February 1951 Czechoslovakia, Hungary, and Poland all announced increases in industrial output, which really meant military production. The previous December Stalin had asked Palmiro Togliatti, head of the Italian Communist Party, to head the Cominform; the international situation was getting worse and worse (Togliatti refused). Western intelligence saw signs that Stalin was preparing for war. Soviet troops seemed to be moving into border areas. It seemed ominous that the Soviets had established a "World Peace Council" in Warsaw as an alternative to the UN. However, no specific preparations for attack are evident (and no war plan has yet surfaced). Stalin did order defensive measures.[13] He may have expected a Western attack but feared demoralizing the satellite armies if he warned them about it.[14]

The NSC turned the logic of the "year of maximum danger" on its head. By 1954 NATO forces in Europe would be strong enough to resist a Soviet attack. Thus the period through 1954 was Stalin's window of opportunity, with 1952 the peak year. The Soviets would have made good important deficiencies both in their atomic and aircraft programs; the West would not yet have geared up for a full war effort.[15]

The Europeans were calmer; their view of NATO was nearly diametrically opposed to that of the U.S. government. The Europeans tended to negotiate down any required force levels. They doubted that the Soviets would intentionally start a war in Europe. It was far too risky, and it would be far too destructive. However, war might begin by miscalculation. To avoid that, they wanted the maximum degree of deterrence. A substantial U.S. presence in Europe was essential. No Soviet leader could lightly contemplate destroying major U.S. forces, for fear of inviting a much larger war, perhaps a nuclear attack. To keep the U.S. commitment alive, the Europeans had to erect enough of a conventional defense to convince the United States that it would not have to use nuclear weapons at the outset. Americans often complained that the Europeans would do just enough to keep the U.S. commitment alive, but no more.[16]

For its part, the U.S. government sought enough of a NATO force to provide a robust nonnuclear defense. That was anathema to the Europeans. Their populations knew exactly what a nonnuclear war would be like; they had just experienced one. Opposition to the Soviets might bring devastation. A protracted conventional war—even if successful—was unacceptable; it was very nearly a direct incitement to neutralism or even surrender.

There was an interesting rub. Eisenhower's estimated requirements were all predicated on assumed Soviet strength. In the 1970s the CIA argued that the U.S. Army should have known that many of Stalin's 1949 divisions were no more than shells, containing a few officers; only reservists would fill the divisions in an emergency. Some of those considered combat-ready were no better than badly under-strength U.S. occupation units in Germany. Stalin could not manufacture adult Russians to replace those he had killed before and during the war, or those Germans had killed. If the CIA were correct, then estimates that Stalin could mobilize much larger forces (320 divisions on M-plus-30, 470 within a year) were specious.[17] The army refused to delete any divisions from the Soviet order of battle unless presented with three independent pieces of evidence to that effect.[18]

At high levels, where the overall U.S. and NATO defense programs were prepared, there was no such quibbling. At the working level, there was every interest in setting high goals. Inevitably they would not be met, but hopefully the lower levels actually accepted would provide forces with a reasonable chance of dealing with whatever the Soviets could mobilize. Any admission that NATO really had enough would encourage the European governments to slash forces. That is why, after 1961, Secretary of Defense McNamara was so surprised to discover that standing NATO forces had an excellent chance of holding off a Soviet attack, and had been in that position for some years.[19]

Meeting at Lisbon in February 1952, the NATO ministers approved German sovereignty and EDC, the prerequisites for German rearmament and integration into European defense. Soon NATO had eighteen ready divisions on the Central Front: six U.S., five French, four British, two Belgian, and several independent brigades. Another seven French divisions could be mobilized at short notice. Germany was expected to provide another twelve (ten infantry, two armored), for a total of thirty divisions on the Central Front, not too far from the 1951 goal. For the flanks, a force goal of twelve divisions (Italian, Danish, and Norwegian) was set, against which seven were in place.

This was less than Eisenhower wanted, but it was not bad. At the least it fore-closed Stalin's military option in Europe. His twenty-two Soviet divisions in place could no longer win a quick victory. To move further divisions up from Eastern Europe and the western Soviet Union would provide significant strategic warning, hence time to mobilize large NATO reserves. For example, numerous Soviet tanks had to be moved to their jump-off areas by rail, on board special "war flats," the appearance of which was a well-known war warning indicator.

In wartime, the Soviet lines of communications would pass through the satellite countries, where resentment was already high. Perhaps a Western guerilla force could capitalize on that potential problem. Preparation seemed urgent, given Stalin's aggressiveness as manifested in Korea. The army resisted; special units tend to drain away the best personnel. The secretary of the army and some within the army staff supported the new initiative, however. On 1 May 1952 the U.S. Army opened a Psychological Warfare Center and formed the 10th Special Forces Group at Fort Bragg. Volunteers fluent in Central European languages were recruited.[20]

The Lisbon conference seems to have prodded Stalin to one last effort to stave off German integration into NATO. In March 1952 he suddenly offered to withdraw Soviet forces from East Germany in return for neutralization of the whole country (with limited rearmament). This would be the classic Communist tactic of accepting a step backward in hopes of taking two steps forward: a neutralized Germany now might become a united Communist Germany later on. By this time the West German government well understood that its Western connection guaranteed its survival in the face of Soviet military power.

Now Stalin had to accept the final failure of a German popular front. Up to this point he had accepted a degree of capitalism in his zone of Germany, on the theory that the Germans were not ready to accept full Socialism. Now he turned the German Communists loose. Within about a year, their drastic imposition of the new system would cause such stresses that East Germany would briefly explode in rioting, particularly in Berlin.

At about the same time that he made his last offer on Germany, in March 1952, Stalin opened a massive anti-American campaign at home. Its propaganda made little reference to Marxism or to class warfare; instead, it sought to stir up "a sheer physical loathing of Americans per se, as people and above all as soldiers." Many foreign observers thought the campaign was intended to prepare the Soviet public for some new stress, most likely war. By late 1952 Stalin was also mounting an anti-Semitic campaign (beginning with the "doctors' plot"). Clearly a big purge was coming; some saw it as a precursor to a planned (or feared) war.[21] The new American ambassador, George Kennan, thought the campaign and the purge were no more than attempts to overcome the "widespread political apathy and skepticism" prevalent (except for World War II) since the purges of the 1930s.[22] Stalin's last major speech, to the Nineteenth Party Congress (14 October 1952) can be seen, however, as a part of war preparation. Foreign Communist parties had to support the Soviet Union in its fight for peace (i.e., domination) and to liberate "people struggling for their liberation."

The ongoing Korean War provided NATO with a sense of urgency. On 27 May 1952 France, Germany, the UK, and the United States all signed the EDC treaty. British Prime Minister Winston Churchill tried to stiffen the Europeans by pledging that the four British divisions and their tactical air arm would remain in Europe for fifty years.[23] However, EDC was doomed. Its sponsor, France, withdrew in 1954. No one had helped enough during the Indochina disaster. French forces locked into EDC might not be available to defend the rest of the French colonial empire. Even the Germans had problems with EDC, since it violated their own pledge to promote reunification.

While the U.S. government tried to convince the Europeans to provide enough men to resist Stalin's hordes, it developed what it considered a complementary nuclear capacity. Unfortunately the Europeans, unwilling to raise large armies, saw nuclear weapons not as a complement but as an alternative to conventional forces. The Truman administration rejected any such idea, for fear that any confrontation in Central Europe might quickly career out of control. On the other hand, several of its 1951 studies showed that, using atomic weapons *and its newly expanded forces,* NATO could finally hold vital areas of Europe.[24] By the mid-1950s the U.S. Air Force Tactical Air Command (TAC) in Europe was armed mainly with the new lightweight bombs. It described itself as SACEUR's sword (his conventional ground force was his shield), flying deep into Eastern Europe to kill off an approaching Soviet force. Two navy carriers in the Mediterranean supplied tactical nuclear fire-power for southern Europe. The U.S. Army began to develop its own family of short-range nuclear missiles.

Because so much depended on using nuclear weapons very early in a war, SACEUR argued that he would have to stockpile weapons in peacetime and that he would also need immediate authority to use them at outbreak of war. To Europeans, instant nuclear attack seemed morally repellant; better to wait until opinion had shifted to support it.[25] SACEUR argued that any European war would inevitably be nuclear. However, contrary to civilian opinion, cities would not be the initial targets. Initial strikes would surely be concentrated on armed forces and military installations.

This turned out to be less than reassuring. In June 1955 a follow-on U.S. Carte Blanche study of a European nuclear war predicted massive civilian casualties (1.7 million dead and 3.5 million wounded), not even counting effects such as fallout. Although considered a success (NATO forces won without requiring support by strategic bombers), Carte Blanche brought home for the first time to ordinary Germans that Germany would likely be a nuclear battlefield in any future war. The German opposition party, the SPD, used this new realization to attack the government's plans for a conventional buildup, on the ground that conventional forces were obsolete.[26]

By this time the Eisenhower administration was announcing that it was pointless to make any sharp distinction between nuclear and nonnuclear weapons, particularly once the Soviets approached nuclear plenty.

U.S. thinking changed quickly due to the advent of nuclear plenty—and lightweight weapons. Thus in 1952 the JCS assumed that, of about one thousand nuclear weapons on hand, no more than eighty—8 percent—could be spared for Europe. They would suffice to deal with advancing Soviet troops. None were needed for deeper strikes. Since the Soviets did not yet have tactical nuclear weapons of their own, airfield strikes were not yet urgent. Once the Soviets got tactical nuclear weapons, the situation would be transformed.

By 1954, the U.S. government no longer made a clear distinction between nuclear and nonnuclear warfare. SACEUR was free to include U.S. nuclear weapons in his strategy. In a July 1954 SACEUR sketch of a 1956 tactical nuclear war, about the same number of weapons (seventy-six, in this case) were used against advancing Soviet troops.[27] However, over six hundred weapons would be used during the first two days in deep strikes to destroy the Soviet tactical nuclear threat at source, such as key airfields and communications.

SACEUR planned to use his troops to mount a stiff nonnuclear defense. To break through it, the Soviets would have to bunch their own troops, creating targets for the seventy-six nuclear weapons. It was assumed that the Soviets still had relatively few nuclear weapons of their own. Following NATO's own logic, they would concentrate them against NATO nuclear forces, and would have few if any to spare to kill NATO troops. Hence the NATO concentrations would not themselves become targets for Soviet nuclear weapons.

Thus the Germans were still vital. The Western Europeans were somewhat less sensitive; the Germans were proving that they had reformed. A German army locked into NATO seemed acceptable. Germany joined NATO in 1955, and the first 101 men were sworn into the new army on 12 November 1955. The first three divisions were raised in 1957, four in 1958, one in 1959, two in 1960, one in 1963, and the twelfth and last in 1965.[28] The Soviets had already raised an army in East Germany. This paramilitary force formally became an army on 18 January 1956.

The Germans, but not their alliance partners, conceived a solution to NATO's paradox. Their powerful mobile force would gain strategic space by attacking east at the outbreak of war. It would try to envelop the advancing Soviet-led force, wheeling around to cut it off from its lines of communication and crush it against more fixed NATO positions. Many within NATO found the idea terrifyingly provocative. Eventually, in the 1980s, it would enter the U.S. Army lexicon as part of a new standard doctrine for AirLand battle, exercised for the first time in Iraq in 1991.

The Soviets responded to German entry into NATO by forming the Warsaw Pact; two alliances now faced each other across the Central Front. There were crucial differences. NATO was and remained very much a voluntary alliance brought into existence by the fears of its independent states. Its senior partner, the United States, could hardly force any of the members to make a desired contribution, nor to take any other action. That was obvious from the long and tortured history of attempts to build up a ground force sufficient to meet the stated desires of the NATO European governments. Disagreements within NATO made it impossible for the United States to force the alliance to adopt its preferred nuclear strategy. Similarly, the United States would find, in the 1960s, that its NATO partners would not endorse actions, in Vietnam, of which they disapproved.

The Warsaw Pact states were already under rigid Soviet control. When the Pact collapsed after 1989, the Eastern European governments discovered, to their surprise, that all lines of military control ran, not to their national capitals and defense ministries, but directly to Moscow. Warsaw Pact strategy was decided in Moscow, to the extent that the subordinate military organizations had little idea of the war plans their forces were expected to execute. That is one reason why, although NATO concepts are now well known, Warsaw Pact war plans are still largely a matter of speculation.

As war broke out in Korea, and as the U.S. government pressed the French to provide divisions for NATO, French fortunes in Indochina continued to decline. The key disaster had been Mao's victory in China. With the border to China open, Ho began to receive masses of equipment. Now he could begin conventional large-unit operations. He formed his first infantry division in 1949; five more followed in 1950. Soon the Chinese were supplying U.S. equipment captured in Korea, as well as their own Soviet-type matériel. In the first large-unit battles, in September–October 1950, six French battalions were wiped out along the northeast frontier of Vietnam. The French now pulled back from the vital border passes, completely opening this supply route. The war became much more expensive for France, and the need for U.S. support increased accordingly.

U.S. military aid to the French in Indochina began at the start of the Korean War, although the two were not connected. However, during the U.S. buildup for Korea so much was produced that it was easy to spare some for the French. That was not enough to save the situation. To the Americans, the problem was French policy. The U.S. government continued to demand real independence for the Associated States, and a true national army for Vietnam. Although the French did found a Vietnamese National Army in 1951, the Vietnamese apparently saw it as no more than an offshoot of the French army. Few of its officers were Vietnamese (an officers' academy was founded in 1949). Many more Vietnamese served in French Union than in "national" units.[1]

From a purely military point of view, the problem was how to entice large Viet Minh formations into battles in which superior French firepower could destroy them. Until the end of 1950, the French had relied on fixed forts, each with a small garrison, which the Viet Minh could overrun one by one. Then a new French commander, Gen. Jean de Lattre de Tassigny, took the offensive, specifically to trap Viet Minh. New fast mobile units (*Groupes Mobiles,* or GMs) were designed to attack the Viet Minh before they could scatter. On 13–17 January 1951 the French forces beat the Viet Minh at Vinh Yen, costing them six thousand dead. In March and

June Viet Minh attempts to break French defenses in the Tonkin delta failed. Then the Viet Minh recovered. They learned to deal with air attacks. The French failed to destroy their supply bases.

Southeast Asia, especially Malaya and Indonesia, was the main world source of natural rubber and tin, and an important producer of oil and other strategic materials. Burma and Thailand were crucial rice exporters to Malaya, Ceylon, and Hong Kong, and were significant to Japan and India. All the states in the area seemed unstable, and beset by Communist subversion; surely the fall of any of them would swiftly cause the others either to submit to or to align with Communism. By early 1952 the U.S. government accepted that Southeast Asia was a key area in an expanding Cold War.[2]

The United States no longer had any leverage to force the French to accept Vietnamese independence, which in the U.S. view was the only real hope of success; the French simply threatened to surrender. However, they were not quite ready to leave. Although popular support for the war was declining, the French feared that defeat would jeopardize the rest of their empire. The U.S. government increased aid in 1953, even though the situation was deteriorating and de Lattre, who alone had seemed aggressive enough to win, was dead.

In May 1953 three Viet Minh divisions invaded Laos. It seemed that they were on the point of enlarging the war, because Laos bordered on Thailand and Burma. We now know that the Viet Minh had only limited objectives: they wanted, simply, to force the French to fragment their forces.[3] However, the U.S. government was sufficiently impressed to demand that the French appoint a new aggressive commander if it wanted continued aid.

The French government sought an honorable way out, which to its mind meant forcing the Viet Minh to accept the new French Union states. To achieve that, its new commander, Gen. Henri Navarre, had to deliver a crushing blow. As the Viet Minh reeled, he would build up local forces to defend the new states after the French left.[4] This was much like Nixon's strategy in 1969. To deliver his blow, Navarre had to find a place where the Viet Minh would have to fight. There he could use his superior firepower to wipe them out. The invasion of Laos suggested that the Viet Minh valued its approaches. They were dominated by Dien Bien Phu, which controlled key roads (actually tracks through jungle) and a key rice-producing area that the Viet Minh needed.[5] Moreover, Dien Bien Phu dominated the approaches to the Laotian capital. Navarre apparently believed that the loss of that capital was unacceptable; it would shock the French public and end the war (it would certainly destroy the fragile French government then in office).[6]

Dien Bien Phu was deep in Viet Minh territory, but French aircraft could supply it. Those planes and the French guns he emplaced could destroy an assault. Initially Navarre planned to use Dien Bien Phu as a base from which to attack Viet Minh lines of communication, but the terrain was terrible and his forces proved inadequate.[7] He soon switched to the idea of using the fortress as bait; the Viet Minh would have to attack it. They initially agreed. They could take Dien Bien Phu, but only by concentrating all their forces, abandoning any hopes for action elsewhere in the country. Early in December 1953 the Viet Minh decided to take Dien Bien Phu, but in January 1954 they decided not to attack.[8]

They reckoned without the French government's determination to extricate itself from the war. In January 1954 the Council of Foreign Ministers (the "big four") reconvened for the first time (at Berlin) since Stalin's death, in theory to plan a Korean War peace conference for Geneva in April. Molotov told the French foreign minister that he might be able to obtain a peace settlement in Indochina if he abandoned the developing alliance with Germany and EDC (the U.S. position had been that further aid to Indochina was conditional on French support for EDC). The French agreed to include Indochina on the Geneva Conference agenda.[9]

For the Viet Minh, the situation had been transformed. If they won a decisive battle, it would be the French who would withdraw. As soon as they were told about the Berlin Conference, they reversed their position.[10] Now Dien Bien Phu was very much worth attacking. Their Chinese and Soviet allies helped build them up for the battle. The Viet Minh were able to risk everything.

Navarre had not known in advance of the French agreement at Berlin. He had therefore committed his troops without realizing just how far the Viet Minh would be able to go. Unsurprisingly, French resources proved inadequate. Air support could not destroy the force being built up, and there were no troops for a counter-thrust on the ground. The incredulous French watched the Viet Minh manhandle antiaircraft guns (provided by the Chinese across the border) into the rough terrain around Dien Bien Phu. Supply flights became more and more dangerous, and French tactical aircraft were unable to knock out the guns. Then the Viet Minh moved mortars and howitzers onto the high ground surrounding the fortress. They smashed through the defenses to overrun the fortress on 7 May 1954. Most of its defenders did not survive the subsequent death march. As the Viet Minh mounted their siege, the French had appealed for U.S. heavy bombers to destroy the antiaircraft guns and thus to reopen air supply. President Eisenhower personally vetoed the idea.[11] The bombers would hardly be enough; large numbers of ground troops would have to follow. As in Korea, the Chinese might well enter the war. They were already powerful enough to drive the French out of the country altogether. Nuclear weapons would have to be used, and ultimately the Soviets would probably join in the war. This was exactly the sort of escalation the Truman and Eisenhower administrations had just avoided in Korea. Indochina seemed to be just another peripheral area, of very limited inherent strategic importance. Secretary of State Dulles was "not very optimistic" about the future of Free Vietnam, Laos, and Cambodia, but reasoned that "these countries are not really of great significance to us other than from the point of view of prestige, except that they must be regarded as staging grounds for further thrusts by the Communist powers."[12]

Dien Bien Phu did not destroy the bulk of the French force in Vietnam, but the

French had seen it as their last chance to win. They were exhausted—and furious that their NATO allies had done so little to help them. As the French later saw it, the United States interfered too much and helped too little. For example, it was never willing to commit troops. The United States was interested in Europe, but not in supporting the empire which made European strength possible. U.S. unwillingness to help in Indochina on French terms bred bitterness. That bitterness would grow as France faced nationalist movements elsewhere in her empire, beginning in Morocco in 1951. Resentment over desertion by the United States would be reinforced by the experience of Suez in 1956 and by U.S. hostility to the French effort to retain Algeria.

While the Dien Bien Phu campaign was being fought, the talks at Geneva opened, with the Chinese and the Viet Minh in attendance. The Viet Minh continued to exert pressure, attacking the French in the Red River Delta around Hanoi and further south. In July 1954 the two sides concluded a truce, to which the Viet Minh reluctantly agreed, under Chinese pressure. They were limited to the northern half of the country, accepting partition at the 17th rather than at the 13th Parallel. The Viet Minh also had to agree to separate settlements neutralizing, rather than partitioning, Laos and Cambodia. In return the Chinese seem to have expected French recognition (which they did not get). They apparently also felt that a compromise solution would limit the extent of U.S. involvement, which they considered inevitable following French withdrawal. For their part the Viet Minh preferred partition to a "leopard-spot" solution (truce in place throughout Vietnam) because it would allow them to consolidate their power in the north. The French were similarly willing to abandon Hanoi and Haiphong in return for the chance to consolidate their position in the south.[13]

The post-Stalin Soviet regime also wanted to end the war. Contrary to U.S. expectations, it actively feared being drawn into a war with the United States via the Sino-Soviet treaty. That was all too possible if the war lasted and the United States effectively took over the French role. Thus the Soviets, too, may have exerted pressure on the Viet Minh. To this extent the truce might be seen as a major victory for the new U.S. strategy of "massive retaliation."

Under the truce agreement, elections would be called in 1956 to unify Vietnam. The two other states of French Indochina (Laos and Cambodia) became independent. The deal the Chinese were offering was so good that the French feared that even a hint of U.S. involvement would upset it and cause the Viet Minh to attack French forces still in North Vietnam. The French negotiators at Geneva thought the best settlement would be neutralization, Indochina forming a barrier between the Communists and the West as part of a "Third Force." This may have been an early example of French hopes that France itself could fill this role.

To the U.S. government, the lesson of Korea seemed to be that U.S. troops should not be committed—as they might have to be, one day, to Vietnam—without congressional approval.[14] Eisenhower and Dulles therefore asked Congress to guarantee the Indochina settlement via a new regional security treaty concluded in Manila. Congressional ratification of a new Southeast Asia Treaty Organization (SEATO) would make future U.S. intervention credible. The former French Indochinese states were not signatories, because in theory the settlement neutralized them. The French negotiators feared that any hint of the formation of SEATO might cause the Chinese to harden their terms. The French government saw matters differently. The Soviets were still a real threat in Europe, and NATO remained essential. France was not strong enough to back any sort of "Third Force," even without the drain of increasing commitments in North Africa. France joined SEATO.[15] So did Britain, which still retained important interests in the area. The other signatories were the Philippines, the United States, and the two ANZAC countries, Australia and New Zealand.[16] Besides Indochina, SEATO guaranteed the security of Malaya, Pakistan, and Thailand.

Many Vietnamese voted with their feet: in 1954 they accepted passage south aboard U.S. Navy ships. Meanwhile Ho began to build a Communist regime, ejecting non-Communist members of the Viet Minh popular front. His doctrinaire measures alienated many North Vietnamese peasants, culminating in a bloody revolt in 1956.

By 1956 neither the North nor the South Vietnamese government wanted to hold the elections mandated in the truce agreement. The Eisenhower administration argued that electors in the North would hardly be free to vote as they pleased; but apparently Ho feared the wrath of his own peasants, should they be permitted to vote freely. When the South Vietnamese said they wanted to defer an election, the North Vietnamese assented.[17]

Critics have suggested that, as a genuine nationalist, Ho inevitably would have won. The exodus south in 1954 suggests that many Vietnamese were not quite convinced. The Eisenhower administration hoped that a self-governing ex-colonial South Vietnam would soon build up enough nationhood to survive on its own. Surely Ho Chi Minh had triumphed in the North not so much because he was a Communist, as because he had led a nationalist revolt against a colonial power. Some in the State Department presumably remembered that the United States had helped finance Ho during World War II (as an anti-Japanese nationalist). They may have wondered whether it would not have been better to support him against the French in 1946, in hopes that his nationalism was stronger than his Communism.

U.S. assistance to the new state of South Vietnam was strictly limited by treaty. Thailand was a different proposition. The Eisenhower administration made it the "hub" of its Southeast Asian position. In many ways it was a much more secure country. No Communist state could claim that it was the true heir to Thai nationalism, and the Royal Thai Army was likely to stoutly defend the country. By way of contrast, any South Vietnamese regime had to prove to its own citizens that it was as strongly nationalist as Ho, the original anti-French rebel.

To the French, Indochina was a new kind of revolutionary war, a social and psychological rather than a purely military struggle. Guerillas like the Viet Minh used psychology to bond with the populace; having done so they could defeat a much more powerful army. Alongside its military effort, the army resisting the guerillas had to conduct social and educational programs. Thus revolutionary war was partisan war plus psychological war. Having learned, they thought, some very expensive lessons, the French thought they were ready for their next struggle, in Algeria.[18]

In fact the lessons were hardly new. Contemporary successes in Malaya and the Philippines and U.S. insistence on true independence for the Associated States showed a clear understanding of the problem. The French may well have wanted to claim a unique (and affordable) capability as opposed to the unaffordable highly mechanized capability then being developed by the United States and Britain. If guerilla war were the wave of the future, then after 1954 France could claim leading expertise (despite its rather conspicuous failure in Vietnam).[19]

17 ENTER KHRUSHCHEV

Any plan Stalin may have had for an early Soviet attack on Western Europe died with him in March 1953. For Communists, most of whom still were members of a unified world movement, Stalin had been a god, and his death left a frightening emptiness. In the Soviet Union, even many of those who had been touched by his horrific crimes mourned him; they refused to believe that he, personally, had been responsible. Shortly after Stalin died, the U.S. intelligence agencies painted him as a brilliant maneuverer, who had extracted maximum concessions from the West without risking war. Surely his successors would be less competent; they might well trip into open war.[1]

With Stalin's death, there were three sets of potential rulers: surviving Stalinists (led by Molotov), technocrats (led by Beria and Malenkov), and younger Party leaders (led by Khrushchev). Stalin had made no arrangements for the succession, and, indeed, he had probably planned to purge all or most of those who now competed for power. These survivors temporarily formed a collective leadership.

Malenkov took over Stalin's title as chairman of the Council of Ministers (prime minister, head of state). Given his feeling that the Party was intellectually bankrupt, he clearly considered Khrushchev of little importance. Beria, already responsible for most military research (including the atomic project), became deputy for internal security. In fact he and Malenkov uneasily shared power. The other deputies were Molotov (foreign policy), and the last two surviving Old Bolsheviks, Bulganin (war), and Kaganovich. Marshal Zhukov, the wartime hero exiled to the Far East by Stalin, was named deputy war minister.

Nikita Khrushchev was Party secretary. Malenkov denigrated him; he seemed to many to be nothing more than a Ukrainian country bumpkin. Western analysts assumed that Malenkov had inherited Stalin's position as Party secretary; they did not even notice Khrushchev. They missed a significant point: Khrushchev was appointed chairman of Stalin's funeral commission. They learned their lesson; henceforth the head of the funeral commission of the last Soviet ruler would be considered his most likely successor.

The country was stagnant, unable to execute the ambitious military plans Stalin had approved. The Soviet Union's condition was, crucially, entirely unknown to the West. A crisis was also developing in East Germany, where in 1952 Stalin had allowed Walter Ulbricht to accelerate "building socialism" in the face of considerable popular resistance. Both problems could be blamed on the sort of dogmatic Party attitudes Stalin had encouraged. Stalin's rigid control had sapped enthusiasm and energy.

Probably Beria, alone of Stalin's successors on the Politburo, had a reasonably accurate idea of conditions both in the Soviet Union and in the Eastern Europe. He proposed liberalization and professionalization; for example, commissarial (Party) control of the military would be relaxed. Surely his program reflected his unhappy knowledge of existing conditions rather than any opposing convictions; he had willingly presided over much of Stalin's pre- and postwar bloodbath.[2] The big purge in preparation in 1952–53 (in connection with the fabricated "doctor's plot") was canceled. Similarly, the virulently anti-American campaign begun a year earlier, in March 1952, was noticeably toned down.

Beria proposed that Ulbricht be reined in, his practices halted and reversed. The cost of supporting East Germany might be too high; perhaps it was time to make a deal with the West and abandon the place. To Beria's colleagues, any such retreat would be a fatal show of weakness and a sign that the horrific sacrifices of World War II had been in vain.

Beria's proposed measures caused riots in East Berlin in June 1953, as well as disturbances in Poland. They seem to have been the first open rebellion in the Soviet satellites. Quite aside from embarrassing the Soviets, the East German uprising quashed Soviet plans to use East German industry and specialists to develop weaponry. For example, plans to build submarines there (and to provide them to the nascent East German navy) were aborted.[3] The Politburo felt that it had no choice: the East Germans might encourage others in the empire. The riots were put down and Beria's liberalization largely abandoned. However, some reforms did proceed in Czechoslovakia and Hungary.

To his Politburo colleagues, Beria was a direct threat. His connections with the secret police made it likely that he could engineer a coup, dispensing with all of them in his predecessor's fashion. Khrushchev arranged a countercoup. Beria was arrested at a Politburo meeting on 27 June (the arrest was not announced until 10 July). Apparently on the day of his arrest he had already assembled secret police troops in Moscow for the coup he planned.[4] Regular troops blocked them. The air defense force (PVO) apparently had a special role in Beria's demise, and it was rewarded afterwards. Secretly tried, Beria was secretly shot in December 1953.

Beria's followers were purged, generally on charges about as truthful as those they had used in purging their own victims. For example, several members of the Leningrad party apparatus were shot on the charge that they had rigged an election. However, nothing done at this time approached the standard practices of the past. Party members would once again enjoy a measure of security. The security forces would concentrate on insuring the Party's control of the rest of the Soviet population. Given stability in their positions, managers and their supervisors could, it seemed, concentrate on their jobs. Anything that made Party members such as factory managers more secure also made the military sector, dominant in the Soviet economy, more secure. Who but Stalin would have dared to shut down a factory, or to change its orders so that its manager would no longer enjoy a bonus?

Ironically, soon after Beria's arrest the nuclear organization he had led produced a major advance, a deliverable 500-kiloton bomb (tested on 12 August 1953). Although advertised as a "super" (an H-bomb), in fact it was a boosted (compound) fission bomb. Even so, it had about twenty times the explosive power of the first weapon the Soviets had tested, in 1949. After receiving a full report on the 1953 test Khrushchev could not sleep for several days. After the 1 March 1954 U.S. test of a fifteen-megaton H-bomb, Soviet nuclear scientists submitted a formal report: such weapons could easily destroy all life on earth. War, at least between major powers, no longer seemed at all practical. Khrushchev and Molotov vetoed publication of the report. However, this and similar papers clearly affected all of those competing for Stalin's throne.[5]

Men like Molotov had served Stalin and his Party apparatus; they wanted to continue as before. Whatever the implications of the new bomb, it was unthinkable to renounce war. As Stalin had said, wars of various sorts were both inevitable and, in a sense, to be welcomed as the catalysts of the desired world change.

Others, like Malenkov, considered themselves realists and technocrats. Having grown up in the 1930s, they had little interest in the Party's ideology.[6] Stalin and the Party had wrecked the country. The Party's war against the West had been extremely dangerous. It might be time to dethrone the Party in favor of the conventional organs of government and the military. Malenkov gave an extraordinary speech to the effect that war was no longer thinkable. The world revolution was now too dangerous to prosecute.[7]

Khrushchev, the Party's general secretary, naturally still considered the Party and its revolutionary mission vital. Party hacks were certainly a serious problem, but not an unsolvable one. He drew an interesting conclusion. The capitalists, too, probably knew that nuclear war, at least on a large scale, would be mutually suicidal, so long as the Soviet Union could deliver its own weapons. General war, which Stalin had considered inevitable, was no longer at all likely. Even in extremis, the West would not commit suicide by attacking the center of the world revolution. Soviet nuclear weapons would be the shield behind which the sword of revolution could safely be wielded.

The problem of Soviet stagnation still had to be attacked. Defense outlays were buying less and less. In August 1953 Malenkov announced that more effort would be devoted to light industry and consumer goods. In hopes of producing more food, the government would look more favorably on peasants' private plots of land.[8] Workers were not producing because their salaries were meaningless: there was nothing to buy. By providing goods to buy, Malenkov was in effect offering them a raise: their existing salaries would finally be worth a bit more.

Stalin's heirs seem to have known little either of his plans or of the military and industrial machine he had built to carry them out. They were probably shocked to discover the extent of Soviet vulnerability, and they moved to reduce tensions to buy themselves breathing space. It was suddenly possible to reach settlement, first in Korea and then in Indochina.

Khrushchev had already gained considerable power by leading the coup against Beria. Then in 1953–54 he allied with Molotov to unseat Malenkov, espousing Stalin's Party-based policies against Malenkov's more pragmatic ones. Malenkov had grossly underestimated the Party's continuing power (and was far too weak to struggle very hard). His fatal sin was to claim that war was no longer possible—a view Khrushchev adopted, once he had used the heresy to unseat Malenkov. Khrushchev was not yet strong enough to make himself sole ruler, so he continued behind a facade of collective rule. A very weak Marshal Bulganin replaced Malenkov as premier late in 1954. Despite his title, Bulganin was essentially a civilian. Marshal Zhukov, the hero of the 1945 victory over Germany (whom Stalin had demoted) became the new defense minister; the professional Soviet military now controlled the Ministry of Defense. They owed Khrushchev allegiance. In October 1954 Khrushchev visited China alone to celebrate the fifth anniversary of Mao's republic and to make crucial deals. Khrushchev's position was not obvious in the West until about 1955.

Khrushchev decided to break out of Stalin's self-imposed diplomatic isolation. He saw little point in continuing the feud with Tito; rapprochement began with Khrushchev's visit in April 1955.[9] Molotov had argued that it was vital to keep Soviet forces in Austria because they would have a valuable flanking role in the event of an invasion of Yugoslavia.[10] To Khrushchev, continued occupation of Austria was merely a liability. He was now strong enough to stand up to Molotov; suddenly, in May 1955 he signed the Austrian peace treaty, ending that country's occupation. He also withdrew from the Finnish bases occupied since 1945. In July, Khrushchev led a Soviet delegation to a summit conference with the U.S., British, and French leaders. Perhaps most remarkably, in September 1955 West German Chancellor Konrad Adenauer was Khrushchev's guest in Moscow as they negotiated to open diplomatic relations. Khrushchev had decided to try to break the Western alliance. On 16 October 1956, he offered the Japanese two of the islands seized at the end of World War II, in exchange for a peace treaty (i.e., Japanese neutrality).[11] Later in the decade he sold underpriced Soviet oil to Italy.

The opening to Tito reflected Khrushchev's generally relaxed view of the world revolution and of his own place in it. Lacking Stalin's paranoia, he was more than willing to befriend anyone who, like Tito, might come over to his side, even though not formally Moscow Communist in orientation. Thus he freed himself to reopen ties to left-wing European parties. Tito himself soon adopted a "middle way" between East and West; his flirtation with NATO was effectively over. Khrushchev's policy was very successful; by the late 1960s many in the European Left were clearly anti-American, to the extent that the Soviets could expect support over issues such as Vietnam and, later, the neutron bomb.

Also in 1955, Khrushchev and Bulganin exchanged state visits with Prime Minister Nehru of India. The Indian visit bore fruit in the 1960s. When India fought China in October 1962, her traditional suppliers, the British (assisted by the United States), replenished her weapons. However, probably because neither country wanted to offend Pakistan, they were unwilling to participate in the post-1962 Indian buildup. The Soviets became the Indians' main arms suppliers for the rest of the Cold War.

With Malenkov defeated, Molotov was Khrushchev's main rival. He and the other Stalinists had to go. Khrushchev turned against Stalin and the past. The Twentieth Party Congress, held in February 1956, was the first since Stalin's death. Planning for it, Khrushchev proposed to investigate Stalin's activities. Molotov was outraged. To question Stalin's work was to question the entire basis of the Party's power.[12] Khrushchev had been part of Stalin's machine; who was he to ask questions now? Khrushchev promised to limit the investigators to "infringements of socialist legality," mostly due to Beria. The Central Committee agreed in December 1955.

Khrushchev headed the investigating commission. He gave his report, the famous four-hour "Secret Speech," on 25 February 1956. Going far beyond what he had promised, he accused Stalin (and, by extension, his surviving supporters) of having betrayed the revolution—of having tried to destroy the Party itself. He condemned the "cult of personality" Stalin had engendered. In effect Khrushchev warned members that if they remained faithful to Stalin's memory, they risked exclusion as a party to terrible crimes.

Party members had been brought up to believe that Stalin was a god, that whatever the he (and the Party) said, whatever emanated from Moscow, had to be true. The line might shift, truth might change, but one could never admit that the Party was not all-wise. The alternative was too terrible to imagine. As word of the Secret Speech spread within the Soviet Union, the Party lost much of its prestige. The Party's ideologists complained that this loss was irreparable. Khrushchev had made deadly enemies. To make matters worse, the text of the speech leaked out and it was broadcast back into the Soviet Union and Central Europe by the Voice of America.

For those who saw him as an opportunist, it seemed that Khrushchev wanted to destroy his remaining rivals, yet limit the effects of the speech by keeping it secret from all but the upper reaches of the Party. To avoid destroying the Party altogether, Khrushchev did his best to ennoble Lenin. Stalinism had been an aberration. It was time to return to Lenin's noble ideas. In October 1961 Khrushchev ordered Stalin's body removed from the Mausoleum, leaving only Lenin's. The city of Stalingrad, whose defense had been so critical during World War II, was renamed Volgograd. Only much later would it become obvious that Stalin had done little more than expand on Lenin's policies.

Khrushchev's detractors point out that his liberalization was limited. Although the gulags were largely dismantled, Khrushchev never publicly apologized for the mass murders of Stalin's time. The Secret Speech was limited to crimes against Party members (presumably shooting nonmembers was far less heinous). A report on Stalin was prepared, but it was never released. Some Stalinists argued that Khrushchev was nothing like the convinced liberal that the West saw; he was quite willing to forge evidence and execute political rivals. As Stalin's enthusiastic lieutenant in the Ukraine, Khrushchev had committed many of the crimes he now abhorred.

It now seems clear that Khrushchev really had come to believe that Stalin had betrayed the country, that unless his methods and his memory were attacked, stagnation could never be overcome. The pervasive fear Stalin had engendered had created a compliant but uncreative citizenry. Who would make a positive suggestion when it might easily be a ticket into the gulag? To restart Soviet society, Khrushchev had to expand personal freedom (the "thaw") while retaining Party control. He was lucky; the shadow of Stalin's terror limited any excesses a thaw might bring out. Even Beria, three years earlier, had realized that something of the sort was needed.

The remnants of the Party led by Stalin were unlikely to be very creative. Khrushchev decided to reform the Party by adding new blood at high enough levels. In this "bifurcation," qualified experts—Stalin's hated specialists—were given senior posts. They had not risen through the ranks. They had not spent much of their youth passing out Party literature ("agitating") or making the endless and meaningless speeches which the Party demanded. Advancement now would depend on expertise, not simply Party loyalty. The new men were hated.

The East European empire was ruled by Stalin's hand-picked men, puppets who had sat out World War II in the Soviet Union (and who could therefore be trusted completely). The Soviets ruled the satellite countries in their name; even the smallest decisions often were made in Moscow. Many East Europeans, including Party members who had spent the war years in local undergrounds, were outraged. Khrushchev seemed to be condemning these local rulers in his Secret Speech.

The Poles took him at his word. Anti-Communist riots erupted in Poznan in June 1956. In October 1956 the Polish Communist Party replaced a Stalinist puppet, Stanislaw Beirut, with Wladyslaw Gomulka, who had spent the war in Poland, and who had been purged by Stalin. Khrushchev went to Poland to demand that Gomulka go. He threatened to invade. The Poles called his bluff; their army also was ready to fight. They convinced him that it was much better to allow them to place their own man in power. Indirect rule was likely to be effective. The old sort of direct rule would have resulted in an uprising. Gomulka pointed out that he was entirely loyal; better to relax rule slightly than to invite disaster. It helped that Khrushchev had known Gomulka since the 1930s.[13]

In Hungary, Soviet rule was less adept, and resentment of the Soviets and their puppets was far more profound. Khrushchev could not afford to let the problem spread.[14] After initially withdrawing from the country, Soviet tanks and troops returned to crush the rebels. The Soviet ambassador, Yuri Andropov, led their suppression. Gomulka protested; he knew he could be next. The Hungarian leaders, including the premier, Imre Nagy, and the defense minister, Pal Maleter, sought refuge in the Yugoslav embassy. The Soviets lured them to their own headquarters, where they were arrested; later they were executed (Tito protested). Stalin had not been altogether wrong. Rule in Eastern Europe depended on force, not on any general appreciation of the virtues of Socialism.

Even so, Khrushchev concluded that it was better to do as the British had in their own empire: to rule through local rulers, rather than almost directly, as Stalin had. His generals told him that they might have found it impossible to contain simultaneous revolts in Poland and in Hungary. The new ruler of Hungary, János Kádár, did institute some reforms. To gain loyalty, he announced that "anyone who is not against us is with us," and avoided the sort of purge that the Hungarian Revolution might have caused.

Elsewhere in the empire, disturbances were limited to minor rioting in East Berlin and to demonstrations in Czechoslovakia. There was some tension: in Romania, Georgiu-Dej apparently feared that Khrushchev would have him unseated. However, Khrushchev made no attempt to eliminate either him or the other Stalinist rulers of Eastern Europe.

Molotov and his friends still had some fight left in them. In July 1957 they defeated Khrushchev in a vote in the Presidium. Khrushchev pointed out that only the Party could oust him as its chief; the Presidium was a non-Party governmental body. He demanded a Central Committee vote. His defense minister, Marshal Zhukov, insured his success by using military aircraft to fly pro-Krushchev Politburo members to Moscow specifically for the vote. The "anti-Party" faction was defeated, its members, including Malenkov and Molotov, ejected (Andrei Gromyko became foreign minister, a post he would hold for the next twenty-eight years, through 1985). The post-Beria rules applied: no one was shot or imprisoned. However, the same senior military men who had helped were potential rivals; in October 1957 Khrushchev retired Marshal Zhukov, whose stature within Soviet society was clearly a threat. He was replaced by Marshal Rodion Malinovsky, also a major World War II professional military figure. In February 1958 Khrushchev made himself prime minister, reviving Stalin's old combination of head of state and head of the Party.

Dwight D. Eisenhower entered office in January 1953 with some enormous advantages. Due to both his wartime experience as supreme commander in Europe and to his more recent duty as SACEUR, he personally knew most European leaders and was very familiar with Allied feelings and needs. At least as importantly, they— including the Soviets—knew him; he did not need to prove himself. His unique depth of military experience made him the only president in modern times who could deal with senior military officers on anything like an equal basis. Moreover, he could trust his military judgement in the face of contrary advice.

He confronted much the same reality that Malenkov and Khrushchev would soon experience: the new H-bomb made general war almost too horrific to confront. To some extent he echoed the Europeans; at a July 1953 NSC meeting he said that "the only thing worse than losing a global war was winning one; there would be no individual freedom after the next global war." To Eisenhower's military sophistication was adjoined a fear that the United States could not long sustain high military spending. The H-bomb virtually guaranteed that there would never be a military end to the Cold War; it might last forty years.

Demanding more and more from the people would require more and more economic controls and, eventually, a garrison state. At the least, continued large deficits might fatally weaken the U.S. economy and with it the entire free world. Eisenhower was not alone in his concern. At a 13 October 1953 NSC meeting, Secretary of the Treasury Humphrey said that "if people begin to think that this Administration is conducting its business in the same old way as the last, the American economy will go to hell and the Republican Party will lose the next election."[1] The buildup had provided a legacy against which Eisenhower could safely make the cuts he wanted—as soon as the drain of the continuing Korean War was over. U.S. forces already had increased to a point at which the Soviets could not lightly start a general war. Moreover, Eisenhower did not intend to cut back to anemic pre-Korea levels; he hoped merely that by FY57 the budget would be $33 billion per year (about twice the pre-Korea figure) rather than Truman's planned

$40 billion. Eisenhower felt he could do as much because war was now quite unlikely.

Could the United States keep up its readiness to fight indefinitely? Soviet nuclear power was growing, but the Soviets did not yet have the power to destroy the United States. The JCS Advance Group proposed that the United States consider deliberately precipitating a war with the Soviets while it was still the only power with the H-bomb. Eisenhower's chairman of the Joint Chiefs, Adm. Arthur H. Radford, said that once the Soviets had the H-bomb (about 1957–60) the United States would find itself either fighting a nuclear war or bowing to the threat of one. After musing that it might be better to do something now than subject untold generations to the cost of maintaining a U.S. deterrent, Eisenhower decided never to consider preventive war; he would not arrogate to himself the choice to try to change the world by killing tens of millions of people.[2]

As SACEUR Eisenhower was well aware of the British proposal to solve that problem, their Global Strategy.[3] The failure of British mobilization during the Korean War might foreshadow U.S. economic disaster due to overspending. The British knew that they could not deploy large enough forces to Germany to stop a Soviet armored thrust. It seemed wiser to use the threat of nuclear attack to deter the Soviets while using conventional forces to solve urgent Commonwealth security problems. If deterrence failed, nuclear weapons might stop advancing Soviet tanks.[4]

The Korean War had been costly partly because President Truman had refused to use nuclear weapons in Korea. At one of his first NSC meetings, President Eisenhower was urged to use a few nuclear weapons in Korea, not least to overcome "civilian hysteria" about the dangers of nuclear attack. He refused: "We could not blind ourselves to the effects of such a move on our allies, [who] feel they will be the battleground in an atomic war between the United States and the Soviet Union."[5]

Eisenhower asked the four incoming members of the Joint Chiefs to suggest ways of drastically cutting costs. On 27 August 1953 the JCS reported that deployed forces could be cut if it were accepted that nuclear weapons could be used freely: U.S. forces should no longer prepare for alternative nuclear and conventional forms of war.[6] Each nuclear warhead might be costly, but it would replace many conventional ones. To generate more firepower was relatively inexpensive, since it involved merely enlarging the single warhead. It would still be mounted on one missile or fired from one artillery piece or dropped by one airplane with one crew and one set of supporting personnel. Conventional forces could never be inexpensive; every added unit of firepower required more weapons.

While the JCS pondered, on 9 May 1953 President Eisehower ordered a strategy study, Solarium (named after the White House solarium). Three task forces would examine the alternatives: (A) continuing containment; (B) containment backed by the threat of general war should the Soviets challenge it; and (C) trying for local success, to produce "a climate of victory, disturbing to the Soviets and their satellites and encouraging to the free world."[7]

Task Force A defended Truman's Korean War buildup and the notion of maintaining sufficient military strength to face down any Soviet threat.

Task Force B suggested that, instead of fighting wherever the Soviets or their proxies might attack, the United States would simply threaten to retaliate massively if matters got out of hand. Relatively small U.S. forces could maintain order along the Eurasian periphery. There was one problem: the American public might reject the risks of general war to deal with some minor Soviet action.

As an example of its strategy, Task Force C suggested deliberately continuing the war in Korea to justify a final war-winning offensive either to end the war on the Yalu or to encircle and destroy much of the Chinese army in Korea. Chiang could be built up to the point where his forces could recapture Hainan. It would provide the base needed to clear out the northern part of Indochina.

Eisenhower chose the JCS option and the Task Force B option to create a "New Look" national strategy. In December 1953 the administration announced that it considered nuclear weapons usable in place of conventional ones. A policy of massive nuclear retaliation "at a time and place of our own choosing" in the event of any further Soviet aggression was announced by Secretary of State Dulles at a meeting of the Council on Foreign Relations in New York, 12 January 1954. Dulles's policy came to be known as brinkmanship. The United States would deliberately escalate a crisis to the point where the Soviets would have to choose between backing down and risking incineration. This policy seemed extremely dangerous, since the Soviets had their own bomb and were building the means to deliver it. Eisenhower's intelligence services certainly thought so, at least until the "missile gap" bubble burst in 1959. We now know that through the 1950s the Soviets had nothing like the capability with which U.S. intelligence services credited them. Brinkmanship was far safer than Eisenhower and Dulles imagined.

The rationale for retaliation at a place the U.S. might choose was based on the Americans' experience in Korea. The war there had been so expensive mainly because it had been fought on a battlefield Stalin had chosen, with mountainous terrain (ill-suited to using tanks and tactical aircraft), against an enemy enjoying short lines of supply leading back to a sanctuary. Moreover, in Korea U.S. and allied forces could not make any threat that would force the Soviets to abandon the war. Threats to places more vital to the Soviets might offer more leverage.

The New Look applied particularly to Southeast Asia, where it was hoped that nuclear-armed air and naval forces might deal with any renewed Communist threat without committing ground forces. Deterrence might not work in Western Europe, which was so valuable that the Soviets might be tempted to seize it even at a considerable risk. Secretary of State Dulles said at a news conference that "there is no comparable situation elsewhere in the world." Critics pointed out that there was no other region where massive retaliation made much sense.

It was never altogether clear exactly what threat the Soviets might find so terrifying as to deter them, given their limited respect for human life. It was assumed that the general destructiveness of H-bombs would suffice. At a 1955 NSC meeting, Vice President Richard Nixon suggested making the Soviets aware of the great nuclear attack capacity of the United States. Eisenhower "observed that it was reasonable to assume that the Soviets . . . had some appreciation of the implications for destruction of their regime and their country . . . the whole prospect of an exchange of all-out blows with thermonuclear weapons staggers the mind. . . ."[8]

Thus, from Eisenhower's point of view the development of a Soviet nuclear arsenal was not too important, as long as the U.S. strategic forces remained effective. Many Europeans felt uneasy. Some feared the new emphasis on nuclear war; would they be dragged in?[9] Others feared that in future the United States would be unwilling to attack the Soviet Union if the latter invaded Western Europe. NATO might not have had the troops, but the Soviets had been deterred by the knowledge that if they moved into West Germany they would suffer nuclear disaster. As the question usually was asked, would New York be risked to save Paris or Bonn?[10] Many Europeans began to wonder whether the Soviets would attack them because they harbored SAC bases; by 1954 some European governments were already demanding a veto over the use of SAC bases.[11]

To Eisenhower, all of this was beside the point. No Soviet leader could be sure that the United States would not retaliate, that a grab for Western Europe would not end with a radioactive Soviet Union. As long as he could credibly threaten to fight an all-out nuclear war, he would never have to fight a major nonnuclear one. Moreover, placing tactical nuclear weapons in Europe improved the situation, because they precluded any cheap quick Soviet victory. He had met many Soviets during World War II; they were not fools. The Soviets would not risk something far more devastating. As long as the United States could threaten the Soviet Union with nuclear devastation, Eisenhower's version of nuclear poker was eminently winnable.

Eisenhower, then, had little use for the big, expensive army he had inherited from Truman, because he could see little chance that it would be used. He could not, however, retire it altogether. He had to keep U.S. troops in Europe and in Korea. But he also had to find some way to justify cutting the army. His solution was brilliant. He ordered his forces to reorganize so as to depend on tactical nuclear weapons rather than conventional ones. That in itself justified massive manpower cuts; one nuclear rocket could replace dozens of artillery pieces, for example. Most students of the New Look took Eisenhower at his word; he was using atomic plenty to save money.

Critics argued that the new policy was extremely dangerous. If war broke out, nuclear weapons would soon be used, and using even a small weapon might trigger a devastating war. To these critics, Eisenhower was foolishly eliminating any U.S. capability to begin a war in Europe without using nuclear weapons. But Eisenhower was anything but foolish. He felt he had precluded war in Europe.

The possibility of U.S. economic meltdown, due to the sheer cost of maintaining an army to fight and win in Europe, was a far greater danger. It was one the new policy was specifically designed to eliminate. If deterrence worked as expected, the Soviets would surely concentrate on economic and political subversion rather than on general war. To resist this type of attack, the United States would need the soundest possible economy. Eisenhower could not, of course, say that he was cutting his forces because they were, in effect, obsolete—that the big war itself could not be fought. That would have been politically suicidal in the United States and dangerous abroad. However, the economic argument explains the New Look perfectly.

Around the periphery of the Soviet Union the New Look largely substituted nuclear-armed U.S. naval forces for troops on the ground. Carrier task forces were particularly valued because they could move rapidly to respond to surprises. The New Look meant the beginning of the sustained forward carrier deployments that are now traditional, in the Mediterranean (Sixth Fleet) and in the Far East (Seventh Fleet). The fleets were not new, and for some time the navy had maintained a nuclear strike group in the Mediterranean. Sustained carrier deployments in the Far East were entirely new; the fleet built up for the Korean War stayed in place. The fleet, moreover, could deliver just the force Eisenhower needed to deal with Third World crises: the marines.

As for the army, late in 1953 Eisenhower hoped to cut the 1.5-million-man army to 1 million; he hoped to cut its 20 combat divisions to 17 by mid-1955 and to 14 by mid-1957. Not surprisingly, the army was unenthusiastic. Eisenhower refused to sponsor the army's main advocate, its chief of staff (1953–55), Gen. Matthew B. Ridgway, for the usual second two-year term (he was replaced by another paratrooper, Gen. Maxwell D. Taylor).[12] The army did develop tactical nuclear weapons, and it tried to ride out Eisenhower's cuts by adopting a new "pentomic" divisional organization in 1956. Its hope seems to have been that by drastically cutting the number of men per division, it could preserve the divisions themselves so that they could be expanded once the tactical nuclear madness had run its course. Not only was the new divisional structure unsuccessful, it failed in its real purpose; Eisenhower cut both the number of soldiers *and* the number of divisions.[13] By 1957 the army had only fifteen divisions. With 41 percent of its strength tied down overseas, it could not easily stretch to any major further overseas deployment. By 1960, at the end of Eisenhower's term, the army was less capable than ever of fighting a major nonnuclear war.

In an echo of the 1949 "Revolt of the Admirals," the army staged a "revolt of the colonels" in 1956.[14] Leaked studies showed just how destructive a nuclear war in Europe could be. The army's position was supported by Truman-era defense and foreign policy officials, many of them Republicans who had left office when Eisenhower won. To bolster its case, the army supported academic nuclear strategists, such as Henry Kissinger. The army's view, that it was dangerous not to have a nonnuclear alternative to nuclear war, was echoed by academics at the air force's think tank, RAND. These strategists, including Herman Kahn (who wrote *On Thermo-*

nuclear War in 1960) and Robert Wohlstetter, developed the theory that the destructiveness of a nuclear war could be limited if escalation was carefully controlled. They saw war as a bargaining process, in which one side might be convinced to limit its own attack in return for a promise that its approach would limit its own. The army embraced such theories because the bargaining would begin with a nonnuclear response to any nonnuclear attack—such as a Soviet thrust into Europe. To make that response credible would require a revived army.

The revolt of the colonels failed. Although it coincided with the 1956 election, unfortunately it also coincided with the air force's campaign against the "bomber gap." Publicity generally went to glamorous aircraft technology. Big articles in popular U.S. magazines such as *Life* showed the terrifying new Soviet aircraft (and miserable-looking U.S. counterparts) rather than maps of nuclear devastation in Europe, or graphs of inadequate U.S. tank and troop strength. The colonels were purged; unlike the naval officers behind the 1949 revolt, they did not survive until better times. However, the army persevered. After retiring as chief of staff in 1959, Maxwell Taylor wrote a book, *The Uncertain Trumpet,* criticizing Eisenhower's policies. It brought him to John F. Kennedy's attention. Taylor was particularly well placed to turn the Kennedy administration away from the "New Look."

The logic of the New Look affected the army on a deeper level. Under Truman, U.S. policy had been to roll back the Iron Curtain, on the theory that the Soviet army in Europe was the main threat to the West. The farther back that army was based, the better the chance that it could never overrun Western Europe. However, shortly after Eisenhower entered office, the Soviets exploded their big compound fission bomb. Clearly it was a step towards a true H-bomb, the sort of weapon that could wipe out an entire country. Now the chief threat to the West was the growing mass of nuclear weapons within the borders of a very hostile Soviet Union. Soviet expansion would endanger the United States only by denying vital raw materials, for example from the Middle East.[15] That would probably be done by subversion rather than armed attack.

Ultimately, the New Look made sense only as long as the United States could credibly threaten to destroy the Soviet Union. The Soviets also threatened the United States. To what extent could Americans be protected? The greater the degree of protection, the more credible the U.S. threat against the Soviets. Otherwise the U.S. threat amounted to a declaration of mutual suicide.

As the Soviets tested their bomb in 1953, a window of strategic advantage, during which the United States but not the Soviets could inflict decisive damage, seemed to be closing. The existence of windows of U.S. or Soviet strategic advantage would be claimed again and again in the 1950s, as U.S. experts tried to guess the outcome of a possible nuclear war. These estimates told President Eisenhower how far he could go in a crisis.[16] Unfortunately, we do not yet know the results of any comparable Soviet studies or, indeed, whether Khrushchev was ever privy to them.

In 1953 there were two key facts. First, the United States was unlikely to have much warning of a carefully designed Soviet surprise attack. Second, the expensive U.S. Continental Air Defense System was unlikely to shoot down more than 7 percent of the attackers (planned improvements might raise this figure to 27 percent in 1955). To achieve surprise Soviet bombers would have to fly precisely, reaching all their targets at nearly the same time; Eisenhower remarked that no one who had flown with the Soviets in wartime would believe in their navigational ability.[17] The first few explosions would alert SAC, and most of its bombers would be able to disperse. Bombs were not stowed at SAC bases; it would take three to six days to collect them and launch the force.[18]

The air defense situation was more worrying. The system consisted of radars that detected incoming bombers, other radars that tracked them, and interceptors that depended on the tracking radars to cue them to destroy the bombers. Exercises showed that it was extremely difficult to track and intercept fast bombers, largely because those coordinating the information involved could not keep up with a quickly changing tactical situation. However, a warning itself might be quite valuable. It could help SAC preserve its own bombers for a counterblow (the threat of which might deter the Soviets in the first place: four hours' warning would save 85 percent of the bombers).

Warning might also save many Americans. Given as little as an hour to flee, people would escape the bomb blasts aimed at the cities. They would still face fallout, but they could be sheltered. Casualties might be halved. Urban sprawl—the flight to the suburbs—also would save many people. In addition, Eisenhower thought, the new interstate highways would help save Americans. Using them, people could evacuate the big coastal cities in a crisis; they might even decide to evacuate themselves. After all, on many holidays, big cities empty themselves quite without government assistance, over a day or two. One of President Truman's last acts in office had been to sign NSC 139 (31 December 1952), calling for construction of sufficient systems in place by 31 December 1955 to provide three to six hours of warning.[19]

U.S. industry was quite concentrated, however, and even a relatively small Soviet attack would be devastating. The first serious U.S. estimate of the effect of a Soviet attack, in 1953, was that it would paralyze a third of U.S. industry (a 1954 attack would paralyze two-thirds). For example, forty-one Soviet bombs could eliminate 90 percent of the U.S. atomic energy production capacity; fifty-five could kill 90 percent of jet engine capacity; ninety could kill half the oil refineries. Yet the country was so rich that enough would be left to provide minimum levels of production not only of civilian goods but also of war material.

In fact the situation was not nearly as bad as portrayed. Due to ignorance (enforced by very successful Soviet security), most U.S. estimates were worst-case guesses. For example, because Stalin had clearly pushed very hard to get his first bomb, it was assumed that he had ordered crash production of further weapons. In

1953 it was estimated that as of the middle of the year the Soviets would have 120 bombs (80 kilotons each). We now know, however, that series production did not begin until 1954, so it seems likely that the Soviet stockpile was only ten or twenty bombs as late as the beginning of 1954. Similarly, the Soviet bomber force was overestimated. In June 1953 the Soviets were credited with 1,600 long-range Tu-4 bombers, copies of the B-29 then being phased out of U.S. service. In fact Stalin had ordered only a thousand, and production ended in 1952 with 847 aircraft completed.[20] These aircraft had limited range, which is why the U.S. Air Force was so interested in obtaining foreign bases from which to launch its own equivalent of the B-29s. It was assumed that a ruthless dictator like Stalin would dispatch his airmen on one-way missions. We now know that he had no such plan in mind; the Tu-4s were intended to attack Eurasian targets. The range problem was so serious that in 1948 the Soviets considered building special assault submarines to seize U.S. air bases from which to attack the United States.[21] For that matter, the Soviet attack postulated in 1953 required extensive use of Arctic bases—but we now know that the Soviets did not even try operational training in the Arctic until the late 1950s. They discovered the problems that, in the 1940s, had deterred the U.S. Air Force from using similar bases on its side of the North Pole. It took the Soviets several years to solve them; for example, lubricants froze, and magnetic compasses were useless.

The Tu-4 was a limited threat; in 1953 the U.S. Air Force was fielding large numbers of jet fighters that could expect to deal with it. The real question was when the Soviets would introduce jet bombers as fast as existing fighters. Radar performance was measured in distance, not time: the faster the bomber, the shorter the warning time. The heavy turbo-prop Bear (Tu-95) was first seen in April 1953. By March 1954 it and a new Tu-16 jet medium bomber ("Badger") were known. In April 1954 a prototype jet heavy bomber (the Myasischev Bison) was clearly seen.[22] Numbers of Bisons and Bears appeared at the May Day 1955 air show. This was very frightening. Although the U.S. Air Force already had large numbers of medium jet bombers (B-47s) more than equivalent to the Tu-16, it was finding production of a jet heavy bomber, the B-52, quite difficult. Somehow, it seemed, the Soviets were telescoping the development process.

Again, the secret seemed to be ruthlessness: surely the Soviets were developing bombers more quickly by skipping development steps and accepting high accident rates.[23] Adm. Lewis Strauss of the AEC argued that the Soviets had managed to concentrate talents much more effectively than the Americans. In 1955 he accurately interpreted the first Soviet H-bomb test as a test of an ICBM warhead; on that basis he correctly predicted that they might have such a missile as soon as mid-1957.[24] It was assumed that the Soviets were producing the bombers as quickly as they could; surely the ultimate weapon, the one which would flatten their main enemy, was their most important program. Thus in 1955 U.S. Air Force intelligence (as reflected in National Intelligence Estimates) guessed that by 1958 the Soviets would have 350 Bisons and 250 Bears. That was a fantasy; the Soviets just could not build big bombers that quickly. They completed only ninety-three Bisons (including prototypes), and only fifty-one bomber versions of the Bear.

The situation was even less ominous than the numbers suggested. Badger medium bombers constituted the bulk of the Soviet bomber force. They could reach North America only on one-way missions—and we now know that the Soviets did not plan to operate them that way; they were intended for Eurasia. Many of these bombers, moreover, were assigned not to strategic attack but rather to Soviet Naval Aviation (to deal with American aircraft carriers, which the Soviets considered a major threat) and to tactical (Frontal) units. Neither assignment seems to have been understood by U.S. intelligence until about 1960.[25] By the time the Soviets had even a fair number of intercontinental bombers, the U.S. air defense system was far better than it had been in 1953. Most importantly, it had been computerized. Ironically, the computer-based system, SAGE, reached maturity about when the Soviets abandoned bombers in favor of missiles, both long-range and air-delivered. Even more ironically, the computer industry that grew out of exaggerated U.S. fears later indirectly destroyed the Soviet Union.

Soviet bomber numbers had real consequences. The more bombers, the more bases—and the more bases, the more SAC attackers were needed to blunt any possible Soviet counterattack. The U.S. Air Force prepared the bomber estimates, and naturally it favored higher over lower numbers. Eisenhower was perfectly willing to buy enough bombers to handle the Soviet threat; they were a lot less expensive than ground troops. However, his whole policy was to control spending. He knew that no commander ever thought he had enough; but he also knew, or thought he knew, that war itself was now unlikely. Like Truman, he believed that the Cold War was much more a political and economic struggle, in which spending too much on the outward appearance of military strength could be fatal.

Thus Eisenhower's every instinct was to avoid making defense a public issue. National security had to be above politics. The parochial desires of the services and of the defense industry could not possibly be allowed to endanger the long-term health of the United States, or of the West. Moreover, much of what Eisenhower decided was based on very sensitive intelligence—which could never be cited in any public way. To military intelligence was added a lifetime of military experience, which often bred skepticism. For its part, the air force had long used public pressure to get what it wanted. It could leak intelligence depicting a rapidly expanding Soviet threat; it could recruit politicians who would use that image to promote themselves. Fiscal consequences, which so exercised the president, were likely to be felt for a long time, beyond the horizons of congressmen and senators.

Moreover, Eisenhower could not play his version of nuclear poker too publicly. He had to be able to bob and weave, to make threats and then very quickly withdraw them. The U.S. public might easily become inflamed. Without much idea of the military balance, or of the likely outcome of a war, it might demand near-term satisfaction. Eisenhower's stance was exactly contrary to normal political behavior; politicians gained support by dramatizing a problem, then by saying they alone could solve it. To Eisenhower, being undramatic was the ultimate civic virtue. Perhaps he had learned that by observing the most melodramatic of generals, Douglas MacArthur, in the Philippines before World War II.

The 1956 crisis over the air force's claimed "bomber gap" illustrated both the problem and Eisenhower's solution. In hopes of getting more B-52s, the air force claimed the Soviet bomber force was expanding very rapidly. Eisenhower already knew that he needed hard intelligence instead of the vague data being thrown about. A panel studying ways to deal with the threat of surprise attack had suggested aerial reconnaissance as the solution. The necessary high-flying airplane, the U-2, flew its first overflight mission in July 1956, about as the air force began its campaign. The Soviets protested these flights, and Eisenhower apparently feared that they would destroy a developing détente. He continued mainly because the first overflight produced evidence almost completely discounting the "bomber gap." U-2 data are reflected in a 1959 CIA report that the Soviets had built only about sixty Bears and 115 Bisons. There were another 1,050 Badgers.[26]

Eisenhower could have announced these data; the air force would have been squelched. He had, moreover, good reason to do so. By 1959 the air force and its friends were announcing, not a bomber gap, but a missile gap. Eisenhower was under intense pressure to buy very large numbers of extremely expensive ballistic missiles. This time, work was proceeding feverishly on another form of reconnaissance, a photo satellite. It would soon reveal that the missile gap, too, was illusory.

However, Eisenhower's instinct was not to reveal intelligence. Better to be attacked as too passive than to damage or destroy vital means of penetrating Soviet secrecy. Eisenhower simply rejected the arguments put forward by the air force and by its congressional allies. He was careful to do so cordially, but he got his way. Probably no other president could have done so; only Eisenhower had the military prestige to stand up to his military chiefs without provoking an open break.

Quite apart from numbers, the great question through the 1950s was whether the Soviets could somehow neutralize SAC, either by destroying it in the air or on the ground. The first might seem paradoxical; if the U.S. Air Force could not hope to block a Soviet attack, surely the more primitive Soviet system would have little chance against SAC. However, many U.S. targets were near the coasts and the borders; it was difficult to detect bombers very long before they arrived. Given the sheer size of the Soviet Union, early detection might be much easier. If the Soviets somehow obtained SAC's attack plan, they would know where to concentrate their defenses. From 1951 on, SAC's commander, Lt. Gen. Curtis LeMay, did not submit his Basic War Plans to the JCS, claiming an urgent need for secrecy.[27]

In 1954 LeMay gave a classified lecture, now often quoted, to the effect that his bombers would never be caught on the ground: it was "inconceivable" that the United States would sit still to be struck. Reconnaissance airplanes, constantly overflying the Soviet Union, would give him so much warning that he could strike before the Soviets even began warming up their airplanes.[28] Perhaps, it might seem, LeMay had classified his war plans because the JCS would have found them an unacceptable approach to Eisenhower's forbidden preventive war.

In fact overflights were anything but continuous; each had to be separately authorized by the president (as was each U-2 flight). The first was flown in 1952, and the only really extensive series began on 21 March 1956, RB-47s flying from Thule over the northern Soviet Union. This series ended with the 6–7 May 1956 "massed overflight" in which six RB-47s mapped all of northern Siberia. In all, 156 missions were flown from Thule. These flights did not penetrate very deeply.[29] Conceivably LeMay relied on intercepts of Soviet radio communications to remote airfields. However, the NSC's intense interest in the effects of a Soviet surprise attack confirms that LeMay lacked any sort of attack warning.

LeMay was defending SAC against a pair of naval officers attending his lecture. If, contrary to his claims, surprise could cancel out SAC, then the United States would need a less vulnerable sort of deterrent, probably launched from aircraft carriers and submarines. Beginning in 1954, LeMay concentrated on developing the ability to strike quickly—on warning. Nuclear bombs were stowed at bomber bases, so that attacks could be mounted much more quickly. In mid-1955 SAC claimed it could launch its first 180 aircraft within twelve hours of an alert, further strikes following every twelve hours, for a total of 880 aircraft launched within forty-eight hours (given three to four days of alert, it could launch over one thousand aircraft in one simultaneous strike). In 1957 SAC claimed that it could launch 134 loaded bombers, given two hours of alert for American bases and thirty minutes for overseas bases; but in an actual test in September 1957, the first airplane was not launched for six hours.[30]

SAC developed a new war plan in which its B-47 medium bombers would fly directly to their targets, rather than to overseas bases from which they could attack. Improved aerial refueling techniques made this new concept viable. SAC retained its overseas bases to complicate Soviet air defenses and also to recover bombers after they had attacked the Soviet Union.[31] To support the new tactics, B-47 bases had to be built up in the northeastern United States, where they became more vulnerable to Soviet attack, including a rather prematurely postulated threat from submarine-launched missiles.[32]

Enough of SAC's war plans did leak out for the army chief of staff, General Ridgway, to charge in October 1954 that the SAC target list was not entirely consistent with approved JCS policy.[33] Nothing was done for a time, because the JCS felt that it lacked the technical capability to evaluate the list. In 1957 SAC seemed to cement its position, buying an IBM 704 computer on which it said it relied (in 1960 Eisenhower's presidential science advisor told him that the computer was virtually useless for this purpose).[34] In 1956, SAC listed 2,997 targets; by early 1957 it listed 3,261.[35]

As the target list grew, SAC needed not only more airplanes, but also more bombs. Early in 1957 it asked the president to approve enlargement of the national bomb stockpile. Eisenhower was wily. Granting the air force's request, he asked the other two services to review SAC's war plan. The result, Project Budapest (briefed to the JCS on 28 August 1957), was shocking.[36] It had generally been agreed that very large numbers of weapons (hence bombers) would be needed to deal with the vast Soviet Union. Hence the sheer size of SAC and its tactical equivalent, TAC. The navy could deliver bombs, but only in small numbers; clearly, it seemed, it had only a secondary role. Now it emerged that many of SAC's targets were so closely bunched that the blast of bombs hitting neighboring targets would probably overlap. So much fallout would be generated that millions in allied countries, such as Japan, might be killed. Many fewer weapons could do the same damage. Moreover, the study exposed SAC's obsession with the Bravo mission and preemptive attacks.

Contrary to LeMay's view, it was virtually certain that the Soviets would get to attack first, or at least to launch first. SAC was ordered to develop an alternative second-strike plan.[37] From the navy's point of view, the situation was transformed. Its forces were already far more capable of survival than SAC's, hence much better adapted to the second-strike war. Now the navy realized that it could deliver quite enough warheads to do SAC's job. Naval strike forces, particularly submarine-launched missiles, could be central rather than peripheral.

Like Khrushchev, Eisenhower was all too aware, by this time, that very large strategic arsenals would buy very little. "There was obviously a limit—a human limit—to the devastation which human beings could endure." Should the entire U.S. stockpile be used, the resulting fallout would destroy not only the United States but also the entire Northern Hemisphere. "We should indoctrinate ourselves that there is such a thing as common sense."[38]

Eisenhower was unwilling, however, to cut SAC. He may have considered its sheer size valuable insurance against losses due to a Soviet surprise attack, the likelihood of which SAC probably underrated. He approved SAC's demand that all U.S. nuclear forces come under a Single Integrated Operational Plan (SIOP-62), for which it was largely responsible.[39] The plan was ferocious, and it drew no distinction between the Soviet Union and China: SAC would hit both simultaneously. That was not just naiveté. Eisenhower knew about the developing Sino-Soviet split, but explained that if it emerged undamaged from a U.S.-Soviet war, China would simply develop into another Soviet Union, that is, into another mortal threat to the United States.[40]

Critics within the government charged that the plan had been rigged to require the largest possible bomber fleet. President Eisenhower asked his science advisor, Kistiakowsky, to evaluate the SIOP. The plan called for an initial attack to be conducted by a ready force. Some hours or days later, a second (follow-on) force would be launched. Kistiakowsky found that this double attack was gross overkill. The planned follow-on forces sometimes killed targets which had already been killed four or five times by the initial attackers. Eisenhower was horrified.[41] In addition, the plan probably could not have been carried out. Satellites later revealed that targeters did not know many target locations accurately enough to be sure of hitting them.[42]

Yet SAC lost the battle it thought it was winning. Eisenhower's decisions on whether to buy new bombers and missiles had nothing to do with the SIOP. By 1960 SAC's most numerous bombers, its B-47s, were aging. A few long-range B-52s each year were hardly enough to make up for the inevitable loss of most of the B-47s in the near future. The missile program could not provide anything like the megatonnage SAC would soon lose, yet a skeptical Eisenhower was not about to buy the next-generation bomber, the B-70.

Whatever the war plan, SAC had to be protected against a surprise attack. On 27 March 1954, Eisenhower asked the Science Advisory Committee of the Office of Defense Mobilization to study ways to reduce this threat. The forty-two-member panel (headed by Dr. James R. Killian Jr.) included an Intelligence Capabilities Panel headed by Edwin Land of the Polaroid Corporation. In mid-1954 it proposed a high-altitude reconnaissance airplane as an interim solution and a satellite as a long-term one. Both might detect early preparations for a surprise attack.[43] As it happened, Eisenhower decided that he had to approve each U-2 overflight personally. The Soviets detected the aircraft, but they could not shoot them down. Eisenhower limited overflights to avoid incidents, so the U-2s never provided enough continuous coverage to detect attack preparations.

Every time a U-2 flew over the Soviet Union, it reminded Khrushchev that his air defenses were toothless. Again and again, Soviet fighters tried unsuccessfully to intercept the airplane. Photographs it brought back documented their humiliating failures. The new anti-aircraft missiles could not quite reach the U-2—until 1960.

Satellites had only limited coverage. They were a very effective means of examining potential targets in the Soviet Union, but they could not scan quickly to see changes in, say, airfields as bombers were prepared for an attack. Satellites carried film capsules which special aircraft could recover in the air. The first such Corona satellite flew in February 1959, but the first film canister was not recovered until August 1960, after thirteen failures.[44] It was just in time to replace the U-2, and it offered far better coverage, since flights, which were unmanned, entailed little or no risk (and the satellite could not, at least as yet, be shot down). Unfortunately the resulting photographs were not nearly as good as those obtained by the U-2.

De Gaulle had chided Khrushchev that a Soviet "space ship" was passing over Paris sixteen to eighteen times a day. Khrushchev's reaction was extraordinary: he said he did not care how many satellites flew over his territory; "anyone could take all the pictures he wished from satellites over Soviet territory." Unfortunately no agreed notes of the conference were taken, but Eisenhower thought Khrushchev's words could be used anyway because the French record would be "comprehensive"—presumably, taped.[45] In recent years there has been considerable speculation that the Eisenhower administration deliberately retarded the U.S. satellite program so as to insure that the Soviets came first, and thus implicitly agreed that sat-ellites could pass freely over any territory on earth. That such points seemed note-worthy as late as 1960 suggests that the administration had had no such ideas three or four years earlier. The U-2 and its successor did have some very important influences on U.S. thinking. The U-2 was operated by the CIA, rather than by the air force (whose attempt to take over the program failed). For the first time, the air force faced independent review of the size of the Soviet bomber force—analysts could count the bombers on photographs. That killed the "bomber gap."

The flood of photographs, first from the U-2 and then from satellites, changed U.S. intelligence. Those relying on human sources (HUMINT) had to concentrate heavily on interpretation of often overwhelmingly subjective information. Even for communications intercepts, context was vital for proper interpretation. A photo satellite provided apparently objective information. Interpretation often amounted to recognizing and measuring what the film recorded. An army of photo interpreters had to be recruited. Their sheer numbers came to dominate the intelligence services. The new "objective" intelligence was very welcome partly because Soviet society was so closed. The Soviet counterintelligence apparatus was so large, for example, that each foreigner visiting the Soviet Union could be tailed and each hotel room separately monitored.[46]

It turned out, however, that the new kind of intelligence was less reliable than had been imagined. Without HUMINT to give it context, the mass of technical data could be quite misleading. For example, when the Soviets were forced to dismantle SS-20 intermediate-range missiles in Eastern Europe in the 1980s, it turned out that substantially more were in place than the U.S. government imagined. Most embarrassing to U.S. intelligence was its poor estimation of the number of Soviet nuclear warheads. Naturally, accuracy in this area was considered particularly important. Late in the Cold War it was estimated that the Soviets had about twenty-eight thousand to thirty thousand nuclear weapons. In the early 1990s the minister responsible for disposing of them pleaded for funds to deal with the *forty-five thousand* he had on hand.

In its 14 February 1955 report, the Killian Committee pointed out that if the Soviet bomber threat were bad, long-range ballistic missiles were far worse. The Soviets were thought to be working on intercontinental ballistic missiles (ICBMs). They seemed to be able to press ahead with really important projects, and the ICBM certainly qualified. Once they had it, they could hit SAC bases, not in five or six hours, but in thirty minutes. The United States desperately needed not only its own ICBM but also some way to reduce SAC vulnerability.

It seemed unlikely that any defense could be erected against ICBMs. At best an attack could be detected early enough to launch bombers. For example, large early warning radars (BMEWS) erected in Greenland and in Scotland could see Soviet ICBMs as soon as they rose high enough; they offered about fifteen minutes of warning. Warning systems, it turned out, were subject to false alarms. For example, on 5 October 1960 the new Thule radar misidentified the moon as a missile attack. Because no impact points were predicted, NORAD and SAC treated this as a false alarm. Modifications precluded any repeat performance, but this and other false alarms were used in the 1980s as arguments that the United States should not buy an automated missile defense system.[47] There was never much possibility that SAC would be launched into combat. Eisenhower once remarked that common sense would keep men from placing nuclear systems on a true hair trigger. He was right.

Given a warning, SAC's bombers had to be able to take off within fifteen minutes. A few minutes after takeoff they would be safe, outside the blast created by a bomb or a missile hitting their bases. That was easier said than done. Bombers were complex, so SAC liked to concentrate them at a few bases, where maintenance could be concentrated. However, each base then became a very attractive target. Moreover, the more bombers that had to flush from the bases, the longer the group takeoff would take.

In October 1957 SAC began to go on ground alert. Ultimately a third of its force was at held at fifteen-minute alert. On any given day, another third was under maintenance, and a third was flying.[48] A warning might be false; but once the bombers were safe in the air, there was time for a decision. SAC developed what it called "Fail Safe" (later renamed Positive Control). As publicized, bombers would hit their targets *unless* recalled; this would discourage the Soviets from any quick attack against the U.S. government. However, a recall message might not get through, for example due to sunspot activity (which affects radio propagation).[49] The actual system therefore was to send bombers out while they listened for a "go" signal. Unless they received it, they would return to base.

The next step was airborne alert. Although it exacted a great toll on aircraft and crews, it guaranteed that some bombers would survive a Soviet strike. Only the B-52 had enough endurance to be suitable. Normally twelve aircraft were kept airborne all the time. SAC ordered its first full airborne alert during the Cuban Missile Crisis of 1962; it kept an average of sixty-five B-52s in the air at any one time, ready to fly to their targets.[50] A few B-52s, a fraction of SAC's force, were maintained on airborne alert through the rest of the Cold War. Most aircraft, however, were still on the ground; SAC could not launch most of them without substantial warning.

SAC also had to be sure of getting to its targets. Through the 1950s the Soviets built up their air defenses, albeit with less impressive technology than the United States had. By the late 1950s they had impressive radar cover—but only against bombers flying above one thousand feet. Much the same could be said of their new antiaircraft missiles.[51] SAC began to practice low-level attacks. B-47s showed that they could flip over like fighters to toss their bombs into Soviet targets without coming within range of the new low-altitude (but short-range) missiles. Unfortunately, low-level flying imposed enormous stresses on airframes. The immense SAC bomber force contracted dramatically as wings began to crack. Much the same happened to the British RAF.[52]

As defensive missiles improved, bombers had to carry their own missiles to attack from outside their range. The first of them were in effect miniature supersonic airplanes, but in 1959 the United States began to develop a futuristic bomber-launched ballistic missile, Skybolt.[53] The missile was important enough to SAC, but to the British it became vital. The U.S. deterrent would continue whether or not the bombers did. The British found that they preferred a Skybolt-armed bomber, which could disperse on warning or even take off to avoid being destroyed, to a fixed ballistic missile, which probably could be destroyed before it was launched. In 1960 they abandoned their own ballistic missile program in favor of Skybolts, which were to be supplied by the United States.

By that time American opinion was split as to the Skybolt's desirability. For example, opponents feared that it would divert resources from other, simpler, ballistic missiles (firing from a moving airplane added considerable complications). The air force was forced to scale down Skybolt's capabilities to limit its cost. The Eisenhower administration deliberately left to the next administration the decision whether to place Skybolt in production. However, it also saw the missile as a very useful bargaining chip; several times during 1960 it assured the British that Skybolt development was proceeding. In return for the promise to provide the missile, the British granted the United States important Polaris basing rights.

From Eisenhower's point of view, the bombers and their weapons served mainly to keep the Cold War cold. Eisenhower harbored no illusions: the war would continue, but on a subterranean level. Having been checked in Europe, the Soviets would concentrate on the Third World. They lacked the means to project military power into it, but there was plenty of discontent to exploit. The obvious pattern for Soviet attacks was the use of popular fronts in Europe in 1947–49. The success in Iran suggested that the CIA was the best way to check the expected Soviet offensive.

In the early 1950s a popular front seemed to be on the verge of taking over the Guatemalan government. For some years before 1954 this government had been headed left. It is often suggested that the Guatemalan government's real crime was to nationalize United Fruit holdings. It was probably far more significant that Guatemala was so close to the Panama Canal. Given Eisenhower's use of sea power, the canal was an extremely important Cold War asset. The Guatemalan government was unique in the Western Hemisphere in observing a minute of silence when Stalin died. A CIA-led coup overthrew Arbenz, the left-wing president. The coup brought a right-wing dictatorship into power, partly because Arbenz had already killed off his right-wing democratic rival, Francisco Javier Arana, during the run-up to the 1952 election.[54]

The effort made in Guatemala seemed anomalous. Many in other Latin American countries were less than pro-American, and through the 1950s several countries nationalized American assets. For example, it was no great surprise that Vice President Richard Nixon was attacked when he visited Caracas in 1958. For all of that, the U.S. government seems to have made little or no effort to control most Latin American governments through the 1950s.

The CIA also attempted a coup in Indonesia, in 1958; the country's leader, Sukarno, seemed to be on the point of going Communist.[55] The country was strategic both in position (on the sea route to the Far East) and in resources (for which the United States tried to defend it against the Japanese in 1941–42). Disaffected colonels in western and northern Sumatra had begun a revolt in December 1956. Other local commanders joined. The CIA saw the revolt as a possible opportunity. Sukarno encouraged the U.S. decision when he declared in February 1957 that all political parties should be abolished; Indonesia would become a "guided democracy" under his leadership. As Sukarno had just toured major Communist capitals, it seemed obvious that he was getting ready to go Communist. It did not help that he then entertained Soviet President Voroshilov for over two months. In September 1957 the CIA was told to go ahead against Sukarno. The hope was that the situation would become so unstable that the United States could reasonably withdraw recognition of Sukarno's government and then land forces to protect American lives and property. Even if the operation failed, Indonesia would probably break up; the view was that a disunited Indonesia was far better than a Communist one. Meanwhile, to distract popular attention from the ongoing military revolt, Sukarno revived an old campaign to wrest West New Guinea from the Dutch. The colonels offered Sukarno peace if he would change his cabinet and abandon "guided democracy." Sukarno turned them down, and in February 1958 the colonels proclaimed an alternative government. It was soon evident that the colonels were not nearly as powerful as the CIA had hoped. Their movement was not sufficiently cohesive. Embarrassingly, a CIA operative flying a supporting bomber was shot down, and his identity papers made it obvious that the agency was backing the rebellion. Part of the price of releasing the operative was a promise of U.S. pressure on the Dutch to relinquish West New Guinea to Indonesia. The failed coup seems to have caused exactly the development Dulles feared. Sukarno was strengthened and he turned to the Soviets for help, and began to receive Soviet weaponry. By 1962 Indonesia really was a problem, a major regional naval power (at least on paper) with an anti-Western orientation.

Covert action was also used against the Chinese.[56] In August 1950 the Chinese army (PLA) conquered Tibet, until then an independent if backward kingdom under nominal Chinese suzerainty. As elsewhere in China, Communist control brought wrenching changes. They were particularly difficult for the theocratic Tibetan society. In 1954 armed resistance began. New roads the Chinese had built to control the country often were blocked.

The CIA probably made contacts in Tibet, mainly for intelligence gathering, as early as 1951. The sustained armed rising was a major opportunity, particularly since the Tibetans soon showed that they were very willing to fight. Effective cooperation apparently began in 1956, with equipment and men dropped in. The CIA trained Tibetan recruits, initially on Taiwan, eventually in Colorado. By 1957, there were about eighty thousand of them, plus about ten thousand bandits and local tribesmen. Some of the weapons came from stocks that had been built up for the abortive Indonesian operation. By 1958, the resistance army was tying down four-teen Chinese (PLA) divisions, a substantial fraction of the force they had used in Korea. Maintaining them in Tibet must have been extremely costly, perhaps limit-ing Chinese freedom of action anywhere else. The Chinese were also uncomfort-ably aware that other border regions were probably restive.

Up to that time the Dalai Lama, the spiritual leader of Tibet, was not yet sup-porting the war. In March 1959, after the Chinese had tried to take him hostage, he fled to India with many of his followers—and reversed his position on the resist-ance. The Chinese shelled the Dalai Lama's summer residence, causing a ten-day battle in which as many as forty thousand people may have died. Elsewhere in Tibet the Chinese claimed that they killed eighty-seven thousand Tibetans that year.

The rebels depended heavily on airdrops, mainly by C-130s flying out of Thai-land. After Gary Powers' U-2 was shot down over the Soviet Union on 1 May 1960, President Eisenhower banned all overflights of Communist countries. The CIA developed alternate overland routes. Then John F. Kennedy became president. His ambassador to India, John Kenneth Galbraith, disliked the Tibetans, and he tried to stop the war. By this time the Tibetans were considered allies; they would not be deserted. The CIA moved the operation to Nepal. Without air drops the resistance weakened, and the Chinese were able to close most of the border routes. However, the Tibetan armed resistance continued through the early 1970s. In 1973 the Nepalese finally agreed with the Chinese to close their border.

The CIA had little hope that the Tibetans would win; the Chinese were just too powerful. To the Tibetans themselves victory apparently did not matter; they often said that, in the face of Chinese atrocities, they would gladly fight to the last man. The fact that they did as well as they did (and lasted as long as they did) in their mountainous terrain must have made a considerable impression. A few years after the Tibetan resistance effectively ended, the Soviets found themselves fighting sim-ilarly dedicated guerillas in somewhat similar terrain, in Afghanistan. In hindsight the Tibetan operation may have had much more potential than was obvious at the time. The Soviets did, in the end, have to leave Afghanistan, and that helped bring down their regime. In 1958–59 the Tibetans were doing better against the Chinese than the Afghans would do against the Soviets, and they were far more united. On the other hand, the Tibetans lacked a supportive rear area across the border; only after the Sino-Indian War of 1962 did the Indians become really friendly. In 1999 Tibet is formally part of China, but it is clear that resentment of Chinese rule is still quite hot; there were, for example, violent demonstrations on the thirtieth anni-versary of the 1959 uprising. There also is apparently strong resentment in nearby Sinkiang. Like the old Soviet Union, China is a multiracial empire—which may yet prove as vulnerable as the Soviet Union to demands for independence.

Khrushchev's situation was not too different from Eisenhower's. He had the same key insight that with the advent of megaton nuclear weapons general war was very unlikely. The struggle would shift to the Third World. Like Eisenhower, he came to the conclusion that sustaining a massive conventional military machine was eroding, rather than improving, his Cold War position. Stalin had worsened the situation by trying to compete with the West in developing very expensive weapons such as heavy bombers and large warships. Khrushchev's style was intuitive, so it is not clear that from the first he realized just what he was doing. However, like Eisenhower, he cut the cost of his forces by emphasizing cheap nuclear firepower. His senior officers came to the same conclusions as their American counterparts: the all-nuclear force was impractical. Khrushchev did not really care, because, like Eisenhower, he never expected to use that force.

Khruschev had had little or no military experience, and according to his memoirs neither he nor his Politburo colleagues had much inkling of the new technology already under development when Stalin died. Khrushchev said that he was shocked to discover, for example, that the new antiship missiles could make quick work of very expensive cruisers. Clearly a few nuclear missiles could replace masses of artillery. Thus, enforcing a nuclear missile revolution could, at the least, drastically cut the cost of the Soviet military machine.

Then, too, the Soviet military of the early 1950s consumed manpower on a vast scale, not only in its uniformed services but also in the mass production of conventional weapons. Yet manpower was becoming scarce, due to the demographic echoes of the mass killings of the 1930s; soon the additional effects of World War II would become evident.[1] In 1955, 5.7 million men were under arms. Khrushchev announced a cut of 640,000 men, followed by 1.2 million in May 1956 (forty-three divisions, to be effective by May 1957), leaving 3.9 million. Another three hundred thousand were cut in 1958–59, and then six hundred thousand in 1960–61. After a pause, there were further cuts in 1962–64. Thus it appeared that by 1965 Khrushchev had cut thirty-five to fifty-five divisions, and some of those remaining had been reduced to cadres. The number of aircraft in Frontal Aviation units assigned to support the Soviet Army was halved in 1960–61.[2] Another six-hundred-thousand-man cut was aborted when Khrushchev was ousted in 1964.[3]

Khrushchev knew that such deep cuts made good propaganda; it seemed that the military threat imposed by Stalin was abating. Social spending that had been deferred in order to buy new NATO forces now regained priority. It became difficult, for example, for countries to replace equipment they had obtained under the U.S. aid program (MDAP) a few years earlier. The British considered making a cut equivalent to Khrushchev's. The Germans considered reducing the term of military service from eighteen to twelve months.[4]

When Khruschev died, Marshal Malinovski, his defense minister—and not one of his admirers—said that Khrushchev had cut the Soviet Army to the point where it could barely keep NATO out of the Soviet Union (he added that he, Malinovski, had restored its striking power after Krushchev's demise). Eisenhower's U.S. Army detractors were saying similar things. In each case, the appropriate reply was that a general war in Europe would inevitably escalate into unlimited strategic war, so the guarantee against it was a sufficient strategic arsenal. Thus it was crucial that on 22 November 1955 the Soviets tested a true H-bomb. To Americans, it was a worse shock than Stalin's A-bomb. Because there was no reason to believe that the H-bomb secret had been stolen, it now seemed that the primitive Soviets had become technological geniuses.

Khrushchev edged into his "new look." In 1954–55 the first post-Stalin Five Year Plan, for 1956–60, was being drawn up. Khrushchev enthusiastically embraced the new missile technology. For example, in 1954, S. P. Korolev, the head of the rocket design bureau, was working on an intermediate-range ballistic missile, which would be effective within Eurasia. He said that it would be just as easy to develop an ICBM with about three times the range. There was some suspicion that he was really much more interested in space exploration. However, championed by Dmitriy F. Ustinov, chief of the Soviet strategic weapons program, Korolev's proposal was approved on 20 May 1954. In 1957 the Soviets thus had the world's first ICBM, the R-7 (NATO SS-6).[5] Money went into a variety of other strategic missiles: the world's first submarine-launched ballistic missile, a heavy bomber standoff missile, and abortive intercontinental cruise missiles.

Given such programs, Khrushchev could cut expensive conventional weapons. For example, he told his navy that antiship missiles, most of them fired from submarines, were the future; in 1955–56 he cancelled a projected fleet of missile-armed cruisers and aircraft carriers. He told a Westerner that he had no use for any submarine that could not deliver nuclear missiles. Production of medium and heavy bombers was stopped, but Khrushchev approved what he called missile carrier versions of many of these aircraft.[6]

Soviet industrial resources were tight; industry had to be realigned to handle the new technology. Managers were just recovering from the terror of working for

Stalin. Now Khrushchev suddenly ordered design bureaus in tanks, artillery, and aircraft to shift instantly to developing the new missiles. All of this change would have been unpleasant in any society. In the Soviet system, it was far worse, because each change in the plan spread chaos throughout it.

No Soviet bureaucrat or factory manager could fail to grasp that Khrushchev was quite as willing as Stalin to inflict pain. Had Stalin ordered the changes Khrushchev sought, managers would have had no choice but to comply. Khrushchev had, however, relaxed Stalin's terror. Further, his managers had achieved their positions through the Party, so each had connections with important Party members, and ultimately with Leonid Brezhnev, the Party's military industrial chief. The managers could, therefore, eventually make their pain felt by complaining to powerful friends. By ordering changes to industry, Khruschev had committed a major sin against the Party.

The nuclear standoff in Europe had left the Third World as a primary battleground. The West was beginning to withdraw from its colonies; the new governments might be recruited to the Soviet cause. In 1955 one of the first newly liberated countries, Indonesia, held a conference of the "nonaligned" countries in Bandung. The Chinese were invited despite their alliance with the Soviets. Their delegate, Chou En-lai, promoted Khrushchev's "peaceful coexistence."

The newly independent countries wanted arms, and some of them chafed under Western-imposed restrictions. Khrushchev offered himself as an alternative, beginning with Nasser's Egypt in 1955. It did not matter that the Egyptians were not Communists.

Khrushchev realized that economic performance was a Cold War weapon. He truly believed that the Soviet system could succeed; indeed, he was deceived by his own overoptimistic figures into imagining that it could outdo the United States within a few decades. Thus his famous 1959 boast that "we will bury you." It was not, as many imagined, proof of his aggressiveness. Rather it meant that capitalism would inevitably fall by the wayside, with Communism as its natural successor—in Khrushchev's earthy phrase, its gravedigger.

In the Third World, local Communist parties were unlikely to win on their own. Rather, Khrushchev had to convince the emerging leaders to go his way. The most valuable thing he could offer was economic development. He had to demonstrate that the Soviet Union, not the West, was the appropriate model for development; that central planning could generate the sort of double-digit growth ex-colonies needed. A successful Soviet-style Third World regime would be an invaluable demonstration.

In January 1959 Fidel Castro overthrew the Cuban dictator, Fulgencio Batista. Although always a Communist believer, he hid his sympathies in what might be considered a popular front. He had sought no Soviet aid for his revolution. Because he was not a member of the Cuban Communist Party, the Soviets did not trust him at first. However, in August 1960 one of his close advisors brought a letter to Moscow: he wanted to announce the creation of a Marxist Party and to seek solidarity with the Soviets. Khrushchev had his military staff investigate the possibility of defending the island against a U.S. invasion.[7] In September–October 1960 both Khrushchev and Castro attended the UN session in New York. By this time Castro had nationalized many U.S.-owned businesses in Cuba and had made other "socialist" moves. The two leaders publicly hugged in New York. When "Che" Guevara came to Moscow in November to sell Cuban sugar (and so to overcome a U.S. embargo), he was invited to stand with the Politburo atop Lenin's mausoleum for the October Revolution parade.[8] Khrushchev recognized in Castro the Third World model he sought.

To make his own economy move, Khrushchev continued the policy Malenkov had begun of producing more consumer goods. That became easier as he cut his military forces, although most of the savings probably went into missile and nuclear programs. Inside the Soviet Union, Khrushchev tried to inspire his work force with promises of improved conditions; his revitalized Party had to show that it was building "Communism," which meant a society of plenty. Unfortunately, the promise of wealth to come from Communism to some extent made him a hostage to his economy's performance.

Coincidentally, Khrushchev's new weaponry was particularly well suited to Third World clients. None of them could afford heavy bombers, or massed supersonic interceptors, or big warships. But a small boat could carry a missile big enough to sink a large, expensive ship, and a man could carry a cheap antiaircraft or antitank missile.

Khrushchev announced his strategy in an open speech at the 1956 Party Congress. War would no longer be considered inevitable. Indeed, given the terrible power of atomic weapons, it was to be avoided. This concept of deterrence ran entirely afoul of Stalin's ideas. Many in the West hoped that the new policy of "peaceful coexistence" marked the end of the Cold War. A self-confident Khrushchev opened the Soviet Union to limited Western tourism. Westerners found that, amazingly, Soviet citizens were humans rather than Stalinist robots. That their views were essentially irrelevant in a totalitarian state seems not to have sunk in.

Closed sessions of the Communist faithful were told that "peace" really meant continuation of the revolutionary struggle by other means (this was not the first time such words had been used). At the least, "peaceful coexistence" had nothing to do with the continuing revolutionary struggle in the Third World—where success might block the West's sources of vital raw materials.

Khrushchev's experience when Hungary revolted in the fall of 1956 seemed to prove that he was right, that the West had no stomach for nuclear war. Despite what seemed to the Hungarians to be unambiguous encouragement by U.S. radio stations (such as Radio Free Europe), the United States refused to back them with armed force.[9] When the East Germans demonstrated a few days later, Khrushchev gave the Soviet Army permission to shoot; he did not fear Western intervention.[10]

In fact, probably unknown to Khrushchev, deterrence went further. After Korea, America's European allies all feared that any U.S. nuclear strike against China would cause a nuclear war in Europe, due to the Sino-Soviet treaty. Their fear limited British support for SEATO and caused the British to protest during the 1955 Quemoy crisis. On the other hand, to an extent unappreciated in the West, Khrushchev, too, was unwilling to risk nuclear war over the Third World. Like Stalin, he wanted gains there, but he considered the world revolution distinctly secondary to Soviet security. His need for restraint would soon embarrass him.

Even after his army was tied down in Hungary, Khrushchev found that his nuclear weapons gave him vital influence. He "rattled his rockets" and the French and British retreated from Suez. No matter that (as described below) they acceded mainly to U.S. pressure, or that he was hardly turning out rockets "like sausages," as he said (after the fall of the Soviet Union, a Russian pointed out that sausages had not been in very full supply, either). The nuclear bluff worked, at least against the West, because it was entrenched in Europe.

At the least, it seemed that the struggle for Europe was over. In failing to support the Hungarians, the West had clearly abandoned any hope of rollback. In announcing "peaceful coexistence," it seemed that Khrushchev had promised in return that his army would limit itself to suppressing dissent east of the Iron Curtain; it would not threaten the West. Khrushchev also showed far more interest in trading with the West. Optimists thought that trade would bind the Soviets into the world economic system. To some extent they were right. Eventually the Soviets badly needed Western grain; to get it, they needed both hard currency and trade agreements.

By 1957 Khrushchev seemed supreme. His defeat of the Stalinists, led by Molotov, meant that he could impose his will on the economy. As if to symbolize his power, he ordered the ongoing Five Year Plan (1956–60) suspended in favor of a Seven Year Plan (1959–65), during which production would shift even more radically towards the new technologies. In a 14 January 1960 speech he announced that the advent of missiles and nuclear weapons marked a "revolution in military affairs."[11]

As in the United States, that meant deep cuts in the army. Large numbers of senior officers—who had important friends—were forcibly retired. Khrushchev took this opportunity to eliminate those still loyal to Stalin's memory or to his surviving supporters. Without much of a pension system, and without hope of senior civilian jobs, retired officers faced a very bleak future. Many in the Soviet military seem to have considered this 1957–59 purge a humiliation comparable to (though more humane than) Stalin's prewar purge. Presumably, the forced retirement of Marshal Zhukov, the most senior surviving World War II commander, seemed to prove their point. Because no one was shot or imprisoned, the victims of the purge remained in position to snipe. In a striking parallel with 1937–38, the purge coincided with the appearance of military power: in the thirties, in the form of large numbers of tanks and modern aircraft; in the fifties, in the form of new nuclear-armed missiles. Opposition could not be stifled altogether, because the Soviet military retained considerable prestige. It was striking that the chief of the general staff and other senior officers did not speak in Khrushchev's support at a January 1960 Supreme Soviet meeting.[12]

Officers who survived Khrushchev's purge had to take his nuclear missile revolution seriously, just as U.S. Army officers of the 1950s had to take the New Look at face value. Both armies claimed that they understood how to fight a nuclear land battle, although it seems unlikely that either ever did. In the early 1960s the Soviets conducted a high-level discussion of the problems and prospects of nuclear ground combat in their professional journal, *Voyennaya Mysl'* (Military thought). Col. Oleg Penkovskiy, surely the most important Soviet defector of his day, handed the articles from this "special collection" to Western intelligence.

The articles were startling. It became obvious that Soviet officers did not realize just how badly nuclear weapons would tear up a battlefield, creating obstacles for their own army. For example, a colleague of the author's at Hudson Institute once said that the Soviet Army thought it could advance even though its men's teeth were glowing from radioactivity. Nor had the Soviets apparently thought through the considerable problem of finding (acquiring) targets in the first place.[13] Americans who had abandoned the New Look said contemptuously that the Soviets were about five years behind the times.

In 1954 the focus of British defense moved from the Middle East to Europe. The informal empire was still extremely important, but it was clearly unlikely that the Soviets would invade it. On the other hand, it was vital that the Europeans be encouraged to accept a rearmed West Germany. British troops permanently stationed there would be a valuable counterweight, an encouragement to the Europeans. Thus Prime Minister Churchill promised that the four British divisions already on the Continent would remain there for the next fifty years, a pledge formally embedded in October 1954 in the revised Western European Union treaty under which Germany began to rearm.[1]

Money also was tight: Churchill had to find £180 million in cuts. The upkeep of the Canal Zone base cost £56 million each year.[2] Then, too, early in 1954 Churchill found it difficult to redeploy troops elsewhere in the Middle East while maintaining the base. In addition, the March 1954 U.S. test of a deliverable H-bomb seemed to demonstrate that no massive base could be useful in a future war. Despite Churchill's reservations and the opposition of the Conservative right wing in Parliament, the Foreign Office concluded a treaty in July 1954. The British agreed to evacuate the Suez bases within twenty months (i.e., by June 1956). They recognized the Egyptians' ASCP defensive pact, which (to the Egyptians) meant supremacy in the Middle East. For the British, the new treaty guaranteed that their troops could return in the event of an attack on any of several Middle Eastern countries, including Turkey.[3]

The agreement seemed to link Egypt to the developing Northern Tier defense arrangement. The arrangement began in April 1954 with a defense treaty between Turkey and Pakistan and a U.S. arms deal with Iraq (which was to be the tier's connection to the Middle East). The treaty with Turkey connected Pakistan to NATO. Iraq joined because the arms deal gave it prestige; Iraq was then trying to revive an earlier campaign to unify the Fertile Crescent (with Jordan and Syria) under the Hashemites. Neither the British nor the Americans seem to have realized just how deeply the Egyptians resented the Iraqis. There was no real chance of any alliance involving the two; the Egyptians would almost inevitably try to wreck any deal that offered Iraq more prestige in the Middle East.[4]

None of this changed the value the British placed on the Suez Canal itself. Once, it had been the vital link to India, the jewel of the British Empire. Now it was the link to the oil of the informal Middle Eastern empire, to places like Kuwait and Iraq. Without Suez, tankers could still get to Europe, but only by steaming around Africa. The flow from the Middle East, which kept Western Europe alive, would be reduced to a trickle.

Meanwhile, in April 1954, Col. Gamal Abdel Nasser, who had probably been the brains behind the 1952 Egyptian coup, came to power. He was a powerful orator with a pan-Arab vision that threatened the vital British informal empire. At first, the British were impressed by Nasser's 1954 book, *The Philosophy of the Revolution*. Then their opinion of Nasser began to sour. Nasser supported Saudi attacks on the British. In June 1955 Anthony Eden, who was then foreign secretary, wrote that "this is gross impertinence by these people who are likely to be attacked and destroyed by Israel before long. I hope we give them no help." Nasser's book came to be viewed as a latter-day *Mein Kampf;* softness on the Canal issue would be equivalent to prewar appeasement (in 1938 Eden had resigned as foreign secretary to protest appeasement at Munich).[5]

With the Canal issue apparently resolved, the U.S. and British governments attacked the root Arab-Israeli problem. Secretary of State Dulles proposed an Egyptian-Israeli peace plan on 26 August 1955. It offered guarantees by the Great Powers in return for visible territorial concessions by Israel. Nasser demanded an unacceptable price, the Negev south of Beersheba. The Negev was the focus of the Israelis' vision, a desert they were making bloom.

Focussed on the Soviet challenge, the Allies did not realize that Nasser did not want a settlement at all, since he gained allies by advertising himself as the Arabs' champion—and the enemy of the Israelis (and the colonialist West).[6] Whether or not he actually planned to fight, Nasser needed arms. He soon discovered that the British would not provide enough. The Americans demanded control over any weapons they supplied, via a Military Assistance Group; they could not be used against Israel.

Khrushchev saw an opportunity; backing Nasser was a way of seizing the Middle East without the unpleasantness of marching there. He offered what the West would not: enough arms for another try against the Israelis. The first shipment, announced in September 1955, came from the Czechs; soon supplies were being delivered directly from the Soviet Union.

The Western Allies misread Nasser. They thought they could woo him with economic aid. In the fall of 1955 Nasser hoped to build a spectacular dam at Aswan, up the Nile.[7] It would provide the electricity to develop Egypt. The British and American governments hoped to trade the dam for Nasser's agreement to a Middle East settlement.[8] The International Bank for Reconstruction and Development used the need for cash flow as an argument against Egyptian arms purchases. How-ever, from Nasser's point of view, prosperity, which the dam might or might not guarantee, was far less important than power within the Arab world—which he could gain by public enmity against Israel and the West.

Both Nasser and his Iraqi rivals saw the Cold War mainly as a way of gaining ground in their much more important regional contest. In February 1955 the Syr-ians allied themselves with Nasser. As a counterweight, Iraq formally joined the Northern Tier, which became the Baghdad Pact.[9] The British joined in April, apparently mainly to maintain influence in Iraq, including access to the important air bases at Shaiba and Habbaniya.[10] Iran soon joined, despite U.S. objections.

Nasser seized what opportunities he could. He advertised the Baghdad Pact as a Western intrusion into the Arab world, a form of neocolonialism.[11] When the Brit-ish seized Buraimi Oasis, which the Saudis claimed, he sided with the Saudis. They signed a five-year defense treaty with him, as did the Yemenis, traditionally the Saudis' satellites. When the British tried to attract Jordan into the Baghdad Pact, Nasser used the Anglo-American peace effort. Much of the Jordanian population consisted of Palestinian refugees; Nasser told them that to join the pact was tanta-mount to accepting the peace plan and thus to recognizing Israel. Jordan's King Hussein could not override the public outrage Nasser was able to generate.[12] Jor-dan joined Nasser's Red Sea Defense Group, along with Saudi Arabia and Yemen.

The U.S. position was tricky. Nasser might be unpleasant, but he seemed to be the wave of the future. He might still be wooed.[13] Moreover, the United States was trying to build up Saudi Arabia as a regional power.[14] With such possibilities in mind, Dulles refused to join the Baghdad Pact.

Toward the end of 1955 the British developed an intelligence source within Nasser's inner circle, codenamed "Lucky Break."[15] Nasser seemed to be moving closer and closer to the Soviets. The British feared that the Soviets might insert "volunteers" to operate Nasser's new weapons. Early in 1956 the British formally decided that Nasser was their enemy; he seemed to prove as much by engineering the dismissal of the British officer, Glubb Pasha, commanding the Jordanian army.[16] The British began to back away from the Aswan Dam project. Early in May 1956 Dulles and British Foreign Secretary Selwyn Lloyd agreed to let the dam pro-ject "languish"; eventually Congress killed it altogether, partly due to Nasser's anti-Western rhetoric.[17] Dulles told an executive session of the Senate Foreign Relations Committee that it might not be a bad thing to dump the project on the Soviets. Paying for the dam would distort the Egyptian economy, and the dam might cause other problems. The Soviets would be blamed.[18]

Meanwhile the Israelis and the Egyptians moved towards war. The Israelis saw the big Czech and Soviet arms deliveries as preparations for an Egyptian attack; they estimated that it would take about six to eight months for the Egyptians to learn to use their new weapons. Other evidence of Egyptian intentions were an intensified blockade and guerilla (Fedayeen) raids mounted from Gaza. As it happened, the raids were Nasser's reaction to an Israeli attack on Gaza in February 1955 that humiliated the Egyptian army, the main prop of Nasser's regime. In December 1955 the Israelis planned an attack on Egypt, but held back.

Nasser had just signed the alliance with Syria, so any war might have to be fought on two fronts. Probably more important, to the Israelis, was the likely attitude of the British—whom the Israeli leaders had fought while Britain still ruled Palestine. Israel thought the British would always favor the Arabs. Under the Canal Treaty, the British guaranteed Egyptian security; they might join the Egyptians in a defensive war. Having just lost the Canal Zone base, they might hope to gain equivalent bases in the Negev. Moreover, Nasser would gain valuable jet bases and masses of equipment as the British pulled out. He would probably strike in the summer of 1956.

Nasser had always talked about wiping out the stain of the 1949 defeat, and now he had run out of excuses; the British were leaving the Canal Zone, and Khrushchev had given him the weapons he would need. Moreover, with Iraq isolated and Nasser's domestic opponents suppressed, Israel was the most serious threat to his regime.[19] In March 1956 the Egyptian army began building up supply dumps in Sinai and distributed battle orders to divisional commanders: their mission would be to destroy the Israeli army.[20]

British intelligence detected these preparations as the new prime minister, Eden, became more and more hostile to Nasser. He personally cabled Eisenhower intelligence information warning of an Egyptian attack against Israel. Under the arms export control arrangements, both powers had guaranteed the 1949 truce agreements, so they were bound to protect Israel against Egypt. To do so, they would need to land enough troops to seize the Canal. On 29 July 1956 Eden told Eisenhower that he had instructed his chiefs of staff to plan to fight Nasser. Dulles advised Eisenhower for the time being to avoid any open break that might turn Egypt into a Soviet satellite; Nasser should be left a bridge back to the West.

However, Dulles refused to understand that Nasser's only interest in the Cold War was to play each side off to get what he wanted. The CIA man on the spot, Miles Copeland, later wrote that no one understood that Nasser would do only what he saw was in either his or Egypt's interest. Copeland played Nasser's part in a U.S. government game designed to project his actions, only to have Dulles upbraid him as "more like Nasser than Nasser."[21]

When the West dropped its offer to finance the Aswan Dam, Nasser saw a golden opportunity to prove his nationalist credentials. To gain the cash he needed, he would nationalize the Suez Canal, which was owned by an Anglo-French company. Nasser also realized the hopes of all Egyptian nationalists by ejecting the British from the Canal Zone. This very shrewd move split the United States from her two principal European allies, Britain and France.

By this time the French, like the British, saw Nasser as a direct threat. They believed—wrongly, as it happened—that the rebels now fighting them in Algeria depended on Egyptian assistance, just as Ho had succeeded due to Chinese assistance (the open Mediterranean would play the same role as the open land border between Vietnam and China). War had broken out in Algeria almost immediately after the one in Indochina ended, with 1 November 1954 attacks by the FLN (Front de la Libération Nationale) on French posts. While the war was being fought, in the spring of 1956 the French government freed the two protectorates bordering Algeria, Morocco and Tunisia. It also granted greater self-government (albeit not independence) to its African colonies. Many in France saw this as a policy of weakness, a continuation of the surrender of Indochina.[22] Humiliating Nasser would demonstrate French determination, and it might save both the Canal and Algeria.

The British and the French began to develop a joint plan, Operation Musketeer, to seize the Canal. Meanwhile the French were backing the Israelis as a way of occupying Nasser's attention and thus of reducing his power in their North African colonies. They were well aware that the Israelis wanted to destroy the Egyptian army before it gained enough strength to hit them. For the Israelis, Operation Musketeer changed everything. Attacking in what Prime Minister Ben-Gurion called "respectable company," they need not fear a British counterattack.[23] The French promised to keep Syria and Lebanon out of the war.

For the British, the situation was more complicated. They still wanted to hold their informal empire; they had mutual defense treaties with Iraq and Jordan. Prime Minister Eden feared that an Israeli attack on Egypt would bring both into the war.[24] Any direct association with the Israelis might be fatal. The British and the French found a solution. The Israelis would attack, threatening the Canal. The French and British would occupy the Canal Zone in order to protect it. The three governments coordinated their plans in secret meetings in a Paris suburb.[25]

Eisenhower was aware that the Europeans planned to act. Through the summer of 1956 Eisenhower tried to persuade the British and the French not to act; Dulles and then Eisenhower explicitly warned Eden that using force would alienate the entire Third World. However, there was no protest when the Allies moved military equipment earmarked for NATO out of Europe.[26]

The Israelis quickly swept across the Sinai Peninsula to the Canal. Khrushchev's big arms shipments had not provided Egypt with real military muscle. As might have been expected, the Anglo-French landing was entirely successful. It was also innovative; the British used helicopters for the first time to land marines. However, the Anglo-French partners had not thought beyond the seizure of one end of the Canal. Their operation stalled. The operation revealed how far the British and the French had fallen. They had to devote virtually all their naval forces to the operation. There were so few amphibious craft that DUKWs (amphibious trucks) used as pleasure craft at seaside resorts had to be conscripted. Many of the amphibious ships had to be civilian-manned.[27]

Eisenhower was aghast. Britain and France were essential allies in Europe. On the other hand, nationalization could not be considered an act of war. To openly back a classic colonial-era attack on a major Third World country would be to throw away any possible U.S. influence there. The United States enforced a truce and withdrawal partly by using financial leverage. The British were vulnerable because in February 1955 the Bank of England made the pound convertible to dollars—to convince holders of pounds that it was safe to keep their cash in that form. Unfortunately British dollar reserves were extremely thin, averaging $2.3 billion in 1954–57 as compared to $22 billion for the United States. As the Canal crisis built up, the Bank of England lost $334 million between August and October as pounds were converted into dollars. After the invasion began, the bank lost $50 million in two days. The cabinet agreed to the cease-fire when Chancellor of the Exchequer Harold Macmillan told it that $280 million (an exaggeration) had been lost since the invasion began. The U.S. government did not join the run on sterling, but it refused to discuss credits for Britain and it blocked action by the International Monetary Fund. The situation worsened because blockage of the Canal cut off oil supplies to Europe.[28]

However, Secretary of State Dulles later said that, had he not been so ill at the time of the attack, he would have delayed U.S. pressure long enough for the British and French to have won decisively. Third World wrath would not have been any worse had the operation been completed.[29] The British must have found it odd that a U.S. administration that had been quite willing to sponsor a coup against Mossadegh in Iran now had cold feet. Surely, they thought, the Canal was as important as Iranian oil.

Khrushchev claimed some credit for aborting the Anglo-French attack. Although his ground forces were tied up suppressing the Hungarian uprising, he threatened Europe with nuclear annihilation by his new ballistic missiles. This was a bluff; he had far too few. However, the NATO European governments felt an unwelcome sense of nakedness.

The Anglo-French failure at Suez demonstrated graphically that neither country could be considered a great power any longer. Although each was quite bitter, neither country's leadership could afford to bolt NATO; the Soviets were a worse threat. However, they had been taught that they badly needed the ability to make their own views heard, both politically and militarily. The European Economic Community was already forming. The French decided that it, and a Franco-German axis, could form a counterweight to the United States. They turned away from the British alliance that had developed during the run up to Suez.[30] Having been impressed by Khrushchev's rocket rattling, the French accelerated work on their atomic bomb; in December 1956 all members of the French parliament except the Communists voted for the nuclear program. Prime Minister Guy Mollet survived, partly because most Frenchmen approved the Suez operation.[31] As for Algeria, initially the population was impressed by French determination, but soon the Suez failure emboldened the rebels.[32]

Suez had been far less popular in Britain; because of it, British Prime Minister

Anthony Eden resigned. Many felt he had behaved irrationally. Harold MacMillan replaced him. It was soon clear that Eisenhower regretted the Anglo-American breach. He made a special effort to rebuild the relationship, meeting MacMillan in Bermuda in March 1957. Eisenhower promised MacMillan U.S. land-based strategic ballistic missiles.[33] The French felt excluded.

The British concluded that the sacrifices they were making for defense had largely been in vain. In 1955, they were spending far more than any other European country: more than 9 percent of their GNP, about two-thirds of all British research effort (mainly for the new deterrent force) and 12 percent of the output of metal-using industries (which were responsible for half of all exports). Even so, the British could afford to maintain their force in Germany only thanks to German payments. Now that the Germans were rearming, they caused a crisis: they wanted to shift spending to their own forces (ultimately they agreed to keep paying half of what they formerly had contributed).[34] In July 1956 Prime Minister Eden ordered a review of defense policy, in hopes of reaching a sustainable level.

Completed in January 1957, the review, conducted by Defence Minister Duncan Sandys, concluded that Britain would have to end the draft (National Service) by the end of 1962; a fully professional force would need much less training. The services would be cut to the number of men expected to volunteer, 375,000 (165,000 in the army). Pre-Suez estimates of the minimum Britain needed to meet her commitments were 445,000 men, including two hundred thousand for the army. Particularly as the Germans armed, the other Europeans wanted the British to stay, as a counterweight. The four armored divisions remained in Germany, but each was cut.[35]

With much less manpower, the African empire was no longer affordable. For the past few years insurrections like the Mau Mau emergency in Kenya had demanded more and more British soldiers. On 3 February 1960 Prime Minister Harold Mac-Millan announced in Capetown, South Africa, that the "winds of change" were blowing through Africa; it was time to accept black majority rule.[36] (The phrase had been used by Stanley Baldwin in 1934, and Macmillan used it as the title of a book on the pre–World War II period.) As he spoke, a committee in Brussels was arranging independence for the Congo, which most considered the beginning of the African whirlwind. Britain had already freed Ghana and Nigeria; MacMillan directed his remarks particularly at the Rhodesians and South Africans, who were determined to maintain white rule. The British were also finding it more difficult to garrison their informal empire. They had to withdraw all forces from Jordan, and within a few years they would also have to withdraw from Libya. What was left of imperial defense would rely largely on mobile forces, supported by aircraft carriers: a garrison in Aden, a carrier task force in the Indian Ocean. In 1960 the hot guerilla war in Malaya was concluded and the country made independent (albeit with a British security guarantee).

The British were hardly alone in their desperate need to cut defense costs.

Throughout NATO, as in the United States, governments saw nuclear weapons as a welcome justification for deep cuts in expensive nonnuclear forces. Reductions were deeper than they first seemed because army strengths were expressed in numbers of divisions. Governments cut the strength of each division, leaving hollow armies, just as Truman's cuts had sapped the U.S. Army in 1950. The average fighting power of a non-U.S. NATO division began to slide towards 60 percent of its U.S. equivalent.[37] In April 1957 Eisenhower offered U.S. tactical nuclear weapons to the Allies, on a two-key basis: both a U.S. officer and an officer of the country operating the weapon had to agree before it could be fired (however, no weapons were transferred). By 1961 the NATO air arms had almost nothing but nuclear capability. Eisenhower found NATO nuclear power perfectly acceptable, but that was because he, like the Europeans (and like Khrushchev), did not believe in war in Europe. However, critics of the New Look in the United States thought otherwise, and they would cause trouble once the Kennedy administration came to power.

The French found themselves in a peculiar double bind. They refused to abandon their expensive draftee army, because they believed in a "nation in arms"; the French Left feared that a professional army might be used to suppress it. As in Britain, draftee manpower was increasingly expensive; the French found it more and more difficult to buy sufficient modern weapons, particularly as U.S. subsidies declined. From 1954 on, moreover, they were engaged in an increasingly expensive hot war in Algeria—which the United States refused to subsidize in any way. The lack of U.S. support was particularly galling because Algeria was legally part of France and thus, in French eyes, should have been a NATO charge (not to mention that it had been included in NATO territory in 1949). By 1957 Algeria was costing France at least $1 billion a year.[38] A weak French government could neither raise taxes nor cut other expenses. France was in a deepening financial crisis, as yet only dimly appreciated by most Frenchmen, who still felt prosperous after four years of steady economic growth (fuelled in part by American assistance).

There was no question of abandoning Algeria, at least at first. It was a department of metropolitan France; millions of French colonists lived there. The French government feared that if they were forced home, they might well undermine the tenuous stability of the home country. Because Algeria was legally part of France, draftees could be sent to fight there. Thus there was no lack of manpower: by mid-1956, France had fourteen divisions in Algeria; only two (each at two-thirds strength) were available for NATO. The draftees, moreover, were a mixed blessing. Ill-trained, they could not be used for anything more demanding than garrison duty. However, at the end of their short tours of duty, they brought the realities of the war home to the French population.

Elite French troops—the Foreign Legion, paratroops, and marine commandos—formed a mobile striking arm. Many were veterans of Indochina. Heeding the lessons learned there, by September 1957 the French had successfully sealed off the borders with Morocco and Tunisia. The organized rebel army sat out the war across the border; it could not challenge the French army.[39] As the elite units struck at the remaining rebels within Algeria, they were uncomfortably aware that, as in Vietnam, whatever the army accomplished in the field could be undone if morale at home was destroyed. For these units, revolutionary warfare blurred the boundary between politics and war. In 1958, fearful of betrayal, the army overthrew the Fourth Republic. It brought back General de Gaulle, who demanded complete freedom of action—which might include exactly the betrayal the army had so feared.[40]

De Gaulle's return to power had important Cold War implications. In 1945–46 he had been quite willing to work with the British and the Americans, because he accepted that France was mortally endangered by the Soviets. However, he considered NATO defense integration incompatible with his intention to restore France to her previous respected and independent position. Thus as early as 1952 he told Eisenhower privately that, if he ever returned to power, he would withdraw France from NATO unless the alliance were reformed: he considered that France had been reduced to the role of an underling carrying out plans decided by others (i.e., by SACEUR).[41]

In 1958 the situation was very different. France was still far too weak, as Suez had demonstrated. She constantly risked humiliation by the Anglo-Saxons—the British and the Americans. De Gaulle vowed to fight back. In so doing, he might split NATO. Probably he considered that risk perfectly safe, since the nuclear balance made a Soviet attack impossible. In all of this de Gaulle was reviving his World War II tactics, by which he had managed to maintain France's status among the Allies despite her defeat in 1940 and her limited resources.

Many in France were already uncomfortable with the realities of guerilla warfare. The intelligence needed for attacks on rebel units and hideouts was often obtained by torture. The large Algerian community in France became involved in the war; its violence spread onto the streets of Paris. In Algeria, too many French conscripts saw too much. Many in France came to see the Algerian war as unacceptably dirty.[42] The war began to tear France apart, even as the French elite units believed they were winning it.

Both European powers paid heavily in the Arab world for their military failure and for their demonstrated connection with the hated Israelis. Nasser cemented his relationship with Syria to form the United Arab Republic (UAR) in January 1958.[43] That frightened conservative regimes; Iraq and Jordan formed their own Arab Federal Union in February. However, the Saudis would not join, because they were hostile to the Iraqis (the Saudi royal family had come to power by ejecting a Hashemite ruler, related to the Iraqi king, from Arabia). The Saudi position became particularly delicate when Yemen, on its coast, joined the UAR. Lebanon could not join the Federal Union because its government, too, was hostile to the Iraqis.

The Iraqi government, Britain's main remaining Arab ally, fell in a bloody 1958 coup to army nationalists who were furious that it was still pro-Western after Suez and that it entertained ideas of supporting a Western intervention in Syria. The day of the coup the Baghdad Pact governments were scheduled to discuss the Lebanese crisis.[44] The Baghdad Pact was destroyed, its link with the Middle East gone (without Iraq, it became CENTO, the Central Treaty Organization, in 1959). Of the conservative Arab governments on which the West had relied, soon only Jordan and Saudi Arabia remained. The British Middle East empire was reduced to small Gulf states, such as Kuwait (a British protectorate until 1961) and Aden (a colony). Eisenhower clearly bought the British charge that Nasser was a Soviet agent. His "Eisenhower Doctrine" (January 1957) offered assistance (including U.S. troops) to any country in the area threatened by any Communist-controlled government, i.e., Egypt.[45] In the wake of the Iraqi coup, Syrian intelligence touched off a brief civil war in pro-Western Lebanon. To bolster its government, marines were sent into Beirut. By the time they arrived, the situation had cooled, and press photographers snapped marines in full battle gear stepping around women relaxing in their bikinis on the Lebanese beaches.[46] They had, however, demonstrated that Eisenhower meant business. That Lebanon was being protected against Iraq's Kassem rather than against Nasser showed that the U.S. focus was shifting to favor Nasser, as a nationalist rather than a Communist. In October 1958 Eisenhower accepted an NSC recommendation that the United States should rely on nationalism to keep the Soviets out of the Middle East.[47] This was much the approach Truman had approved in 1952, when he had backed Mossadegh against the British.

The two most populous states in the region, natural rivals, were both now governed by radical Arab nationalists—each of whom hoped to gain wider power. The new Iraqi dictator, Kassem, convinced the Soviets that he was the better revolutionary, more in tune with Communism. At the January–February 1959 Party Congress the Soviets announced that they would support local Communist parties (i.e., Kassem), rather than bourgeois nationalists (i.e., Nasser).[48] Kassem used the Iraqi Communist Party to destroy an Iraqi movement for union with Nasser's UAR. To reduce his dependence on the Soviets, Nasser moved towards the Americans, and Eisenhower made Egypt the focus of his Middle East policy. Kennedy would follow suit. Despite Khrushchev's blandishments, Nasser attacked the Soviets as little more than colonialists.

Then Nasser destroyed his own creation, the UAR. Like any other Third World dictator, he worked by patronage; he rewarded political loyalty with plum jobs. They included many in Syria. However, the Syrian Ba'athists who had brought their country into the UAR maintained power the same way: those jobs were an important way to buy support. Unintentionally, Nasser was fatally weakening his local allies. Syria withdrew from the UAR after the inevitable military coup (September 1961). Both of the rivals for Nasser's friendship, the Soviets and the Americans, quickly recognized the new Syrian regime. Nasser felt isolated. Yemen soon also left the UAR, so quite soon only Lebanon, fearful of Syria, remained friendly with Nasser.[49]

Nasser had to reestablish his nationalist credentials. He proclaimed a new revolution at home (October 1961) and a new National Charter (May 1962). It was now declared Egyptian policy to support liberation movements abroad. Nasser was in effect claiming a license to exploit any instability that showed itself in the very fluid Arab world. The Socialist principles embodied in the charter encouraged the Soviets to think that Nasser might later lean their way.[50] They had just fallen out with the Iraqis.

Nasser blamed his Syrian problem on the two remaining conservative governments, Jordan and Saudi Arabia. To hit back, he supported a coup in Yemen (begun 26 September 1962).[51] The Saudis had always considered Yemen important to their own security. A radical republic there would encourage their domestic enemies. The coup proved indecisive; a civil war followed. In it, the Saudis supported the Yemeni royal family. To fight the war, Nasser needed weapons—and, as in 1955, he found it much easier to get them from the Soviets than from the United States (which did not want to become involved in an intra-Arab fight). Western-sponsored attempts to broker a peace failed.[52] The Saudis were driven into a closer embrace with Britain and with Iran to make up for the lack of U.S. support.[53] Meanwhile Nasser backed uprisings in Aden (against the British) and in Oman.

Nasser had to pour much of his army into Yemen. The war was frustrating; by 1963 he was saying that U.S. policy was to weaken Egypt by tying him down in Yemen. That was not true, but as late as 1967 a third of the Egyptian army was still in Yemen. The troops were withdrawn following the Egyptian defeat that year.[54]

Coups in Damascus and Baghdad (February and March 1963) brought the pan-Arab Ba'ath Party—a rival to Nasser—to power in Syria and in Iraq. The Ba'athists immediately proposed union to Nasser, on a collective basis which would have submerged him.[55] The overthrow of the Iraqi Ba'athists in November left the Syrians isolated. To gain friends in the Arab world, they concentrated on the most emotive Arab issue, Israel. Burned badly in 1956, Nasser saw little point in inviting a new war. The Syrians painted him as a coward, unworthy of leadership in the Arab world.[56] He could no longer afford to be nearly as friendly to the United States. Moreover, U.S. policy began to shift after President Kennedy died in November 1963. His successor, Lyndon Johnson, was warming towards Israel and cooling towards nonaligned governments. The U.S. attempt to court Nasser, who had been so successful for a time, was failing.

The men who made the early Cold War pose at their last friendly meeting, at Potsdam in July 1945. Seated, left to right, are Clement Attlee, the newly elected British Prime Minister; President Harry S. Truman; and Josef Stalin. Stalin was shocked at how quickly Winston S. Churchill, the wartime British prime minister, had been displaced after the first British postwar election. Behind the national leaders are advisors who played major early Cold War roles: Adm. William D. Leahy, a very senior survivor of President Roosevelt's wartime staff; Ernest Bevin, the British foreign secretary (and a prime architect of NATO); James Byrnes, Truman's first secretary of state; and Vyacheslav Molotov, Stalin's foreign minister. Molotov had precipitated World War II by negotiating the 1939 Non-Aggression Pact with Germany. *U.S. Naval Institute*

The Bomb kept the Cold War cold. Here an underwater bomb explodes among target ships at Bikini Atoll, 1946. The ships' silhouettes give some idea of the sheer size of the ascending water column, which is a measure of the power of the explosion—of what was, in the post-war context, a relatively small bomb. Most Americans, unaware of just how few such bombs their country had, thought through the late 1940s that their monopoly on the bomb check-mated Stalin's mass army. Indeed, it is often suggested that the Bikini tests were conducted to show the Soviets that the United States still had a nuclear arsenal and that it was still very usable. Stalin's successful explosion of a Soviet nuclear bomb in August 1949 was a terrifying shock. *U.S. Naval Institute*

Marshal Josip Tito of Yugoslavia posed a special problem for Stalin. His revolutionary enthusiasm made him too much a hero to European Communists. Here Czech Communist schoolgirls parade past a portrait of Tito in Prague, en route to a pro-Tito rally, in July 1948. Czechoslovakia had just fallen to a Communist coup the previous February, and the new leaders were not yet fully attuned to Stalin's line. As these girls marched, the Cominform was already attacking Tito, who would soon be ejected from the world Communist movement. *U.S. Naval Institute*

Mortal enemies toast each other on the eve of the Chinese civil war. Mao Tse-tung (left) and Chiang Kai-shek (right) celebrate victory over Japan in the wartime Chinese capital, Chungking, August 1945. It would take only about three years for Mao to win the civil war; Chiang was forced back onto Taiwan. *U.S. Naval Institute*

Mao Tse-tung and Ho Chi Minh toast each other in Beijing, 7 July 1955. Mao's 1949 victory had led directly to Ho's five years later, because China had become the essential sanctuary for Ho's forces. For his part, Mao considered Ho's North Vietnam to be a valuable buffer against his Western enemies. A decade later, Ho would be able to wage war against South Vietnam mainly because Mao was supporting world revolution in the face of Soviet reluctance. To the end of his life, Ho remained grateful to the Chinese; his successors felt otherwise. Later, they accused the Chinese of forcing them to keep fighting in hopes of bleeding Vietnam, which in the past had been China's enemy. *Eastfoto*

Above all, it was never clear during the Cold War whether the Soviet threat was political or military. To President Truman, money spent to rebuild Western Europe (so that the appeal of Communism would recede) was as much part of the defense budget as money spent on troops or ships or aircraft. The purely military budget had to be squeezed brutally; unavoidably, the United States came to rely heavily on nuclear deterrence. Its great symbol was the B-36 bomber, which could attack Soviet targets from the United States. In theory, once the U.S. Air Force was equipped completely with B-36s, the United States could have fought a nuclear war without any overseas bases. That day never came, partly because the B-36 was so expensive. Moreover, the B-36 attained its great range because it was powered by piston engines (it also had four jets to give it higher speed over the target), and thus was too slow to deal with the new jet interceptors. *U.S. Naval Institute*

The outbreak of war in Korea showed that deterrence was not enough; even without very many bombs of his own, Stalin seemed very willing to fight (albeit using proxies). Even worse, the lightly equipped Chinese managed to defeat mechanized U.S. units. Here marines rest in the snow during the retreat from the Chosin Reservoir in North Korea, 8 December 1950. *U.S. Naval Institute*

By the time he became president in 1953, Dwight D. Eisenhower was extraordinarily well prepared for the job. Thanks to his wartime service as supreme commander in Europe and to his postwar service as the NATO military chief, he was personally acquainted with most of the major world leaders of his time. Here he relaxes with three of them at the Four-Power Conference in Geneva, August 1955: Soviet Prime Minister Nikolai Bulganin (left), French Prime Minister Edgar Faure, and British Prime Minister Anthony Eden. Westerners did not yet realize to what extent Bulganin's supposed partner, Nikita Khrushchev, already actually ran the Soviet Union. Eden and the French had not yet begun to plan the attack on Suez that, in late 1956, would nearly split NATO. *U.S. Naval Institute*

SAC, the U.S. Air Force's Strategic Air Command, was Eisenhower's big stick. He believed that nuclear deterrence, based mainly on SAC, made wars in Europe very unlikely. As long as SAC was secure from Soviet attack, Eisenhower could concentrate on Communist threats around the periphery of Eurasia. Here SAC B-47 jet bombers line up at Thule, Greenland. *U.S. Naval Institute*

Eisenhower used the marines and the U.S. Navy to enforce peace around the unruly edge of Eurasia. Given the deterrence enforced mainly by SAC (with considerable naval help), he saw little chance of a war in Europe. There was, therefore, little point in maintaining a large U.S. Army. The marines were best equipped to deal with quick crises. If much more was needed, the United States should never act alone; allies should always provide much of the force. Eisenhower's successor, President Kennedy, ignored this advice, building a U.S. Army powerful enough to intervene in Vietnam. Here, the Marines land in Lebanon in 1958, in support of the Eisenhower Doctrine. *U.S. Naval Institute*

When Krushchev attacked Stalin's "cult of personality," he indirectly attacked all the Soviet puppets—the little Stalins—ruling the East European empire. Poles and Hungarians took him at his word. Here Hungarian revolutionaries destroy a giant statue of Stalin in Budapest, 29 October 1956. To some extent the Hungarian Revolution might be considered proof that the West's strategy of containment worked; the Soviet system built up extremely dangerous internal pressures. However, in a nuclear-armed world, it was far too dangerous for the West to exploit the results. Hopeful Hungarians waited in vain for Western intervention. *Associated Press*

The ballistic missile became the great emblem of the Cold War. Here a Soviet RT-2 (NATO designation SS-13 Savage) is paraded through Red Square during the May 1965 parade commemorating the twentieth anniversary of victory over Germany—an event the Soviets used as a unifying theme in their country. The missile was the first even moderately successful Soviet solid-fuel strategic missile (the United States had had such weapons in service for some years). Its poor performance was symptomatic of the difference between a militarized command economy and the consumer-driven U.S. economy; U.S. solid fuels succeeded because they embodied chemistry taken from the mainly civilian plastics industry. RT-2 also embodied another Soviet theme, the political power of the major weapons designers. As bad as the missile was, it was produced only because its design bureau, Korolev's, was far too important to disband. Ultimately Soviet internal politics, as practiced by Leonid Brezhnev, made it impossible for the Soviets to cut back excessive military industrial organizations in order to build new industries like those needed to produce computers in the 1980s. *U.S. Naval Institute*

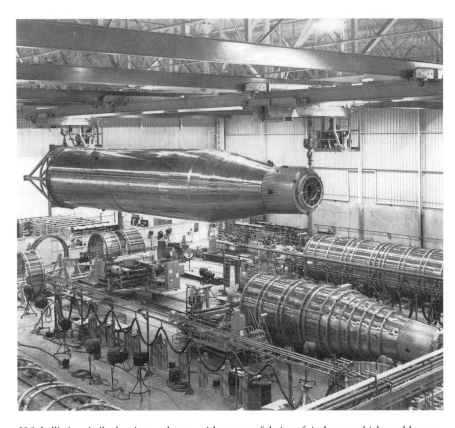

U.S. ballistic missile dominance began with a powerful aircraft industry, which could mass-produce the new weapons, as shown here. These are Atlas missiles, the first U.S. intercontinental ballistic missiles. Despite the popular perception that the United States was falling dangerously behind in the "missile race," in fact U.S. weapons soon outperformed their Soviet counterparts. Much more importantly, the United States—but not the Soviet Union—had the industrial capacity to go quickly from prototypes to masses of operational weapons. The structure shown in this picture is the missile's thin-skinned fuel tank, whose shape was maintained by the pressure of the fuels within it (gas was substituted on the assembly line); incomplete tanks were supported by external metal rings. *U.S. Naval Institute*

New U.S. President John F. Kennedy and Soviet leader Nikita Khrushchev meet the world press in Vienna, 4 June 1961, after Khrushchev had devastated Kennedy in private talks. Kennedy's embarrassing mistakes in Vienna helped convince Khrushchev to press him on Berlin and then to precipitate the Cuban Missile Crisis. Andrei Gromyko, the long-time Soviet foreign minister, is visible behind the two. *Associated Press*

In Fidel Castro, Khrushchev found an ideal Third World revolutionary who would serve the Soviet Union for the rest of the Cold War. Castro and Khrushchev are shown at the United Nations late in 1960. *Associated Press*

Khrushchev's public humiliation at the close of the Cuban Missile Crisis probably helped unseat him less than two years later. The Soviets had to display the missiles they were withdrawing to watching U.S. pilots. Two missiles are shown (their tail fins are visible) aboard a Soviet merchant ship. Kennedy was able to conceal his quid pro quo, which was to remove U.S. ballistic missiles from Turkey and Italy. The Soviets found Kennedy's violent reaction to their Cuban missile adventure surprising and irrational, and for a time their fear of similar irrationality limited their enthusiasm for other Third World adventures, as in Vietnam. Behind that fear lay their respect for overwhelming U.S. military superiority. Americans, who did not (or would not) see Kennedy's reaction as irrational, did not realize its effect on the Soviets. *U.S. Naval Institute*

Helicopters made war in Vietnam much easier to fight for Americans than for the French a decade earlier, because they could move troops quickly even over a trackless jungle. Among the first Americans to fight in Vietnam were U.S. Army pilots seconded to the South Vietnamese by order of President John F. Kennedy (much was later made of whether they had actually engaged in combat). By mid-1963, they had done well enough transporting government troops to convince President Kennedy and his advisors that the war might be over within two years. Then progress collapsed, perhaps partly because Kennedy and his administration began to back a series of coup attempts directed at the South Vietnamese government. The success of a U.S.-backed coup, which killed President Ngo Dinh Diem, bound the United States to the war, well before very many Americans were involved. *U.S. Naval Institute*

Kennedy's successor, President Lyndon Baines Johnson, inherited Kennedy's advisors, most notably Secretary of Defense Robert S. McNamara (foreground, left). President Johnson is at right. At the table, to the left, is Secretary of State Dean Rusk. Behind Rusk is Marine Corps Maj. Gen. Victor H. Krulak, who served as special assistant for counterinsurgency and special activities for the Joint Chiefs of Staff between February 1962 and January 1964. In this position he was especially responsible for policy on Vietnam. He was then promoted to lieutenant general, commanding the Fleet Marine Force until he retired in June 1968. To the right of President Johnson is Ellsworth Bunker, who became U.S. ambassador to South Vietnam in 1967 (he left in 1973). Next to him is Assistant Secretary of State William Bundy. On the sofa, next to Rusk, is Under Secretary of State George Ball, who drafted the Tonkin Gulf Resolution. Next to him is Joseph P. Califano, Johnson's advisor on domestic affairs. This photograph must have been taken late in 1963 or early in 1964, before the commitment to Vietnam was entirely firm. At this time Johnson still wondered whether the war was winnable.
U.S. Naval Institute

In the Soviet system, economics and politics were two sides of the same coin. Economic reform automatically meant political change—unacceptable change. When the Czechs tried this path, the Soviets sent tanks into the country and installed a new hard-line government. Here a Czech youth carries his flag in front of a Soviet tank invading Prague, 21 August 1968. The invasion demonstrated that Soviet troops and their tanks were the ultimate bulwarks of the Communist regimes of Eastern Europe. Understanding this, in mid-1989 the regimes fought Mikhail Gorbachev's plan to reduce Soviet troop strength in Eastern Europe to save money and to reduce tensions with the West. *Associated Press*

Given growing Soviet military superiority, President Nixon had to accept Soviet attacks with a smile. It was his particular misfortune that, having been tutored by a master, President Eisenhower, he was painfully aware of the significance of various Soviet military and political moves; he knew just how badly the United States was doing. Here Nixon presents Soviet Party chief Leonid Brezhnev with a plaque signed by U.S. astronauts, on 24 June 1973. Brezhnev was at the height of his own powers, and Watergate was not yet taking a toll on Nixon. Each had yet to face the strain of the major Mideast War that fall. *U.S. Naval Institute*

In China, Nixon saw a possible balance to growing Soviet strength. In Nixon, the Chinese saw a balance for the Soviet strength threatening them. Dr. Henry Kissinger negotiated the opening between the United States and China—which Stalin had so feared as early as 1950. Here Mao Tse-tung (right) meets Kissinger in Chungnanhai, China, 17 February 1973; Chinese Premier Chou En-lai is in the background. Given his larger interest in an "American card," Mao was no longer an enthusiastic supporter of the North Vietnamese attack on the South Vietnamese (but the Soviets stepped in, in hopes of gaining bases to use against the Chinese). The Sino-American relationship warmed as Mao's successor, Deng Xiaoping, opened the country to American business and to Chinese free enterprise—most likely in hopes of building enough strength to face down the Soviets. In so doing, he risked weakening the control his Communist Party exerted. With the end of the Cold War neither China nor the United States retains much interest in facing down the Soviets' Russian successors. The Sino-American relationship is, therefore, much less valuable to both former partners, at least at the strategic level. *Associated Press*

Disaster in Saigon: South Vietnamese try to escape the oncoming Communists by climbing the wall of the American Embassy, 29 April 1975. The remaining question is whether South Vietnam might have survived had U.S. aid been forthcoming during the 1975 North Vietnamese attack. As proof that it could not have been enough, the South Vietnamese army generally did not fight very effectively. On the other hand, its morale had been sapped partly because it had far too little ammunition—thanks to congressionally enforced limits. It may also have been significant that the South Vietnamese population did not rise in revolt to support the invaders. The Nationalist message of the North Vietnamese apparently was not attractive enough. Instead, millions fled, often at the cost of their lives. *Associated Press*

Computer-guided missiles were, in important ways, the nuclear weapons of the 1980s—the new technology in which the West led, and in which Soviets could not easily follow. In this test a Tomahawk cruise missile explodes above an obsolete bomber, destroying it. An earlier-generation missile with a relatively crude seeker would have been hard-pressed to detect the revetment, let alone the bomber inside; only a nuclear-armed missile would have been sure of destroying the bomber. With its onboard computer, however, the Tomahawk could be sent to exactly the right spot, just above the bomber, and the bomber could be destroyed without any need for a nuclear strike. *U.S. Naval Institute*

For the Soviets, Poland in the 1980s was a particularly disastrous place. Here one of the two architects of the disaster, Lech Walesa, kisses the hand of the other, Pope John Paul II, 8 June 1981. A few months later the Polish government, under Soviet pressure, would try to suppress Walesa's independent Solidarity trade union movement by declaring martial law. The Soviets themselves would try to kill the pope, who was entirely too popular in Poland. Both men were mortal threats because they refused to accept that the Communist system would necessarily survive much longer; their own survival carried that message to growing numbers of people. *Associated Press*

In the end, collapse in Eastern Europe came out of panic. The East German government suddenly opened its border to the West in hopes, apparently, of convincing the West Germans to lend it money it desperately needed to keep operating. Like its counterparts in other Communist countries, East Germany had spent earlier loans buying consumer goods to keep internal dissent down—and to pay off the elite who supported the governing Communist Party. The one thing the money had not bought was industrial modernization, which might have translated into an effective export industry capable of earning Western currency to pay off the loans. Real modernization would have required deep political change—and the destruction of the Communist state. As soon as the border opened, East Berliners poured through, for fear that the arbitrary East German regime might soon reverse itself—and soon the Berlin Wall itself, the greatest symbol of the Cold War, was torn down. Here East Berliners pour over the wall on 10 November 1989. *Associated Press*

Victors and vanquished: Vice President George Bush (soon to become president) and President Ronald Reagan meet with Soviet ruler Mikhail Gorbachev, 7 December 1988. The Soviet empire in Eastern Europe still had about a year to run, and Gorbachev's Soviet Union was still a superpower—with only about three more years of history left. Even so, it was clear that Gorbachev had little leverage. Like Nixon in the 1970s, he knew that his military forces were grossly inferior; he could do little but smile while the United States and her allies pressed ahead on many fronts. *U.S. Naval Institute*

PART FOUR

STALEMATE

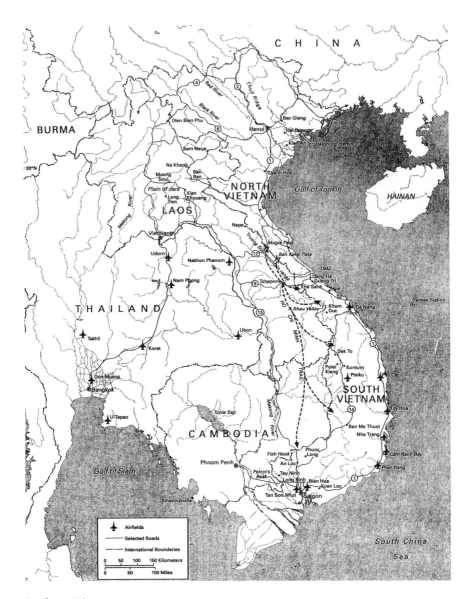

Southeast Asia

The key to the Vietnam War was the Ho Chih Minh Trail, which ran through neutral Laos and Cambodia. The Nixon Administration argued that it could legitimately attack the trail because neither neutral was preventing the North Vietnamese from using its territory to prosecute the war. The Laotian and Cambodian governments privately agreed, but feared that to say so openly would cost them neutral status (and would risk overthrow by the Communists). Hence the U.S. attacks had to be secret—which seemed, to many Americans, yet another hypocrisy in an unjustifiable war.

Map created by Bowring Cartographic for Darrel Whitcomb, *The Rescue of Bat 21* (Annapolis, Md.: Naval Institute Press, 1998), facing page 76.

The enduring symbol of the Cold War from the 1960s on was the intercontinental ballistic missile, the ICBM. Quite aside from its military value, at the start it was a symbol of modernity, as airplanes had been before World War II. Rockets caught the public's imagination in a way that no airplane could. Khrushchev bought them in a conscious attempt to end-run the United States, which had invested heavily in the now-stodgy technology they apparently were making obsolete, manned bombers. Early American failures to match Khrushchev's rockets seemed to prove that the United States had gone soft. For that matter, the race to build and deploy the first ICBMs was probably the closest the Cold War ever got to an arms race between the superpowers. Between about 1955 and 1960, both tried to build much the same kind of weapon. At all other times during the Cold War one side generally built weapons while the other, for a wide variety of reasons, did not. Even the missile race was not the action-reaction situation so often imagined. Both sides realized at about the same time that they wanted ICBMs, and each pursued its goal knowing very little about what the other was doing.

Big, long-range rockets were part of the heritage of German World War II research. The German V-2 was probably the most futuristic wartime weapon. In 1946, a book on rockets was titled *The Ballistics of the Future;* in the past, ballistics had been the science of gunnery. The great question was when the rockets would mature to the point that they could replace earlier weapons such as aircraft. To get there, rocket designers had to build a rocket with enough power to loft H-bombs. To do that, the rocket had to be immense. The Soviets pushed hard to build the first such missile (before they developed lightweight H-bombs). U.S. H-bombs were lighter, so the first U.S. missiles were much smaller than their Soviet equivalents, and easier to deploy. Missile guidance and the design of reentry vehicles that could protect a bomb during the fiery descent into the atmosphere were other problems facing designers.

In 1946 Stalin imported German experts to develop new weapons, including big rockets. Americans found out what the Soviets were doing when those experts began to return home from the Soviet Union in the early 1950s. The U.S. Air Force already was developing its own long-range missile, Atlas, under a program begun during the Korean War, but now it seemed a race was on. For two years the air force's ballistic missile program had a high priority, but no higher than several others. Compared to a bomber, a missile had a much smaller payload and was far less accurate.

In 1955, however, the Killian panel emphasized to the NSC that a Soviet ICBM could have devastating effects. That December the ballistic missile program was assigned the single highest U.S. national priority. It was so important that a backup missile, Titan, was financed alongside the first air force program, Atlas. To back up both of them, a pair of shorter-range missiles (intermediate range, IRBMs), was ordered: Thor and Jupiter. IRBMs were simpler than ICBMs, so it seemed almost certain that they would succeed. Based in Europe or even in Alaska, they could reach Soviet industrial areas. If the Soviets did no better than an IRBM, they would find it much harder to hit American targets. Perhaps most important, it seemed likely that the U.S. IRBM program could match the predicted Soviet IRBM.

Above all, a missile was terrifying in a way that a bomber was not. A bomber could be shot down; a missile seemed unstoppable. The State Department argued late in 1955 that if the Soviets successfully tested even an IRBM before the United States, NATO would be badly weakened. At best, allies betting on U.S. technological superiority would be dismayed. Those advocating accommodation with the Soviets would feel strengthened. If the Soviets got an ICBM first, allied governments also would wonder whether the United States would risk destruction *for them*.[1]

Few understood that missiles did not quite live up to their advertising. The big first-generation missiles took hours to set up to launch. An alert bomber could fly out before enemy missiles arrived, but missiles would probably be caught on the launch pad, still being readied for flight. Once in the air, the missile would arrive very quickly, but the bomber might take less time from "go" order to arrive at the target. Missile launch facilities were massive, and anything but invulnerable. The missiles' limits all would be overcome, but not for a few years.

That the United States was desperately racing the Soviets, that failure was among the administration's worst nightmares, was secret. That was the Eisenhower administration's style, and usually it was the best choice. In this particular case, however, secrecy gave the administration no way to deal with its vociferous critics. Eisenhower's great strength, that he was above politics, did not serve him well.

Khrushchev's missile men moved faster than the West expected. On 26 August 1957 he announced the successful firing of an R-7 intercontinental ballistic missile (ICBM). Most U.S. intelligence analysts were then predicting that the Soviet ICBM would not appear until about 1960; the R-7 flight was more in line with predicted IRBM progress. No one in the West knew that in fact in 1954 the Soviets had decided to develop R-7 instead of an IRBM.

The engine was the critical problem. In the West, it was assumed that a missile would have a single main engine. The key to the Soviets' success was to cluster large numbers of less powerful engines in a "bouquet." That design made R-7 an even more massive missile than it might otherwise have been—but, crucially, it drastically shortened development time.

Khrushchev's R-7 claim was not taken too seriously at first. The CIA had no way of independently confirming the missile had been fired, and Khrushchev liked to boast about his rockets (soon the CIA would place a long-range radar in Turkey to observe Soviet rocket tests).[2] We now know that he was exaggerating in this case, too. The rocket was not a full prototype of the planned R-7 ICBM, which may not have been fired until January 1958. Nor did it reach anything like its full planned range of fifty-five hundred nautical miles (NM). We also now know that as yet the Soviets lacked a reentry vehicle to preserve the missile's warhead as it came down out of space.[3] For the moment, their weapon was toothless.

On the other hand, the Americans were discovering that long-range missiles were difficult to build. A few weeks before Khrushchev's announcement, the U.S. ICBM, Atlas, failed its first test flight.

On 4 October 1957 Khrushchev very publicly demonstrated that he had an ICBM. A modified R-7 launched Sputnik, the world's first satellite. By beating the United States to a major technological advance—a satellite—Khrushchev seemed to be demonstrating Soviet superiority. U.S. allies were unnerved. The administration's very reasonable rejoinders—one test did not prove that a whole arsenal existed; SAC could still obliterate the Soviet Union—seemed hollow. Khrushchev rubbed in his success: Sputnik had been launched, he said, by a *production* ICBM. In fact it was an early and unreliable prototype.[4] Since it had been unable to monitor most of the Soviet launch program, the CIA could not tell. Many in the West confused a test flight with an operational missile force. Later President Eisenhower would point out that the Soviets' first few missiles were the most important, because (at least for now) their effect was primarily psychological.

Sputnik was the beginning of an odd era, in which achievements in space, many of them absolutely unrelated to military capability, became tacit demonstrations of scientific, and hence of military, power. At first the two were connected, since a rocket capable of lofting a heavy satellite obviously could also loft a heavy H-bomb. That capability applied, for example, to Laika, the "space dog," which the Soviets orbited late in 1957, and also to early manned flights, beginning with Yuri Gagarin in 1961. Lunar and planetary probes were somewhat less clearly related to military issues, although it could be argued that merely hitting the moon or Mars was a remarkable demonstration of missile accuracy. The ultimate space stunt—President Kennedy's declaration that within the decade of the 1960s an American would land on the moon—was clearly mainly a matter of prestige. All of this was quite separate from the intense military use of space for roles such as navigation, communication, and reconnaissance, which became very important early in the 1960s.

Ironically, the U.S. scientific satellite program had been badly delayed because it could not be based on any of the big missiles under development. By avoiding any missile connection, Eisenhower hoped to conceal his intense interest in a reconnaissance satellite. The navy's modified Viking research rocket (Vanguard) was chosen. Modification proved difficult; Vanguard suffered a series of embarrassing failures. Fortunately the army's missile team at Huntsville, Alabama, already had proposed using the existing short-range Redstone missile; it got an unofficial go-ahead when Sputnik went into orbit. As Jupiter C, in February 1958 it launched the first U.S. satellite—which weighed far less than Sputnik, let alone the Soviet follow-ups.

Sputnik seemed to prove that the regimented Soviets could develop military technology more quickly than the soft United States. Much was made of how many more Soviet than U.S. citizens were taking advanced degrees in the hard sciences. Congress passed a National Defense Education Act providing special grants for graduate work. The U.S. school curriculum was revised, with much greater attention paid to science in elementary and high schools. As part of the new public emphasis on science, the Science Advisory Committee of the Office of Defense Mobilization became the President's Science Advisory Committee; its head became the president's science advisor. Americans did not know that much of the Soviet system of higher education was quite unsophisticated. Many of the graduate engineers were so narrowly specialized that they were roughly equivalent to U.S. technicians. Far from being a weight dragging down the Western defense effort, civilian-oriented technology offered important military spin-offs.

Sputnik seems to have taken Eisenhower aback. He had little use for stunts, which he feared the services would use to generate the publicity needed to escape his attempts to control spending. Knowing just how valuable the reconnaissance satellite already under development could be, and just how little capability Sputnik had, he dismissed the Soviet satellite as militarily irrelevant. It irked him that almost no one else did. Eisenhower was able to ride out the storm, partly because he was unflappable and partly because he was able to sense the reality behind the inflated claims of Soviet prowess.

With its own ICBMs not yet ready, the United States could offer only IRBMs to counter Khrushchev's new weapon. Their ranges matched those of the medium bombers already based in Britain. Indeed, as early as March 1956 the U.S. Air Force planned to base them there.[5] Moreover, the British wanted missiles. In the fall of 1956, Khrushchev rattled his missiles (actually IRBMs) at the British to force them out of Suez. They badly wanted something to rattle back. At Bermuda in March 1957, Eisenhower offered the British the U.S. IRBM, Thor, as soon as it was ready. Missiles entered British service (under a dual-key arrangement) two years later. They brought Moscow and Leningrad within missile range, but overall they were psychological rather than practical weapons; they could not be prepared and fired quickly enough to escape incoming enemy missiles. As news of the British deal came out, in July the French asked for equivalent weapons.[6]

To other NATO governments, Khrushchev's IRBMs seemed much more impressive than NATO's nuclear-armed bombers. NATO IRBMs were the obvious solution. To reassure NATO governments upset by Sputnik, Eisenhower upgraded the planned December 1957 NATO Council meeting to what amounted to a summit conference. It approved SACEUR's October request for ballistic missiles to counter Khrushchev's.[7] It is unclear to what extent SACEUR was simply making it easier for the United States to obtain IRBM bases within range of Soviet targets. By the fall of 1958, the U.S. government was negotiating to place Jupiter IRBMs in France, Italy, and Turkey. The French proved too difficult, but Jupiters were emplaced in Italy and in Turkey. Missile development moved extremely fast; by the time the Jupiters were in place, U.S. ICBMs were operational, so these IRBMs no longer seemed nearly as vital.

In fact in 1957 Khrushchev still had very few rockets to rattle. His 1,000-nautical-mile rocket (R-12) was not deployed until 1958. Not until 1961 did the first four soft launchers for a true IRBM, the 2,200-nautical-mile R-14 (SS-5), became operational. U.S. experts found it difficult to understand why Soviet missile deployment was so slow. Khrushchev had announced a crash missile program. No one realized that the Soviet Union still had to develop the industry needed to mass-produce missiles. Khrushchev also had a problem, which was unknown to the Americans, and which was rooted in Soviet politics. In 1946, when the Soviet rocket program was established, Stalin purged his aircraft industry in retaliation for imagined political disloyalty. Missile development therefore was awarded not to aircraft makers, but to the artillery industry, which had much cruder standards.

The Americans were more logical. The expertise developed by the U.S. aircraft industry translated almost directly into missile capability. Thus a U.S. crash program quickly produced long-range missiles. As early as 20 September 1956, a modified version of the army's Redstone achieved a range of 3,400 nautical miles. This was about what Khrushchev's ICBM achieved nearly a year later, albeit with a lighter payload; it proved that the army could have orbited a satellite a year before Sputnik. This achievement had little or no impact at the time, nor was it brought up when Americans felt so humiliated in 1957. An Atlas flew 6,325 nautical miles on 28 November 1958. Not until 30 May 1959, six months later, did the Soviets fire an ICBM beyond 3,500 nautical miles.[8]

Early missiles were quite unreliable; even successful programs were plagued with failures. Because U.S. missiles were generally tested from Cape Canaveral, in Florida, the failures, which tended to be spectacular, were generally very public. Often they appeared on the nightly television news. The Soviets had similar—but much less public—problems. For example, the first four R-7 shots all failed, and the missile came close to cancellation (Khrushchev would later insist on having two parallel programs for each missile class, specifically to protect against failure). The Soviet missile ranges were well inland, safe from prying American eyes; but the CIA's radar trackers sometimes did notice that what went up often did not get all the way downrange. Because the entire tracking project was secret, so, unfortunately, was its knowledge of Soviet failures.

Then, too, the administration could not trumpet a key reality. By late 1957 the big liquid-fuelled missiles, many of them not yet successfully tested, would soon be obsolete. American chemists, using techniques developed by the plastics industry, had developed successful solid fuels. They were not as energetic as the liquid fuels used in existing missiles, but they were far safer, and they were easy to store; a solid-fuel missile did not have to be fuelled just before it was fired. By this time it was clear that bombs would soon be light enough for solid-fuel missiles to loft. In effect, then, in 1957–58, public pressure to build more missiles was pressure to build very expensive, obsolescent weapons.

The advent of solid-fuelled missiles transformed U.S. strategy. Such weapons were relatively easy to emplace in silos, so protected ("hardened") that enemy weapons could not easily destroy them. Missiles could, then, ride out an enemy attack. Alternatively, since a solid-fuelled missile needed much less servicing, the missiles could be dispersed so that they could not all be destroyed in a single attack. The United States took both approaches. Beginning in February 1958, the air force developed the inexpensive mass-production Minuteman, which sat ready to fire in a silo (hence the name), with a guaranteed ten-year lifetime. Each squadron of fifty missiles (five times the number in an Atlas or Titan squadron) could be ripple-fired (within thirty seconds) from a single launch control center. Each missile had a single target preset in its guidance system. To maintain full readiness, the guidance gyros were kept running at full speed for the entire life of the missile.[9] Given the relative inaccuracy of existing Soviet weapons, the silos were unlikely to be destroyed even by direct hits.

Solid fuel also made a new kind of missile possible: the navy's Polaris, which a submarine could carry and fire underwater. Earlier U.S.—and Soviet—submarine-launched missiles had been clumsy, and could be fired only by a surfaced—hence very visible—submarine. A Polaris submarine could remain underwater, virtually undetectable, posing a constant threat to a potential attacker.

Solid-fuel chemistry drew not on U.S. military investment, but much more on the power of the American consumer industry. Plastics chemists developed the key binders that held the motor together and protected it from cracking.[10] Equivalent Soviet additives were either too heavy or too bulky, or both. The Americans' success could be attributed, not to more money or sophistication, but to the fact that so much of the U.S. economy was driven by consumer demands—which had unexpectedly useful consequences.[11] Eventually the Soviets would achieve somewhat comparable performance using missiles fueled with storable liquids, but that took some years, and the weapons were always somewhat difficult to handle. For the moment, they had to make do with massive weapons that were very vulnerable to a preemptive attack.

With little understanding of the limits under which Khrushchev labored, and with little hard intelligence, the sense grew that there was a missile gap: Khrush-chev would soon have ICBMs in service, and that for some years afterwards he would have the United States at his mercy. The very depressing available data were reflected in a blue ribbon report issued in November 1957, with Sputnik and the new Soviet ICBM very much on official minds. The Gaither Commission reported that although for the moment SAC held the balance of power, that could not last much longer.[12] The report itself was fairly sober (its most important recommenda-tion was that the Polaris submarine-launched missile system, invulnerable to a Soviet first strike, should be accelerated). However, a much more sensational ver-sion leaked, fueling public fears.

Early in 1958 the president's science advisor, George Kistiakowsky, estimated that the Soviets were about a year ahead in propulsion, a year behind in warheads (the one area where there was hard evidence, because Soviet bomb tests could be monitored), and slightly behind in guidance. In fact the United States was well ahead in all these areas. Kistiakowsky assumed that the Soviets would be deter-mined to make all their missiles mobile, to limit their vulnerability. It was known that Soviet missile launchers were associated with railroad lines. The interpretation was that the Soviets would move their missiles constantly along these lines, so that they could not easily be attacked. That was the sort of sophisticated basing scheme Americans would have chosen. In fact the Soviet ICBM was so heavy that it had to be transported to its fixed launcher by rail.[13]

In August 1958 the official estimate (NIE) was that the first ten Soviet ICBMs, with 5,500-nautical-mile range, would be ready for service the following year. A year later the Soviets would have one hundred missiles. It seemed unlikely that any corresponding U.S. missiles would be ready until 1961, when Khrushchev would have five hundred.[14] Moreover, SAC would not have adequate warning of a Soviet ICBM attack until 1962 or later.

Fortunately Eisenhower was unflappable. Given his experience with the U.S. missile program, he knew that ICBMs were difficult to develop, and in his expe-rience the Russians were not superhuman. Estimates of when they would have ICBMs in service were probably unrealistic.[15] SAC already was widely dispersed. A few ICBMs would not change the situation; for at least the next five years bombers would still be the main strategic weapons. Until the Soviets deployed enough ICBMs, the increasingly powerful U.S. land-based bomber force could destroy its Soviet rival, albeit at the cost of considerable damage to the United States. Even after the Soviet ICBMs were in place, the United States had a very powerful sea-based force they could not destroy in a surprise missile attack. After Project Buda-pest, it was clear that even that force could inflict terrible, unacceptable damage on the Soviet Union.[16]

Khrushchev did his best to keep up the pressure. For example, in 1959, he pri-vately told several Western officials that he had ordered studies of how many mis-siles it would take to destroy the "vital centers" of the United States and Western

Europe. Late in 1960 he privately told "important Bloc officials" that it would take three hundred missiles to destroy the United States, and two hundred to destroy Europe. The CIA reported that that talk of hundreds of ICBMs already in existence was pretense, but that Soviet factories were gearing up to produce such a force.[17]

It already was clear that Khrushchev valued his big missiles. Thus in December 1959 he created a new independent arm of the Soviet services, the Strategic Rocket Forces (RVSN in Soviet parlance, but always SRF in Western publications).[18] Its first chief, Marshal Nedelin, was the man who had personally approved rocket development in 1951, overcoming the opposition of his predecessor (he was soon killed in a missile explosion). The creation of a separate RVSN contrasted with U.S. practice, in which the earlier bomber force, SAC, also was responsible for land-based missiles, so that there was an inevitable conflict between advocates for the two weapons.

Eisenhower found that he could not stave off political pressure to buy more missiles. Congress was too eager to do something about the new menace. Eisenhower's fears that politicians were irresponsible were being graphically demonstrated. Congress was perfectly willing to buy more missiles, but it preferred not to authorize missile sites, which were unpopular. But missiles in warehouses contributed little. With missile technology changing very fast, by the fall of 1958 Eisenhower wondered whether he had approved expensive production orders a bit too early.[19]

In 1959 Sen. Stuart Symington, a Democrat long sympathetic to the air force and to its alarmist views of Soviet capabilities (he had been secretary of the air force), publicized the "missile gap." He hoped to ride that issue to the 1960 Democratic nomination.[20] Another presidential hopeful, John F. Kennedy, took up Symington's cry. At open and closed hearings in January 1959 administration officials convinced several Democrats that the gap was irrelevant, given overall U.S. strategic superiority. Neither Symington nor Kennedy cared.

Soon evidence began to accumulate that Khrushchev had been bluffing. In November 1959 the CIA pushed the operational date for the Soviet ICBM back to 1 January 1960 because as yet there was no evidence that it was operational.[21] January 1960 passed without a visible deployment. However, the CIA credited the Soviets with fifty ICBMs (thirty-five of them on launchers), based on their supposed needs.

By the spring of 1960, Eisenhower was reasonably sure that the gap was opening in favor of the United States—at great expense. Meanwhile the Democratic candidates' attacks became particularly shrill after the FY61 budget was presented in January 1960. Eisenhower was appalled: "These men lack the judgement required for such responsibility . . . [Symington] lack[s] sense of responsibility."[22] A 1960 campaign advisor, Harvard professor (and air force consultant) W. Barton Leach told Kennedy to "keep hammering" at the administration's policies.[23] Eisenhower refused to say what he was doing to solve the missile problem.[24] He never spelled out his reasons for rejecting intelligence estimates of Soviet forces or for maintaining that the U.S. deterrent sufficed. Probably he was too aware of just how sensitive his own sources of information were—the U-2 and communications intelligence, for example. This supreme self-control, exercised in the face of enormous provocation, unfortunately left the field open to those who argued that the strategic balance was precarious at best. The two best-known proponents of this view were Henry Kissinger of Harvard and Albert Wohlstetter of RAND, the air force's think tank. In an article, "The Delicate Balance of Terror," in the January 1959 issue of *Foreign Affairs*, Wohlstetter argued that in its "deep pre-Sputnik sleep" the administration had allowed SAC to become dangerously vulnerable. Wohlstetter was far readier than Eisenhower to imagine that the Soviets would chance a first strike; in his world no one took much interest in Murphy's Law. Supported by the U.S. Army, Kissinger used the missile gap (which he agreed, in 1961, was unavoidable for 1961–65) to argue that the United States could no longer rely on nuclear force as a deterrent to conventional attack. A larger non–New Look army was needed.

Early in 1960 the intelligence picture was still confusing. Eisenhower authorized a U-2 flight over the Soviet missile range, in hopes of catching a missile on its launcher.[25] Flown from Pakistan by Francis Gary Powers, the U-2 took off on 1 May 1960. A Soviet missile shot Powers down near Sverdlovsk. The flimsy U-2 was sometimes described as a jet-powered glider. Eisenhower was assured that Powers had been killed and the airplane destroyed. He bluffed, telling Khrushchev that a U.S. weather airplane had strayed off course. Khrushchev produced not only a live Powers (who later said that he had been shot down because his airplane descended too low) but also cameras and developed film. A planned summit meeting in Paris collapsed. The U-2 was never again used over the Soviet Union, but it flew extensively everywhere else.

Fortunately the U-2's replacement, the new satellite film retrieval system, finally worked a few months later. By mid-1961 the new reconnaissance satellites showed why deployment had been so slow. The Soviet R-7 ICBM was shockingly large, about twice the size of an Atlas or half that of the Saturn being developed for the moon shot. It had to be transported mainly or even exclusively by rail; it could not be deployed to any sort of hardened site. To fuel each missile, the launch site had to store the equivalent of about five large rail tank cars. Crucially, the missile could not be maintained in a fuelled state. It had to go through a laborious checkout before launch. This was hardly the terrifying first-strike weapon described by the Gaither Commission. The CIA estimated that at least two to four sites were probably under construction in 1957–59. By 1961 they had to be presumed operational. No others were known, although the agency refused to say that none existed. Later only one operational site was identified. A second, begun in 1957, was abandoned. Four more, started by mid-1958, were redesigned to accommodate later missiles, tests of which began in 1960.[26]

To Eisenhower's disgust, John F. Kennedy hammered at the bomber gap throughout the 1960 election. It was good politics, and Kennedy seemed not to let facts get in the way. Classified briefings from Gen. Earle Wheeler, then chief staff officer to the JCS, had no impact at all.[27] In his last State of the Union address, on

12 January 1961, Eisenhower said that "the 'bomber gap' of several years ago was always a fiction and the 'missile gap' shows every sign of being the same."[28]

The facts caught up with Kennedy after he entered office. At his first background briefing for the press, Secretary of Defense Robert S. McNamara admitted that the gap seemed to be opening in favor of the United States.[29] His admission was embarrassing; too many Democrats had gotten too much out of the "missile gap" during the previous election. Kennedy's news secretary, Pierre Salinger, soon contradicted the story. McNamara understood. He reversed himself. Although his first classified report to the president showed that the gap had closed, a little over a month later he told George McMahon, chairman of the House Appropriations Committee, that "estimates" showed that the gap might not be closed until 1963.[30] The Washington press corps concluded that McNamara was untrustworthy.

During the campaign, Kennedy also had charged that the administration was making no real effort to protect Americans from (nonexistent) Soviet rockets. The U.S. Army, which had developed the Nike missiles protecting U.S. cities from Soviet bombers, was now working on an antimissile equivalent, Nike Zeus. Bomber defense was barely practicable, using computers to handle radar data and to control fighters and missiles. In a dramatic test, an army Nike Hercules intercepted an incoming Thor IRBM.[31] The question was always how much it would cost to protect a city from numerous missiles, particularly if they were accompanied by decoys. In January 1960 the president's science advisor, Dr. Kistiakowsky, told Eisenhower that the United States would have to spend ten dollars to defend against every dollar's worth of missiles the Soviets bought. The Zeus project could not, however, be killed altogether: Khrushchev was boasting that he had rockets which could "hit a fly in space."[32] The Soviets had begun antimissile tests in 1957.[33] Like the Americans, they could not produce an entirely satisfactory system. However, they never said so, and some new Soviet air defense (antibomber) systems were mistaken for missile defenses.[34] Thus for Kennedy in 1960 missile defense was a valuable political opportunity.

Eisenhower could not bring himself to defend his record; he would not reveal the secret information that would have justified his decisions. Thus he could not back the Republican candidate, Richard M. Nixon, his vice president, effectively. He had benefited enormously from his military reputation, and until the missile gap had managed to keep politics out of national security.

After Nixon lost the election, Eisenhower gave a farewell address. He attacked the "military-industrial complex," the combination of the services, which demanded too much, and the companies that he thought helped push their extravagant programs. His real but unnamed target was Congress, which irresponsibly demanded and bought more and more, and might bring the national economy down in the process.[35] To Eisenhower, the winner, Kennedy, typified Congress in his brazenness and his preference for publicity over honesty.

To an extent unappreciated in Washington at the time, by 1958 Khrushchev badly needed to prove that he was neither soft nor naive.[1] Mao, his erstwhile ally, was contesting his leadership of the world movement. In many ways Mao was an Asian Charles de Gaulle, the leader of a proud but weak country, determined not to be submerged by a stronger ally. Nominally, the feud broke out over Khrushchev's February 1956 Secret Speech denouncing not only Stalin but also the "cult of personality." As Stalin's successor, Khrushchev defined the party line not just in the Soviet Union but throughout the Communist world. The Chinese party downgraded Mao in favor of the "collective leadership" Khrushchev was then espousing. Mao was furious. He backed Khrushchev's enemies on the Soviet Central Committee during the 1957 fight.[2] He later said that, had Khrushchev had the sense to create a cult of personality around himself, he would not have been overthrown. As for his own cult, Mao said that it was too soon for China to discard a thousand years of imperial tradition.[3]

To Mao, Khrushchev was selling out to the Americans for fear of nuclear war. In 1954–55 Khrushchev had advised him to pull back from invading Quemoy, a Nationalist-held island off the Chinese coast, after Eisenhower threatened nuclear war (in an early application of his New Look doctrine).[4] In fact Khrushchev had also shielded Mao from any U.S. attack. Eisenhower retreated from his own campaign promise to "unleash" Chiang Kai-shek (he had signed a mutual defense treaty which gave him a veto over any Nationalist attack on Communist China). In part, Eisenhower's retreat was due to pressure from the British and other Europeans; they feared that a U.S. attack on China would cause Mao to invoke the Sino-Soviet treaty, thus triggering a war in Europe. Some of Eisenhower's advisors pressed for action that would make up for the loss of Western prestige in Asia due to the Dien Bien Phu disaster, but Europe was far more important than Asia. German entry into NATO was being negotiated. It was no time to frighten the Europeans. Eisenhower's advisors, moreover, had estimated that U.S. strikes against Chinese bases would have killed twelve to fourteen million Chinese—insuring that any subsequent war would be long and bitter. A few islands off the Chinese coast were hardly worth that.

Mao already distrusted the Soviets. In 1950 Stalin had levered him into the Korean War to bleed as a Soviet proxy. Worse, the war had bound his army to the Soviets, since its experience in Korea seemed to demonstrate the need for help in modernization. Mao could not tolerate that idea; China was the center of the world, not a Soviet dependent. When Stalin died in 1953, the Chinese argued that Mao, the authentic revolutionary hero, should replace him as the head of the world revolution.[5] They took the horrified Russian refusal as proof that the Soviets would not treat them as equals. Khrushchev was well aware of the problem. He tried to mend fences when he visited Beijing in September 1954 for the fifth anniversary of Mao's republic. He softened some of Stalin's hard bargains, turning over two of the classic symbols of Soviet power over China (which the czarists had held): Port Arthur (and the ships there) and the Manchurian railroad.[6] To the horror of his Presidium colleagues, Khrushchev also turned over the Soviet shares of many joint-stock companies then operating in China, and he offered much more generous aid. To the Chinese, this was too little, since he refused to renounce the Chinese debt, which then stood at $2 billion.[7] Most of the money had paid for weapons used in Korea—where the Chinese had fought Stalin's battle.[8] Tension increased. Symbolically, Gao Gang, who had been so friendly to Stalin during the 1949–50 treaty negotiations, was purged in April 1955.[9] However, for the moment, relations remained warm.

In the aftermath of the 1955 Quemoy crisis, Mao was alarmed when the 1956 Party Congress declared that war now had to be averted. Khrushchev seemed to be abrogating the Sino-Soviet treaty Mao had sacrificed so much to gain in 1950. On the other hand, during the winter of 1955–56 Khrushchev unofficially promised the greatest prize of all, the bomb, in return for the uranium he badly needed to make his own weapons. In August 1956 the two leaders signed a first agreement to help build a Chinese nuclear industry.

Mao was further distressed when the 1957 Party Conference passed a resolution enjoining Communist parties from revolutionary warfare. They were to limit themselves to subversion and political activity. That applied to North Vietnam, whose governing party was pledged to reunite the country by taking over South Vietnam. The Soviets were so firmly opposed to armed action that in January 1957 they proposed UN membership for both Vietnams—without consulting Hanoi. In Moscow in October, Ho Chi Minh did manage to extract an admission that sometimes Socialism must be achieved by other than peaceful means (i.e., by revolution), but the Soviets still refused any formal support for a war in the South. Moscow's decision held because the Chinese also had no interest in supporting a war on their border. Thus Ho could not play off the two Communist superpowers—yet.[10]

When Mao attended the celebrations of the fortieth anniversary of the October

Revolution in Moscow in 1957, he terrified the Soviets. He welcomed a future nuclear war in which half of mankind might die, but so would imperialism; in fifty to one hundred years the world would make up its losses.[11] Mao's attacks were particularly painful for Khrushchev because the celebrations were to have marked his triumph over the "anti-Party" group. Khrushchev needed Mao. He wanted Chinese support in the wake of the Polish and Hungarian disorders. The New Defense Technical Accord (to provide bomb data and a bomb) was signed on 15 October 1957. On the Politburo, Mikoyan argued against supplying a bomb while Bulganin argued in its favor.

Relations between Khrushchev and Mao worsened. By about 1960 Khrushchev needed the Eastern European parties as allies against Mao and a possible revolt within the world Communist movement. He had, in effect, to buy their loyalty. Khrushchev opted for economic integration, a concept called "economism." That was a natural equivalent to Khrushchev's Third World strategy. Superior Socialist economics would hold the Soviet bloc together.[12] That was clearly a facade, but it was an important one. The existing Council for Mutual Economic Assistance (Comecon, to the West), which had been formed in 1949, was strengthened as a counterweight to the new European Common Market (now the European Union). To some extent Khrushchev tried to force different countries to specialize; for example, he tried to halt Romanian industrialization and to make Romania an agricultural supplier to the designated industrial powers (a move resisted by the Romanians). Overall, however, Khrushchev did little to integrate the Eastern bloc economies with that of the Soviet Union; that task fell to Brezhnev.

Economism was only part of the political contract between Khrushchev and the Eastern European ruling parties. Ultimately each of the parties knew that it depended on Soviet force to back it up. It had to be able to call in the Soviet tanks to protect itself against its own population. For that matter, undue liberalization in any one country could threaten the others. When Brezhnev ordered the invasion of Czechoslovakia in 1968 he was acting partly at the behest of other frightened satellite governments, not, as in 1956, entirely on his own.

For the moment, the main economic tie was in the form of subsidies, which began in the 1950s, probably first for Czechoslovakia, with its highly developed machine tool industry. East Germany was in effect subsidized as soon as reparations were stopped in 1954, and Poland and Hungary began to receive subsidies in 1956–57.[13]

Meanwhile Mao clearly demonstrated that he was master of China. His course, not too different from Stalin's, must have reminded Khrushchev of the horrific past he was explicitly rejecting. First he purged the Party. In 1956 he encouraged potential opponents to speak out and then arrested them (the "Hundred Flowers of Thought" campaign). As the campaign ended in 1957, Soviet officials reported that Mao was calling his enemies "Soviet agents."[14] Like Stalin, Mao tried to use his followers' enthusiasm to speed industrialization—to make him independent of the

Soviets. His disastrous "Great Leap Forward" (Three Red Banners Movement) began in 1957. The peasants would create a modern industrial country, making pig iron in their fields.

Mao was building a "cult of personality" every bit as grandiose as Stalin's was. His underlings told him that the Great Leap was succeeding brilliantly; for example, as his train crossed China, fires were lit to simulate the supposed backyard iron works. The reality was far grimmer. Not only did the forced industrial revolution fail, but also peasants trying to make iron did not produce the food China badly needed. As many as fifteen to sixty million died in the resulting famine.[15] Mao eventually had to face failure. Like Stalin, he blamed specialists with insufficient revolutionary faith. Sterner measures were needed. For the moment, however, he could not afford a purge. He faced too many external threats.

Overall, however, perhaps the most important parallel between Mao and Stalin was Mao's belief that revolution should be permanent, that the country and the Party had to be in a constant state of tension. External hostility helped. The Korean War had been a success in this sense: to many Chinese it was the first time that Party and nationalism had come together. However, in its wake had come reconstruction and revival of prerevolutionary attitudes. The revolution had to tear up traditional China. Critics often said that Mao had gone too far, that traditional values, such as respect for the elderly, were well worth preserving. Mao's rejoinder was that most Chinese were ignorant peasants, and that they would be much better off discarding their ignorance and starting afresh.

Khrushchev secretly visited Mao between 31 July and 3 August 1958.[16] According to the Soviets, Mao again upbraided Khrushchev for being afraid to fight a nuclear war to destroy capitalism and insure the victory of communism (the Chinese denied the charge).[17] Khrushchev felt compelled to approve Mao's plan for a new attack in the Taiwan Straits. He announced (falsely) that he had given Mao nuclear weapons. From the last crisis, Chiang had learned that U.S. support might well be lukewarm; the Americans had estimated that, in the end, the islands could not be held unless Chinese invasion bases opposite them were wiped out (by nuclear attack). He was a good poker player: he deployed about a quarter of his army to Quemoy and Matsu, his two remaining islands just off the Chinese coast. Thus, if he lost these islands, he would lose so much of his army that Formosa itself would be in danger.[18] Unwilling to risk that, Eisenhower provided new U.S. weapons.

On 23 August the Chinese Communists began shelling Quemoy intensively. As in 1955, the United States warned that it might have to use nuclear weapons; as before, Eisenhower privately doubted that was practical.[19] Khrushchev replied that the Soviet Union would use nuclear weapons of its own to answer a U.S. nuclear attack on China.[20] As in 1955, he convinced Mao to back down. Mao charged that Khrushchev had not threatened Eisenhower until he knew it was safe to do so, with the crisis already winding down. Probably Khrushchev concluded that Mao would be quite willing to draw him into a nuclear war.

According to the Chinese, Khrushchev unilaterally abrogated the bomb agreement in June 1959, after having supplied production facilities.[21] The last Soviet technical experts left on 1 August 1960, 40 percent of the promised nuclear-industrial material having been withheld. For their part, the Soviets argued that they could supply neither a prototype bomb nor blueprints and technical data while negotiating a test ban treaty. To the Chinese, this was a simple sell-out: the Soviet reversal was a gift Khrushchev brought for his 1959 visit to the United States.

Mao later said that he feared that Khrushchev's détente with the United States might convince people in China that they could relax their vigilance. He was using the existence of Chiang's hostile regime just offshore to keep tensions high within China, to maintain the country's unity. In this sense Chiang's regime was quite valuable. Mao said that he had concocted the crisis specifically to dramatize the conflict with Chiang, not to resolve it.[22]

Eisenhower certainly did not yet consider Khrushchev his friend. It appeared that Khrushchev thought his missiles had bought freedom of action, even in the most sensitive place in Europe, Berlin. Khrushchev announced that he was going to sign a peace treaty with the East Germans. That would void the occupation arrangements under which the Western powers maintained troops in West Berlin. They would no longer be able to deal with the Soviets there; they would have to recognize the East German regime. But rejection of East Germany was central to the West German government. Its own legitimacy rested largely on its claim that it was the rightful heir to German nationalism, which meant that its central purpose was to reunify the country. Membership in NATO was justified partly on the alliance's tacit promise not merely to preserve West Germany, but also eventually to unite it with East Germany. Although it was well understood that this might be a very distant prospect, for the major Allies to recognize East Germany would be to abandon it altogether, and thus to weaken the West German state unless it left NATO (particularly if the East Germans were allowed to espouse reunification). Without West Germany as its European core, NATO might well break up.

For Khrushchev, West Germany, the "economic miracle," was now a major threat. East Germans were already streaming to join it, mostly through the open gateway of Berlin. Khrushchev feared that economism might collapse if the East German satellites found a connection with the Germans more lucrative than one with the Soviets. He greatly overstated the danger; he apparently did not realize the extent to which the East European regimes realized that they could not survive without Soviet help. Moreover, Khrushchev considered it essential to keep East Germany Communist as a justification for terrible Soviet wartime sacrifices. Unless East Germany was propped up, the Soviet army there would be "surrounded by fire."[23]

The East German ruler, Walter Ulbricht, demanded relief. The experience of the June 1953 East German revolt tied Khrushchev to him. Khrushchev had refused to drop Ulbricht's tough Stalinist regime. Ulbricht now convinced Khrushchev that the East German economy lagged that of the West mainly because the Soviets had not been able to match Western aid.

Although symbolically important, militarily Berlin was indefensible. At a 1 May 1958 NSC meeting, Secretary of State Dulles announced that he would soon go to Berlin to repeat the "ritual declaration": an attack on the city would be an attack on the United States. He "did not know whether he himself quite believed this or, indeed, whether his audience would believe it."[24] President Eisenhower saw no alternative to a nuclear defense of Berlin. Allied forces there could not resist a serious attack. They could bluff their way into Berlin, but they could not fight their way out. Berlin was, moreover, a key symbol. If the United States backed away, then soon all of Western Europe would be lost. The balance of power would tip, perhaps decisively. Dulles "indeed hoped that the President would order a nuclear war if the Soviets attacked Berlin, but he doubted very much whether the President's successor would issue such an order."

For the moment, Khrushchev had to back down. He and Eisenhower both knew that although he might have a few ICBMs, he did not have enough to make a difference. NATO rode out the storm. Eisenhower had gambled, correctly, that Khrushchev would not risk a nuclear war over Berlin.

To Mao, it seemed that Khrushchev had gone soft. It was infuriating that Khrushchev visited the United States first before stopping in Beijing for the tenth anniversary of the republic in 1959. Mao made sure that the reception was cold; no crowds greeted the Soviet motorcade.[25] Khrushchev offered very unwelcome advice. Mao should accept "two Chinas"; he should stop taking chances over the offshore islands. He should settle his ongoing border dispute with India, even if that meant ceding territory. That was unacceptable; restoring Chinese territorial integrity had been at the center of Mao's revolution. Khrushchev was clearly favoring the Indian leader, Nehru, because he was also leader of the nonaligned movement and therefore an important potential client.[26]

Overall, Khrushchev could no longer command the foreign Parties. He had to lobby them for support against the Chinese; they could easily wriggle out of his strictures against revolution. That particularly applied to Vietnam; without the Sino-Soviet split, there probably could not have been a Vietnam War. In 1956–57 the South Vietnamese government was quite successfully suppressing the Communists there; victory, even bare survival, depended on armed support from the North. Hanoi did allow its cadres in the South to fight back, but that only brought forth more effective suppression. Party membership in the South fell by about two-thirds, to only about fifteen hundred.[27]

The North Vietnamese were still consolidating their position (witness the big 1957 peasant revolt).[28] They also were beginning reconstruction (with a Three Year Plan, in 1958). Most important of all, they could convince neither the Soviets nor the Chinese to support a new war in the South. Then things began to change. After a secret trip to the South in late 1958, Le Duan, who advocated the revolution there, reported that Diem was fatally weak; despite his success in suppressing the Party in the South, he could be overthrown if sufficient support were provided.

Khrushchev's 1957 dictum no longer applied. In January 1959 the North Vietnamese Central Committee decided formally to support a revolution in the South.[29] Some of the ninety thousand "regroupees" who had gone North in 1954 were infiltrated back into South Vietnam. Two guerilla bases were created, one near the Cambodian border and one in the western Central Highlands. The armed struggle was formally begun in October 1959, and the National Liberation Front for South Vietnam was officially formed on 20 December 1960. The North Vietnamese decisions had to be communicated on paper to the Party in the South, and early in 1959 the CIA was well aware of what was happening.[30]

Americans did not realize how badly Khrushchev's control had been eroded. They thought he was encouraging militancy in the Third World. In June 1960 the Soviets circulated criticisms of Mao among world Communist parties. The Chinese replied in kind. On 16 June the Soviets recalled all their experts from China. Later in the year the Chinese and the Soviets aired their differences at the Moscow International Conference of Communist Parties, which was attended by every Party except Yugoslavia's. An attempted reconciliation failed.[31] The Albanian party took the Chinese side, breaking with the Soviets and evicting them from a potentially valuable submarine base near the mouth of the Adriatic Sea. The Albanians were apparently afraid that as Soviet-Yugoslav relations warmed the Soviets might support a Yugoslav attempt to absorb Albania (Tito had tried to do just that in 1948).[32]

At about the same time Khrushchev turned up the heat on Berlin, but Eisenhower was not fazed. He was fairly sure that Khrushchev would not fight in Europe.[33] "For example . . . he simply could not believe that if the Soviets tried to seize Austria we could fight them in . . . a nice, sweet, World War II type of war." As for any alternative to a nuclear holocaust, "the President expressed bewilderment. What possibility was there, he asked, that facing 175 Soviet divisions, well armed with both conventional and nuclear weapons, that our six divisions together with the NATO divisions could oppose such a vast force in a limited war in Europe . . . ?"

On the other hand, there was evidence that Khrushchev thought that as his missile program matured he really would gain freedom of action outside Europe. The previous year he had told Vice President Nixon and Gov. Averell Harriman that he was building enough ballistic missiles to paralyze the vital centers of both the United States and Europe. To the director of central intelligence, these conversations showed that Khrushchev understood not only the concept of mutual deterrence but also that his own military power was increasing. Once his program matured, he would push the West harder and harder because he doubted that he would be risking war.[34]

Quite aside from mutual deterrence, Khrushchev might choose to exploit the natural paralysis of a U.S. election year. This one, 1960, was particularly critical because a new president would have to be chosen. For the first time the two-term limit applied, so Eisenhower could not run again.[35]

That year the Congo (later renamed Zaire) degenerated into chaos soon after Belgium granted independence. Not only was the Congo valuable for its mineral wealth (for example, 67 percent of Western cobalt supplies), it bordered on nine other countries. It was so central that in 1964 Mao told a Chinese diplomat that "if we can take the Congo, we can have all of Africa."[36]

The Belgians had made little effort to prepare the Congo for independence. Fewer than twenty Congolese had college educations. The Belgians offered a form of independence in which they would have to remain to operate the country. The Congolese could not help but be furious. To make matters worse, the constitution the Belgians wrote established six provinces, each with powers similar to those of the central government (the Belgians planned to retain control of the mineral-rich provinces). Patrice Lumumba was elected prime minister with a plurality of the vote, just before independence. Soon after independence the army mutinied, and Moise Tshombe, the leader of Katanga (now Shaba) province, which supplied about 80 percent of the country's national income from minerals, accused Lumumba of being a Soviet agent. He soon seceded. In July 1960 both Lumumba and his president, Joseph Kasavubu, asked the UN to intervene, to put down Tshombe's rebellion and also to replace Belgian troops who were still in the country. Lumumba combined his own strong personal appeal with loyal strong-arm squads. To the U.S. government, it seemed that he was setting the country up for a takeover. The local CIA station reported that, although he might not actually be a Communist, he would use Communism to gain and maintain power. Soon after the call for UN intervention, CIA Director Allen Dulles called him "a Castro or worse" at an NSC meeting.[37]

In August Lumumba openly sought Soviet help. It was not clear whether he was a committed Communist or an opportunist, but that did not matter. The U.S. interpretation was that he was about to ask the Soviets to intervene directly. Khrushchev seemed quite responsive. The CIA was ordered to kill Lumumba.[38]

With the UN in place, in September Lumumba was ousted by the Congolese president. U.S. policymakers considered that Lumumba was still a threat, because he retained both his appeal and his followers. Col. Joseph-Désiré Mobutu, the army chief, took power and his associates captured and killed Lumumba. It was widely, but unfairly, claimed that they did so at CIA instigation.[39]

Soviet interest continued. Another of their friends, Antoine Gizenga, tried to secede with another province, Orientale. The Soviets announced that the UN operation was a sham to cover U.S. designs on the Congo as a whole. They offered the central government their own aid to end the secession—by one of their own men.[40] For his part, President Kennedy, Eisenhower's successor, saw the Congo as a possible showcase for his new anticolonial policy. In the end, the UN force remained in a deteriorating Congo through June 1964.

As soon as it left, former Lumumbists staged a major rebellion, proclaiming the People's Republic of the Congo in September. Support from the "socialist" world included Chinese equipment and advisors who came through Tanzania and Uganda, and instructors from Egypt. By this time Tshombe had made himself prime minister. He asked for and received U.S. help (largely involving the transport of Belgian paratroops). The war was largely over by mid-1965, and in November Mobutu, the kingmaker, staged a coup and became dictator. Over the next three decades he received continuous Western support, both to keep the Congo open to the West and to allow it to be used as a conduit to attack leftist regimes in surrounding countries.[41]

Closer to home, Khrushchev was clearly backing a dangerous Western Hemisphere revolutionary, Castro; Eisenhower ordered the CIA to develop a plan to overthrow him.[42] At an NSC meeting, the CNO, Adm. Arleigh Burke, suggested that "we would have to face a series of annoying little actions in many places . . . and would have to be prepared to act rapidly."[43]

The Eisenhower administration seemed largely unaware of the impact of the deepening schism in the world Communist movement. Probably the most important new reality was that the 1957 stricture against armed revolution no longer held. That dramatically changed the situation in Vietnam. There, the Communists began to impose their own violence on South Vietnamese society, both to destroy support for the local government and to gain adherents. The pattern was not new; the Communist terrorists slipped into villages by night, killed government-supported headmen, and then slipped away into the jungle, where they were indistinguishable from the rest of the population. Success depended on their ability to reach sanctuary—and on the fact that they were more ruthless than their enemies. The Communists' promise of social revolution (reform) and their nationalist vision helped, but the violence gained them control and kept their supporters in line.

For Westerners, this reality was confusing. The Communists' rhetoric stressed social reform, so sometimes it seemed that the only way to compete was to develop an alternative social revolution. Yet on the other hand guerilla warfare often seemed to be more a matter of efficient police work. The more totalitarian a Western-oriented regime was, the better it might resist being undermined by guerillas—yet the more unacceptable it might be to Westerners. A famous British novelist, Eric Ambler, caught the violent aspect in his novel of the Greek civil war, *The Schirmer Inheritance.* A German sergeant wakes up surrounded by Communist guerillas. They ask him whether he is a true democrat or a Fascist. What is the difference? Democrats live, Fascists die. His choice is simple. To prove he is sincere, he is told to kill the woman with him. When he does so, he shows he is committed to the revolution.

The other reality, that people need something in which to believe, formed the basis of another popular novel of the time, *The Ugly American,* by Eugene Burdick and William Lederer, in which the Communists often gained adherents simply by outsmarting the clumsy Americans, who had far too little understanding of the local culture. A deeply conservative Eisenhower apparently saw little point in imposing a competing U.S.-sponsored social revolution; Communist insurgency was mainly a military or police problem. The United States certainly had a point in demonstrating to the Third World that it could outperform the Soviet economy, but that was quite different from tearing up local societies. Eisenhower had not—perhaps significantly—had a hand in the main recent U.S. experiences of that type, the Marshall Plan and the early phase of the U.S. occupation of Japan.

Another, subtler, factor may have been more important. Ho claimed that he was the authentic heir to Vietnamese nationalism. To Eisenhower, as to other Americans, nationalism was very dangerous. It might lead a U.S.-backed regime into an attack on North Vietnam, with disastrous consequences: the Chinese might enter the war, nuclear weapons might be needed, the Sino-Soviet treaty might be invoked. In this sense Eisenhower was unknowingly paralleling Khrushchev's 1957 decision: even in the Third World, war was very dangerous. The difference was that U.S.-backed regimes could not play Eisenhower off against some Western equivalent to Mao. Ngo Dinh Diem, president of South Vietnam, was clearly a nationalist, just as Syngman Rhee was in South Korea. He talked about a desire to go north; he even said, in 1956, that he could have won the promised election. Whether or not that was a fantasy, by 1959 he had been outflanked, because the Americans, who would have had to provide the necessary weapons, had no intention of backing him.

The level of violence in South Vietnam rose noticeably late in 1959. The North Vietnamese cared little that in attacking a Western client state they might be endangering the Soviet Union. Stalin had excommunicated Tito for exactly these sins, but neither Khrushchev nor his successors could afford to punish the Vietnamese.

The South Vietnamese government thought it had a special claim on U.S. sensibilities. Alone of the countries in Southeast Asia, it had a large Christian (in fact, Catholic) population. As in Europe, the Communists threatened the church; priests were among the victims of the rising violence. The connection naturally interested Sen. John F. Kennedy, who was about to run for president. Vietnam became an issue in the 1960 election.

To Eisenhower, the problem was the same as that in Greece: insurrection depended on sanctuary. The promise of social progress was far less important. As in Korea, the border between the two Vietnams was fortified. The United States had built up a conventional Army of the Republic of Viet Nam (ARVN) specifically to block any North Vietnamese invasion across the border. However, both countries bordered on Laos. With its dense jungles and mountains and its lengthy portion of the Mekong River, Laos was the natural supply route between North Vietnam and South Vietnam and Cambodia. It also bordered Thailand, which Eisenhower considered the "hub" of the U.S. position in Southeast Asia.[44] The North Vietnamese therefore greatly valued Laos, through which ran the Ho Chi Minh Trail, the key to their fight in South Vietnam.

Laos had been neutralized under the 1954 Geneva Accords. The Communist Pathet Lao had been given two provinces, and in 1956 it was allowed into the government and the army. The U.S. government protested. After the Pathet Lao won most of the assembly seats up for election in 1958, the CIA set up an opposition front, which gradually took control of the government. However, it was unwilling to risk civil war by trying to crush the Pathet Lao. In 1960 the neutralist government was overthrown in a pro-Western coup. Prodded by the North Vietnamese, the Pathet Lao fought back. Khrushchev airlifted the supplies they needed. By early 1961 the Pathet Lao had occupied the country's main agricultural area, the Plaine des Jarres. Unfortunately, the Royal Laotian Army was grossly unwarlike (according to intelligence reports, the Pathet Lao, who were winning, kept fighting only because they were prodded by the North Vietnamese).[45]

Shortly before he left office, Eisenhower told Kennedy that Laos was the key to Vietnam and, indeed, to all of Southeast Asia. He had refrained from putting troops into Laos only because he did not want to commit a new administration to combat. Laos was important enough to be one of five places included in the Eisenhower administration's last evaluation of limited war. Eisenhower felt that, to be effective, intervention in Laos would have to be a SEATO operation.[46] He remembered how reluctant Congress had been to send more U.S. troops to Europe in 1950. Allied participation had been absolutely essential. The same would certainly be true in a more obscure place, Laos. This reasoning had helped justify deep cuts in the U.S. Army. They made unilateral adventures very difficult. Eisenhower thought he could count on troops from Thailand, the Philippines, and Pakistan, all of whom counted on SEATO to protect them. The British and French had already said that they would quit SEATO rather than send troops to Laos.

Somehow Khrushchev had to match Chinese radicalism while maintaining a measure of peace with the West. That confused many Westerners. In January 1961 he gave a speech supporting "Wars of National Liberation."[47] He seemed to be abandoning a relatively mild policy of peaceful coexistence for revolutionary ardor. Eisenhower understood that his bluster was nothing really new. His successor, John F. Kennedy, did not—with terrible consequences. He read portions aloud at his first NSC meeting. On the advice of his ambassador to Moscow, Llewellyn Thompson, he gave copies to all his senior officials and told them to "mark, learn, and inwardly digest" it.

John F. Kennedy fought and won the 1960 election with a promise to break with the stodginess of the past to get the country "moving again." He called his program the New Frontier, and above all he espoused "vigor." According to Kennedy, the Eisenhower administration had done too little, not only for national security but also for the national economy. It is not clear just how well this message had sold; Kennedy won by a margin so narrow that the charge that the election was stolen was never entirely discredited. On the other hand, as a Catholic, he faced immense prejudice. It may be that without his message he could not even have come close to election.

Once in office, Kennedy presented himself as the leader of a new generation, fit to take over from the giants who had won World War II. He said, both during and after the campaign, that his generation faced similar challenges, and that it could do what the giants had not: prevent a new world war by dealing with the aggressor before matters got out of hand. There would be no Munich on his watch. Kennedy expected that in 1964 he would again face Nixon, a man who had made his entire reputation as a Cold Warrior. Any charge that he had lost free territory—like the Republicans' charge that Truman "lost" China—would be disastrous.

Compared to, say, Franklin D. Roosevelt, Kennedy clearly was not a born politician.[1] He lacked political instincts, and he showed a strange lack of confidence. He depended very heavily on his advisors. Indeed, it might be said that in important ways his administration *was* his advisors. With little innate feeling for what to do, he tended to follow the last, or the loudest, advice he received. To obtain that advice, he tended to try out alternative policies on different listeners, so that it is sometimes difficult in retrospect to know what he actually intended to do. The issue of whether he really planned to disengage from Vietnam in 1964 is a major case in point.

In conversations Kennedy seemed to display intense concentration and a hunger for information, but he apparently retained remarkably little of what he heard.[2] For example, just before giving his first major foreign policy speech Kennedy had received an extensive briefing on the Sino-Soviet split, yet he spoke then and later as though world Communism was a single, seamless entity. Perhaps Kennedy concentrated much less than he seemed to; sometimes he showed a very short attention span, and he was easily bored.[3]

Moreover, Kennedy's undeniable glamour and charm could not make up for inexperience when dealing with tough foreign leaders old enough to be his father, such as Charles de Gaulle and Nikita Khrushchev.

Unfortunately, given his dependence on advisors, Kennedy discarded Eisenhower's elaborate military-style staff system, which had been centered on the National Security Council (NSC). When Kennedy met him just before entering office, Eisenhower explained that the staff filtered out the mass of relatively trivial issues that would otherwise flood his desk. He apparently did not emphasize the staff's other role, that it automatically evaluated all the policy alternatives open to the president, bringing in the views not only of his close advisors, but also of career civil servants and military officers.

As a politician, Kennedy had little use for such formal arrangements. He relied mainly on a few trusted friends. He favored those who charmed or impressed him sufficiently; their titles and training meant very little. He preferred ad hoc task forces of advisors with whom he personally felt comfortable.[4] Inevitably his advisors competed for attention and authority. Lines of reference were tangled at best. Some senior cabinet officials, such as Secretary of State Dean Rusk, never entered Kennedy's inner circle at all. Formal staff meetings, such as those of the NSC, were used to announce decisions already taken. Since military officers were generally present only at these meetings, they had little input. That was one reason the Joint Chiefs' uneasiness had no impact on the decision to mount the Bay of Pigs attack. Moreover, as a politician without reliable political instincts, Kennedy had to trust others to tell him, not only the military or economic consequences of his actions, but also the political ones, at home and abroad. Since he preferred relatively inexperienced men, some of the advice on which he acted was disastrous. Kennedy himself often seemed aggressive but indecisive—a very bad combination.

Too much of Kennedy's thinking throughout his term in office seemed to reflect the rhetoric he had learned to use during the 1960 campaign. He seemed unable to absorb contradictions between his rhetoric and fact. According to his campaign rhetoric, the United States was in crisis, faced with a rising tide of Communist aggression, rather than with a few fairly local incidents. For that matter, because he had taken a personal interest in Vietnam, he could not accept that it was a minor place in Southeast Asia rather than a focal point of Communist aggression.

As a politician, Kennedy liked to grandstand; he often overdramatized problems to gain public support. In his Inaugural Address, Kennedy said that the United States would not shrink from confrontation in defense of freedom, that his presidency would be a time of national sacrifice. ("Ask not what your country can do for you, but what you can do for your country.") Defense plus sacrifice suggested that Kennedy expected war. Not long afterwards, in his first State of the Union address, Kennedy said that Communist pressure abroad was "relentless" in Asia (Vietnam and Laos), in Africa (the Congo), and in Latin America (Cuba). The "hour of maximum danger," at which time the Soviets would have such superiority that they could blackmail the West, was rapidly approaching. This was a conscious reference to the "year of maximum danger," referred to in NSC-68. The language was hysterical; no president had spoken so grimly in a decade.[5] It was also entirely unwarranted—as Kennedy should have known, having just been briefed on, among other things, the Sino-Soviet split. Kennedy also had just been told that, apart from his "wars of national liberation" speech, Khrushchev had been quite conciliatory.

There is, remarkably, no evidence that Kennedy thought about the effect of *his* speech on Khrushchev—who apparently took it as a slap in the face. Khrushchev had been signaling that he wanted better relations, lauding Kennedy in public as another Roosevelt.[6]

As the first Democratic president since Truman, Kennedy naturally inherited many of Truman's advisors, such as Dean Acheson and Paul Nitze. The experience in postwar Western Europe showed that Communism was a dual political-military threat. Throughout the Third World, it appealed because it promised social justice. Unless the United States could offer a competing kind of social revolution, the Communists might well be unstoppable.

Certainly in postwar Western Europe those disenchanted with capitalism could literally have voted the Communists into office. The Third World was somewhat different. Few peasants were free to vote, either by ballot or by even by foot (i.e., by simply deserting societies they disliked). Many were deeply conservative, supporting the system in place simply because it was there. They would not see the Communists as a serious alternative until they had demonstrated that they could win, perhaps by killing many of the local notables. In much of the Third World, the social system had not been torn apart by war. Those running intact societies might not share the Kennedy administration's sense of crisis. In addition, they might not be too enthusiastic about accepting the sort of radical solutions they were soon offered.

The new administration envisaged a dual approach to the threat of Communist expansionism in the Third World. The political appeal of the Communists would be overcome by nation building (American-supported economic growth) while Special Forces dealt with Communist guerillas. That seemed to apply as much to Latin America, threatened by Castro, as to Southeast Asia. This combination of political-economic and military or paramilitary approaches recalled the two-track approach the United States used in Europe in the 1940s: NATO to shield governments from external threats, the Marshall Plan to build them up enough to resist internal ones.

In the case of Cuba, it might also be possible to deal with the threat at its source by unseating Castro. Kennedy inherited the Eisenhower administration's CIA operation: an amphibious landing by Cuban exiles.[7] Adlai Stevenson, Kennedy's UN ambassador, advised him to avoid any obvious U.S. involvement. Kennedy ordered that only aircraft readily available to Cuban exiles could be used, and they had to fly from Central America rather than from Florida. None of Kennedy's personal advisors had enough military experience to understand how significant these choices were, and no one wanted to tell him he was wrong. Thus Kennedy did not learn that, coming from such distant bases, the bombers could cover the strike force only intermittently. The site of the landing was shifted suddenly from a promising area near the Escambrey Mountains (into which the invaders could melt, to join with existing anti-Castroites) to the Bay of Pigs, which had no nearby refuge. Landing tactics had to be changed drastically. On the eve of the operation, Kennedy personally decided to cut air support, which was crucial, by 80 percent.[8] The remaining air strikes failed to destroy Castro's air arm, which cut off the invaders by sinking two of their supply ships. The invaders were denied air cover over the beach, an essential in any modern amphibious operation. On Kennedy's orders, U.S. warships and aircraft which were available to support the operation were held offshore, silent.[9]

After the disaster Kennedy told Eisenhower that he had canceled a bombing attack for fear of revealing U.S. involvement that would trigger a Soviet counteraction in Berlin. Eisenhower found his fears ludicrous: "If [the Soviets] see us show any weakness, that is when they press us the hardest. The second they see us show strength . . . that is when they are very cagey." Eisenhower also scoffed at the idea that American involvement could be concealed.[10]

Allen Dulles, the CIA director, who had to resign afterwards, felt that Kennedy lacked the political courage necessary to win at the Bay of Pigs. Kennedy was too focussed on possible unpleasant repercussions.[11] He refused to blame himself (and the CIA wisely produced an evaluation exonerating him). Nor did he admit (or, probably, realize) how much support he had denied himself by discarding the NSC staff.[12] He was furious to discover that his Joint Chiefs were well aware of the problems inherent in the operation, yet had not spoken out—probably because he had never really elicited their views.[13] To the end of his life Kennedy continued to prefer ad hoc decisionmaking. Probably the main effect of the Cuban failure was his obsession with wiping out his failure by killing Castro.[14] The administration kept mounting plots against the Cuban leader, and in 1963 it was planning an invasion. When Kennedy himself was assassinated, there was serious speculation that Castro was exacting revenge.

Kennedy soon discovered the real consequences of failure. The U.S. public was furious.[15] On the other side of the world, American allies were embattled in Southeast Asia. Would they conclude that Kennedy had too little nerve to save them? Among Kennedy's first acts after the failure at the Bay of Pigs were attempts to reassure President Diem of South Vietnam and Premier Sarit of Thailand.[16] To make his point, Kennedy sent more U.S. advisors to train the South Vietnamese army. He also immediately established a Vietnam Task Force, to be run by Gen. Edward G. Lansdale, his expert on that area.

The Bay of Pigs gave Khrushchev his first opportunity to measure the new and apparently truculent American president. With Presidium support, he wired Kennedy that the Cuban invasion jeopardized world peace, that he should "avoid the irreparable," that if the invasion continued, he might start a war elsewhere.[17] It seemed that Kennedy lacked Eisenhower's skill at nuclear poker: he had blinked. Perhaps, Khrushchev concluded, his threat had doomed the Bay of Pigs operation by causing Kennedy to deny the rebels U.S. fire support.

Overall, Kennedy's White House ran U.S. policy in Latin America; none of the senior State Department policymakers was interested in the region. Already, in an October 1960 campaign speech, Kennedy had proposed a nation-building Alliance for Progress, modeled on the Marshall Plan.[18] In the past, the Communists had held a monopoly on sympathy towards change. Kennedy hoped that by offering an alternative way of growing towards a better future, the United States could beat off Castro and his Soviet allies. Once Kennedy was in office, his officials realized that to be seen to impose U.S. nation-building ideas on Latin America would make for a disastrous collision with the strongest force in the area, nationalism. They took pains to claim that the alliance derived from a Brazilian idea, Operation Pan-America.[19]

The region was thought to be in a state of chronic crisis because its population was growing faster than its income. As people inevitably lived worse year after year, clearly they would find Communism more attractive. Past U.S. policy, influenced by the International Monetary Fund (IMF), had been to promote financial stability rather than development (the theory was that development would come later, as a stable economy attracted foreign capital). That policy had caused drastic deflation and falling living standards in Argentina, Chile, and Bolivia. The result was that the elected president of Argentina, Arturo Frondizi, was in deep trouble (he would soon fall to a military coup); the Communists were gaining in Chile (under Allende); and they were penetrating the ruling MNR in Bolivia. By way of contrast, the Brazilians, having defied the IMF, had enjoyed considerable economic expansion despite inflation.[20] It was time, then, to promote development, particularly industrialization, despite any risks.

Increasing Soviet economic power complicated the situation. In the past, whenever a new government had come to power in Latin America, it had quickly turned to the United States for support. Now the Soviets increasingly presented a real alternative.[21] For that matter, several major governments in Latin America also wanted to demonstrate their independence from the United States.[22]

As the Kennedy administration saw it, the main barrier to modernization was the entrenched landholding oligarchy of countries like Chile, Peru, Ecuador, and Colombia, which in effect shut large numbers of people off from the national economy. The cure was a middle-class revolution, that is, the creation of a large, dominant middle class. If it failed, worker and peasant revolutions would probably prevail. These probably would be either Communist (Castroite) or Nationalist and thus anti-American (Perónist, as in Argentina).[23] Some Latin Americans were already trying to promote such middle-class revolutions. Important examples were Kubitschek in Brazil and Betancourt in Venezuela. Their still incomplete revolutions had to be encouraged. U.S. aid should not be discouraged by the nationalist-populist rhetoric the early stages of these revolutions often entailed.

It was assumed that only middle class–oriented democracies were stable enough to stand up to the combination of internal subversion and foreign pressure the Communists offered.[24] Early in 1962 it seemed that Mexico, Uruguay, and Costa Rica, and to a lesser extent Venezuela and Argentina, met this criterion. This belief was somewhat disingenuous, since Mexico was (and in 1999 still is) essentially a single-party state, and in Argentina the Perónists the army had ousted a few years earlier (1955) were still extremely strong. Brazil, Chile, and Colombia seemed to have reasonable prospects for a transition to democratic stability.

The key to the desired revolution was a stronger government, which could promote literacy and agrarian reform. These programs in turn would create jobs for the rising middle class. At some point there would be a large enough middle class to transform society altogether. The stronger governments would be financed by modernized tax systems. In the past, governments had relied mainly on import duties and on excise and sales taxes. Land was little taxed, so it attracted money, and land prices were bid up. That situation alone blocked any sort of agrarian reform. A reformed tax structure, including both land and income taxes, would both support a stronger government and would reduce the power of the oligarchy blocking larger reforms.[25]

U.S. economic leverage was limited. The United States lacked the disposable income to pay for a new Marshall Plan. Then, too, many of the problems of the Latin American countries were due to mismanagement rooted in the local social structure. Reform would entail major dislocation. The oligarchies in power might not quite see Castro's threat the way the U.S. government did. Their instinct would be to tighten control. The Kennedy administration was arguing, against the oligarchies' common sense, that by giving up power to create a viable middle class they would be ensuring long-term stability.

In many cases problems were the immediate consequences of periodic crashes in commodity prices. For example, in 1962 the administration perceived that Brazil was in crisis, so badly that it might go Communist. The problem was mainly that coffee accounted for half of Brazilian exports.[26] There was no short-term solution; in the long term, Brazil had to find some way of diversifying its economy. Kennedy's central dilemma was that he wanted to promote change without obviously intervening in local internal affairs—a great sin of past administrations. The alliance would certainly support democratic regimes, but how would it deal with the coups endemic to Latin America? How would it deal with friendly dictators?

Kennedy demonstrated his sincerity by helping to oust the Trujillos after Rafael Trujillo, the dictator, was assassinated in May 1961. The Eisenhower administration already had imposed political and economic sanctions after Trujillo had tried to have the president of Venezuela assassinated. The CIA even had tried to help overthrow him.[27] To Kennedy, the Dominican Republic was the "show window" of the Alliance for Progress. Accordingly, he threatened sanctions and provided economic support to ensure that free elections were held in 1962.[28]

However, to many Latin Americans, U.S. acceptance of a 1962 Peruvian military coup, which overthrew a pro-U.S. regime, seemed to show that immediate security was more important than democracy.[29] In October 1963 Assistant Secretary of State Edwin Martin said that the administration had abandoned its attempt to promote democracy. It would oppose only those coups originating outside the hemisphere, i.e., Communist ones. In some cases only a coup could prevent a Communist takeover.[30] Latin Americans who had been struggling to keep their armies out of politics were outraged. President Kennedy soon said publicly that he remained opposed to governments imposed by coups.[31] However, Martin's statement probably better expressed the administration's ideas. It applied not only to Latin America but also to Vietnam, where for months the administration had been actively promoting a coup to topple President Ngo Dinh Diem.

In all, between March 1962 and June 1966 there were nine military coups in Latin America, eight of them against governments considered too weak to deal with local Communists or else, as in Brazil and the Dominican Republic, considered too leftist.

There was no question but that Latin America had been restive for years, with active Communist parties in every country. Nor was there any question but that Castro wanted to spread revolution. Like Tito, he considered it a duty rather than a choice.[32] For example, at the second conference of the Alliance for Progress (1962), both Colombia and Peru charged that Cubans were trying to subvert them. Ultimately neither Castro nor the non-Cuban Communists proved particularly effective. Because it exploded into a war involving large U.S. forces, in retrospect Southeast Asia seems more important than Latin America. Strategically, it was far less vital. But failure in Vietnam is far better remembered than success in Latin America.

In line with the newly perceived threat, U.S. military aid shifted towards counterinsurgency, including counterguerilla and civic action training.[33] To make that aid effective, Latin American governments had to be convinced to accept a military role in their internal security—which naturally could mean encouraging coups later on. The administration's ideas about the need for social transformation seeped into war colleges throughout Latin America.[34] A coup against a regime sliding to the left could be justified by an army bent on strengthening the social system and maintaining its democratic potential. In Cuba, Castro certainly had demonstrated that once a state went Communist any possibility of democratic development was over.

Brazil experienced just this sort of coup in 1964. It is interesting as a prelude to the military coup that overthrew Allende in Chile in 1973. Like several of its counterparts in the region, the Brazilian military thought of itself as the guarantor of a Brazilian democratic system; in 1954, it had thrown out populist nationalists (similar to the Argentine Perónists), who had had strong Communist connections. In 1961 Brazil had both a very high rate of growth and high inflation, as well as a large foreign debt. The new president, Janios Quadros, was expected to solve the country's very serious problems. His vice president, João Goulart, led the Brazilian Labor Party (PTB). He was considered a leftist radical, a protégé of the Vargas government, which had been thrown out in 1954. In August, Quadros suddenly resigned. He apparently expected that the Brazilian Congress and the military would ask him to stay in office, offering him the increased powers he sought, rather than accept Goulart.[35] Initially the Brazilian military announced that Goulart was unacceptable. However, a compromise was found: the constitution was changed, making Brazil a parliamentary democracy in which a prime minister took over many presidential powers.

Goulart was already well known for his associations with the Communists and for his anti-U.S. positions. The U.S. government was placed in a difficult position. If it provided new aid, it would be showing that it did not punish its enemies in the hemisphere. If it failed to go ahead with existing agreements, it would be supporting Communist propaganda, which already blamed the constitutional compromise on the United States.[36] Goulart was clearly unwilling to back the U.S. attempt to isolate Cuba diplomatically; in late 1961 he seemed increasingly Soviet-oriented. The U.S. ambassador reported that the Goulart government showed "Communist infiltration and influence exceed[ing] anything of the sort previously known in this country."[37] The United States funneled money to Goulart's opponents in the 1962 congressional elections.[38] In their wake Kennedy sent a counterinsurgency assessment team to Brazil. Ties to the Brazilian military were strengthened.

At this juncture came the Cuban Missile Crisis (see below). The Kennedy administration concluded that Cuba was much less of a threat. Indeed, it seems to have lost interest in the Alliance for Progress.[39]

Conversely, Brazil, the largest country in Latin America, was now much more important. In 1962–63 its economy was in crisis; inflation exceeded 50 percent a year. The problem was growth—exactly what the alliance had been designed to promote. In Brazil's case, headlong development had been paid for largely by loans. Development had not yet produced the sort of exports that might have paid them off. Goulart had to choose between shutting down growth (to cut his costs) and seeking more loans. Early in 1963 the U.S. government guessed that he could not get what he wanted. The result would be a crash, which he would blame on the United States and the West; Brazil would then adopt an ultra-leftist Soviet-oriented foreign policy. Probably Goulart's Soviet friends would be unable to provide the aid he needed; in the end he would have to impose an authoritarian regime—which the Brazilian military might oppose. At the very least Brazil would face a crisis within two years.[40]

It did not really matter that Goulart was outwardly friendly (and indeed had been supportive during the missile crisis).[41] The potential for crisis was too threatening. He would turn left, opening the way for something much worse. The Brazilian Left built up its own army as a screen against possible military intervention. It also tried to subvert the Brazilian army (for example, sergeants revolted in Brasília in 1963). Many Brazilian opposition leaders as well as military officers became convinced that Goulart was planning a leftist dictatorship. The U.S. ambassador reported that, given ongoing economic problems, there was "substantial imminent danger" of a Communist takeover. To avert it, Goulart had to be replaced. This was not too different from the U.S. reaction to Mossadegh a decade earlier.

Paradoxically, Kennedy's death increased U.S. interest in a coup, since his successor, Lyndon Johnson, had no use for the reform concepts inherent in the alliance. In March 1964 his new assistant secretary of state for Inter-American affairs, Thomas Mann, announced that he was interested mainly in economic growth and would not demand social reform.[42]

Liberals who considered they were defending the existing (1946) constitution designed the March 1964 coup.[43] They established an authoritarian state with ultraliberal (as opposed to socialist) economic policies. Ironically, the post-coup state dramatically expanded what amounted to state capitalism. That the liberals and the generals soon fell out did not change the reasoning that had produced the coup in the first place; Brazil became a formal dictatorship in 1968. However, given the nature of the coup, the military never quite eliminated elections. All emergency legislation was repealed in 1978.

As in Chile in 1973, the U.S. government clearly sympathized with the coup plotters. Certainly it quickly recognized the new Brazilian government. Moreover, reportedly the coup had been planned in close coordination with U.S. diplomats.[44]

At about the same time the Brazilian army overthrew Goulart, a Chilean Marxist, Salvador Allende, was running for president. The United States helped finance his opponent, who lost.[45] At this time Kennedy's counterinsurgency ideas were still very much in vogue in the United States, and social science was in fashion. This combination proved quite embarrassing. The U.S. Army let a contract for a study of what amounted to the stability of major Latin American armies, Project Camelot. In Chile, and probably elsewhere, many local academics contributed to the study, ignorant of its sponsor. It was, however, soon revealed.[46] This scandal reverberated in Chile when the United States was again accused of trying to tamper with the presidential electoral process (against Allende, again), in 1970.

Kennedy told his staff that the United States needed its own guerillas (Special Forces), who might take on the enemy directly at home, or who might train friendly local guerillas to do so. The Special Forces already existed, but Kennedy supported them enthusiastically. He made their green berets—their unofficial symbols—official. The regular U.S. military disliked such elite units; Kennedy thought it was uninterested in guerilla warfare, and created a special task force to develop an U.S. version of guerilla warfare.[47]

Kennedy's administration also created a new kind of U.S. military force, based on France's experience in Algeria. To make quick attacks on rebel hideouts in complex, almost roadless, terrain, the French needed the sort of mobility that only helicopters could provide. Helicopters also offered a degree of surprise which neither ground vehicles nor paratroops could match. It was possible to imagine a complete army division transformed, with helicopters to move troops and to provide fire support. The U.S. Army was fascinated.[48] The army and the marines already were using helicopters, but the French seemed to understand them in a new way— which offered, as it turned out, vital advantages. Helicopters would dominate U.S. tactics in Vietnam a few years later. The U.S. Army formed its first experimental Air Assault Division in February 1963.[49]

These new kinds of forces were particularly important in another area directly threatened by the Communists, Southeast Asia. In 1961 Vietnam was the only place in the world where the local Communists seemed to be using outside help (from North Vietnam) to overthrow a pro-Western government.[50] Like his predecessors, Kennedy argued that Vietnam was worth saving. A Communist victory there would encourage revolutionaries in much more vital countries in Southeast Asia: Burma, Malaya, Singapore, Thailand, and, above all, Indonesia, whose president, Sukarno, was already flirting with the Communists. A defeated South Vietnam would be a valuable sanctuary leading into Thailand, just as China had served Ho in 1949.

Gen. Edward G. Lansdale was the key U.S. expert on Vietnam. He had advised Ramón Magsaysay, who won the war against the Huk rebels in the Philippines, and in 1954–56 he was advisor (and friend) to Ngo Dinh Diem, the Vietnamese president. Lansdale helped arrange the 1954 exodus from North Vietnam, and he also helped Diem consolidate his power in the South. He probably was personally responsible for Kennedy's perception that success against the Communists demanded both armed intervention and nationbuilding. That matched well with the experience of Kennedy's older advisors, who had staved off Communist penetration of postwar Europe using a combination of NATO (military deterrence) and the Marshall Plan (nationbuilding).

Lansdale was the hero of an extremely influential novel, *The Ugly American;* Kennedy was one of six senators who signed a full page advertisement for it in *The New York Times*. The novel described how Communists in a thinly fictionalized Vietnam (a country called Sarkhan) constantly outwitted clumsy Americans. In Asia "we stand relatively mute, locked in the cities, misunderstanding the temper and needs of the Asians. . . . America [spends] vast sums where Russia expends far less and achieves far more. We have been losing—not only in Asia but everywhere." Lansdale also featured in Graham Greene's *The Quiet American,* as Alden Pyle, a naive U.S. official.

Through the spring of 1961, the situation in Laos, which Eisenhower had called the key to Vietnam, was desperate. Kennedy said that he could not bring sufficient strength to bear. Laos was too far from the sea and dominant U.S. naval forces. That the country bordered Thailand, a U.S. ally, seems to have been irrelevant to him. His administration had cut itself off from those who had built Thailand into Eisenhower's "hub." The Joint Chiefs told Kennedy to move in a large force of U.S. troops, but he distrusted them after the Bay of Pigs fiasco.[51]

To end the war, he had to bluff Khrushchev. Radio traffic was used to indicate that U.S. Marines boarding ship in Okinawa were headed for Laos. Kennedy was lucky; Khrushchev preferred Laotian neutrality to Chinese influence. Ho Chi Minh wanted to keep feeding the South Vietnamese rebellion via Laos, but he feared a U.S. presence. A May 1961 cease-fire divided the country into Pathet Lao and royalist areas. This was not quite what Kennedy had wanted. In their part of the country, the Pathet Lao kept the Ho Chi Minh Trail going, to feed the growing war in Vietnam. Kennedy protested, but he could only bluff.[52] In early May 1962, with North Vietnamese support, the Pathet Lao broke the cease-fire. Now they threatened the Thais, who accepted U.S. and SEATO forces, including contingents from Britain, Australia, and New Zealand.[53] Eisenhower's pact worked: if the Americans got Allied support, they could escalate the war. Khrushchev backed off, convincing the Pathet Lao to accept a cease-fire and a coalition government. However, the North Vietnamese had other ideas. They were determined to overrun South Vietnam, and for that they needed the trail through Laos. The Pathet Lao soon withdrew from the coalition.

To Kennedy, Laos had been a disaster largely because the Laotians lacked the stomach to fight. Surely the Catholic Vietnamese, with so much to lose if the Communists won, were much more willing to fight. Under the Geneva Accords, which had ended the Indochina War in 1954, foreign assistance to both North and South Vietnam was strictly limited; that was one reason Eisenhower had concentrated his efforts in Thailand. From 1959 on, the North Vietnamese were clearly violating the rules by helping their Communist brethren in the South. Kennedy began his own covert support of the U.S.-backed South Vietnamese government of Ngo Dinh Diem. Secretary of Defense Robert S. McNamara became the administration's point man for South Vietnam. He provided both arms and U.S. advisors to train and stiffen its troops, developing South Vietnamese Special Forces to take the fight to the North.

To Diem, Kennedy's pullback in Laos proved that he might just as easily sell out Vietnam. As a nationalist, he had always opposed the presence of foreign troops in his country. But his best guarantee of continued U.S. support was U.S. casualties. Therefore, in October 1961 Diem asked for U.S. troops.[54] The JCS proposed a 22,800-man SEATO force (including 13,200 Americans) specifically to cut the Ho Chi Minh Trail. If the North sent in regular troops, the total would rise to two hundred thousand (129,000 Americans); if the Chinese attacked, the SEATO force would rise to 350,000 (150,000 Americans). Tactical nuclear weapons might have to be used against China. In October 1961 the consensus was to send in ten thousand men; Kennedy preferred leveraged action by Special Forces.[55] Kennedy sent Gen. Maxwell Taylor, his military advisor, and Walt Rostow, his counterinsurgency man, to Vietnam. Probably prodded by Diem, Taylor told Kennedy that he doubted South Vietnam could hold on for three months without U.S. troops; eight thousand combat troops could be disguised as a civic action unit, to stiffen the South Vietnamese. Probably mindful of the JCS estimates, McNamara thought that ultimately as many as six divisions (205,000 men) might be needed. It was time to decide whether to commit the United States to the Vietnamese fight.[56] Kennedy had already lost in Cuba and in Laos. He would fight in South Vietnam, he said, because he could not handle three defeats in a single year. There he would at least have the advantages of access from the sea and of natives who were willing to fight.[57] He had already committed a few U.S. pilots to action, for covert reconnaissance flights called "Farmgate." By 1964 these aircraft were bombing the Ho Chi Minh Trail in Laos.[58] Thanks to Eisenhower's cuts, the army had so thin a strategic reserve that Kennedy did not have large numbers of combat troops to commit, whatever he wanted to do. He sent support troops, including, crucially, about three hundred U.S. Army helicopter pilots. They provided the South Vietnamese with such mobility that by mid-1963 they seemed to be winning their war.

As in Latin America, Kennedy's brand of antiguerilla warfare included social revolution—which Diem, quite understandably, resisted. He did not want to commit political suicide. He could always choose to eject the Americans, which he increasingly threatened to do as they applied more pressure for reforms. The only reason not to do so was that the alternative—defeat at the hands of the North Vietnamese and their guerilla allies—was worse. Kennedy did not realize that if he ever overthrew Diem, that act would make South Vietnam an American dependency, and bind the United States to the war there. He, too, was free to disengage only as long as he treated the South Vietnamese as independent.

Virtually all U.S. writers on Vietnam dwell on the corruption and incompetence of both the South Vietnamese government and its Army of the Republic of Viet Nam (ARVN). Bitter experience in both Vietnam and in China more than a decade before seemed to show that pro-U.S. regimes would inevitably be both corrupt and weaker than their Communist enemies. Somehow the North Vietnamese sustained a war effort despite gruesome casualties.[59] Somehow their soldiers continued to march down the Ho Chi Minh Trail in the face of enormous U.S. firepower. Stalin had evoked much the same sort of effort during World War II. What did the Communists have that the rest of the world lacked? This perception may be less meaningful than it seems; there is no recent example of a society that collapsed as a result of horrific human war losses. Americans ignored the lesson of the Chinese civil war, that soldiers often fought well, and that military disaster was usually the fault of their corrupt officers.

Overall the question was whether the Communists had somehow overcome the basic facts of human nature, such as greed and the desire for self-preservation, which seemed so unpleasantly evident in South Vietnam. Had they somehow built societies in which the whole really was more important than the individual, in which self-sacrifice was second nature? The Communists certainly talked about creating a new type of individual (the Soviets called him Soviet Man). The reality seems to have been that a ruthless police state can enforce a high degree of self-sacrifice, because the individual has little real alternative. As everywhere else, society operates on a mixture of idealism and self-interest. However, because a Communist society is so different from a Western one, at first blush it seems not to use self-interest. That is only an illusion.

The North Vietnamese certainly did benefit more from a very potent brand of Vietnamese nationalism, developed under decades of French rule. It certainly brought them valuable adherents in places their forces could not reach, such as cities and even the South Vietnamese army. Moreover, many South Vietnamese, unfamiliar with conditions in the North since the 1954 exodus, did not realize to what extent their economic self-interest lay with the U.S.-sponsored South Vietnamese regime. For most South Vietnamese, democracy seems to have been too abstract a virtue—until it was lost. Even so, vast numbers of South Vietnamese risked their lives to flee their supposed liberators from 1975 on, mostly as "boat people."

It was at least as important that the North Vietnamese showed a full understanding of how to exert social control through absolutely ruthless police power. Ho's first major exercise in that direction was the bloody suppression, by an army division, of a major peasant revolt which broke out on 2 November 1956 in his own home province, Nge An, a Communist bastion. The revolt was a reaction to a bloody "land reform" program begun in 1955, that is, as soon as Ho's power had been consolidated in the North.[60]

It seems naive to have seen South Vietnam and Nationalist China as uniquely corrupt. Government corruption in Third World countries is the visible end of the social contract through which their governments secure the loyalty of those who exercise power in the society. That is a universal fact of life. The details, however, can vary dramatically. In a conventional Third World country, power centers on local magnates, such as landowners, and on the army, which can overthrow the central government. The magnates are paid for their loyalty, sometimes by being given the right to tax or to steal. The government secures the magnates' acquiescence by distributing its favors (including permission to exploit the country) among them. Magnates in turn secure the support of lesser notables by paying them off. In effect all of this is a tax on the population, but it does not look like one.

Perhaps the central fact of life in such a country is that power is pyramided. Buying off a magnate insures that those under him will acquiesce. Because there are relatively few major magnates, the government can make deals among them. In the case of the army, buying the commander of a division buys the division.

An army coup is often a much more serious threat than foreign attack: the loyalty of the army is more important than its combat competence. Americans saw much the same factors at work in 1991 in Iraq; Saddam Hussein had destroyed all his most aggressive army commanders for fear that they would overthrow him. He had also created a separate army, the Republican Guards, specifically to protect his regime against his regular army.

American advisors often criticized the division protecting Saigon as weak and corrupt. They rarely appreciated why: the regime feared a coup by the divisional commander. Thus, like many other Third World armies, ARVN was heavily politicized. Officers, particularly senior ones, were loyal because they owed their positions not to their own competence but to the government's largesse. Americans were shocked that the best young ARVN officers were interested mainly in staff jobs, which offered political and hence financial rewards, rather than in combat. That should not have been a surprise; in most of the Third World, many officers join the army for its material rewards rather than out of patriotism. Having joined for material gain, they see no point in risking their lives.

By guaranteeing against a North Vietnamese victory, the U.S. presence encouraged continuing politicization and other forms of gross inefficiency. ARVN performance was important to the U.S. government because its failures might be symptomatic of future failures by other U.S.-sponsored Third World governments. Conversely, if ARVN could beat the North Vietnamese and the Viet Cong, then the United States might have a Cold War–winning formula. Curiously, something did work. When put to a real test at Tet in 1968, ARVN fought well.

In Vietnam the Communist troops were much more aggressive. The North Vietnamese enforcement system made it difficult for officers to evade field service or to protect themselves once they were there. The system worked because, as in other Communist states, power did not flow down in stages; the police and the army exercised it. The police could ensure obedience marching to the front in World War II, or down the Ho Chi Minh Trail in 1967. The Party's representatives—commissars and informers whose power cut across normal military lines of authority—guaranteed the army's loyalty, at least in theory. This system seemed honest because it was the government, not the policemen or soldiers, which seized virtually everything and redistributed it to supporters. In the Soviet Union and China, the system's reputation was maintained partly by carefully suppressing any account of the luxury with which senior officials had surrounded themselves. Poverty helps the state (i.e., the Party) maintain a monopoly on rewards. Even so, it is difficult for the small group at the top to control the greed of those in key positions further down.

Perhaps, then, it is fairer to say that corruption was better hidden in an impoverished Communist state, in which most people (like most in a non-Communist Third World state) could only hope for a better life, perhaps for their children. As these countries got richer, rewards had to be provided at lower and lower—and more visible—levels. Quite soon petty officials demanded either direct rewards or else the ability, as in the worst non-Communist systems, to squeeze rewards out of the population at large. That was very obvious both in the Soviet Union and in China.[61] Eventually Vietnam fell into the same category. It seems that the Communists' only real brake on corruption—idealism—did not survive the first generation of Communist rule.

The Communist system made for aggressiveness (to hold back might be considered treasonable) but also for stereotyped tactics and very high losses. It was also inefficient; all significant decisions had to be approved by politically reliable but often militarily ignorant commissars. This combination also makes for discontent among professional military officers, and thus probably cannot be sustained for very long. In 1966–68 the North Vietnamese army was still run by men who had fought with Ho from the first; they accepted Communist Party discipline. In two analogous cases, the Soviet Union and China, ultimately the Party had to agree to free the military from full control, in return for important political support. It was beginning to tread the same path of politicization that made other Third World armies inefficient.

Advanced Western-style societies are very different from both Third World systems because there are many centers of economic and, therefore, political power. Corruption is frowned upon because it makes the society less efficient. The government's end of the social contract is to guarantee the impartial rule of law, under which all of those individuals and companies can flourish. Until there are many individuals powerful enough to demand equal treatment, this kind of social contract has little meaning. Thus in East Asia the demand for democracy (i.e., for a Western-style social contract) went hand-in-hand with the economic growth which created large numbers of economically powerful people in each country. Favoritism was no longer particularly acceptable, and it carried real dangers—as the recent crashes in East Asia have demonstrated.

Thus it would seem that the ultimate answer to the social ills of South Vietnam, which were many, would have been the sort of development seen elsewhere in East Asia since the end of the war—which might well have happened, had South Vietnam not fallen in 1975. The region's history strongly suggests that social development is an inevitable consequence of economic development, but that it cannot be otherwise imposed.

Obviously this is an idealized picture. For example, in many American cities a single party maintained its power by catering to different groups, in much the same corrupt way that the South Vietnamese government worked. However, local government in the United States controls only a limited portion of the economy and the society. Enough depends on other levels of government for major companies and individuals to operate despite the local government's extortions.

Americans, who came from an advanced society, however imperfect, did not understand how Vietnamese society worked, or that it was typical of a Third World country. To the extent that they had worked abroad, their experience generally had been in Europe, in societies not too different from the United States. U.S. counter-insurgency strategists thought economic development would give the South Vietnamese population a stake in their country, and would motivate them to reject the Communists. However, prosperity would attack the social structure that supported the South Vietnamese government, since the locals would have a way to become prosperous without obeying the local magnates. Inevitably the South Vietnamese government resisted what the U.S. government saw as anticorruption or local development efforts. Kennedy's interest in revolutionary development implied a willingness to throw out the existing government if it failed to democratize Vietnamese society. In 1963 that sort of thinking led to American support for the coup that overthrew President Diem. But the problem was never one man; it was the country's social system—which affected all of Diem's successors.

In the 1980s these issues were revived. Dr. Jeane Kirkpatrick, who became President Reagan's UN ambassador, distinguished between authoritarian governments, like Diem's, and totalitarian ones, like the North Vietnamese or the Soviets.[62] An authoritarian government brooks no dissent, but it does not try to intrude into every area of economic or civic life. Ultimately it can evolve into democracy, because distributed economic power and independent social organizations eventually become alternate centers of political power. A totalitarian state understands that, and demands control of all aspects of every citizen's life. It cannot change without shattering. It is also inherently far more oppressive than even the worst authoritarian regime.

Neither type of government is democratic, but it can be argued that unless democracy is already deeply rooted only an authoritarian state can deal with a guerilla movement. Opening up such a state merely destroys the existing mechanism that fights the guerillas, without providing any substitute. Americans who drew no distinction between authoritarian and totalitarian systems condemned Diem as a straightforward dictator. They were shocked that he (and his successors) saw so little difference between Communist and non-Communist domestic opponents. In the U.S. view, the Communists were agents of a foreign power (North Vietnam), hence easily distinguishable from disaffected but anti-Communist South Vietnamese. Diem was probably wiser; many Vietnamese Communists were entirely homegrown. Diem had no reason to make a distinction, since his main goal was to keep himself in power, not to avoid a specifically Communist takeover.

With the helicopters in place, South Vietnamese fortunes seemed to improve. Overoptimistically, the U.S. mission in Saigon predicted that the war might largely be won in 1964. The last region, the Mekong Delta, would be cleared of rebels during 1965. On 4 April 1963 Robert G. K. Thompson, a guerilla warfare expert who headed the British Advisory Mission to Vietnam, suggested that if the South Vietnamese continued to succeed, an announcement, out of the blue, that the U.S. was withdrawing one thousand advisors would (1) show that it was winning, (2) deflate Communist claims that South Vietnam was an American satellite, and (3) reaffirm the honesty of U.S. intentions.[63]

The situation continued to seem good through most of 1963, perhaps largely because Diem and his friends were able to doctor the evidence. Kennedy's style of government hardly helped; a brief trip to South Vietnam by a few trusted advisors could hardly uncover what Diem did not want to show.[64]

Diem had problems other than the Communists. In mid-1963 Buddhists in South Vietnam began to agitate against him. He imprisoned many of them. The Buddhists knew that the Americans were watching; some of them publicly burned themselves to death in protest. To Washington, Diem was showing the unacceptable face of dictatorial power. Averell Harriman, undersecretary of state for political affairs, had Ambassador Lodge (in Saigon) encourage a coup; he demanded changed policies from the Vietnamese generals.[65] Kennedy suddenly discovered what tangled lines of authority meant. At Harriman's urging, two more junior officials, George Ball and Roger Hilsman, joined him in signing an approving cable *in the name of the secretary of state,* but without Rusk's approval.[66] In effect the anti-Diem faction within the U.S. government had taken over. To make matters worse, the Voice of America broadcast the contents of the cable.[67] Kennedy dithered, and the Vietnamese generals backed down, unconvinced that the United States was really supporting them. Kennedy ordered all coup cables destroyed, but he did not give up on the idea that a coup—leading to radical reform—would solve the Vietnamese problem.[68]

Coup talk continued in Saigon, where Diem considered the CIA responsible. Both McNamara and Secretary of State Rusk wondered whether the Viet Cong might not be the true winners in a coup. To find out, Gen. Victor Krulak, the JCS special counterinsurgency expert, was sent to Vietnam early in September, accompanied by Joseph Mendenhall of the State Department (who McNamara feared would simply push State's preference for a coup). As might have been expected, the two gave such divergent reports that Kennedy asked whether they had visited the same country.[69] Meanwhile, in Saigon, Ambassador Lodge continued to foment the coup that Harriman ardently backed in Washington.

McNamara and General Taylor returned from Vietnam on 2 October 1963 with an optimistic report.[70] The military situation now seemed so good that the Viet Cong could not possibly exploit the confusion of a coup. Moreover, Ambassador Lodge managed to convince McNamara that a coup was essential. The McNamara-Taylor report to Kennedy was full of information on prospects for a coup. The U.S. government adopted an explicit policy of letting coup plotters know that they would neither be thwarted nor denied assistance once they gained power.[71] Covertly, plotters were encouraged.

To continue pressuring Diem, Kennedy decided to withdraw a thousand advisors. The number was large enough to be noticeable but small enough not to affect the course of the war.[72] The announcement of withdrawal (possible, Kennedy said, because the war was going so well) was *also* the first public acknowledgement of the number of U.S. advisors in the country (16,370 as of 30 October), which was far above the 888 permitted by the 1954 Geneva accord.

This was hardly, as some have supposed, a decision to pull the United States out of the war. Kennedy's explicit interest in changing the Vietnamese government proves that he still hoped to win. Diem was the problem, and he had to go. There were dissenters; for example, at a 29 October 1963 NSC meeting Robert F. Kennedy argued against placing faith in an unknown replacement for Diem: "We do know Diem is a fighter who will go down fighting." By that time a coup could have been thwarted only by warning Diem, i.e., by betraying those whom the United States already was encouraging. If they won anyway, matters would be even worse. If they lost, Diem would surely blame the United States for the attempt. Probably the key argument within the U.S. government was that a coup being prepared in late October was the "best chance for success that we are likely to have."[73]

The coup went ahead; Diem and his very powerful brother-in-law, Ngo Dinh Nhu, were both killed. Kennedy was very upset to find blood on his hands, yet the United States was clearly responsible. It had made no effort to dissuade the plotters from killing the brothers, and on the day of the coup the acting CIA chief in Saigon said that it would take twenty-four hours for him to get an airplane to take them out of the country. That as good as guaranteed that they would be killed to preclude any rally around them.[74]

Probably the most important consequence of this American-sponsored coup was that it solidly committed the United States to Vietnam. That was the view expressed by Presidents Johnson and Nixon and by General Taylor.[75] There was no longer a way out. Thus, after President Kennedy was shot, his last Vietnam directive was superseded by the Johnson administration's first; it repeated the planned initial withdrawal, but included a paragraph calling for plans for different levels of possible increased U.S. activity.[76]

Kennedy himself had said several times late in 1963 that it was vital to stay the course in Vietnam. In an oral history, Robert F. Kennedy said that his late brother "felt that he had a strong, overwhelming reason for being in Vietnam" and that it was generally accepted that all of Southeast Asia would be lost if Vietnam was lost. His brother had never planned a withdrawal without victory. In fact Kennedy increased and never reduced the number of advisors.

Later, when the Vietnam War was going disastrously wrong, there were claims that Kennedy had planned to pull out after the 1964 election, even if that meant losing Vietnam. It has been argued that his public statements were all a smokescreen, and that Kennedy felt that he could not act freely until after he had been reelected in 1964.[77] This argument was made at a time when the Kennedy family and its supporters wanted to show that they were opposed to President Johnson's policy. Michael Forrestal, the NSC Vietnam specialist staffer, said that he had been told that an intensive review of Vietnam policy was needed, but Kennedy may well have wanted the staff to examine options to escalate the war.

In the aftermath of the coup, Washington learned that Diem had been deceiving the U.S.; the situation in Vietnam was much worse than had been imagined.[78] Existing programs would not save it. The troop withdrawal no longer made much sense.

In fact the coup made matters worse, in a way the United States government did not expect. The officers who overthrew Diem also removed most of those he had appointed, which meant most of the experienced province chiefs and senior military officers. That was inevitable in a politicized army, in which the posts all carried valuable patronage. Throughout the war, Americans frustrated with ARVN performance often argued that it should be transferred to American command. That was impossible, because it would have confirmed the Communist charge that the war was nothing more than an expression of U.S. colonialism.

The wars of national liberation were not Kennedy's only Communist problems. His habit of overdramatization and his ignorance of nuclear reality caused near-disaster, first in Berlin and then in Cuba. By 1961 Walter Ulbricht of East Germany really was facing a crisis. Due to its four-power status, a relic of the 1945 peace settlement, Berlin was the one gap in the wall that contained the East Germans. About four million East Germans left between 1948 and 1961, including the best engineers and technicians. By 1961 so many workers had left that the ratio of workers to children was only four to three, and only 45 percent of the East German population was male.[1] For example, an attempt to gain prestige by developing an East German airliner failed when too many of the engineers involved went West. In the spring of 1961 it seemed to Khrushchev that East Germany might collapse. A wag on Khrushchev's staff told him that soon the only one left in East Germany would be its unpopular ruler, Walter Ulbricht.[2]

The situation was aggravated by efforts to prop up the East German economy: Westerners were buying goods the Soviets were subsidizing, taking advantages of the low prices and the low exchange rate. Ulbricht demanded foodstuffs, such as butter, which was in short supply within the Soviet Union. Khrushchev refused to provide replacements for the fleeing East Germans: "We won the war; our workers will not clean your toilets."[3] However, Ulbricht knew that an East German collapse would be a disaster for Khrushchev, who badly wanted to announce some sort of victory at the Twenty-second Party Conference in October 1961.

Khrushchev tried once more to obtain a peace treaty, which would cut off West Berlin by ending its four-power status. In February 1961 he told the West Germans that a peace treaty must be concluded before their fall elections. As the crisis deepened, Kennedy met Khrushchev in Vienna on 4 June. Khrushchev demanded a settlement by December. After that the United States would have to fight for access to the city. That would mean nuclear war.[4] Unlike Eisenhower, Kennedy would not bet that Khrushchev did not consider Berlin worth that price.

Kennedy spoke to Khrushchev as though the two countries were at rough strategic parity. His words probably echoed his missile gap campaign rhetoric. Khrushchev was astounded. He knew Kennedy enjoyed crushing superiority. If Kennedy behaved so weakly when he held most of the cards, he would really become cooperative as Khrushchev's forces grew. It did not help when Kennedy spoke of Sino-Soviet forces to a man under attack for alienating the Chinese.[5] Kennedy had completely forgotten his recent briefings on the developing schism. To his advisors, Khrushchev stressed Kennedy's ignorance and narrowness; he could not match Eisenhower.

Khrushchev seems to have been little affected by what Westerners considered Kennedy's disastrously weak demeanor in the face of Khrushchev's threats and his self-confidence. Kennedy said that Khrushchev had "treated him like a little boy." He told *New York Times* reporter James Reston that the meeting with Khrushchev was the "worst thing in my life. He savaged me." Khrushchev knew that Kennedy was sensitive about wars of national liberation: he called them holy wars. He clearly felt he had won the summit; he was in very high spirits when he returned to Moscow.[6]

Thus Kennedy was partly defeated by a combination of poor U.S. intelligence (the JCS figures he got grossly overestimated Soviet forces) and by his continuing belief in a nonexistent missile gap.[7] Khrushchev managed to conceal his gross weakness from a very uncomfortable Kennedy. His bluff paid off; Kennedy emerged badly frightened. In much the same way he later justified his decision to fight in Vietnam, he told Fred Dutton, secretary of the cabinet, that he had to fight for Berlin; he could not tolerate a third defeat after the Bay of Pigs and Laos. Dutton translated: "It's more than the Cold War. It's saving Kennedy's presidency."[8] However, he must already have been nervous. Dean Acheson, a key advisor, argued that in the past Berlin had been protected by U.S. nuclear threats, but that in the wake of the summit they were no longer credible. He concluded that Kennedy ought to prepare for nuclear war.[9] Kennedy probably doubted that Berlin was worth that much.

A Berlin Task Force developed a contingency plan to send a force down the autobahn to the city. It would fight if necessary, even though it would be destroyed. Larger forces would then be drawn in. The Soviets had at least one spy on the task force; Khrushchev knew about the plan, and about its likely consequences.[10]

Khrushchev was more realistic than Kennedy was. He wanted a tactical victory, not nuclear chaos. If he signed the threatened separate treaty with the East Germans, Ulbricht was just foolish enough to try to throw the Westerners out of the city. Late in July Khrushchev decided to solve the problem by closing the border, despite physical and political problems raised by his German experts and by his ambassador to East Germany.[11] This should not have been a total surprise. As early as March, in a Top Secret eyes-only cable for the president and the secretary of state, Ambassador Llewellyn Thompson had predicted from Moscow that sooner or later the Soviets would seal off East Berlin to stop the flow of refugees. Thompson asked what the U.S. would do if the Soviets acted without disturbing Allied access.[12]

What happened next is puzzling. Probably Khrushchev managed to let Kennedy know what he intended to do. On 25 July Kennedy made a belligerent speech, almost threatening nuclear war—but he referred to West Berlin, rather than to Berlin itself. He seemed to imply that there would be no reaction as long as West Berlin was left undisturbed.[13] The speech can, therefore, be read as posturing, cloaking Kennedy's retreat. On a 30 July television show, moreover, Sen. William Fulbright, chairman of the Senate Foreign Relations Committee, in effect suggested that Khrushchev close off East Berlin. Kennedy remarked simply that the U.S. neither encouraged nor discouraged refugees, which was hardly the usual anti-Communist stance.[14]

Khrushchev had probably already made his decision. On 13 August the East Germans began to wall off East Berlin. Kennedy later admitted his relief; with the wall up, it was no longer nearly so urgent for Khrushchev to threaten West Berlin. His weak response probably encouraged Khrushchev to keep the threat of a separate peace treaty alive.

Probably in September, Kennedy learned that he might have a real window of opportunity. New studies confirmed that the Soviet early warning system had little chance of detecting low-flying bombers. A small force of twenty-one such aircraft might virtually disarm the Soviet Union by destroying forty-two key targets. Few civilians would be killed. The first bombs to go off would tell the Soviets they were under attack, but their ICBMs, at standby status, would take one to three hours (according to the JCS) to get to launch status—more than enough time for SAC bombers to destroy them. A surprise attack plan was prepared as a response to possible Soviet action over Berlin.[15]

In fact, after August, the crisis was an illusion. Khrushchev took until November to withdraw his December deadline for a settlement, but from his point of view the crisis had ended with his decision to build the wall and thus end Ulbricht's own problem. Berlin had never been worth dying for.

Meanwhile McNamara learned that NATO already had much of the nonnuclear capability Kennedy wanted, particularly since the Soviets were moving troops to the Chinese frontier in view of the continuing schism. He was surprised at the cool reception he received. The Europeans feared that if the wild Americans realized that the NATO army could stand off a Soviet attack, they might be encouraged to precipitate a war out of some random crisis like Berlin. There was no sign that the Kennedy administration understood the problem.

With the Berlin crisis still in bloom, Americans were surprised late in August 1961 when Khrushchev announced that he would resume atmospheric nuclear testing. He had agreed to a moratorium after discussions with Eisenhower in 1958. The 1961–62 series was unusually intense. Some Americans took it as a particularly nasty way for Khrushchev to apply pressure, comparable to the ICBM and Sputnik.

However, the new series seems more explicable in terms of the ongoing weapons program. To be producible and deployable, his new ICBMs had to be much lighter than the original missile, R-7 (SS-6). They could not throw heavy warheads, and initially that meant less powerful warheads. To develop a new lightweight warhead as powerful as the older, heavier one required a new series of tests. The Soviets also needed new warheads for a host of tactical weapons (developed for Khrushchev's military revolution) and for new antiballistic missile (ABM) weapons. Without testing, none could be fielded. Probably Khrushchev had not realized just how important testing would be when he negotiated the 1958 agreement.

There was certainly an element of propaganda. The 1958 moratorium had precluded tests of a new one-hundred-megaton bomb, by far the largest ever designed. Now Khrushchev ordered it exploded at reduced yield, fifty-eight megatons, which is still the most powerful in history. Khrushchev saw the bomb mainly as a propaganda device, to cow the West; American analysts suggested that it might destroy a target leaving minimal fallout (a high altitude blast would flatten an area without raising much dust). Very high yield bombs might create subtle nuclear effects and secondary thermal radiation. Multiple high-yield explosions might do disproportionate damage to a hardened target. Because the United States had never built as powerful a weapon, no hard data were available. An ICBM was designed to deliver it. Another new ICBM warhead (twenty-five megatons) also was tested.

Meanwhile, Khrushchev was getting some very depressing news. At a conference at Gagra in February 1962, he learned that the U.S. edge was likely to last a long time.[16] The new Soviet missile industry was finding it very difficult to produce key components like inertial guidance mechanisms. All of the ICBMs under production were affected.[17] Because the Soviets were fielding large numbers of MRBMs, the CIA missed the production problem with ICBMs, which required better subsystems.[18] Khrushchev had said that he needed hundreds of ICBMs; surely his command economy would soon provide them. Not understanding just how deep Soviet industrial poverty was, U.S. analysts tended to see apparent cuts as reflections of policies of restraint rather than as symptoms of brutal reality.

Khrushchev ordered a new generation of ICBMs in April. As a backup, he ordered a new submarine-launched missile, to be carried on board a submarine the West nicknamed "Yankee" because of its superficial resemblance to American Polaris submarines. This missile, an IRBM, could hit American targets because its submarine could take it into range. Unlike earlier Soviet submarine-borne weapons, it did not have to get so close that it risked detection by the increasingly effective U.S. underwater surveillance systems.

Through the spring of 1962, Kennedy seemed increasingly assertive. He rebuffed Khrushchev's offer of a nuclear test ban treaty despite a major concession, a limited number of on-site inspections (many fewer than Kennedy wanted). More likely Kennedy feared that signing a treaty would have political consequences at home; he could not seem soft with the fall 1962 congressional elections coming. In addition, Kennedy continued to threaten Castro's regime in Cuba. A defeat for Castro would be the first rollback of a Soviet-backed regime, and thus a very serious defeat for Khrushchev, and disastrous in the ongoing struggle with China.[19] Khrushchev seems to have guessed that Kennedy had finally awakened to his impotence. He did not realize just how obsessed Kennedy was with Castro.

Khrushchev badly needed an equalizer. His MRBMs and IRBMs worked, and his factories were turning them out at a satisfactory pace. Cuba offered him what Italy, Turkey, and the United Kingdom offered the United States: IRBM bases within range of the main enemy. Moreover, if the missiles were sold as a deterrent to U.S. invasion, they would bind Castro to Khrushchev. Khrushchev would later flit between the two explanations of his deployment, and would give different versions of its timing. Sometimes he said that he got the idea while walking on a Black Sea beach near Sofia. An aide pointed across the sea to Turkey, where U.S.-supplied Jupiters were emplaced. Khrushchev apparently broached the idea to his foreign minister, Gromyko, on the flight back to Moscow.[20] At about this time Khrushchev was told that the Soviets lagged so far behind the Americans in ICBMs that it might well take at least a decade to catch up. The idea was ratified unanimously at a 24 May 1962 Presidium meeting. The Cubans were told soon afterwards.[21]

Because Khrushchev feared that U.S. forces might abort the missile installation, Operation Anadyr (after a Polar air base) was conducted in secret. Ships carried missiles and other equipment below decks, with agricultural machinery visible topside. Their captains knew nothing until they opened their sealed orders at sea. Because Khrushchev feared that the Americans would find out and board the ships at sea, he ordered them fitted with antiaircraft guns. Captains were ordered to flood their holds (where the missiles were) if their ships were boarded.[22]

Veterans of the Kennedy administration have said that they would have found it difficult to oppose open Soviet deployment, given U.S. missile deployments in Britain, Italy, and Turkey.[23] Castro wanted open deployment, on the ground that Cuba had nothing to be ashamed of in accepting Soviet weapons. Khrushchev seems to have thought that the missiles would not be an effective deterrent unless they were kept secret until ready. His view was satirized in the movie *Doctor Strangelove,* in which the world is destroyed because the Soviets have built and started up—but not announced—a "doomsday machine" which will explode in the event of a U.S. attack.

In October 1962, as the missiles were being set up in Cuba, the Twenty-second Party Congress opened in Moscow, with Chinese Premier Chou En-lai in attendance. Chou obliquely criticized Soviet policy. He left before the end of the Congress, telling his Chinese colleagues that it had been "revisionist." The Chinese demonstrated their anger by refusing to accept delivery of Soviet and East European equipment already on order.

Word of the Soviet deployment began to leak. During the run-up to the November 1962 congressional elections, the Republicans adopted Kennedy's 1960 strategy. They charged that he was doing nothing about Soviet missiles going into Cuba. Kennedy vigorously denied the charge. He may have felt personally embarrassed—and endangered at the polls—when denial became impossible. He reacted violently. When the Soviets continued to deny that missiles were being deployed, he displayed U-2 photographs. Kennedy justified his angry reaction on the rather quaint basis that it was unacceptable to be lied to in the Oval Office. In fact the crisis presented him with an opportunity. He could now justify an invasion of Cuba, to wipe out the shame of the Bay of Pigs. Plans were drawn, but virtually at the last minute Kennedy drew back. He substituted a blockade. The situation recalled that in Berlin: Kennedy built up the crisis, then backed away as he was forced to confront the danger in which he had placed himself.

The solution seems to have come out of a chance conversation. Kennedy remarked that Khrushchev's deployment was as outrageous as if the United States had deployed missiles to Turkey. He was surprised to find that the United States already had missiles—the Jupiters—in that country. The previous year he had asked that they be withdrawn—and then had forgotten about the whole subject.[24] He offered Khrushchev a deal: he would withdraw the missiles from Turkey in return for withdrawal of the Soviet missiles and a pledge not to invade Cuba. To avoid the appearance of a sellout, Khrushchev agreed to allow Kennedy to delay the Turkish withdrawal for a few months. The agreement remained secret for many years because it was privately agreed between Kennedy and Khrushchev rather than between their governments.[25]

SACEUR, Gen. Lauris Norstad, pointed out that Kennedy was as much as admitting that his position on the Cuban missiles was weak. Moreover, it was a clear sellout of the Turks. To camouflage the deal, the administration pulled the analogous missiles out of Italy.[26] In his FY63 DoD Annual Report, McNamara falsely claimed that Britain, Italy, and Turkey had decided on their own to phase out the missiles.[27] The Turks did manage to extract a quid pro quo: nuclear-capable F-104G fighter-bombers as well as other military aid. Polaris submarine patrols in the Mediterranean were no substitute for seminational control of the Jupiters. The British had already agreed to give up their missiles, on the ground that they were obsolete; they could never be fired quickly enough in the event of an attack.[28]

Castro had been sold out. Soviet missiles supplied, in theory, to protect him from invasion had been quickly withdrawn in the face of U.S. threats, without any attempt to consult him. He was furious that virtually nothing had been extracted from the Americans: not recognition, not withdrawal from Guantánamo. The Soviets also had withdrawn the bombers they had offered, so Castro could not threaten the bases in Central America from which another attempt to unseat him could be mounted. For the moment, Castro's instinctive reaction was to befriend the Chinese, at the least to show how angry he was.[29] However, the Chinese could not supply the fuel and other goods on which he depended.

Castro was not the only one shocked by the Missile Crisis sellout. At the open-ing of the UN session in the fall of 1963, Romanian Foreign Minister Manescu pri-vately told U.S. Secretary of State Dean Rusk that his country had not been a party to Khrushchev's decision. His country would remain neutral in any future conflict so ignited, and he wanted U.S. assurances that it would not be struck due to any mistaken U.S. assumptions. He offered assurances, including an inspection, that there were no Soviet nuclear warheads on his soil. Romania had begun the with-drawal from the Warsaw Pact, which it announced in April 1964.[30]

Khrushchev seems to have been shocked to discover that Kennedy seemed will-ing to risk nuclear war to deal with the sort of threat he had been living with for years. In retrospect, it is difficult to understand why Soviet weapons in Cuba were worth a global war. Quite soon, Soviet submarine-launched missiles would impose much the same sort of threat. Kennedy seems not to have understood what was happening.

Both leaders spoke darkly of the imminence of global nuclear war; of how close the world had come to catastrophe. Probably it was in everyone's interest to laud the statesmanship shown at the time. To make communication easier, a special "hot line" was installed between the Kremlin and the White House. To avoid ambi-guities and translation errors, the line was a teleprinter, not a telephone. By all accounts it was almost never used.

Kennedy did not want to seem weak; his retreat (from a fairly absurd position) could be seen as strength only if the alternative were utter destruction. Later, when participants met to discuss the crisis, the Soviet Union was collapsing, and Mikhail Gorbachev badly wanted Western support. To insure that support, he emphasized the danger of nuclear miscalculation. He alone could make sure that no subordi-nate got the wrong ideas. It should not have been a surprise, then, that a senior Soviet officer said that those on the spot had had the authority to use the tactical nuclear weapons brought in to cover the Soviet missile installation. Later it became clear that the opposite had been the case, as many at the time had suspected. Khrushchev was daring, but he was hardly insane.

For Kennedy, even crushing strategic superiority had not been enough to encourage a U.S. nuclear attack. In October 1962 Khrushchev was thought to have fewer than fifty operational ICBM launchers (4 SS-6s, about forty SS-7s, plus per-haps half a dozen test launchers at Tyuratam). Actually he probably had only the four SS-6s plus at least one test missile at Tyuratam (fitted hurriedly with a nuclear warhead and programmed to hit New York). Unless these missiles were on alert, they could easily be destroyed by a relatively small surprise attack of the sort that had already been discussed during the Berlin crisis the previous year. Khrushchev also had about thirty submarine-launched cruise missiles and one hundred short-range submarine-launched ballistic missiles, few of which were at sea. During the crisis, few if any managed to reach stations off the U.S. coast. During the naval quarantine, the U.S. Navy forced six Soviet submarines, none of them missile-equipped, to surface. As for the shorter-range weapons aimed at Europe, given sluggish Soviet alert rates, NATO aircraft might well have been able to eliminate the threat. Kennedy never seems to have been tempted to try his luck. Like Eisenhower, he was probably a devotee of Murphy's Law.

Kennedy drew a rather egocentric lesson. He thought he had limited the risks of the crisis by his rigid control of U.S. forces. In future no low-level commander, misunderstanding the delicate shading of a White House decision, could be allowed to send a disastrously wrong signal to the other side. The national command had to be able to control local commanders on the scene, bypassing the usual military echelons.[31] The resulting national command system made practical the detailed (most would say, grossly intrusive) control the Johnson administration exercised over bombing in Vietnam.

There was an unexpected consequence. Beginning in 1968, the Soviets were able to read many U.S. military messages because of the treachery of the Walker spy ring. Codebreaking paid off because so much had to be transmitted back from field commands to Washington. The Soviets now enjoyed the sort of advantage the Allies had gained by breaking German and Japanese codes during World War II. Many operations in Vietnam failed to achieve surprise despite heavy security (for example, despite having been concealed from the South Vietnamese, who were always suspected of harboring North Vietnamese agents).

There seems to have been no U.S. suspicion that high-grade codes were being compromised. The Soviets seem to have used their information quite freely, in distinct contrast to Allied World War II practice, when it was feared that operating on the obvious basis of codebreaking information would have tipped off the Germans and the Japanese. U.S. suspicions were apparently raised only after the Walker ring was broken in 1985. Possibly few thought of code failures because the secret of World War II Allied success against the Germans had been kept so well.

On a less cosmic level, centralization badly hampered operations. Because so much had to be transmitted, traffic moved slowly. For example, in January 1969 slow communications made it impossible for anyone to react in time when the North Koreans seized the U.S. Navy intelligence ship *Pueblo* in international waters. Centralization encouraged the National Command Authority in Washington to micro-manage, for example by giving rudder orders to the Sixth Fleet during the October 1973 Middle East War. In a famous 1975 incident, the White House learned that the carrier *Constellation* had just arrived on station off Cambodia (as part of the reaction to the *Mayaguez* incident). Someone thought the reference was to a Constellation, a radar plane; the ship was told to "orbit at 35,000 feet."

Khrushchev drew the lesson that even the Third World could be a very dangerous place. Kennedy was unpredictable, but in the wake of the crisis he seemed friendly. Rapprochement was much safer than continued tension. That was not particularly good news for those, like the Vietnamese, who wanted his support for further revolutionary adventures.

Castro refused to accept this message; he continued to try to export his revolution. He extended support to guerillas trying to overthrow the Venezuelan government.[32] The democratic system, set up in 1958, was still weak, and the Venezuelan Communist Party disdained Soviet orders to refrain from revolution. After it failed to gain agreement on a popular front, it joined the guerillas in 1963. Had Castro succeeded, he would have gained access to Venezuelan oil and thus drastically reduced Soviet control. However, it seems more likely that he was acting out of revenge. In 1959 the Venezuelans had spurned Castro's request for $300 million in oil, which would have made him independent of the United States.[33] Castro's revenge attempt fizzled; the Venezuelans fought back and the local Communist party lost its backers.

More importantly, Castro and his close aide Ernesto "Che" Guevara publicized the idea that the rural-style Cuban revolution could easily be exported. That was not entirely popular in a Moscow which was still nervous after the Cuban Missile Crisis, but Cuba was not quite a satellite.[34] Thus the ELN movement, intended to use Guevara's tactics in Colombia, was founded in Cuba in 1963–64.[35] Neither it nor several other movements in Colombia, many inspired by Castro's success, was particularly successful.

By 1965, Castro was explicitly attacking the Soviet preference for peaceful change over armed revolution. Revolution was, he said, the only possible way to attack the entrenched social systems of Latin America. The soft urbanized Communist parties of the area were entirely incapable of rising to the occasion.[36] Castro threatened to make the Andes into a guerilla sanctuary like the one he had used in the Sierra Maestra mountains of Cuba.[37] There were no takers. In February 1965, however, Guevara visited central Africa and made initial contacts with several revolutionaries. This effort would bear fruit in the 1970s, as will be recounted later.

The U.S. government certainly was impressed, probably more than it should have been. It was sufficiently spooked to send troops into the Dominican Republic in April 1965 to put down a coup. The situation was ironic; the coup was intended to restore Juan Bosch, who had been elected in December 1962 (in the election Kennedy had insured) and deposed in September 1963. At that time, in accord with its new policy, the U.S. government had refused to intervene unless the country was threatened by a Communist coup. In 1965, as the pro-Bosch forces seemed to be winning, a junta of anti-Bosch colonels asked for U.S. help. In 1963 the U.S. government had considered Bosch a demagogue who might inadvertently open the country to a Communist takeover. In 1965, as the rebels won, the U.S. Embassy warned that "Castro-type elements" were involved. President Johnson became personally involved. The CIA identified efforts by three left-wing groups in Santo Domingo to bring in a Castroite government. Johnson ordered intervention specifically to preclude a Communist takeover, although publicly he emphasized the danger to American lives. The issue was not whether Bosch was a Communist; he was not. It was whether a coup mounted in his name would be used to bring in a

Communist-dominated popular front.[38] On that the evidence was murky. Johnson was well aware, from the beginning, that Latin American governments would see his intervention as a reversion to old and discredited patterns of U.S. behavior. Only very careful U.S. statesmanship, in which the Organization of American States (OAS) was brought into the situation, kept the Dominican operation from alienating many otherwise friendly Latin American governments. Bosch lost a 1966 election supervised by both the OAS and the United States.[39]

The second Cuban offensive was an attack on Bolivia, conceived during the 1966 Tricontinental Conference in Havana.[40] In October 1966 Guevara and fifteen followers went to Brazil, entering Bolivia that November. Advance men from Cuba had already contacted Bolivian dissidents and prospected for promising sites.[41] Guevara believed that his small force could be effective: Castro himself had won Cuba after starting from just such beginnings. The Cubans took the venture seriously; four of Guevara's comrades were members of their Central Committee.

The Soviets still espoused peaceful coexistence, and the Bolivian Communist Party was loyal to Moscow. It promised help, but did little.[42] Then, too, the area which Guevera hoped to make his sanctuary offered little cover and few of the local peasants spoke Spanish. Guevara's revolution never caught on, and his own carelessness betrayed him. He was run down and killed on 9 October 1967 by Bolivians trained by U.S. Special Forces, that is, by counterguerillas. Guevara's failure seems to have been symptomatic of a more general defeat of left-wing rural movements, which also fought in Peru and in Guatemala. Cubans were involved in both of those countries.

Because the CIA had missed Khrushchev's missile production problems, no one in the United States realized just how little strategic firepower Khrushchev had in 1962. The Cuban deployment thus elicited fanciful attempts at explanation. Americans imagined that they were attempts to supplement an already substantial force. For example, the Cuban missiles were interpreted as an attempt to threaten U.S. strategic command and control systems, the missile flight times being too short for the United States to react effectively.[43] There is no evidence of this sort of sophistication in Khrushchev's thinking.

Many have suggested that Khrushchev's fall began with his misadventure in Cuba. However, he had already committed so many deadly sins that Cuba is unlikely to have been a decisive disaster. He argued that he had achieved much of what he sought in the U.S. agreement never to invade Cuba. Foreign policy was brought up at the Presidium session which unseated Khrushchev, but not at the Central Committee plenum which explained that decision to senior Soviets.[44]

Too, many have traced the rise of a modern Soviet Navy to the humiliation wrought by the U.S. blockade of Cuba, the act that, in theory, drove the Soviets to withdraw their weapons. However, the missile-firing surface ships and attack submarines identified with this crisis in the West were, we now know, conceived before 1959 as part of a big 1959–65 shipbuilding plan which was not, in the event, fulfilled.

For Kennedy, the Cuban crisis confirmed that strategic war, not a Soviet invasion of Europe, was the central issue. The retreat from disaster in Cuba seemed to show that Khrushchev shared his desire for mutual survival. Remarkably unmindful of Khrushchev's continued support for wars of national liberation and indeed of the entire logic of Cold War, Kennedy became interested in ways of making nuclear weapons less dangerous. He and Khrushchev signed a Limited Test Ban Treaty with considerable fanfare in 1963. Nuclear explosions would no longer pollute the atmosphere or the seas or space. They would be confined to special tunnels dug deep underground, from which their debris was unlikely to spread.

To many Europeans this agreement seemed to demonstrate that the Cold War was over. Not only was further exertion unnecessary, but also to some it seemed that the United States and the Soviet Union were moving towards some sort of deal which might betray them. They had always feared that the superpowers might somehow agree to confine a fight to their own territory (Americans often said that in the event of war the Europeans would prefer to look up and see U.S. and Soviet rockets passing over them, to hit only the superpowers).

In their escalating campaign against Khrushchev, the Chinese charged sellout. They began to broadcast anti-Khrushchev propaganda into the Soviet Union. They also began to demand the return of territory seized by the czars over the past hundred years, including Khabarovsk and Vladivostok (under earlier "unequal treaties" the czars had taken Siberia itself). Trade between the two Communist superpowers effectively ceased. In the United States, President Kennedy called the widening schism a "great hope" for the United States. He was apparently unaware that, at least for the moment, its main effect was to reduce Khrushchev's ability to exert any sort of control—and therefore to make the world more, not less, dangerous.

A second consequence of the test ban was more technical. On 9 July 1962 the United States exploded its first and (due to the treaty) only nuclear weapon in space, 280 miles over the Pacific, near Hawaii. The islands experienced a massive power failure. Circuit breakers jumped. Telephones failed. It turned out that the radiation released by the bomb, hitting the atmosphere, caused what amounted to a massive electrical storm (electromagnetic pulse, EMP). The effect, or at least its magnitude, was unexpected. It was suddenly discovered that EMP could disable several important U.S. strategic missile warheads at ranges up to one thousand miles. EMP promised a new kind of nuclear warfare. A single bomb exploded at high altitude might knock out NATO's entire communications and warning system, without killing anyone.

With the Test Ban in place, EMP could never be fully tested again. It could be simulated, on a small scale, and devices could be placed in underground chambers to receive bomb blasts. It became the accepted wisdom that solid-state electronics was very vulnerable to EMP, whereas earlier vacuum-tube equipment would fare better. When a defector landed a Soviet MiG-25 in Japan in 1976, U.S. and Japanese experts found that its electronics relied heavily on tubes. They concluded that the Soviets took EMP very seriously. Whether it was because of EMP or for industrial reasons, the Soviets continued to make vacuum tubes long after the West abandoned them. (In an ironic twist, many Western music enthusiasts believed that tubes were much better than solid-state components in stereo systems. In the West the Soviet-supplied tubes they bought were advertised as "Commie virgins.") For years, U.S. experts thought the Soviets would begin a war with a big EMP attack, disabling U.S. command and control. EMP finally made it into the public eye in 1996, in the James Bond movie *Goldeneye;* the evil mastermind intended to use a nonnuclear EMP weapon to wipe out all of the computers of the City of London.

THE McNAMARA BROOM

Robert McNamara built the army President Kennedy wanted to use in the Third World. To pay for it, he reversed Eisenhower's priorities: the strategic nuclear forces were cut drastically. McNamara concealed his dramatic changes as attempts to enforce efficiency in defense. Like Eisenhower's secretary of defense, he came from the country's largest industrial sector, the automobile industry. Historians of the automobile industry later characterized him as part of a new generation of "whiz kids" concerned mainly with the bottom line. Totally uninterested in cars and their production, they brought in high profits but opened the way for the industry's collapse.[1] McNamara had an enormous appetite for statistics, but little concept of strategy or, indeed, of the other human factors which are often so critical in war.[2] He seems to have regarded crucial details as irrelevant; he was described as politically tone-deaf.[3] Nor did he seem to understand the wider political environment in which the Cold War was being fought.

Unfortunately McNamara enjoyed far more influence than Secretary of State Dean Rusk through the Kennedy and Johnson administrations. His annual posture statements, issued from January 1962 onwards, always included relevant statements on U.S. foreign policy. Since they appeared earlier than any State Department equivalent, McNamara in effect issued the definitive annual statement of U.S. foreign policy.[4] Because President Kennedy was uncomfortable with the Joint Chiefs he had inherited from Eisenhower, all of whom had held senior commands during World War II, he generally deferred to McNamara.

Given Kennedy's style of governance, McNamara could block any of the Joint Chiefs' advice from reaching the president. Kennedy valued quick responses to his questions, and McNamara collected a staff that could provide them. Editing draft papers became a "competitive sport" which McNamara, as well as his staff, played.[5] By way of contrast, the JCS was necessarily a consensus organization; papers had to be laboriously staffed before they could receive what amounted to collective approval.[6]

Even before the campaign, Kennedy and some of his key advisors were much impressed by *The Uncertain Trumpet*, an attack on the Eisenhower defense policy written by former Army Chief of Staff Gen. Maxwell Taylor. Taylor repeated his points when, in February 1960, he testified before Lyndon Johnson's Senate Preparedness Subcommittee. He was so forceful that Eisenhower considered reprimanding him, but did not do so for fear of creating a martyr.[7] Taylor apparently did not join the campaign, although he was impressed that another former army officer, Gen. James Gavin, became one of Kennedy's campaign advisors.[8] He was, however, apparently closely associated with Kennedy's inner circle. For example, when he suffered a car accident, Dean Acheson sent him a card (which referred to his Senate testimony).[9]

Clearly Kennedy was much impressed by both Taylor and Gavin.[10] In mid-January 1961 Taylor was offered the ambassadorship to France, which he turned down. This plum offer suggests a close relationship with Kennedy. Most importantly, Taylor had introduced Kennedy and his circle to the army's preferred strategy. At the outset of a crisis, a strong army would offer the administration an alternative to Eisenhower's nuclear option. Taylor and the strategists the army had supported appealed to the Democratic party national security advisors Kennedy inherited, such as Paul Nitze and Dean Acheson, who had espoused just such ideas during the Truman administration.

The new strategists drew a different conclusion from the observation, which the Eisenhower administration had accepted, that it was no longer possible to protect the United States by attacking Soviet strategic forces (and vice versa). Eisenhower had concentrated on the fact that the Soviet Union, too, was now so unacceptably vulnerable that war was very unlikely. The new strategists argued that Khrushchev might be willing to take chances.

It might still be possible to limit damage to the United States by controlling the escalation of a war, holding combat to the lowest possible level of violence. The army could, therefore, argue that it was extremely relevant to the nuclear world, even if it could not fight a successful nuclear battle. Eisenhower had laughed at such arguments, because they might convince an enemy that it was safe to fight, that the United States would avoid escalation.

The new academic strategists thought, moreover, that if nuclear war could not be avoided altogether, the United States could limit escalation by sending the Soviets a signal. It could deliberately limit its initial attack to Soviet military targets, trying not to kill too many Russians. The Soviets would have a clear incentive to practice similar restraint, because if they failed to do so the next U.S. strike (or strikes) would wipe out their population and industry. For example, in May 1962 McNamara described a 1966 war, in which an unrestrained Soviet attack would probably kill seventy-five million Americans and 115 million Europeans. An attack limited to military targets, however, would probably kill about twenty-five million people in the United States and another fifty million in Europe. A restrained U.S. attack would kill twenty-five million Soviet citizens; but a U.S. urban-industrial attack would kill at least one hundred million people. McNamara apparently missed what was obvious to Eisenhower, that few national leaders would find much difference between these horrific options.[11]

If military actions were messages, operations had to be very tightly controlled. The wrong message might have terrible consequences. The Kennedy administration would be particularly fond of a new history of the outbreak of World War I, Barbara Tuchman's *The Guns of August* (published in 1962), which described mechanical escalation to an unplanned catastrophe.[12] Eisenhower would have said that both sides' good sense made it unlikely that either would destroy the world because of some random incident. In 1914 no one had any idea of where escalation might lead, whereas in 1961 the prospect of nuclear destruction was very obvious to everyone.

Again and again in NSC meetings, Eisenhower said that a unit facing destruction should be free to use its tactical nuclear weapons. Fearing loss of control, the Kennedy administration wanted locks—permissive action links (PALs)—to prevent the unit from firing unless it had received specific permission to do so.[13] After the Cuban crisis, the administration offered PALs to the Soviets.[14] Without them, they could not, in theory, ever go on alert, for fear of unauthorized use—not so much against NATO, as against the Soviet government itself. Once the Soviets had PALs, they could place their strategic force on permanent alert. They could also deploy tactical weapons under far less settled conditions, for example in the somewhat restive countries of Eastern Europe. Neither consideration seems to have been high on Washington's list of concerns. As it happened, the Soviets did deploy armed ballistic missiles, but in Eastern Europe they demanded that all nuclear weapons remain under their own armed custody. PALs were not quite enough reassurance.

The new strategy applied to NATO, as laid out in NSAM (National Security Action Memorandum) 40, issued on 21 April 1961.[15] Nuclear war could be contained only if one actor (which clearly had to be the United States) controlled all the nuclear signals on each side. Independent Western nuclear arsenals, like Britain's, were anathema. To conceal that policy, Kennedy offered all the Europeans, including the British and the French, membership in a new Multi-Lateral Nuclear Force (MLF).[16] It would replace the existing NATO arsenal. All the members, including the United States, would have vetoes. The Europeans would have nuclear weapons, but the Americans would now hold the key. It was fairly obvious that MLF would never fight, since some country would always object.

Kennedy should have known how unacceptable this idea would be. The British believed their force gave them a voice in American decision making. Past experience had shown just how irresponsible the Americans could be. For de Gaulle, an independent nuclear force was an essential trapping of French power. He could not possibly give it up. Thus MLF never had much of a chance, but it took several years to die. Ironically, a form of MLF had been suggested late in the Eisenhower administration, but as a way of increasing NATO nuclear firepower.

The new administration espoused a concept it called Flexible Response. If the

Soviets attacked, they would be met with nonnuclear firepower. If they did not stop, NATO would fire a few nuclear weapons (the "shot across the bow") to illustrate how much worse things could become. If the Soviets failed to get that message, nuclear weapons would be used on a larger scale, but still within Europe. If NATO were still losing, in the words of a later NATO document, the Soviets would "pay the ultimate price": U.S. strategic weapons would destroy them. There was a certain illogic here. Until the final stage, NATO governments would suffer, but not the Soviets—only their satellites, which presumably they regarded as expendable. Moreover, both the Soviets *and* the Americans would pay the "ultimate price." Would the Americans really be willing to trade Washington for, say, Paris?

The theory, then, had real consequences. As Soviet strategic forces grew, Flexible Response became less and less credible, because the price the Americans, its ultimate guarantor, would have to pay rose. As their defense became less credible the NATO Europeans became more interested in whatever deals the Soviets might offer. As it happened, that development paralleled a palpable reduction in Cold War tension, which allowed the Europeans to think that deals were something better than simple appeasement.

Where Kennedy thought that a stiffer nonnuclear defense made everyone safer, to the Germans it merely encouraged the Soviets to believe that the consequences of invasion, at least at the outset, would be limited. The Europeans understood that as long as the NATO alliance credibly threatened the Soviets with nuclear disaster, the Soviets would not consider war worthwhile. They absolutely did not want to let the Americans withdraw their nuclear umbrella. Many of them suspected that the Kennedy administration had a secret agenda. It wanted to cut the nuclear risk to the United States. It would, however, be quite willing to fight a nonnuclear war—in Europe.

Moreover, signaling required of both sides an exquisitely tuned awareness of what was happening, in detail, in a very confused situation. Both sides would also have to be reading from the same book. Even two decades later it was by no means clear that the system then in place could clearly distinguish, for example, between a missile attack on the ICBMs in North Dakota and a strike designed to level Chicago. Yet the two strikes would have had vastly different strategic meanings. Nor does it seem that the Soviets ever had much interest in such niceties. Military actions, such as attacks, were just that, rather than messages in some larger game.

Much would be made of debates over the new nuclear strategy, and of the new administration's purchases of particular strategic weapons to implement it. In some very important ways, these issues were secondary. The main beneficiaries of the administration's defense policies were Gen. Maxwell Taylor—and the almost completely nonnuclear U.S. Army. Kennedy asked Taylor to come to Washington shortly after the Bay of Pigs, to help investigate the disaster. This project was extremely sensitive, since it might well have focussed on Kennedy's own responsibility; Taylor must have been very well trusted by this time. In this post he became friendly with Bobby Kennedy, and was offered the CIA directorship. Then there was interest in reviving the old post of military advisor to the president, held during World War II by Admiral Leahy—who was often referred to, incorrectly, as chairman of the Joint Chiefs (a post which did not yet exist). General Taylor was appointed to the new post of military representative to the president on 1 July 1961.[17] Taylor's was usually the only military voice Kennedy heard.[18] His style fitted well with Kennedy's—and, as it turned out, with McNamara's. Taylor flattered McNamara, telling him that throughout his term as army chief of staff he had yearned for just such a strong secretary of defense. Indirectly he sold both McNamara and Kennedy the new strategists' flexible response strategy. The key briefing is supposed to have been given in February 1961 by William W. Kaufmann of RAND, who (among others) had been developing this sort of strategy for years. However, McNamara was probably already familiar with the new ideas, since his 20 February 1961 notes on proposed changes to the FY61 and FY62 budgets already incorporated a good deal of the new strategy, in quite polished form.[19] Taylor was made chairman of the Joint Chiefs on 1 October 1962; his old post lapsed. He continued to cultivate McNamara, and continued to back the secretary in blocking JCS access to the president.[20]

Eisenhower had rejected U.S. Army modernization on the theory that a few divisions could hardly make much of a difference. However, during the Berlin crisis Dean Acheson found that NATO was much closer to a sufficient nonnuclear defense than had been imagined. A few U.S. divisions really might matter.[21] Many in NATO apparently already knew as much, but they had not said so; NATO governments were too prone to cut forces. Acheson's revelation was important because it justified the program Taylor had in mind, for a more powerful U.S. Army.

McNamara found that individual U.S. and NATO units were already far more powerful than their Soviet counterparts. He eventually estimated that a U.S. division was equivalent to 1.75 to 2.3 Soviet ones.[22] About 1965 it was typically assumed that one U.S. division equaled two Warsaw Pact divisions, and that one non-U.S. NATO division equaled 1.2 Warsaw Pact divisions. According to a secret June 1961 report, NATO would have to use nuclear weapons because it could not match Soviet numbers: on the Central Front twenty-two ready NATO divisions (equivalent to eighteen U.S. divisions) faced fifty to fifty-five Soviet divisions. However, if that really meant a ratio of thirty-six to fifty, then the situation was much less bleak—particularly since it was generally agreed that an attacker needed a three-to-one advantage over the defender.[23]

Eisenhower would have said ratios were irrelevant; given the terrible power of thermonuclear weapons, "any threat [in Europe] could safely be treated as bluff."[24] Stiffening conventional forces sent the wrong signal: something short of thermonuclear catastrophe was being contemplated. Nor had Eisenhower any interest in fighting World War II in Europe again. Neither Kennedy nor McNamara understood.

McNamara's analysis justified the bigger and more modern army Taylor wanted. The Berlin crisis provided the occasion. The three training divisions were made combat-ready and two National Guard divisions were mobilized (soon replaced by regular units), the army growing from eleven to sixteen combat divisions and from 860,000 to over one million personnel. All army divisions in Germany were mechanized. Symbolically, the weak garrison in Berlin was permanently reinforced to full combat strength. This sort of expansion was very expensive; in FY64 McNamara spent more than twice as much on army equipment as in the five years prior to the Kennedy administration.[25]

The growing U.S. Army was most useful outside Europe, in the Third World, which exercised Kennedy's imagination. The Berlin growth provided divisions that could be used anywhere in the world. They could not be based in Europe, given Truman's old pledge. They were five of the six divisions McNamara thought, in the fall of 1961, the United States might eventually need in Vietnam. Conversely, without the Berlin-driven growth, the army could not possibly have put large forces into that country. McNamara demonstrated, moreover, that he understood the connection. In October 1962 Secretary of the Army Cyrus Vance asked for an additional infantry division, which would be based in the Philippines, within easy range of Vietnam. McNamara used the money instead to establish an experimental air-mobile division—which would be even more useful in Vietnam.[26] Certainly there was much talk within the administration about limited wars in remote places. McNamara paid enormous attention to the need for more strategic mobility for the army—for aircraft to lift the troops and for fast ships for their heavy equipment.

McNamara probably understood that he could not sell Congress or the U.S. public an army intended to fight in the remote reaches of the Third World; it was much easier to base everything on the accepted need for NATO forces. NATO demanded heavy firepower. It can also be argued that the U.S. Army's new prosperity oriented it towards a firepower- and technology-intensive style of war and against Third World subtleties such as nation building and police-style counterinsurgency. The much leaner and poorer U.S. Army of the 1950s might have found itself forced to adopt tactics more like the ones the relatively impoverished British did in Malaya in the 1950s, perhaps with far better results.

The force already in NATO was becoming more and more expensive. The Kennedy administration convinced the Germans to buy U.S. equipment, including nuclear-capable missiles (a sale which, incidentally, undermined the administration's policy of turning the allies away from their nuclear emphasis). Unfortunately, that was not enough to pay for the U.S. troops. Yet the Europeans were very sensitive to any possibility that the United States might withdraw troops. For example, in the fall of 1961 McNamara came up with a plan to make it easier to reinforce the army in Europe. Heavy equipment would be stored there, packaged so that U.S. units whose men arrived by air could quickly form up.[27] To nervous Europeans, the idea was a way to withdraw troops (as many as five of the six divisions) from Europe without admitting as much; troops in the United States could, it would appear, very quickly return as needed.[28] Leaks of an October 1963 plan for major cuts in 1963–66 caused such an outcry that Kennedy had to promise to keep all six divisions in Europe as long as needed. A secret decision to withdraw the Berlin round-out units was rescinded within a week.

Although a Democrat, Kennedy had been raised to fear inflation; he was as much addicted to budget balancing as his predecessor. Kennedy's Council of Economic Advisors, led by Walter Heller, fought to wean him away from such ideas; a tax cut might cause a small deficit in the near term, but it would stimulate growth, which in turn would raise revenue. Kennedy had no idea what they meant. Fortunately for him, the buildup for the Berlin Crisis had much the effect his advisors sought, creating a small deficit.[29] Even so, Kennedy could not possibly have accepted a deficit large enough to fulfill all the promises he had made during the 1960 campaign. McNamara had to kill enough programs to make the books balance.

McNamara was very lucky; Eisenhower had enormously strengthened the Office of the Secretary of Defense, in a 1958 attempt to reduce interservice rivalry.[30] The significance of this Defense Reorganization Act had been hidden; Eisenhower's secretaries of defense had been wise enough not to intrude on service prerogatives. They worked for the most senior military man of all, who to some extent was his own secretary of defense. McNamara was different. As evidence of the shift, before 1962 the annual report of the Department of Defense consisted mainly of reports by the different service secretaries. Beginning in 1962, with McNamara firmly in power, the annual report was prepared entirely by his office. Instead of dividing forces by service, the report divided them by function—strategic, general purpose, and so on—the implication being that different services' contributions to each function were being integrated. Now the chain of command ran directly from the president through the secretary of defense to the unified commanders. The service chiefs lost their command status; the secretary now shared their role as military advisors to the president.

The obvious source of money was the air force, previously the richest of the services. In 1960 it was already feeling the pinch, having lost its initial battle for a new bomber, the B-70. Kennedy had promised not only the bomber but also to close the nonexistent missile gap. To break those promises, McNamara used a rationale, "system analysis." Alternative solutions for each military task were compared, and the most economical selected. Systems analysis seemed far more rational than the past practice of allowing each service to make its own choices based on the often unquantified judgement of senior officers. In fact it was a means of justifying decisions in ways the services could not easily challenge. Very few military systems were designed for sharply defined tasks. Their value often lay in their versatility, which was very difficult to quantify. McNamara seemed masterful at framing his systems analysis questions to elicit particular answers. He became famous for his arrogance and, later, for his disregard for the truth.[31]

Nor, it seems, did McNamara always understand what he said he wanted. For example, in line with the directive to strengthen the army, he wanted the air force to devote more effort to ground support. To force it to buy the appropriate aircraft, he contrasted its purchase of multipurpose fighters with the marines' use of special-purpose attack aircraft; he replaced the air force's F-105 with the marines' airplane. In reality neither service was buying close support aircraft; no such aircraft existed. The F-105 was a light nuclear bomber. The marines' alternative, developed with the navy, was the F4H (later F-4) Phantom—which was more general-purpose than the F-105. McNamara seems never to have understood; he used the incident as an example of his ability to force the services to be more logical.

Although weapon development could be costly, production was far worse. As a former Ford executive, McNamara was used to projecting costs. Henceforth no weapon system would go into full-scale development without a thorough analysis of its likely costs. McNamara's computer-based Programming, Planning, and Budgeting System (PPBS) became standard throughout the federal government in 1965.[32] Remarkably, time was not a parameter in choosing optimum programs.

The new strategy was McNamara's other key to evaluating programs. For bargaining to work, many U.S. strategic weapons had to be able to ride out a Soviet attack. Their command and control systems had to do much more than insure that forces got the order to fire during the first chaotic minutes of a Soviet attack. They had to endure so that subsequent strikes could be intelligently delivered. Decision-makers needed sufficient information to interpret the signal given by a Soviet strike. The strategy, moreover, had to be made public, as otherwise the Soviets might not realize what was intended. Hence McNamara's famous speech at Ann Arbor on 16 June 1962, which seemed to proclaim that in future the United States would concentrate on attacking Soviet forces rather than their cities (counterforce rather than countervalue).

In fact much was driven by the need to cut costs. McNamara could not afford to concentrate on Soviet strategic weapons (the Bravo, or blunting, targets of the past) because as the Soviets built up their missile force the number of such targets, already large, would explode. In 1962 strategic forces already consumed a third of the defense budget.[33] McNamara had to reverse course, concentrating on the much smaller number of Soviet cities, which was unlikely to grow; the 170 largest Soviet cities, the Delta targets, contained about 80 percent of the country's industrial floor space. There were then about 150 bomber bases (Bravo targets) plus about two hundred air defense targets that SAC had to destroy to hit the others. Yet it was expected that in 1965 the Soviets would have two hundred to five hundred missile silos (each a Bravo target), and perhaps as many as eleven hundred in 1967.[34]

He therefore announced that it was pointless to attack Soviet missiles at all; they would surely be launched before the bombers arrived.[35] Unknown to him, poor Soviet command and control (and the sheer clumsiness of the missiles) made just this mission quite feasible.

The services rejected McNamara's ideas as infeasible; the necessary technology simply did not yet exist. McNamara did not care.[36] The JCS agreed to develop a more flexible SIOP, which in the end offered five alternatives instead of Eisenhower's single all-out attack, ranging from a strike against Soviet strategic forces or Soviet tactical forces, up to an all-out attack. One of them seems to have been a preemptive attack. All were designed to minimize civilian casualties and civil destruction in allied and satellite countries. The president could withhold some attacks, for example against China and the satellites and against enemy governmental control centers. The other side had to be allowed to continue to make decisions during the protracted war.

Probably the most important fruit of McNamara's attempt to harden U.S. nuclear command and control was the Internet. He asked the Defense Department research arm, ARPA, for a command system so redundant that it could survive a nuclear attack. A network of computers, connected to each other by numerous separate phone lines, could automatically reconfigure to work around breaks in those lines. ARPA tested the concept in an ARPANET connecting its university consultants.[37]

The new strategy clearly favored survivable weapons: the planned Polaris force more than doubled (from nineteen to forty-one submarines) and Minuteman prospered (ultimately Eisenhower's eight hundred Minutemen grew to about one thousand, although the Air Force had wanted eighteen hundred more, plus three hundred mobile versions). Over the next two decades, the total number of Minutemen and submarine-launched ballistic missiles would change very little from those McNamara planned in 1961, although individual missiles would be replaced by far more capable ones. Having pulled far ahead of the Soviets, the United States in effect ceased adding to its strategic numbers. Instead, individual missiles were replaced by much more capable successors.

In theory, bombers, if they could survive Soviet air defenses, most closely met McNamara's needs. They were survivable, because they could be launched on warning, before Soviet missiles arrived. Yet they could still be held back to await confirmation that the warning had been real. Unlike existing missiles, they were flexible: their crews could be told to attack alternative targets. Moreover, a bomber crew could find a target that had not yet been accurately located—and few target locations were really known in presatellite days.

Yet McNamara disliked bombers, because they were expensive; a wing of B-52s armed with Skybolts (forty-five bombers, 180 missiles) cost as much as 250 Minuteman missiles or six Polaris submarines (ninety-six missiles). McNamara's real mandate was to cut strategic weapons costs. Solid-fuel missiles were cheap both to buy and to operate (they needed very little maintenance). McNamara quickly retired nearly all the expensive liquid-fuelled missiles, retaining only a few Titans for their ability to carry very heavy warheads.

Then it was time to kill the bombers. McNamara moved in stages. First he killed off the B-70, on the ground that it was less effective than a B-52 armed with Skybolt standoff missiles. This was disingenuous; McNamara had already been told that Skybolt was too difficult technically, that it deserved cancellation. With the B-70 dead, McNamara killed Skybolt—on the ground that it could not enter service much before the B-52 would have to be retired (in fact B-52s are still in service, almost four decades later). McNamara had no successor to the B-52 in mind; he simply assumed that it could be written off as soon as he had enough Minutemen.

The air force's friends in Congress added B-70 money despite McNamara's wishes. McNamara and Kennedy cited a tradition of executive refusals to spend some funds voted by Congress.[38] Congress won. This was much worse than Eisenhower had feared. Now Congress would be able to force the president to spend money as it wished. Not until 1997 would a president, in this case Bill Clinton, try to reverse the situation with a bill providing a line item veto, and even then the Supreme Court overturned it.

The death of Skybolt had important international implications. It would have insured the viability not only of U.S. heavy bombers but also of the British bomber force. The British read that cancellation as a direct attack on their independent deterrent—on British independence itself. They had already abandoned development of alternative missiles in its favor. The result was the opposite of what Kennedy wanted. He found himself offering the British a much more effective missile, Polaris, which they had sought for some years.

There was an unexpected Cold War consequence. Once the Royal Navy got Polaris, the Royal Air Force would lose its central deterrent role. At the same time the Royal Navy was planning a new class of aircraft carriers, which would provide the main British firepower in the increasingly unstable area "East of Suez." They were also justified as a mobile tactical force for NATO, on the theory that Soviet missiles could vaporize fixed air bases. They would take over the RAF's remaining tactical role. To pay for both carriers *and* strategic submarines, the British defense budget would have to squeeze down the RAF. In the subsequent fight, in 1965 the RAF convinced the British government to kill the carrier replacement program. Within two years the commitment east of Suez—which had become, if anything, more valuable to a U.S. government enmeshed in Vietnam—had to go.

McNamara's other target was the army's expensive ABM program. Like the B-70, Kennedy had supported it during the 1960 campaign. For several years McNamara stalled, saying again and again that he was on the point of authorizing production as soon as some problems were solved. Unlike the B-70, ABM was potentially a very hot political issue. It seemed to promise the American public protection from a mortal threat, Soviet missiles.

Inside the Defense Department, McNamara killed successive versions of the army missile with technical arguments. Thus late in 1963 he claimed that new studies showed that the defense would have to spend three dollars for every one the attacker spent. No one seems to have realized that, given the much smaller size of the Soviet economy, the United States might well have many more than three dollars for every one the Soviets had. Nor did anyone realize just how difficult missile production was proving for the Soviets. Each Soviet missile might well cost, in effect, three or four or more times what the United States would pay.[39]

McNamara also linked ABM with a truly unpopular subject, fallout shelters. Thinking about shelters implied that nuclear war was possible. Many found it better to imagine that its effects could never be alleviated, hence that it had to be avoided at all costs. Logically, shelters had to be associated with ABMs: fallout from enemy missiles exploding outside ABM range might kill many of those in cities downwind. Congress refused to approve a national shelter program, however.

Neither Kennedy nor his successor, Johnson, could afford to tell Americans that he had no interest in protecting them. The Soviets were developing their own ABM system. In 1966 the army convinced the JCS to recommend deployment of its new improved Spartan ABM system. Congress appropriated money for ABM production for the first time since 1959. Many in the Defense Department favored deployment. The Chinese demonstrated an IRBM; surely soon they would have an ICBM, too. Even if ABM could not protect against an all-out Soviet attack, it might still be quite useful.

McNamara still did not want to deploy an ABM. He found a new argument: it was in neither U.S. nor Soviet interests to deploy such a missile, since both sides would merely spend a bit more to overcome it. In January 1967 he asked President Johnson to authorize immediate negotiations with the Soviets to limit ABM deployments. Unknown to him, the Soviets were well aware of the severe limits (and high cost) of their new system.[40] McNamara thought the Soviets were already somewhat interested in banning ABM altogether and in limiting offensive forces. U.S. deployment could be a useful bargaining chip. In fact, however, the Soviets had a system in place.

By this time, moreover, a presidential election was approaching. How could Johnson, Kennedy's successor, face the electorate without any American ABM? Johnson offered McNamara a six-month deadline; without a Soviet response by mid-1967, he would order deployment. The topic was raised informally at the 23–25 June 1967 summit at Glassboro, New Jersey. Soviet President Kosygin later said that he could not understand why anyone would oppose defensive weapons.[41] Johnson ordered deployment.

McNamara was hardly the cool rationalist he claimed to be. He had vetoed ABM; he had hated it from the start; and he would not be thwarted. He tried to sabotage Johnson's decision by ordering protection only for ICBMs, not for the citizenry.[42] An entirely new system was needed, because at that point the army's ABM was designed for a very different mission. The interceptor had been designed to kill its targets at high altitude (to protect a soft city), whereas it was most economical to kill an incoming missile quite close to a hardened ICBM. Eventually a rationale was constructed for a light defense against a projected Chinese threat.[43] The twelve-site Sentinel system was announced on 18 September 1967. McNamara made it clear that he resented what he considered an essentially political choice by President Johnson (i.e., one that reversed him).

From a Cold War point of view, the main impact of ABM was indirect. Once the Soviets were working on ABMs, U.S. missiles had to be modified to overcome them. The obvious solution was decoys to accompany the warheads.[44] They had to be as far from the warhead as possible, so that one ABM could not destroy both decoys and warhead. In 1962–63 several U.S. designers proposed that the missile launch a powered post-boost vehicle or bus. As it maneuvered in space, it would throw its warhead plus decoys along separate paths. Additional warheads could be substituted for the decoys, and a powerful enough bus could throw them at several widely separated targets. The key was a computer to maneuver the bus.

This new MIRV (for multiple independently-targeted reentry vehicle) technique transformed the economics of ICBMs. Now they could easily swamp defenses. Each missile could destroy several enemy missiles in their silos. The services adopted different approaches. The air force placed three large warheads on each Minuteman III, the MIRVed version of that missile. The navy was satisfied with much smaller warheads, ten of which could fit on board a modified Polaris (called Poseidon, so that President Johnson could advertise it as a wholly new missile). The navy's logic was that, because the missile was not too accurate, it had always been aimed at soft targets; smaller warheads would be perfectly adequate. About half the Minutemen and three quarters of the submarine missiles were MIRVed. The balance between the two services' contribution to American strategic firepower tilted dramatically. After MIRVing, the navy had many more than twice as many ballistic missile warheads as the air force (the air force bombers made up some, but not too much, of the difference).

Nuclear strategists argued that once both sides MIRVed, either side could wipe out the other's ground-based missiles using only a fraction of its own; there seemed to be a tremendous incentive to strike first.[45] The reality was different. Several missiles had to be aimed at each target. They had to arrive in a very tight sequence. If they exploded at too short an interval, they might interfere with each other (fratricide). A missile passing through dust thrown up by earlier explosions might be destroyed. It might also be disabled by radiation or electromagnetic pulses produced by other missiles. There were other problems; without a large-scale test, no one could be sure that all of them had been solved. Overall, it was soon obvious that quite minor timing errors could totally upset an attack, leaving the attacker open to horrific return damage. Moreover, the first strike would deal with neither bombers nor submarines. Murphy's Law still reigned. No one would cheerfully gamble away his whole country on a coordinated missile strike which had never been practiced beforehand, using a technology which, however often tried out, was always tested in very artificial ways.

For Kennedy, Dean Acheson drew up a new European policy, which became the administration's Grand Design.[1] Its theme was European integration, both military and economic. Military integration meant the Multi-Lateral Nuclear Force (MLF) and the abandonment of the independent British and French nuclear forces. Economic integration meant weakening the Special Relationship between the U.S. and Britain and thus forcing the British into a closer relationship with the continental Europeans, who were forming the new European Economic Community (now the European Union). To reduce the cost of U.S. forces in Europe, the new policy included an attempt to lower tariffs so as to increase U.S. exports and thus improve the balance of trade.

Like Mao, de Gaulle deeply resented his junior position within his alliance, in this case NATO. France already dominated the new European Economic Community (in partnership with Germany); de Gaulle thought she should also run NATO. The new American policy was a prelude to withdrawal from Europe. A triumvirate that included France should replace the Special Relationship. De Gaulle had first floated this idea in 1958; it had always been rejected because it would have destroyed NATO. Now that he had the bomb (first tested in 1960), surely the Kennedy administration would provide him the sort of technical help the British already were getting. De Gaulle also wanted a veto over U.S. nuclear use; he mistakenly thought the British had one.

Kennedy refused de Gaulle, turning him into a ferocious enemy.[2] He decided that Kennedy's new strategy was proof that the United States would not risk Soviet nuclear retaliation over some European crisis.[3] The U.S. government did offer the French the same Polaris deal as the British (missiles but no warheads). Unfortunately, the French were so far behind in nuclear technology that they could not have supplied a warhead for such small missiles.[4]

In demanding more French authority, de Gaulle was actually making a subtler point, which had animated French strategists for some years. The front in Europe was the least likely to erupt; Kennedy's new policies were largely irrelevant. Eisenhower had understood as much when he gutted the U.S. Army. The Soviets needed some way to evade that stalemate. In places like Indochina and Algeria and the Congo they had found it. Thus in future the West would be defended, not so much in Europe, as outside, beyond NATO's writ.

Even with North Africa gone, France retained a massive African empire. Her colonies were nominally independent, but they retained very strong security and economic ties to France. Through the 1980s much of French strategy revolved around the need to support local regimes in places like Chad and Djibouti. French Foreign Legionnaires, for example, would support the Congolese (Zairean) government against a Cuban-backed 1978 invasion. They would defend Chad against a Soviet proxy, Colonel Qaddafi of Libya, in the 1980s.

Given these circumstances de Gaulle could reasonably equate his own situation outside NATO with Britain's. He therefore expected the Americans would give him special treatment. None of the other NATO members had any major territory outside NATO Europe. Kennedy's rejection was therefore more than a blow to de Gaulle's considerable pride; it was a tacit admission that the U.S. government had no idea whatever of the changing reality of world power. To de Gaulle, that realization must have been deeply unsettling.

De Gaulle's Cold War policy was largely dictated by his need to unite France in the aftermath of the Algerian defeat. De Gaulle decided to withdraw from what he considered an unwinnable war. The French elite forces felt that he had abandoned them even though they had won the revolution. The loyal Algerians with whom they had bonded all would be sacrificed; the Frenchmen living in Algeria would be sent, penniless, into exile. On 22 April 1961 three French parachute regiments staged a coup in Algiers.[5] De Gaulle managed to rally support; the coup collapsed. However, de Gaulle and his enemies in the OAS (Organisation Armée Secrète) then fought a subterranean battle for some time, so that France was substantially less stable than, say, Britain or Germany.

De Gaulle fixed on French nationalism to unite his country. An attack on NATO—a foreigners' alliance, which had not helped France in any of her desperate colonial wars—was made to order. Nuclear weapons offered the sort of independent power that de Gaulle so badly needed. Nothing else—certainly no subordinate role within NATO—could have been nearly as useful. De Gaulle set the standard French posture for the next three decades: any Soviet attack would be met with instant nuclear retaliation. Even a small French force could so damage the Soviet Union (mainly by wiping out Moscow and Leningrad) that the Soviets would not risk invading France. De Gaulle announced a deterrent for "*tous azimuts*" (all directions).

He had little alternative. Procurement had largely stopped during the Algerian War. After it ended, the French nuclear program consumed a fifth of the procurement budget (about half in 1968). These were much higher percentages than in Britain and the United States. A weak French economy could not provide a large enough defense budget; there just was not enough left over to equip the French mass army with modern weapons.[6] Moreover, in 1963 much of the French officer corps was disloyal due to the trauma of Algeria. The better equipped the mass army, the worse the threat it presented to de Gaulle himself. Because the nuclear force required few officers, its loyalty would not be a problem.

Weapons development and production was largely paid for by Third World customers.[7] The weapons were, therefore, shaped to the needs of those customers, rather than to those of a NATO war in Europe. The standard French tank of the 1960s, the AMX 30, was a case in point. Conceived as a fast tank destroyer for deserts, it lacked the heavy armor of main battle tanks designed for Europe. It could not keep out anything larger than a 20mm automatic cannon shell.

On the other hand, the French could reasonably claim that, in a nuclear Europe, ground combat was less than likely. This was much the view Eisenhower had taken—and Kennedy had rejected. A force armed with the sort of weapons Third World customers wanted probably would also be effective in combat against them. In this, de Gaulle's main frustration was probably that he had to spend far too much on a mass army he did not really need. The symbols of his—and France's—continued concentration on the Third World included a pair of expensive aircraft carriers, and the decision to replace them with nuclear-powered ships when they approached the ends of their lives in the 1990s. Similarly, from the late 1960s on the French navy paid much more attention than, say, the British, to the needs of power projection, such as shore bombardment and amphibious ships.

The Germans felt Kennedy had whipsawed them. Under Eisenhower's guidance, they had just decided to buy the second largest nuclear delivery capacity in Europe (using dual-key weapons), at a considerable domestic political cost. Now Kennedy was telling them, in effect, to cancel the order; but even they could not afford to buy enough new conventional weapons.[8]

De Gaulle saw an opportunity. In 1963 he offered the Germans a strategic partnership outside NATO. He may have seen the German army as a conventional shield for his evolving nuclear force. The French spread the rumor that U.S. proposals for the new flexible response strategy were part of a larger plan for U.S. withdrawal from the Continent.[9] De Gaulle's timing was bad; in past years, the Germans had depended much more on the relationship with France. They had needed French goodwill to convince other states in Europe to help defend Germany against the Soviets, rather than themselves against Germany. Now, however, well integrated into Europe, they refused de Gaulle's offer unless the Special Relationship remained within a NATO context.[10] For them, the U.S. presence in Europe still was the most valuable deterrent of all.

However, many Europeans were no longer sure that any deterrent was needed. By late 1963 it seemed that the Soviet military threat was in steep decline. Everywhere governments were feeling intense pressure to cut military spending.[11] Then, too, there was a real fear that Kennedy's close relationship with Khrushchev was undercutting the Europeans. De Gaulle's attacks continued. It was all Kennedy's successor, Lyndon Johnson, could do to keep the alliance from unraveling. Probably it was no accident that two NATO members, Greece and Turkey, came to blows in 1964 over Cyprus.

Thwarted by the Germans, de Gaulle resented NATO all the more. Under the NATO treaty, he could withdraw completely in 1969, on the treaty's twentieth anniversary. In April 1964 he announced that the French would drastically curtail involvement in NATO naval activities.[12] In June 1965 the French announced that they would offer specific proposals after their December 1965 presidential election. The other NATO governments soon decided that the alliance could survive even without French participation.[13]

Early in March 1966, de Gaulle announced that he would withdraw all French troops from NATO as of 1 July 1966. All foreign installations were to leave France as of the following April. They included the NATO headquarters, which had to move to Brussels.

However, de Gaulle did not abandon NATO altogether. He assured the NATO heads of state that, in the event of war, arrangements would be made for the cooperation of French forces (skeptics pointed out that a war might move much too fast for those forces to be effective).[14] Thus France withdrew from the alliance's military policy-making bodies, the Nuclear Planning Group and the Defense Planning Committee. However, she did continue to participate in its early warning system (NADGE), which helped insure the survival of her own deterrent force. On the other hand, France pulled out of the NATO-wide communications system, which she needed, mainly because it was called the NATO *Integrated* Communications System.[15] Nor did France participate in the NATO purchase of U.S.-built AWACS airborne radar aircraft. She did later buy similar aircraft, but because they were her own they could be dedicated to the Mediterranean mission, which the French considered more important. Two French divisions stayed in Germany. It was generally assumed that they would be available in the event of a deliberate attack, and that NATO troops would be able to retreat into France after absorbing a Soviet attack in Germany. There were no formal agreements on either point. However, there was still considerable informal cooperation; the French certainly were kept informed of changes in NATO war plans.

Even so, de Gaulle's departure drastically reduced NATO's strategic depth. When he came into office, Nixon realized as much; he tried hard to mend fences during his first year in office.[16]

PART FIVE

THE WEST ON THE DEFENSIVE

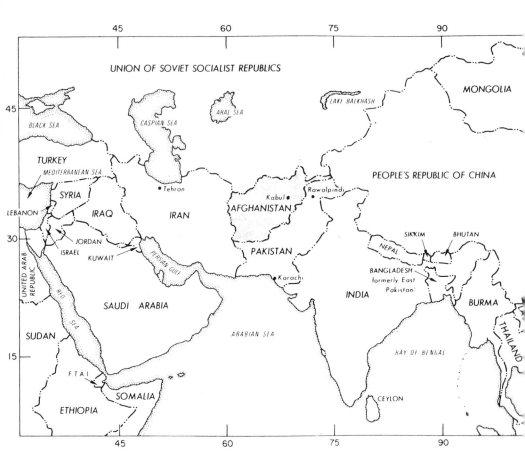

Afghanistan

Afghanistan was the Soviet Union's Vietnam: a war undertaken at the high point of national power, the failure of which helped dramatize deeper problems at home. Like the attack in Korea in 1950, the Soviet invasion of Afghanistan convinced many Americans that the Soviets were indeed on the march—ironically so, since the Afghan adventure was probably anything but intentional aggression. However, as this map shows, once Afghanistan was in Soviet hands the way would seem clear for the Soviets to realize the classic czarist ambition of reaching warm water, in this case the waters of the Arabian Sea and the Persian Gulf. It also seemed that the position in Afghanistan might be directed at a later takeover of oil-rich Iran. The fear that Soviet forces in Afghanistan would eventually march into Pakistan recalls the old British fear that the Russians would push through Afghanistan into India, the subject of the "great game" of the late nineteenth and early twentieth centuries.

Reprinted from Harvey H. Smith et al., coauthors, *Area Handbook for Afghanistan,* fourth edition (Washington, D.C.: Government Printing Office, 1973), page lvi.

27 THE BREZHNEV COUP

Khrushchev was Stalin's only real heir, the last Soviet ruler to enjoy what amounted to total power. He formulated military and economic policy, and he was able to make sure that those policies matched reasonably well. His ouster led inexorably to the economic imbalance that helped destroy the Soviet Union. Conversely, his attempts at control and balance infuriated all three key sectors of Soviet society: the Party, the industrial complex, and the military. The Secret Speech, bifurcation, and the thaw all attacked the basis of the Party's power. Crash programs and cancellations were deeply resented by the industrialists and factory managers. The Soviet military chafed at being relegated to almost a cosmetic role. The retreat from Cuba could be interpreted as a consequence of Khrushchev's all-nuclear strategy.

Khrushchev had, moreover, fallen victim to the classic Soviet sin, economic fraud. For example, he thought that he could release funds for development by reducing the unit costs of many of the weapons in production. These figures were meaningless because what counted were the resources and manpower needed to make a weapon. To make up for lower weapon prices, plants simply raised the prices of civilian goods they also were producing. The military burden did not change much, but it did become far less visible.

As with other Soviet leaders, Khrushchev's agricultural policy failed. He ordered Central Asian grasslands turned over to cereal crops, even shifting some aircraft production to provide the necessary transports and crop dusters. Unfortunately, topsoil and rain ran out. With food scarce, on 31 May 1962 he personally announced that prices would double, having courageously refused to let some subordinate do so for him. His reward was handbills calling for strikes in all the big cities. The KGB averted all but a 1–3 June strike in Novocherkassk. The strike spread; the local Party could not regain control. Khrushchev had to send in troops.

Similarly, Khrushchev's attempt to provide enough housing for Soviet urban citizens failed. People continued to live several families to an apartment. Privacy was almost unknown. Birth rates fell in the urbanized parts of the Soviet Union, such as Russia, Byelorussia, and the Ukraine. Only in rural areas, particularly in

Soviet Central Asia, did the birthrate remain high. In the 1970s and 1980s the demographic echoes of the purges and World War II were further exacerbated by these postwar failures. An increasingly sophisticated military machine had to make do with less and less sophisticated draftees from pre-industrial areas of Central Asia. Having entered the army with little love for the Great Russians who dominated their lands, the Central Asians found their feelings reinforced by what amounted to blatant racism. Moreover, the best of the draftees were siphoned off into the more technical branches of the service, the strategic rocket troops, the air forces, and the navy, leaving the army short of technicians and potential noncommissioned officers.[1]

The 1964 plot was possible because in 1957 Khrushchev had failed to kill the plotters he defeated.[2] Each of Khrushchev's three classes of victims was represented among the plotters who gathered at Stavropol in 1964: the Party, by Mikhail Suslov, its chief ideologist and kingmaker; the military-industrial complex by Leonid Brezhnev, the Party's industrialist; and the military by Marshal Malinovskiy, the minister of defense.[3] Suslov led the coup. Its organizers included Aleksandr Shelepin, whom Khrushchev had made head of the KGB in 1958 (its first from outside its ranks) and then deputy prime minister as head of the new Party-State Control Commission (overseeing police and legal agencies) in 1961. The plotters' host at Stavropol was Mikhail Gorbachev, later the last ruler of the Soviet Union. He was connected to the KGB, but was far too junior to serve as that service's representative to the plotters.

This was not the first threat to Khrushchev's power after 1957. On 4 May 1960, three days after the U-2 incident, Frol Kozlov, then considered Khrushchev's main rival, was made second secretary of the Central Committee (two of Khrushchev's men, including Brezhnev, were demoted). In February 1963 Khrushchev had to admit that consumer needs must surrender to defense needs, i.e., that his Seven Year Plan had failed. In March, he had to accept a new Supreme Economic Council, headed by D. F. Ustinov, a senior defense production expert unfriendly to Khrushchev. Fortunately for Khrushchev, Kozlov suffered a severe stroke in April. It took more than a year for Suslov to find another candidate.

Khrushchev announced a November 1964 Central Committee meeting at which many changes at the top would be announced; younger men suitable for the succession (such as Yuri Andropov) would be added. Senior Party positions would all be subject to term limits. The plotters had to act. As early as June or July of 1964, Brezhnev had explored the possibility of having Khrushchev assassinated or arrested. By the fall of 1964 Khrushchev could be blamed for popular unrest, as his many promises of more consumer goods had gone unmet.

Khrushchev was unseated by a vote of the Central Committee, which he had used to defeat the "anti-Party" group in 1957. The committee members tried to hobble any successor by permanently separating the positions of prime minister and first secretary. Thus on 16 October 1964 Khrushchev was replaced by Alexei

Kosygin (prime minister: head of the Council of Ministers) and by Leonid Brezhnev (general secretary, head of the Party). Kosygin was initially largely responsible for foreign policy and Brezhnev for domestic. Thus it was Kosygin who met President Johnson at Glassboro in 1967. Kosygin was also interested in the Soviet economy; beginning in March 1965, he embraced market reforms. That proved a great mistake; in 1968 Dubcek's Czech regime seemed to demonstrate just how dangerous such thinking was. Kosygin's star set, although in 1973 he was still important in Soviet foreign policy.[4]

Since the Party ran the country, Brezhnev was de facto head of the government. The plotters had been chosen him because he was so malleable; in the prewar Ukraine he was nicknamed "the ballerina" because he was "easy to turn."[5] Khrushchev had made Brezhnev chairman of the Presidium of the Supreme Soviet (i.e., titular head of state) in 1960. To Brezhnev, that made him Khrushchev's designated successor. However, in July 1964 Khrushchev asked Brezhnev to step down in favor of Mikoyan; that may have convinced him to join in the coup. Brezhnev may also have heard that Khrushchev had told his son that he lacked the strength of character to succeed him.[6]

Brezhnev's backers seem to have seen him as little more than a transitory figure. Aleksandr Shelepin ("Iron Shurkik"), chairman of the KGB and secretary of the Party's Central Committee under Khrushchev (and intimately involved in the plot) apparently expected to succeed him.[7] By the time of the coup, Shelepin had his people in both the KGB and the Interior Ministry (in effect, the domestic police), as well as in the army, the important departments of the Central Committee, and the Soviet media. Shelepin's confidence apparently alerted Brezhnev, who warned his own cronies that this strongman might well become a new Stalin. In 1965 he maneuvered Shelepin out of control of the Party cadres (which had been Stalin's road to power) and into the minor role of responsibility for food and for consumer goods. Brezhnev also managed to maneuver Kosygin out of power.[8] That had real consequences for the Soviet economy: Kosygin had championed economic reforms, which Brezhev rejected simply as a way of disposing of Kosygin's threat to his primacy. Typically Soviet leaders could adopt their victims' policies once the victims had been destroyed; but Kosygin managed to survive into Brezhnev's dotage, so he never could adopt the economic reforms.[9]

Brezhnev seems to have epitomized a successful Party bureaucrat (*apparatchik*), elbowing out of place all who might in future oppose him. In his emphasis on the use of the Party bureaucracy to gain and maintain power, he might be seen as a less sinister equivalent to Stalin, using the same political techniques Stalin used at first, without the accompanying paranoia.[10] Too, at first Brezhnev was quite modest about his ideological abilities, in marked contrast to Stalin's posturing. However, Brezhnev soon learned the value of a cult of personality, and through the 1970s he sought to create one, awarding himself numerous Soviet decorations. This effort coincided with the gradual rehabilitation of Stalin and with the adoption of some

Stalinist techniques, though not the kind of mass repression Stalin had so liked.[11] Instead of open repression, the practice grew, particularly after late 1968, of attacking anyone who attacked the new Stalinism, by firing them from jobs and expelling them from the Party. This was quite aside from the growing practice of throwing dissidents into psychiatric hospitals (rather than into prisons).[12] More generally, the bounds of legal expression contracted; as in Stalin's day, people learned that it was necessary to be very careful about what they said.[13]

As time passed, Brezhnev demanded primacy. For example, he was very unhappy that the UN invited heads of state to its twenty-fifth anniversary in 1971: although he was de facto head of state, Kosygin or Podgorny (president) would have gone. He became much more interested in foreign policy, particularly in the détente he built up with President Nixon from 1969 on. He was supreme by 1974, but at about the same time began a physical decline, becoming dependent on drugs. He edged out Podgorny in 1977 to become titular head of state; Kosygin retired in 1980.

Like all other major Soviet figures, Brezhnev had his own clique, the "Dnepropretovsk gang." It included Dmitri Ustinov, the military industrialist, and Konstantin U. Chernenko (later head of state). There were also important wartime associations. That was how Brezhnev had become friendly with Khrushchev. Both had worked with Adm. Sergei Gorshkov and with Gen. (later Marshal) A. A. Grechko (commander of Warsaw Pact forces from 1960 on). His association with Brezhnev explains why Gorshkov survived Khrushchev's fall and why, for the Soviet Navy, Brezhnev was far more generous than his predecessor. Chernenko became Brezhnev's personal assistant as head of the Party's General Department. In 1967 the defense minister, Marshal Malinovskiy, died. Brezhnev was not yet strong enough to move his own man, Ustinov, into that position. Instead, the next senior military officer, Marshal Grechko, was named (Ustinov succeeded him when he died in 1976).

Brezhnev's mandate was to end Khrushchev's excesses, which might more fairly have been described as attempts to direct and discipline the Soviet system (in effect, managers and other highly placed *apparatchiki*) without undue use of gulags and executions. The policy was inherently painful. Brezhnev would end the pain; he promised "stability of the cadres," which meant job security. Khrushchev's bifurcation was abandoned. Because the Party's strength was concentrated in the country's military-industrial sector, placating the Party meant removing any constraints on military production. Heavy defense spending was nothing new, but Brezhnev knew that he served, in effect, at the pleasure of his defense industry. He made no real attempt to control the direction or the quantity of defense spending.

The big ministries Khrushchev had broken up were restored.[14] Each was now powerful enough to resist any future attempt to reshape Soviet industry by creating new enterprises at the cost of existing ones. Brezhnev made what turned out to be a more devastating mistake. He failed to recognize that advancing computer technology was creating a new "revolution in military affairs." The Soviets did invest in military computers, but not on the immense scale on which Khrushchev had invested in missiles. To do so, Brezhnev would have had to raid the ministries—thereby infuriating the industrialists on whom he depended. The effect of this nondecision would not be felt until the 1980s, when the United States began to field weapons based, not on a few large computers, but on an emerging flood of microcomputers. By then the entire Soviet electronic industry was in trouble. For example, late in the 1970s new warships began to go to sea with empty platforms in place of many of their planned electronic systems. The ships would have been ineffective in wartime. That was a sign of larger problems: in the 1980s Ustinov had to cancel some programs as unaffordable.

The general staff's reward was to be freed of serious political interference.[15] It was free to plan for war and to raise the forces needed to fight and win, without any sense of limited resources. No one challenged it; Khrushchev's talk of the devastating consequences of nuclear explosions was abandoned. Soviet spokesmen went so far as to claim, after Chernobyl, that they had never before taken into account delayed nuclear effects such as fallout.

Crucially, Brezhnev had no intention of abandoning the power to decide war or peace. His Politburo controlled most military operations, and certainly those involving weapons of mass destruction.[16] Brezhnev seems to have been altogether unaware of the effects of the general staff's new nuclear belligerency on the West. Westerners assumed that he had to know exactly what he was doing, as he prated about peace and détente while his military industry cranked out more and more terrifying weapons, in seemingly endless quantities. Was he reflecting chronic Russian insecurity, simply buying insurance? Or was he buying what it would take, one day, to fight and win a nuclear war? Now it seems that Brezhnev simply found it easiest to go along with his marshals and his industrialists, buying whatever they wanted and enjoying the influence that powerful military forces inevitably bought. There was no particularly good reason *not* to do so. Unlike Stalin and Khrushchev, Brezhnev was simply uninterested in the details of war planning. He could, therefore, talk détente with apparent sincerity while his general staff developed ferocious war plans—which could be unleashed only on his approval.

Brezhnev ended the domestic thaw, which had caused the Party's authority so much damage. Stalin was not formally rehabilitated, but there were sly hints that he had been unjustly attacked, and his "positive parts" were extolled.[17] However, Stalin could not quite be restored to his former status; it proved impossible to restore the name of Stalingrad. Brezhnev's attempt to create his own cult of personality suffered both from the population's increasing cynicism and from television coverage that demonstrated his declining capabilities.

Those who had spoken out under Khrushchev, such as Aleksandr Solzhenitsyn, came under attack.[18] However, Stalin's techniques could not be revived; now the police harassed only chosen individuals. An American State Department observer saw Brezhnev's crackdown as part of a sort of sclerosis, an inability by an elderly ruling group to provide novel solutions or to react to novel situations. Contact with the outside world, which Russian rulers historically considered threatening, was largely shut down, to the extent that direct-dial telephoning was nearly abolished and it became impossible to send packages to Soviet citizens.[19] There was one particularly shocking example of dissent: in January 1969 2d Lt. Viktor Ivanovich Ilyin tried to shoot Brezhnev as he left the Kremlin in a motorcade. He failed, but it was considered "inexpedient" to put him on trial, so he was locked up in psychiatric institutions.[20]

The new repression was somewhat affected by Western radios. Jamming had been reduced drastically in 1963, as Khrushchev sought détente with the United States. In February 1966 the Soviets put Andrei Sinyavsky and Yuli Daniel on trial for sending their works abroad for publication. Their supporters soon discovered that by giving Western reporters news of the trials they could insure that Western radio stations broadcast this information back into the Soviet Union. The dissidents soon realized that they could spread their ideas effectively despite Soviet censorship. This was quite apart from attempts to generate pressure in the West to reduce the scale of repression within the Soviet Union.[21]

China was Brezhnev's great foreign policy disaster. Mao's scientists exploded his first atomic bomb about when Khrushchev fell. Fortunately for Mao, he got his bomb not long after the U.S. government realized how deep the Sino-Soviet split actually was, hence how little the Sino-Soviet treaty still counted. With a bomb in hand, Mao had his own deterrent. He no longer had to tolerate a professional military high command or, indeed, specialists in charge of producing military equipment. Chinese embassies showed a movie about the threat of nuclear war. It began with mice in a cage. A nuclear explosion was shown; the cage was shattered. The message: Nuclear war would set people free by destroying imperialism. Not everyone agreed. In 1965 the PLA's chief of staff, Marshal Lo Ruiqing, argued that China had to mend fences with the Soviets to gain both technology and time in which to develop nuclear forces. Mao disagreed violently; politics was everything. He had, after all, beaten a well-equipped Chiang Kai-shek, starting with nothing but enthusiastic peasants.

Brezhnev clearly hoped that his new regime, which was much closer to Stalinist lines, would be more attractive to the Chinese. They were interested. In November 1964, shortly after Brezhnev's coup, they sent a delegation headed by Chou En-lai to the annual celebration of the Russian Revolution. They demanded that the Soviets admit that they had been wrong throughout the 1960–64 dispute; Soviet foreign and other policies should be reversed. This was far too much. Soon the Chinese press would call the new Soviet leaders "Khrushchevians without Khrushchev" and worse.[22] When war broke out in Vietnam, the Chinese initially refused to coordinate their aid with that of the Soviets. An 11 November 1965 editorial in the official *People's Daily* announced that the two governing parties had nothing in common except for their mutual opposition. The "chief task" of the Chinese Party was now to mark itself off from the Soviet Party. The Soviets symbolized economic development conducted by experts, rather than by Mao's politically motivated peasants.

The Sino-Soviet split made the war in Vietnam possible. In 1964, when the North Vietnamese first sent regular troops south, they feared that the United States would retaliate. A supply of Soviet air defense weapons became a prerequisite for war. The Soviets valued détente. They also remembered the violent, apparently irrational, U.S. reaction to their missile deployment in Cuba. Any crisis might explode. Despite lengthy entreaties in January–February 1964, they turned the North Vietnamese down.[1] The North Vietnamese found that the Chinese would support them as long as they tilted towards China within the larger world Communist movement.[2] In the summer of 1964 the Chinese offered a billion yuan if Hanoi agreed to reject any further assistance by the Soviets (the North Vietnamese refused).[3] Parroting the Chinese, the North Vietnamese accused the Soviets of "revisionism."[4] The Soviets withdrew their ambassador from Hanoi during the spring of 1964 (he was absent during the Tonkin Gulf incident). In November 1964 the North Vietnamese ejected Soviet military advisors.[5]

By 1965 the Vietnamese were skillfully playing off the two Communist superpowers. The Soviets found themselves supplying the wherewithal for war without enjoying very much power over its course. Americans who did not understand the depth and the meaning of the schism were surprised that the Soviets could not be convinced to turn off the arms spigot and thus to end the war.

The Chinese saw the war as a valuable opportunity. In August 1965 Mao told his Politburo that it was necessary to seize Southeast Asia—including South Vietnam, Thailand, Burma, Malaysia, and Singapore—in order to gain sufficient strength to face down the Soviets. The Chinese had recently formed "national liberation fronts" in Thailand and Malaysia; in January 1965 they openly declared "Thailand is next."[6] Later, when they had fallen out with the Chinese, the North Vietnamese charged that the Chinese wanted to protract the war because as long as it continued they could present themselves to revolutionaries in Asia, Africa, and Latin America as the champions of an active revolution. They also claimed that the

Chinese saw the war as a valuable opportunity to sap Vietnamese strength, given their "thousand-year enmity."[7]

As President Johnson entered office late in 1963, the situation in South Vietnam was deteriorating rapidly, partly due to the effects of the recent coup against Diem, and hence the removal of his experienced subordinates. Meanwhile radio intercepts made it quite clear that, despite their denials, the North Vietnamese controlled the Viet Cong fighting in the South, even though Viet Cong personnel were South Vietnamese. It might, then, be possible to solve the South Vietnamese problem by discouraging the North Vietnamese. Moreover, the North Vietnamese had painstakingly built up their fledgling industry. In February 1964 Walt W. Rostow, chairman of the State Department Policy Planning Council (i.e., heir to Kennan and Nitze, and the main U.S. counterinsurgency strategist) pointed out that surely they could not ignore a mortal threat to it. This approach was far more attractive than risking large numbers of American troops in a frustrating ground war.[8] Johnson added another element, a carrot: economic assistance. A seasoned politician, he was used to bargaining.

Moreover, Johnson saw the developing war in Vietnam as a distraction. He was far more interested in reviving and extending President Roosevelt's social revolution. To do that, he needed the support of social conservatives, who would vote for Johnson's Great Society programs only if he continued to fight the Communists abroad. Moreover, the Great Society was expensive. Whatever he did in Vietnam, Johnson had to limit its financial cost. At the outset, Johnson also was faced with the 1964 presidential campaign. Kennedy had seen a threat from the hawks: he could not seem too soft. Johnson was a much more instinctive politician than Kennedy had been. He sensed that the American public, having tasted real danger in the Cuban Missile Crisis, was not in a very hawkish mood. He therefore had to emphasize his own moderation, compared to the hawkishness of his Republican challenger, Barry Goldwater—who was much more extreme than Nixon would have been.

Thus, like Kennedy, Johnson had, at least at first, to fight a covert war. With only limited interest in military affairs, he deferred to McNamara, to a far greater extent even than had Kennedy.[9] McNamara in turn kept the Joint Chiefs at arm's length. Inevitably the new strategists' ideas of gradual escalation, developed to deal with the threat of nuclear annihilation, dominated the administration.[10] The Joint Chiefs were unable to present Johnson with the traditional military wisdom: a quick sharp overwhelming attack is much more likely to end a war. With each turn of gradual escalation, the North Vietnamese and their Viet Cong allies found they could adjust. It would have taken bigger and bigger shocks to shatter them. Only after McNamara was gone did Gen. Earle Wheeler, the chairman of the JCS, attend the president's Tuesday lunches, where Vietnam policy was discussed and made. By that time the cost of any sharp escalation massive enough to matter was far too high for Johnson to contemplate.

As before, Maxwell Taylor was an important factor. In 1963 Johnson made a Republican, Henry Cabot Lodge, ambassador to South Vietnam, to insure bipartisan support for his policy. However, Lodge wanted to run for president in 1964. Maxwell Taylor replaced him. Taylor clearly saw himself as the key figure in saving South Vietnam; he wanted full authority to run the war from Saigon. That was never forthcoming, and Lodge returned to the ambassadorship in 1965.

Unfortunately, for the North Vietnamese the fight for reunification was their justification for maintaining power. The human or industrial cost of the war was irrelevant, so long as it did not break their grip on power in the North. Conversely, the North Vietnamese could not imagine that the United States would fight for territory of little or no inherent value. They were right: South Vietnam itself did not matter. What mattered was the likely effect of its fall on other governments in the region. For example, in a June 1964 National Intelligence Estimate (NIE) the CIA predicted that, except for Cambodia, all of Southeast Asia would probably quickly fall if the Communists won in South Vietnam and Laos. Moreover, Chinese prestige in the world Communist movement would rise at the expense of the more moderate Soviet Union. This was the famous "domino theory."[11] The following March, when the cost of U.S. intervention had risen dramatically, McNamara's assistant secretary for international security affairs, John McNaughton, wrote that 70 percent of the U.S. aim in Vietnam was to avoid a humiliating defeat (which would cause other governments under U.S. guarantee to fall, i.e., to become dominoes).[12]

This perception was widely shared in Asia: several times during the war, Lee Kwan Yew, prime minister of Singapore, emphasized the importance of the U.S. effort in preventing a Communist sweep in Asia. Australia, New Zealand, the Philippines, South Korea, and Thailand all supplied troops. With two divisions and a marine brigade, South Korea provided the largest expeditionary force after that of the United States.[13] Thailand allowed free use of air bases despite Chinese threats of insurgency. This coalition aspect was never much emphasized, perhaps because too many, both in the United States and Europe, found it difficult to distinguish between different Asian armies, friendly and enemy. Had the war turned out better, it might have cemented SEATO into a strong alliance reminiscent of NATO in its better days.

The U.S. hope was always that if the North Vietnamese attack could be contained long enough, the people of the South could build up enough of a stake in its survival to want to stand up to, and ultimately defeat, subversion. It is often argued that this strategy was ultimately pointless, since populations north and south shared a common nationalism. Certainly the central role of nationalism seems to have escaped the successive Kennedy, Johnson, and Nixon administrations. The Korean situation was somewhat similar, yet ultimately South Korea was certainly strong enough to stand up to the North and to develop on its own. A Korean-style outcome would have stopped the Communist bandwagon. As it was, the beating administered to North Vietnam apparently discouraged potential imitators.

The wet season in Vietnam stopped most combat during late 1963 and early 1964, so Johnson did not have to plan his first moves until January–February 1964. The five-month dry (campaigning) season would test the post-coup South Vietnamese government. In February 1964 Johnson decided to pressure the North via a covert program, OPLAN (Operations Plan) 34A, under which it assisted South Vietnamese raids on North Vietnamese coastal installations.[14] Initial plans to use South Vietnamese aircraft to bomb North Vietnam were abandoned.[15] As the JCS warned in January 1964, these minor attacks were ineffective. The United States had to take over the war, commit troops to combat in South Vietnam, and, if necessary, attack North Vietnam directly. None of this was even remotely practical in the spring of 1964.[16] As it was, OPLAN 34A was to have been followed with covert support of overt air attacks (including mining) and then with overt U.S. and South Vietnamese naval displays, bombardments, and air attacks.[17]

In March Johnson did approve Secretary McNamara's request to plan a bombing campaign, which was to have been part of a larger combination of stick and carrot. The Joint Staff estimated that all the targets associated with infiltration into South Vietnam could be destroyed within twelve days.[18] For the moment, Johnson held back. Mindful of Truman's problems in Korea, he would not act without a Joint Congressional Resolution.

For their part, the North Vietnamese had seen their hopes for an easy victory fade. They had assumed that, given Diem's unpopularity, the South might well collapse without much military effort. The post-coup government was (as it turned out, temporarily) very popular. Moreover, by late 1963 it was clear that the United States would not simply withdraw and allow North Vietnam to take over. U.S. troops surely would enter the war. To deal with them, the North Vietnamese would have to send in their own regular troops. Yet without Soviet support, North Vietnam would be vulnerable to American retaliation by bombing. Thus a December 1963 Party plenum rejected, for the moment, a proposal to introduce North Vietnamese regular troops.[19] However, Col. Bui Tin was sent down the Ho Chi Minh Trail the same month to evaluate the fighting qualities of the Viet Cong and the possibility of moving in large units ahead of the expected U.S. deployment. In April 1964 North Vietnamese units began training for possible deployment south.[20]

Meanwhile, in February Rostow suggested that Johnson might get authority to escalate in the form of a congressional resolution, which would be easier to obtain than a declaration of war.[21] The resolution would be broadly patterned on one Eisenhower had extracted from Congress in 1955 to authorize the use of force to protect Quemoy and Matsu; he had used it to apply the pressure which ended the crisis. A resolution would entail fewer domestic problems than a declaration of war. There was some fear that the debate over a resolution would provide an opportunity for Americans pressing for what would amount to surrender. Under Secretary of State George Ball drafted a broadly worded resolution, to be held in reserve until it was needed.[22]

In March 1964 MacNamara and Taylor brought a very pessimistic report back from Saigon: the Viet Cong controlled about 40 percent of the territory; there was widespread apathy; and the situation had worsened noticeably since the coup. Johnson now made it official U.S. policy to maintain a free South Vietnam. He ordered plans developed to cut off infiltration across the borders with Laos and Cambodia and to retaliate against North Vietnam. He explicitly rejected introducing U.S. troops into combat (e.g., to protect Saigon) or placing South Vietnamese units under U.S. command.[23]

OPLAN 34A attacks were still going on. In addition, U.S. warships patrolled just outside North Vietnamese territorial waters in a program code-named De Soto, mapping out North Vietnamese coast defense radars and intercepting signals.[24] The North Vietnamese knew what they were doing; during a February 1964 patrol, for example, they shut down all communications as the ship passed. In August the De Soto patrol was made to coincide with a South Vietnamese OPLAN 34A naval raid; to deal with the raid, the North Vietnamese would have to turn on their radars and communicate.[25] None of this was very different from the cat-and-mouse game played around the world to probe and define coastal and air defenses. Sometimes aircraft collecting just such intelligence were attacked and even shot down. Nothing like that had yet happened to ships, which generally collected intelligence from just outside territorial waters, where they were considered safe.

Perhaps the North Vietnamese did not understand these rules. On 1 August the U.S. destroyer *Maddox*, on De Soto patrol, intercepted and interpreted a North Vietnamese order, from high authority, to attack an enemy warship at her position.[26] Three torpedo boats duly attacked the next day; with the benefit of warning, the ship drove them off. U.S. carrier aircraft also attacked the torpedo boats. One was left dead in the water. The U.S. Navy already feared that De Soto ships might be attacked because they might be mistaken for support for OPLAN 34A attacks.[27]

The North Vietnamese may have wanted to demonstrate to the South Vietnamese that their U.S. ally was a "paper tiger." The attack may fit a pattern of strikes against U.S. personnel and installations, none of which had triggered retaliation: a 3 February attack on the U.S. compound at Kontum City, a 7 February bombing of Americans in a Saigon theater, the 2 May sinking of the aircraft transport *Card*, and 4 and 6 July attacks on Special Forces camps.[28]

Johnson accepted that the attack was a North Vietnamese mistake. He may have hoped for a pretext to fight, but he certainly did not use this one. He did order the De Soto patrols to continue. On 4 August NSA flashed an attack warning to the destroyers *Maddox* and *Turner Joy*, based on an intercepted North Vietnamese message.[29] Relying on radar (but not visual) contacts, the ships reported they were being attacked; they were not hit. In fact radar conditions were bad, and the operators on board the ships were not familiar with them. They almost certainly picked up false targets.[30] The North Vietnamese may have wanted to attack (the intercepted message was real), but it seems certain that they did not do so.

Privy to NSA's very secret intercept of the North Vietnamese message, President Johnson felt sure that the attack had been planned. It was apparently so far out to sea that it was a clear act of North Vietnamese aggression. Johnson ordered a retaliatory air strike. Officers in the western Pacific, more familiar with local conditions, generally doubted that the second attack was real, but the higher command in the Pacific felt much more confident; it had the NSA intercepts. President Johnson apparently developed doubts a few days later.

Johnson saw in the pair of incidents justification for Congress to pass Ball's resolution.[31] Under this Tonkin Gulf Resolution the president could use whatever force was needed to assist South Vietnam and other allies in the area. He later said that, remembering Truman's problems in Korea, he wanted Congress to declare its support for the war. This was disingenuous. The resolution's floor chairman, William Fulbright, told Congress that Johnson planned no war, although he did acknowledge that the resolution could be read as authorization for war.[32] Furious at what he later saw as Johnson's deception, Fulbright would become one of the war's early critics.

A week after the Tonkin Gulf incident, North Vietnamese Party leaders convened a special meeting. Troops were already training to go south. In Mao's theory of revolutionary war, which the North Vietnamese followed, there was a point at which the rebels had to form large conventional units to win their war. The regular North Vietnamese army would supply them. The North Vietnamese had, however, a special twist on Mao's theory. They romanticized the events of 1945 into a "general uprising" in which Ho's Viet Minh had triumphed in the cities of Vietnam *without* having large armed units. For Mao, the central event was an assault *on* the cities. This difference helps explain why the U.S. Army found the Tet Offensive of 1968 so unexpected. Mao would not have escalated nearly as quickly or with as much risk. In South Vietnam the general uprising clearly needed the backing of large units if it was to succeed; otherwise the South Vietnamese army could crush it.

The North Vietnamese seem to have seen Johnson's rather limited responses to the Tonkin Gulf incident (and his lack of response to earlier incidents) as proof that he was not yet ready to intervene in the war. The longer they waited, the better the chance that Johnson would change his mind. It would be much better to send in troops to spearhead a quick victory, rather than to depend on slow guerilla warfare, which would risk later American action. Presumably the North Vietnamese were aware of the pledges Johnson made during the summer of 1964 not to expand the war. They decided to send in regular North Vietnamese units. They must have thought that was safe; as yet they had failed to extract air defense weapons from the Soviets, which they would have needed to fend off U.S. retaliatory air strikes.[33] It is also possible that the North Vietnamese read the aftermath of Tonkin Gulf as a warning that the United States was gradually turning towards intervention, and thus that they had better end the war before that happened.[34]

The first regular North Vietnamese unit, a small regiment, arrived in the South early in December 1964.[35] It had probably left its base at Vinh in September or early October 1964. By mid-1965 the North Vietnamese had 5 regiments in South Vietnam; by the end of the year they had 12, and during 1966 another 15 (5 divisions, 58,000 men) were sent south. This infiltration changed the war from an insurrection supported by the North to an invasion by the North. In December 1964 the Chinese agreed to move up to three hundred thousand troops (five infantry and five antiaircraft divisions) into northern Vietnam to free North Vietnamese troops to go to South Vietnam.[36] When the North Vietnamese began to send army units south they appointed a local commander for that zone, Gen. Nguyen Chi Thanh. He was made equal in rank to Gen. Vo Nguyen Giap, the North Vietnamese commander. In the fight that followed, Thanh generally preferred a more aggressive strategy; Giap always feared putting North Vietnam itself at risk.

The actual dispatch of regular North Vietnamese units coincided roughly with the fall of Khrushchev. To wean North Vietnam away from the Chinese, his successors finally offered Hanoi what it needed to face the United States: modern air defenses. The Soviets got remarkably little in return for becoming the main arms suppliers to the North Vietnamese.[37] During the war a Vietnamese journalist told a Soviet counterpart, Mikhail Ilyinski of *Isvestia*, that the Soviets were providing 75 to 80 percent of total assistance, but gaining only 4 to 5 percent of political influence (Ilyinski thought the true figure was 15 to 20 percent).[38]

The North Vietnamese relationship with China was far warmer.[39] For example, Chinese anti-Soviet propaganda was widespread in North Vietnam despite Soviet protests, and Chinese diplomats had more freedom that their Soviet counterparts. The Soviets did extract a Vietnamese promise to decrease their own exposure by limiting the war to South Vietnam. They would also stop criticizing Soviet foreign policy.[40] The Vietnamese knew that the Soviets still valued their relationship with the Americans; they feared a sellout. The Soviets hoped to resolve their dilemma by promoting a negotiated settlement, an idea the North Vietnamese rejected.[41] The U.S. government never realized just how little leverage the Soviets had over the North Vietnamese.

By late 1964 the Communists controlled half the land area and more than half the population of South Vietnam. Only the cities remained under government control. In the past, the Viet Cong had limited themselves to hit-and-run raids, fading away after overrunning a town. They now felt far bolder; in their first divisional attack, the Viet Cong destroyed two elite South Vietnamese units at Binh Gia, only forty miles from Saigon. They held the town for four days.[42] It seemed to be time for a final push; the Viet Cong began training the elite teams they would need to destroy key government installations as part of a "general uprising." The North Vietnamese had the troops for the initial attack, but lacked the regional forces (Viet Cong) for a follow-through. The North Vietnamese therefore rejected a "general uprising" in South Vietnam as premature.

Reelected on 2 November 1964, Johnson no longer had to prove that he was a moderate. The next day he formed an NSC working group to study ways to keep South Vietnam from collapsing. The three options were to continue existing policy but also to react to attacks on U.S. targets; to impose heavy military pressure on the North; or to escalate slowly. In each case, the objective was to force the North to negotiate, rather than to overrun it altogether. None of the three options would bring quick results. It would be best to wait, to see whether conditions continued to deteriorate so badly early in 1965 that dramatic escalation was necessary.[43] In December 1964 President Johnson approved the first phase of a two-phase air campaign: armed reconnaissance of infiltration routes through Laos, then air strikes on North Vietnam.[44]

Johnson's moves were covert: it must have seemed that the United States was unwilling to stop the slide towards disaster. The Communists had won in Laos, and they would soon win in Vietnam. Sukarno, the ruler of Indonesia, concluded that Communism was the wave of the future. He publicly embraced the Indonesian PKI, which in 1965 was the largest Communist party outside the Communist world, with more than three million members.[45] Many outside observers expected Indonesia to become formally Communist by 1966.

For some years Sukarno had depended on foreign successes to buttress his power. The Kennedy administration thought he was a Far Eastern Nasser, so it backed his claim to take over West New Guinea (West Irian) from the Dutch in 1962. Sukarno then decided to "liberate" Malaysia.[46] The Malaysian Federation comprised Malaya, Singapore, and British Borneo (Brunei, Sabah–North Borneo and Sarawak). Beginning in 1962 Sukarno supported rebels against the sultan of Brunei; the PKI pressed for war against Malaya and Singapore. Sukarno publicly attacked the new Malaysian Federation as a British neocolonialist outrage. In 1963 he equipped Chinese-oriented guerillas operating in the Malaysian parts of Borneo. After the Chinese guerillas in Brunei were crushed in 1964, Sukarno fed in his own troops.[47]

The British were obligated by treaty to defend Malaysia, just as they had defended it (as Malaya) against Chinese-sponsored terrorists since 1948. For a time in 1964 the British had more troops "East of Suez," mainly in Borneo and Malaysia, than the United States had in Vietnam. Sukarno had already adopted Communist rhetoric; he said that the way to defeat imperialism in Southeast Asia was for China to strike Vietnam from the north, while Indonesia struck Malaysia from the south.[48] The U.S. government supported the British in this "Confrontation."

Between the PKI and power stood the Indonesian military.[49] Veterans of the fight for independence, they hated the PKI for its old treachery; even as the Dutch had attacked the fledgling Indonesian government, the PKI had revolted, on 18 September 1948 at Madiun, East Java. The military was, moreover, infuriated by Sukarno's expensive and unsuccessful fight in Malaysia.[50] The PKI had a solution:

in January 1965 its chief proposed that Sukarno form a mass militia, which the Chinese, their allies, could arm. Their ally within the Indonesian armed forces was the air force, which began training the militia.[51]

Sukarno had no designated successor, so it was clear that when he died the PKI and the Indonesian army would fight for power. By the summer of 1965 Sukarno had been ill for some time. He was being treated in China; the Chinese told PKI chief Aidit that Sukarno was gravely and probably fatally ill.[52] The Chinese may have wanted to precipitate a PKI coup. On 28 August the PKI Politburo unanimously agreed to kill the Indonesian general staff.[53] The operation went awry: the raiders missed one key prize, Chief of the Joint Staff Gen. Abdul Haris Nasution (who was also minister of defense). Armed units did seize key points in Jakarta and an Indonesia Revolutionary Council proclaimed itself, with Sukarno under its protection. Senior army ranks were abolished. The PKI newspaper announced that the army had been purged.[54]

With Nasution free, Sukarno apparently lost his nerve and failed to make the necessary statement of support for the PKI-led coup.[55] The army could counterattack without seeming to be against Sukarno, who was still very popular. The PKI tried to distance itself from the murders of the generals, but was tied to them by the presence of large numbers of its paramilitary troops and then by the statements of its own newspaper the next day. It was virtually destroyed in a bloodbath.[56] With the end of the PKI, the Confrontation collapsed. The tension, the coup, and the bloodbath are recalled in the movie, *The Year of Living Dangerously*.

The Indonesian army was not anxious to put Sukarno, the "father" of the country, on trial. Although in effect ousted in 1965, he was not formally removed from the presidency until 11 March 1967. Major General Suharto, leader of the main counterattacking force, who lasted three decades as chief of state, replaced him.

The Indonesian army countercoup was only loosely related to an emerging U.S. intervention in Vietnam: the Indonesian army acted because the PKI tried to destroy it, not because it suddenly became emboldened. The PKI itself was reacting to U.S. weakness, as demonstrated in 1964. On the other hand, the growing U.S. commitment to Vietnam had encouraged the British to fight the Confrontation. Had they withdrawn, had Sukarno won an easy victory, the army would have found it impossible to oppose him. The PKI might not even have found it necessary to decapitate the army.

Indonesia was an illustration of a domino effect, in this case only narrowly averted. It certainly was a great Cold War prize, not only because of its vast natural resources, but also because of its strategic position, athwart the tanker route between the Middle East and Japan. To jittery Indonesian generals, the massive U.S. commitment to Vietnam begun in 1965 helped prevent any PKI resurgence.

Through early 1965 the situation in South Vietnam continued to deteriorate. The North Vietnamese troops were making themselves felt. If they could seize control of the central and northwest highlands, they would cut South Vietnam in two.

The South Vietnamese army seemed incapable of dealing with attacks on the new scale; South Vietnam could not withstand another year of this sort of combat. Johnson feared that losing South Vietnam would destroy his presidency and his prized domestic programs.[57]

On 7 February 1965 the Viet Cong hit a U.S. Special Forces base at Pleiku, in the Western Highlands. U.S. National Security Advisor McGeorge Bundy was then visiting South Vietnam; he suggested immediate retaliation. Explaining why the U.S. had retaliated against Pleiku but not against other, similar attacks, Bundy said that these incidents were "like streetcars. If you missed one, another would soon arrive to go to the same place."[58] The Pleiku attack also triggered the eight-week air campaign (against bases in southern North Vietnam associated with infiltration south) which Johnson had considered the previous December.

The Soviets were already supplying antiaircraft weapons, initially guns, but soon missiles as well. Once U.S. bombing began, the North Vietnamese backed this hardware with a propaganda campaign, which many in Vietnam believed stopped the air campaign in March 1968. They successfully sold a double standard: the destruction of a bridge by Viet Cong in South Vietnam was acceptable, whereas the destruction of a similar bridge by bombing in North Vietnam was not. Air power perfectly acceptable in, say, the Middle East was not at all acceptable in Southeast Asia.[59]

Once Soviet-supplied missiles were in place, U.S. pilots found it very difficult to get close enough to hit important objectives. To get hits, they had to make dozens or even hundreds of attacks, at a terrible cost. The situation recalled what SAC bombers would have faced in a big war, and the solution was the same: guided weapons. In some cases they could be fired beyond the range of the worst antiaircraft fire. At the least, they drastically reduced the number of passes needed to get a hit. This development of relatively inexpensive "smart" bombs (precision-guided munitions, PGMs) was very significant for the sort of war NATO might have to fight in Europe, in which Western fighter-bombers would probably be the main counter to massed Soviet tanks. They would face air defenses similar to those erected for North Vietnam. Given the new bombs, the NATO aircraft would not have to use nuclear weapons.

As the North Vietnamese system developed, the United States deployed more and more sophisticated electronic countermeasures. As U.S. aircraft were shot down, their modern electronic systems fell into North Vietnamese hands. Under an agreement with the Soviets, Soviet experts were allowed to examine the wrecks and to send whatever they wanted north (however, they were often obstructed).[60] Under the pressure of heavy air attacks, particularly late in the war, the North Vietnamese got many of the best Soviet air defense weapons and radars. As the U.S. learned to neutralize them, the Soviets realized that SAC was learning how to overcome their own national air defense system. Yet in their struggle against the Chinese, the Soviets could not afford to be seen denying the best defenses to a beleaguered Communist ally. Simply by shipping that equipment by rail through China, the Soviets made it possible for the Chinese to steal it and copy it. That must have been galling as the Sino-Soviet split moved towards possible war in the late 1960s.[61]

Soon Johnson began a program of continuous air attacks against North Vietnam, Rolling Thunder, which would last through March 1968. In line with current nuclear escalation ideas, Johnson and McNamara treated air attacks as messages to the North Vietnamese.[62] They personally selected the targets in order to control the messages they were sending. The area attacked gradually was extended towards Hanoi. To Johnson and his advisors, Hanoi was being given a choice either to negotiate an end to the war, or to suffer worse pressure. Johnson halted bombing seven times to allow the North Vietnamese a chance to negotiate. The North Vietnamese saw the pattern of restraint as proof of Johnson's weakness.

The bombing pauses were McNamara's idea.[63] The JCS strongly resisted them, because they gave the North Vietnamese time to repair damage and recover.[64] However, they were not invited to the meetings which discussed the first one, in December 1965. Chairman Gen. Earle Wheeler was told only just before he left for the Far East. The cable ordering the pause was drafted in McNamara's office; both the chief of the Air Staff and the CNO refused to sign it. McNamara told them that the president was aware of their objections; he sent the cable in the name of the JCS. To appease the JCS, he offered a major escalation early in 1966.

McNamara tried to kill the bombing altogether, arguing that in 1965 it cost the United States about $6.50 in aircraft lost for every one dollar of damage inflicted on North Vietnam; in 1966, the cost rose to about $10.40. This was disingenuous; if the whole point of the bombing was to send effective signals, it did not really matter whether it was cost-effective on its face. Moreover, McNamara had rigged the figures, because his target choices limited damage to North Vietnam. Nor did McNamara take into account the diversion of North Vietnamese manpower to make good bomb damage. U.S. intelligence estimated that one hundred thousand North Vietnamese worked full-time to repair damage to roads and railways; others worked part-time.

The JCS demanded attacks that would do real damage; it had no use for signals. Destroying North Vietnamese oil storage would paralyze the country, and thus would probably dislocate its support for the war in the South. However, most oil tankers were around Haiphong, the port of the North Vietnamese capital, Hanoi. Bargaining required that at each stage of bombing the Americans had to be able to threaten something worse if the North Vietnamese refused to negotiate. Attacks on their capital seemed to be the worst the United States could do. It took Johnson about seven months to agree to the JCS attacks (in June 1966). Washington was so leaky that the North Vietnamese were undoubtedly forewarned; they dispersed their oil.[65] Overall, American pilots found it obscene to brave North Vietnamese air defenses merely to attack obviously secondary targets. The rules included a prohibition against attacking air defense sites under construction, for fear of killing Soviet and Chinese technicians.[66] (A quarter century later, U.S. forces hit Saddam Hussein's palace on the first night of the Gulf War, to announce that this time no such political limits would be imposed.)

While their country's air defenses were built up, North Vietnamese soldiers in the South attacked the main air base, Da Nang, from which the U.S. air attacks were being mounted. Two marine battalions were ordered to Vietnam to secure Da Nang. The U.S. military commander, Gen. William Westmoreland, probably saw them as the beginning of a major buildup; bombing would not dissuade the North Vietnamese, and the situation was deteriorating fast.[67] Johnson refused an army request for a full U.S. division, but he added more marines. Much more significantly, on 1 April 1965 he changed their mission from airfield defense to "more active use" against the Viet Cong.[68]

Johnson wanted Congress to show that it approved. In May he asked for a $700 million supplemental specifically to demonstrate congressional support for "our basic course." It passed 408:7 in the House and 88:3 in the Senate, and Johnson signed the bill on 7 May, less than fifty-three hours after he had requested it.

Johnson had passed the point of no return, although for the moment he kept that decision secret.[69] Like Eisenhower, he wanted any war to be a coalition affair; he ordered "urgent exploration" of ways of getting "significant" combat units from Korea, Australia, and New Zealand.

At first it seemed that U.S. troops would be used only to defend coastal enclaves. In May 1965, however, the Viet Cong made a series of successful attacks. By late June it seemed that the enemy could cut South Vietnam in two or else form an enclave in which the Viet Cong might establish a government.[70] Unless the U.S. Army entered combat, the country would surely collapse.[71] The first major U.S. ground action was a 27–30 June search and destroy mission near Saigon by the 173d Airborne Brigade, an Australian battalion, and Vietnamese forces.[72] Johnson enlisted a group of senior advisors, the "Wise Men" (led by Dean Acheson), who told him that he had no choice but to escalate.[73] He sent Westmoreland more troops.

Later many would say that Johnson's decision violated a fundamental lesson of the Korean War by becoming involved in a land war in Asia, where the enemy would have limitless manpower. However, as long as the Chinese did not intervene, Vietnamese manpower was not limitless. Moreover, the objective was precise: to keep South Vietnam from collapsing. Hopefully blocking a Communist victory in the South and punishing the North (by bombing) would convince the North Vietnamese to accept a settlement.

U.S. troops could not invade North Vietnam. Mao still considered North Vietnam either a buffer or a threat on his border; he could no more tolerate U.S. conquest of North Vietnam than he could the U.S. conquest of North Korea in 1950.[74] U.S. representatives secretly assured the Chinese that the United States would not

invade North Vietnam, and in the spring of 1965 the Chinese offered not to introduce combat troops into Vietnam unless U.S. or South Vietnamese troops invaded
the North. Through the summer of 1965 the Chinese hotly debated just how much
help they would give the North Vietnamese.[75] By November 1965 they had a tacit
understanding with the Americans.[76]

Meanwhile the Chinese were insuring against U.S. attack, relocating key facilities inland from coastal areas. This Third Front program consumed as much as
two-thirds of industrial investment in 1965–71. The program raised the cost of
production by dispersing plants; many were built in narrow canyons, to complicate air attack.[77]

The North Vietnamese were apparently unaware of the U.S. assurances to
China; perhaps the Chinese wanted to maintain their own leverage in Hanoi. They
thus supported a U.S. bluff: during much of the war the United States maintained
an amphibious force in the South China Sea. This tacit threat of invasion was
intended to keep part of the North Vietnamese army at home. It may have inspired
Giap to organize for "people's war," i.e., for the home defense of every village in
North Vietnam.[78]

In mid-1965 the North Vietnamese got the Chinese to agree to intervene if the
United States invaded North Vietnam. The North Vietnamese could never be
entirely sure they were serious. For example, in January 1965 Mao said that he
would not intervene unless Chinese territory was attacked.[79] In September Lin
Biao gave an important speech, "Long Live the Victory of People's War," which was
widely seen as an incitement to world revolution. It could also be read as a warning
to the North Vietnamese that they would have to win with their own resources;
China would not help.[80] In July 1965, for example, it refused a North Vietnamese
request for fighter pilots. The Chinese did move construction and air defense
troops into North Vietnam, beginning in September (there were 60,000 to 100,000
in place by 1967, according to the Soviets).[81] Between September 1965 and March
1968 a total of 320,000 Chinese troops rotated through North Vietnam (of whom
twenty thousand may have become casualties). The Chinese built a base at Yen Bat
to use if the U.S. invaded North Vietnam.[82] They also built a southern air defense
radar system which tracked targets over North Vietnam and reported them to the
North Vietnamese, supplementing their own radar net. On occasion Chinese aircraft engaged U.S. aircraft that strayed over the border.

Although he decided to commit U.S. troops, Johnson also decided deliberately
not to stir up enthusiasm for the war.[83] An aroused U.S. population might well
demand exactly those steps, such as an invasion of North Vietnam, which would
widen the war disastrously. The Joint Chiefs disagreed. They pressed for a patriotic
war, for mobilization of reserves and for a declaration of war—and the sort of
offensive tactics that would have destroyed the North Vietnamese army and, probably, its government. Mobilization would have afforded the opportunity for the
public debate that should have surrounded the Tonkin Gulf Resolution. Johnson

would have had to explain just why it was vital to preserve South Vietnam. He preferred to minimize political danger—in 1965—by minimizing public awareness and debate. He was following Truman's 1950 course, and he would suffer as Truman had when the war went bad.

McCarthyism had devalued the crusade against Communism; it was easy for Americans to see the Viet Cong and North Vietnamese as local nationalists rather than as agents of an enemy empire. It was difficult to see why Americans should die to protect the obviously corrupt South Vietnamese society. Worst of all was the sense that the war would last forever. The government clearly had foresworn the one way of ending it: destroying North Vietnam itself.

The war coincided with the rise of a powerful youth culture throughout the West, probably mainly because the first of the huge wave of baby boomers had reached adolescence. Inevitably the youth culture challenged adult authority, which in the United States was responsible for the ongoing and apparently senseless war—apparently senseless largely because of the refusal to raise passions and also because of the way the war was being fought. Some have seen in this challenge the end of the belief, born in the Great Depression, that government could cure American problems. Now it seemed that government *was* the problem.

Johnson's advisors saw Vietnam as the first of many small wars the United States would have to fight against Communist insurgents. There could be no thought of raising special taxes to pay for this one. Johnson particularly feared that Congress would cut his prized domestic programs rather than raise taxes.[84] At first that was no problem: in FY65 the war cost only $100 million. However, in 1966 it cost $14 *billion*. While deficit spending can do considerable good when the economy is in recession (as during Kennedy's term), it causes inflation when the economy is already running at or near full capacity. Although inflation hit only 3.4 percent in 1966, voters were already so nervous that they counted it third among their problems, behind only Vietnam itself and race relations. When Johnson tried to raise taxes in 1967, Wilbur Mills, the conservative chairman of the House Ways and Means Committee, refused to approve his proposed 10 percent tax surcharge until he offered spending cuts (i.e., dismantled the Great Society)—which he would not do. Partly due to the deep U.S. deficit, the gold problem worsened.

McNamara tried to buy only enough to meet the war's requirements. Thus, unlike World War II or Korea, Vietnam left no vast surplus of military hardware or ammunition to be used during the inevitable postwar crash in military funding. Equipment and weapons had to be withdrawn from Europe or from European war reserves, and a great deal was left behind when U.S. forces left Vietnam.

To minimize the impact of the war, soldiers' tours of duty were limited to one year. That applied to individuals rather than to whole units. Each unit thus combined very inexperienced soldiers and soldiers who, though experienced, had a short service time remaining, and hence were concerned mainly with surviving the rest of their tour of duty. Officers generally served six-month tours in combat and six months on the staff. It was widely believed that this policy had been adopted so that as many as possible could "punch their tickets" with some combat experience.[85] With so little time to prove themselves, officers concentrated on short-term successes. This policy also attacked vital small-unit cohesion. Colonels and even generals took a short-term view and therefore concentrated unduly on the activities of platoons and companies in firefights rather than on the larger issues of the war.

Also to limit pain, soldiers were given lavish support. As a result, in 1968 only 15 percent of U.S. Army personnel were available for ground combat; many soldiers were employed in rear areas.[86] Those in the field were heavily outnumbered by the enemy; firepower became an essential equalizer. Unfortunately guerillas and even North Vietnamese regular troops were difficult to distinguish from ordinary South Vietnamese civilians. U.S. firepower killed numerous civilians—and convinced others that U.S. forces were anything but their friends.[87]

Lavish support had another, unexpected, consequence. Money poured into the South Vietnamese economy, particularly in the cities. South Vietnamese therefore flocked from the dangerous and relatively impoverished countryside to the artificially prosperous cities. This depopulation hurt the Viet Cong, because it affected their sanctuaries. However, because prosperity depended entirely on the Americans, the South Vietnamese economy virtually collapsed when they withdrew, with terrible consequences.

Through the 1950s, the U.S. draft pool consisted of those born in the lean years of the Depression. Because the pool was small, most Americans of draft age served. The Vietnam War coincided with the maturing of the "baby boom" generation born from 1946 on. The draft pool exploded. Most men of draft age were not needed. A system of deferments had long been in place, on the theory that it was in the country's interest that men enter certain vital careers (such as teaching) and that they go to college and university. In the past, the pool had been thin: most who enjoyed deferments later served. Now a deferment often became an exemption. Those too poor to go to college served; the well-off avoided service legally. The combination of a national feeling of injustice and a sense that the war was being conducted pointlessly was devastating. Angered by student demonstrations against the war, President Johnson cancelled deferments for graduate students early in 1968. Students rioted. Presumably they assumed that they would be drafted; they decided to display their feelings before they went. Ironically, few of them actually were drafted.

Deferment policy made the army much blacker than the country as a whole, since far fewer blacks than whites could claim college deferments. The war coincided with the growth of the civil rights movement in the United States. Working-class men, many of them black, occupied a disproportionate fraction of the most dangerous combat assignments, such as infantry. The combination of an increasingly vocal civil rights movement at home, which increasingly identified injustices, with a feeling of injustice in the field, proved explosive.

Johnson's decision to send in U.S. combat troops coincided with his fight for his cherished Great Society programs.[88] In mid-1965 the divisions for Vietnam had to come from the general reserve Kennedy had built up. Chief of Staff Gen. Harold K. Johnson assumed that Johnson would mobilize reserves to replace them (he expected to add about seven divisions).[89] The president decided not to mobilize. He feared a fight that would derail the Great Society program.[90] Johnson told the NSC and the JCS that he feared full mobilization would raise the "noise level" so high as to bring in the Chinese and perhaps the Soviets; better to do everything as quietly as possible. His opponents charged that he was more interested in the domestic noise level.

The U.S. Army later considered Johnson's decision to avoid the pain of mobilization the key to disaster in Vietnam. After the war, with the Total Force concept, they sought to make the reserves so integral to combat units that no president could deploy large forces without first engaging public support.

Moreover, when on 28 July Johnson announced publicly that he was sending troops, he emphasized his desire for negotiations. This was hardly the sort of war message that was likely to motivate the country.[91]

Once he got his troops, Westmoreland thought he could stabilize the situation by the end of 1965. Given more troops, he could begin an offensive in 1966.[92] McNamara told Johnson that, with extra troops, he stood a good chance of winning. This was his last private optimistic statement on the war, although in public McNamara continued to be quite optimistic.[93]

The Viet Cong and their North Vietnamese allies were elusive. To be effective, Westmoreland's troops had somehow to come to grips with them. Westmoreland ordered them out on "search and destroy" missions. In effect he hoped to attract the enemy by offering the possibility of ambushing U.S. troops. Once they showed themselves, they could be destroyed by heavy U.S. firepower. At the least, the search and destroy missions would, it was hoped, force the enemy to use up ammunition and personnel. To keep up the effort in South Vietnam, more would have to come down the Ho Chi Minh Trail—where, it was hoped, they would be subject to attack by the U.S. Air Force. The U.S. Navy and U.S. Coast Guard enforced a complementary coastal blockade, Market Time.

In October 1965 the North Vietnamese suffered a sobering defeat. Units of their 325B division besieged the important crossroads of Plei Mei in hopes of attracting and then ambushing a South Vietnamese force. The South Vietnamese fought well; the North Vietnamese withdrew into the sanctuary of the trackless Ia Drang Valley. They thought they were safe. U.S. helicopter assault troops followed them in, and they were crushed.[94] Even so, this battle was bloody enough to make senior Defense Department civilians think that they had underestimated the North Vietnamese; much more escalation would be needed.

For his part, Giap learned that U.S. units could be shockingly effective. Seven to nine North Vietnamese battalions would be needed to deal with each U.S. battalion.[95] The Southern commander, Thanh, still thought it was time to use large units; he did not want to retreat to small-unit guerilla war. Giap won his fight, but his victory was not immediately apparent; Thanh got one more offensive, a failed two-division attack through the DMZ into northern South Vietnam in February 1966. Other units attacked from Laos. The objective was to pull U.S. forces from more heavily populated areas.[96] Westmoreland feared that the North Vietnamese hoped to seize the two northern provinces to create a defendable puppet state. The U.S. Marines occupied a former Special Forces base at Khe Sanh, overlooking a key road.[97]

Overall, the big North Vietnamese formations vanished. They refused even to defend base areas they needed to fight future battles; trained men were more important to Giap than supplies, however painstakingly built up. To some extent simply moving them underground, where the American troops failed to find them, protected the supplies. On the other hand, the U.S. attacks spoiled planned enemy strikes, and the North Vietnamese had to withdraw their forces from anywhere near populated areas. Captured documents showed that they considered the new U.S. attacks a disaster.[98]

This war was eerie; it seemed that there was no particular territory the enemy so prized that he would stand and fight for it. He had to be sought out. Critics argued that the U.S. Army should have been split up to protect the villages and thus the South Vietnamese population. Westmoreland feared that his troops would simply be destroyed in detail. Moreover, once his army was broken down into small units, it would be very difficult to weld them back into larger units to fight large enemy units.

The war was inevitably confusing, since it was impossible to say how close the enemy was to defeat. There was no natural indicator of U.S. success or failure. Often ground declared friendly in daylight was hostile at night. All reporters—and the U.S. public—saw was the chaos of day-to-day fighting, a sequence of apparently pointless firefights.

In theory, the measure of success was the degree to which the enemy was being ground down. The U.S. government offered a body count, but too many of those killed were not enemy troops. Because the enemy rarely wore a uniform, it was easy to kill real civilians, or to be killed by Viet Cong wearing civilian clothes. U.S. ground commanders fastened on the body count as a measure of their success, and even encouraged their subordinates to kill indiscriminately in order to inflate it. By 1966 it was clear that although the North Vietnamese and the Viet Cong were suffering, they were not noticeably weakening. That must have been partly because Giap had won his debate: North Vietnamese units were avoiding combat—for the moment. There was an uncomfortable sense that the enemy's supply of manpower was bottomless.

The same problem—that it was difficult to assess progress in the war—had another effect. U.S. commanders tended to sum up their contribution to the war effort, not in terms of what was achieved, but in terms of input: of how many sorties, or shells, or bombs, were expended. Commanders even were chided for not using as much firepower as they had. There was no incentive to economize, since the productive U.S. economy could always provide more.[99]

By the fall of 1966 it seemed to the U.S. government that the war had reached a stalemate. In October 1966 McNamara returned from Vietnam and told President Johnson that it was time to negotiate. Victory seemed impossible. Giving Westmoreland more troops was pointless. The North Vietnamese had shown no interest in the signals implicit in the bombing campaign. It would be best simply to try to cut off supplies, by bombing near the DMZ and by emplacing electronic sensors (called Igloo White) to cue attacks on the Ho Chi Minh Trail.[100] The Joint Chiefs rejected all of McNamara's suggestions, but Johnson agreed to limit the air war to the 1966 level.

By this time Vietnam, the peripheral war, was at the center of Johnson's interest. The Europeans were uninterested; they could not imagine how a war in so distant a place could affect them. Many in Europe openly opposed the war. Except for the British, they had lost their Asian empires; the threat, if there was one, was only in Europe. The French went much further. Having been ejected from Vietnam a decade earlier, they resented U.S. involvement.[101] Knowing that they could not convince the United States to withdraw, the French promoted negotiations in which they hoped to play the leading role. In this they were encouraged by the Soviets. The British and the French undoubtedly remembered Suez. Only West Germany strongly supported the United States: it read the U.S. engagement in Southeast Asia as proof that the commitment to Europe would be honored. It was caught between its two main allies, the French and the Americans, neither of which it could really afford to offend.[102]

Johnson offered the Soviets concessions in Europe—a far more important Cold War theater—in return for reduced support for North Vietnam. For example, in 1966 the Hungarians claimed that the U.S. government was offering to recognize the western boundary of Poland (which the Germans still rejected) and also to end German involvement in NATO nuclear policy making.[103] American arms control offers, which began in November 1966, may fall into the same category. The Americans tried to tempt the Soviets out of Vietnam; the Soviets tried to link the talks to American withdrawal.[104] The Soviets could not deliver North Vietnamese concessions; nor could they accept such deals, however attractive, for fear of losing their own standing in the world revolutionary movement. The West Germans, uncomfortably aware that the United States was losing interest in them, smelled a sellout by both the Americans and their European allies.[105]

The Europeans were already interested in some form of détente with the Soviets. Brezhnev and Kosygin saw their way to a great prize, formal Western acceptance of the post-1945 partition of Europe. The West Germans stood in the way, with their demand for eventual reunification and, therefore, their refusal to recognize East Germany as legitimate. Moreover, they had long refused to deal with any state that recognized East Germany as legitimate. That blocked Western recognition of East Germany as well as German relationships with the satellite states—which were a potentially lucrative market for the export-driven German economy. This market must have seemed even more important in 1966, when West Germany suffered its first postwar recession. In October 1966 Johnson made a speech about building "bridges to the East." He hoped to conciliate the NATO governments, but the Germans feared they were being sold out. In effect the Soviets offered the other West Europeans continued détente if they would desert the West Germans. To avoid being isolated, in March 1966 the West Germans had offered the Soviets and the Eastern European satellites a treaty renouncing the use or threat of force. That came very close to recognizing East Germany. At Soviet instigation, in July the satellites revived an earlier proposal for a European security conference to discuss unresolved questions, i.e., to legitimize the post-1945 settlement in Europe.

The Germans' Christian Democratic government, under Adenauer, had depended on the votes of many refugees from areas taken by Poland and the Soviet Union in 1945. A famous sign in the West Berlin railroad station announced that trains to Koenigsberg—now Kaliningrad, in what was the Soviet Union, but had been German East Prussia in 1945—were merely suspended, the implication being that some time soon they would resume. Although Adenauer retired in 1963, his old party continued his policy. The German Social Democrats and the German Protestant churches both supported an "opening to the East." They argued that recognition of East Germany might make it possible to alleviate the condition of its population. In December 1966 the Christian Democrats had to join with the Social Democrats in a "Grand Coalition" government. They accepted cooperation with the East Germans to promote the desired détente and to ease living conditions there.[106] The "opening" convinced the Soviets that the West would not interfere in their empire. It made mounting the 1968 invasion of Czechoslovakia much less worrisome.[107] On the other hand, some Soviets saw the "opening" as an act of political aggression, the beginning of a return to German economic dominance of Central Europe.

Détente and the Soviet and German 1966 initiatives made many Western Europeans question the value of NATO itself. De Gaulle's pullout badly weakened the alliance militarily, not least by eliminating much of its strategic depth behind the Central Front. In 1967 Pierre Harmel, the Belgian foreign minister, proposed a study of NATO's future. At the least, it would demonstrate faith that the alliance, newly based in Harmel's country, would last past 1969, the twentieth anniversary of the founding treaty—at which time members could withdraw on one year's notice. The U.S. government backed Harmel. The French reluctantly agreed to participate. The report concluded that the two apparently contradictory policies of détente and military security were actually compatible.

Without France, central NATO military policy was decided by the United States, Britain, and Germany—all of whom agreed during November 1966 talks to a form of the Flexible Response first proposed by the Kennedy administration; the NATO ministers formally accepted the new strategy in December 1967.[108] The U.S.-sponsored stiff conventional defense had to be watered down to meet the Germans' preference for deliberate and ambiguous escalation. In theory a Soviet attack massive enough to overrun the NATO force would have to tear Europe up so badly that NATO governments could reasonably threaten to use tactical nuclear weapons. This doctrine would remain in force through the end of the Cold War. The 1967 policy declaration supported détente as a parallel to military preparedness. To many Europeans, the obvious way to combine the two was to negotiate balanced troop reductions with the Soviets. NATO forces were expensive. If the threat was declining, governments wanted them cut. However, they could not justify doing so unilaterally; that would have been obvious surrender. They therefore became interested in negotiating mutual cuts with the Soviets (mutual and balanced force reductions, MBFRs). For the Germans, the new policy justified the growing opening to the East, and it formed the basis for their foreign policy through the 1980s.[109]

The war was exacerbating the economic problems the U.S. military presence in Europe caused. The $3.5 billion trade deficit in 1967 was the worst since 1960. In 1966 the Germans felt compelled to stop buying U.S. weapons (which cost nearly $700 million per year) and to halve the $250 million annual subsidy for the British army in Germany. After a run on the pound in July 1966, the British threatened to withdraw their whole army by 1968. The Johnson administration feared Americans would demand similar cuts. The British were persuaded to limit their cuts. Some U.S. units were withdrawn, but to soften the blow, they were dual-based, returning to Europe for annual exercises. Even so, the Europeans saw a loss of U.S. commitment. Other NATO nations cut their own forces.

All of these problems were not so obvious from outside the United States and NATO. To the Soviets, rising U.S. involvement in Vietnam seemed to mean that the United States was on the march. They saw an American bandwagon: the Americans had intervened to spoil the expected victory in Vietnam. Sukarno had been defeated (in the Confrontation) and overthrown. The Chinese were defeated in the valuable Congo. In 1965 the Greek military overthrew a potentially left-leaning government. This was the domino theory from the other side.

The Middle East gave the Soviets an opportunity to stop the onward march. As always, in 1967 it was quite unstable. A third of Nasser's army was still in Yemen, and his friendship with the United States had faded; the Americans were no longer entranced with Third World nationalists. The Soviets were still friendly; they saw Yemen as a potential base in a very strategic place, at the mouth of the Red Sea. Despite generous Soviet aid, by 1967 Egypt was nearly bankrupt.[110] Nasser badly needed some sort of victory.

In 1966 the situation in the Middle East had been further complicated when leftist officers staged a successful coup in Syria. Like some of their predecessors, they adopted a radical and anti-Israeli agenda to legitimize themselves. Nasser was still at war, in effect, with conservatives led by King Feisal of Saudi Arabia. He aligned himself with the Syrians.[111] In May 1966 the Soviets convinced him to repair relations with the Syrians and to form a defensive pact. Nasser was in trouble.

The Israelis also were touchy. To some extent their own leaders may have been inclined to posture so as to improve their positions in internal Israeli politics. The usual raids and counterraids gained significance.

The Soviets decided to convince both Nasser and his Syrian friends that they needed much closer friendship. They planted a false story on the Syrians that the Israelis had concentrated troops on their borders. The Israelis hotly denied it. The report meant war: it seems unlikely that it was fabricated without high-level approval. The then-head of the Egypt Department of the Soviet Foreign Ministry, Evgeny Pyrlin, later said that the Soviets wanted a war; even if the Egyptians lost, it would have demonstrated the extent of Soviet support and thus have insured Nasser's continued loyalty.[112] Moreover, in 1967 the majority belief in the Kremlin and in the Soviet high command was that Soviet equipment and training had transformed the Egyptian forces, so that Egypt, backed by Syria and Jordan, was likely to do well in a war (a negative report was ignored).[113]

The Soviets told Nasser to honor his commitment to Syria. If he did nothing, he faced renewed charges of cowardice that would have destroyed his position in the Arab world. Deeply engaged in Yemen, he had only limited forces. Privately he warned the Syrians not to fight.

Then the Soviet message changed. Probably that reflected disunity in the Kremlin. The Party (Brezhnev) and the Soviet military (Grechko) tended to play up the massive amount of equipment provided to the Egyptians; they kept telling the Egyptians that they now had the most powerful army in the region. They deliberately ignored human failings in the Arab forces. Kosygin was much warier.[114] In any case, the Soviets apparently warned Nasser against dangerous initiatives such as blockading the Strait of Tiran. He refused to consult them.[115] On 16 May Nasser demanded that the UN evacuate its buffer force, in place since the 1956 war, from the Sinai. He probably expected to be turned down. Later he said that he was surprised when the UN secretary general, U Thant, agreed immediately.

By this time Israel depended on oil from Iran, which was shipped through the Strait of Tiran. The Israelis also feared that, without a buffer zone, Egyptian troops would invade their country. Within a few days, Nasser closed the Strait of Tiran (one of the causes of the 1956 Israeli attack) and proclaimed his readiness for war. The Israelis found the situation intolerable. They were further alarmed when King Hussein of Jordan, formerly Nasser's deadly rival, signed a joint defense treaty with Egypt and Syria. He apparently feared that Nasser would foment a civil war in Jordan (as he nearly had in 1955) if he failed to do so.[116] Apparently Nasser expected the major powers to intervene before any war could break out. The Soviets were also nervous: about 28 May, just before war broke out, they told the Egyptians that they had just won a great victory (regaining sovereignty over the Sinai) and that they should not destroy it by going too far.

The Egyptian army wanted to make up for the disasters at Suez and in Yemen. Soviet defense minister Grechko told Egyptian war minister Badran that the Soviets would provide all the arms needed and would stand by Egypt in case of attack *by the United States,* but Badran told Nasser that the Soviets would intervene to keep other powers out, even fighting for the Egyptians.[117] Thus the Egyptians imagined a commitment that the Soviets had never made. They discovered as much when the Soviets rejected their frantic appeals for help once the war had begun.[118] Disunity in the Kremlin probably made it possible for Grechko to offer more than the Politburo approved. The 1967 experience probably explains the Politburo's insistence, in 1973, that a formal decision be made that the Soviet Union would not fight.

The Israelis believed that the key to any Egyptian attack was the massive air force stationed mainly in the Nile Delta. In a carefully planned air attack they wiped out most of the Egyptian air arm on the first day of the war. Israeli armor gained control of the Sinai Peninsula. Despite these disasters, Nasser boasted of nonexistent victories, drawing in both Syria and Jordan. Israeli forces defeated both. This "Six Day War" provided Israel with defensible borders: the Suez Canal in the west, the Jordan River in the east, and the Golan Heights in the north. Israel now controlled all of Jerusalem.

Unable to accept the truth, that the Israelis had beaten him unaided, Nasser charged that they had had U.S. support.[119] Henceforth he would rely on the Soviets. He granted them the base facilities they wanted. This was a major disaster for the West. U.S. and British strike carriers still provided much of the air striking power on the NATO southern flank. Until 1967 the main threats they would have faced in wartime were Soviet strike aircraft and submarines. To get at the carriers from their Black Sea bases, the strike aircraft had to fly over NATO territory, where they could be shot down. The submarines had to come from the Soviet Northern Fleet (the Black Sea Fleet had few submarines, because the passage through the Turkish Straits was considered virtually impossible). In wartime they would probably have been blocked at the Straits of Gibraltar and at the Sicilian Narrows. Now they could be based at Alexandria, the old British naval base. Moreover, in the wake of the 1967 war, the Soviets began to operate a major surface fleet, the Fifth Eskadra, in the Mediterranean. Quite aside from any direct impact on allied operations, it helped offset the peacetime effect of allied naval presence. The Soviet naval message, that henceforth the Mediterranean would be extremely dangerous for U.S. carriers, was reinforced by the new practice of "tattletaling," in which Soviet destroyers followed U.S. carriers so as to help direct missile strikes against them in wartime.

The Israelis won the war with aircraft the French had supplied as part of a relationship begun to distract Nasser from supporting the rebels in Algeria. Now, however, Algeria was no longer a problem. The French badly wanted closer ties with Arab governments. General de Gaulle cancelled aircraft deliveries. The United States took his place. Johnson hoped that aid to Israel might help limit Soviet penetration of the entire Middle East by tying down Nasser and Syria, the other Soviet client. For other Arab countries, the United States was now in effect confirming Nasser's propaganda, to the effect that it was the enemy. Nor was the U.S. decision to back Israel popular in Europe, which depended on Arab oil. On the other hand, as Israel's only important arms supplier the United States gained considerable leverage. It now had something to offer the Arabs.

With the Israelis encamped on one of its banks, the Suez Canal was shut. The cost of oil in Europe suddenly escalated, since tankers had to steam all the way around Africa. There was another run on the pound. The British government had to abandon operations "East of Suez," withdrawing from Aden (at the mouth of the Red Sea) in 1968. Stretched by the demands of the Vietnam War, the United States could not take over the British burden. It supported Iran as the guarantor of the Gulf. Because the Saudis rejected Iranian ambitions to control the whole area, they had to be supported as a complementary ally. However, Iran was far more populous and could support far larger forces.

The British area of responsibility "East of Suez" had included the gulf (with its oil) and Southern Africa (with its minerals). In 1962 the British headed off an Iraqi threat to Kuwait. In 1964 they began a struggle to curb a rebellion by Rhodesia's white government against a grant of black rule. The British hoped that by aligning themselves with the black majority they could moderate its politics. Otherwise, when the inevitable happened, the successor Rhodesian government was likely to be pro-Soviet.

Nasser could not tolerate his defeat. In January 1969 he began a "war of attrition" against the Israeli troops encamped on the canal; the Israelis hit back with air attacks. When Brezhnev hesitated to offer aircraft and antiaircraft missiles to attack Israeli aircraft, Nasser threatened to resign in favor of a pro-American president.[120] The war of attrition against the Israeli air force began in January 1970. Many of the personnel involved were Soviet.

The 1967 Israeli victory created an important Soviet asset: a new generation of subversives and terrorists. The PLO and other radical Palestinian organizations took donations (which often meant control) from governments such as those of Syria and Egypt, which were allied to the Soviets. They also enjoyed the protection of oil-rich states such as Saudi Arabia, in which many Palestinians now worked. The rulers of those countries were uncomfortably aware that, for all their posturing, they were doing little or nothing to eject the Israelis. The PLO was a possible nucleus for local revolution. It was far easier to pay what amounted to tribute, encouraging the PLO to limit its activities to Israel.

Western European governments badly wanted to curry favor with the oil-rich states, so they (particularly the French) turned a blind eye to terrorists passing across their borders. Through the 1970s a network of terrorist organizations grew throughout Western Europe, using PLO and other Arab training bases. Examples included the German Red Army Faction (the Baader-Meinhof gang) and the Italian Red Brigades; links were established with older nationalist groups such as the Irish Republican Army. The satellite states in Eastern Europe provided sanctuary. For a time in the 1970s and 1980s, it seemed that German and Italian society in particular were under siege. Terrorists could destabilize governments and they could also impose pressure to throw American bases out of Europe. Soviet involvement was proven when terrorism virtually collapsed upon the collapse of the Soviet Union and its East European empire.

In an echo of 1956, the West lost further influence in the Arab world. The Israeli victory helped weaken pro-Western King Idris of Libya.[121] In 1969 young army officers overthrew him, establishing a radical regime. Although by no means a Soviet satellite, Libya was now strongly sympathetic. Since World War II, it had been under strong British influence, to the point where the British army used it as a training area. The United States had a large air base, Wheelus, there. The new Libyan ruler, Colonel Qaddafi, soon ejected the U.S. Air Force.

Now all of the North African coast was in either neutral or hostile hands. To the extent that wartime passage through the Mediterranean would still be still vital (for example, to reach the NATO southern flank countries), this was a disaster. The Soviets could now base naval strike aircraft in both Libya and Egypt. For a time, for example, they "wet-leased" aircraft to Libya; Soviet crews flew bombers in Libyan markings.

In mid-1967 the Vietnam War seemed to have reached stalemate. From the outset, the great disappointment had been the failure to close the Ho Chi Minh Trail. Later a prominent North Vietnamese officer said that the United States had missed its opportunity to win the war by not occupying a stretch of the trail, in nominally neutral territory, between 1965 and 1967.[1] As it happened, that idea had been proposed—and vetoed—several times, because the key part of the trail was in neutral Laos.[2] Other key targets—the NLF headquarters, the Central Office for South Vietnam (COSVN) and important Viet Cong base areas—were in neutral Cambodia, which also was untouchable.

As the United States poured in troops, so did the Communists, who in each quarter of 1965 added fifteen battalions to the Americans' seven. The North Vietnamese could not match American firepower, so the strength ratio still was estimated as 2.8 to one (rather than the expected 3.2 to one). On this basis Westmoreland kept asking for more troops; by January 1966 he was up to a total of 459,000. Probably Westmoreland really wanted a million men in the beginning, but knew that number was politically impossible. Hence his constant demands for more troops—which soon became equally unpalatable.[3] McNamara became pessimistic; within a year the war might still be undecided, but at a much higher price for the United States. Finally, in October 1966 McNamara vetoed Westmoreland's request for more men, which would have brought the total to 542,588 in 1967.[4]

Westmoreland's generals told him that they were wearing down the enemy, and that enemy attacks had declined, but it was clear that the U.S. Army had been unable to destroy the regular North Vietnamese units. Most importantly, the North Vietnamese were showing no real interest in negotiation.

Something had to be done to break the stalemate. The Joint Chiefs listed options they believed would win the war, singly or in combination: an airborne-amphibious landing just north of the DMS (the "right hook"), a corps-size operation to cut the Ho Chi Minh Trail in Laos; invasion of the enemy sanctuaries in the DMZ, Laos, or Cambodia; or bombing vital targets in Hanoi and Haiphong.[5] By this time the Cultural Revolution was sapping Chinese energies; the Chinese might have found it impossible to intervene effectively. Since none of the Joint Chiefs' options was being discussed seriously, in August 1967 they reportedly briefly considered resigning, then having a press conference. But the Joint Chiefs pulled back.[6] Later, with McNamara gone, they warned President Johnson that progress in Vietnam would be slow unless their proposed operations were approved.

Johnson thought he did not have to take such drastic steps. Reports told him that more aggressive U.S. tactics had increased reported Communist battle deaths from about five thousand to about fifteen thousand per month in the first half of 1967. Against that, the Viet Cong could recruit about thirty-five hundred men per month, and the North Vietnamese could infiltrate about seven thousand per month. After Tet, in February 1968, a senior Viet Cong prisoner said that losses in his region between September 1967 and January 1968 could not be made up.[7] Then, too, an improved pacification program removed up to a million Vietnamese from Communist control, complicating Viet Cong recruiting.

On 1 November 1967 Johnson's "Wise Old Men" met at the State Department to hear an optimistic briefing by Gen. Earle Wheeler, chairman of the JCS. They included Dean Acheson, retired Gen. Omar Bradley, Clark Clifford (who would soon succeed McNamara as secretary of defense), Douglas Dillon, Averell Harriman, retired Gen. Maxwell Taylor, and former Ambassador to Saigon Henry Cabot Lodge. The next day Acheson told Johnson that the country could and would win the war; the North Vietnamese would give up when they realized they could not win. The Korean War had ended the same way.

Acheson was far less optimistic in private. He wrote former British Prime Minister Anthony Eden that Johnson was in trouble. He could handle Vietnam, but not the other crises breaking out: race riots at home, pressure by de Gaulle in Europe, and a continued threat by Nasser in the Middle East. "Americans aren't used to this, and LBJ is not a loveable type. He is the one to blame."[8] In January 1968 Acheson told Johnson that he feared the Pentagon was sanitizing its reports. Four weeks later, Tet seemed to show that he was correct.

Unfortunately, U.S. intelligence was excluding Viet Cong irregulars from its estimate of enemy strength, while including them in its body count. The irregulars provided vital logistical and intelligence support to the enemy. They also defended enemy-held villages and planted many of the mines and booby traps that accounted for about a fifth of U.S. casualties.[9] In 1967 there were probably about as many irregulars (three hundred thousand) as Viet Cong and North Vietnamese regular troops. U.S. intelligence thought the lull in combat was due to the enemy's destruction; it was actually to allow the enemy to build up for the coming decisive battle.

The North Vietnamese, too, sensed stalemate. By late 1966 they knew that they were unlikely to win the kind of quick victory which had seemed so close early in 1965. They and the Viet Cong were becoming demoralized.[10] They were coming to realize just how limited Chinese and Soviet aid was likely to be. Neither was likely to want to confront the United States directly. Protracted war seemed less and less attractive. Continued U.S. bombing of North Vietnam caused some in the North Vietnamese government to advocate abandoning the fight altogether, at least for the time. The dissenters were argued down.

In January 1967 the North Vietnamese formally adopted a new strategy of "fighting while negotiating" instead of the earlier one of people's war. They had used this strategy in 1954; in Ho's words, "military action is the bell, diplomacy is the sounding of the bell."[11] Once negotiations were in train, a devastating military blow could be decisive, in political though not in military terms. But it was pointless to begin talks until a military blow was almost ready. Thus the North Vietnamese suddenly pulled back from a series of talks with the Americans (codenamed Marigold).

A new U.S. initiative began a series of negotiations early in 1967 (Sunflower). The Vietnamese may have seen Sunflower as the negotiations during which they would wage a decisive battle. Certainly by the spring of 1967 the Vietnamese were far more confident of victory.[12] The Tet plan was being framed.

Apparently the Chinese believed that negotiations were the cover for a virtual surrender by the North Vietnamese. In October–November 1966 Chou En-lai asked Le Duan, the Viet Cong leader, to promise to continue fighting at least through 1967.[13] In April 1967 the Chinese extracted a "solemn promise" to continue the war. This was Korea all over again: the Chinese were playing Stalin's old role, and the Vietnamese were bleeding for them.

As the North Vietnamese saw it, the combination of battlefield stalemate and the run-up to the 1968 U.S. election were their window of opportunity. A sharp blow might particularly affect an administration facing the time limit represented by the primaries and the election.[14] The U.S. government misinterpreted what was happening. It thought it had forced the North Vietnamese to bargain. For their part, the North Vietnamese misjudged the strength of South Vietnamese society and of the ARVN itself.

The North Vietnamese hoped that a general uprising in the South Vietnamese cities would, at the least, convince the U.S. government that it should withdraw. That would be easier if power could be handed to a popular front rather than directly to the Viet Cong. The North Vietnamese therefore created a popular front in the South in May 1967, which contested the September 1967 South Vietnamese election.

Giap, still cautious, argued against using regular units in the big attack. The U.S. might retaliate against North Vietnam itself. Thanh saw the coming offensive as an opportunity for Main Force units (including those built up by the Viet Cong). He died in Hanoi about 6 July 1967. At about the same time a North Vietnamese Party plenum approved the attack.[15] All the North Vietnamese ambassadors were recalled for the plenum; the U.S. government thought they were being given new instructions for the peace talks it sought. Ambassadors avoided any stop in China, which opposed any compromise settlement. In September 1967 over two hundred senior Party officials, including the North Vietnamese intelligence chief, were arrested for harboring doubts.

To test U.S. reactions, Giap's regular forces, equipped with new Soviet weapons, attacked across the demilitarized zone (DMZ) into South Vietnam in September 1967. This was the type of war the U.S. had been waiting to fight; Giap's men met unprecedented firepower. However, the Americans did not pursue them across the border. The North Vietnamese concluded that, whatever else might happen during the forthcoming offensive, their home base would not be endangered. The probing attack was also the beginning of a campaign to draw U.S. forces out of the cities. The Viet Cong would then infiltrate those cities in preparation for the "general offensive/uprising." This phase would last through December 1967. Viet Cong forces also began large-scale attacks, which by November were being coordinated across provinces and regions. As in the past, the Viet Cong did not seize territory; instead, they hit outposts, captured weapons, and then pulled back.

The second phase (January–March 1968) would begin with a general uprising in thirty-five South Vietnamese cities. Viet Cong regular forces would attack from the countryside. The Viet Cong would call for a popular uprising. In the third decisive phase, the North Vietnamese army would strike across the DMZ, attacking U.S. units that by now would be engulfed in a sea of hostile people. Another attacking wave would seize the population centers of South Vietnam. The third phase probably was conditioned on the success of the second.

The "general offensive" came on 30 January 1968, during the Tet holiday. A total of eighty-four thousand Viet Cong attacked Saigon, thirty-six of forty-three provincial capitals, five of six autonomous cities, and sixty-four of 242 district capitals. The most spectacular attacks in Saigon were executed by five special shock battalions, who had been training since 1965.[16] One puzzle of the attack was that the Viet Cong did *not* hit the many officers' billets, despite the fact that they knew where those billets were, and that they were lightly protected. The Viet Cong thus missed the opportunity to decapitate the U.S. force.

In most cases the attackers achieved complete—and, for the U.S., embarrassing—tactical surprise. Some great enemy thrust had been expected, but no one had thought the Viet Cong would risk disaster by concentrating in the cities, or that they could coordinate their forces well enough to mount so many nearly simultaneous attacks.[17] According to the official investigation (March 1968), overly optimistic reports (not only on casualties but also on enemy recruitment and morale) contributed heavily to the false sense of security before Tet.

Despite some dramatic successes, such as penetration of the U.S. embassy in Saigon and the capture of the old imperial capital, Hue, the attacks failed. Not only the U.S. Army but also the much-despised ARVN held and fought well. In the cities, the population the Communists had expected to inspire instead rejected them.

Many actually fought the invaders. South Vietnam experienced a marked patriotic surge. The Viet Cong revealed themselves and so attracted the sort of firepower Westmoreland had always wanted to use. Most of their main force units and infrastructure were destroyed; forty thousand to fifty thousand Viet Cong were killed. It was estimated that 40 percent of the NLF cadres were killed or immobilized during Tet.[18] The Viet Cong never recovered.

Overall, Tet failed because the attack plan was too complex; its coordination broke down. Giap had failed to realize just how mobile U.S. forces were; Westmoreland could deal with his border attacks and yet move forces back in time to deal with the big urban attacks. Then, too, the North Vietnamese believed their own propaganda and ideology and expected the South Vietnamese to crumble; in fact the South Vietnamese army fought better than it ever had before or would again.[19]

Many of those who survived Tet defected when their political leadership told them to try the same tactics again.[20] Moreover, the replacements moved into South Vietnam after Tet were of relatively low quality; in October 1967, before Tet, 82 percent of enemy prisoners had had more than six months of service; by May 1968, that number had fallen to 40 percent, and 50 percent of prisoners had had less than three months of service, including time spent infiltrating south. The May attempt to repeat Tet was mounted without tactical surprise and with much less capable troops. Many of the attacks were preempted. Saigon was penetrated, but the Communist troops were soon driven out. Moreover, many Viet Cong survivors believed that they had been placed in the forefront of the attack because the North Vietnamese wanted to destroy their organization, leaving the North Vietnamese supreme.[21] Overall, the damage Tet did to the Viet Cong became a major opportunity for the pacification program.

As Giap had intended, the North Vietnamese army did not participate in the Tet attacks, and thus survived. However, the Tet plan did include follow-up attacks, after which the North Vietnamese army would have poured through the DMZ to link up with the Viet Cong in the cities. As it was, U.S. intelligence did not appreciate the scope of the North Vietnamese plan.[22]

The North Vietnamese acknowledged that Tet had been a disaster. In May, after an internal debate, they decided to retreat to protracted guerilla operations, and to emphasize negotiations rather than combat. They began to speak of rebuilding the North while continuing the struggle at a lower level in the South.[23] With the Viet Cong virtually destroyed, gaps in nominally Viet Cong units were generally filled by North Vietnamese regulars. During the 1968–72 guerilla phase larger North Vietnamese units regularly attacked.[24]

This was success, at least in the field; but it was not seen that way in the United States. The U.S. media reported Tet as a defeat. That was natural; the simple fact that the Viet Cong had been able to attack on such a wide scale made it terribly clear that earlier claims of progress by the United States had been misleading at best. Reportedly President Johnson, who was extremely sensitive to press coverage, found it difficult to decide whether to believe the official account of success, which was so different from that the he saw in the press and on television. He refused to take his advisors' positive reports to the country at large. That mission he left to his generals. Given their poor credibility, the generals' statements fell flat. The U.S. public was already war-weary, though it did not yet strongly favor withdrawal.

Johnson's generals did not help. In March, Westmoreland asked for 206,000 more men, a 40 percent increase. His request seemed to belie his statement that the U.S. had won Tet. In fact, Westmoreland's request had nothing to do with Tet. The army saw Tet as an opportunity finally to get the reserves it needed. Vietnam had whittled its general reserve down to a single airborne division, the 82d, which was being stripped to send troops to Vietnam. The country was becoming restive, partly due to the unpopularity of the war; in his darker moments Army Chief of Staff Gen. Earle Wheeler knew that he did not have enough troops to maintain order.[25]

Visiting Saigon, Wheeler conned Westmoreland into his 206,000-man request. To make his story convincing, he had to describe the post-Tet situation in shockingly gloomy terms. The request proved to be a catalyst for change in the Johnson administration, partly because it was promptly leaked to the *New York Times*.

By this time Johnson considered McNamara defeatist. Clark Clifford, a veteran Democratic strategist, replaced him. The JCS saw Clifford as their man, the antidote to McNamara's surviving "whiz kids." However, Clifford had begun to have doubts. In the late summer of 1967 he and General Taylor had found it difficult to convince other countries in Southeast Asia to contribute troops. Now Johnson asked Clifford to find ways to reinforce Westmoreland. Wheeler's pessimistic report troubled Clifford's task force. The sheer size of the demand for troops would have severe economic and social consequences; it would probably finally kill Johnson's Great Society program.

McNamara was gone, but many of his "whiz kids" remained. Among them was Assistant Secretary of Defense for International Security Affairs Paul Warnke, who disliked the war and was responsible for assembling information for Clifford. The CIA supported the whiz kids, and Clifford listened to their opinion: current policy had failed, and ARVN was nearly useless. The excellent ARVN performance during Tet went unheralded. The CIA's projection of the *least likely* course of enemy action—the expending of forces so completely as to be unable to stop a steady U.S./South Vietnamese advance—was what the enemy actually had done at Tet. Overall, the CIA thought there was a good chance of a South Vietnamese defeat within a few months.

The JCS failed to convince Clifford that 206,000 more men would be enough. All Westmoreland could offer was that, given additional troops, he could cut the Ho Chi Minh Trail in Laos and perhaps in Cambodia and that he could threaten North Vietnam itself by establishing an enclave just north of the DMZ.[26] Clifford decided that Westmoreland could not win; he could only delay a North Vietnamese victory. He recommended shifting the burden of combat to the Vietnamese.[27]

The "wise men" had been badly shaken by Tet (and by the domestic reaction to it). Clifford may have convinced some of them personally. Paul Nitze worried that the effort in Vietnam was weakening the much more important Western alliance. The "wise men" told Johnson to withdraw. Johnson was furious; he felt Clifford had betrayed him by abandoning his administration's policy.[28] However, he made no attempt to replace Clifford, and he did not follow the Joint Chiefs' advice. He adopted Vietnamization (i.e., he placed more of the burden of the war on the South Vietnamese) and a gradual troop withdrawal. Under the new plan, U.S. troops would form a shield behind which ARVN and the South Vietnamese government could develop. Bombing would be limited to the area of North Vietnam relevant to infiltration, near the DMZ, and this limitation would, it was hoped, entice the North Vietnamese to negotiate. The South Vietnamese feared that the U.S. government was planning to sell them out.

Johnson barely won the New Hampshire Democratic primary. On 31 March he announced that in hopes of negotiating a settlement he would stop bombing North Vietnam (actually, the area north of the 20th Parallel) and that he would not run for president in 1968. Negotiations began in Paris on 10 May—just before Johnson planned to resume bombing in northern North Vietnam if the negotiations had not started. They led nowhere. Probably Ho remembered his bitter experience in 1954; he was interested in victory, not compromise. Moreover, Johnson's retreat gave him hope.

On 31 October Johnson announced a total halt to bombing North Vietnam. He apparently hoped to get the talks moving in order to give his vice president, Hubert H. Humphrey, a better chance in the coming election. Although the North Vietnamese also preferred Humphrey to his opponent, Richard Nixon, they stalled the talks. Plenary sessions began only on 25 January 1969, after Nixon had already been sworn in. The South Vietnamese, who did want Nixon, did their best to stall the process. The talks went nowhere for nearly four years; the North Vietnamese were well aware that Nixon could not withdraw from the talks. They felt free to violate a series of "understandings" Johnson had tried to impose: that they had to accept the South Vietnamese government as a party to the talks; that they would stop attacking major South Vietnamese cities; that they would stop sending troops across the DMZ; and that they would allow unarmed aerial reconnaissance of North Vietnam.

Thus when Johnson left office in January 1969 the military situation in South Vietnam was better than it had been for many years, thanks to the Viet Cong's self-inflicted wounds in the Tet Offensive. However, as the North Vietnamese well knew, the U.S. public and its Congress were, to put it mildly, tired of the war. The North Vietnamese still believed that striking a blow during negotiations could be decisive. Moreover, the talks had given them some badly needed breathing space.

On the other hand, after Tet, and perhaps particularly after Johnson's announcement of negotiations, the U.S. Army began to disintegrate. Like the North

Vietnamese and the Viet Cong, American soldiers thought that the war would soon end. No one wanted to be the last casualty. In addition, the antiwar movement, which was becoming quite effective, was beginning to affect the army in Vietnam. The lack of support from home was discouraging; it made the war seem pointless and dishonorable. Probably many were furious that they received no recognition for the Tet victory—which the U.S. media did not even consider a victory.

Discipline began to decline in 1969, reaching its lowest level by 1971. By 1969 the quality of NCOs and junior officers was noticeably lower than it had been, leading to incidents like the My Lai Massacre. For example, "fragging"—attacks on officers by enlisted men—were first reported in 1969. Offenses within the army in Vietnam rose 13 percent between 1968 and 1969 even though the army was shrinking; cases of mutiny rose by about a third during the same period. The figures do not include very common forms of insubordination such as "search and evade"—refusing to find the enemy when on patrol. The rate of drug arrests rose by about 75 percent. In 1970, hard drugs appeared in the army for the first time.[29]

The war also had badly weakened the U.S. economy. In the spring of 1968, after Tet, the projected FY69 deficit was $24.2 billion, more than the total of the last five years. The deficit could be attributed entirely to the war, which was costing $25 billion annually. It was impossible to cut the deficit by raising taxes, due to the crisis in public confidence (as reflected in Congress). De Gaulle, who already opposed the Vietnam War, attacked the now-vulnerable U.S. economy by demanding gold for dollars held by France, as permitted under the Bretton Woods agreement. The British, de Gaulle's other nemesis, were already in economic trouble. Both governments had to scramble to keep the Bretton Woods arrangements alive.

Kim Il Sung of North Korea apparently saw the Vietnam War as an opportunity to renew his own fight. This time he ordered diversionary (special forces) attacks on South Korea, initially to keep South Korean troops from going to Vietnam, and then to exploit the fact that the U.S. *and* South Korean armies were tied down in Vietnam.[30] The attacks began during President Johnson's 1966 visit to Seoul. Troops infiltrated across the border using both tunnels and small craft. In January 1968 a thirty-one-man unit went into South Korea specifically to kill President Chung Hee Park. It was destroyed only eight hundred meters from the presidential palace, the Blue House. At about this time Kim seized the U.S. intelligence ship *Pueblo* off his coast. The incident, unexplained at the time, may have been intended to prevent discovery of the North Korean infiltrators.

Kim's attacks were worrisome because the Koreans had sent a very large contingent to Vietnam; those forces might be recalled if the threat from the north escalated. In 1969 North Korean fighters shot down a U.S. RC-121 reconnaissance aircraft. Tied down in Vietnam, the United States could not respond effectively. Kim's infiltration across the border effectively ended that year.[31] However, Kim continued to build up his special forces for a further attempt at infiltration.

Besides being the year of Tet, 1968 was also a terrifying year for Western stability. Probably the basic reason was the wave of baby boomers who were of university (or military) age throughout the West. The postwar economic recovery had made it possible for an unprecedented proportion of those adolescents to go into college rather than into the work force. University facilities in France and Italy were grossly inadequate. There were not nearly enough teachers. One consequence was that, far more than in the past, students listened to each other, rather than to older or more conservative voices. Student movements could thus become extremely powerful. The French and Italian economies were not nearly flexible enough to accommodate the graduates the universities were churning out. In both countries, student discontent merged into a kind of revolutionary romanticism. The Soviets had been discredited, so many students spoke instead of Mao's Cultural Revolution—which was attractive because it was so little understood. It offered what they most wanted, which was to tear apart a social system that they felt was strangling them.

In France, social policies that had been designed, before World War II, to guarantee the rights of workers made it very difficult for businesses to risk hiring new employees. That was all very well as long as the population was stable, but it could not accommodate the baby boom. In May 1968 an attempt to prohibit a student demonstration soon caused a strike and then a battle with the Paris police.[32] The French left-wing unions called a general strike to protest police brutality. The movement gathered momentum; its strength seemed huge because few spoke out against it. In France, probably more than in any other Western European country, governments were sensitive to the threat of mob violence in the capital. Paris mobs had overthrown French governments before, beginning with the monarchy in 1789.

When de Gaulle ordered an end to the unrest, the students were unmoved. Premier Pompidou actually seemed to surrender to the students, because he considered the general strike a much more serious threat. The Communists who were running the strike had little use for the anarchist student movement, which challenged the Communist power base in the unions. For example, the Communists found that workers rejected the deal they soon extracted from Premier Pompidou. In the end, de Gaulle asked the faithful to join a monster demonstration—which succeeded—and dissolved parliament, calling new elections. The crisis subsided, having demonstrated just how fragile France was. De Gaulle himself ordered constitutional reforms, subject to a referendum. He made it clear that the vote would actually be a vote of confidence. When his reforms were defeated, on 27 April 1969, he resigned. His anti-NATO policy, however, survived, proving that it had much deeper foundations than his own resentment of his wartime and postwar allies.

Italy was in an even worse situation, because in effect it was a one-party state; by definition, the Communists were excluded from power. As in the Soviet Union, patronage and, therefore, corruption flourished, albeit without the police horrors of the Soviet version. The sclerosis of Italian society was reflected in a grossly inadequate university system. Still, admissions were allowed to explode. To a growing number of students, the problems they saw in school proved that the larger society was incapable of modernization.

Student protests began in Italy in 1967. Perhaps because there was no single dramatic explosion, the protests lasted for years, with two major consequences. One was the growth of a left-wing terrorist movement, beginning in 1970. The other was a wave of strikes in 1969–70, which ended a long period of labor peace.[33] As in France, the strikes demonstrated a loss of Communist control of the labor unions. To Italian students, the events in France in May and June 1968 proved that there was a real hope of revolution if they could wrestle control of the labor movement from the Communist Party—which they saw as an accomplice of the existing social and economic order. The Italian "Red Brigades" were worse than any other in Europe. Violence from the Left engendered further violence from the Right. Eventually the Maoist Red Brigades attacked not only Christian Democrats but also Communists they accused of collaborating with the state.[34]

Because the new movement was so fragmented, it could not make national wage agreements that would hold. The level of wages ratcheted up, so that by 1974 wage increases greatly exceeded any growth in productivity. Inflation exploded.

German students also rioted, partly because of the same problems as those encountered by the French and Italian students. There was also a political dimension, rooted partly in perceptions of the country's Nazi past. Protests began in the spring of 1966, when the Social Democrats joined with the formerly governing Christian Democrats in a "grand coalition" which would control 90 percent of the votes in the Bundestag, precluding any sort of effective opposition. To the West German Left, this development justified formation of an extraparliamentary opposition—an opposition to the German governing system. Using its overwhelming parliamentary power, the coalition proposed emergency laws to be activated in the event of invasion—or internal unrest; given Germany's past history, they could be described as an enabling act for a new dictatorship. The Left also opposed West German support for the United States in Vietnam and for Israel in 1967. In 1967–68 the German students demonstrated and ultimately rioted, culminating in Easter riots in West Berlin in 1968 and in riots in all the major cities in April 1968. The demonstrations ended with a May 1968 march on Bonn to protest ratification of the emergency laws—whose passage undoubtedly had been helped along by the earlier disorders. Much of the rioting centered on Axel Springer, a conservative who nearly monopolized the German press.

Germans student protesters saw in Vietnam, as it was presented to them, a reminder of the Nazi past; they equated the Springer press with the Hugenberg press of the early 1930s, which had helped bring Hitler to power; and they saw in the new emergency laws a parallel to the Enabling Act with which Hitler had scrapped the Weimar constitution. They saw the Grand Coalition as a parallel to the coalition of nationalists and Nazis that had brought Hitler to power (ironically, it brought Willy Brandt, the architect of *ostpolitik,* into power as foreign minister; thus it was a halfway house towards exactly the foreign policy the students espoused). The State's intense anti-Communism was dismissed as a way of diverting attention from the depredations of German industrialists, and it was also a dangerous way of exacerbating tension between East and West. Springer fought back, mobilizing much West German opinion against the students. He was unique in this regard in the countries affected by student disorders; no other press magnate made the attempt. He argued that during the Weimar period Hitler had successfully exploited disorders just like those the students were now causing; they were trying to destroy a valuable democracy. He also demanded that Communism be equated with Nazism, exactly what the left-wing student radicals were trying to deny. Thus he and his followers implied that the student movement was an attempt to subvert the West German democracy.

Overall, the student movement failed because West German workers were far too prosperous to be interested in revolution, and because many West Germans still realized just how dangerous Communism could be. Even so, the students did indirectly force the government to limit Springer's press monopoly. Moreover, the Grand Coalition did not last. The 28 September 1969 election eliminated the Christian Democrats' majority, although that party was still the largest in the Bundestag. Now the Social Democrats, Brandt's SPD, could rule by making an alliance with the small Liberal party (FDP). Because some members of both parties opposed the new policy of *ostpolitik,* the new coalition had only a very thin majority with which to pursue its new policy (it received a comfortable majority in 1972). The new government took office in October 1969. Presumably its emergence, and thus the success of *ostpolitik,* can be traced in part to the emotions and thoughts stirred up by the students the previous year. Certainly the new policy fulfilled, in effect, the students' demands for less anti-Communism and for an accommodation with the Soviets.

There was one darker outcome. In April 1968, supposedly inflamed by Axel Springer's propaganda, a twenty-three-year-old student tried to kill Rudi Dutschke, leader of the German League of Socialist Students. A small group took this attempt as proof that terrorism was the only solution to German problems. Led by Andreas Baader, Gudrun Ensslin, and Ulrike Meinhof, they formed the notorious Baader-Meinhof Gang (Red Army Faction), which terrorized the upper levels of German society through the 1970s and early 1980s. It also attacked U.S. military installations in Germany. Victims included the head of the Deutsche Bank, the president of the West German employers' association, the leader of the Berlin CDU Party, and the president of the Berlin Supreme Court. The Red Army Faction also collaborated with the PLO, for example in a December 1975 attack against oil ministers. The East German government provided the PLO with support, and it was a haven for escaping members of the Red Army Faction. It also provided them with essential training; it is not clear to what extent it directed their efforts. Certainly the East German government saw terrorism as a valuable means of attacking its West German enemy.[35]

All of the protests were, in the end, attacks on the governing establishments of the countries, and the students generally seem to have associated those establishments with the United States, as the prime mover of the Cold War. It seems arguable that whatever political protests might otherwise have ignited in 1968 were dramatically strengthened because the apparent success of the Tet Offensive in Vietnam seemed to demonstrate that the Western establishment might actually be overthrown, that the revolution might have a chance of winning. Each disorder was tied to local conditions, and each ran its course nearly independently. The students and other radicals involved did communicate with each other. For example, a key figure in the French student rising was Daniel Cohn-Bendit, a German. To some extent disorders sparked each other because each received international publicity via television. Once protests reached a critical mass, they attracted television coverage that made them seem far larger and more significant. That was certainly true of the disorders in Chicago, at the 1968 Democratic Party convention. This impression in turn inspired protesters in other countries, who (wrongly) scented success. In 1968 truly global television coverage on a current basis, which was possible mainly because communications satellites had come into service, was still quite new. In earlier times film would have been carried from country to country, and television news would have spread relatively slowly. Preparations might have been made for quick coverage of a particular event, but not of an entirely unexpected series of disorders such as those which rocked Paris—or Chicago. Even so, it is striking that while there were student disorders throughout the West in 1968, nothing approached the intensity of those in the United States, France, Italy, and West Germany.

The difference in outcome was striking. In France, the social fabric was strong enough to withstand the shock, and a new election ended the crisis. Much the same could be said of Germany, where the crisis seems not to have been as deep. In Italy, a weaker social fabric suffered protracted strain, to the point where it seemed for a time that it would tear.

The combination of demographics and stagnation applied to Eastern Europe as well. It explains why, for example, the Czechs were willing to take such desperate chances in 1968. In Eastern Europe, the mere threat of disorder was so frightening that governments tried to appease potential opponents—but could not go far enough to solve their problems.

The Soviets' political victories were marred by economic failure. Given Brezhnev's new laissez faire approach, his military ate whatever growth the Soviet economy could generate. Yet, like Khrushchev, Brezhnev felt that he had to offer his population a higher standard of living. To do that, he bought grain from the West. Using it, he converted much of Soviet agriculture from grain to meat production, increasing the proportion of meat in the Soviet diet. Grain had to be paid for in hard currency; the main thing Brezhnev could sell the West was raw materials, principally oil. Thus oil production became crucial as a way of making up for the inefficiency and militarization of the Soviet economy. A Soviet economist later called it the drug to which the economy became addicted.

The 1976–1980 and 1981–1985 Five Year Plans both failed, and between 1979 and 1982 the Soviet economy either did not grow or actually declined.[1] A Soviet economist, G. I. Khanin, estimated that the economy had grown only 5 percent in all between 1976 and 1980 and 3 percent in 1981–85, compared to 17 percent in 1971–75 and 22 percent in 1966–70.[2] Growth had been exaggerated for years; Khanin estimated that the Soviet economy was less than two-thirds as large as the CIA imagined, or about a third as large as that of the United States.[3] A major crop failure (1975) seemed to prove the system itself was failing. Much worse than economic failure was a disastrous loss of morale, a loss of interest in work, and a growing awareness of corruption and abuse of power.[4] People became aware of just how prosperous the West was, and of how badly the Soviet Union was falling behind, despite various official promises. None of this was likely to upset the regime, but it did make people more pessimistic and less likely to work hard. Beginning in 1975 Yuri Andropov, the head of the KGB, began sending Brezhnev reports of hard times to come. They were sealed into special envelopes that only Brezhnev could open. Andropov's prescription was a tougher (and more honest) regime under which people would work harder.[5]

The base cause of this economic disaster—the cost imposed by the military buildup—was not discussed. Instead, Brezhnev's enemies focussed on corruption.

His pledge not to punish the Party had meant that it could expand out of control. Although the corruption of power had always characterized the Soviet state, Brezhnev's coincided with obvious national stagnation. To his enemies, the corruption of Brezhnev's own family was symbolic of the problems of his regime. Brezhnev's daughter, Galina, was married to Deputy Minister of Internal Affairs Gen. Yuri Churbanov; one of her lovers was a Bolshoi opera company singer, Boris ("the Gypsy") Buryata. During the summer of 1982, shortly before Brezhnev died, the KGB revealed that Boris the Gypsy was part of a vast diamond- and currency-smuggling operation. It had been covered up by Churbanov and by another Brezhnev crony, Deputy Chairman of the KGB Gen. Semyon Tsvigun (Churbanov's brother-in-law). Boris the Gypsy died in KGB hands and Tsvigun apparently committed suicide. Further corruption scandals involving Brezhnev's inner circle were investigated in the fall of 1982; among those arrested were the manager of the main Moscow food store (which served the Party elite) and an executive at GUM, the department store. It was widely believed that, as chairman of the KGB, Andropov had ordered the investigations as a way of undercutting Brezhnev.[6]

In Eastern Europe, economic growth stalled just as the baby-boom generations of the satellite countries reached maturity. Expanded educational systems produced many more educated people than shrinking economies could absorb. It became, if that was possible, even more obvious that the system was fundamentally corrupt; all the good jobs went to Party members. That left a growing dissatisfied class. They could not overcome the Party's raw power and its secret police, but they would celebrate when the crisis eventually struck.

Czechoslovakia was the first case in point. With the country beset by economic troubles, in 1967 its Central Committee voted out Stalinist ruler Anton Novotny, replacing him with a newcomer, Aleksandr Dubcek. Chosen as a decidedly conservative Communist, Dubcek rather suddenly decided on a Khrushchev-like thaw, which became known as the "Prague Spring." He seems not to have realized that any sort of tolerance of alternative ideas could be quite dangerous; he thought that it was enough to reassure the Soviets that, unlike Imre Nagy, he did not intend to quit the Warsaw Pact. However, Dubcek's "socialism with a human face" was coming to look a great deal like an alternative to the more or less monolithic system followed elsewhere within the Soviet bloc. The Soviets found that threatening enough. Moreover, there were important links (and a fairly open border) between Czechoslovakia and the western Ukraine; Ukrainians could see and hear Czech broadcasts and could read their newspapers.[7] Prominent Soviet dissidents began to find inspiration in the Czech reforms. Discussions in Czechoslovakia of past excesses by the security police naturally made the KGB nervous.

Brezhnev's notebooks show that he considered a military solution as early as April 1968, after having attended a Warsaw Pact meeting in March; it concluded that Socialism was disintegrating in Czechoslovakia. After a May meeting with Dubcek, he told the Politburo that the Czech party was "headless." Marshal Grechko returned from a trip to Prague saying that "the army has disintegrated. Liberalization and democratization are in essence counterrevolution." The situation was so bad that, for the first half of 1968 the Politburo spent most of its time on the Czech crisis. Andropov compared Czechoslovakia to Hungary in 1956.[8]

The European satellite rulers also were nervous.[9] As they had since the beginning of the Sino-Soviet schism, their views counted. The first Pact leader to denounce the "Prague Spring" was Gomulka of Poland (19 March); Ulbricht of East Germany soon followed him. At a conference in Dresden in late March they denounced the Czech reforms as "counterrevolution." At another conference in Moscow early in May 1968 they demanded immediate action. The Bulgarians, who initially favored the Czech developments, began to sour in April. The Hungarians joined the anti-Czech bandwagon in June.[10] The agreement among the Pact governments apparently changed the Soviet attitude from wait-and-see to "extreme measures."

Plans for a Warsaw Pact training exercise, which could be turned into an invasion, went ahead. In June Brezhnev approved the exercise. The Politburo began to discuss armed intervention. Brezhnev received a letter from Czech hardliners asking for help, but the Politburo considered it an inadequate pretext for action. Finally he obtained a letter from five senior Czechs. It took the Politburo three days to decide to act. Andropov had been the strongest advocate of intervention.[11]

The Soviet Union would preserve what it called Socialism by force. That was an inevitable extension of the political contract Khrushchev had developed after 1957. The Soviet Union would back up its client Communist governments in Eastern Europe when their own populations threatened them; in return, those client states would become the Soviet Union's vassals. It seems noteworthy that it took pressure by the other Pact governments to push the Politburo to action. It was, then, appropriate that the armed forces of the entire Warsaw Pact (except for Romania), led by the Soviets, poured into Czechoslovakia. As in Hungary, massed tanks were the symbols of repression. Dubcek was deposed. It was now obvious that the Soviets were an imperial, not an ideological, power.

The Czech invasion was not undertaken lightly. Given their ideology, the Soviet leadership assumed that Dubcek was a Western agent, and they warned their troops that they might well encounter NATO armored forces. If they did, they were instructed to back off. Dubcek might be a disaster, but a war in Central Europe would be worse. Since Dubcek was not a Western agent, there was never any possibility that NATO would intervene when the Soviet tanks appeared. The Soviets no longer had to fear any NATO attempt to roll back the Iron Curtain.

By failing to participate, the Romanians in effect broke with the Warsaw Pact, although they retained membership and continued to receive new weaponry. Apparently the Soviets, long irritated by the Romanians' independence, seriously considered a second invasion.[12] The Romanians carefully avoided any provocation. It probably helped that Nicolae Ceausescu, the Romanian dictator, combined his independent foreign policy with a Stalinist domestic policy, much sterner than that the Soviets had adopted. Romania could not provide an example to subversive forces within the Soviet bloc.

For Brezhnev, the invasion was a resounding success. Unlike the Hungarians in 1956, the Czechs hardly resisted; there was very little bloodshed. Perhaps that was because Dubcek had applied reforms from above. Czechs had been grateful, and they certainly liked the reforms, but that was very different from a popular uprising (as in Hungary), which might have triggered a Soviet invasion. By mid-1968, moreover, the worrying Vietnam crisis had largely been tamed. The U.S. government was clearly finding less and less popular support for the war, and its interest in talks showed that it would not expand the war in any dangerous way.

Western leaders acted as though the invasion was a normal measure to restore order to a Soviet empire that they fully recognized. Thus as early as 10 September President Johnson said that he hoped this "setback" (to détente) would be only temporary, and French Foreign Minister Michel Debre called the invasion "an unpleasant incident along the road." Johnson was apparently reacting to continuing Western European pressure; everyone wanted some sort of agreement.[13]

The general nonreaction to the invasion presumably demonstrated that Western morale was slipping. The Cold War surely had a long way to run, but, to Brezhnev, victory was in sight. After the invasion, at the Czech spa of Karlovy Vary (Karlsbad), he told his fellow Warsaw Pact rulers that within two decades the United States would be beaten.[14] Brezhnev soon proclaimed a new doctrine, named after him: each Socialist country had a duty not only to preserve Socialism at home but to protect it abroad—which meant helping to crush any regime trying to reverse Socialism.

In the long run, the invasion caused the Soviets real problems. It demonstrated that innovation would not be tolerated—not only in the satellite countries but also, by extension, within the Soviet Union itself. Dubcek had, it seemed, shown that any attempt to open politics (hence economics) would threaten the system itself. Some members of the Soviet elite became disenchanted; the invasion provided a pretext for protests by dissenters.[15] It seemed that Stalinism was creeping back; with it inevitably came economic stagnation in the Soviet Union. That stagnation would begin to cause real problems within a decade. For the moment, Khrushchev argued that the crisis would never have come had Novotny, the previous Czech ruler, had the sense to denounce the Stalinist crimes committed in his own country; such denunciation would have reduced the pressure released when Dubcek opened up Czech society.[16]

To Castro, the invasion showed that Brezhnev was serious, that it was time to stop flirting with heresies such as exporting violent revolution without permission. The Soviets had been trying to bring Castro to heel for some time. They had imagined, wrongly, that it was enough to be Castro's only important oil supplier. Thus in 1967 they offered a 2 percent increase in oil deliveries when Castro urgently needed eight.[17] But the Soviet Union's ability to limit Cuba's oil supply was not enough. Initially the Cuban media attacked the invasion; if the Soviets could crush Czechoslovakia, why not Cuba as well? Castro soon realized how weak his position was. Without Soviet backing he could hardly expect to hold off the Americans. He spoke out in favor of the invasion; the Soviets would never invade Cuba because they would never question his loyalty. In 1969 and 1970 he got the oil he needed, as well as additional Soviet technicians. Henceforth his troops would be available to support Soviet operations.

As in 1956, a Soviet invasion caused problems in the larger Communist world. To the Chinese, it showed that the Soviets really might attack, so it exacerbated the Sino-Soviet schism. The Italians, who had been losing members since 1956, broke with the Soviets over the 1968 Czech invasion. For some time they had been seeking a position independent of both the Soviets and the Chinese.

Poland suffered from much the same problems as Czechoslovakia. December 1970 price increases led to worker riots in Gdansk and to student demonstrations, which were violently repressed. Edward Gierek, who promised "goulash Communism," replaced the Polish ruler, Wladyslaw Gomulka, who had been installed to avoid a disaster in 1956. The Czech example was far too dangerous to follow. Structural reform could not be considered. Gierek convinced the Soviets to allow him to borrow money from the West. With some of it he could buy consumer goods, which could be sold at low prices to keep Polish workers happy. For example, in Warsaw in 1974 a bottle of imported Coca-Cola could be bought for the equivalent of eight cents.

The rest of the borrowed money would modernize Polish industry. In theory, profits from exports produced by that industry would pay off the debt. That was impossible. New machinery might be bought, but without serious reforms the industrial system could not really improve. No new export sector was created. Too much of the money was spent on political patronage—in effect, stolen by the Polish party elite.

After 1968 the Czechs tried much the same tactics. For example, in 1971 there was one car for every seventeen Czechs; that number rose to one car for every eight Czechs in 1979.[18] As in Poland, no economic reform was allowed, for fear that the 1968 virus would return.

After the 1973 oil shock money flowed into Arab hands. To encourage the Arabs to place that money in their banks, Western bankers had to offer high rates of return. To earn them, they sought customers for enormous loans at high interest rates. Only governments qualified. Suddenly it became very easy for the satellite governments to borrow money (Third World governments did the same). For the bankers, the loans seemed perfectly safe; no government would ever declare bankruptcy. In the case of Eastern Europe, Western governments encouraged the loans because they seemed to be part of détente. Communist bloc debt increased from $13 billion in 1974 to $50 billion by 1977. Very high interest compounded the problem. In 1981 East European and Soviet debt to Europe and the United States was fifteen times what it had been in 1970.[19] The situation escalated as the Soviets raised their own oil prices within their empire.

These problems affected all of Eastern Europe, most significantly, from the point of the Cold War, Poland. The Polish hard-currency debt grew from $700 million in 1971 to $6 billion in 1975. After a bad grain harvest in 1976, the government decided to import grain, paying for it with meat exports. It found that it had to raise meat prices to keep the Poles themselves from buying all of the available meat. To Poles, even the suggestion of a price increase meant that the 1970 agreement not to raise prices had been cancelled. There were riots and strikes. The standard of living began to collapse.[20] That disaster led in turn to the creation of a truly independent union, Solidarity, which would undermine the Polish government.

Yet the government could not afford to squeeze hard enough to pay off its debt. By 1979 interest payments consumed 92 percent of Polish export earnings. The Poles had to borrow to pay their interest; their debt snowballed. By 1989 it had reached $40 billion. Quite soon only the Soviet Union, with its oil income, could pay enough to keep Poland solvent. The Romanians recognized that piling up debt would ultimately mean handing control to the Soviets. Ceausescu chose to pay off his debt by squeezing his economy, relying on what amounted to Stalinist control to avoid problems. That worked through the 1970s and 1980s, but it probably worsened the explosion in 1989.

Hungary had a somewhat more efficient economy, because its government had accepted some private enterprise; it had relaxed some controls to avoid any danger of another uprising like the one in 1956. However, its tentative steps towards a free market could not protect Hungary from the combined effects of rising Soviet oil prices and falling world prices for the raw materials it exported (aluminum and grain).

In economic, and therefore political, trouble, the East European governments forced Brezhnev to put Khrushchev's economism into practice, ultimately with serious consequences for the Soviet Union. Following up a Polish initiative, in 1971 Brezhnev set up a Comprehensive Program for Socialist Economic Integration.[21] To prop up their economies, the East Europeans needed cheap energy (at sub-sidized prices, from the Soviet Union) and markets for their products. Market forces were irrelevant: the terms of trade—even how much was traded—were negotiated by Eastern European politicians who had long ago understood what economism meant: the Soviets had to continue to buy their loyalty. Satellite exports, machinery and consumer goods were grossly overpriced, because their prices were set equal to those of much superior Western goods. The Soviets felt compelled to sell the satellites raw materials, particularly fuels, at low prices. The satellite governments therefore always tried to increase the volume of trade, whereas the Soviets tried to hold back; the materials they were sending to Eastern Europe could have been sold to the West for the hard currency they needed. Thus satellite-made consumer goods were always in short supply in the Soviet Union. The heavily militarized Soviet economy could not provide any alternative. Because the Soviets had to take whatever they shipped, the satellites generally sent their worst products, reserving anything better for less forgiving Western markets.

The Soviets knew they were in trouble, but they saw no way out, as long as they held Eastern Europe by economism. In 1971 they calculated that it was 32 percent more expensive to import machinery from Czechoslovakia and East Germany than to make it in the Soviet Union, 28 percent more expensive to import it from Hungary, and 20 percent more expensive to import it from Poland.[22]

Later the satellites got into worse trouble. Eventually the Soviets raised the price of the energy they were providing. At the same time the price of Western machinery began to fall. Now the satellite states had to export more and more in return for each unit they imported—28 percent more in 1984 than in 1980. In the Warsaw Pact as a whole officially calculated growth slowed from 4.1 percent per year in 1976–80 to 3.1 percent in 1981–84. In Hungary and Romania (and in some parts of Czechoslovakia) the standard of living fell. The Soviets had to extend loans to make up for the imbalance of trade; the estimated subsidy involved was 18 billion rubles in 1981–84.[23]

None of these figures was particularly meaningful in Western terms, but to the Soviets they gave some idea of the scale of the disaster. Trade was conducted by barter or by fictitious "transfer rubles." For example, in the 1980s the Soviets shipped refrigerators to Poland. The Poles shipped back food or raw materials or requested manufactured goods of an equivalent value in "transfer rubles," whether or not the refrigerators found a market. After the collapse, it would be estimated that the Soviet subsidy to the satellites amounted to $87.2 billion between 1960 and 1980.[24]

To some degree the satellite and Soviet economies really were integrated. For example, Poland built a large steel complex at Katowice, specifically to handle Soviet ore. Polish finished steel was shipped back. Particular satellite countries became important producers of weapons for the Soviet Union and the entire bloc (and also for export). Poland built most Soviet amphibious warfare ships. Hungary became the main computer maker. East Germany made precision equipment, including optics. Hopefully each satellite would become so dependent on the Soviets and on the other satellites that breakup would become inconceivable. Much the same thing had been done inside the Soviet Union. When the system did break up, it certainly caused profound dislocation. However, when the crisis came, political passions were far too intense for that to matter. Perhaps this was yet another example of Communist wrong-headedness; politics trumped economics, rather than the other way around.

From a military point of view the Czech invasion was frightening because the Soviets had achieved so high a degree of tactical, if not strategic, surprise.[25] It was no longer possible to believe that NATO would enjoy sufficient warning to mobilize in the face of a Warsaw Pact attack. Then, too, once the invasion was over, the Soviets gained a permanent military presence in Czechoslovakia (which they had long wanted), complicating NATO defense.[26] The Soviets had been particularly concerned that the Prague Spring would disrupt nuclear storage arrangements.[27]

By the early 1970s it seemed that the Soviets could attack with no more than forty-eight hours of visible preparation. In the past, NATO had assumed a "23/30" scenario: the Soviets would take thirty days to mobilize, and NATO would take a week to decide to respond, leaving it twenty-three days to mobilize its defense. The shorter warning time was due to a buildup in Soviet numbers. In the past, battle tanks stored in the Soviet Union had to be moved up to attack positions. As the Soviet tank inventory grew, however, tanks could be stored in ready condition in forward areas while others were worn out in training. The appearance of the special warehouses probably was the key evidence that the Soviets were moving towards a standing-start posture. As in Czechoslovakia, the Soviets could use a large-scale exercise as cover for final mobilization, then turn west.

Early in 1968 McNamara was still blithely announcing that NATO could stand off the Warsaw Pact, that it enjoyed rough parity on the ground and a significant edge in the air. Unaware of the depth of Khrushchev's force cuts, he and his staff also were unaware of force increases. It takes time to form units and to reopen factories, and it takes even more time for the fruits of such actions to become visible, even to satellites. Thus, despite the shock of the invasion, the European allies saw little point in increasing their contributions to NATO.[28] The consequences of McNamara's misplaced optimism would become obvious in the 1970s, when in the aftermath of Vietnam Congress would not provide the money needed to rebuild U.S. forces.

Overall, the decline of apparent U.S. commitment in the face of growing Soviet power made Western Europe much more vulnerable to Soviet blandishments. Throughout the Vietnam War, the Soviets made much of the fact that they were at peace, whereas the United States was fighting a hot, dirty guerilla war. Their usual peace propaganda suddenly seemed meaningful. The Western Europeans began to think more about accommodation with the Soviets.

As an early indicator of an important trend, the Czech invasion had remarkably few political consequences in the West. Instead, Western youngsters were immersed in protest against the reigning system (albeit not in support of its Soviet alternative). In the United States that summer, the Democratic National Convention was conducted amid unprecedented scenes of rioting and police brutality. Few of the protesters were particularly interested in foreign affairs, other than in Vietnam. In France, disorders, which at times seemed to approach revolution, in effect toppled General de Gaulle. Again, there was little interest in events farther east.

NATO arms reduction proposals did have to be abandoned after the invasion, but the underlying Western European sentiment survived. Moreover, the Czech invasion did not keep the Germans from moving to the left. In 1969, the first German Social Democratic government, under Willy Brandt, succeeded the Grand Coalition of 1966. *Ostpolitik* had arrived.

While all of this was happening in Europe, Mao was tearing China apart. With the bomb in hand, and with the Americans tied down in Vietnam, he was relatively safe from foreign attack. Mao could now purge the Chinese Communist Party. In 1966 he created the teen-aged Red Guards, telling them to overturn their elders and smash anything that was not "red" enough. The Soviet enemy became a focus of this Great Proletarian Cultural Revolution. For example, the Beijing street on which the Soviet embassy lay was renamed for the Struggle against Revisionism. Anti-Soviet slogans and portraits of Mao surrounded the embassy. For a time it was blockaded day and night by Red Guards shouting slogans through loudspeakers. Chinese still living in Moscow demonstrated against the Soviet Communist Party.[29] The Chinese Army (PLA) was ordered not to interfere with the revolution. As in the Soviet Union of the 1930s, individuals whose main qualification was loyalty to Mao replaced many officers. For example, Mao's orderly was made a divisional commander.

Some local commanders tried to restore order. In Wuhan, the military district commander formed the "Million Heroes" to join his troops against the Red Guards. In effect, he mutinied. An airborne corps sent by Beijing attacked him in turn.[30] Regional commanders were ordered once more not to interfere, and the Red Guards began to attack their headquarters. By August 1967 the Red Guards were fighting the army throughout China. The radicalization of the army was officially halted on 5 September 1967, when it was instructed to restore order. More than half of the PLA troops were used in this effort. On National Day, 1 October 1967, the generals stood with Mao atop the Gate of Heavenly Peace in Beijing, and two weeks later Chinese youth were ordered to return to their studies. However, some fighting continued into 1968.[31] Millions of people may have been killed, the PLA suffering hundreds of thousands of casualties.[32] Perhaps as importantly, by 1971 the PLA was performing most police functions in China, dissipating its strength. Overall, it seems fair to equate the Great Cultural Revolution to Stalin's purges of the 1930s.

By 1968, moreover, Mao badly needed to regroup his forces; the August invasion of Czechoslovakia showed how real the Soviet military threat might be. To Mao, the Great Cultural Revolution had been particularly provocative to the Soviets because its purpose had largely been to root out Soviet sympathizers within the Chinese party and the military, which Mao considered threats to his own authority. For the first time, the Chinese focussed on the ongoing military buildup in Siberia. For example, in September 1968 they began to protest Soviet overflights, which had been going on for some time.[33] On 26 November Chou En-lai invited the United States to resume contacts in Warsaw, which had been suspended in May; clearly there was some interest in finding a new ally to balance against the increasingly powerful Soviet enemy. This was despite evident Chinese discomfort at the mildness of U.S. protests against the Czech invasion; if the Americans so valued their relationship with the Soviets, how far would they go to help China in the event of a Soviet attack?[34] The Chinese also sought improved relations with the two countries in Eastern Europe most threatened by the aggressiveness Brezhnev had shown in Czechoslovakia: Romania and Yugoslavia. The rapprochement with Yugoslavia in particular showed that Mao was now much more interested in national security than in ideology, since the Yugoslavs were, if anything, more revisionist than the Soviets.

Mao had seen the Cultural Revolution as a way of keeping his Communist Party pure, of maintaining what he called a continuous revolution. Once it had run its course, however, few Chinese retained much of the idealism of the 1950s.

Few in the West immediately realized just how chaotic and bloody the Great Proletarian Cultural Revolution had been or, for that matter, just how squalid Chinese life was. Given their almost total ignorance, Western radicals could imagine China as a kind of Promised Land, a better alternative to both Western consumerism and bureaucratic Soviet-style Communism. The Cultural Revolution seemed to be just the sort of romanticized revolution that Western left-wing students imagined they wanted. It certainly seemed—quite misleadingly—to place those of the students' own age at the center of power rather than, as in the West, at its periphery, unable to influence events. Western students also responded to the moral fervor that seemed to inspire the Chinese Red Guards. Mao was popular as a symbol of that alternative. He and his "Little Red Book" became fixtures in the mass Western student protests of the late 1960s and early 1970s. Mao also seemed to symbolize the attack on "colonialism" and hence on the greatest symbol of the hated Western establishment, the Vietnam War. Often Mao's image was accompanied by that of Che Guevara, the anti-imperialist guerilla, students having little or no interest in the extent to which Guevara's Cuba was a Soviet satellite.

The Cultural Revolution stopped Chinese industrial development. For nearly a decade no new technicians were trained. Many of the best educated were humiliated or even killed, in a kind of parody of Stalin's insistence that Party spirit could always trump knowledge. When, in the 1980s, the Chinese began to publish accounts of the development of their military programs, it was striking how long those programs had taken to reach maturity, and how badly many of them had gone awry.[35] Access to Western military technology became far more attractive.

Richard Nixon won the 1968 election. As Eisenhower's vice president, he had attended nearly every NSC meeting, learning a great deal about strategy at various levels. Although the president's contributions naturally overshadowed his, transcripts make it clear that he played a substantial role. Compared with his contemporary, Kennedy, Nixon seems to have been far more serious, and far more interested in international affairs. But he came into office with an important disability. The methods he had used in his early career as a domestic Cold Warrior had left a very bad taste among liberals. They considered him totally unscrupulous in his pursuit of power; he was always "Tricky Dick."

Nixon badly wanted the liberals' affection, perhaps because he knew that he had narrowly won the election in 1968.[1] He expanded U.S. domestic programs well beyond anything Johnson had proposed. Examples included the Philadelphia Plan, which established minority quotas for federal hiring, and Wilbur Mills's bill providing automatic increases in Social Security to compensate for inflation, the first U.S. entitlement law. Thus, like Johnson, Nixon badly wanted to escape from the financial burden of the Vietnam War. He was surely much more aware than Johnson had been that the cost of fighting in Vietnam was destroying the U.S. ability to fight the Cold War everywhere else. Nixon earned no credit for his social programs and, ironically, gained the liberals' contempt for his inability to do what he and they both wanted, which was to extricate the country from Vietnam.

Nixon won in 1968 partly on the basis of a supposed "secret plan" to end the Vietnam War. His campaign promise recalled Eisenhower's 1952 pledge that he would go to Korea and end the war. He felt that he could not end the war simply by abandoning South Vietnam.[2] An alternative was some sort of decisive blow against North Vietnam. Nixon examined and rejected three possibilities. The first would destroy the dikes in North Vietnam (which would flood most of the country). The second would use tactical nuclear weapons. The third would escalate the war by renewing bombing of the North (including mining Hanoi-Haiphong to cut off supplies), allowing the free pursuit of Communist forces into Laos and Cambodia, and threatening invasion of North Vietnam.

Nixon then was left with the option of negotiating some sort of settlement. The settlement Nixon proposed would provide for mutual troop withdrawals by the United States and North Vietnam; a political settlement within South Vietnam (between the South Vietnamese government and the National Liberation Front [NLF]); and international guarantees.[3] Nixon thought he could maneuver the North Vietnamese into such a settlement if he could convince them that they could not win the war. At the same time, he would use diplomacy to isolate them from their backers in Moscow and Beijing and strengthen South Vietnamese forces so that they could take over the war.[4] Nixon hoped that the war could be settled during his first year of office.

The North Vietnamese insisted that peace was possible only if the United States withdrew all its troops. To make their point, they launched a large-scale offensive throughout South Vietnam on 22 February 1969, aimed mainly at U.S. forces rather than at the pacification program (which attacked the NLF directly). Special Forces (sapper) attacks on over 125 targets were combined with two regimental and sixteen battalion attacks. The offensive failed so badly that by mid-1969 more North Vietnamese and Viet Cong had defected than in the whole of 1968.[5] Giap's view, that large-unit attacks had to be abandoned, was confirmed.[6]

Nixon decided that he could negotiate effectively only if he proved his strength by retaliating. He needed an appropriate target. It seemed pointless to resume bombing North Vietnam; the attacks apparently had been ineffective, and many Americans believed that the bombing halt had made negotiation possible. Nor would it be appropriate to mount a major ground assault into the enemy sanctuaries of Laos and Cambodia to counter a failed Communist offensive. However, a really interesting target now presented itself. A defector revealed the location in Cambodia of the Communist headquarters from which the war was being directed (COSVN). Nixon agreed to bomb it.[7]

His secretaries of state and defense argued that Congress and the media would be furious at this expansion of the war into nominally neutral territory. Nixon later wrote that the previous year Prince Sihanouk of Cambodia had said that he would not object if the United States retaliated against Communist use of his country. News of the secret raids was leaked, and published by the *New York Times.* The area hit by the first B-52 raid was apparently the COSVN base area; afterwards COSVN withdrew deeper into Cambodia.[8] Neither the Cambodians nor the North Vietnamese protested the raids.

In May, Nixon offered a peace plan: all foreign troops (U.S. and North Vietnamese) would be withdrawn from South Vietnam, after which an international body would supervise free elections.[9] The key was "Vietnamization," a term the South Vietnamese hated, because they had been fighting from the first (they preferred "modernization," missing the point that the plan was preparation for an American pullback). The U.S. hope was that initially ARVN would be able to take over responsibility for ground combat, the United States continuing to provide air and naval forces. Then South Vietnamese air and naval forces would be built up to the point of self-sufficiency.

In fact there was never enough time or investment to build up the necessary infrastructure. In addition, ARVN units were essentially immobile local defense forces, tied to specific areas, and burdened by numerous dependents who made maneuvers, including combat withdrawals, impossible.

As it happened, 1969 was a good time to propose Vietnamization because in the wake of their failure the North Vietnamese were winding down the war to small-unit actions, giving the South Vietnamese a respite. With the virtual abandonment of search-and-destroy tactics the U.S. Army could concentrate on training the South Vietnamese armed forces. Then, too, Tet had given the South Vietnamese valuable self-confidence. Nixon's new secretary of defense, Melvin Laird, returned in March with an optimistic account of the progress of South Vietnamese training. Nixon decided to begin pulling out U.S. troops in May after both the North and South Vietnamese had rejected his peace plan. The pullback of the first twenty-five thousand troops was announced on 8 June 1969. It was opposed by the South Vietnamese and even by U.S. commander Gen. Creighton Abrams (who had replaced Westmoreland).[10]

As a wider application of Vietnamization, in July Nixon announced that in future the United States would provide its Asian friends with matériel rather than with armed force; it would help only those countries that were clearly willing to help themselves. Later the policy was amended: the United States would continue to supply the air and naval support which no small country could be expected to provide for itself. Unfortunately, the policy was widely misinterpreted as a U.S. plan to pull out of Asia altogether. Rather, it was Nixon's attempt to remain in Asia on sustainable terms.[11]

Nixon feared that in the fall, with students back on American campuses, the antiwar movement would regenerate. It would be much more difficult for him to apply any stick to goad the North Vietnamese into an acceptable settlement.[12] In secret meetings Kissinger threatened "measures of the greatest significance," which clearly meant a nuclear attack; Nixon recalled (incorrectly) that Eisenhower's nuclear threat had broken the stalemate in negotiations over Korea in 1953.[13] The package of threats, called Duck Hook, drawn up by Gen. Alexander Haig, one of Kissinger's assistants, included mining Haiphong, through which most of Hanoi's war matériel came; blockading the port; renewing and intensifying bombing of Hanoi (population centers, military targets, and key roads and bridges); and attacking the Red River dikes.[14] Nixon also leaked a threat to invade North Vietnam.[15] These measures had already been rejected on the ground that they would outrage American public opinion; Nixon was bluffing. He set 1 November 1969, the anniversary of Johnson's bombing halt, as a deadline.

Nixon feared, correctly, that the North Vietnamese would call his bluff, knowing that he could not carry out the threats in the face of U.S. public opinion.[16] He later wrote that, had the antiwar movement been less active, he might have been able to offer just what protesters wanted, a quick peace.[17]

On the other hand, through the summer of 1969 enemy morale suffered. The North Vietnamese government found it difficult to explain to its war-weary troops that negotiations did not necessarily mean that peace was at hand; few, particularly in the Viet Cong, were anxious to be the war's last casualties. Dispersed in small units, troops were more difficult to control. Defections increased.[18] Moreover, in October 1969 Sir Robert Thompson, who had won the Malaysian fight against the Communists, told Nixon that he could win within two years. Either the South Vietnamese would be able to fend for themselves (using U.S. matériel) or the North Vietnamese would have to offer a satisfactory negotiated settlement.[19]

Like Johnson, Nixon tried and failed to link continued détente with the Soviets to progress in the Vietnam War.[20] Unknown to him, the fact of ongoing formal peace talks had relieved the Soviets' worst fear, that the war would somehow widen into a confrontation with the United States. They were therefore no longer nearly as interested in restraining the North Vietnamese.[21] For that matter the Soviets still had virtually no leverage over the North Vietnamese. They were still very suspicious of the Soviets. According to the 1970 political report of the Soviet Embassy in Hanoi, the North Vietnamese limited Soviet ideological influence and "rationed" information about events in the Soviet Union and Eastern Europe; they treated Soviet citizens working in Vietnam with suspicion. They often "forgot" to inform Moscow of their foreign policy initiatives. The KGB considered setting up its own network in North Vietnam, to provide information on the leadership there and on its relations with the Chinese.[22] Nixon knew none of this; he could not imagine that the country which supplied its crucial air defense could not control its client.

Probably most important of all, Ho Chi Minh remembered how helpful the Chinese had been during his war against the French. He died on 3 September 1969. About this time the Vietnamese became more interested in negotiations, which the Soviets badly wanted as a guarantee against a wider and more dangerous war; at its January 1970 plenum the North Vietnamese Communist Party for the first time placed diplomatic and political efforts at the same level as military ones. The Soviets regarded this step as a rejection of the Chinese antinegotiation posture. As a measure of continued North Vietnamese hostility, the Soviet leadership learned of this shift in advance from intelligence sources, *not* from the North Vietnamese leadership.[23]

By this time the Sino-Soviet schism had reached the point of open hostility. The Czech invasion seemed to prove to the Chinese that the Soviets were willing to fight. The schism might degenerate into war. In October 1968, for the first time,

Mao referred to the Soviet Union as China's primary enemy.[24] On 2 March 1969 Chinese border guards secretly occupied a disputed island (named Zhenbao by the Chinese, Demansky by the Soviets) in the Ussuri River on the Siberian-Chinese border. When Soviet border guards tried to eject them, the Chinese wiped them out. On 14 March the Soviets made a major counterattack. Fighting continued through August.[25] The Chinese government told its people to prepare for the "inevitable" war against the Soviets. Border populations were relocated and Red Guards sent in their place. Industry was relocated to central China. Bomb shelters were built on a large scale.

For their part, the Soviets rebuilt border fortifications they had blown up, on Khrushchev's orders, in the 1950s. The Soviets deactivated MRBM and IRBM sites in the Far East because they were too close to the Chinese border, and therefore vulnerable. Americans noticed that 190 SS-11 ICBM sites (one-fifth of the total), among the last to be built, apparently targeted China.[26] In 1970 there was another border incident. Soviet troops were ordered to open fire ten kilometers into Chinese territory as a "preventive" strike.[27]

The Soviets began to take war with China very seriously. Old Russian fears of a "yellow peril" revived. Now Mao's hordes, his "blue ants," were clearly a threat rather than a potential asset. Grim jokes circulated. In one of them, on the first day of the Sino-Soviet War, a million Chinese surrender. On the second day, another million surrender. On the third day, the Soviets surrender. Brezhnev became more interested in détente. To dissuade the Chinese, the Soviets began to float rumors that they were planning a preemptive strike against the developing Chinese nuclear force.[28] To preclude a Chinese rapprochement with the United States, some of the rumors had the Soviets approaching the Americans with the strike plan. Whatever the truth of the rumors, by 1973 the Soviets had decided that the moment had passed; the Chinese had emplaced their missiles in hardened positions.

From a Cold War point of view, it was probably much more significant that the Soviets now had to maintain a very large army in the Far East. They were probably well aware that the Chinese still resented the czarist seizure of Siberia (from which large numbers of ethnic Chinese had been driven). Since 1965 the Soviets had increased the number of ground divisions on the Chinese border from fifteen to forty, the number of tactical aircraft from two hundred to over one thousand, and the number of tactical nuclear missile launchers from about fifty to over three hundred. At the end of 1971, the only Soviet field commanders with four-star rank commanded the three military districts bordering China, although the new commander of the forces in Germany was expected to attain a similar rank in the near future. About four hundred thousand Soviet troops and associated tactical airmen faced China.[29] This buildup removed resources from Europe. In this largely undeveloped territory, they had to create the infrastructure, such as roads and even a second main line railroad (the Baikal–Amur Main Line, or BAM) merely in order to support massive armies. Then they moved in the troops, simply because there would be no time to do so in an emergency. A Soviet historian later estimated that in the late 1970s a third of Soviet military strength was concentrated against China.[30] These troops could not possibly have moved West quickly in an emergency.

In this developing context Vietnam became much more valuable to the Soviets, because it could be used as a base from which to threaten China.[31] By mid-1970 they were planning to gradually reorient North Vietnam towards the Soviet Union. It became even more important to court the North Vietnamese by providing them with whatever weapons they wanted. Pressuring them to accept U.S. terms was out of the question. It must have relieved Soviet fears considerably that Nixon demonstrated that he considered the developing relationship with the Soviets more important than Vietnam.

In Chinese eyes, the Soviet Union now formally replaced the United States as the chief enemy. The United States might become a shield against the Soviets. Nixon was already interested in an opening to China. In 1967, while out of office, he published an article, "Asia after Vietnam," in *Foreign Affairs*. It was irrational to try to isolate China; better to bring it back into the international community, where its revolutionary ardor might dissipate. The Chinese were intrigued. At an NSC meeting in mid-1969 Nixon decided to move secretly towards normalizing relations. The initiative had to be taken quietly because the Chinese government might draw back if it were publicly embarrassed. Nixon took a series of small steps: he lifted the ban on travel to China, he allowed foreign branches of U.S. firms to deal in "non-strategic" goods with China, and in December he ended the Seventh Fleet patrol of the Taiwan Straits. Then the trade embargo was further eased and Congress was asked to permit sale of U.S. grain to China. In October 1970 Nixon called Mao's republic by its official name, the People's Republic, for the first time.[32]

Publicly, the Chinese kept up their anti-American propaganda. During secret talks, however, they laid out their price for conciliation. Mao told his own Central Committee about the talks at a meeting at Lüshun on 25 August–6 September 1970. Slogans about preparing for war now applied only to the Soviet Union, not to the United States. His heir apparent, Lin Biao, disagreed violently. Early in December Chou En-lai sent a message: the Chinese would be glad to meet a special U.S. envoy. Henry Kissinger arrived secretly in July 1971.

In September, Lin, probably the chief opponent of the opening, died, and was posthumously accused of having attempted a coup. He was probably intended as Mao's scapegoat for the disasters of the Cultural Revolution, which was then ending. All aircraft in China having been grounded on 13 September 1971, Lin's airplane nonetheless took off, headed for the Soviet Union. It crashed in Mongolia. The Soviets later said that Lin had been shot before his airplane took off.[33]

While all this was happening, Nixon continued to withdraw U.S. troops from Vietnam. The Viet Cong never recovered from their losses during the Tet offensive.[34] The North Vietnamese army had largely withdrawn into sanctuaries deep in

Laos, Cambodia, and the DMZ. By the spring of 1970 nominally neutral Cambodia was a vital enemy base area; many supplies were flowing through its port of Sihanoukville rather than down the Ho Chi Minh Trail. The North Vietnamese in Cambodia threatened U.S. forces, particularly around Saigon. Cambodia's ruler, Prince Norodom Sihanouk, tolerated both a major Communist presence and secret U.S. raids directed against it. While he was in France in March 1970, the Cambodian National Assembly replaced him with Premier Lon Nol, who promised to drive the Communists out. As in Laos in 1961, a vigorous Communist reaction threatened to take over the whole country. Even so, many of Nixon's advisors argued against aiding Lon Nol.

Nixon decided otherwise. Initially he refused permission to use U.S. troops, but gave it when Abrams refused to promise success without them. On 1 May 1970 South Vietnamese and U.S. troops attacked across the border into the two principal enemy base areas, the "Parrot's Beak" and the "Fish Hook." Sir Robert Thompson, the British guerilla expert, claimed that the raid and the loss of a Cambodian port, Sihanoukville, set back any North Vietnamese offensive plans by at least eighteen months, possibly by as much as two years; Kissinger thought it bought fifteen months.[35] Good South Vietnamese performance in the raid encouraged proponents of Vietnamization.

In the United States the raid brought widespread protests, including the famous one at Kent State University in Ohio, where four students were killed. On 24 June the Senate repealed the Tonkin Gulf Resolution. Later it passed the Cooper-Church Amendment prohibiting the use of U.S. ground troops in Laos or Cambodia. Nixon could very reasonably have said that what seemed a gross escalation was actually badly needed cover for winding down the war, but no one wanted to listen.

Nixon continued the raids. Without Sihanoukville, the North Vietnamese operating in central and southern Vietnam had to depend on the Ho Chi Minh Trail through Laos. Aware of its significance, the North Vietnamese reinforced the area in the fall of 1970. Their presence there apparently was a surprise; the North Vietnamese had never before strongly defended their base areas.[36] The trail was attacked in Operation Lam Son 719 (30 January–25 March 1971). For the operation, the South Vietnamese supplied their two best divisions; the United States supplied air transport and air support but it could not provide troops.

It was hoped that the destruction of North Vietnamese base areas and supplies, coupled with the effects of the previous year's Cambodian raid, would delay any major Communist offensive by at least a year. Although large quantities of supplies were captured, the South Vietnamese did not stay through the 1971 rainy season as they had planned. Thus the Ho Chi Minh Trail did not remain closed for long. Had the South Vietnamese held the bases and part of the Ho Chi Minh Trail as planned, all Communist operations in South Vietnam would have been crippled. Moreover, the buildup to the 1972 attack would have been impossible.

The operation failed partly because South Vietnam still had a Third World political system. Its best units were its president's palace guard; he personally could not afford their destruction. The Americans, who thought very differently, forced President Thieu to use exactly those units. He very naturally told their commanders to avoid casualties. Even so, the casualties they incurred shocked many in South Vietnam.

The North Vietnamese were trying to break the stalemate, as in 1967. In May 1971 their leadership formally approved another big push. This decision was not unanimous. As in 1967, Giap preferred to continue low-level warfare. When he lost the argument, Giap was made responsible for planning the attack. As in 1967, the strategy would be "fighting while negotiating." To provide sufficient matériel, the North Vietnamese extracted aid from both the Soviets and the Chinese.[37] Soviet diplomats in Hanoi warned their hosts that the planned operation was too risky, but the North Vietnamese went ahead anyway.[38]

Meanwhile, Nixon made a state visit to China in February 1972. Mao got warmth but not the modern weapons he wanted. Moreover, to Mao's disgust, Nixon saw no problem in maintaining good relations with both the Chinese *and* the Soviets. Even so, Mao now had a potential "American card" to play to limit Soviet expansionism in the Far East. Nixon had a "Chinese card" that would make it more difficult for the Soviets to concentrate their forces in Eastern Europe.

To some extent this was poker; to get more out of Nixon, Mao had to eliminate the remaining barrier, the North Vietnamese. Thus before Nixon arrived the Chinese pressed the North Vietnamese for permission to discuss the ongoing war during the upcoming summit. The Soviets thought the Chinese were about to make a deal. The Vietnamese vetoed the discussion, but they realized that the Chinese might be preparing to sell them out. They would therefore tip towards the Soviets, giving them the prize they sought.[39]

The North Vietnamese invaded at Easter 1972 (the end of March). They massed every North Vietnamese unit in North and South Vietnam and everything in Laos except one division and four regiments. This force was probably far more powerful than ARVN, but it could not be concentrated; roads and logistics were limited. With few American combat troops still in the country (only 6,000 out of a total of 76,000 Americans), everything depended on the South Vietnamese. As at Tet in 1968, they fought well. Eventually ARVN regained the initiative and threw out most of the invaders. Air strikes by U.S. aircraft helped considerably. With very limited battlefield logistics, the North Vietnamese had to stop every few days to regroup. That gave the Americans time to shift air power among the threatened areas. North Vietnamese generalship was often poor; they did not yet know how to integrate tanks with their infantry. As a harbinger of the future, a few hundred TOW antitank missiles, which had been sent to Vietnam for operational tests, proved very effective in stopping North Vietnamese tanks. The North Vietnamese lost 450 tanks and more than 190,000 troops (killed and taken prisoner).[40] The attack was reminiscent of the North Korean invasion of June 1950; this time the defending army (with critical U.S. air and naval support) proved adequate to stop it.

In May, with the battle in the balance, Nixon ordered retaliation: air attacks on Hanoi and the mining of Haiphong Harbor. Johnson had refused to permit the latter for fear of hitting Soviet ships. Now North Vietnam was cut off from its Soviet suppliers. Perhaps most significantly, the North Vietnamese discovered to their horror that Nixon paid no diplomatic price to either the Soviets or the Chinese for this escalation. With most American troops out of Vietnam, the U.S. antiwar movement was drastically weakened. The big offensive had bought virtually nothing, and the North Vietnamese had lost so much that there could not be another offensive for three to five years.[41] U.S. bombing, moreover, demonstrated that the Vietnamese air defense system was no longer effective.

Neither the Soviets nor the Chinese had enthusiastically supported the offensive, and the Soviets were particularly angry that it came on the eve of the Moscow Summit (Nixon-Brezhnev). They did not allow Nixon's escalation to derail détente. For his part, Nixon blamed the Soviets, who had provided the necessary weaponry, for the Easter Offensive. At the presummit conference, Kissinger was instructed to concentrate on Vietnam; the United States would escalate unless the North Vietnamese withdrew. Brezhnev lied: he told Kissinger that the Soviets were not behind the offensive, that the North Vietnamese had been hoarding weapons for two years, and that the Vietnamese and Chinese were trying to break détente.[42]

Nixon still wanted to end the war. At the summit, Kissinger told the Soviets that the United States would accept any government, even a Communist one, which might be elected in South Vietnam. Kissinger proposed an electoral commission, in effect a coalition government, that might be one-third Communist, one-third neutral, and one-third selected by the current South Vietnamese government. However, the U.S. government would not overtly surrender by destroying the South Vietnamese government.[43] The Soviets agreed to press the North Vietnamese to accept Kissinger's plan.

Now the North Vietnamese had a real incentive to deal. They could rely on neither the Soviets nor the Chinese. Kissinger was offering to remove all remaining U.S. forces from Vietnam. Once the Americans were gone, it might be far easier to deal with the Thieu government. Moreover, the North Vietnamese needed some time in which to rebuild. Between July and September 1972 they agreed to most of the U.S. conditions.

South Vietnam, however, was not a U.S. colony. Nixon had to reassure President Thieu that U.S. forces would return as needed to police the settlement. The North Vietnamese were pressed to accept Thieu's added conditions. They added their own. Even so, by late 1972 the North Vietnamese thought an agreement was imminent.[44] Then talks broke down. Like the South Vietnamese, the NLF feared being sold out. For example, the treaty did not require that their prisoners in South Vietnam be freed at the same time as the U.S. pilots imprisoned in the North. The U.S.

government had never recognized the Communists in South Vietnam as an independent entity. The North Vietnamese seemed to be reneging.

In December Nixon ordered another round of attacks on Hanoi and Haiphong, beginning with a second mining of Haiphong Harbor. Targets would not be restricted; Nixon ordered the North Vietnamese warmaking capability knocked out. That would buy invaluable time for the South Vietnamese. It would also demonstrate to the North Vietnamese just how destructive U.S. air power could be. After twelve days no targets were left to strike. The loss rate was far less than in previous attacks on Hanoi-Haiphong, and in the final series of these "Linebacker" raids the North Vietnamese were unable to destroy any B-52s at all.[45] The Soviets were being forced to see that their own national air defense system, after which the Vietnamese system had been modeled, might prove ineffective against SAC.

Propaganda was still an antiaircraft weapon: much was made of "barbaric carpet bombing." In fact the strikes were carefully targeted away from civilians: 1,318 died in Hanoi and 305 in Haiphong, hardly the sort of figures implied by the antiwar media at the time (U.S. activists in Hanoi advised the mayor to claim ten thousand deaths).[46] Negotiations resumed once the bombing was over, and a treaty was signed on 27 January 1973, ending U.S. participation in the war. The final terms were not too different from those the North Vietnamese had considered acceptable earlier in 1972. Probably Nixon and Kissinger wanted to impress the North Vietnamese with U.S. power to discourage them from breaking the agreement. The bombing also was calculated to impress the South Vietnamese with the lengths to which the United States would go, and thus made the final compromise more acceptable to them.[47] The North Vietnamese blamed the NLF for the bombing.

The agreement was a cease-fire in place. U.S. troops were withdrawn, and U.S. prisoners of war were repatriated. Under the agreement, neither the United States nor North Vietnam could send more troops into South Vietnam, but North Vietnamese troops already in place stayed there, inland towards the Cambodian and Laotian borders. To avoid an arms buildup by either side, equipment could be replaced only on a one-for-one basis. The South Vietnamese in particular benefited from major U.S. arms deliveries late in 1972, under a program called Enhance Plus.[48] However, the period of Vietnamization training had not created the necessary corps of maintainers.

Very significantly, the Joint Military Commission (South Vietnam/North Vietnam/Viet Cong) and the International Commission on Control and Supervision (Poland, Hungary, Indonesia, Canada), which were created to police the accords; both included Communist members, and required unanimity. Thus the North Vietnamese had effective vetoes in both organizations.[49]

The North Vietnamese did not give up their determination to conquer South Vietnam. The only effective deterrent to a new invasion was the threat of defeat—which in 1972 had come largely, though by no means entirely, from U.S. air power. However, by the spring of 1973 Congress was heavily against both Nixon and the

Vietnam War, and it was about to legislate the United States out of the war by literally prohibiting combat operations in or over Vietnam—as it already had with
Cambodia.

For the Soviets, the outcome of the Vietnam War carried a profound lesson.
Until about 1970 they had regarded Third World instability mainly as a source of
danger to themselves, because (as in Cuba) a local crisis could suddenly become a
superpower standoff. Then Brezhnev watched the United States and the West visibly weaken.[50] The considerable Soviet role in Vietnam had cost nothing in terms
of the Soviets' relationship with the United States. Even better, the Soviets had captured the prize, North Vietnam, which needed them even more as it tried to
rebuild itself from 1973 on. The Soviets became interested in further adventures,
both in Africa and in the Middle East. Brezhnev included support for national liberation movements in his 1977 Soviet constitution.[51]

The war had also apparently strengthened a classic Soviet weapon. The Soviets
had long tried to use tame peace movements to move Western governments. The
U.S. involvement in Vietnam inspired a new worldwide protest movement. The
Soviets saw in it a new generation of sympathizers in Europe, who could be
counted upon to resist further Western assaults on the "socialist commonwealth."
Although the movement was largely spontaneous, the Soviet leadership believed
that it could be guided to support other Soviet goals. The Soviets had subsidized
numerous "peace movements" for their own purposes.[52]

Since Vietnam was a hot war, the U.S. public came to see it, rather than the Cold
War as a whole, as the only struggle in which the United States was engaged. When
the war ended, the public expected to enjoy the benefits associated with peace;
surely the money previously spent on the war would become available for other
things. Yet the end of the Vietnam War did not end the larger Cold War, and the
cost of the war had largely been met by foregoing other Cold War spending. The
"peace dividend" could be provided only by continuing to forego needed military
investments. It was impossible, for a decade, to remedy the *military* costs incurred
during Vietnam.

The draft had been, in the end, a root cause of opposition to the war. Perhaps
the war had really shown that the United States could not deploy a draftee army
against any country with propagandists as imaginative as the North Vietnamese. In
any case, by 1972 it was time to abandon the draft. A study purported to show that
the United States could maintain sufficient forces on a volunteer basis. To no one's
real surprise, the study turned out to be unduly optimistic. Because there was no
money for greatly increased pay, through the 1970s the military was unable to
attract enough able volunteers. Critics pointed to a more fundamental problem.
Recruiters generally offered job skills saleable in civilian life. Yet many really vital
military skills, such as those of an infantryman, could not possibly be valuable in
the nonmilitary world. Then, too, to attract and retain volunteers, the harsher elements of military life would have to be toned down. Could volunteers be shaped

into a usable force? In Korea all-volunteer formations had been badly mauled. Ultimately the volunteer force did work, as Desert Storm would demonstrate in 1991.

The latter stages of Vietnam coincided with Nixon's attempt to head off what he feared would be a Communist takeover closer to home, in Chile. In 1970 Salvador Allende, an avowed lifelong Marxist, won a 36.3 percent plurality in a three-way election against the Christian Democrats and the conservative Nationals. That was much the sort of percentage the Communists had achieved in postwar Czechoslovakia. In Chile it meant that nearly two-thirds of the voters did not want the Marxist society Allende and his popular front allies of the UP (Unidad Popular: Socialists, Communists, and Radicals) offered.

The election had to be decided by the Chilean Congress. The U.S. government considered Allende (a member of the Socialist rather than the Communist Party) probably a Communist, and in 1964 it had helped finance the opposition that had defeated him in an election. This time the CIA warned that although Chile could hardly be considered a strategic prize, a Communist victory there would have devastating political and psychological effects throughout the hemisphere.[53] Kissinger did not "see why we need to stand by and watch a country go Communist due to the irresponsibility of its own people."[54] Nixon ordered a covert campaign against Allende. It failed; the Christian Democrats backed him in Congress after passing a statute limiting his power. He agreed in writing not to abandon democratic methods, and also not to form a workers' militia. The Christian Democrats thought that, however Marxist Allende might be, they had guaranteed against a takeover. However, the UP included not only the professedly legalistic Allende but also much more raucous revolution-minded elements.[55] In any case, Allende could claim to be the first Marxist president elected anywhere in the world in a free election.

Allende's victory could, moreover, be seen as part of a larger left-wing movement in much of Latin America. In Peru, a left-wing military junta seized power in October 1968, and in Bolivia an extreme left-wing government took power in October 1970. Neither the Bolivian nor the Peruvian regime seemed nearly as threatening to the U.S. government as the Chilean one, presumably precisely because Allende had gained office by constitutional means and was thus far more legitimate than the other rulers. Moreover, as the hopes raised by Kennedy's Alliance for Progress failed, it seemed to many in Washington that only Chile, with its democratic government led by Eduardo Frei, was left as the last best hope in Latin America. Allende's success thus seemed particularly devastating. Now the Left appeared to be the wave of the future. The ongoing U.S. failure in Vietnam seemed to show that the country had lost that quality of decisiveness or aggressiveness that impressed those in Latin America. Fidel was macho; the U.S. government evidently was not.[56] This view was reinforced by the traditional and very widely held view throughout the continent that the United States was the key exploiter and the cause of most problems. In a popular Chilean joke, for example, the natural reaction of a man who finds his wife in bed with another man is to break the windows of the American embassy.[57] On this basis, it was much easier for Chileans who resented Allende's downfall to blame American intervention than to accept that the coup was essentially a local phenomenon, supported by (but not caused by) the U.S. government. U.S. power over events was much more limited than many wanted to imagine.

As elsewhere in Latin America, the Left was divided between what might be called a Communist Establishment, personified by Allende, and much more radical groups espousing immediate revolutionary action: Maoists, Guevara-ists, Trotskyites. A British historian, Alistair Horne, visiting Chile in 1971, thought that Latin America would be the ultimate battleground where the Soviets would have to fight the Maoists for domination of the world Communist movement.[58] His perception may explain some of the unwillingness of established (Moscow-oriented) Communist parties to help Allende and others on the left in Latin America during the 1970s.

Chileans soon learned that the presidency had enormous powers. Allende exploited heretofore-obscure laws to control the Chilean economy.[59] For example, under a 1932 law, a government arbitrator (*intervenor*) could be imposed on a business which could not meet its obligations, or which was accused of "financial irregularities." This bankruptcy law was used creatively to seize control of private businesses. The private banks were quickly nationalized under this law, no additional legislation being needed. In the case of *Ercilla*, a leading weekly unfriendly to the new government, an *intervenor* was brought in after a three-week strike. He imposed an increase in wages that the parent company said would force it to declare bankruptcy. The *intervenor* vetoed this. As a consequence, other, healthier publications owned by the same company were bled white to keep the magazine afloat. The law was also, of course, applied to U.S.-owned companies.[60] Ultimately Allende's government controlled 60 percent of the Chilean GNP.

A Marxist state was quickly created. Allende redistributed income to the UP's generally impoverished supporters.[61] Expenditures on social programs rose from an average of $562.8 million in 1965–69 to $1,012.6 million in 1972.[62]

Opponents found themselves virtually powerless, although there was a widespread sense that Allende was systematically violating the constitution. By late 1971 they were taking to the streets in protest, most famously housewives in Santiago banging their empty pots in December 1971, during a visit by Fidel Castro. Allende's left-wing followers began to attack his opponents. The two parties that had opposed Allende in 1970 were forced into alliance. They represented a clear majority of Chilean electors.

Nixon and Kissinger had never abandoned their enmity for Allende. They proposed support for a military coup, but the CIA pointed out that the Chilean commander in chief, Gen. Carlos Prats, was a strong believer in the constitution; the military was unlikely to intervene. Instead, they attacked the Chilean economy.

Even without any action on their part, the effect of rapid nationalization and politicization would have been to damage the Chilean economy very badly. In effect Nixon and Kissinger exacerbated the effects of Allende's policies. For example, farms nationalized under a policy much like Soviet collectivization could not produce enough food, so Allende had to import it.[63] In 1970, Chile imported 19 percent of her food ($193 million). In 1972 that rose to about 35 percent ($400 million). The projected 1973 import cost was $650 million. There were also acute shortages of consumer goods.[64]

Chile's main source of hard currency was copper, which before Allende was produced in U.S.-owned mines. When the mines were nationalized, key technicians left, but numerous UP political workers were hired. The result recalled what had happened in the Soviet Union, where Stalin had imagined that political spirit could be substituted for expertise. Between 1970 and 1973 employment increased by 45 percent, but per capita production fell by 19 percent (by 28 percent in one mine).[65] It did not help that the U.S. ex-owners sued the Chilean government, drastically reducing export sales of the copper that was mined, or that the miners themselves were furious to discover that their new government could not provide them with the increased wages agitators had promised in pre-Allende days.

It was never clear just how devoted Allende was to the limitations he had accepted in 1970. For example, a few months after taking office he told a French revolutionary, Régis Debray, that he had signed as a "tactical necessity."[66] Throughout his regime, he attacked the opposition press and television stations, although he could not quite close them down. For example, as he nationalized the Chilean economy, he was able to starve most newspapers of advertising. He also tried to starve them of newsprint; orchestrated labor problems and plant seizures; juggled prices to attack them; and tried to dry up their finances.[67] Presumably much of the U.S. money spent in Chile was used merely to keep the opposition press alive. In addition Allende moved to replace the judicial system with one based on "socialist legality," in which neighborhood tribunals could seize property.

Allende now tried to temper his revolution to convince the Christian Democrats to form an alliance. That failed, and through 1972 the Chilean economy continued to deteriorate. It probably did not help that beginning in 1971 radicalized workers began to demand that the government expropriate their plants. In October 1972 Chilean truck drivers and small shopkeepers struck, afraid that even their very small firms would be seized. By the end of 1972 the Chilean balance of payments was $400 million in debt, compared to the $28 million in surplus when Allende took office.[68]

Allende now made a key mistake. He invited the Chilean military into his cabinet in hopes that the army could quell growing disorders. Up to that point, in keeping with a long-held tradition, the army had carefully avoided political involvement (several attempted coups had ended in farce largely because of this attitude). Now some form of military rule became quite conceivable.

New congressional elections were due in March 1973. The Chilean army's view was that its role was to establish order so that the elections could proceed. The elections produced another anti-Allende majority, roughly 56 to 44 percent, even though Allende had tried to bring more supporters into the electorate by enfranchising the illiterate (and younger voters).[69] The Chilean Supreme Court and the congress both declared that Allende had violated the constitution, yet Allende seemed unstoppable.

Allende's UP included the MIR, which had begun as a guerilla movement in 1965. Like the Vietnamese Communists, it had advocated revolution via a general strike and uprisings by "popular militias" in the cities, coordinated with a protracted guerilla war in the southern provinces.[70] Its central committee had gone underground in 1969, but Allende had pardoned them when he came to power. In theory his election should have made such action unnecessary, but the MIR strengthened once Allende took power. Allende himself clearly was close to the MIR; he made some of its members part of his personal bodyguard.[71]

The movement's chiefs told its followers that Allende's victory had been no more than a temporary setback for the ruling class; he was no Lenin. By mid-1972 it had built a power base, including its communal governments and its militias, in the belts of nationalized plants in Santiago, the Cordon de Curillos.[72] To many middle-class Chileans, the MIR was the illegal arm of Allende's revolution. While his government used existing laws to squeeze them, it winked as the MIR evicted landowners from their properties. The government ordered the police to stand aside.[73] There was a widespread belief that the government hoped that its conservative enemies would go outside the law to deal with the MIR, giving it an excuse to crush them.[74] Through 1972 Chilean society increasingly polarized, right-wing militias forming to oppose the MIR. In January 1973 Allende said that if the military tried a coup he would go underground in Chile rather than flee to Cuba.[75]

Allende certainly showed no interest in curbing the MIR, and his government helped arm it. Late in 1971 unmarked Cuban aircraft began arriving at the airport in Santiago every Saturday night, their deliveries bypassing customs. These shipments ended after they attracted attention. In 1972, however, it was reported that the Chilean national airline, LAN, was shipping in weapons.[76] Two government-owned metal companies began making bazookas, and rubber truncheons and government-made gas masks were in evidence at many left-wing rallies from late 1972 on. Huge caches of mostly Czech-made arms were found after the coup, and the government claimed that over two thousand foreign weapons instructors (including Cubans, Czechs, and East Germans) were in the country (the government had covered their arrival by not releasing immigration statistics for the past two years). The instructors' presence in the industrial belt had first been reported early in 1973. The MIR militia seemed to be Allende's private army.

Having brought in the army to restore order, Allende had to allow it to search for the illegal arms the MIR had cached. Through the summer of 1973 there were frequent clashes as this was done. However, Allende refused the army's demands that the guerilla bases, many of them in the cities, be eliminated or that the MIR be outlawed.[77]

Allende had curbed leftist guerillas only twice. In July 1971 an extremist group, the VOP, whose members Allende had pardoned, killed an ex-minister of the interior. The Christian Democrats demanded that VOP and other paramilitary groups be crushed, but Allende attacked only the VOP; he did not touch the MIR. About a year later a previously unknown "16 July Commando" unsuccessfully attacked Allende's home. There was speculation that the real motive had been to give Allende an excuse to attack Chilean conservatives.

Castro had known Allende for years. When he visited in November and December 1971 he chided Allende for his constitutionalism; Socialism, for Castro, required a dictatorship backed by real fear.[78] Castro made his Santiago embassy his largest in the world; its personnel outnumbered those of the Chilean foreign ministry. Reportedly Castro supplied Allende's personal bodyguard, which was distinct from the detectives surrounding him. One of his men, who had been in Bolivia with Che, married Allende's daughter Beatriz. The Cuban DGI was active in Santiago. Given Castro's rapprochement with the Soviets after the 1968 Czech invasion, the visible Cuban activity was surely carried out with Soviet agreement or even encouragement. Czech arms and Czech and East German advisors meant Soviet involvement, but at a slight distance. That the Chilean Communist Party within the UP advised caution also suggests that the Soviets did not want to be held responsible for the coming takeover.

To many on the right, Allende seemed to be Sukarno in 1965. He was not quite a Communist, but he was the Communists' (or radical leftists') path to power. His private army would destroy the last barrier, the constitutionalist military. The word "Jakarta" began to appear on walls in Santiago.

To many on the Left, Allende was the best chance in years to establish a new "socialist" regime. Allende welcomed refugees from the many failed left-wing operations throughout South America. Ultimately Chile would presumably have become their base. Nixon and Kissinger had been right: Chile might not have any direct strategic value, but its fall would probably have had important effects throughout South America.

The Soviets provided support in the form of about $400 million in project aid and import credits through late 1972.[79] Unfortunately what Allende needed was imports from the West, and for that he had to have more hard currency—which, before the fall 1973 explosion of oil prices, the Soviets lacked. They had, moreover, just made a huge wheat deal with Nixon, which may have consumed what hard currency they could have spared. Thus in December 1972 Allende asked the Soviets for $500 million in credits and hard currency, and got only more useless trade credits and an offer of $50 million in arms (which was not made public). Chilean foreign exchange had been exhausted by April 1973. It is not clear to what extent

Allende's government managed to obtain Western European, Latin American, and even Chinese credits, but clearly they were not enough.[80]

The March elections and the subsequent court and congressional actions split the Chilean military. Initially its commander, General Prats, wanted to continue within the government. The army was by no means wedded to the existing social system. Like many others in Latin America, it had absorbed the American idea that society had to be reformed to survive. However, the MIR presented a distinct threat, and by 1972 its agitators were trying to undermine military discipline. Moreover, the military had failed to control rising violence, partly because radicals in Allende's government refused to control violence from the Left.

Tension increased; Allende's friend, Régis Debray, said that "everyone knew" that the president was playing for time "to organize, to arm, and to co-ordinate the military forces of the UP parties."[81] In June 1973 a right-wing militia, Patria y Libertad, tried to coordinate a coup with a Santiago-based armored regiment. Word leaked, and the coup fizzled. One column did make for the center of the city. It was noteworthy that Allende's supporters, the Santiago workers, did not come out, as Allende expected, to oppose the coup. Prats resigned in August after a delegation of generals told him that he no longer had their confidence. Allende appointed another constitutionalist general, Augusto Pinochet, to replace him.

Pinochet believed that the military had to save the constitution by overthrowing Allende. In September 1973 Allende was planning a plebiscite to endorse his presidency, and presumably to give him a mandate to overturn Congress. That alone would have alarmed the Chilean military. Later the military claimed that after the March election left-wing ultras in the government had been working to complete their takeover; a detailed death list was supposedly found in the safe of Communist Deputy Minister of the Interior Daniel Vergara. The generals claimed that the takeover plan would have been executed on Chilean Independence Day, 18 September. They themselves planned to use forces assembled for a parade that day to take over Santiago, but then moved the coup up a few days, perhaps as a result of discovering an attempted naval mutiny at Valparaiso. The coup actually began when ships there bombarded leftists in the town.

As the coup began, Allende appealed to the workers supporting his government. As in the earlier attempted coup, they refused to rise. Allende found himself isolated in the presidential palace with his closest associates. Refusing to surrender, he was attacked by air force jets and by army tanks. The situation having proved hopeless, Allende died, probably by his own hand.

In the past, the Chilean army had sometimes stepped in to halt what it considered an unconstitutional government, then quickly removed itself from power. This time it stayed; Pinochet made himself president in 1974. He never formed any mass movement on the theory that Chile really needed to be depoliticized so that it could recover economically. Perhaps the Left demonized him because it had seen Allende as the beginning of a future in which the people would sweep it into power in many countries. Surely it would take something (or someone) very unnatural to disrupt that popular trend. It was unacceptable that it was Pinochet who was riding a popular wave. The Left claimed, for example, that during the coup the Chilean military killed thirty thousand people. The true figure was probably no more than a few hundred.[82]

As for Nixon and Kissinger, unquestionably they exacerbated the crisis in which the Chilean military acted. However, they spent very little money and probably had little influence.[83] It was the Chileans who ousted Allende. That was much the same situation as in Indonesia a decade earlier; the United States was clearly friendly to the coup, but it did not cause it.[84]

After the coup, Pinochet created a police state. He sought to destroy the UP altogether; his secret police hunted down (and often tortured and killed) its adherents.[85] They also went abroad to reach out to kill enemies such as Orlando Letelier, Allende's former ambassador to Washington. Hundreds of thousands of Chileans left the country. Democracy was not restored until 1990. Nine years later, many Chileans credit Pinochet with saving them from chaos and Communism, but others feel that he deserves punishment for the "dirty war" which followed the coup, and for a repressive dictatorship.

From a Cold War perspective, Chile offered both sides some very important lessons. Communist parties elsewhere in the world, particularly in Italy, learned that equivocal victories could be quite dangerous. For Americans, Allende's acceleration to the Left and his support by the Soviets and their proxies suggested that Nixon and Kissinger had been right: Communists would abandon democracy whenever it suited them, and they would never renounce armed struggle. Moreover, the destruction of Allende's economy and the crucial role of hard currency may have foreshadowed Reagan's economic attack on the Soviet empire in the 1980s.

That the Chilean Communists, presumably following Soviet instructions, had counseled against radicalism and the MIR, meant little; Moscow did not want to be implicated directly in a left-wing coup. If the reports of Czech arms and Czech and East German instructors were correct (and they predated the coup), then the Soviets clearly supported the MIR and its radical friends. That Allende was, and continues to be, a hero to the liberal Left may demonstrate yet again that the Western liberal Left never quite understood that the Communists were not its brethren.

What is clear is that the United States did not oppose Allende simply because he expropriated U.S. property. By the late 1960s several Latin American armies had accepted (or invented) Kennedy's earlier idea, that economic revolution was necessary and inevitable. They rejected the complementary idea that linked such changes with democracy. They put left-nationalist systems in place to preempt Communist takeovers. The main examples are Peru (October 1968), Panama (October 1968), Bolivia (September 1969, against another military regime), Ecuador (March 1972), Honduras (December 1972), and Uruguay (June 1973). In the case of Peru, the army essentially adopted much of the platform of the MIR guerillas it fought down: it attacked an "unjust social order," and the "abandonment" of sources of national wealth; it instituted agrarian reform.[86] In Uruguay the impetus was a fight against Tupamaro urban guerillas, much of whose platform the army took over.[87]

These armies were by no means necessarily pro-American. In most cases left-nationalism meant expropriating U.S. property. In no case did the U.S. government try to overthrow such regimes. It had probably learned the lesson of Nasser: a true nationalist is preferable to a puppet that will be vulnerable to Communist attack. In the case of Panama's Gen. Omar Torrijos Herrera that meant a foreign policy centered on recovering sovereignty over the Panama Canal.[88]

When Nixon entered office, the United States held a very important, if little-known, ace. He might be able to win a nuclear war. Within the highest levels of the U.S. government, it was common (though secret) knowledge that a U.S. first strike might disarm the Soviets.[1] The Soviet strategic command system was clumsy and slow; the Soviets could not effectively react to a U.S. attack.[2] Then, too, Soviet first-generation missiles took time to prepare to fire. The combination of clumsiness and slow communications also applied to the Soviet missiles that threatened Europe and Japan. U.S. land-based ballistic missiles enjoyed far better communications, and by about 1965 they were so accurate that they could probably destroy even hardened Soviet missiles. There was no real temptation to attack, because much might go wrong. However, a U.S. attack could have been mounted had it been clear that the Soviets were getting ready to strike.

In 1970 the Soviets placed a new semiautomatic command system, Signal, in service. Their new missiles could be launched much more quickly, and they were emplaced in much harder silos.[3] Without the gross sluggishness of the Soviet command system (and of the missile launching process itself), the United States no longer had a first strike option.

A master, Eisenhower, had tutored Nixon for eight years. It was Nixon's tragedy that this advantage, which he understood far better than his predecessors, evaporated during his term of office. Now the best possible outcome of a nuclear war could no longer be victory, but merely prevailing or enduring. There was no longer much of a point in multiplying the number of U.S. missiles, since increased numbers would have been useful mainly to attack the growing number of Soviet missiles—which were no longer nearly as likely in their silos waiting to be destroyed.

In addition, the Soviets were building many more missiles than anyone had expected, consistently exceeding U.S. expectations. For example, in 1966 it was estimated that the Soviets would have 420 to 476 ICBMs in 1967; they actually had 570. That year it was estimated that they would have 505 to 695 in 1969; they actually had 1,028.[4] Two factors were at work. One was Khrushchev's April 1962 decision to order a new generation of strategic missiles to supersede the unsatisfactory ones then in production. He was simply determined to match U.S. numbers.[5] The other was Brezhnev's laissez-faire attitude towards the Soviet military-industrial complex. At least through the late 1960s the Soviets made no effort to develop any sort of U.S.-style strategic theory which might have linked numbers or characteristics of missiles with desired political effects.[6]

When Americans saw the Soviets turning out missiles like Khrushchev's sausages, they sought some deeper explanation. In this they were driven by the elaborate strategic rationales which McNamara had espoused. Numbers equated to a first-strike option: the ability to disarm an enemy by hitting first. As it happened, McNamara had made this equation (and made it evil) largely in order to limit the number of missiles he had to buy. Ironically, he had done so just as the United States had developed a very real first strike capability. Since very few Americans in the defense community were aware of the first strike option, they accepted McNamara's reasoning.

The only possible explanation for the big Soviet program was that, unenlightened by anyone of McNamara's caliber, the Soviets were seeking a first-strike capability. That the Soviets simply thought that more was better, and that their industrialists liked that sort of choice, was inconceivable to the Americans. Nor could it be suggested that, given the poor performance of so much of their equipment, the Soviet military leadership thought it needed a great many missiles to insure that enough of them worked. Surely, too, nuclear war was far too serious for missile programs to be used as little more than political pork.

Thus the great question for the next decade was whether the Soviets were actually developing the ability to disarm the United States in a first strike. The CIA argued forcefully that no first strike by the Soviets was feasible. The Soviets lacked two keys, the ability to detect and sink American strategic submarines and any real ability to shoot down incoming U.S. warheads. They were very unlikely to solve these problems. No matter what they did to U.S. land-based missiles, those at sea would survive to destroy the Soviet Union. The U.S. Air Force downplayed the rival U.S. sea-based force, arguing that communication with it was inherently unreliable and that the missiles were not accurate enough to destroy some vital Soviet targets. It now appears that the Soviets wanted to be able to win, but that there were always many in high positions who knew they could not.[7]

Khrushchev's demand for increased numbers of missiles had an unintended consequence. His favorite missile designer, V. N. Chelomey (who had hired Khrushchev's son Sergei as an engineer), was ambitious; he wanted to replace *all* existing missiles with a series of "universal" weapons. Up to that time Chelomey had designed naval cruise missiles, essentially unmanned airplanes. He told Khrushchev that he could solve the production problem because the aircraft industry, with which he was associated, knew how to build precision equipment in quantity. He sold a mass-producible missile, UR-100 (NATO SS-11), not only as the next ICBM, but also as a replacement for existing shorter-range IRBMs aimed at Europe and, later, at China.

To Americans, it was unimaginable that the Soviets would make the effort to build the longest-range missiles for any purpose other than to destroy the United States. As Khrushchev had known, IRBMs were much easier to make. Using an ICBM as an IRBM would be a waste of resources. However, Soviet economics were different. Waste was not too important. Chelomey had Khrushchev's ear, and the more of his missiles that were built, the better off he was.

Because UR-100s had to replace both ICBMs and IRBMs, the Soviets built them in large numbers—which, to Americans, exaggerated the size of the missile threat they suddenly faced. Because there was no new IRBM, they mistakenly imagined that the Soviets were uninterested in maintaining a missile threat against Western Europe; they apparently were satisfied with the obsolete missiles already in place, on their unprotected launch pads. The Europeans found that very comforting, so they did not think through the possible implications of the UR-100. When, in the late 1970s, the Soviets replaced the UR-100s aimed at Europe with a new missile, the Europeans thought that entirely useless ancient weapons were being replaced. The result was the "Euromissile" crisis.

From Nixon's point of view, if a first strike was no longer possible, he had to turn to some form of arms control to limit what the Soviets could do to the United States. Unaware of the underlying change in the situation, American conservatives attacked Nixon's arms control initiatives as softness in the face of Soviet power.

Nixon needed some carrot to convince the Soviets to stop building more missiles. Since the United States was not producing new missiles, he could not offer a corresponding halt in U.S. production. Probably he would have to offer to accept superior Soviet numbers. To the U.S. public, or at least to anyone interested, that would look like surrender. There was one saving grace. The United States had MIRVed missiles, but it seemed the Soviets could not follow that path, because they lacked the necessary onboard computers. Thus, even if the Soviets exceeded the number of missiles the United States had, the United States would be able to project many more warheads at the Soviet Union. The U.S. edge in numbers of warheads would make an agreement more palatable to Americans.

The newly tipped strategic balance turned Nixon against the ABM system he had inherited. McNamara had ignored the system's greatest virtue. If the United States could indeed wipe out the bulk of the Soviet missile force, then fairly simple ABMs could handle whatever survived. Now any U.S. ABM would have to face the full threat that had always been advertised. Such defenses might still be useful. For example, deployed around U.S. missile silos, they would force the Soviets to devote more weapons to destroying the U.S. missile force. Missiles used that way would not kill American civilians. The smaller the overall Soviet force, the less would be left over to kill civilians.

Nixon badly needed money. ABM was likely to be quite expensive. Yet Johnson's experience had shown that Americans would hardly accept killing it off unless the Soviets followed suit with their own "Galosh" system. Nixon opened ABM negotiations in November 1969. He revived McNamara's argument that it was too easy to counter ABMs simply by adding more attacking missiles. As at Glassboro, the Soviets were incredulous. How could defenses be bad?

Their system had been sold on the strength of experiments showing that one explosion outside the atmosphere could destroy many missiles with its EMP effect. Unsurprisingly, the Americans had learned to harden their own missiles against exactly such effects. By the mid-1960s the Soviet scientific community doubted that any ABM could be successful.[8] The Soviet ABM system was suddenly just as horrifically expensive as its American equivalent, and, given the level of Soviet technology, probably far less effective.[9] Americans counted it as a great triumph that they converted the Soviets to a belief in MAD and thus to drastic limits on ABM deployment. The ABM Treaty signed in 1972 limited each side to protecting either its capital or some of its strategic missiles.

U.S. politicians could not afford to be seen protecting themselves in Washington while allowing the rest of the country to be atomized. They opted for the missile field option, using a missile system called Safeguard. Congress killed it in 1975 just before it became operational, leaving alive only its big radar, which became part of the U.S. strategic warning system. The Soviets took the idea much more seriously; they kept and improved the "Galosh" system around Moscow.

Nixon decided to associate ABM limitation with limits on offensive weapons. There had been vague talk about controlling offensive weapons since 1966. An opening by President Johnson in 1968 elicited Soviet interest but was aborted after the August 1968 invasion of Czechoslovakia.[10] Apparently by November the Politburo badly wanted some agreement, apparently because it was becoming aware of the heavy financial burden the strategic missile program imposed. The Soviet Foreign Ministry announced its interest in negotiations on Nixon's inauguration day, 20 January 1969.[11]

Nixon put them off until November. Once negotiations began, he managed to head off a Soviet attempt to include U.S. long-range bombers and forward-based strategic weapons, such as carrier aircraft, in both of which categories the United States clearly led. The Soviets also failed in their attempt to include British and French strategic weapons.[12] In the end, the Strategic Arms Limitation Treaty (SALT) was limited to ABMs, ICBMs, and submarine-launched ballistic missiles. Signed on 26 May 1972, the treaty was to run five years.

This seemed to be a great achievement: the number of offensive missiles had been frozen; the strategic arms race had been capped. In fact there had never been a race. McNamara had capped U.S. missile numbers in about 1964. No new U.S. long-range bombers had been built since 1962. The Soviet buildup had left a distinct imbalance, which the treaty ratified: 1,618 Soviet ICBMs versus 1,054 U.S., 950 modern submarine-launched missiles versus 656 U.S. The point of Nixon's perception—that a first strike was no longer possible—was that even the U.S. had more missiles than it needed. The United States already had what it needed to wipe out the Soviet Union, with a considerable margin to overcome any Soviet counter-measures.

The treaty had a time bomb in it. At some point the Soviets would develop their own MIRVs, and then the much greater throw power of their missiles, particularly the few very heavy ones, would allow them to fire many more warheads than their nominal U.S. equivalents. Once that happened, the treaty would seem too lopsided for Americans to tolerate. To contain this threat, Nixon's negotiators convinced the Soviets to distinguish between light and heavy missiles. Light missiles (and the survivors of the pre-1964 generation) could be replaced only by other light missiles. For their part the Soviet negotiators managed to make sure that medium missiles already under development would be counted as light ones, hence could be built in quantity.[13]

SALT seemed to symbolize a new stage in Soviet-American relations. Nixon said that during the SALT negotiations a new and more cooperative relationship with the Soviets had been built. His national security advisor, Dr. Henry Kissinger, described it as détente. It was warmer than the Cold War, but was not any sort of alliance (entente). Nixon and Kissinger probably oversold détente to themselves because they so badly needed a breathing space as they wound down the war in Vietnam. Its high point was probably a May 1972 U.S.-Soviet agreement to defuse crises by consultation.[14]

Brezhnev also found SALT extremely valuable. The United States had finally been forced to acknowledge the Soviet Union as its equal. Both Gromyko and Usti-nov, the Party's military industrialist, agreed. The military thought otherwise. Marshal Grechko, the defense minister, refused to provide Soviet data: his colleagues spoke of his "guerilla war" against arms control.[15] The head of the general staff, Gen. Viktor Kulikov, considered the treaty process a deception by the Americans. On the other hand, by 1973 Brezhnev felt that he had built a personal relationship with Nixon.[16]

Without Soviet data, the treaty had to be based entirely on what satellites ("national technical means") could see. Missiles in their silos were invisible, so the distinction between light and heavy was the measurable size of silos; the rule against replacing light missiles with heavy ones meant simply that silos were not allowed to grow by more than 10 to 15 percent.

Nixon was uncomfortably aware that he had very few new strategic programs underway, whereas the Soviet strategic weapons program seemed to be flourishing. Largely to prove to other Americans that SALT did not equal surrender, he approved two weapons with enormous later significance, the cruise missile (sea-launched Tomahawk and air-launched ALCM) and the submarine-launched Trident. They could, it was thought, be deployed within the five-year term of the treaty. Nixon also approved a longer-term plan to develop a new heavy missile (MX) whose design would emphasize accuracy and hitting power. Probably Nixon saw it as a threat to help convince the Soviets to keep their end of the new SALT treaty.

For the moment, the U.S. government continued research on ABM technology, nominally to insure that U.S. missiles could continue to penetrate the new Soviet system. Periodically developers were asked whether it might be worth while to deploy missiles; the other side of the question was whether (and how soon) the Soviets might react with systems of their own. Since the Soviets were also continuing ABM development, there was also considerable interest in whether they were planning their own breakout from the treaty. Republicans would later charge that a Democratic Congress had been far too happy to approve a suicidal agreement to limit U.S. defenses. President Reagan's advocacy of Star Wars slightly over a decade later was a declaration that the whole idea of a MAD-driven strategic balance was, indeed, mad.

About when SALT was signed, the Soviets began to launch their land-based missiles in a new way. In the past, they had ignited the missile in its silo. Much of the volume of the silo was needed to allow the hot missile exhaust to escape. Now the Soviets began to cold-launch: as in a submarine, a gas generator under the missile produced just enough gas to pop it out of its tube. Space was no longer needed for exhaust; in fact, the more of the tube the missile filled, the more efficient the process. Suddenly the treaty's clever distinctions based on observed silo dimensions seemed far less meaningful. Had the Soviets slyly accepted them in the knowledge that they would be pointless?

In addition, because the missile does not damage the silo when it is fired, it can quickly be reloaded. The cold-launch innovation roughly coincided with much better U.S. satellite coverage of missile fields. Satellites sometimes saw the Soviets reloading their silos. Were they planning a protracted nuclear war? It now seems that they were periodically pulling missiles out for factory maintenance, then returning them.[17] A significant number of Soviet silos were unoccupied at any given time (or were occupied by defective missiles awaiting repair). Had Grechko been more open, much later tension might have been avoided.

During the negotiations, the Soviets warned their U.S. counterparts that a new generation of missiles was already very close to fruition. It was inconceivable that a nebulous change in spirit, reflected in a treaty, would abort them. The planned Soviet economic system naturally turned out new missile designs in time for production under the Five Year Plans; the Americans had to be naive to imagine otherwise. They were; when the new missiles appeared, it seemed to Americans (for whom it was easy to cancel programs) that the Soviets had been hypocrites, talking peace while preparing for nuclear war.

It should, moreover, have been clear that the missiles were being developed to specifications framed about 1969, long before the treaty had taken shape. All were

MIRVed, and the program included a new kind of ICBM, which was fully mobile because it used solid fuel (Temp-2S/RT-21, designated SS-16 by NATO). The previous generation had included only two ICBMs, Chelomey's UR-100 and the heavy SS-9. This generation comprised four separate missiles; not only were the Soviets not taking the new spirit of SALT seriously, they were pressing ahead.

This impression was somewhat misleading. The Soviets bought two different medium-weight missiles (UR-100 successors) because they could not choose between two competing designs; they had been developing competitive ICBM prototypes for years. The mobile ICBM was the largely unsuccessful successor to a long series of mediocre solid-fuel designs. The fourth missile was the direct successor to the heavy SS-9.

Since ICBMs but not IRBMs were limited by treaty, there was no longer any point in using the same missile for both ICBM and IRBM roles. To get the logistical advantages of the earlier common missile, the Soviets chose to use the upper and lower (without the middle) stages of the mobile ICBM as an IRBM, Pionir (SS-20). It was a lot more successful than SS-16. Americans were still convinced that only the United States was worth incinerating. Had SS-20 been conceived to exploit a loophole in the treaty? Would all the SS-20s one day be converted into ICBMs? In fact the Soviets badly needed something to replace SS-11s used as IRBMs. That was much more important than having a new lighter-weight ICBM. Moreover, given the failure of the new SS-16, it was more likely that they would convert solid-fuel ICBMs into SS-20s than the other way around.

Alongside the strategic missile buildup Brezhnev approved a program Khrushchev would have disowned, a buildup of tactical forces for a war in Europe. Even before Khrushchev was ousted, the leading Soviet strategist, Marshal Sokolovskii, published a classified article raising the possibility that war might be protracted and nonnuclear.[18] Work on a new strategy soon began. Its objective would be to seize as much NATO territory as possible without reducing all of Europe to radioactive waste. The new strategy was announced in the 1968 edition of a standard handbook, Sokolovskii's *Military Strategy.*

Westerners who read the book were fascinated and horrified. For all its supposed interest in the tactics of a war in Europe, NATO was designed as a deterrent; no one expected actually to fight. Khrushchev had shared that attitude. Now the Soviets were laying out the methods they planned to use. Within a few years, moreover, it became clear that they were buying the much larger army they might need to execute their new plans.

NATO nuclear forces might wipe out the advancing Soviet force. The NATO nuclear arsenal became the initial Soviet target. Moreover, once NATO had lost its nuclear firepower, it would also lose much of its nerve. A dramatic change in the nuclear balance (which in Soviet eyes largely determined the "correlation of forces") might cause NATO to surrender.

If that did not happen, the Soviets would be free to use their own nuclear weapons to smash through any NATO defense. A mobile striking force would follow through. It was frightening that the Soviet generals writing about such combat seemed to think that their new armored vehicles could operate freely amid nuclear devastation. Other newly important parts of the Soviet military machine would contribute to the strategy. Airborne troops could land in the rear of the NATO force to seize key points, including stocks of nuclear weapons. Special forces (*spetznaz*) would help disrupt the rear of the NATO forces as the breakthrough was mounted.

As Khrushchev had realized, such operations required immense—and very expensive—ground forces. However, it very much to Brezhnev's political advantage to reward Soviet industry by increasing production. The West saw a dramatically growing Soviet army. In 1965 the Soviets had ninety motor rifle divisions (plus fifty tank divisions and seven airborne divisions). In 1974 there were 110 motor rifle divisions; by 1983, 134; by 1987, 150.[19] As in the past, many of these units were cadres; total personnel strength rose much more slowly. However, all the divisions had their full complements of weapons.

Moreover, as time passed the units were packed with more equipment. For example, the tank battalions of motorized rifle divisions of the late 1960s contained thirty-one tanks; that of the early 1970s and beyond contained forty. Each division still had as many tank battalions, so a motorized rifle division grew from 186 to 240 main battle tanks. The Soviets introduced a new tank (the T-72) and replaced their towed artillery with self-propelled guns. A new tracked infantry combat vehicle, the BMP, was deployed. In 1976 the U.S. secretary of defense estimated that each Soviet division had 25 percent greater combat strength than in the preceding period. Overall artillery strength in Eastern Europe grew by 50 to 100 percent.[20]

The modernized units had very high firepower but they could not fight for very long. To Westerners, that seemed to mean that the Soviets planned to fight and win a very short, extremely violent war. Those worried about NATO's chances in a war pushed for it, too, to be able to develop as much firepower as possible, albeit for a short time. In fact, although each Soviet division was designed to fight a very short war, the Soviets planned to replace each division altogether as it was expended. There were enough divisions, echeloned back into the Soviet Union, to keep a much longer war going. When East Germany collapsed, Westerners would be shocked at the immense quantity of ammunition that had been built up. It was NATO that notoriously on the whole turned out to lack ammunition to fight beyond about thirty days.

The Soviets seemed to be adding another important capability. They revived their naval infantry (marines) and began to build new amphibious ships. They also restored an earlier emphasis on airborne units.[21] In 1965 the CIA read these two developments as the beginnings of an attempt to project Soviet power into the Third World. They were actually parts of the buildup in Europe. Short-range amphibious forces might be very useful in the Baltic, to turn the northern flank of the Central Front. The big airborne units could land well behind NATO's defensive line.

In Soviet eyes, looming strategic superiority and increased capability in Europe were closely linked. NATO used the threat of escalation to deter the Soviets. Once they had enough strategic weapons, no American president could cheerfully order any sort of attack on the Soviet Union. NATO would have to fight and win in Europe. Soviet nuclear weapons would probably deter alliance politicians contemplating nuclear attacks on advancing Soviet forces. If the Soviets limited themselves to a few very discrete attacks, which produced only very localized damage, would the Europeans risk much greater damage by retaliating? With NATO's nuclear weapons effectively crippled, surely the powerful Soviet ground force could sweep across Europe. NATO showed little interest in buying the expensive conventional force needed to deal with it.

To hopeful Europeans, SALT and Nixon's détente were part of the larger process they had been pursuing at least since 1966: the end of the Cold War. In effect they bought the Soviet propaganda line that they and their satellites maintained powerful forces in Europe to defend against the West. After all, German reunification was practically written into NATO. Once the West Germans gave up on it, NATO could give Brezhnev what he badly wanted, formal recognition of the Soviet empire in Eastern Europe. Both sides could then begin to demilitarize the border by agreeing to mutual and balanced force reductions (MBFRs). It took about a decade for these ideas to be recognized as the fantasies they were. In March 1969 Brezhnev revived a July 1966 Soviet proposal for a Conference on Security and Cooperation in Europe (CSCE).[1]

To the Soviets, the conference would offer the possibility of replacing NATO with a collective security arrangement embracing all of Europe. The two are radically different. NATO was designed specifically to defend its members. Military action is triggered by an attack across the alliance's border. A collective security system, on the other hand, seeks to avoid any disruption of agreed borders. One member cannot easily deal with an attack by another, since the aggressor can easily charge that it has been attacked—and the collective security system cannot make any clear distinction between the two claims. As a consequence, a collective security system was most unlikely to secure Western Europe against any future Soviet attack, yet it might seem very attractive to the Western European population disenchanted with the Cold War. [2] Moreover, Western acceptance of any collective security system would automatically ratify Soviet control of Eastern Europe, since any attempt to undermine that control could easily be presented as aggression contrary to the spirit of the arrangement. Initially the Soviets hoped that the conference would exclude the United States (to drive a wedge into NATO) and that its agenda would include the dissolution of NATO. The formal Soviet proposal called for a conference to improve East-West relations, recognize the inviolability of the European frontiers, and for both East and West Germany formally to recognize the inter-German border (at this time the West Germans did not yet recognize East Germany; Willy Brandt was not yet chancellor). Soviet Ambassador Dobrynin delivered the conference proposal to the White House on 3 April 1969, offering as "concessions" that the United States would be invited to attend and that the demand to dissolve NATO would be dropped.[3]

The European allies were eager to participate in the proposed conference; Nixon and Kissenger saw it as an opening to disaster. When he came to power in October 1969 the new Social Democratic chancellor of West Germany, Willy Brandt, apparently saw the general agreement to accept CSCE talks as valuable cover for his new policy of *ostpolitik*. Thus he accepted some important Soviet aims, negotiating a nonaggression treaty with the Soviets in 1970, recognizing as "inviolable" existing frontiers. They included both the Oder-Neisse line (the post-1945 western border of Poland) and the border between the two German states. In December 1970 he reaffirmed the Oder-Neisse line and formally abandoned earlier West German claims to Polish territory wrested from Germany after World War II. That caused considerable bitterness in West Germany.[4] In 1972 he signed a treaty with East Germany, explicitly accepting that Germany was one nation in two states. At the least, the West Germans hoped that by cooperating they might alleviate the more unpleasant features of the East German regime.

Brandt argued that as tensions were reduced, the East might allow itself to be drawn towards West Germany. Henry Kissinger, Nixon's national security advisor (and later secretary of state) found that argument naive. The West seemed weak; the Communists had iron self-discipline. Why should they abandon their ideals in return for West German goods and money? Brandt had abandoned the moral high ground.[5] Now the West Germans in effect collaborated with the East German regime. They excused the horrors of the East German regime and acted as though it had softened (which was anything but the case).

Brandt had to abandon any support for dissidents in East Germany. To this moral aid he added economic aid to the Communist regime. The East Germans also managed to extract considerable payments, for example, to allow elderly citizens to emigrate to the West. These transfusions of West German hard currency helped the East Germans avoid reforms. Although Brandt fell in 1974, his *ostpolitik* lived on through the 1980s.

To Nixon and Kissinger, then, Brandt was demonstrating just how damaging CSCE could be. At the least, they could extract something from the Soviets in return. On the theory that no CSCE conference could open without U.S. participation, they managed to extract two concessions. In 1971 the Soviets finally signed a treaty guaranteeing Western access to West Berlin, thus ending the periodic crises of the past decade. The Soviets were also forced to begin negotiations on Mutual and Balanced Force Reductions in Europe (MBFR: January 1973).[6] The existence of ongoing (though futile) MBFR negotiations neutralized European demands for unilateral arms reductions, on the reasonable ground that they would leave the

Soviets no incentive to cut their own forces in Eastern Europe.

For similar reasons, Nixon was able to use the MBFR talks as a way of stalling U.S. congressional pressure to cut forces in Europe. He told the Senate that unilateral U.S. force reductions would undercut MBFRs, since the Soviets would not have to make any cuts in order to buy decreases in the U.S. force. In November 1970 Nixon had the NSC endorse a decision not to cut U.S. forces in Europe except in the context of MBFRs. Later Nixon claimed that unilateral cuts would undermine SALT by removing U.S. pressure on the Soviets.

These concessions having been made, the CSCE conference opened in July 1973.

A principal architect of *ostpolitik* told Kissinger that the Germans were simply reacting to U.S. strategic vulnerability; they were no longer nearly so sure that the United States would risk destruction by going to their aid.[8] Brandt was saying that NATO had to recognize that it was never going to win the Cold War. Better to reach some sort of accommodation. The West Germans were on a slippery slope; as long as Brezhnev was adamant, accommodation meant accepting at least some of what Brezhnev wanted, never the opposite. Americans called that "Finlandization."

For Brezhnev, *ostpolitik* was a clear symptom of a tipping "correlation of forces." The Soviets' measure of the East-West balance included the usual military factors but it emphasized popular morale and staying power. For example, whereas conventional measures of power had favored France over Germany in 1940, in terms of the correlation of forces the Germans had the edge. Now the West seemed to be losing its collective nerve. In the United States domestic protests (in Soviet eyes, a pro-Soviet political movement) apparently were forcing withdrawal from Vietnam; could the United States ever hope to fight a Communist country again? Nixon had willingly supported détente despite Soviet support for the North Vietnamese, who were killing Americans. Kissinger reportedly said privately that he was trying to manage the inevitable decline of the West in as graceful a manner as possible (later he hotly denied the report).[9]

The U.S., however demoralized, was still the core of NATO. By the early 1970s the country was in economic trouble, partly due to the enormous costs it had imposed on itself by fighting the Vietnam War. With the Soviet threat apparently reduced, the NATO allies were unlikely to solve U.S. problems. Congress pressed Nixon to pull U.S. troops out of Europe. Nixon did not want to do so; he harbored no illusions about Soviet intentions. Ironically, European pressure for (MBFRs) gave him a valuable advantage.

In 1971, for the first time in a century, the United States suffered a trade deficit; its exports were falling. Nixon feared the deficit would trigger a recession, which would cost him the 1972 election. He therefore took short-term measures, including floating the dollar (in August 1971), to maintain American economic growth—at the expense of the Europeans and the Japanese. For example, allowing the dollar to float made U.S. exports cheaper but made other countries' exports more expensive. Moreover, the Bretton Woods agreement, still in effect, made the value of the dollar much more than an American issue; many countries used the dollar as their reserve currency. The Europeans and the Japanese were furious that Nixon could so lightly attack them.[10] By this time the European allies felt free to criticize the United States over such events in Vietnam as the 1970 invasion of Cambodia and the 1972 Christmas bombings.

Nixon had always considered Europe central and Vietnam peripheral to U.S. interests. Finally, as he began his new term in January 1973, he thought he could concentrate on repairing the badly frayed European alliance. Unfortunately he was almost immediately engulfed in a scandal he had caused: Watergate. The previous June, during the run-up to the 1972 national election, operatives working for him burgled the Watergate office of the Democratic National Committee. It has never been entirely clear why. Nixon apparently did not order the break-in. He did soon realize that he might lose the 1972 election if the break-in were connected to him. His crime was to use all of his considerable presidential power to cover up high Republican involvement in the burglary. Having lost the presidential election, the Democrats in Congress were in no mood to offer Nixon any quarter. They smelled blood.

Quite aside from the cover-up, Nixon had been involved in a wide variety of power abuses, such as spying on (and sometimes disrupting) opponents of the war. In a sense he was a victim of Johnson's decision to fight a war without declaring one. Many of Nixon's major sins were not too different from measures that previous U.S. governments had taken during war crises. They had been legitimized by declarations of war, i.e., by the outcome of public debate *before* the government could act. In Nixon's case, the decisions not to make the war a patriotic issue (as the Joint Chiefs had wanted) had contributed to the worst division of the United States since the Civil War. As a consequence, official assaults on critics of the war were much less acceptable. In addition, Nixon and his associates probably grossly overestimated the meaning of ongoing domestic (largely antiwar) disorder. He and Kissinger talked about how domestic unrest had, for example, played into the hands of the Nazis in early 1930s Germany. In this sort of atmosphere a proposal to break into the Democratic headquarters would not have excited enormous opposition within Nixon's organization.[11]

The Europeans showed little interest in Nixon's announcement that 1973 would be "the year of Europe."[12] For example, French President Pompidou sarcastically observed that for Europeans, every year was "the year of Europe." The developing European Economic Community seemed more important than a worn-out military alliance. Many Europeans resented Kissinger's speech emphasizing (and deploring) the gap between America's global responsibilities and Europe's regional interests.

Moreover, Nixon was forced to admit that the United States could not afford to keep its troops in Europe forever.[13] As the year wore on, the growing Watergate scandal eroded his authority in Congress. Nixon could no longer effectively argue that troop strength had to be maintained pending progress with arms control and European security negotiations.

Overall, Americans found détente puzzling. They were gratified that Brezhnev seemed to prize détente over Cold War. Yet he was still buying all of those threatening new missiles. The problem was crystallized in the events of a single day, 9 July 1973. That day, the Soviets first tested their MIRVed SS-17 ICBM. The same day the Soviet Communist Party's journal, *Kommunist,* published an editorial which the CIA called the most optimistic assessment of the future of U.S.-Soviet relations printed in the Soviet Union over the last decade. U.S.-Soviet relations had passed a fundamental turning point; "considerable obstacles" already blocked a reversion to Cold War relations. The editorial did contain the usual language: peaceful coexistence did not weaken the class struggle in the "international arena" and it promoted Soviet interest in national liberation and in the war against "bourgeois ideology."[14] Surely that language was boilerplate; the key was that détente was permanent. Surely the missile test was some sort of anomaly.

It took about five years for realism to set in. In Soviet-speak, permanently friendly relations meant that the United States would no longer oppose the world revolution (the "class struggle in the 'international arena'"). The successful MIRV test was one reason why that could be taken for granted. There was no contradiction, unless the article was read from a U.S. point of view. The Soviets could not possibly abandon the struggle with the West, although they could hope that it would not explode into global war.

In the midst of détente, the Yom Kippur War broke out in the Middle East in October 1973. It proved that the clients could maneuver the superpowers that nominally were their masters. Nasser had died in 1970 without wiping out the shame of the 1967 defeat. His successor, Anwar Sadat, also refused to accept the Israeli presence on the shores of the Suez Canal. In 1971 he signed a military assistance treaty under which he had to inform the Soviets of any plans to start a new war against Israel.[15] He offered to restore relations with the United States and to make peace with the Israelis if the latter withdrew to the Passes in Sinai. The Israelis refused, despite Kissinger's urging, perhaps because of divisions in their government.[16]

In July 1972, however, Sadat ejected his Soviet military advisors. Nixon thought that the Egyptians were interested in some sort of deal; he had Kissinger open a "back channel" to Sadat.[17] For his part, Sadat probably thought that, with no advisors in his country, he could hide preparations for war from the Soviets. He may have thought that his "back channel" to Nixon would limit U.S. aid to Israel in a crisis. In 1973 Sadat obtained Syrian agreement to mount a coordinated surprise attack on Israel.

When war broke out, Brezhnev was still cementing his position in the Kremlin. He had planned a World Peace Congress for late October specifically to celebrate his primacy in foreign relations.[18] Cooperation with the United States helped

Brezhnev in his internal war. Conversely, any demonstration that détente was empty would hurt Brezhnev at a particularly delicate time. On the other hand, détente had to be weighed against the danger that Soviet pressure to maintain or restore peace would drive the Arabs, their allies, into the hands of the Chinese.[19] For his part, Nixon was increasingly focussed on the Watergate scandal (the "Saturday Night Massacre" was conducted during the Yom Kippur War).[20] His secretary of state, Henry Kissinger, gained much more latitude than the Soviets realized.

Brezhnev did not want open war in the Middle East. If the Arabs lost, as he expected, they would blame the Soviets (never themselves, of course) for having supplied inferior hardware. The Egyptians were already turning towards the West (though the Soviets were unaware of Sadat's back channel). If they won, they would no longer need the Soviets to supply weapons, so they would turn away altogether. Better for the existing hostile truce to continue.[21] Unbeknownst to the Soviets, on 30 November 1972 Sadat had decided to go to war.[22]

About 4 October 1973 the Soviets learned that the Egyptians and Syrians planned to attack Israel at 2 P.M. Cairo time on the sixth.[23] Neither government had been particularly candid; the information presumably came from moles within the Arab governments. Brezhnev could not veto an attack, although he did say that it would be much better not to resort to war. Perhaps most importantly, he and the Politburo decided that, no matter what, the Soviet Union would not go to war to support the Arabs.[24] Just before war broke out, Syrian President Hafez al-Assad told the Soviet ambassador that he planned a brief offensive to retake the Golan Heights. As soon as he had succeeded, he expected the Soviet Union to ask for a cease-fire, so as to keep the Israelis from retaking the vital area.[25] Sadat was evasive.[26] However, the Soviets favored Egypt, which they regarded as more strategic, and with which (under Nasser) they had had a close relationship. Assad represented the nationalist, rather than the internationalist, wing of his ruling Ba'ath Party, and as such he was much criticized by the Syrian Communists—who had a very friendly audience in Moscow.

Given strategic warning, the Soviets flew their nationals out of Egypt. Asked whether this airlift might not tip off the Americans and the Israelis, Foreign Minister Gromyko replied that Soviet lives were much more important.[27] It seemed to a senior Foreign Ministry official that Brezhnev hoped to abort the war by giving exactly the warning the airlift would provide. If so, he may have fallen afoul of U.S. self-deception. The U.S. government was trying to negotiate a peace settlement, and presumably it did not want to imagine that the Egyptians were serious about war. Kissinger personally assured the Israelis that the Egyptian preparations did not mean war. Later he showed unalloyed admiration for Sadat's decision to fight, not to win territory but rather to administer a psychological shock that would cause both the Arabs and the Israelis to make peace.

Israeli intelligence did little better.[28] After Sadat entered office in 1970, he often spoke of 1971 as the "year of decision," when he would liberate the Sinai, even at the cost of a million Egyptians. When the year passed uneventfully, many Israelis wrote Sadat off as an ineffectual braggart.[29] Sadat had planned an air attack on Sharm-al-Sheikh, in the south, but had abandoned it due to the outbreak of the Indo-Pakistan War.[30] The Israelis had partially mobilized, and then felt embarrassed. They were also aware of Sadat's abortive December 1972 plan to land a paratroop brigade in the Sinai, to seize and hold territory until the UN could be induced to intervene.[31] Each false alarm convinced the Israelis that Sadat would not act.

They were certainly aware of an arms buildup by the spring of 1973; they actually saw the Egyptians practice the move to the canal.[32] Sadat said publicly that the key to an attack was the supply of long-range (180-mile) Scud missiles, with which Egypt and Syria could threaten Israeli population centers. This threat would cancel the Israeli air threat, which the Egyptians took very seriously, and which had been demonstrated during the War of Attrition. The first missiles arrived in Egypt in April 1973.[33]

In fact the Egyptians planned an attack that May, but they abandoned it. The next propitious time for an attack (based largely on tides in the Suez Canal) would come in the fall. Israeli intelligence dismissed the preparations as an exercise or, at worst, brinkmanship. The army commander ordered mobilization anyway. That proved very costly; the Israelis concluded that their intelligence assessment had been correct. They would be reluctant to mobilize again. This experience carried a lesson for NATO, which expected to mobilize if warned of an imminent Soviet attack. For NATO, too, mobilization would be quite painful. Like the Israelis, it could be lulled into a false sense of security.

In the end, Israeli assessments were colored by too much self-confidence. The Egyptians seem to have been aware of Israeli thinking, and ran a misinformation campaign to match.

By late September 1973 there was an unmistakable buildup on both the Egyptian and Syrian fronts. The Israeli intelligence chief insisted that preparations were defensive: the Arabs feared an Israeli attack. It was inconceivable that, after the beatings they had received, they would again go on the offensive. Even so, the Israelis prepared to mobilize if necessary, for the first time since 1967.[34] There was some nervousness that the alert might have been an overreaction. In the heated atmosphere of the Middle East, it might have touched something off.

Again, the lesson for NATO was that a government could easily refuse to believe a fairly clear war warning, out of incredulity. Later several governments sponsored studies of surprise attacks. The conclusion was almost always that the victim had had sufficient notice; surprise was achieved largely due to self-deception.

On 4 October, the same day the Soviets learned that war was imminent, Israeli intelligence alerted Prime Minister Golda Meir.[35] She decided to mobilize twice as many troops as had been planned, but rejected a proposal for a preemptive strike.

She, too, did not want to believe what was coming. It has also been suggested that she feared such a strike would alienate the United States. U.S. intelligence may have been a bit slower to react: Kissinger sent the Israelis a war warning a few hours before the attack (the Soviets received their Washington ambassador's version just as the attack began).[36]

The Egyptians and the Syrians struck before Israeli mobilization was complete, achieving tactical surprise. Moreover, the local commander in the canal area had not moved his force forward, apparently to avoid provoking the Egyptians.[37] The Arabs attacked on the afternoon of Yom Kippur, the holiest Jewish holiday. As it happened, because everyone was home, mobilization was probably quicker and more complete than it otherwise would have been. The Egyptians and the Syrians claimed supposed Israeli attacks as pretexts, possibly to excuse their failure to provide warning under the 1971 treaty.[38] Egyptian troops crossed the Suez Canal and penetrated deep into Sinai. The Syrians overran much of the Golan. With limited reserves of equipment, the Israelis seemed to face disaster.

The Israelis counterattacked with their most mobile forces, fighter-bombers and tanks. Aircraft were shot down by the heavy air defenses the Egyptians had built up along the canal, mainly as part of the earlier 1969–70 War of Attrition. Others fell victim to hand-held antiaircraft missiles. Tanks were attacked from the rear by dug-in infantrymen brandishing rocket-propelled grenades and longer-range wire-guided missiles. The Israelis would later say that they had suffered from their own arrogance.[39] They had been aware of the existence of the Egyptian weapons, but had not grasped their significance.[40] Had they sent troops in support of their tanks, the Egyptian infantry would have been flushed out (they soon learned to surround their tanks with a barrage, which wiped out the missiles). Artillery should have been used to destroy many of the surface-to-air missiles. This sort of combined-arms approach, which was standard in Western armies, had not seemed so important in the face of the much less sophisticated Arab armies of the past.

To the Egyptians, the Soviets had provided the margin of victory, in the form of new weapons. To the Americans it seemed that inexpensive guided missiles, particularly antitank weapons, could drastically reduce the value of an attacker's investments in expensive tanks and aircraft. That might well apply to Europe, where the Soviets had such a preponderance in armor. The Americans recalled that their own TOW antitank missiles had made an enormous difference during the 1972 Easter offensive in Vietnam.

The Syrian attack ran out of steam (inexplicably, to both the Soviets and the Israelis) on the second day; Assad asked the Soviets to call for a cease-fire, as he had planned. Sadat refused to do so; he felt his war was going very well. The Soviets thought that Sadat was deluding himself. His troops had not done well enough because they had stopped without seizing the key passes in Sinai.[41] But no one could tell Sadat that he was doomed unless he quickly ended the war.

The U.S. government decided to resupply Israel by air. It soon discovered that the European allies had no interest in helping; they banned the U.S. aircraft from their bases and their airspace.[42] The only exceptions were Portugal, the Netherlands, and Germany; the Portuguese base in the Azores proved critical.[43] Aircraft carriers in the Mediterranean launched tankers to refuel the transports flying to Israel. As in 1967, NATO was proving that it could not agree on policy outside Europe.

The Israelis changed their tactics. Their second attack punched through the Egyptian army. The Egyptians could not stop them because they had no way of attacking the Israeli units assembling to pour through the breach in their line. Within two weeks, the Israelis were at the canal, breaking the Egyptian front. The Soviets again approached Sadat; surely it was time to ask for a cease-fire. Given their satellites, they could see the scale of the Israeli attack. Within a short time the Israeli army might well be able to seize Cairo. Sadat was still deceiving himself. He spoke of a few Israeli tanks across the canal, when the Soviets knew a division had crossed.[44]

Then, on 21 October, Sadat suddenly realized just how desperate his situation was. Brezhnev invited Kissinger to Moscow, and the two worked out a UN resolution.[45] Kissinger's strategy was to preclude either an Israeli defeat or another Arab humiliation, in longer-term hopes of rapprochement with Sadat.[46] To Brezhnev, this was détente in action; the two superpowers were guaranteeing world peace. Sadat wanted one last flourish. His short-range Scud ballistic missiles were under Soviet control. He had the Soviet ambassador call the minister of defense, Andrei Grechko, to ask for permission to fire, as a demonstration against the Israelis. Without asking either Brezhnev or Foreign Minister Gromyko, Grechko approved a single firing (into waste ground)—which Gromyko vetoed, minutes *after* the missile had been fired.[47]

The Israelis were encircling the Egyptian Third Army. Once they had destroyed it, the road to Cairo would be open. Egypt would have to surrender. They therefore stalled, refusing to honor the UN cease-fire resolution. Sadat cried for help. It is not entirely clear whether he already knew that the Soviets had decided not to fight. The Soviets saw the continuing Israeli offensive as American duplicity: Kissinger was not delivering the cease-fire he had promised. They sent a fairly stiff note to Washington threatening unspecified unilateral measures if the cease-fire was not enforced. To Brezhnev, the note called for Nixon to do what he had promised; the threat was deliberately toned down.[48] The note arrived in Washington after Nixon had gone to sleep. His national security advisor, Gen. Alexander Haig, refused to wake him. He apparently considered Nixon too distraught (due to talk of impeachment since the Saturday Night Massacre) to make serious decisions. Kissinger convened the National Security Council. They answered the note by placing U.S. forces worldwide on nuclear alert.[49]

The Politburo was bewildered. The next day, Nixon claimed that he had put forces on alert to match a Soviet alert; but the Politburo had ordered nothing of the sort. Kissinger and Haig may have read the note as referring to observed alerts of airborne units and the Soviet fleet in the Mediterranean (which Grechko could have ordered on his own initiative), but a Soviet diplomat reviewing the record thought that the U.S. alert was grandstanding (an NSC officer, however, recalled solid evidence).[50] It seems noteworthy that among the evidences of Soviet posturing later cited by Nixon was the Scud firing—which Grechko had approved as a minor sop to Egyptian honor.

Kissinger had often used military movements and alerts to convey his messages.[51] He badly wanted to convince the Israelis that some cataclysm would follow if they did not halt their forces. Kissinger had a considerable stake in the outcome. Had the Israelis completed the destruction of the Egyptian Third Army, Sadat would probably have fallen, to be replaced by some radical pro-Soviet ruler.[52] Conversely, if Kissinger could deliver, he would be proving to Sadat that the United States, not the Soviet Union, was the more valuable ally in the Middle East. Kissinger's goal was to shut the Soviets out of the region. To do that, he had to keep the Soviets from putting any force into Egypt to monitor the cease-fire. He tried to avoid leaking news of the alert so that only the Soviets would get the message; of course it was impossible to do so, when so many in the military had to be placed on notice. NATO Europeans saw the alert as yet another example of U.S. irresponsibility.[53] Some were angry because they had received little or no notice.[54]

Nixon later said that the two superpowers had come close to war. Brezhnev and the Politburo had the good sense not to raise the stakes after the alert had been ordered and widely publicized. As a reward, in effect, Brezhnev's World Peace Conference was very successful, offering him valuable prestige.

For once the major Arab oil producers were able to agree to use oil as a weapon. They embargoed oil destined for the United States. However, the Arab suppliers provided only 17 percent of U.S. oil imports, which then accounted for only 6 percent of US oil consumption; the United States was still a major oil producer in its own right. Even so, every day Americans had to acknowledge what seemed to be the power of the Arab oil states when they lined up to obtain gasoline. In effect they felt the decline in U.S. power. Brezhnev had counseled the Arabs against the embargo, on the theory that it would encourage NATO forces to seize the oilfields (in fact there was much talk in the United States of fighting an oil war, but nothing came of it).

More significantly, the Europeans (except for Britain and France, who backed the Arabs) were to have their oil supplies reduced 5 percent per month until the Israelis withdrew. The European Community urged that the Israelis withdraw. In December it was rewarded with a suspension of the planned reductions. The Japanese reacted (and were rewarded) similarly. Both soon adopted more strongly pro-Arab positions.

There was also a major price shock: on 16 October six gulf producers raised the price per barrel from $3.01 to $5.12, and on 22 December the OPEC ministers raised it to $11.65. A massive transfer of wealth to the oil-producing states began.

By early 1974, reeling under the effect of the oil shock, the West was in a recession that lasted a decade. The recession lessened any chance of U.S. military recovery after Vietnam. For their part, the Europeans showed that they were less than unified under economic pressure. For the Soviets, selling their own oil at high prices brought in more of the foreign currency they badly needed—among other things, to finance covert attacks on the West, such as those mounted by the new terrorists.

The Egyptian success, limited as it was, gave Sadat sufficient prestige to consider a peace settlement. As Brezhnev feared, he turned to the West; the United States would broker the 1978 settlement in which Israel withdrew from the Sinai in return for recognition and a formal peace treaty. Sadat also abandoned Nasser's pan-Arab mantle in favor of Egyptian nationalism; it was in Egypt's interest to reduce the burden of military power.

The war demonstrated that détente had its limits; the world was still quite dangerous. Congressional pressure for cuts changed to pressure on the allies to pay their share of U.S. costs. The MBFRs talks went nowhere. Nixon's desperate arguments against cuts had paid off handsomely.

The Yom Kippur War was fought as the scale of Brezhnev's buildup of conventional forces became evident. Many saw it as the first missile war, the first time small, often hand-held, weapons showed their potential against expensive aircraft and tanks. Many of the new weapons had already been used in quantity in Vietnam, but with far less public impact. It seemed that at least for a time they could make up for the obvious material and skill advantages of the Israeli army and air force. In Western hands, perhaps they could make up for the vast new Soviet investment in tanks and other armored vehicles.

In an odd sort of way, the decisive phase of the war—the battle between Egyptians entrenched after having crossed the Suez Canal, and Israelis bent on breaking through to the canal—was a NATO war in miniature, with the Egyptians playing the NATO role and the Israelis the Soviet one. To NATO planners, then, the initial Egyptian success in stopping an Israeli breakthrough demonstrated a tantalizing possibility. Antitank missiles were already far cheaper than tanks, so NATO could afford to build a first-echelon defense. Missiles could be carried by attack helicopters or light vehicles or fired by dug-in troops.

However, that defense was not quite enough. The initial attack exhausted the defenders; the next echelon broke through. That was exactly what the Soviets were now practicing.[55]

The new antitank missiles could not destroy the follow-on force the Soviets would project through the exhausted defense. The problem was technical. A human eye can distinguish a tank easily enough, but simple missile sensors find that quite difficult. The designers of the antitank missiles being deployed by the Soviets and by NATO solved this problem by having a human operator, who could see the tank, control the missile until it hit. An operator on the ground could not see, hence could not deal with, a distant target, in the follow-through echelon.

A pilot using the new "smart bombs" might do better, but here the lesson of the war seemed ominous. The crack Israeli air force had failed to destroy the Egyptian bridgehead at the canal protected by Soviet-supplied antiaircraft missiles. They had been static, unable to accompany the Egyptians as they moved forward. However, one of the fruits of Brezhnev's buildup was a family of mobile antiaircraft missiles.

That left nuclear weapons, which could be fired from a distance at an ill-defined target such as a mass of tanks. In the past, it had generally been assumed that both NATO and the Warsaw Pact would use such weapons. Now, however, the Soviets were developing the ability to fight without them, or else to use them very sparingly. The onus of deciding when and whether to go nuclear would rest much more clearly on NATO. NATO governments found the idea less and less attractive; they could hardly advocate destroying their countries in order to save them. Moreover, given the emerging combination of Soviet nuclear and nonnuclear firepower, in the late 1970s it was increasingly said that if NATO chose to go nuclear, it would only lose a war in a more devastating way.

Obviously NATO governments did not spend their time, in the 1970s or later, thinking about how to fight a war they hoped would never come. However, when the Soviets pressed them, they were uncomfortably aware that they had no credible defense. The Americans periodically reinforced that point by pushing the Europeans to do more, to buy enough to be able to fight.

For a little while, the antitank missile lesson of the Yom Kippur War did help. It allowed the U.S. Army to change orientation to match the generally defensive posture of its allies, under the rubric of "what can be seen can be hit; what can be hit can be killed." In the past, the U.S. Army had always argued that NATO had to attack the Soviets, if only to spoil their own assault. Its allies had found that sort of orientation yet another frightening manifestation of American irresponsibility and aggressiveness. Now a badly shrunken U.S. Army fell into line. In fact, without some nonnuclear way to deal with the follow-on Soviet force, all of this was still fantasy.

As the war in the Middle East was being fought, Nixon was being destroyed. Threatened with impeachment for Watergate, he resigned the presidency on 9 August 1974. His successor, Gerald Ford, was badly weakened. His prospects for reelection in 1976 probably were fatally damaged when he provided Nixon with a blanket pardon. Moreover, in the wake of Watergate, an unusual number of new congressmen were elected in November 1974. Most were idealistic Democrats deeply suspicious of the Cold War and the U.S. military.

The new Congress took part in two disasters, the final loss of Vietnam and the loss of Angola, which seemed to symbolize the onward march of the Soviets and their proxies. Both disasters began under Nixon but ended after his downfall. The North Vietnamese began to violate the 1973 peace treaty as soon as it was signed, moving men and equipment into South Vietnam to rebuild the force so badly damaged in 1972. For example, in February 1973 they moved 223 tanks from Laos and Cambodia into South Vietnam; tank strength there was increased from one hundred to five hundred. Roads to the South were modernized and airstrips built. During 1973 over seventy-five thousand troops moved to the South.[1] Treaty violations were so serious that in March 1973 Henry Kissinger recommended that Nixon order bombing of the Ho Chi Minh Trail or the DMZ or both. Nixon ordered some limited attacks in Laos and Cambodia. In June Congress cut off any funds for additional operations. On 1 July an amendment sponsored by Senators George McGovern (the 1972 Democratic candidate for president) and Mark Hatfield prohibited direct or indirect combat activities over, on, or near Laos, Cambodia, and both Vietnams.

Later Congress cut the FY74 military aid bill to South Vietnam from the requested $1.6 billion to $1.126 billion. The effect of the cut was exacerbated in that Thieu, expecting further U.S. supplies, sent his forces into the Mekong Delta and to the Cambodian border. They used up supplies and ammunition—which later proved difficult to replace.[2] In addition, the 1973 Middle East War caused a drastic increase in oil prices—and with limited cash resources South Vietnam could buy less and less fuel. Yet its U.S.-style war machine relied heavily on the logistics that oil should have fuelled. Congress passed the War Powers Act over Nixon's veto; the president had to obtain congressional approval to use troops for more than sixty days.

The North Vietnamese concluded that the United States would not intervene were they to mount a 1972-style attack. Rumors of a planned North Vietnamese "blitzkrieg" began to circulate.[3] However, the Communist troops in the South still were too weak. The Communists also had to overcome their own troops' expectation that, the war having ended, they could go home. Thus in 1973–74 the Communists concentrated on political warfare. It produced few results. However, there also was a military campaign, against ARVN outposts, in response to an October 1973 decision to shift back to combat. Unfortunately, Thieu had ordered every outpost held, so each defeat in an outpost cost valuable troops. Meanwhile the sharp cut in military aid reduced ARVN capabilities.

Congress became ever more reluctant to support South Vietnam, in part due to effective North Vietnamese propaganda. For example, the administration's FY75 aid request was more than halved. Inflation (largely due to the oil price shock) further reduced the buying power of the money that was available, so that in the end only about 20 percent of what the South Vietnamese needed could be bought. According to the North Vietnamese, South Vietnamese firepower was reduced by nearly 60 percent and mobility was halved.[4] The North Vietnamese also were very effective in presenting U.S. air attacks—the likely form of intervention should they invade the South—as barbaric carpet bombing.

The South Vietnamese economy began to collapse. The war had made refugees of millions of peasants. They had survived in the cities mostly on the largesse of the big U.S. Army in Vietnam. It provided jobs and even the goods that stocked the black market. Now the army was gone, and so was a good deal of the U.S. aid money. Wartime Vietnam had never had a chance of building up a self-sufficient economy. In 1974 a third of the urban labor force was unemployed. Urban per capita income had fallen 36 to 48 percent between 1971 and 1974. Oil-driven inflation made matters much worse; inflation in Saigon was 26 percent in 1972, 45 percent in 1973, and 63 percent in 1974.[5]

Military pay was now nearly worthless. Corruption grew enormously. For example, quartermaster units demanded payment to supply troops; officers obtained the needed funds by squeezing villagers. The wartime prosperity had bred considerable corruption, but the post-1972 version was far worse than that experienced earlier.[6]

Aid reductions undercut South Vietnamese President Thieu because they were the source of the patronage that guaranteed loyalty to him. Now many of his former supporters decided that neutralists in the South could reach agreement with the essentially South Vietnamese Viet Cong. In 1974 Pope Paul VI urged Thieu towards an accommodation. When Thieu refused, the Catholics, in the past the best-organized anti-Communist force in the country, deserted him. The Hoa Hao sect in the Mekong Delta, previously loyal, turned on Thieu and armed military units (built around ARVN deserters) to oppose him. The Montagnards in the highlands, who had fought the North Vietnamese, also turned on Thieu. The An Quang Buddhists, the sect that had fought Diem, increased their resistance to Thieu.[7] None of these reversals in themselves destroyed South Vietnam, but inevitably they did reduce the loyalty of the forces on which Thieu soon would have to depend.

In 1974 the North Vietnamese began a series of what they called strategic raids, intended to regain the initiative, wear down ARVN, and sharpen their forces for a big future attack.[8] The raids proved surprisingly successful. When in July–October 1974 the North Vietnamese politburo debated the action to take in the coming dry season (1974–75), it tentatively decided to concentrate on the Mekong Delta in 1975 and to make a major attack in 1976. The politburo was understandably cautious after the 1967 and 1972 disasters. Stockpiles of weapons and ammunition were still very low. On the other hand, after analyzing the U.S. political situation, in October 1974. the politburo in Hanoi decided that, whatever it did, the Americans would not intervene.[9]

Gen. Tran Van Tra, commanding the force in South Vietnam, was more ambitious.[10] An attack concentrating on Saigon might win the war. His preliminary attack, which took the provincial capital of Phuoc Long, seventy-five miles from Saigon (7 January 1975), had a vital secondary effect. It demonstrated that the United States would not intervene. That encouraged the North Vietnamese and appalled the South Vietnamese. Now the South Vietnamese were short of ammunition (thanks to Congress) and had little hope of U.S. help.

The Chinese had advised the North Vietnamese to abandon the conquest of South Vietnam; they valued the developing "American card."[11] Knowing this, the Soviets realized that generous support would buy them the North Vietnamese. In December 1974 Marshal Viktor Kulikov, chief of the Soviet general staff, visited Hanoi with promises of fresh matériel. The Soviets would replace whatever the North Vietnamese lost or expended in what they saw as the run-up to a decisive 1976 offensive.[12]

In March 1975 the best South Vietnamese divisions were in the north, facing the DMZ. The North Vietnamese struck from Laos, to cut South Vietnam in two. South Vietnamese President Thieu could not decide what to do. When the strategic town of Ban Me Thuot fell on 10 March, he first ordered a withdrawal to the south, which contained most of the country's people and resources. Then he reversed himself: he wanted the old imperial capital, Hue, and the main northern port, Da Nang, held as enclaves. Neither survived for long, but Thieu's orders lost him the northern divisions, which had streamed into the enclaves.

This was much better than the North Vietnamese had imagined. They raced to get to Saigon before the South Vietnamese could regroup to defend it. The administration asked for $700 million in emergency aid, to help defend the southern rump. By that time the situation was nearly hopeless, and some have seen the request as little more than an attempt to put the onus for disaster on Congress—which, as might have been expected, forbade any sort of involvement.[13] Thieu resigned on 21 April. General Minh, a neutralist and former head of government, replaced him. The Communists were not interested in negotiation; only the military situation mattered. The South Vietnamese did manage to block the road to Saigon (at Xuan Loc) for two weeks. However, on 30 April the North Vietnamese rode into Saigon, their tanks crashing through the gate of the Presidential Palace.[14] The war was over. Americans were treated to the humiliation of watching the last few dependents climb onto helicopters from the roof of their embassy. For the first time, the United States had lost a war.

Having backed the North Vietnamese, the Soviets gained air and naval bases—built by the United States—uncomfortably close to the vital tanker route from the Middle East, through the South China Sea, to Japan.

Could the United States and the South Vietnamese have won? If the stream of North Vietnamese men and supplies had been cut off, if more attention had been paid to local development during 1965–68, maybe Tet would have been impossible. Americans might then have tolerated a lengthy military presence in a clearly improving situation. The North Vietnamese peace faction might have won out after Ho died in 1969. None of that happened. Even so, had U.S. bombers come back, as in 1972, the attacking North Vietnamese might have been beaten off.

By that time the indigenous rebellion was over; the Viet Cong were finished. Perhaps North Vietnam itself would have collapsed if its army had been destroyed during the 1975 offensive. By then, given their increasing interest in the "American card," the Chinese probably would not have intervened.

Ultimately the Americans left South Vietnam open to conquest because an endless guerilla war exhausted them. The key to disaster was President Johnson's decision, in 1965, to fight the war "in cold blood," and thus not to engage the American public in the decision to fight. Gradualist tactics did not help.

The war in Vietnam makes an interesting comparison with that which the Soviets faced in Afghanistan a decade later. Without a main force to back them up, the Afghan guerillas could ultimately exhaust the Soviets and force them out of the country. However, it took them a very long time to overrun the rump government the Soviets had left behind. The North Vietnamese army did much better against Saigon.

To the extent that the U.S. government tried to elicit popular support, it portrayed the Vietnam War as a fight against a brutal totalitarian empire. Domestic critics scoffed; the North Vietnamese and the Viet Cong were simple nationalists, and national reconciliation would surely follow their victory. The desperate postwar exodus of Vietnamese boat people proved otherwise; probably one or two million left by sea, many perishing there; at least another half million escaped from

Laos and Cambodia. In all about a million Southeast Asian refugees settled in the United States.[15] In Cambodia, the Communist victory was followed by a far more brutal rule. The Khmer Rouge killed about two million of their own people (nearly half the population), including nearly all its educated people, in a grim echo of the Chinese Cultural Revolution, a bizarre attempt to cleanse the country of non-Communist ideas and influence.

In the larger context of the Cold War, Vietnam was a campaign rather than a war. The decade of armed resistance to the North Vietnamese bought the time other governments in the region, particularly Thailand and Malaysia, needed to grow to the point at which they would not easily fall in the wake of South Vietnam. They felt free to be both nationalist and anti-Communist. From the beginning, the resource-rich states south and west of former French Indochina had been the great prizes, and none of them fell to Communist rebels. The time bought by U.S. involvement may well have been the reason the feared bandwagon or "domino" effect never happened, apart from Laos and Cambodia. Perhaps Vietnam was well worth the effort, after all.

The war shattered the U.S. Army, and to lesser extent the other services. American officers who survived this period vowed to rebuild the army. Over the next two decades they did so. The results were spectacularly demonstrated in the Gulf War.

Another result of Vietnam was a widespread belief that the United States could not risk intervention in a Communist-sponsored war, at least on land: the "Vietnam syndrome." Many Americans, including those in Congress, drew the lesson that guerilla war in the Third World was both inherently dirty and fundamentally unwinnable. Whatever their supposed orientation, the guerillas were likely to be nationalists first and Communists second.

Vietnam badly damaged the main instrument of the U.S. military presence, and therefore U.S. influence, in the Third World: the navy. Its numbers fell badly. In 1963 the U.S. Navy operated about a thousand warships, many of them products of the big World War II building programs. Ships last twenty to twenty-five years, so many were due for replacement in the mid-1960s. They had already seen hard Cold War service, and Vietnam was harder still. At the end of the war, the new CNO, Adm. Elmo Zumwalt, agreed to accelerate retirement of older ships (whose running expenses were increasing) in return for new construction. But few new ships were built, and the active navy was more than halved, to about 450 ships. This reduced fleet had to cover the same overseas commitments. Ships had to remain on station much longer than in the past. They wore out. Sailors, who resented the additional time away from their loved ones, failed to reenlist. The net level of experience in the fleet declined, which made it less effective, and resulted in more accidents and worse maintenance. There was far less money for spares and even for weapons. The fleet hollowed.

As fewer U.S. ships operated in the Third World, the Soviets could point to their own more visible fleet. Admiral Gorshkov, their naval commander, claimed that his ships had deterred the United States from intervening in Angola, and that they could do the same again. Gorshkov commissioned the Soviet Navy's s first aircraft carrier, *Kiev,* in 1975. It was widely (but incorrectly) interpreted as a means of projecting Soviet power into the Third World.

Overall, Vietnam was the reverse of Korea. Its outcome would have warmed Stalin's heart. In each case, it could be argued that local nationalism was the driving force—but that the nationalists could not have fought effectively without the backing of a Soviet Union driven by Cold War ambitions. In Vietnam, the U.S. government focussed on the local at the expense of the global. Instead of using a local war as a starting point for global strengthening, the United States allowed the local war—the local campaign—to draw down its global forces. Yet the larger war was far from over.

The Soviets seemed to be on the march. The KGB developed an "African strategy," which the Politburo approved in the summer and fall of 1970.[16] The regimes and guerilla movements of Southern Africa were looking for allies; their attempts to gain American aid had failed. KGB Chairman Andropov argued that the West did not yet suspect that the Soviets could move in, and that this was a good reason to do so.

Portugal controlled the last big European colonies in Africa, all of them in the south: Angola and Guinea-Bissau on the west coast, Mozambique on the east coast. Guerilla wars raged in all three, and the Portuguese army was slowly losing ground. The whites in Rhodesia, backed by the South Africans, were also fighting guerillas. KGB Deputy Chairman Viktor Chebrikov emphasized the strategic value of Angola and Portuguese Guinea (Guinea-Bissau).

To some extent the Soviets seem to have thought they were in a race for Africa against the Chinese, much as the Europeans had raced for Africa at the end of the last century. They said that unless they acted, the Chinese (possibly in collaboration with the Americans) would control the continent.

From the point of view of Cold War strategy, southern Africa was valuable on two counts. First, it was the West's source of vital raw materials, such as cobalt and chromium. Without them, it might be impossible to produce key items such as jet engines. Brezhnev once called Africa a "storehouse" of just such treasures.[17] Second, after 1967 (when the Suez Canal was closed, due to Israeli occupation of one of its banks) the vital tanker route between the Middle East and Europe passed around Africa. Based on the African coasts, a growing Soviet Navy could threaten that route. To these considerations the Soviets added a third. Southern Africa presented possibilities for cheap victories over the United States. If the Soviet Union could present itself as the liberator of the Third World (in competition with the Chinese), then a bandwagon would form. The correlation of forces would tip further in its favor.

Fidel Castro was already involved in southern Africa, albeit on a small scale, as part of his self-imposed revolutionary duty.[18] After involvement in the Algerian

War, he sent Che Guevara to Africa in December 1964, and early in 1965 he met various revolutionaries to decide which ones to back. For Castro, this policy of spreading revolution would gain him stature in the nonaligned world, and hence gain him some immunity from Soviet power, as in the missile crisis.

Guerillas were fighting in Angola and Portuguese Guinea (later Guinea-Bissau); another guerilla war was beginning in Mozambique, and in Zaire a guerilla war threatened the U.S.-backed regime. By the summer of 1965, four hundred Cuban volunteers were in Zaire (the former Belgian Congo) and in the former French Congo (Congo Brazzaville). The Zairian rebellion failed; the Cubans had to withdraw in November 1965. In Congo Brazzaville, however, the Cubans saved the government from a June 1966 military coup. Then they found a worthwhile cause, PAIGC (Partido Africano da Independência da Guiné e Cabo Verde), which U.S. reports considered the most effective rebel organization in Portuguese Africa. The president of Guinea-Bissau later thanked the Cuban technicians who commanded his artillery for his success. Because only forty to fifty Cubans were in Guinea at any one time, this operation was little discussed in the West. None of these operations received any publicity in Cuba.

In 1970 the Soviets focussed on Angola. The rebellion had begun in 1961, and in 1970 there were three rebel groups: Agostinho Neto's MPLA (Popular Movement for the Liberation of Angola), Holden Roberto's FNLA (National Front for the Liberation of Angola), and Jonas Savimbi's UNITA (National Union for the Total Independence of Angola). The MPLA was tied to the Soviets, the Cubans, and the Portuguese Left; its support was mainly urban. The CIA had supported the FNLA since the Kennedy administration; its leader was related to Mobutu of Zaire (Congo), and it relied on Zairian military aid (plus some Chinese aid after 1973). UNITA had split from the FNLA in 1964. In the summer of 1970 the Soviets made their move: they offered Neto aid on a scale which startled him.[19]

The Soviets had bet wisely. On 25 April 1974, Portuguese army officers radicalized by their experiences in colonial warfare (in Angola, Guinea, and Mozambique) overthrew the long-standing Salazar dictatorship. The Portuguese Communist Party was hard-line, almost Stalinist. It saw its chance. For a time, each succeeding provisional government was further to the left than its predecessor. Many ministers were either Communists or close sympathizers.[20] For a time Portugal had a far-left president, Francisco de Costa Govies; a Moscow-oriented prime minister, Vasco Gonçalves; and a Maoist security chief, Gen. Otelo Saraiva de Carvalho. A right-wing countercoup failed. The main Lisbon bullring became a political prison. Portugal seemed destined to become a Soviet satellite. Left-wing officers aligned with the Communists fought moderates within the ruling Armed Forces Movement. At the same time that Portugal was moving towards Communist control, the Italians were considering a coalition with Communists. Kissinger feared that Communist victory in either country would create a sense of inevitability, leading to Communist penetration into other NATO governments.

This trend was even more worrying given the energy crisis (due to the 1973 Mid-East War) and the loss of U.S. leadership due to Watergate and the collapse of congressional and domestic support for Vietnam and other Southeast Asian operations.[21] The Portuguese were denied access to sensitive NATO intelligence.[22]

Portugal would have been a considerable prize. Although poor, it controlled the Azores, islands which were vital to NATO antisubmarine operations in the Atlantic. The United States had used them in 1973 to resupply Israel.

Partly due to large-scale financial help to the Portuguese Socialists by European Socialist parties, a Communist victory was averted. Kissinger warned the Soviets off, and there apparently was significant CIA covert activity. Both the prime minister and the security chief were ousted, and the left-wing Armed Forces Movement was put down. In November 1975 the Portuguese government beat off a left-wing coup attempt by paratroopers and other troops.[23] Even so, the Soviets had come very close to winning; they had proven that they were hardly averse to adventures in Western Europe.

The post-coup Portuguese government opted to rush its African colonies to independence. Angola and Mozambique formed a buffer between black African countries and the remaining white-dominated ones, Rhodesia, South–West Africa, and South Africa. As long as Portugal maintained control of its two big colonies, guerillas operating in the white-dominated countries had no viable sanctuaries. Once the Portuguese were gone, it was unlikely that the white regime in Rhodesia could last much longer. Their protective barrier gone, the South Africans immediately decided to develop an atomic bomb.[24]

In Luanda, the capital of Angola, the high commissioner, the "Red Admiral," Antonia Rosa Coutinho, made sure Neto's MPLA received the weapons the Portuguese left as their army departed. He considered this the key to their later success.[25] The Soviets began airlifting weapons to the MPLA through friendly African countries. Che Guevara had met Neto in 1965; the Cubans in Brazzaville had trained his troops in 1966–67. After two senior Cubans met Neto in Dar es Salaam late in December 1974, they reported that his movement could win. The next summer Neto asked for help, and in July the Cubans provided a few instructors. They were far more welcome than the Soviets might have been, because Cuba was so clearly part of the Third World. They must have proved very effective, because the MPLA soon drove its rivals out of Luanda, the capital. The Cuban presence was too small for Western intelligence to detect.

Mobutu of the Congo (Zaire) and Kenneth Kaunda of Zambia both asked the United States to help UNITA and the FNLA, and on 18 July 1975 President Gerald Ford approved secret supplies of both money and weapons.[26] By August, the MPLA controlled twelve of the sixteen Angolan provinces.

In October UNITA brought in the South Africans, who feared a radical black republic on their border (a potential sanctuary for their own black rebels). MPLA was not nearly professional enough to stand up to them. Neto asked for Cuban troops. In deciding to provide them, the Cubans calculated that they need not fear U.S. intervention due to factors such as the ongoing investigation of the CIA and the continuing fallout from the debacle in Vietnam.

By Independence Day (11 November 1975) the MPLA was already in possession of enough of Angola to proclaim itself the government. The Cubans fought the South Africans to a standstill late in December.

The U.S. government naturally assumed that the Cubans had acted as the Soviets' proxies. Certainly it was in Castro's interest to show the Soviets how valuable he could be; surely Castro was aware of the Politburo's 1970 strategy decision. Castro's actions in Southern Africa were consistent with the Soviet concept of a "socialist commonwealth" whose members would know how to act for the common good. In April 1977 Castro said as much; he told Erich Honecker, the ruler of East Germany, that future moves in Africa "must be discussed with the Soviet Union. We follow its policies and its example." To the extent that Soviet support was vital to the Cubans' African operations, the Soviets always had a veto; they provided support because Castro was doing something of which they approved, rather than because he was following their orders.

Americans were aware of Cuban presence in the Congo and in Guinea-Bissau, but the numbers were too small to excite interest. The sheer size of the Angolan operation was a shock. It had been assumed that any foreign Communist support for the MPLA would have come from East Germany.

By late 1975 the Soviets saw Portugal slipping into their hands. It was a much greater prize than Angola. They seem to have feared that continued action in Angola might justify a Western reaction that would also sweep away their chance in Portugal. Castro was like Tito a generation earlier: he was too enthusiastic, and he would not take orders. As Angolan independence approached, the Soviets tried (but failed) to keep him from inserting troops.

For their part the Cubans badly wanted to present the Angolan adventure as their own effort. That was in the Soviets' interests, since it protected them from Western wrath. The Cubans later claimed that, until January 1976 Cubans were transported to Angola solely by Cuban aircraft and ships. On 16 January 1976 Cuba and the Soviet Union signed a protocol to provide weapons to the Cuban troops in Angola. Castro himself exercised detailed control over the operation in Angola.

The MPLA victory had not been a foregone conclusion. In November 1975 it was estimated that UNITA was supported by 40 to 65 percent of Angolans, while the MPLA had only about 33 percent support.[27]

Kissinger personally protested the Cuban intervention, and by December 1975 the Soviets may have been willing to pull back. Then the story of the covert U.S. involvement leaked out. Sen. John V. Tunney amended the FY76 defense appropriation to ban aid to the Angolans (the ban was later made permanent, as the Clark Amendment). It was argued that the Soviet intervention had been nothing more than a reaction to the initial U.S. aid, or to Chinese aid. The United States would have been on the same side as the clearly unacceptable South Africans. Then, too, somehow Americans proved largely unable to recognize Castro as a direct Soviet proxy; they saw a difference between Cubans in combat and Russians in combat. However, the memory of Vietnam overrode everything else. There was also considerable animosity towards Kissinger himself, for his association with Nixon and with the secret diplomacy and attacks (in Laos and Cambodia) of the Vietnam War.[28]

From a Cold War point of view, perhaps the most striking feature of the Angolan war was the new Soviet ability to support operations at a very great distance; previously only the United States had that ability. The Soviets maintained a force of sixty thousand Cubans at a distance of six thousand miles from both the Soviet Union and Cuba. The means included both a large merchant fleet and new long-range airlift aircraft.[29]

The Soviet victories in Angola and in Mozambique had wider implications. These countries controlled the access to the sea from mineral-rich Zaire and Zambia, as well as from Rhodesia (now Zimbabwe). Evident U.S. unwillingness to become involved had to demonstrate to southern African governments that in future they would have to turn to either China or to the Soviet Union for both economic and military support. Other southern African governments would inevitably move to the left, away from the United States.

Once the MPLA had won in Angola, it was free to attack Zaire, from which its enemy, the FNLA, had operated. In May 1977 it sent Congolese dissidents (the National Front for the Liberation of the Congo, or FNLC, including former Katangese gendarmes) across the border into former premier Moise-Kapenda Tshombe's old province of Katanga, now called Shaba. The province was still being "punished" for Tshombe's earlier attempt to break away, so there was much discontent for the invaders to exploit. The new U.S. president, Jimmy Carter, did not react; the French saved the day by flying in twelve hundred Moroccan troops. The FNLC attacked again in May 1978, and this time the United States provided an airlift for the twenty-nine hundred French and Belgian troops, who won.

Shaba was a valuable prize, and there was evidence of Soviet bloc involvement. At least in the second case, Cuban troops stood by to exploit any victory by the invaders. There was some evidence that East Germans had trained the FNLC for the second assault. Even though the assault failed, the Shaba mining operation was seriously disrupted, and many key technicians fled.[30]

In the end the Politburo saw Angola as an easy victory, which the Americans would swallow without too much resistance. Warned that Angola was hardly worth undermining détente, Brezhnev replied that the Americans were getting what they deserved.[31] He could happily go further in Africa. The ultimate prize was South Africa. There the main opposition movement, the African National Congress (ANC), was tied closely to the Soviet-oriented South African Communist Party, whose chief, Joe Slovo, was a senior ANC officer.

As it happened, the Angola story was not over. UNITA in particular kept fighting, partly on the strength of South African support. It was therefore in position to receive U.S. aid in the 1980s, when U.S. policy changed again.

In Mozambique, the only likely successor was the Marxist FRELIMO, which the United States recognized in 1975. Rhodesia lost its outlet to the sea. Anti-Rhodesian (ZANU) and anti–South African (ANC) guerillas gained a valuable sanctuary. To deal with them, the Rhodesians formed their own organization, RENAMO, among Mozambicans.[32] Both Rhodesia and South Africa periodically raided Mozambique. After Rhodesia collapsed in 1980, RENAMO continued to operate; South Africa became its patron, hoping to dislocate ANC guerillas based in Mozambique.

The Soviets did suffer a defeat in another ex-Portuguese colony, East Timor, which the United States and Australia encouraged neighboring Indonesia to seize after a left-wing FRETILIN (Frente Revolucionaria de Timor Leste Independente) movement had proclaimed the Democratic Republic of East Timor (28 November 1975). They feared a Soviet presence on the vital sea routes around Indonesia. FRETILIN resisted, but by 1978 it had lost. Subsequent Indonesian rule was brutal, and in 1999 the East Timorese were allowed to vote for independence.

To limit the radicalizing effect of the Soviets and their Cuban proxies in Africa, in April 1976 the Ford administration publicly committed itself to majority rule in Rhodesia and also, by implication, in South–West Africa and in South Africa itself. After Ford lost the 1976 election his successor, Jimmy Carter, favored the radicals Ford had tried to block. They won in 1980; Rhodesia became Zimbabwe.[33]

The left-wing victories in Portuguese Africa seemed to continue a larger pattern, in which the Soviets were winning power further north. As the British prepared to leave Aden, a Marxist National Liberation Front defeated an Egyptian-backed rival in a bloody civil war. It proclaimed a People's Republic of South Yemen in Aden and the surrounding territory (formerly the South Arabian Federation) in 1968.[34] Yemen, over which Nasser had fought, became North Yemen. The new rulers announced their goal: to overthrow all the traditional regimes of Arabia—which meant, ultimately, Saudi Arabia itself.

Although South Yemen had few natural resources, it was in a very strategic place, at the mouth of the Red Sea, and on the Saudi border. The British had prized the port of Aden largely because of its position on the route between the Mediterranean and the Far East, through the Suez Canal. With the canal shut (by the 1967 Israeli victory), Aden lost much of its income as a port. The Soviets bound its new rulers to themselves by offering fees (and arms) in return for Aden's naval and air facilities. For example, the Soviet aircraft lifting arms to southern Africa stopped in Aden to refuel.

From a Western perspective, with the canal shut, South Yemen was important mainly for its potential as a sort of Arabian Cuba, exporting revolution throughout the Arabian Peninsula. Oman was the first step. For years the Saudis had backed a rebellion against its sultan. Now the South Yemenis took over control of the rebels, who formed the Marxist-Leninist Popular Front for the Liberation of the Occupied Arab Gulf (PFLOAG). Like Aden, Oman had few natural resources but a very strategic location. It lay at the mouth of the Persian Gulf (the Straits of Hormuz), through which tankers had to pass. In addition, a successful rebellion in Oman would likely spread to the oil sheikdoms of the gulf itself. The situation was particularly difficult because, in addition to withdrawing from Aden itself, the British were abandoning their long-standing role as protector of the sheikdoms. The two local powers in the gulf, Western-backed Iran and Soviet-backed Iraq, began to move into the resulting power vacuum. As it happened, the British and the Iranians jointly helped the Omanis beat off the PDRY-sponsored rebellions of the 1970s.

That still left two anti-royalist Yemeni regimes bordering Saudi Arabia. The Saudis tried to overthrow the North Yemeni regime (which had become more vulnerable as Egyptian troops withdrew after the 1967 Mideast War), the hope being that North Yemen could then be sponsored to deal with the more radical South Yemen. That failed, and the Saudis tried to neutralize South Yemen by fomenting war between it and North Yemen. There were also direct attempts to foment rebellion in South Yemen, ending about December 1968. In June 1969 a Marxist-Leninist faction led by Abd al-Fattah Ismail took over South Yemen from somewhat more moderate leaders. Abd al-Fattah ruled as one of a triumvirate, alongside President Salim Rubaya Ali and Prime Minister Ali Nasser al-Hassani. In classic Communist fashion, the new government consolidated its power by purges and repression. It invited and received considerable Communist bloc aid: Soviet arms and technical assistance, East German help with internal security, Cuban help with air force training and with agriculture. This was not quite a Soviet satellite, because it also received Chinese aid, in this case a key road (from Aden to Hadramaut) and medical assistance.[35] The National Front which ran South Yemen was an offshoot of the larger Arab Nationalist Movement, another of whose arms was the Popular Front for the Liberation of Palestine (PFLP). Thus the South Yemeni government was able to strike back at the Saudis, who were attacking it, by having the PFLP blow up a section of the Tapline, the oil pipeline which carried twenty-three million tons of Saudi oil to the Mediterranean (30 May 1969). In the fall of 1969, the South Yemenis went so far as to invade Saudi Arabia, the Saudis using their army for the first time since 1934 to eject them from a strategic position.[36]

In 1971 the South Yemenis changed the name of their country to the Popular Democratic Republic of Yemen (PDRY), indicating both their radicalism and their determination to unite both Yemens under their leadership. As Soviet clients, the South Yemenis received support from a nearby Soviet client, Iraq, which in the early 1970s was fighting a low-level war against Kurds supported by the United States and Iran. Saudi efforts to foment conflict between the two Yemens continued, the main effect being to cause the South Yemenis to harden their regime and to ask the Soviets for more help. From a Saudi perspective, any permanent union of the two Yemens (which both governments espoused) was a threat, because it would place a poor country with a relatively large population (larger than that of Saudi Arabia) on the border of their wealthy country. Yemen had, moreover, claims on Oman and on parts of Saudi Arabia itself, including the country's richest agricultural province, Asir. The worst nightmare was of course union under the radicals of South Yemen. There were to be several fruitless attempts to unify the two Yemens, frustrated partly by differences between the two countries and partly by the Saudis themselves.

After a Saudi prince assassinated Saudi King Faisal in March 1975, his successor, King Khalid, abandoned the attempt simply to destroy the National Front ruling South Yemen. The Saudis came to hope that South Yemen could be weaned away from its revolutionary ideology and from the Soviets. Other forces were also at work. In March 1975 the Iranians and the Iraqis reached an agreement, under which the Iranians withdrew their support from the Kurds. In the wake of the agreement came a Saudi-Iraqi rapprochement, under which the Saudis expected the Iraqis to withdraw their support from the South Yemenis. It seemed to the Saudis that, just as the Iraqis had moderated their own behavior (and as the Syrians and the Egyptians had done before them), the South Yemenis might be expected to do the same. In that case, instead of being used against South Yemen, the slightly more moderate North Yemen might be induced to function simply as a counterweight.[37]

For his part, the Yemeni president, Salim Rubaya Ali, favored a more moderate policy in which he would play the Saudis off against the Soviets to obtain more aid.[38] He also saw moderation as a way of ending his country's isolation within the Arab world. Rubaya had, however, to be content with Adb al-Fattah Ismail, the hard-line chief of his country's only political party. Moreover, he knew that ultimately he had to favor the Soviets over the Saudis. That became evident when the crisis in the Horn of Africa (between Ethiopia, the current Soviet client, and Somalia, the former one) blew up in 1977. As a moderate, Rubaya had to fear the charge that he was selling out the Yemeni revolution. He could not, therefore, abandon the goal of union with North Yemen (which the Saudis much feared) nor could he abandon the revolution in Oman (which was supported by Iran, a Western-backed imperial power detested by the revolutionaries).

Across the Red Sea, Siad Barre took office in Somalia in an October 1969 coup. Already Soviet-oriented, in 1974 he signed a treaty under which the Soviets set up a naval arms depot in Berbera, the main Somali port. The Suez Canal having been closed, tankers from the Persian Gulf to Europe had to pass near the Berbera base. After the Suez Canal reopened in 1975, the combination of Aden and Berbera gave the Soviets control of the mouth of the Red Sea, the Bab-el-Mandeb, through which ships had to pass en route from the Indian Ocean to the Mediterranean. The canal having been widened and deepened, it now could accommodate the new supertankers—which had been built in the first place because smaller tankers could not economically transport oil around Africa, the route made necessary when the canal had been closed. Thus Suez—and South Yemen—became, if anything, more vital than they had been when the British had ruled Aden. On the other hand, given the hard-line Marxist policies undertaken by the South Yemenis, the merchants who had made the port prosperous in the past did not return. Aside from Soviet aid, the country's main sources of income were its aging oil refinery and remittances from its many citizens living abroad.[39]

At about the same time an even better opportunity opened up. Ethiopian officers overthrew Emperor Haile Selassie. The Soviets were slow to approach the new Ethiopian regime, perhaps because their recent bad experiences in Egypt and Sudan had shown that even massive aid did not buy continuing influence. Worse, their current ally, Somalia, contested Ethiopian control of the Ogaden region. No amount of common world revolutionary zeal could bring the Ethiopians and Somalis together on this issue. The Soviets had to choose. They discarded Siad Barre.

Ethiopia was a much more populous country, and much better situated. It was ruled by an extremely unstable junta, which went through bloodbaths once in 1974 and twice in 1976. In 1976 an Ethiopian delegation visited Moscow to prepare for closer relations. The Soviets' key move was to warn the Ethiopian dictator, Mengistu, that his colleagues planned to unseat him. In February 1977 he had them killed; the Soviets had ensured that he would stay in power.[40]

Fearing a sellout by the Soviets, the Somalis began talks with the United States. They then successfully attacked Ethiopia (in July–August 1977) believing that the Carter administration would back them up. By the fall of 1977 the Ethiopians had been soundly defeated. Infuriating Somalia's regional allies (Saudi Arabia, Egypt, the Sudan, and Iran), the Carter administration then announced that it would send the Somalis no arms until they pulled back across the border. It also prevented the Iranians from transferring Phantom jets, which might have been decisive.[41] That gave the Soviets time to save their new ally, Ethiopia, by shipping in an enormous force of fifteen thousand Cubans. They hoped to win quickly, before the UN—hence the West—could get involved. In November 1977 the Somalis abrogated their 1974 friendship treaty with the Soviets. Following their rescue, the Ethiopians signed a Treaty of Friendship and Cooperation in Moscow in November 1978. The Soviets having switched sides, the United States became the Somalis' backer.[42] The presence of the Cubans, so soon after the victory in Angola, raised the level of this Horn of Africa crisis. It seemed to be one more Soviet conquest.

Soviet access to South Yemen made support of the Ethiopians possible; the Soviets had no other staging post anywhere nearby. After Siad Barre ejected Soviet advisors in November 1977, the Soviets pressed South Yemen for access to its ports and airfields, and Rubaya agreed. His attempt at rapprochement with the Saudis had brought too little gain. For their part, the Saudis justified breaking diplomatic relations with South Yemen on the ground that it was becoming a Soviet base.[43]

Neither Somalia nor Ethiopia nor Aden offered much in the way of natural resources. All, however, had enormous strategic significance. Aden was close to the oil fields of the Persian Gulf, and all lay on the key tanker routes. Soviet interest in African coastal states seemed to parallel the rise of the Soviet blue-water surface fleet. It is still not clear whether the apparent pattern was real.

It could be argued that the fundamental problem in Portugal had been détente, which had convinced too many Portuguese military men that Communism itself was not an unalloyed evil. In July 1975 the Spanish and Italian Parties announced Eurocommunism: they foreswore the use of force to gain power. They also denounced the Soviets. The French, who were invited to join the declaration, refused; they stood with Moscow.[44] To Kissinger, Eurocommunism was like the old popular front: it made Communism respectable. Once that happened, Parties could slip into power. It did not matter whether the Party was Moscow-oriented; it would still be Communist. Americans would find it difficult to retain their commitment to a Eurocommunist NATO. Inevitably these regimes would fall under Soviet domination.

Italy seemed ripe for such penetration. The country was already quite unstable, suffering from waves of strikes and from internal violence. Since 1958 her economy had been transformed from a largely agricultural one producing mainly for the home market to a heavily industrial export economy. The rapid increases in wages (due to industrial anarchy), unaccompanied by rapid improvements in productivity, made for inflation. The oil shock made matters considerably worse. Italy was particularly vulnerable, because in 1973 she relied on imported oil for 75 percent of her energy needs (compared to 33.6 percent in 1955). The world recession drastically reduced demand for her manufactures. Through the 1970s, Italy suffered from the highest inflation in the West.[45]

Early in 1974 the Red Brigades began "an attack on the heart of the state."[46] There were also Fascist terrorists, and for some time Leftists and Fascists had been fighting each other on the streets of major cities such as Milan. Many Italians feared that some sort of civil war was imminent. There was also a sense of economic crisis due to continuing student and worker unrest.

Even before the Red Brigades began their campaign, the head of the Italian Communist Party, Enrico Berlinguer, told his comrades that an alliance with the other two main Italian parties, the Christian Democrats and the Socialists, might be essential as a way of avoiding a coup (and consequent annihilation) something like that which had just happened in Chile.[47] He told the other parties that they were safe: even if they won a majority, the Communists and the Socialists could not govern alone; they had to join the usual governing party, the Christian Democrats. Meanwhile, as the economic crisis deepened, the independent workers' councils (who had, in effect, broken the Party's power over labor) lost much of their power. They found it less and less possible to win local strikes. The Party then reasserted control. It now had something to bargain with.

Moreover, the Party's own showing in opinion polls was rising. As an election approached in 1976, one showed the Communists with 34.5 percent, against 27.6

percent for the Christian Democrats.[48] It seemed that a Communist-led government might emerge. Many Italians were still infuriated that the previous September the American ambassador, John Volpe, had given an interview strongly opposing any Communist participation in a NATO government. It did not help that Berlinguer declared he would not pull Italy out of NATO if his party won. That could be read as a declaration that he would destroy NATO from the inside.

The situation throughout the Mediterranean seemed grim. Greece and Turkey were still locked in their dispute over Cyprus. The right-wing Greek colonels' junta had been overthrown in 1974 as a result of the Cyprus crisis; it was by no means clear that its successors would remain pro-Western. In Spain, Franco's rule was clearly almost over, and the Spanish Eurocommunists obviously thought they had a fair chance of gaining power. In France a united Left (Socialist and Communist) seemed to be gaining ground in the wake of serious economic troubles engendered by the 1974 oil shock. If Italy went Communist, it would clearly inspire the others.

In the June 1976 Italian national elections, the Communists received 34.4 percent of the vote, close to what they had gained in the last free Czech elections. The ruling Christian Democrats did little better, with 38.7 percent. However, as a whole the Left (Socialists and Communists) had polled about 47 percent. It was crucial that the Socialists decided that they would do better in a center-left than in a Left coalition; they decided to join with the Christian Democrats. The United States, Britain, and West Germany kept the Communists out of the Italian cabinet by threatening not to provide loans to any coalition government.[49] In fact neither Left party was represented in the new government. Instead, they agreed not to cause its downfall by a no-confidence vote as long as they were consulted in its decisions. This rather odd coalition was called the "historic compromise." Given a stake in the government, the Communists demonstrated their power by drastically reducing strikes and helping to stabilize wages.

That solved one problem, but not the ongoing one of terrorism. Elsewhere in Europe terrorism declined in 1976; in Italy it grew. In 1977 the Red Brigades tried to become a mass organization. Had they succeeded, they would probably have brought down the Italian republic. As it was, they recruited enough new members to increase the level of terrorism, against both the state and its U.S. allies. The most shocking manifestation was the kidnapping and murder of former Premier Aldo Moro in 1978. This act triggered a general strike; the Communists condemned it. However, through 1979–80 the level of violence rose: from eight people killed in 1977, to twenty-nine in 1978, twenty-two in 1979, and thirty in 1980. In 1980 the Italian police finally broke the Red Brigades.

It did not take too much imagination to see something like the pre-1948 Czech situation in these developments. The Communists would enter the government, and they would offer to help put down left-wing violence. In the wake of the near miss in Portugal the situation was quite frightening. As Gerald Ford's secretary of state, Kissinger saw the Italian compromise as an interim step before Italy went

Communist.[50] This time, unlike 1947–48, the Italian Communists were dealing with an exhausted Christian Democratic Party and a West demoralized by détente—and, though Kissinger did not say so, by a U.S. government no longer willing to adopt tough covert measures to survive a continuing Cold War.

As a presidential candidate in 1976, Jimmy Carter attacked Kissinger's policy. However, once he was president Carter's national security advisor, Zbigniew Brzezinski, made much the same argument. Carter approved firm resistance to a coalition but barred direct interference. The "historic compromise" ended in January 1979. Brzezinski claimed this as a little-known Carter administration success.[51] The Italian Communist Party began to decline at the polls, apparently because voters considered it compromised by its demand for a direct role in the government. To prove its independence it condemned the invasion of Afghanistan and the imposition of martial law in Poland.

That was not quite the end of the story. When the French Left won the 1981 elections, the new president, François Mitterand, appointed four Communist ministers. They were, moreover, Moscow-oriented hard-liners rather than Eurocommunists. In this case the United States did not protest, because it was soon apparent that Mitterand was taking a very hard line against the Soviets, and that he was using Socialist-Communist alliances to maneuver the Communists out of power. For example, Mitterand pursued a rapprochement with NATO and pressed the Germans in 1983 to accept U.S. medium-range missiles. It seems arguable that, just as in the United States, it took a conservative—Nixon—to open to China, in France it took a Socialist to open to the United States and NATO. Had he taken similar measures, a conservative French president would have been destroyed by the French Left.

Trouble also was brewing in Greece. A military dictatorship had collapsed in 1974 due to a disastrous fight against Turkey over Cyprus. By that time many left-wing Greeks associated the dictatorial colonels, who had seized power in 1967, with the United States. It did not help that the colonels had seized power in the name of anti-Communism. In the first post-dictatorship elections a new left-wing nationalist party, PASOK (Panhellenic Socialist Movement), did quite well, winning 14 percent of the vote. It was an old-fashioned one-man party built around Andreas Papandreaou, the son of a veteran Greek prime minister, who had served in the U.S. Navy during World War II, and who had later worked as a professor in the United States. In the 1960s he had precipitated a crisis when right-wing military officers accused him of heading a secret left-wing group within the Greek military, Aspida (Shield). In a simmering crisis with Turkey, Papandreaou boosted himself by calling for an attack on a Turkish survey ship operating in disputed waters. He demanded that Greece drop out of NATO and eject vital U.S. bases. In 1977 PASOK roughly doubled its share of the Greek vote, an impressive achievement.[52] In 1981 Papandreaou gained the largest share of the vote, 48 percent, a truly astonishing jump in only seven years. He won partly because, although his slogan was "change," Greek voters were reassured that their strong conservative president, Konstantinos Karamanlis, could limit his excesses. For his part, Papandreaou moderated his rhetoric, though not his ultimate goals. Papandreaou was sworn in as prime minister in October 1981.

Papandreaou announced a policy of national reconciliation, which meant renouncing the anti-Communism of the Civil War. He was clearly sympathetic not only to the Soviets but also to the new generation of Soviet-supported terrorists. Within a few years the U.S. government would list Athens airport as particularly unsafe. Classified documents would be marked "NATO except Greece." Papandreaou refused to join in the sanctions against Poland, and was the first Western leader to break that country's isolation, by making an official visit in 1984. Later it would be reported that the KGB itself owned the largest Greek newspaper. In 1983, when Greece held the European Community presidency, its foreign minister prevented the community from condemning the destruction of the Korean airliner, KAL 007, by Soviet fighters. The Greeks showed their left-wing tendencies in other matters, too, such as their condemnation of the Israelis in Lebanon in 1982 and the presence of Hortensia Allende, Salvador Allende's widow, at the 1984 PASOK party conference.[53]

Yet Papandreaou never quite took the steps he threatened. He never left NATO, and he never ejected the U.S. bases (tenancy was renegotiated in 1983, to run through 1988). Nor did he sap the Greek electoral process; he was run out of office in 1988. His fall was due to the fact that PASOK was a one-man party. It lost strength dramatically when Papandreaou had to leave the country for seven months of medical treatment. When he returned, he was engulfed in personal scandals, including his decision to leave his wife in favor of an airline stewardess. There was also a major Greek financial scandal. When Papandreaou died, PASOK did not survive him.

Papandreaou's Greece and Mitterand's France make interesting contrasts with the Italy of the "historic compromise." All three offered the Soviets real opportunities. Only in the case of Italy did the U.S. government apparently take direct action. Arguably, had he remained in power, Andreas Papandreaou would have taken Greece into the Soviet orbit—but the Soviet Empire disintegrated as he himself lost power.

None of this seemed to have much impact on U.S. willingness to negotiate strategic arms treaties, which were the centerpiece of détente. The SALT I agreement of 1972 had specified that a second treaty would be signed five years later, in 1977. President Ford signed a draft agreement at Vladivostock on 24 November 1974. Within a few years the draft SALT II treaty would become a major target for increasingly vociferous opponents of détente. They argued that it precluded any American attempt to overcome a lengthening Soviet strategic lead.

Meanwhile Congress hobbled the CIA, the main weapon the United States actually could use in a nuclear world. The new congressmen elected in 1974 were furious that the CIA had illegally helped President Nixon investigate Americans protesting the war in Vietnam. The CIA was forced to divulge many of its past covert activities, which had been conducted with tacit presidential approval: subversion of foreign governments and even assassination. On 10 June 1975 a commission led by Vice President Nelson Rockefeller recommended that Congress create a joint oversight committee to approve proposed clandestine operations. Rockefeller had been deeply involved in past U.S. intelligence operations and probably hoped that his suggestion would limit damage.

The Europeans had seen neither the October 1973 Mideast war nor events in Africa as proof that the Soviets remained hostile. Thus they were still willing to give Brezhnev his long-desired ratification of the postwar division of Europe. CSCE talks opened in 1973. Thirty-five governments (the Canadians and Americans plus all of the Europeans except Albania) signed a CSCE Final Act in Helsinki in August 1975.

At least from Kissinger's point of view, the Western governments entered the CSCE process hoping to avoid disaster. However, as the conference proceeded, the Western powers gradually realized that they had considerable leverage. Brezhnev badly wanted his ratification of the postwar borders, a demand Kissinger would later deride as somewhat ludicrous.[54] He had the most powerful military machine in the world, and the borders had been ratified in separate agreements reached either immediately after World War II or, in the case of Germany, in 1970–71. There was, however, an important exception. The treaty in effect ratified the Soviet annexation of the Baltic republics, to which the United States and her allies had never agreed.

To get ratification, Brezhnev made concessions. To critics of the CSCE process, the concessions were pointless; Brezhnev never intended to live up to them. The treaty itself was drafted so as to deny that any of its clauses was legally binding. Thus it could well be argued that any concessions extracted from the Soviets were merely cover for the Western governments, which could not admit that the entire process had been one of appeasement. To those responsible for the treaty, the concessions were important limitations on future Soviet action.

The treaty was divided into three "Baskets." Brezhnev's ratification was part of Basket I, the security section. This basket included a clause allowing for changes of frontiers "in accordance with international law, by peaceful means and by agreements," inserted at the behest of the West German government, with strong U.S. support. Thus borders were not quite as inviolable as Brezhnev wanted—or as the West Germans themselves had agreed in 1970–71. This clause eventually provided the legal basis for German unification. The same clause affirmed the right of each country to enter or leave alliances. At least in theory, the treaty prohibited the sort of invasions the Soviets had staged in Hungary in 1956 and in Czechoslovakia in 1968—except that in the latter case they had arranged an "invitation" from hardline Czech Communists. Kissinger later claimed that the governments of the East European satellites privately told him that the treaty would make it more difficult for the Soviets to invade them, and thus would provide them with valuable maneuvering room. That was particularly true, according to Kissinger, of Poland, Hungary, Czechoslovakia, and Romania; the Yugoslavs were also keenly interested in insurance against Soviet invasion.

The United States also managed to extract an agreement on "confidence-building measures" (CBMs) which would make it more difficult for the Soviets to stage an attack on Western Europe under the guise of a sudden exercise. The Soviets eventually agreed to give thirty days' notice of the movement of any army division.

Basket II offered trade improvements.

Basket III guaranteed some important human rights. It seems to have been included in the treaty mainly to satisfy Western, particularly U.S., public opinion, which otherwise would have rejected the entire CSCE exercise as a surrender to the Soviets.

For some time U.S. enemies of détente had concentrated on human rights issues. They argued that Soviet repression was at the heart of the Soviet threat: the Soviet Union was dangerous because its rulers could not be called to account by those they ruled. Only if the Soviet system was fundamentally reformed could there be a prospect of lasting peace. Otherwise what the West called peace would be no more than a period of less warlike aggression by the Soviets.

Against this view, "realists" like Dr. Kissinger argued that the Soviet Union, including its repressive political system, was an immovable fact of life. There was no point in seeking utopian changes. All that diplomacy could accomplish was to regulate relations *between* states; serious attempts to interfere in the internal affairs of other states were, at the very least, quite dangerous. Moreover, the Soviets were most unlikely to agree to valuable concessions if they felt that the point of those concessions was to destroy their own internal power. Brezhnev clearly wanted détente, but only at an acceptable price. If Nixon and Kissinger also wanted détente, they had to accept that price. Their problem was that Americans tended not to accept their argument. To the extent that they distrusted the Soviets, most of them instinctively associated the Soviet threat with Soviet internal repression.

Congress reflected this more common American perspective. For example, late in 1974, in the Jackson-Vannik Amendment, it tied trade conditions to Soviet willingness to allow Jews to emigrate. Brezhnev found himself permitting the emigration of prominent dissidents, such as Alexander Solzhenitsyn (expelled from the Soviet Union in February 1974)—who spread the word that his government was much more totalitarian than many Westerners liked to imagine.

Brezhnev signed the Helsinki Final Act because he did not consider its "third basket" a problem. Whatever he signed, the KGB would control anyone too interested in his rights. Western critics of détente long argued that the "third basket" had been no more than a sop to Western conservatives. Certainly the Soviets did not take it seriously; if anything they were harder on human rights after Helsinki, and they refused to participate in the mandated meetings to monitor compliance.

The Soviets were even able to plead détente to gain agreements from some Western governments and newspapers to cease encouraging dissidents in their bloc.[55] However, the Helsinki agreement had to be publicized quite widely within the Soviet bloc. Groups suddenly formed to "monitor" Soviet bloc compliance with the accords. KGB crackdowns on the Helsinki groups proved embarrassing, but they were not abandoned. For the moment, these groups, heavily penetrated by the KGB, were insignificant.[56] However, once controls were relaxed under Gorbachev, dissidents who had begun their careers under Brezhnev became much more important, and their contacts grew. At the time of the Helsinki agreement, however, the Soviet system seemed indestructible.

In December 1975 the U.S. State Department adopted the "Sonnenfeldt doctrine" (named after Kissinger's aide): the Soviets were dangerous because they now no longer had genuine friends in Eastern Europe, except perhaps Bulgaria. This seemed to be nothing more than a new version of the old doctrine that Soviet aggressiveness in the Cold War originated with insecurity. If only the insecurity could be dealt with, the Soviets were unlikely to want (or to cause) military problems. The more secure the Soviets felt in their East European empire, the more willing they would be to forego any other adventures. Henceforth U.S. policy would be to encourage a more organic relationship between the Soviets and their satellites (now that any attempt to detach them had been formally abandoned) so that the emerging Soviet imperial power would develop along friendlier lines. By "organic" Sonnenfeldt meant that the East European states should develop sufficient ties with the Soviet Union to keep them content within the Soviet sphere of influence. The Poles had already learned their lesson, abandoning their past "romantic political inclinations," which had caused disasters, to develop means of satisfying their need for national identity without disturbing their Soviet masters. This was very much what Brezhnev had hoped to get.[57]

Conversely, resistance to Soviet rule might well cause crises—like those in Hungary in 1956 and in Czechoslovakia in 1968—which could touch off a general war. Sonnenfeldt clearly assumed that the Soviet occupation of Eastern Europe was permanent, but that had been accepted by the U.S. government since the days of Eisenhower; it would take Ronald Reagan to say that the Soviet empire might not be permanent. It was Sonnenfeldt's misfortune that he made his speech just as Reagan and other conservatives began to ask just why the United States had acquiesced in Soviet expansion.

To American conservatives, Sonnenfeldt was sounding a defeatist note typical of the Ford administration. Many years later, Henry Kissinger defended Sonnenfeldt.[58] He argued that a more peaceful relationship between the Soviets and their East European satellites would remove Soviet military forces (required to dominate the satellites) and thus would allow much more autonomy in Eastern Europe, a status more like that of Finland than like that of, say, newly occupied Czechoslovakia. This view entirely avoided the reality, that governments without real popular support needed Soviet troops as their final guarantors. Kissinger also pointed out that, as a contemporary Japanese observer said, the United States had to appear to acquiesce in the status quo in order to change it. Direct attacks on Soviet hegemony in Eastern Europe would simply cause the Soviets to dig in, whereas apparent acceptance might make for relaxation.

As the 1970s wore on, American conservatives began to attack détente as appeasement comparable to what the British and French had offered Hitler in the 1930s. The Soviets were willing to face the realities of actually fighting, where the United States and the West seemed paralyzed by the fear of nuclear weapons. Under Brezhnev, the effects of nuclear war were deliberately played down, so that a nuclear attack seemed far more conceivable. We can now see that this was a consequence of his laissez-faire attitude towards the military and Soviet military industry. It reversed Khrushchev's attitude, which in turn had justified limited spending and limited forces.

SALT seemed less and less attractive. The Soviets were fielding monstrous ballistic missiles while the United States was developing only cruise missiles and the naval Trident (which seemed to be a warmed-over Poseidon). The strategic arms imbalance gained enormous political significance in the United States. Simple comparisons could be made between Soviet and American strategic forces: numbers, yields, accuracies. It was far more difficult to gauge how well NATO would do against the Soviet Army and its allies. As the Soviets improved their missiles, they seemed to be gaining the ability to knock out the entire U.S. land-based force with a single strike. Once it became sufficiently accurate, each MIRVed Soviet missile could destroy several U.S. silos. Endless numbers of diagrams ("drawdown curves") showed that the U.S. land-based missile force was doomed. Once it had been destroyed, the Soviets could stop firing and threaten U.S. cities if the United States dared retaliate. Kennedy's strategic logic had been turned on its head.

This reasoning was a rather questionable relic of McNamara's strategic sophistry. Even a strike limited to missile silos would create immense fallout, killing millions of Americans. An American president might feel compelled to avenge them using the very considerable resources, such as submarine-based missiles, which the Soviet strike would not destroy. For that matter, he might fire everything he had in hopes of destroying enough Soviet missiles (as yet unfired) or command systems to negate a second Soviet strike. Nor was it likely that the Soviets could be sure of wiping out U.S. strategic warning systems, such as satellites in orbits so high as to be nearly untouchable.

In retrospect it is not at all clear that a Soviet first strike would have worked or that anyone ordering it should have expected it to. Enormous technical problems had to be overcome. For example, several warheads had to be aimed at each hardened silo in order to insure success. They could not arrive in very close succession, because the debris and nuclear effects from one might well destroy another (an effect called fratricide). Any attack thus had to extend over a considerable time. The first few explosions would surely tell the U.S. government that an attack was under way, no matter what had been done to the other warning systems. Much of the U.S. force then could be fired in retaliation. Given the sheer size of the U.S. force, the Soviet Union would be subject to terrible damage.

For a Soviet strike to succeed, every one of hundreds or even thousands of missiles had to arrive on target within a fraction of a minute on a fixed schedule. That could not be practiced in advance. Even the quick firing of ten missiles, which the Soviets tried, could not test the disarming attack. Would a Soviet leader chance such an attack, which had never been practiced in any way? Surely Murphy's Law, an overriding fact of everyday Soviet life, would have made itself felt.

In fact the Soviet strategic missile force provided the Soviet leadership with the option to strike first in the event that a U.S. attack was inevitable. That was not too different from the U.S. position on blunting attacks. In such circumstances, deterrence does not apply; the attack is mounted only after it is clear that the other side is attacking. Clear evidence is, of course, a tricky proposition. When the Soviets fielded their first infrared warning satellites, they received a false alarm of a massive U.S. attack. They were well aware of the possibility of a false alarm; the chain between the alarm sensors and those deciding to launch included a human being. That individual applied the common sense to which Eisenhower had appealed more than a decade before, and cancelled the alert. Much the same thing happened several times in the United States.

There are also real questions as to just how seriously the Soviets were planning to wipe out the Minuteman missiles in U.S. silos. In 1981 the Soviets had no fewer than nine different missile subtypes in service, including single-warhead versions of each MIRVable missile. Programming an attack by such a mixed force would be extremely complex. Although their SS-19 came closest to an ideal Minuteman-killer, the number of these missiles was cut by one hundred after 1975, leaving only a marginally sufficient force.[59] Russian accounts now emphasize turmoil in the RVSN as new weapons, particularly SS-19, were introduced.

To win a nuclear war, the Soviets would have to do much more than knock out most U.S. missile silos. They would have to insure against U.S. early warning, and they would have to destroy the bombers and the submarines. Since some missiles would surely be launched, they would need an effective missile defense. Even then some weapons would probably get through. The Soviets would need the backup insurance of effective civil defense. The great questions of the 1970s were whether the Soviets had an integrated program to achieve these ends, and whether it was succeeding.

As the 1976 election approached, a new Committee on the Present Danger was formed. It would help elect Ronald Reagan in 1980. It charged that the Soviets were seeking, not parity or security, but the ability to win a nuclear war. The CIA felt compelled to offer some of its members, formed into a "Team B," an opportunity to write an alternative to the CIA's National Intelligence Estimate (NIE) on Soviet strategic forces. Dr. Richard Pipes, a Soviet expert teaching at Harvard, headed Team B. The team included Dr. William van Cleave, who would be Reagan's campaign advisor on defense in 1980. Advisors included Paul Nitze.

The United States had added no entirely new missiles since 1967, although those in service had been drastically improved. As early as 1967, Soviet land-based missiles could throw as great a weight as the entire U.S. missile arsenal; in 1976 the Soviets could throw about 75 percent more. For the moment, U.S. missiles could deliver many more warheads (about 6,000 vs. 2,500), but the more powerful Soviet missiles would surely soon be MIRVed to more than make up the difference. For a long time, U.S. bombers had made up the difference in the megatonnage they could deliver, but the CIA estimated that the Soviets had reached equality in 1974, and were now pulling well ahead.

Perhaps the most contentious issue was civil defense. The Soviets planned to evacuate their cities in an emergency. The U.S. strategic deterrent was aimed at just those cities, the theory being that their destruction would, in effect, kill the Soviet Union. What if most people left the cities? If the others were protected by blast shelters? Visitors to Moscow began to report blast doors in strategic places on the subway. They had been in place for some time, but Western observers had missed the program because they had not known how to recognize it. Dr. Edward Teller, an inventor of the H-bomb, asked what the U.S. government would do if the Soviets *preemptively* evacuated their cities, then threatened U.S. cities full of people.

Should U.S. citizens receive similar protection? As in the past, government studies suggested that simple fallout shelters could make a considerable difference, particularly to those relatively far from the explosions. They might become more effective as MIRVing made individual warheads smaller. Even simply evacuating big cities might be useful.

Most Americans imagined, wrongly, that nuclear war would wipe out virtually everyone in the United States, and that defense would be pointless. War therefore seemed remote. A big national shelter program would make it seem far too real. Many in cities like Washington, which would clearly be hit, rejected shelters as an obscenity; they thought, in Herman Kahn's phrase, that survivors would surely envy the dead. They did not say, perhaps more honestly, that they refused to help protect anyone else when their own deaths seemed inevitable. Some argued that, by providing shelters and by making evacuation easier, the government could falsely convince itself that it could fight a nuclear war without destroying the country. Later it seemed that the Soviets felt compelled to make whatever preparations they could against the possibility of war, even though they had limited confidence in those preparations. Americans would not have made the investment *unless* they expected it to be worthwhile. Nor was it at all clear how the Soviets would maintain control of their population after evacuation. Blast shelters, which were essential for anyone caught near where a warhead exploded, had quite limited capacities. Soon there was evidence that internal security troops were being specially trained to limit access to these shelters if the time came.

The CIA argued that the Soviet leaders could not count on the United States' allowing them to achieve, within a decade, the ability to devastate it without suffering similar damage in return. Probably the Soviets hoped that in the event of a war they would emerge in somewhat better condition than the U.S. would. Their visible strategic edge would, they expected, cause the U.S. government to back away from confrontation. The State Department pointed out that the Soviets had considerable respect for U.S. capabilities and might therefore doubt their own ability to win an arms race. It doubted that the Soviets were seeking anything like a "war-winning" or "war survival" capacity.

The CIA's case rested mainly on Soviet failures in two areas: antisubmarine warfare (ASW) and ballistic missile defense. No one really knew how well the Soviets were doing in either field. In ASW, they were pursuing approaches so different from those used in the West that intelligence was difficult to evaluate. The CIA knew that Soviet ABMs were unimpressive, but the Soviets also were interested in beam weapons (lasers and particle beams). The air force argued that in both areas the Soviets were making "extraordinary" advances. That argument was somewhat self-serving. If the Soviets could solve their ASW problem, then the navy's fleet of missile-firing submarines would no longer be terribly valuable. A major thorn would have been taken out of the air force's side. If beams could wipe out missile warheads falling on the Soviet Union, then only bombers would still be effective. The Soviets were upgrading their air defenses, but in 1976 stealth technology was well advanced. A stealthy bomber could overcome anything the Soviets were installing.

Later it would become apparent that the Soviets had not done nearly so well as the air force imagined. Their exotic ASW methods seem not to have been terribly successful (after the collapse, they tried quite hard to sell what they had developed to the U.S. Navy). They never fielded any sort of beam weapon. None of this was for lack of trying. Under Brezhnev, the Soviet general staff was getting whatever the Soviet economy could provide, plus whatever could be bought or stolen from the West. It was intent on building what it took to win a nuclear war. That did not mean that it was succeeding; the laws of physics that hampered Western military scientists also applied to the East.

The Soviet economy could stretch only so far, but in 1976 its weakness was just beginning to show. The CIA grossly underestimated the Soviet defense burden. In 1976 it had just accepted that Soviet defense industry was no more efficient than civilian industry, and thus that the burden was 11 to 13 percent of Soviet GNP, compared to 6 percent for the United States. However, the Soviet GNP was actually only about half or even a third as large as the CIA supposed. Thus the Soviets were actually spending something more like 25 to 39 percent of their national product on defense.

Much more importantly, the *structure* of the defense economy could not be changed without infuriating the industrialists. As long as the marshals wanted improved versions of much the same products, that was no problem. However, to win a nuclear war the Soviets needed something entirely new, masses of high-performance computers and other electronics. They could get some, but apparently never enough. To get more, they had to forcibly convert existing firms, imposing real pain on the military industrialists. The CIA seems to have missed this issue altogether.

The U.S. services rejected the CIA view. They claimed that the Soviets were building up forces that could enable them to fight and survive a nuclear war with enough resources left intact to dominate the postwar world. That did not necessarily imply that the Soviets planned to start a world war, because probably there was not (at least as yet) a set target date to achieve the desired capability.

The air force argued, moreover, that overall Soviet policy was carefully coordinated. Western loans to the Soviet Union and Eastern Europe were propping up inefficient sectors of their economies and, in effect, subsidizing the strategic program. The loans were so massive that many Western banks were becoming hostages to the Soviets. SALT, détente, and arms-control diplomacy were slowing down the U.S. defense program while providing the Soviets better access to crucial U.S. technology.

The 1976 National Intelligence Estimate (NIE) was much starker than its predecessors, but the air force argued that it still "fell far short of grasping the essential realities of . . . the most extensive peacetime war preparations in recorded history." This was the 1930s all over again, the Free World failing to recognize what the totalitarians were preparing to do. For years, the air force had dissented from NIEs, and now its dire predictions were being borne out. The air force blamed SALT on blithe NIE claims that the Soviets sought nothing more than strategic parity, and the ABM treaty on American intelligence's disbelief in a big Soviet civil defense program. These widely shared judgements explain why the Committee on the Present Danger was so influential.

Team B concentrated on what it believed the Soviet objective was, and on what it considered systematic deficiencies in past NIEs. Too much attention had been paid to technological details and too little to cultural factors. It was no accident that Richard Pipes, who had spent a lifetime studying Russian and Soviet history, led Team B, or that the team included Paul Nitze, whose education in Soviet realities had predated the flood of data from satellites. Team B claimed that its analysis had deeply affected the official NIE (the CIA director, George Bush, denied that).

The drafters of the NIEs had been far too willing to "mirror-image," imputing U.S. thinking (which rejected nuclear war altogether) to the Soviets. They assumed that, much like its U.S. counterpart, the Soviet government was driven mainly to provide its citizens with a better life. For example, mirror imaging had convinced Americans that the Soviets were interested in shifting competition from military to civilian areas so their citizens could have more consumer goods. The reality—that the state existed to serve the Party and to extend its power—was too unpleasant or too alien to contemplate. Similarly, the NIEs missed the nature of defense in Soviet thinking—that it included defense of the gains the Soviets thought would fall into their hands as history favored their Socialist cause.

To Americans, the military was a peripheral factor in society; peace was the natural state of affairs. To Team B, the Soviet Union was "a giant conglomerate in which military, political, and economic institutions—and the institutions appropriate to each of them—are seen as part of a diversified arsenal of power, all administered by the same body of men, and all usable for purposes of persuasion and coercion. The distinction between the civilian and the military sectors of society and economy, appropriate to capitalist societies, is not very meaningful in the Soviet environment." This view now seems to have been essentially correct.

Team B argued that the Soviets were true heirs to Clausewitz; all weapons, including strategic ones, were part of "a varied arsenal of means of persuasion and coercion." Thus the Soviets might well see their nuclear missiles as a way of coercing the United States and the West as a whole, without risking actual war. To Americans, such coercion was far too dangerous to risk; actual nuclear war would be mutual suicide. For the Soviets, too, nuclear war was to be avoided. However, since it might occur despite deterrence, it was essential to prepare to fight and to win.

Team B pointed out that when the "correlation of forces" was in the Soviets' favor they were *obligated* to solidify whatever gains they could make, lest the balance tip the other way. Soviet internal audiences were already being treated to accounts of what had been gained by means of détente and the positive correlation of forces. The Soviet Angolan adventure certainly seemed to prove this case.

Perhaps most importantly, Team B argued that the NIE writers consistently watered down their estimates for fear of upsetting Congress, détente, and the SALT process. They were far too willing to take détente at face value. It was instead part of an overall strategy to attack the West without using the military while strengthening military forces so that the West could not hope to reply. The team thought the Soviets were well advanced toward their goals of isolating the United States from her allies, and the rich Western nations from the Third World and its resources.[60] One way NIEs minimized the Soviet threat was to examine each weapon program in isolation rather than as part of an overall plan. Individual developments which seemed insignificant might be much more threatening when taken together.

The argument was so divisive that Director of Central Intelligence George Bush charged in a covering memo that Team B selectively leaked both details of the process and its conclusions; the team had not, as it claimed, shaped the official estimate. In the end, he issued one more NIE merely outlining the alternative arguments that Team B had developed.[61]

In 1976 the Republicans nominated President Gerald Ford and wrote a platform that, although mild, avoided any reference to détente. Team B needed another four years before its advocates could take over the party. However, its advocates disliked Ford for what they saw as a soft policy towards the Soviets, culminating in the apparent surrender of the Helsinki Final Act (treaty). Many Democrats disliked Ford for his blanket pardon of former president Richard Nixon. This combination proved deadly. The Democratic Party's winner in 1976, Jimmy Carter, clearly hoped to continue détente. During his campaign, he pledged to try to eliminate nuclear weapons altogether. Soon after entering office he asked whether it might be possible to cut the deterrent to a few hundred weapons. Although he was soon advised that any cut this deep would be suicidal, he was determined to achieve something. For example, he delayed making the new Tomahawk cruise missile operational, and he rejected production of the B-1 bomber. Later Carter would leak news of the new generation of stealthy aircraft, hinting that the B-1 had been killed because something much better (which became the B-2) was being developed.

Soon after having been inaugurated, Carter pronounced himself free of the "inordinate fear of Communism" which had brought about not only the Vietnam War but also the embarrassment of embracing too many dictators merely because they pronounced themselves anti-Communist.[1] He accepted that the Soviets were still a military threat, but he did not accept that Communist movements in the Third World were per se threatening. This view showed, for example, in his distaste for the navy's traditional power projection role, which had been justified by the need to deal with exactly such hostile Communist Third World states. In Carter's view, regimes or rebels in the Third World were almost certain to be nationalists first and Communists only second or third. After all, the key U.S. mistake in Vietnam had been—it was widely argued—to mistake a genuine nationalist movement (the Viet Cong) for the mere tool of an aggressive Communist power (North Vietnam). On this basis the main issue in the Third World was redressing the very serious injustices which had made for Third World poverty. The great divide in the world was between North (industrial) and South (Third World), not between First (capitalist) and Second (communist) worlds.

This is not to say that Carter entirely discounted the Soviet threat, as a national threat. He chose Zbigniew Brzezinski, a tough Pole who viscerally distrusted the Soviets, as his national security advisor.[2] On the other hand, Carter's secretary of state, Cyrus Vance, was dedicated to preserving détente. For example, Vance opposed any attempt to link increasing Soviet aggressiveness in the Third World with the central strategic relationship with the Soviets. For his part, Brzezinski often espoused covert operations specifically to deal with the Soviets both at home and in the Third World.[3] Although President Carter formally approved a number of such operations, they were generally stymied by Vance's State Department— and by opposition from the CIA bureaucracy. It may be fairest to say that Carter himself was too obsessed with detail to be able to command his government to action. Examples included not only the Cold War but also Carter's attempt to make the United States self-sufficient in energy, a program he had called the "moral equivalent of war." It was also, incidentally, the only way in which the United States could have insulated itself from the increasing problems of the Persian Gulf area.

Carter's director of central intelligence, Adm. Stansfield Turner, personally wrote much of the next strategic NIE, issued in 1980. It generally followed past analyses: the Soviets were serious about developing new weapons, but their advantages were not decisive. Moreover, they were entering a more difficult time. Their economy was slipping, and their air and underwater defenses were unlikely to cope with the new U.S. systems, such as Trident, MX, Pershing, and the cruise missile, all of which would come into service in the 1980s. Whatever window of opportunity the Soviets had opened in the 1970s would begin to close in the 1980s—thanks to programs the Carter administration had sponsored and to the SALT agreements. As for civil defense, Turner was quite skeptical. The Soviets could certainly protect their key leaders. With a few hours' warning, they might save a quarter of the workforces of key industries. However, their economy and their society still would be horribly damaged. Even with a good civil defense, the Soviets could not chance a war. Moreover, their most potent form of civil defense, mass evacuation, would inevitably tip off the United States that they planned an attack.

This time the services were furious. They echoed Team B: the estimate did not take Soviet thinking into account. It mirror-imaged and emphasized bare numbers. It minimized a threat that could not be faced unless the United States rearmed on a serious scale. All of the services formally dissociated themselves from the entire NIE, an unprecedented step.[4]

In his last NIE, Turner was forced to publish the services' views, and to admit that he had not coordinated his own view with them. He argued that, while the Soviets certainly wanted to be able to win a nuclear war, their definition of victory included emerging relatively unscathed—which they could not reasonably hope to do. He had to admit that for the first time the newest Soviet missiles were more accurate than the best U.S. ones. They could now destroy most U.S. missile silos. However, for the Soviets the future was not nearly as rosy as it had been. Industrial productivity was falling; the satellites demanded more support; the work force was no longer growing. The U.S. public was aroused (Turner probably was writing before it proved just how aroused it was by electing Ronald Reagan). The Soviets had considerable respect for U.S. technical prowess and so might well fear that the United States could develop some very effective weapons. Then, too, they might feel restrained by the Chinese threat.

The services were less sanguine.[5]

In Carter's view, the Cold War essentially was limited to Europe. There he was willing to invest to cure NATO conventional-force deficiencies. Like Kennedy fifteen years before, he wanted NATO to be able to stand up to the Soviets without having to resort to nuclear weapons. The steady rate of increased spending he sold to NATO had already been proposed in 1970, but had been aborted because of the oil shock and the recession which followed it.[6] Carter's program did not last long, but his effort did publicize the idea that NATO could cure its problems if only every member government increased defense spending by 3 percent each year.

NATO still faced the problem of stopping a massive Soviet follow-up tank force. A new possibility emerged: a revived neutron bomb. It would neither kill sheltered civilians nor destroy buildings, but it could destroy tanks, which could not be fitted with effective anti–neutron bomb shielding. A defense that used the neutron bomb need not devastate Western Europe. Perhaps a neutron bomb was not quite an atomic weapon, so it really was usable.

The Soviets found the neutron bomb extremely threatening. They tapped the well of anti-military and anti-American sentiment in Western Europe. The bomb's virtue, that it would destroy neither property nor properly shielded people, was turned against it: it was the "capitalist bomb," designed to kill people without harming property. The European peace movement took up the cry. By 1977 Brezhnev was offering a bilateral pledge not to be the first to use nuclear weapons (he made a unilateral pledge in June 1982).[7]

President Carter handled the issue ineptly. Before the weapon could be developed, he wanted an assurance that the Europeans would accept it on their soil. Apparently he actually wanted them to absorb some of the developing criticism.[8] The question was put to the NATO Council. NATO Secretary-General Joseph Luns warned that was a mistake: the United States, the alliance's nuclear shield, should develop weapons as it saw fit, after which the Europeans surely would accept them. That had always happened in the past. Opening the question before deployment was courting political disaster. The anti–neutron bomb movement had time to apply considerable pressure. For example, the Dutch parliament went into emergency session. The Americans had to exert enormous pressure on the Europeans. Then, just before the crucial council vote, Carter suddenly reversed himself. His reversal may have been at the insistence of his UN ambassador, Andrew Young, who disliked the neutron bomb. Carter's NATO ambassador, Tapley Bennett, thought it was the worst national security error of his entire administration. Carter had destroyed his credibility almost completely.

It must have seemed to the Soviets that the morale portion of the correlation of forces was very much on their side. Everyone seems to have been blissfully unaware that most of the army's tactical nuclear warheads, such as those on the Lance missile and artillery shells, were *already* very similar to neutron bombs. Most of their energy was expended as radiation (a true neutron bomb would have expended nearly all of its energy that way). Nothing happened to those weapons.

There was also another twist. By the late 1970s northwest Europe had been very thoroughly urbanized. It was not really clear that there were very many open spaces through which masses of tanks could pour. That was evident, for example, when the U.S. Army in Germany tried to exercise. In the event of a war, the roads an invading army would use would also be crowded with refugees fleeing in cars. Drivers would find it quite difficult to get out of the way of Soviet tanks (in 1940 refugees had simply run to the sides of the roads). It was not, therefore, entirely clear that the Soviets' favorite attack instrument would have worked quite as they (and NATO) imagined.[9]

Documents found in East Germany describing a major exercise (Soyuz-83) show Soviet plans to reach the French border thirteen to fifteen days after war broke out. Soviet forces would reach the Pyrenees in thirty-five to forty days. Shades of 1948! German officers reviewing the documents doubted that operations could have gone as quickly as outlined unless nuclear and chemical weapons were used freely. To break through the NATO defensive line in Germany, the Soviets would have used twenty-eight to seventy-five nuclear strikes in the first wave and thirty-four to one hundred in the second. For example, the Soviet forces supporting the Fifth East German Army had sixty-five missiles and about twenty nuclear bombs. None of this shocked NATO officers, but few civilians probably realized quite how serious the Soviets and their allies were.[10]

Plans were quite detailed; the attack would have been made on four separate fronts, three from East Germany and one from Czechoslovakia. A fifth front would have been formed if Soviet and Hungarian forces were not occupied in a separate attack into northern Yugoslavia and Italy. Forces would have violated Austrian and Swiss neutrality while heading into France. An interesting feature of the plan was that East German forces would stop at the West German border, to occupy West Germany, while Soviet, Czech, and Hungarian troops pressed on through France.

German readers were surprised that a large force (six to nine divisions) was assigned to encircle the small allied garrison in Berlin. The allies had a contingency plan to cut the main rail line running near Berlin. The Soviets feared that they might be able to stop vital traffic for as much as twenty-four to seventy-two hours. The Soviets also considered a break to the east, along the Warsaw-Minsk axis, a real threat, and they would have placed at least four divisions in a blocking position. Probably they feared that any thrust east would raise anti-Soviet enthusiasm in Poland.[11]

In a global scenario tried in June 1982, Soviet forces in the Far East remained on the defensive until the fortieth day, then began their own counteroffensive (presumably after the war in Europe had been won).

These exercises envisioned the use of large Soviet forces. Perhaps the new strategy was actually the result of the general staff's desire for more forces and of Brezhnev's laissez-faire approach. The U.S. government estimated in the mid-1970s that Soviet military spending had grown by 4.5 percent annually since the mid-1960s, i.e., since Khrushchev's demise. Overall Soviet spending in Europe matched U.S. spending in 1968, and from that year through 1972 the Soviets spent 21 percent more than the United States on defense. Between 1972 and 1976, the U.S. government estimated that they outspent the United States by 28 percent (their estimated budget increased by more than 65 percent). By 1976, by U.S. estimates, total Warsaw Pact defense budgets matched those of NATO. Between 1968 and 1977 the number of Soviet ground troops in Eastern Europe grew by a quarter, to five hundred thousand.

Evidence of the sheer magnitude of Soviet programs emerged with the collapse of East Germany. The 160,000-man East German army had more ammunition than its 500,000-man opponent. A special road network was built in East Germany to support a three-pronged attack, and vehicles and rolling stock suitable for Western roads and railroads were stockpiled. A mock Western city, Scholzenslust, built for exercises, was found thirty miles from Berlin. Detailed operational plans were found, as well as new street signs to be used in occupied West German cities and even medals to be given to victorious East German troops. In addition, occupation currency had been printed.

Examination of East German intelligence documents showed, unsurprisingly, that accurate information was limited to a very narrow circle. For everyone else, NATO was quite falsely credited with a strong nuclear policy, in which it would deliver a massive first strike (2,714 weapons without France, 2,874 including France) plus a follow-on (1,528/1,624 weapons). This fictitious NATO also had very strong ground forces, sufficient for it to strike towards Berlin with four attack groups. West Germany had sufficient organized reserves to double its army instantly. Thus NATO was credited with a six-to-one advantage in the "Berlin direction."

The official German report notes dryly that there were often conflicts between East German intelligence and the main army staff because NATO numbers were insufficient for planning, i.e., for justifying the size of the East German forces. To help the main staff, intelligence became very ingenious; the West was full of hidden military assets, such as seventeen (largely nonexistent) French divisions. A chart of war plans showed an overall four-to-one NATO advantage (the reality was a two-to-one advantage for the Warsaw Pact). Briefing documents for senior politicians showed the grossly inflated numbers. According to the Germans, "no doubt . . . the highest-ranking commanders" of the East German army knew the truth, but is that necessarily so?

Would it all have worked in practice? The Soviets certainly had enormous fire-power and mountains of ammunition. They lacked maintainers, but their practice of discarding and replacing weapons and vehicles might have overcome that prob-lem. Westerners seeking solace for their own lack of preparedness tended to concen-trate on two Soviet weaknesses: the lack of initiative and problems of unit cohesion.

The Soviet system generally deadened personal initiative. It developed elaborate rulebooks and detailed plans. Units probably would attack "by the book" even if NATO showed that it understood and was exploiting the stereotyped tactics. Then, too, the Soviets would probably find it very difficult to react if their plans began to unravel. Soviet military magazines regularly called for special efforts to develop initiative. Clearly the problem was never solved. That made sense; two years in the army would hardly change the behavior drilled into a Soviet citizen from the earli-est age.

During the 1970s Western military analysts became more and more interested in just what makes soldiers fight. In a widely accepted book, *The Face of Battle*, a British military historian, John Keegan, argued that the key was the close relation-ship between the soldiers of each small unit. The Soviet Communist Party, how-ever, found such cohesion quite dangerous. Loyalty to a sergeant or to a lieutenant could reduce loyalty to the Party. The next step might be loyalty to a colonel or general who might challenge the State itself. But, as Western scholars knew, it was suicidal to destroy unit cohesion. The Soviets found that out in Afghanistan. One reason the Afghan veterans were so subversive was that, to win, the Soviet army fostered just the kind of unit loyalty the Party feared. Perhaps partly to avoid the loyalty problem, the Soviet army did not form any core of long-service noncom-missioned officers. Instead, it relied entirely on draftees serving two-year terms.

For all its rhetoric, the Soviet Union was still an empire, in which ethnic Great Russians ruled many subordinate peoples, particularly the Moslems of Central Asia. Racism was widespread. Many of the Moslems resented Russian rule and could not be used as first-line troops. Probably the paper strength of the army was quite deceptive, as divisions from the Central Asian military districts could not have been fleshed out in an emergency (if they could have been trusted at all). In addition, many Central Asians did not speak Russian, so commanding them pre-sented real problems. The situation was complicated by the fact that the Mos-lems—the least satisfactory troops, and probably the least loyal—tended to have a much higher birth rate than the ethnic Russians did.

There was another, subtler, problem. In 1967 the Soviets changed their draft policy, cutting the term of service from three to two years, with two call-ups each year. Probably the changes reflected the reality of a shrinking pool of draft-age men (in 1982 student deferments were eliminated). It was not only that sheer numbers were down, but that the declining quality of Soviet life was reducing the health of draft-age men, more and more of whom had to be rejected as unfit for service. Whatever the reasoning, the change had a corrosive effect. Draftees had less time to learn their military trades. The Soviets had never had a strong cadre of noncommissioned officers, so the second-year soldiers were able to dominate the new recruits, hazing them mercilessly. Army life became substantially more brutal. Soldiers from ethnic minorities often bore the brunt of the violence. Suicides became quite common.

Paralleling the Soviet army buildup was naval expansion well beyond what Khrushchev had approved, ultimately including aircraft carriers (albeit far less effective than U.S. ones). Americans sometimes described the new Soviet fleet as a "luxury" like the kaiser's World War I High Seas Fleet—an unnecessary irritation to the West. In 1918 many Germans argued that the resources poured into building the High Seas Fleet could have bought just enough additional troops to have won in 1914. The postwar Soviet Navy was a heavy consumer not only of steel but also, more importantly, of modern technology such as electronics. Was this expensive and irrelevant investment a major contributor to the Soviet economic collapse?

Carter planned to draw down U.S. forces in South Korea and in the Pacific to reinforce those in Europe. He doubted that his budget could maintain both areas simultaneously. Sensing an opportunity, the North Koreans became considerably more aggressive. The South Koreans began to build up their own forces and, more importantly, their own military industry. That gave them considerably more bargaining power, since in the future the United States would no longer be able to control them by cutting off supplies. On the other hand, only U.S. troops in Korea possessed nuclear weapons, which still seemed to be the only real counter to masses of invading North Korean troops.

In the spring of 1978 the Carter administration reviewed its foreign policy, looking towards the fall congressional elections. It decided that the American public liked arms control. However, the public was also worried by American weakness. Like Kissinger, it read détente as a way of managing American decline, which it rejected. The administration was deeply divided. Secretary of State Cyrus Vance favored negotiation and détente. National Security Advisor Zbigniew Brzezhinski demanded strength in the face of Soviet pressure.

Like earlier presidents, Carter believed that arms control (in his case, SALT II) should be pursued regardless of Soviet behavior in other areas. Although the SALT agreement lapsed in 1977, he continued to abide by it while his negotiators developed SALT II. The perceived weaknesses of the earlier agreement show in the enormous level of detail in the later one.[12] The Soviets were forced to provide some data (they invented a fictitious system of missile designations for just this occasion).[13] Carter signed the treaty, subject to congressional ratification, in Vienna on 18 June 1979.

By this time considerable Soviet aggression in the Third World and the Soviet Union's gross violation of the Helsinki accords had convinced many Americans that SALT was strategic surrender in disguise. A senior American diplomat of this period later wrote that Carter had lost sight of a fundamental in U.S.-Soviet relations: the public wanted both negotiation *and* U.S. strength, not one or the other.[14]

Carter did increase the defense budget for FY79, but here he felt quite limited.[15] There seemed very little hope that U.S. defense spending would rise to counter the growing Soviet threat. Depressing graphs charted the inexorable rise of fixed obligations, many of them social. The defense budget was by far the largest item of discretionary spending, so surely it would fall in priority as the fixed items rose further. Low post–baby boom birthrates would be reflected, later in the century, in a drastic reduction in the military-age population. The military would find it more and more difficult to compete against the civilian economy for fewer people. It would have to raise pay and amenities, further reducing funds for weapons and other essentials.

U.S. defense analysts wondered whether the United States had any leverage to exert. One idea circulated during the late 1970s was to buy some (ideally inexpensive) weapon that the Soviets would feel bound to counter, despite having to pay a horrendously high price. They might then be unable to invest in those weapons, such as the tank army, which so threatened the West. The favorite candidate was the B-1, a new supersonic bomber. The Soviets maintained an enormous national air defense system, even though SAC believed it was unlikely to be effective. A new threat might bring forth new Soviet defensive systems no more effective than their predecessors. They might sop up the limited Soviet capacity to produce defense electronics.

Another idea was industrial mobilization. In the past, the great American strength had been the ability to turn the civilian economy into military muscle. That was why the United States, with perhaps the nineteenth-largest army in the world in 1939, was able to supply much of the wherewithal needed to defeat two highly militarized Axis powers only six years later. Interest in wartime mobilization had died off; any future war would probably be a quick nuclear disaster in which only forces already in existence would matter. Peacetime was a different proposition. Could preparations be made so that, once ordered, the production machine could right the balance? How well could the Soviet economy match a U.S. mobilization?

Studies revealed important U.S. industrial bottlenecks. Increasing the defense budget would be little more than symbolic, because supply could not quickly rise to meet higher demand. It seemed likely that any drastic increase in defense spending would go mainly into higher defense prices. World War II mobilization, moreover, had required production pooling. Given existing antitrust laws and a generally antimilitary atmosphere, the government might find it difficult to get major companies to cooperate. For example, a federal judge broke up AT&T, the national telecommunications company, on antitrust grounds. The Defense Department desperately tried to stop him. It argued unsuccessfully that AT&T had invested heavily in features (such as EMP hardening) which, although not justifiable on commercial grounds, had important defense implications. No company facing competition could justify that sort of expense.

Civil defense studies convinced President Carter that a large, modern country might well survive an initial salvo. Therefore a war could be quite protracted. The Soviets might really imagine that they could win such a contest. Perhaps deterrence had to be rethought. Carter therefore signed Presidential Directive 59 (PD 59) in the summer of 1980. It called for ways to make U.S. forces endure longer, so that they could fight a protracted nuclear war, whatever that might mean.

Perceived weakness in the U.S. deterrent was matched in Europe, as the Soviets deployed the new mobile solid-fuelled SS-20 (Pionir) MIRVed missile. The replacement of earlier MRBMs and IRBMs missiles by SS-11s having been misperceived, it seemed to Europeans that the Soviets suddenly were replacing very elderly and hardly usable missiles with a modern weapon. With its low-yield warheads and its very short reaction time, SS-20 could destroy not only NATO's nuclear-armed aircraft but also the NATO command system. SALT did not cover SS-20, because it was limited to those Soviet weapons that could threaten the United States. Some Europeans concluded that the United States was not particularly interested in limiting the nuclear threat they faced. The missiles appeared as the Carter administration was trying to negotiate a SALT II agreement that, Europeans guessed, would do nothing more to restrain this new threat.[16]

The United States offered a counterdeterrent, Poseidon ballistic-missile submarines assigned specifically to NATO. The Soviets soon announced that they would regard an attack by U.S. forces, wherever located, on missiles in the Soviet Union as cause for a retaliatory strike at United States territory.

Chancellor Helmut Schmidt of West Germany hit upon a two-track solution to the SS-20 problem. While comparable (intermediate-range) missiles capable of hitting SS-20 sites were emplaced on European soil, NATO would offer to negotiate controls over both sides' intermediate-range weapons. Willingness to consider elimination of the weapons made it easier to deal with the NATO populations' natural fears, that the new missiles would become new nuclear targets. The Carter administration announced the decision to deploy these new Intermediate Nuclear Forces ("Euromissiles") in December 1979. They were to be placed in Britain, Belgium, Germany, Italy, and the Netherlands. To avoid the charge that it was escalating nuclear weaponry in Europe, NATO announced that a thousand older weapons would be withdrawn when the new missiles were emplaced.[17]

The weapons selected were longer-range versions of the army's Pershing and the air force's ground-launched cruise missile (GLCM), a land-based version of the navy's Tomahawk. Both weapons were extremely accurate. Pershing could reach and destroy Soviet command centers after a flight so short that the Soviets might not be able to launch any of their own weapons before it arrived. The Pershing might be able to end a war by destroying the Soviet leaders. In the mid-1980s the annual U.S. Defense Department booklet on the Soviet threat began to include detailed drawings of the system of bunkers under Moscow. The message was that those who initiated a new world war would not survive it; U.S. missiles could find them.

The missiles' existence seemed to demonstrate renewed U.S. dedication to European security. Because some of the missiles were deployed well forward in Germany, they would be in the path of a Soviet ground attack. They would have to be used quite early in a war, if they were to be used at all. Given the Soviet threat, by deploying the missiles the United States was demonstrating its willingness to risk nuclear destruction rather than allow Europe to be overrun.[18] The Soviets could not contemplate overrunning Western Europe without risking attacks by the new missiles; they would have to preempt them, using nuclear missiles of their own. Once the Euromissiles were in place the Soviets could no longer expect to defeat NATO without using nuclear weapons.

Carter's national security advisor, Zbigniew Brzezhinski, considered China a very valuable counterweight to increasing Soviet power. The Chinese had gone so far as to enshrine their struggle with the Soviets in the new constitution adopted in 1975; the struggle against "social imperialism" (i.e., the Soviet system) was made a key role of the Chinese military.[19] There was evidence that by the late 1970s the Soviets had much the same view of the Chinese.[20]

In December 1978 the United States and the People's Republic announced that they would open full diplomatic relations the following January. As the Communist Chinese had demanded, the United States formally broke relations with Nationalist China (Taiwan), although informal relations survived, and the United States continued to supply defensive weapons. Moreover, the United States extracted a promise that the People's Republic would not mount an invasion of Taiwan.

President Carter believed that the chief world problem was the relationship between the developed North and the undeveloped South, the Third World. He resolved to remove humiliations the United States had imposed on the Third World, chief among them the Panama Canal, in effect a U.S. colony. Carter negotiated a treaty returning the canal to full Panamanian control by the end of the century.

On the Panamanian border, Nicaragua was in turmoil; the Carter administration and most Latin American governments agreed that only the removal of the Somoza regime could end it. The Cuban-backed Sandinistas, who were Leninists, led the popular front that overthrew Somoza.[21] As in the case of Cuba two decades earlier, the revolutionaries initially gained Western backing, and it was some years before their sympathies were generally understood. The administration distrusted the Sandinistas but maintained relations in hopes of gaining influence. That was wishful thinking; it was soon evident that the Sandinistas planned to dominate their popular front just as Stalin's men had in Eastern Europe after World War II.[22] In March 1980 the Soviet Communist Party established party-to-party ties with the Sandinistas, a sign of common ideology. In May 1980 the new Council of State, a quasi-legislative body, convened with forty-seven rather than the planned thirty-three seats, the Sandinistas (who were to have had thirteen seats) receiving all fourteen new ones, for a majority. They soon announced that elections would be postponed until 1985. The Cubans sent numerous advisors.

Another guerilla war was already being waged in neighboring El Salvador. In mid-1980 the Nicaraguans decided to provide arms to the rebels, and they continued to do so despite the Carter administration's September warning that they were jeopardizing economic aid to their country. Late in 1980 Cuban-backed guerillas began a "final offensive" in El Salvador. President Carter did not feel that it was worth intervening to keep a Cuban-backed movement out of power.[23] By the beginning of the 1980s Carter's inaction had placed a potential Soviet ally at the borders of Panama just as U.S. control over the canal itself, an immensely important strategic asset, was about to decline.

The Cubans also were active in the Caribbean, on the island of Grenada. Maurice Bishop, who had had a close relationship with Cuba for six years, seized power there on 13 March 1979. It was soon clear that the island was being built up as a Cuban military surrogate.[24] It seemed that the Cubans planned to use Grenadians to gain power in other Caribbean countries, such as Jamaica.

Overall, the Carter administration was well aware of the Cubans' role as Soviet surrogates. By 1979, the U.S. official judgement was that Soviet arms shipments begun in 1975 (i.e., before the Cubans had begun to function as Soviet surrogates in Africa) had transformed the Cuban military from a home defense force into a powerful offensive weapon for use in both Latin America and Africa.[25] However, the U.S. government was not about to attack Cuba. It did try unsuccessfully to bribe the Cubans, promising an end to economic sanctions (which had impoverished Cuba) if they abandoned their Third World offensive.[26] This was a fundamental misreading of the Cuban (and, more generally, Communist) situation; general prosperity was by no means attractive to such governments, because it did not reinforce their grip on political power. Moreover, Castro personally believed that his life's mission was to support the world revolution. He would not abandon it merely to give the average Cuban better living conditions.

Carter revived a classic U.S. theme: support for human rights. He seemed unable to press the Soviets on this topic, but he quite readily attacked Third World regimes loosely allied to the United States. Iran was the most prominent case in point. In 1979 popular discontent with the shah boiled over into riots. President Carter sent an envoy specifically to advise the Iranian military not to put down the riots. It is not clear to what extent the military's inaction tipped the scales. Within a short time the shah, the main U.S. ally in his region, was in exile.[27] President

Carter's enabling role bought him very little; the Iranians were still sure that the United States was the "great Satan." Some of them were so sure that they raided the American embassy in Teheran and seized its occupants. President Carter's failure to assure the prisoners' release, including a botched rescue attempt, helped cost him the presidency in 1980.

To Jeane Kirkpatrick, who was later UN ambassador, writing in 1980, Carter's crucial mistake had been to confuse totalitarian with authoritarian regimes. By damning both equally, he had been unable to realize that the shah and Somoza were not nearly as bad as the fundamentalist and Communist regimes which replaced them. This naive human rights approach made it impossible to support embattled friends like the shah. It also abandoned any hope that U.S. leverage could cause those friends' regimes to evolve. Kirkpatrick argued that as long as an authoritarian regime was not fighting for its life, it would be amenable to U.S. pressure for human rights reforms. It could evolve into the desired democracy. Totalitarian regimes were a different proposition altogether. Since, except for El Salvador, Latin American regimes were not fighting for their lives, U.S. pressure did help cause a gradual transition to democracy. During the Carter administration that happened in the Dominican Republic, Ecuador, and Peru. During the next administration it happened in Argentina, Bolivia, Brazil (which was on the point of holding its first free election in years in 1980), Chile (Pinochet lost a key plebiscite in 1988), El Salvador, Guatemala, Honduras, and Uruguay. Many other factors were at work, and perhaps the widespread transitions to democracy prove Kirkpatrick's basic point, that authoritarian regimes are far more likely to evolve in that direction than totalitarian ones.

The Soviets were not involved in the Iranian revolution, but they benefited from it. They gained access to the advanced military technology with which the United States had showered the shah. For example, they obtained an F-14 fighter, with a very advanced radar and air-to-air missile system. They certainly also benefited from the destruction of the U.S. position in the Persian Gulf. The principal remaining U.S. client, Saudi Arabia, was not nearly strong enough to stand up to the local Soviet client state, Iraq. Moreover, the historical rivalry between Iran and Saudi Arabia persisted. The Iranian revolution having become fundamentalist, the Iranians tried to destabilize Saudi Arabia, whose government's legitimacy depended in large part on its claim to be the appropriate guardian of the main shrines of Islam. Thus, after the revolution, there seemed to be a fair chance that the West would be ejected altogether from the oil-rich Persian Gulf.

As it turned out, this particular threat was not realized. As the Iranians purged their army, Saddam Hussein, the president of Iraq, saw an opportunity: he attacked Iran. The West was placed in the ironic position of supporting a Soviet client state, Iraq, against a former U.S. client, Iran. It turned out that even with most of their experienced officers dead the Iranians were more competent than Saddam had expected, and the Iran-Iraq War dragged on for nearly a decade.

The war was fought mainly around the big Iranian refinery at Abadan and the nearby Iraqi oil port of Basra. The resulting price shock caused a new Western recession (which helped abort the NATO buildup Carter had advocated). The Soviets offered the Europeans natural gas from new Siberian fields. Conservative Americans feared that, once the Europeans came to depend on the Soviets for much of their energy, they would again show their cravenness, as they had toward the Arab oil suppliers in 1973. At the least, the Soviets would be able to extract whatever technology they needed, as well as a massive supply of hard currency, both in payment and as loans.[28]

It was less obvious to the West that Islamic fundamentalists in power in Teheran endangered the Soviets. They were likely to inflame passions among the Moslems of Soviet Central Asia. These areas had been conquered by the czars only in the last century, and many residents still resented the loss of independence and the attempts to Russify them. Soviet efforts to contain local nationalism merely strengthened it.

The U.S. government discovered that late in 1979 the Soviets prepared contingency plans to seize northern Iran in the event either that the disintegrating situation there seemed to threaten their control in Soviet Central Asia, or if the United States intervened. A major exercise in August 1980 apparently tested the plan.[29]

Not too far away, on 27 April 1978 a Communist-oriented coup had overthrown the neutral government of Afghanistan, on the Soviet border. In the past, British and Russian agents had competed there in what was called the "great game." The British resisted czarist advances into Central Asia and ultimately into Afghanistan on the theory that the country was the gateway to their richest colony, India. By this time the country was of little strategic importance. It was very mountainous, and it offered little in the way of highways to more interesting targets such as Pakistan. Moscow did not inspire the coup, although the Soviets knew about it and assured the plotters that they would receive support and recognition.[30]

The rather conservative Islamic Afghan population resented the modernization the Soviet-backed government was trying to impose. For example, female schoolteachers were sometimes burned alive. Matters came to a head after a March 1979 Shiite rising in Herat. Over one hundred Soviets were killed, some being tortured. The Soviet advisors insisted that the Afghan government restore order, using its own troops against the rioters. When government troops retook Herat, they killed several thousand Afghan civilians. Civil war began in earnest. Soviet Minister of Defense Ustinov told his men in Kabul to "arm the working class."[31] Early rebel successes inspired offers of support from Islamic governments, particularly neighboring Pakistan. The Carter administration became interested in aiding the rebels as early as the beginning of 1979, and on 5 March the CIA presented it with a series of possible covert actions. Likely possibilities for the Soviets in Afghanistan were predicted in a 28 March 1979 paper by Andrew Horelick, the national intelligence officer for the Soviet Union (i.e., the officer responsible for U.S. estimates of Soviet behavior). Horelick suggested that if the Taraki regime deteriorated badly enough, the Soviets might conclude that only extensive and direct assistance could save it, and that they would choose to do so. Such assistance would cause Pakistan, Iran, and possibly China to aid the Afghan rebels; as U.S. allies the Pakistanis in particular might well ask the United States to protect them from Soviet attempts to intervene in Pakistan itself. The United States would feel pressure to help the Afghan rebels. Horelick commented that such aid, leading to a protracted guerilla war, would inspire Moslem and Arab opinion against the Soviets and might also make possible a U.S. rapprochement with the Iranians.[32]

At a 30 March 1979 preparatory meeting for the Security Coordinating Committee (SCC) concerned with such covert operations, Under Secretary of State for Political Affairs David Newsom stated that it was official U.S. policy to eject the Soviets from Afghanistan. That in turn would demonstrate to key governments (particularly the Pakistanis and the Saudis) U.S. resolve to resist the Soviets. Walt Slocumbe of the Department of Defense specifically asked whether it might be worthwhile to keep the insurgency alive to trap the Soviets in their own Vietnam; Brzezinki's deputy, David Aaron, asked whether assistance to the rebels would risk provoking the Soviets. Horelick argued that covert action would increase Soviet costs and would inflame the Moslem world against them. The CIA reported that a senior Pakistani official had offered to help the rebels, but that Pakistan could not risk "Soviet wrath" without a firm U.S. commitment. According to Gates, at this time (nine months before the Soviets invaded) a senior Saudi official raised the possibility that the Soviets would invade Afghanistan, and offered financial aid and encouragement to the Pakistanis. The U.S. government might have been deterred by fear of Soviet reaction, but the Soviets were already attributing Taraki's problems to U.S. and Pakistani assistance to the rebels.[33] In the end, the SCC proposed nonlethal aid, and on 3 July President Carter authorized a combination of cash assistance and propaganda support. By that time the Chinese were offering arms to the Afghan rebels.

Horelick's guesses proved accurate. On 18 March 1979 one of the two main Afghan Communist leaders, N. M. Taraki, asked Soviet Premier Alexei Kosygin for men and weapons to retrieve a critical situation, invoking the Brezhnev Doctrine. Kosygin turned him down: introducing Soviet troops would be a "fatal mistake" which would "outrage the international community," providing their common enemies with a pretext for intervention. Brezhnev agreed. The Soviets did provide aid, mainly three hundred thousand tons of grain; the airfield through which it came was guarded by seven hundred Soviet troops.[34]

Early in April 1979 a Soviet mission visited the country to meet its two leading Communist politicians, Taraki and Hafizulah Amin. Each represented one of Afghanistan's two main (and bitterly opposed) ethnic groups.[35] One of the Afghan officials said that he could spread the revolution to Pakistan, providing the Soviets with access to the Persian Gulf and the Indian Ocean—if only they would help. But the Soviets rated the regime as weak.

Soon there were Soviet advisors in Kabul, and the regime was using its aircraft to strike at rebels. However, in April and May 1979 it was still possible for a foreigner to drive through the country without meeting much violence.[36] A British journalist, Martin Walker, recalled an April–May 1979 drive through Afghanistan during which he saw only sporadic fighting. He did see Soviet advisors in Kabul, and air strikes were often being made around the city.

The U.S. government was well aware of Taraki's problems, and the CIA even predicted that the Soviets might decide to overthrow him. However, the CIA also was well aware of the dangers such intervention would carry, so through 1979 it doubted that the Soviets would take any such action.[37]

Four Politburo members (Gromyko, Andropov, Ustinov, and Ponomarev) soon signed a letter urging "intensified" struggle against counterrevolution and stronger national authority. The Soviets provided an airborne battalion plus GRU and KGB advisors. At first they tried to convince Taraki to reconcile with Amin. That was impossible; bands of their followers began to fight each other. In September Amin overthrew Taraki. On 9 October Taraki was killed. Brezhnev was shocked; only three weeks earlier he had welcomed him to his study. Amin sent a telegram professing his loyalty and offering to explain all.[38]

After Amin's coup the Politburo formed a special committee on Afghanistan, consisting of Ustinov (Defense), Andropov (KGB), and Ponomarev (International Department). The KGB station chief in Kabul reported that by imposing a harsh rule Amin would animate and unite the opposition.[39] On 29 October the Soviet special committee argued for intervention. They made the kind of argument the Politburo would buy: Amin was purging his opponents within the Afghan party preparatory to moving towards non-Soviet powers; he could no longer be considered loyal.[40] He was becoming friendly with both Pakistan and China, who were already supporting anti-Afghan rebels. Almost certainly the committee members made their decision for the same reason that Kennedy had decided to unseat Diem sixteen years earlier: the problem was the local ruler. A new ruler and some competent (in this case, read Soviet) troops would solve the problem. As in Washington in about 1963, there was little or no recognition that failure was even possible.

The KGB leadership pressed Brezhnev to save the situation by finding a new ruler. Surely basic reforms, such as literacy programs and improvements in women's rights, would make a Soviet-imposed government popular. Soviet troops would overthrow Amin and remain in Afghanistan to stabilize the country while a new broader-based government took shape (it would distance itself from the revolutionaries by abandoning the red flag in favor of a traditional one). The Soviets chose a new Afghan ruler, Babrak Kamal. The Soviet special forces who were to overthrow Amin were slipped into Kabul in November, to act if necessary.

As of November 1979 those in the Politburo formally pressing for action were Brezhnev, Suslov, Andropov, Ustinov, and Gromyko. Marshal Sergei F. Akromeeyev, then deputy chief of staff, said in 1989 that the army had opposed invasion, since the troops were not ready (the Uzhbek and Tadzhik units available in the area were considered unreliable; after the invasion they were quickly replaced by Slavic units). On 6 December 1979 the Politburo voted to approve an intervention proposed by Andropov (KGB) and Marshal Nikolai V. Ogarkov (chief of the General Staff). On 12 December all members of the Politburo were obliged to sign a document drafted by Konstantin Chernenko, authorizing "measures" to be taken in country "A."

To preclude any demonstration in Moscow, the physicist and civil rights campaigner Andrei Sakharov was ordered confined to Gor'kiy, a city off-limits to Westerners.[41]

On 27 December 1979 Soviet special forces overthrew and killed Amin, installing Kamal. The Soviet Union was now directly involved in the Afghan civil war. By the time it pulled out on 15 February 1989 the Soviet Union would have lost 13,826 dead and 49,985 wounded.[42]

The Soviets took over an ongoing war against guerillas. They thought they were defending "socialism" against the forces of "reaction." To the rest of the world the invasion and coup looked like a grab for power in a small country. No one in Washington thought the Afghans had any chance of actually ejecting the Soviets. However, some military supplies were soon secretly provided to them.

Afghanistan demonstrated to President Carter that his Eurocentric ideas were wrong. He swung the other way, telling Congress that the Soviet invasion of Afghanistan was the worst threat to world peace since World War II. Iran and Afghanistan were on a new "arc of crisis." Surely the Russians were headed for the Persian Gulf and its vital oil. Once they had secured Afghanistan, they could penetrate either directly into Iran (a Russian goal since czarist times) or into Pakistan en route to Iran and the warm waters of the Indian Ocean. The dramatic growth of the Soviet Navy and the moves in Africa and in Arabia (Yemen) seemed to confirm this idea.

As an indication of U.S. thinking, on 16 January 1980 the CIA sent President Carter and the NSC an "Eyes Only" study of "Soviet Options in Southwest Asia After the Invasion of Afghanistan." It was unlikely that the Soviets had planned the invasion, and it might well have been authorized only reluctantly; but the Soviets did want a wider sphere of influence in Southwest Asia, and the invasion presented them with a valuable opportunity. The invasion placed their forces on the eastern border of Iran, as well as on the northern border they had previously occupied. They were now in a good position to help the main Iranian separatist movements: Baluchis (who were also in Pakistan), Azeris, and Kurds. Moreover, Soviet oil production was about to run down; surely expanded influence over oil-rich Iran was a major Soviet priority. In March, another CIA study suggested that although the invasion of Afghanistan might be no more than an aberration in Soviet behavior, "the possibility that Afghanistan represents a qualitative turn in Soviet foreign policy in the region and toward the third world should be taken seriously." The CIA director, Admiral Turner, went further. In a covering letter to the March study, he saw the invasion as a direct extension of the Third World aggressiveness the Soviets had been demonstrating over the past six years. Détente had had no effect on their efforts in places like Ethiopia, Kampuchea (Cambodia), and Yemen; "how assertive the Soviets will be in the future will very likely depend upon how 'successful' the Soviet leadership views their intervention in Afghanistan to have been."[43] The sense of alarm deepened when it became clear that the Soviets had a contingency plan to invade Iran.

Meanwhile Carter faced yet another crisis in Arabia. The long conflict between the two Yemens came to a head in 1978. On 24 June a messenger from the president of South Yemen (the PDRY), Salim Rubaya Ali, brought a bomb into the office of the president of North Yemen, killing him (the attribution to Rubaya may have been part of a South Yemeni plot to discredit him).[44] Two days later Rubaya Ali himself was killed in a coup; his followers were also killed. The much more revolutionary Abd al-Fattah Ismail, formerly only the leader of the ruling party, now became president as well.[45] The coup moved the PDRY even closer to the Soviets. Early in 1979 it attacked North Yemen. The U.S. government suspected that the Soviets, the Cubans, or possibly the Ethiopians were involved. U.S. policy, decided at the same 30 March 1979 pre-SCC meeting that discussed covert action on Afghanistan, was to reinforce both North Yemen and Oman, which the PDRY threatened. However, it was agreed that none of these measures could succeed until something was done to neutralize the PDRY. No solution was found. The interim measures were approved by President Carter on 3 July 1979, at the same time that he approved initial measures for Afghanistan.[46]

In an irony of the Cold War, the Soviets themselves provided the solution. While the two Yemens fought, the United States was sponsoring the Israeli-Egyptian peace talks (at Camp David) that ended the state of war between those two countries on 26 March 1979. The other Arab countries, including Saudi Arabia, rejected this peace process. To maintain their power in the Middle East, the Soviets sided with the rejectionists—which included both the Saudis and the Yemenis. Rejectionism improved Arab unity, to the point that the two Yemens were able not merely to make peace but, for the moment, to agree to unite. On the other hand, it now became important to the Soviets to maintain the unity of the rejectionist bloc, which meant that they had to keep the Saudis friendly. By this time war had broken out in Afganistan, and the Saudis were cooperating with the United States to aid the Afghan rebels against the Soviets. For their part the Soviets feared that the Saudis and the Americans might now pressure the South Yemenis to eject them. They became interested in a warmer relationship with the Saudis. To cement it, they fomented a coup in Yemen in March 1980, in which the radical Abd-al Fattah Ismail was ousted; he spent the next five years in Moscow.[47]

These arrangements were soon overtaken by the strains of the Gulf War between Iran and Iraq, in which the Saudis found themselves siding with the

Soviet-oriented Iraqis. Suddenly they badly needed American help. Moreover, as the war in Afghanistan intensified, the Saudis became far more interested in aiding the rebels. The U.S. government made its initial approaches in February 1980, at about the same time the Soviets were improving Saudi security by fomenting the coup in South Yemen.[48]

Given his new sense of crisis, on 3 January 1980 President Carter withdrew the SALT II treaty (which the Senate was probably going to reject) from Senate consideration. It seemed to favor the Soviets. On 7 January he embargoed grain exports to the Soviet Union. On 20 January he told the U.S. Olympic Committee that if Soviet troops remained in Afghanistan the games should be moved from Moscow (which was impossible) or boycotted; the boycott was announced on 28 March. In a bizarre moment, at a 12 June news conference Carter said that, despite the invasion of Afghanistan, he still supported the policy of détente.

With SALT II dropped, Carter was in the embarrassing position of having no major strategic program to accelerate when the planned treaty limits were abandoned. Thus the United States found itself abiding by a treaty it had not signed. One of the main projected treaty benefits had been a ban on encryption in missile telemetry to make it easier to measure the characteristics of new missiles during their tests (e.g., to help insure that new weapons were really modified versions of existing ones, as claimed). Without signatures on the treaty, no such ban could be demanded. The Soviets agreed to abide by most treaty provisions, so through the early 1980s both sides found themselves discussing claimed violations of an agreement neither had signed.

On 23 January the president proclaimed the Carter Doctrine: any attempt by an outside power to gain control of the Persian Gulf would be regarded as a "direct assault on the vital interests of the United States," to be repelled, if need be, by force.[49] That was all very well, but none of the countries in the area was likely to welcome a major U.S. base. The Defense Department came up with the Rapid Deployment Force. The mass of matériel needed for an initial lodgment would be stored on board ships stationed at the existing U.S. Indian Ocean base at Diego Garcia. Surely some country in the gulf area would allow the U.S. to unload. That country also certainly would have an airport. U.S. troops would be flown in to use equipment landed from the sea. Even though the Persian Gulf was about eight thousand miles from home, the U.S. Rapid Deployment Force probably would arrive well before Soviet troops driving over very bad roads from northern Iran. Once the lodgment was secure, heavier forces could be brought from the United States. Initial air support would come from aircraft carriers. To emphasize the importance of the area, an aircraft carrier was permanently stationed in the Arabian Sea, within striking range of some specified Southwest Asian targets. A decade later these preparations made it possible for the United States to protect a Southwest Asian country (Saudi Arabia) against a serious armed threat (by Iraq).

The European allies were not nearly as shocked by Afghanistan. They liked détente, and they refused to declare it dead. To U.S. critics of détente, that proved that the Europeans were too inclined towards appeasement to care. They seemed unable to accept that their security could be affected by events so far away, in Central Asia, whereas to the more globally oriented Americans they clearly were threatened.

France, Italy, West Germany, and Japan all opened bilateral trade talks with the Soviets in the summer of 1980. In effect they shifted some large contracts from American firms to their own, such as a $350 million specialty steel plant. U.S. exports to the Soviet Union, mainly grain, were halved in 1980. That year exports from France, West Germany, and Britain all increased by more than 30 percent. French Premier Valéry Giscard d'Estaing fawned so completely on Brezhnev that his critics both in France and in the United States accused him of self-Finlandization, i.e., of swinging towards a Finnish-style accommodation with the Soviets even though France was not under any direct Soviet threat. [50]

The Siberian gas project was far more significant. Soviet gas reserves were a third of the world total. By 1979 the Soviets were already supplying the Austrians, the West Germans, and the French. Now they planned a cooperative project for a five-thousand-kilometer pipeline to supply West Germany, France, Italy, Belgium, Austria, Finland, the Netherlands, Switzerland, Sweden, and Greece. The pipeline would be financed by loans to be paid back in gas; it would earn the Soviets $8 to $10 billion a year beginning about 1985.

In 1979 oil exports provided more than half of the hard currency that the Soviets badly needed to buy grain.[51] Cheap oil exports propped up the East European empire. However, oil fields in the European Soviet Union were being exhausted, to the point that in 1977 the CIA predicted that by 1985 the Soviet Union might be a net oil *importer*. The Soviets needed Western technology to exploit new fields in Siberia. The gas project would provide it.

Americans feared that the project would also provide leverage over the West Europeans. In a crisis, a European buyer could switch from one oil supplier to another by welcoming one oil tanker rather than another. Since gas came through a pipeline (in this case), switching gas suppliers was a very different proposition.

The Europeans found the deal very attractive, not least because it would provide work for their engineering firms, which were suffering in the recession due to the oil price shock. The Carter administration was uneasy, but it did not press the Europeans very hard. That was left to its successor, the Reagan administration. It must, however, have seemed ominous that German Chancellor Helmut Schmidt went straight to Moscow to sign the first pipeline contract after an unpleasant June 1980 meeting with President Carter.[52]

Roughly parallel with Afghanistan, another crisis erupted in the Far East. Vietnam was a Soviet client state. To balance it, the Chinese tightened their ties with the Khmer Rouge in Cambodia. The two countries had a long history of rivalry.

The Vietnamese joined Comecon, the Soviet economic union, in June 1978, and that November signed a Friendship Treaty with the Soviets. In December they crossed the border. Under the terms of a secret annex to the treaty, in exchange for access to Cam Ranh Bay the Soviets provided the $15 billion of aid needed to maintain the Vietnamese regime in Cambodia.[32] The Vietnamese made a special point of seizing Cambodian crops to feed themselves. They used weapons they had seized in South Vietnam to fight the Khmer Rouge.[53]

The Cambodian Communists (Khmer Rouge) were certainly murderous butchers, but that is not why the Vietnamese attacked. The invasion was apparently the culmination of border conflicts, which began with Khmer Rouge raids in 1977. Ultimately the Khmer Rouge hoped to take back areas Vietnam had seized from Cambodia centuries earlier.[55] Enough Khmer Rouge survived to mount a lengthy guerilla war, supported by the Chinese via the "Deng Xiaoping Trail" through neutral Thailand. Vietnamese occupation of Cambodia became one of "three obstacles" to normalizing Sino-Soviet relations (the others were the Soviet presence in Afghanistan and the Soviet military threat on the Chinese border).[56]

To the Chinese, the Vietnamese invasion was an assault on a client state. To "teach the Vietnamese a lesson" they sent six hundred thousand troops across the border.[57] Because Vietnam was a Soviet client, they placed their northern border on alert. Women and children were evacuated to shelters.[58] The result was ludicrous. The Chinese, once masters of the art, complained that the Vietnamese had resorted to guerilla warfare.[59] They lost a tenth of their troops and five hundred armored vehicles. Ironically, China had supplied many of the North Vietnamese weapons and vehicles during the Vietnam War.

The Chinese government was forced to confront the obsolescence of its army. Clearly it would have fared much worse in the event of war against the Soviets, a possibility that it still took quite seriously. The Chinese would have to modernize. An alliance with the United States now seemed much more valuable. It is interesting in retrospect that the Chinese did not use the Vietnamese example to claim that some more modern version of "people's war," i.e., guerilla war, which Mao had espoused, would be effective against their main enemy, the Soviet Union.

By this time the United States was deeply interested in the Chinese "card." Zbigniew Brzezhinski suggested that the Vietnamese invasion was connected to the push south through Afghanistan, part of a Soviet attempt to gain control of both ends of the Bay of Bengal, the eastern part of the Indian Ocean.[60]

In 1980 Secretary of Defense Harold Brown visited China to discuss modernizing the PLA. China was permitted to import technology normally granted to NATO members. The Chinese agreed to allow U.S. installation of listening stations to replace those lost in Iran. They became interested in promoting nuclear proliferation as a way of handling the Soviet threat.[61] Later China would provide a bomb design to Pakistan, which felt threatened both by the Soviets (through Afghanistan) and by India, a Soviet client, which had its own bomb. This clearly ran counter to U.S. policy, which was to resist any spread of nuclear weapons. The

United States did not protest; China's role in reducing the Soviet threat to NATO was too valuable.

The Soviets were having their own problems closer to home, in Poland. An organization, KOR, was formed to assist workers arrested after the wave of strikes in 1976. It was soon transformed into the committee for social self-defense (KOR/KSS). Its main spokesman, Jacek Kuron, began to advocate withdrawal from Soviet control. Moreover, in Poland, unlike anywhere else in the Soviet empire, there was another focus for dissent, the Catholic Church. Karol Wojtyla, archbishop of Cracow, led the attack on Communism. Elected pope on 16 October 1978, he attracted huge crowds when he visited Poland in June 1979.[62] It was unpleasantly clear that the church rather than the Party dominated the country.

The problem got worse. On 1 July 1980 the government raised the price of meat; there were new strikes. Strikes in Gdansk in August soon led to the formation of Solidarity, the first free trade union in the Communist world. The Gdansk shipyards were the main source of Polish export earnings. By letting things come to such a pass, the Polish Communist Party chief, Eduard Gierek, had created the nightmare of all Communist regimes, a movement, Solidarity, which united intellectuals (dissidents) and workers under a nationalist banner.

On 28 August Suslov, Gromyko, Andropov (KGB), Ustinov (Defense Ministry), and Chernenko all signed a proposal to immediately mobilize four divisions (later increased to five to seven) to support the Polish Communist Party, that is, to occupy Poland.[63] Troops would have come from Czechoslovakia and East Germany as well as from the Soviet Union. A large-scale exercise on the Polish border, West-81, was intended as a warning. The Politburo approved the invasion plan in November. On 2 December a Soviet column actually crossed the border to reconnoiter the route to Wroclaw. At least one Polish officer remarked that his troops might shoot back, despite any effort he might make to restrain them; it would be better to let the Poles take care of their own problem. The Carter administration, which had a spy on the Polish general staff, warned the Soviets off. Two years later Chief of Staff Marshal Ogarkov told Dmitri Volkogonov, the military historian, that he had been worried that combat in Poland would stretch Soviet forces too thin while they were fighting in Afghanistan. He was also mindful of the possibility that the Poles would manage another "miracle on the Vistula," as in 1920, when they had stopped a Soviet army.[64]

Stanislaw Kania, the general secretary of the Polish Party in December 1980, was shown a map of the planned route of a Soviet invasion. He convinced Brezhnev to desist; an invasion would have triggered a national uprising.[65] In February 1981 the minister of defense, General Wojciech Jaruzelski, became prime minister. The Soviets had decided that Kania was indecisive; Jaruzelski was their man. In June they demanded that he replace Kania, and that was done in October. Jaruzelski thus combined the two top Polish offices in his own person.

By the fall of 1981 the Politburo had given up on an invasion. At its behest Jaruzelski declared martial law in December 1981. The Carter administration's spy was still in place; the CIA had notice of Jaruzelski's plan. However, it never informed the White House. Before declaring martial law, General Jaruzelski sent the deputy chief of the Polish general staff, Eugeniusz Molczyk, to Washington. Lacking information from the CIA, Vice President George Bush told him that self-declared martial law was preferable to a Soviet invasion. Jaruzelski interpreted Bush's words to mean that the U.S. approved his plan to impose martial law in Poland—of which Bush was ignorant.

For the first time in the Communist system a military man was head of state. The Party was no longer predominant. What would the Soviet military think? In addition, Jaruzelski's action implied that he badly wanted to preserve Polish sovereignty. For example, reportedly he formed a special military unit, which might be used to resist any Soviet invasion.

For the allies, the Polish crackdown was too close to ignore. They were willing to impose economic sanctions when Carter's successor, Ronald Reagan, suggested them early in his first term.

PART SIX

COUNTERATTACK AND VICTORY

(Overleaf) **Soviet Union**

The Soviet Union was a multiethnic empire, and its imperial character eventually brought it down. This map shows the republics that made up the old Soviet Union. Geographically, the Russian republic was by far the largest, and Russians dominated the empire. The impression given by this map is distorted by the emptiness of much of central and northern Russia.

Reprinted from Raymond E. Zickel, editor, *Soviet Union: A Country Study,* second edition (Washington, D.C.: Government Printing Office, 1991), facing page lvii.

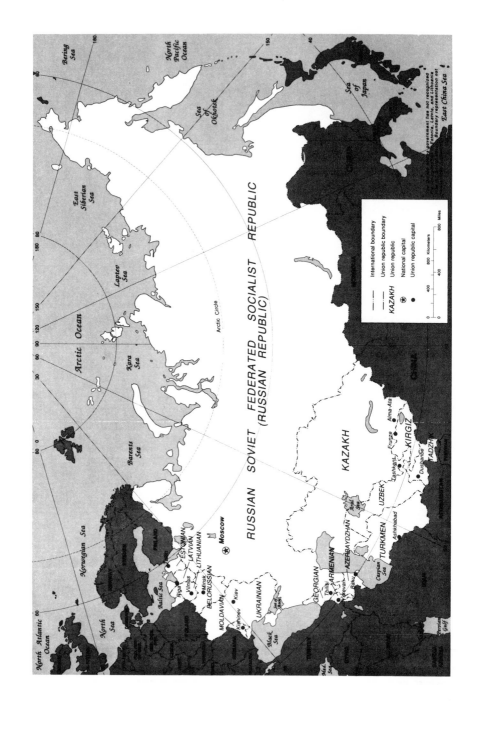

While the Soviets wrestled with political problems in Poland, they also faced a reversal of their military position, due to a new military revolution, computer proliferation. Few if any in the West seem to have realized just how quickly the balance of military power was tipping, probably because in the late 1970s most analysts concentrated on nuclear weapons, which were relatively easy to count and to understand. Yet, once both sides were heavily armed, once a first strike was no longer practical, nuclear weapons were essentially unusable. The Soviet buildup in Europe was terrifying because it created a vast conventional force that NATO seemed unable to match. By the early 1980s, however, Western microcomputers provided a potentially winning edge—which the Soviets found they could not match. Computers and the related "brilliant" weapons matured just as Ronald Reagan decided to boost U.S. defense spending.

The enormous impact of computers was obscured because the boundary between precomputer and computer warfare was far less visible than that between prenuclear and nuclear warfare. Also, the advent of programmable digital computers was easily confused with the advent of "robot" weapons (homing missiles and torpedoes) using analog circuitry. Such weapons had first appeared during World War II. Most missiles now use digital guidance systems, which make them substantially more flexible.[1] However, the really revolutionary application of computers is in organizing, displaying, and transmitting information among tactical users. Computers could assimilate enormous amounts of information much more quickly than had ever been possible before into a usable picture of a military situation. The most common case in point is air defense. The radars of an air defense system produce lists of the targets they detect. The heart of the system is a map (a tactical picture) showing where the targets are and where they appear to be going. On the basis of that picture, a decision maker (which may be a computer) identifies the most threatening targets, selects those weapons that can intercept them, and often commands the interceptors into position. All of these functions can be done by human beings. As the targets move faster, and as more of them pop up, human operators find it more and more difficult to deal with the swelling river of information coming out of the radars. The picture they draw up bears less and less resemblance to what is really happening. The system collapses.[2]

Computers solve the problem by dealing with the radar data much more quickly. The computer in which the tactical picture is assembled can be programmed to choose targets and to decide which interceptors (or missiles) can deal with each target. Such an operation is now so familiar that it seems trite. That is because it was developed in the 1950s to solve what seemed to be the impossible problem of defending against modern bombers armed with nuclear weapons. In 1952 MIT's Lincoln Laboratory proposed using a digital computer, Whirlwind I, to deal with air defense data.[3] Its proposal suddenly reversed the NSC's pessimistic view of air defense. Lincoln Labs' experimental air defense center at Cape Cod proved so successful that in 1954 the NSC ordered a national version, SAGE (Semi-Automatic Ground Environment).[4]

SAGE was not a single national computer, since no computer could cover all air traffic over the United States. Instead, the country was split up into sectors, each with its own SAGE centers (with computers and backups). For the first time, the United States needed a large number of very powerful computers. The program required many of the developments that made the commercial computers of the 1960s viable. For example, in 1958 IBM announced the first solid-state computer, proposing it as a replacement for the vacuum tube FSQ-7 that SAGE then used.[5] The first SAGE sector entered service in October 1958, and all were complete by December 1961. SAGE led to similar NATO (NADGE) and Japanese (BADGE) systems; Britain developed an analogous UKADGE.[6] Many other countries followed suit. Ironically, SAGE was completed just as the threat shifted from bombers to missiles.

A SAGE center filled a large building. By the late 1950s the same sort of computer capability could be packaged tightly enough to fit on board a major warship. The U.S. Navy's equivalent to SAGE was NTDS (naval tactical data system), which became the basis for most NATO naval command and control systems.[7]

Overall, SAGE might be considered a counter to the previously dominant nuclear weapons technology; it made a credible air defense possible.

Like nuclear weapons, computers went from a situation of scarcity (in which machines were assembled by hand) to one of plenty (mass production). As this second stage began, in the 1950s, their potential was widely recognized on both sides of the Iron Curtain. The Soviets sometimes wrote that cybernetics, the science of computers, was part of a second revolution in military affairs.[8] However, they were unable to produce computers on anything like a Western scale. Although they could make small quantities of very sophisticated circuits, generally they could not advance to mass production.

It turned out that computerization, like the adoption of nuclear weapons, had an inexorable logic. The sensors feeding the central computer had to provide their data in computer-readable form, since otherwise human operators would slow down the data river. Similarly, the central computer had to command its weapons via computer-to-computer links, as otherwise the system would not respond quickly enough. Thus the sensors and the weapons needed their own compact computers. For that matter, it was soon obvious that the computer-generated tactical picture had to be shared among many commanders, who needed their own tactical computers even to keep their display of it current.

In Vietnam, the SAGE concept was applied to stopping supplies running down the Ho Chi Minh Trail into South Vietnam. Instead of radars, ground sensors were strewn (by air) along the trail, under a program called Igloo White. They picked up such signatures as truck noises and even the urine of draft animals. As in SAGE, a central computer (in this case, in Saigon) correlated the sensor data and directed air attacks.[9]

In theory an enormous number of troops permanently stationed along the Ho Chi Minh Trail could have done the job, but that would have been unaffordable. Partly because it was only one of many campaigns being waged as part of the Cold War, Vietnam could not possibly attract the sort of resources needed for conventional (i.e., precomputer) techniques. This time the technology was pushed too far.[10] The North Vietnamese learned to fool the sensors. Vast amounts of bomb tonnage fell on the trail, with limited results. The technological revolution had not yet quite occurred.

By the late 1970s the U.S. Army faced another terrible numerical problem in Central Europe. Again, there was no real hope of matching the sheer size of the enemy army. The solution of the 1950s, tactical nuclear weapons, seemed less and less attractive. The only really mobile asset available to NATO was a very powerful tactical air force. It had to be concentrated on the attacking spearhead. To do that, the axis of advance of the Soviet force had to be identified as soon as possible. A big Soviet attack into Western Europe would involve tens or even hundreds of thousands of vehicles. While assembling into attack formations, they would seem to be heading in many directions. Which was the right one? Airplanes attacking in the wrong areas would not survive long enough to change course.

The U.S. Army's solution was to feed all its available intelligence into a computer, which it hoped would automatically identify the axis of advance. Initial trials were encouraging, although there was a real fear that the Soviets would manage to confuse the system by decoying. This was much the same idea as Igloo White, but using a much more sophisticated computer and more reliable sensors (including large numbers of human observers). Although the BETA (Battlefield Exploitation and Target Acquisition) system of the late 1970s and early 1980s was dropped, the idea survived.[11]

Systems like BETA were possible because by the 1970s Western computers were so small and so inexpensive. Roughly like nuclear weapons, they went from massive devices that could be used only for the most vital functions to machines that could be used tactically, on board medium-sized warships and aircraft.

Just as tactical nuclear weapons changed the face of ground combat, plentiful tactical computers made possible a new kind of warfare. Netted together, they could share a common picture of a tactical situation and could quickly execute complex plans. Forces could be made far more agile and could be far better integrated. The next stage was extreme plenty and portability. Minicomputers were replaced, in the 1980s, by microcomputers small enough and cheap enough to be made by the million. The new computers had another virtue: because they were controlled by software, which could be changed radically without altering the computer itself, they offered enormous flexibility.

Microcomputers brought a new revolution in weaponry. A bullet or a bomb is a "dumb" weapon; it cannot correct its course once it has been aimed. The "smart" bombs of the Vietnam era locked onto a laser spot or part of a target image chosen by the bomb's operator. They were, therefore, much more accurate than their "dumb" predecessors. However, it still took the operator's brain to decide what was and was not a target. The step beyond was a "brilliant" weapon capable of making such decisions. That is not too difficult when the target stands out against a featureless background, as in the case of a ship or an airplane. Ground targets are a very different proposition. They require considerable effort on the part of the weapon, hence the use of the word "brilliant"—and hence the need to place a very powerful microcomputer in the weapon.

In the 1970s this technology promised to replace the neutron bomb with a usable weapon, a system called Assault Breaker. New surveillance systems (in effect, outgrowths of SAGE) would direct long-range rockets at concentrations of tanks deep behind the battle line. Instead of nuclear bombs, the rockets would carry masses of "brilliant" bomblets (submunitions), each of which would fix on and kill a tank. This was infinitely more efficient than firing one long-range missile at each tank. It was a revolutionary advance over earlier bomblet weapons, which scattered unguided devices over a limited area—and which often missed their targets altogether. Now, even if the tanks spread out, the self-guided bomblets were likely to hit them. As it turned out, initial attempts to develop the submunitions, during the 1980s, were less than successful; the first really effective weapon of this type, BAT, did not appear until well into the 1990s. However, what mattered was that the Soviets knew about the program—and they assumed that it would be made to work. To an extent unappreciated in the United States of the 1970s, the Soviets believed that their American rivals were scientific magicians; what they said they could do, they could do. To the Soviets, Assault Breaker was a disaster. Once in place it would neutralize a major threat they could deploy against NATO, a conventional armored attack. Unlike its predecessor, the neutron bomb, it was entirely immune from any political counterattack; it did not entail nuclear weapons of any sort.

In addition, Assault Breaker seemed to be a radical kind of weapon, what the Soviets called a "reconnaissance-strike complex," a single system that searched for targets, selected them, and attacked them. It could support war at a very much faster tempo. In an earlier era an air force had mounted reconnaissance flights to find enemy units. They reported back, attack plans were developed, and the attacking pilots were briefed. The whole process was lengthy, and so was ill adapted to dealing with moving targets. It took nuclear weapons to make up for the inevitable errors due to time lags. Now the reconnaissance aircraft fed computers that maintained a picture of the tactical situation, and automatically directed weapons to attack targets before they could move very far.

Without comparable computers, the Soviets would have to fight a slower war. In the 1970s, a U.S. Air Force officer, Col. Richard Boyd, pointed out that tempo could be decisive. His reasoning was widely accepted, at least in the United States. Boyd described combat as a cycle, beginning with observation of an enemy action, followed by a decision, and then by a reaction. He argued that forces won, not by sheer weight, but by running faster cycles than their enemies could. If the enemy could only react to something several cycles back, ultimately he collapsed in the military equivalent of a nervous breakdown. Boyd attributed the German victory over France in 1940 to exactly such a breakdown.

The Soviet military was well aware of the cycle principle. In 1977 Marshal Nikolai Ogarkov was appointed head of the Soviet general staff specifically to modernize the Soviet armed forces. That meant computerization. He was particularly interested in reconnaissance-strike complexes, i.e. in fast-tempo war.[12]

If he needed a practical demonstration of just how devastating the new technology could be, Ogarkov found it in the Israeli aerial victory in the Bekaa Valley of Lebanon in June 1982. In four raids on 9 June Israeli aircraft knocked out at least seventeen of nineteen Syrian surface-to-air missile sites. The Syrian system had been installed by the Soviets; the Israelis used mainly U.S. equipment. The clear implication was that the U.S. Air Force could inflict a similar defeat on the systems defending the Soviet Union. Once the missiles had been destroyed, the Israelis wiped out the defending Syrian fighters. Again, it was modern U.S. computer-controlled weaponry against modern Soviet-supplied systems. In all, the Israelis shot down ninety-two Syrian aircraft at the cost of no more than six aircraft (possibly as few as three). Soon it emerged that the key to the very one-sided Israeli victory had been a computer-driven Air Battle Management System, which provided Israeli commanders with a complete and current picture of air and ground activity in the Bekaa Valley. It was the heart of exactly the sort of reconnaissance-strike complex Ogarkov espoused.

What Ogarkov apparently did not realize was that the missile-building organization created by Khrushchev and Brezhnev already sopped up most of the country's capacity to develop and mass-produce new kinds of electronic devices. Much work was done, but mainly on a laboratory scale. To create new industries it was necessary to tear apart existing ones. The pain that caused had helped destroy Khrushchev. A leadership unwilling to follow suit could not impose a new military-industrial revolution from above. The Soviet system did not provide incentives from below in the form of demand for computers (or, for that matter, for anything else).

Within the Soviet Union, the existing ministries had no use for new industries. By the mid-1960s, some Soviet economists were arguing that an ongoing scientific-technological revolution would have enormous consequences for the Soviet economy.[13] Not only were calls for new industries rejected, but the very term "scientific-technological revolution" was censored from all public documents. The leadership, which could not accept the need for such a change, could not publicly admit that it was failing to match the West. There was some internal interest; in 1973 the Politburo planned a special Central Committee plenum on the subject. A special report was delivered in May 1973—and was ignored; the plenum was never held.[14] Re-industrialization—creating or fostering the new technology—seemed at the time to be tied to improvements in overall Soviet economic performance. The dramatic rise in oil prices after the 1973 Middle East War increased Soviet national income without demanding any sort of reform or industrial reorganization, and so made it possible for Brezhnev to avoid the problem. Apparently he and his colleagues were unaware of the military implications of failing to build modern computer and other new industries.

The Western situation was very different. Not only was the electronics industry bigger (due in large part to civilian demand), but by the early 1960s civilian computer applications provided an incentive to build up productive capacity. In addition, Western industry was more open to the kind of restructuring that would be necessary to produce the new weapons and systems.

The Soviets understood what was happening; they had been writing about the potential of what they called military cybernetics since the early 1960s. Probably far more than their American adversaries, the Soviet strategists knew that they were losing a new revolution in military technology. To get the new kinds of weapons, they needed another Soviet industrial revolution. Somehow the Soviet economy had to be reshaped to provide what the general staff, led by Marshal Ogarkov, needed. Ogarkov had no idea of what it would cost. Therefore he never made the case for any alternative. The obvious fallback position—which the Soviets never took—would have been to abandon hopes of an armored thrust and rely instead on the deterrent effect of a large nuclear arsenal.

Ironically, Westerners accustomed to Soviet military largesse tacitly assumed that the Soviets would do whatever they had to; they did not realize just how badly the system's structure constrained them. Perhaps they did not realize just how much Western computers and command/control systems contributed to military effectiveness. Computers just did not seem as important, or as pervasive, as they were. Nor, apparently, did Westerners realize just how badly the Soviets suffered from their lack of computers. It was widely known that the Soviets could produce excellent prototypes, but that their computers typically never appeared in numbers. The Soviets had once bought a thousand electronic calculators specifically to put their chips into MIRV guidance packages. What now seems the obvious conclusion—that the Soviets were so far behind in computer production technology—typically was not drawn in the West.

In 1980 Ronald Reagan won a landslide election. He promised to revive American power and the American economy and to stop the Soviet advance. Carter obviously had failed to do either. Reagan was popular partly because his outlook was that of the optimistic general public, rather than of the pessimistic Washington elite: it was "morning in America." He seemed sure of himself, and he had a remarkable ability to communicate his ideas. That combination made him relatively invulnerable to the propaganda offensives the Soviets mounted against him. It also made Reagan confident that he could negotiate effectively with the Soviets; from the beginning, he sought talks.[1]

The president insisted that the issue was not long-term competition, but what it had been in 1946: a fight to the finish between the free West and a Soviet Communist system bent on enslavement, what he called the "Evil Empire." Reagan was the outsider who had never learned to fear upsetting the Soviets, the man who did not realize that the Cold War—or the Soviet Union itself—had to be a permanent fact of life.[2] He reversed the goal of previous administrations, which had been simply not to lose the Cold War (in the hope that in the long run something would improve). It was time to play to win.[3] Reagan's entire policy flowed from that perception. The Soviets almost immediately sensed this profound change in American policy.

The president was fond of reminding Americans of the deep difference between their own system and that of the Soviets. For example, the Soviet constitution might seem to be as liberal as any other, but its powers were given from above; in the United States the people had the power, some of which they might give to government. Such comparisons were distinctly unfashionable in Washington in 1980. Reagan's view absolutely rejected the dream many shared, that somehow the Cold War would disappear as the two world systems became more similar.

Reagan believed that he could win the Cold War partly because he personally believed that the free market system was so much more productive than the Soviets' planned economies. It followed that the U.S. could win a competition to produce a new kind of military power based on new technology: SDI and the new computer-dominated weapons.[4] Reagan had an important ally in another outsider: Britain's Conservative prime minister, Margaret Thatcher, who had entered office in 1979. Both leaders shared an explicit faith in democracy (which they associated with a free market). Both were far less sympathetic to declared Soviet ideology than their predecessors had been. Both were disgusted with what they saw as national decline in their respective countries, and both were determined to reverse it. Mrs. Thatcher seems to have played an important role in encouraging President Reagan to follow his own instincts rather than those of his sometimes less determined (and much more conventional) advisors. Later, having met Mikhail Gorbachev in 1985, she was probably the one who told Reagan that Gorbachev was a man "one could do business with."

Reagan fought the 1980 campaign advised mainly by Dr. William van Cleave of the B Team, who argued that the United States was in imminent danger because the Soviets were building a nuclear first-strike capability. Unlike Kennedy, Reagan was able to discard this view once he won the election and discovered that it was too narrow. Certainly it was time to improve the nuclear balance, but even the existing balance was far more stable than van Cleave and other Team B veterans had said. Reagan reasoned roughly as Khrushchev had. The nuclear balance could liberate rather than constrict him. The Soviets would not risk a general war to stop him. And he added something new. The point of whatever he did would not be simply to improve the U.S. position within a long-term competition; it would be to win the war altogether.

The president and George Shultz, his secretary of state, revived the old idea of the 1940s and 1950s, that the Soviets were expansionist abroad because they were unaccountable at home. A Soviet regime that had to recognize the rights of its citizens would be accountable, and could not be aggressive.[5] Thus human rights in the Soviet Union—irreversible domestic liberalization—became the central policy goal, far more important to the administration than arms control.[6]

Reagan probably was convinced that he could win the Cold War by his new director of central intelligence, William Casey, a veteran of the World War II Office of Strategic Services. Even before Reagan was inaugurated, Casey was chairman of his Interim Foreign Policy Group. He convinced Reagan that the Soviets were already in such deep economic trouble that, if enough stress was applied, they might, in the president's words, "implode."[7] Reagan's nuclear perception told him that such an attack was reasonably safe. So was another strategy long since discarded: covert action to detach the satellites from the Soviet Union. These forms of attack became two of four themes in the administration's formal strategy, enunciated in May 1982. The others were military modernization (including increased Allied spending) and political persuasion/propaganda.[8]

The idea that the Cold War might be won in the short term was radically new. The possibility of winning changed Reagan's perception of what he could do. If he was fighting a relatively short war, he could afford to run up enormous deficits—for the duration. He could not afford to let the Soviets realize that he thought the war would be short and intense, because in that case they might survive simply by waiting him out.

The new administration had a typically American global outlook. The satellites included the entire "socialist commonwealth," not merely the states of Eastern Europe. For example, in March 1981 the administration approved covert action against the Sandinistas.[9] By November there was an official Central American policy: El Salvador would be supported in its fight against the Cuban- and Nicaraguan-backed rebels, while whatever democratic forces survived in Nicaragua would be backed against their leftist government.[10] This was not the simple anti-Communism of the past, under which any non-Communist regime, no matter how unpleasant, deserved U.S. support. It was shaped in large part by UN Ambassador Jeane Kirkpatrick's perception that the ultimate U.S. goal was democratic government, which in many cases required support of non-Communist authoritarians. Regimes not under immediate Communist threat were to be nudged towards democracy. For example, the Reagan administration continued the Carter administration's pressure on Bolivia, where the military had deposed the left-wing winner of the 1980 election.[11]

The next step was the Reagan Doctrine: The administration would support any resistance movements fighting the Soviets or their proxies. That applied, for example, to Angola and Mozambique, where the Cuban army was engaged. About fifteen years before, Che Guevara had described a way to bring down the West: "two, three, many Vietnams," which could not all be fought at the same time. Now Reagan was promising more Afghanistans.[12]

Afghanistan, where rebels fought the Soviet Army itself, was clearly the key theater. One of the administration's advisors, a Russian-area expert (and a former member of Team B), Dr. Richard Pipes, had pointed out many years before that the czarist regime came closest to grief (before its fall) when it suffered military disaster in the Far East in 1904–5.[13] That war was fought so far from Moscow that defeat there had not excited the sort of strong patriotic feelings Stalin had exploited during World War II. Military disaster threatened the stability of the Soviet regime, because ultimately the regime was based on terror and coercion. The police and the KGB cowed the Soviet population, but the army was the ultimate guarantor of the regime.

At first Reagan, like Carter, assumed that the Afghan rebels were no more than an irritant to the Soviets; they could not possibly win. Then he reversed himself, ordering increased aid in March 1985. Stinger missiles were supplied to counter Soviet air power. They had such an impact that the Soviet Defense Ministry offered the "Hero of the Soviet Union" decoration to whoever brought back the first one.[14] U.S. satellite data were provided to the Afghan rebels, to help them target attacks.[15] They were encouraged to disrupt the extraction of Afghan natural resources, which the Soviets apparently were using to help pay for the war.

While supporting the guerillas, the administration supported negotiations in Pakistan, aimed at Soviet withdrawal. It also pressed for the withdrawal of all foreign forces from Angola and Namibia (South–West Africa), and for the withdrawal of the Soviet-backed Vietnamese from Cambodia.

It took several years for the Soviets to realize just how deep the Afghan morass was. At least until 1985 they thought they could stabilize the situation.[16]

The Democratic-controlled Congress did not always see eye to eye with the Reagan administration. The Nicaraguans convinced many in Congress that they were independent progressives rather than Soviet stooges. The jungle war there and in El Salvador seemed reminiscent of Vietnam. Foiled, the administration convinced some of its foreign allies to fund anti-Sandinista guerillas, the "contras." Congress was outraged; its control over foreign adventures, first exercised in Southeast Asia in 1973 and then in Angola in 1975, was being evaded. Some Democrats thought Reagan's crime exceeded Nixon's, and it could bring him down. The Nicaraguan operation was linked to a bungled attempt to trade arms to Iran in return for American hostages. Hearings were inconclusive; the special prosecutor's few convictions were overturned on appeal. It was never proven that the president had personally ordered any of the acts Congress regarded as violations. Moreover, it was clear that the American public supported Reagan in a way they had never supported Nixon. The net effect of the Iran-Contra Affair was to leave ambiguous Congress's power to control U.S. foreign policy in the face of presidential prerogatives.

Poland was the other area of major covert action. The Soviets could not afford to lose it, because the front-line forces in East Germany were supported through it. Without Poland, the Soviets could no longer credibly threaten to overrun Western Europe. Moreover, in 1981 Poland's Solidarity movement was a threat to Soviet stability. It united the few surviving dissidents with a much broader workers' movement, which could contest the Party's claim to be the workers' representative. In effect Solidarity revived the Party's old fear that workers would vote Democratic Socialist instead of Communist. If Solidarity could survive, it might spread through Eastern Europe and even into the Soviet Union. The lesson of 1981–82 was that Solidarity was too entrenched to be destroyed even by a military crackdown.

The Carter administration had supported Solidarity, but had been nervous about doing so openly, for fear that the movement would be compromised.[17] Reagan ordered more (covert) help: money (about $8 million per year); advanced communications equipment and training (so that Solidarity could continue to function even under martial law); and intelligence.[18] In effect he was reviving the old idea of supporting resistance movements within the Soviet bloc.

The rise of Solidarity coincided roughly with the accession of the Polish pope, John Paul II. Like Reagan and Thatcher, he was an outsider, the first non-Italian pope in centuries. He was also an outsider in that he rejected the Catholic Church's trend towards an accommodation with the Communists, the wave of the future. That had been exemplified by an earlier pope's attack on the South Vietnamese government in 1974, and by the church's support for "liberation theology" in Latin

America. As a Polish Catholic priest, the pope had fought the Communists personally. He saw the Communists as mortal enemies. Most important of all, he did not accept that their rule was necessarily permanent. To the Soviets, the combination of a Polish pope and Solidarity was too explosive to tolerate. By 1981 the Soviet leadership ordered him assassinated.[19] The attack failed. Reagan joined forces with the pope.

The situation in Poland gradually worsened through the 1980s as the military government tried but failed to destroy Solidarity. Instead, it demonstrated that Poland could only barely be held down. Dissident movements elsewhere in the Eastern European empire, many of them created by the 1976 publication of the Helsinki accord (with its human rights "basket"), began to grow.

The beginning of political persuasion was convincing the Soviets that Reagan and his advisors were serious, not merely a slightly less friendly Carter administration. To that end Reagan would act slightly mad, adopting an aggressive "cowboy" image. (Nixon similarly had used the appearance of irrationality to restrain the Soviets from exploiting their strategic edge.) To buttress that image, Reagan ordered, for example, U.S. reconnaissance aircraft to act much more aggressively when operating near the Soviet Union.[20]

Reagan shocked the Soviets. They thought the West had accepted that the correlation of forces had tipped in the Soviets' favor, that the advance of "socialism" was virtually guaranteed. Soviet diplomats spoke of "rough parity" in military power and of "equality" in international affairs. Soviet propaganda emphasized the nuclear side of the U.S. program, harking back to Reagan's campaign rhetoric and exploiting the general fear of nuclear war. Reagan was presented as irrational, a danger to world peace. Unrestrained, he might destroy the world.[21] It is not clear to what extent the Soviets believed their own rhetoric.

In 1984 senior Soviet officers told some Westerners that the Soviet Union could no longer afford to compete. If that was true, why should the West try to overtake them? Soviet sympathizers in the West argued that Reagan's buildup was crippling the U.S. economy, that it was being paid for by the poor, whose social programs were being slashed (which generally was not true). Their audience was unaware that Soviet military production was still accelerating.

Much has been made of Operation RYAN (in Russian, the letters stand for Warning of Surprise Nuclear Attack), begun in November 1981, after Yuri Andropov denounced Reagan's policies at a secret May 1981 KGB meeting.[22] The KGB in key Western capitals was told to report preparations for nuclear war, even though they knew that nothing of the sort was being planned. For example, they were to make daily checks on whether offices in key government buildings such as the Pentagon were fully lit at night, on the bizarre theory that workers would stay late to prepare for a strike. The KGB told its overseas chiefs that "actual or impending" deployment of Pershing II could mean war. Interest in new Western technical developments was downgraded, which might suggest that the Soviets expected war in the near future (new technology would not be available in time to make a difference). The KGB's American experts considered Andropov alarmist, and thought the pressure for RYAN had come from the military high command, probably through Defense Minister D. F. Ustinov, who would later support Andropov's bid to succeed Brezhnev in power.

In fact each side had long known that a successful surprise attack could be extremely profitable (though also extremely risky). Each therefore carefully monitored the other. RYAN seemed bizarre because those discussing it had no experience with its U.S. equivalent and because the indicators were alien to U.S. practice, which was said to rely on satellites and on communications intercepts. In the past, attack warning had been the province of Soviet military intelligence (GRU); it is possible that Andropov was poaching this GRU function for his own service, the KGB. The RYAN order suggests that the Soviets wanted human-intelligence confirmation of what their attack sensors might tell them. Unsurprisingly, RYAN continued at least through 1991.

Mrs. Thatcher helped Reagan make his point. Early in 1982 the Argentines seized the Falklands Islands, a British possession that they had long claimed. Many in Britain assumed that their country would not fight. Instead the British retook the islands. Argentina was not the Soviet Union, and the Falklands conflict was not World War III. However, the war was an extremely unpleasant shock for the Soviets. It demonstrated that morale in a key Western country was not nearly so low as they had imagined. That lesson was reinforced when Mrs. Thatcher was returned to office with a large majority soon after the war. The increasingly left-leaning opposition Labour Party, with which the Soviets might have been far more comfortable, was being marginalized. Its opposition to British assertiveness and rearmament, positions the Soviets had hoped would help neutralize Reagan, were proving fruitless.

In 1983 a Communist coup in the small Caribbean island of Grenada provided the Reagan administration with a valuable opportunity. U.S. forces overran the island and overthrew its Cuban-backed government. Critics said that the operation was ludicrous, but the other two potential Caribbean targets, Cuba and Nicaragua, would have been far more difficult. The administration knew that the Cubans (and, for that matter, the Russians) had received its message: the U.S. would keep its possessions, and could take away Russia's.

In 1981–82 it was widely understood that the Soviet economy was in trouble, that it was spending far too much on its military. What was special about Reagan and Casey was their belief the economy's troubles might be terminal. Almost all other observers assumed that, as in the past, the Soviet State could accept poor economic performance, and the KGB could hold down any discontent; the system surely could remain in power indefinitely. On this basis the Soviet crisis seemed mainly to offer the United States a chance to catch up with the Soviet military expansion of the previous decade. What was new, beginning in the late 1970s, was the urgent Soviet drive to match the U.S. computer threat, a drive comparable to Stalin's quest for the atomic bomb. The Soviets could not match Stalin's achievement because they were unable to mobilize their economy; Brezhnev had already mobilized it to make tanks and airplanes and missiles and nuclear warheads. Reagan did not realize it, but the form of military modernization he chose was itself a kind of economic attack. Had he followed the campaign advice given by Professor van Cleave, Reagan would have spent most of his money on nuclear weapons, in effect playing to Soviet industrial strength. Richard Allen (who soon became his national security advisor); Ray Cline of the CIA; and Dr. John F. Lehman Jr., the secretary of the navy, convinced Reagan that a strong conventional defense was affordable; new U.S. technology provided enormous leverage.[23] It was emblematic of this understanding that van Cleave, who expected to become secretary of defense, or at the least national security advisor, became a member of the insignificant General Advisory Committee of the Arms Control and Disarmament Agency. Rearmament emphasizing nonnuclear weapons meant buying the fruits of the emerging computer revolution, which the Soviets could not match. Their attempt to do so subjected their economy and their society to terrible and ultimately fatal strains.

The defense budget had begun to grow under Carter, but Reagan drastically increased the amount to be spent: $6.8 billion more in FY81, which was a quarter over when Reagan entered office, and then $25.8 billion in FY82. Reagan consistently overruled his budget director, David Stockman, who feared that his program was bankrupting the country. He also beat back the opposition of much of the Washington bureaucracy (Congress generally supported rearmament) and that of many NATO leaders and bureaucrats.[24] The buildup should be put in context. In the 1950s and early 1960s the United States often spent 10 percent or more of its GNP on defense. The last budget entirely prepared by the Carter administration, for FY80, spent 5.3 percent on defense. Reagan spent 6.3 percent in the first budget for which his staff was completely responsible (FY82), and the highest percentage was in FY86, 6.5 percent. However, between the early 1960s and 1980 the U.S. economy grew enormously. Each percentage point represented far more money, in absolute terms, even though many weapons also cost much more than their predecessors.

The Reagan team did consciously try to make U.S. rearmament costly for the Soviets by applying special "black" (above Top Secret) classifications, formerly used only for intelligence projects, to a few weapons projects. To some extent it hoped to conceal weapons until they were fielded; when they were suddenly revealed the Soviets might begin crash programs—which would particularly damage their highly programmed economy.[25] The most famous "black" programs were low-observable ("stealthy") aircraft (the F-117 light bomber and the B-2 heavy bomber) and missiles. They might be able to penetrate Soviet air defenses so effectively as to destroy the Soviet land-based missile force and, probably, the command centers. Few would doubt that the sudden revelation of the program was likely to panic the Soviets into a crash antistealth program. "Blackness" would inevitably attract Soviet espionage. Penetrating it would sop up their hard currency.

"Blackness" made it easier to mount deception operations, which had proven so valuable during World War II. A secret technical disinformation program began in 1984.[26] Measures included deceptive leaks to journalists. False information included performance and operational achievements. The program covered "six or seven" projects, including stealthy aircraft and missile defense, which it was hoped would lure the Soviets into wasteful efforts. Probably some of the accounts of exotic U.S. military aircraft tested in Nevada can be traced to this program. The program produced falsified plant designs and computer chips. The chips were particularly important because the Soviets depended so heavily on imports (often illegal) from the West. Sabotaged chips were sold in the knowledge that the Soviets would have to spend a great deal of time testing the chips to verify that they matched their supposed designs.[27]

The key to these attacks was that the Soviet leaders believed that the West, particularly the United States, could do almost anything technological. In some important cases, such as "Star Wars," they apparently persisted in this belief even when their own scientists told them that the U.S. programs were totally impractical. The situation recalled that of 1945: the conquering Allies considered the Germans technological supermen. Anything the Germans had sketched, the Allies believed—often wrongly—could be made to work. The more secret the U.S. project, the more likely the Soviets were to believe it would work, and the more resources they would expend to duplicate it.

Drastically restricting access to information within the defense establishment made oversight difficult. "Black" programs evaded McNamara's system of program reviews; too much exposure would breach their security. The normal procurement process was universally recognized as slow and cumbersome, largely because it entailed so many reviews. It was tempting for a program manager to protect his program by escaping into the "black" world. Yet there was a point to the reviews. The navy's vital A-12 bomber, a largely "black" airplane because of its stealthiness, probably failed as expensively as it did because no one caught it (or fixed it) early enough. Similarly, because "black" programs did not figure in budget estimates, they were unpleasant shocks when they reached the production stage. Production was considerably more expensive than it might otherwise have been because tens of thousands of production workers needed special stringent clearances. Many of the Defense Department's fiscal problems towards the end of the Reagan administration and early in the Bush administration can be traced to the sudden emergence of "black" programs such as the B-2 bomber. They crowded out more conventional programs.

How well did "blackness" work against the Soviets? Perhaps the Soviet military used the mass of American initiatives to convince the leadership that industrial

460 COUNTERATTACK AND VICTORY

rebirth was vital—with ultimately disastrous results. Perhaps more open aspects of the U.S. rearmament program, such as the proliferation of tank-killing precision weapons, exerted enough pressure.

The U.S. also used direct economic warfare. By the 1980s the Soviets badly needed hard currency. They increasingly depended on technology bought (often illicitly) from the West (for which they budgeted $1.4 billion in 1981).[28] The Reagan administration tightened export controls on critical technology; at the least they raised the price the Soviets paid for what they had to get. To keep their own population more or less contented, the Soviets had to buy Western grain. The countries of the Eastern European empire still were buying off its citizens with Western consumer goods (paid for with borrowed hard currency). In addition, they had at the least to pay off the interest on the loans taken out during the previous decade, also mainly to keep the population from rioting. By 1981 it was clear that none of the East European economies had managed to develop the ability to sell much to the West. The bloc's only significant source of hard currency, vital for so many reasons, was Soviet oil and gas sales, which brought in $300 billion during 1973–83. In effect, oil sales allowed the Soviets and the satellites to put off any sort of real reform, which would have had political consequences: Stanislav Shatalin, a Soviet economist who later advised Gorbachev, compared oil to a drug, which destroyed the Soviet economy while giving it the appearance of strength.[29]

In the summer of 1981 Poland seemed to offer an interesting opportunity. It needed to borrow $10 to $11 billion, of which $7 to $8 billion would roll over the huge existing debt.[30] Financial pressure might force the Poles to seek Western help, and thus to detach themselves from the Soviet bloc. The Reagan administration arranged to have the Western banks demand immediate payment of about $2.7 billion. Poland was so vital that the Soviets paid instead. Between August 1980 and August 1981 they transferred $4.5 billion in hard currency to the Poles. In the process they wiped out much of the money they had in Western banks (deposits fell from $8.5 billion to about $3 billion); the Soviet trade surplus, $217 million in 1980, shifted to a $3 billion deficit.[31] The Soviets would not be able to afford a few more such attacks.

Reagan's writ was limited, because most Soviet income came from energy sales to the Europeans. They certainly did not agree to his assault on the Soviets. Differing perspectives were illustrated by the sanctions Reagan ordered in June 1982 against exports of gas pipeline equipment to the Soviet Union, in hopes of stopping the Siberian project. The Europeans pointed out that Reagan already had reversed Carter's embargo on grain sales, merely to fulfill a campaign promise to American farmers. Now he wanted European manufacturers to forgo valuable contracts. Reagan saw no contradiction. The grain sales extracted hard currency from the Soviets. The technology would make it possible for them to earn more hard currency, and moreover would bind U.S. allies to the Soviets. European profits would be quite incidental. Some pipeline construction went ahead, but only one of several planned lines was built. Most Western European energy needs continued to be met from outside the Soviet Union; the Soviets never got the leverage they sought.

The administration convinced the Saudis to increase production and thus reduce the world price of oil from a peak of about $40 per barrel in 1980 to $10 or $12 in 1986. Soviet income fell. The Saudis agreed partly because they felt threatened by the Soviet attack on Moslems in Afghanistan.[32] This damaging cut coincided with a decline in production within the European Soviet Union. The price of Siberian development was very high.

Reagan also took some major military initiatives. As a candidate, he had visited the Colorado headquarters of the North American Air Defense Command (NORAD). There he learned to his surprise that, despite its name, the command could do nothing whatever to protect the country in the event of a Soviet nuclear attack.[33] Because he had not learned the orthodox version of nuclear strategy, that mutual vulnerability bred stability, he found the lack of protection horrifying. Dr. Edward Teller later told him that a new technology, the X-ray laser, would make a full missile defense both possible and affordable. In 1983 President Reagan announced that the United States would develop and deploy a missile shield, which he called the Strategic Defense Initiative (SDI). He saw SDI as a way of eliminating the threat of nuclear war; he offered the new technology to the Soviets. Detractors called SDI "Star Wars."[34]

Although their scientists told them that SDI was impractical, the Soviet leadership took Reagan at his word. At the least, they had to have SDI first—and not from proffered American technology. After the Cold War was over, the Soviets described their own attempt to develop an SDI—which probably cost them far more than SDI cost the Americans. If the Americans did get SDI first, their own nuclear weapons would be unusable. Then the Americans would have the upper hand due to computer supremacy. Without usable nuclear weapons the Soviets could no longer cow a NATO that would soon, they imagined, be able to use computer weapons such as Assault Breaker to stop their tank army.

The Soviets activated the only countermeasure they had, an intense propaganda campaign to convince Americans that SDI was a cover for the administration's insane plan to fight a nuclear war. U.S. intelligence knew that the Soviets already were spending very heavily on SDI, and that the administration was goading them to spend even more. The Soviets had their physicists urge Americans not to waste money on SDI; the CIA knew that most of those who signed the physicists' advertisement in the *New York Times* actually were working feverishly on a Soviet equivalent.[35]

The administration's new ideas were reflected in its two main military initiatives. Secretary of the Navy Lehman publicized a Maritime Strategy, which had been evolving at the Naval War College since 1979, but it had never been articulated publicly.[36] It was a return to the more aggressive concept of operations the navy had espoused in the 1950s and 1960s. Instead of concentrating on directly protecting the sea route to Europe, the United States would seize maritime supremacy by destroying as much as possible of the Soviet fleet, including its land-based aircraft, in their bases. U.S. submarines would attack Soviet strategic submarines, their most valuable naval assets, in their protected holding areas. At the least, that would tie down much of the Soviet submarine fleet, which would try to protect the strategic submarines. All of this was practical because the new administration was buying enough of the new systems developed over the previous decade, such as the F-14 fighter and Aegis.

Once the fleet had triumphed, it could change the dynamics of a war in Europe. It could, for example, afford to undertake risky attacks on the Soviet flanks, for example in the Baltic or on the North Sea coast as a Soviet army advanced through the Netherlands. Thus threatened, a Soviet army might have to stop or even pull back. By this time it was known that the Soviets took the threat of amphibious operations, even in places like the Kola Peninsula in the north, and near Leningrad, quite seriously. A credible threat would force the Soviets to hold back large forces, which would otherwise be usable on the Central Front. To make the point, the U.S. Navy bought new air-cushion landing craft, which could operate over a far wider variety of beaches than could their predecessors, hence could more easily threaten the areas the Soviets considered most sensitive.

The Maritime Strategy created a sensation. Never since the late 1940s had the navy explained what it would do in wartime. Few realized that what they were hearing in the early 1980s was not new. It had evolved quite steadily from the thinking of the 1940s into the late 1960s; it reversed some thinking of the 1970s. Critics of the new strategy feared that pressure on Soviet strategic submarines would lead a panicky Soviet leadership to fire before they were lost. They did not realize that the Soviets planned to hunt down U.S. strategic submarines from the outset. Others, many of them veterans of the European NATO navies, thought that convoy operations (i.e., direct protection of shipping) surely sufficed; why the dangerous run north?

The Soviets understood. Their naval exercises began to concentrate on home defense against an attacking U.S. fleet rather than on open-ocean attacks on Western shipping. They strengthened their coast defenses—which meant reducing the threat they could deploy against the NATO army on the Central Front. The new U.S. naval strategy was associated with a new force goal: fifteen operational carrier battle groups (which meant more than fifteen carriers) and a six-hundred-ship fleet. The desired fleet size was not new (Congress could provide up to twenty ships each year, and ships last about thirty years) but its composition was; it reflected the needs of the new strategy. Reagan personally supported the new force goal.[37]

The U.S. Army's more aggressive doctrine, AirLand Battle, was formally adopted in August 1982. Instead of waiting for an attack, the army would advance to gain battle space on the enemy's side of the inter-German border. Some saw in

AirLand Battle something much more like current Soviet tactics than earlier NATO defensiveness. However, any advance would have been limited; there was no plan for the U.S. Army to run east the way the Soviets planned to advance west. The U.S. Army triumph in the Gulf War, using AirLand Battle concepts, was sometimes described as the victory of Soviet methods. To support the new doctrine, the army was enlarged, and it got new weapons. Perhaps as importantly, it was given the National Training Center. It was often said, in the early 1980s, that American armies performed poorly at the outset of a war, then learned their lessons and won. The National Training Center, in which battles could be simulated on a large scale (using lasers to simulate firing), was a way of learning those early-war lessons without losing. It was much criticized at the time, on the theory that Central Europe was unlikely to resemble the Western desert terrain of the Center. Ironically, the war the Cold War–bred army actually fought, in the Persian Gulf, was on exactly the sort of terrain the center had used.

Both Maritime Strategy and AirLand Battle showed an aggressiveness hitherto absent in NATO. As might have been expected, NATO Europeans were less than enthusiastic. On the other hand, the offensive emphasis in AirLand Battle must have suggested to many in Eastern Europe that, in the event of war, Allied forces might liberate their countries. That message was certainly widely understood in the United States of the early 1980s. If the Soviets wanted to preserve the status quo, they had better avoid war.

To go with all these sticks, the Reagan administration extended the carrot of arms control negotiations, initially as part of NATO's two-track missile program in Europe. On 18 November 1981, before any missiles had been emplaced in Western Europe, President Reagan offered the Soviets the "zero option": all such Intermediate (Range) Nuclear Force (INF) missiles, on both sides of the border, would be eliminated. The Soviets refused. Having offered this sort of deal, Reagan and his European allies could overcome the protests the Soviets helped organize.

Reagan saw little point in the SALT treaties, which merely perpetuated a very high level of nuclear armament on both sides. In May 1982 he announced that he would seek a 50 percent reduction in Soviet land-based ballistic missiles, which were considered most threatening. To distinguish the new concept from SALT, he called it START (Strategic Arms Reduction Treaty).

Leonid Brezhnev died in November 1982. From the mid-1970s on Brezhnev no longer took any active part in Party or state activity, yet still demanded that he be shown daily on television; everyone could therefore see his gradual physical decline. For example, it took obvious physical exertion for him merely to lift the heavy SALT II treaty book at Vienna in 1979.[38] With Brezhnev effectively incapacitated, the Soviet Union was ruled by a triumvirate: Mikhail Suslov, the Party's ideologist; Marshal Ustinov, the minister of defense and the Party's former head of Soviet military industry; and Yuri Andropov, chief of the KGB. Suslov and Andropov were, in effect, competitors for the succession. Brezhnev favored his assistant,

Chernenko. In 1982 Suslov died. Andropov was allowed to leave the KGB and return to the Central Committee, hence to seek the succession for himself. The situation recalled that in 1953, in that the Party's man, Chernenko, was opposed by a bureaucrat, Andropov, impatient with the Party's corruption. This time the Party's man was quite feeble.

To get the new weapons the Soviet military needed, Ogarkov and Ustinov threw the military's weight behind Andropov, whose prescription was to end the corruption.[39] He seems to have been entirely unaware that corruption—patronage—was integral to the Soviet social contract, just as it had been for the South Vietnamese a decade or more before. Just as in Vietnam, to root out corruption would be to destroy the system itself.

Andropov became general secretary of the Party on 12 November 1982, Brezhnev having died two days earlier. Despite earlier practice, on 16 June 1983 he was made prime minister (chairman of the Presidium). To solve the factional problem in the Politburo, he made Brezhnev's favorite, Chernenko, his deputy.[40] A next generation waited in the wings. Andropov's main protégé was Mikhail S. Gorbachev, the minister of agriculture. The Party's Moscow and Leningrad bosses, Viktor G. Grishin and Grigoriy Romanov, were allied to Chernenko. Romanov had ties to military industry, much of which was based in Leningrad. Grishin had been head of the trade unions.

In Andropov's view, productivity was down because workers had no good reason to work. He decided to give them one by arresting any found on the street during working hours. He also attacked the alcoholism rampant in the Soviet Union, which others might have seen as a symptom of years of very low morale. Despite early Western press reports, he showed no interest whatever in opening Soviet society. If anything, under his tenure the KGB worked harder to suppress dissent.

As an example of "socialist legality" at work, Andropov brought some members of Brezhnev's family to trial. He attacked Brezhnev's interior (police) minister, Nikolai A. Shchelokov, whose organization had failed utterly to root out corruption. Shchelokov probably committed suicide. According to one account, his widow took her revenge. Andropov lived in the same apartment bulding as she did, and one night she shot him as he climbed the stairs. Although the shot was not immediately fatal, it incapacitated Andropov and apparently hastened his death.[41]

By the middle of 1983, the Reagan administration seems to have felt that it had made up much of the ground lost by earlier administrations.[42] For example, on 31 August l, the Soviets shot down a Korean airliner (KAL 007). The U.S. reaction was strong but it was nothing like the across-the-board boycott President Carter had felt compelled to impose over Afghanistan. Reagan felt he did not have to prove anything.

At about the same time the administration demonstrated that NATO could stand firm in the face of a strong Soviet propaganda campaign: In the fall of 1983 cruise and Pershing missiles finally were deployed to Europe as planned. The protest campaign had begun with twenty thousand people massed in Hyde Park in June 1980. On the eve of deployment, West Germany saw the largest street protest in its history.[43] Polls showed, for example, that a majority of West Germans opposed deployment. There were significant pacifist wings in the British Labour Party and in the German Social Democratic Party. However, the missiles were deployed as planned. Later, Mikhail Gorbachev would upbraid his generals: They were useless; they had failed to intimidate even the Belgians. The Soviet propaganda weapon, so effective in the past, apparently had been blunted. It had not been destroyed; the antimissile campaign, and later ones against "Star Wars," certainly raised the level of Western anxiety about nuclear war. Overall, Europeans found the new toughness of the Reagan administration frightening.

The Soviets advertised a new submarine-launched cruise missile, SS-N-21, as an equivalent, capable of suddenly destroying U.S. command centers from a position just off the U.S. coast. In the fall of 1983, when the U.S. Pershing II missile was being deployed to Europe, a Soviet Victor III submarine, a candidate launch platform for SS-N-21, reportedly operated for a time off the U.S. coast. There was speculation (presumably inspired by the Soviets) that it represented the first SS-N-21 deployment. That was a bluff; the Soviets had not yet perfected their weapon.[44]

The KGB was alerted that the mere appearance of Pershing IIs in Europe might be a war warning. The Soviets appeared to be panicking. The most famous case in point was the reaction to a command post exercise, Able Archer-83, conducted on 2–11 November 1983. It was the first exercise to involve Pershing II missiles (simulated ones—real ones had not yet arrived). Simulated nuclear forces in Europe were raised to high readiness to prepare for a simulated strike. It seemed inconceivable that a command post exercise, conducted many times in the past, would have much impact on the Soviets. Possibly because word of RYAN had been leaked, plans to include the president and other senior officials were cancelled. Probably the Soviets reacted because they had not previously associated NATO signaling in Europe as a strategic tip-off: Pershing was aimed, not at their troops, but at their own command posts deep in the Soviet Union. What had been of interest only to the Group of Soviet Forces in Germany might now be significant on a much higher level. At that level, Soviet intelligence was not used to NATO command post exercises.

The Soviets seem to have misinterpreted the nominal alert in the exercise as a real one. They thought they saw signs of real alerts at NATO bases. On 8 or 9 November Moscow warned KGB residents that war might be imminent. About twelve nuclear-armed aircraft were placed on strip alert in Eastern Europe. Remarkably, the Soviet alert was not noticed in the West until records were reviewed months later. The very limited Soviet strip alert was probably precautionary. One can conclude that the Soviet general staff did not take Able Archer terribly seriously. President Eisenhower had been right. Common sense restrained both sides from attacking on flimsy evidence.[45]

The Able Archer alert seems to have been connected with a major Soviet propaganda campaign, mounted in November–December, to the effect that the United States was preparing for a nuclear war. It was a last attempt to derail missile deployment in Europe. In December Defense Minister Ustinov called the scare off. An American diplomat speculated that it may have backfired, causing undue panic within the Soviet Union.[46]

Andropov announced that any illusions of improved relations with the United States had been dispelled. A confident Reagan continued to offer opportunities for better relations, but Andropov did not live long enough to change his mind. He last met foreigners in August 1983 and died the following 9 February. He tried to place his protégé, Gorbachev, in line to succeed him by having him chair sessions of the Central Committee during his illness. However, neither he nor the two alternative candidates—Grishin and Romanov—had sufficient strength to win.

Ustinov was still kingmaker; he chose a very elderly and infirm Konstantin U. Chernenko, whom he preferred to Romanov and Grishin.[47] Despite Andropov's efforts, Gorbachev was not in the running because Andropov's successor as KGB chief, Chebrikov, was not powerful enough to have a say. Then, too, since September 1983 Chernenko had chaired Politburo meetings in Andropov's place. Throughout his career Chernenko had been a nonentity; only through Brezhnev did the Central Committee's clerk become its chief. On the other hand, under Brezhnev he had been responsible for bugging the senior Soviet party officials, hence knew more than anyone else about intrigues within the Party.[48] Clearly Chernenko was unlikely to last; he was almost unable even to read his speech at Andropov's funeral. However, many of the words attributed to him foreshadowed those of Gorbachev; some on Chernenko's staff apparently realized that the country was stagnating, and that orthodox cures would not work.[49] There was a general feeling of malaise among the ruling elite. For example, in the summer of 1984 Army General Yepishev, certainly no malcontent, remarked that "things feel sticky, congealed. I don't know what's going to happen, but something must."[50]

In March 1985 Andropov's protégé, Mikhail Gorbachev, became Party chairman. He had been carrying out the duties of the chairman for some time, because Chernenko had been so sick. Of two possible alternatives, Romanov was considered too untalented. Grishin was a member of the old guard, but apparently lacked allies. The selection was the quickest in the Politburo's history. It met at 2 P.M. the day after Chernenko died, and announced the result at six. Andrei Gromyko, the veteran diplomat, ensured Gorbachev's success by making his nomination the first speech of the meeting; no one in the Politburo "would dare to break the golden rule by opposing the first candidate named."[1] Gromyko told the Politburo that Gorbachev would be another Andropov, healthy enough to last the course: "This man smiles, but he has steel teeth."

Americans tended to agree. When he first met Mikhail Gorbachev in 1985, at Chernenko's funeral, George Bush considered him far more dangerous than any of his predecessors. He was slicker, with "a disarming smile, warm eyes, and an engaging way of making an unpleasant point and then bouncing back. . . . He can be very firm." Gorbachev soon learned to say just what Westerners wanted to hear. Through the latter half of the 1980s was a real fear that he would be able to disarm the West without having to make any real sacrifice of his own forces.[2]

Gorbachev understood that his mandate was the same as Andropov's: to make up for the yawning gap in Soviet military technology. He told the Politburo that the country had fallen behind the West by an entire generation of technology, as reflected, he said, mainly in machine tools. He planned to devote the entire 1986–90 Five Year Plan to producing modern machinery. Probably he meant computers and the means to make them. Machine building was often a euphemism for a particular segment of military industry, such as missiles or nuclear weapons.[3] Gorbachev's first Five Year Plan increased military spending by 4.5 percent at the cost of the Soviet standard of living.[4] This choice—to favor industrial investment over investment in consumer goods—had not been made since Stalin's day.

Gorbachev was in roughly the same position Nixon had occupied in 1973. His general staff told him that it would take years of intense effort to redress the military balance. In 1973 Brezhnev had regarded his growing military superiority as a guarantee that U.S.-Soviet relations were irreversibly friendly, i.e., that the United States would accept the tipped balance of forces. Nixon had had to accept Soviet attacks in the Third World. Now Reagan was in much the same position Brezhnev had occupied, and Gorbachev soon understood that he had much the same agenda. The United States was on the offensive, often in the same places Brezhnev had claimed a decade before.

There was one immense difference. The Western economic system had been flexible enough to support the military comeback of the Reagan years. Gorbachev's attempt to redress the military would sink the Soviet system. He failed not because Reagan outspent the Soviets, but because what he was buying involved a revolution in military technology.

Gorbachev is unlikely to have realized how badly the Soviet economic system had deteriorated, because, like other favored citizens, he could still get the consumer goods he wanted. A decade of declining living standards, which were already worse than drab, left people with little hope for the future, and with even less willingness to accept more sacrifices.

Gorbachev also faced mounting hard currency debts throughout his empire. He knew that the relatively cheap oil in the European Soviet Union, which had provided so much hard currency, was being exhausted. Soon the cost of extraction would rise. Production began to decline steeply in 1988; exports were halved between 1989 and 1991. When the decline was first predicted (about 1981), the Soviets cut their oil exports to Eastern Europe by 10 percent.[5]

Gorbachev probably inherited from Andropov the view that the Party bureaucracy was the problem. He also inherited some of Andropov's experts on economic reform, such as Nikolai Ryzhkov and Yegor Ligachev. Ryzhkov became Gorbachev's prime minister (chairman of the Council of Ministers). Ligachev became Gorbachev's chief assistant, chairing Secretariat meetings in his absence. He broke with Gorbachev when reform became radical in 1988.

To compete with the West, Gorbachev had to rouse the Soviet public to new efforts. He was a creature of the Party on which he sometimes blamed his country's problems, an *apparatchik*, used to obedience and fawning underlings. He had little concept of leadership, because he had never had to convince people who had real alternatives available. In the Soviet Union, the first rule was to eliminate any alternatives to the Party. The Party gained obedience by using a stick; it had long had little hope of gaining enthusiasm, because it did not have enough carrots to attract the vast Soviet population. Those at the top rarely understood just how demoralized the people were, partly because their underlings lied about how avidly the Party's orders were being followed. Thus Gorbachev did not realize that a cynical public had long since learned to discount slogans.

To make matters worse, the war in Afghanistan was going badly, and its failure was undermining Soviet authority in Central Asia, not to mention public confidence in the power of the Soviet state (as reflected in its army). The war also was beginning to create a generation of angry veterans.

In 1985, Gorbachev's problem was simply to grasp power firmly enough that he could not soon be unseated. Like his predecessors, he concentrated on personnel, immediately firing Grishin and Romanov. He pursued Andropov's attack on corruption, which wiped out many remaining Brezhnev supporters. Thus by the beginning of 1986 only 172 of the 307 Central Committee members of 1980 were still serving, and half the *nomenklatura* (those holding the main patronage jobs) had been fired.[6] As in Brezhnev's time, summit meetings with the Americans reflected back into the Politburo, to prove that the Soviet partner was indeed head of state. Thus it was to solidify his still somewhat shaky position within the Politburo that Gorbachev agreed to meet Reagan in Geneva in November 1985.

For Gorbachev, the summit was a minefield. On the one hand, he had to extract something to show the Politburo. On the other hand, he could not afford for Reagan to cancel. Reagan was the better poker player. He rejected Gorbachev's attempt to trade SDI for Reagan's desired deep cuts in strategic missiles and Euromissiles. To Reagan, SDI and the cuts were steps in the same direction. To Gorbachev's military, they were both steps to disaster.

Gorbachev apparently hoped that he could still operate freely in the Third World—where he could win, where his less adventurous predecessors had lost. Thus in 1985 he greatly escalated the war in Afghanistan—just as U.S. aid made the Afghan rebels considerably more formidable. He also escalated in Angola; Soviet advisors became more involved in combat, and sometimes directed Cuban-Angolan forces. There was also a buildup in Nicaragua. In the cases of Angola and Nicaragua, the buildups sufficiently impressed Congress for it to reverse previous bans on U.S. assistance.[7]

At the Party Congress, Gorbachev won a solid majority in the new Politburo, but only enough of the new Central Committee to protect himself against a Brezhnev-style coup—for the moment. He had to build coalitions for each step he took. He could not take Khrushchev's path and gain the capital he needed (for example, for Ogarkov's new weaponry) by canceling major programs. The Party chairman's power had eroded too badly for that.

Naturally Gorbachev tried to solve his problem with minimum pain. He seems to have imagined that the stagnation he faced was a temporary problem; a minor adjustment would tune the "Socialist engine" well enough to carry it forward to ultimate victory. He called for reform (perestroika, meaning restructuring) imposed from above, for greater efficiency. His mass media began to publicize better Western ways of doing business, but it was impossible to say that they worked because of the incentives built into capitalism. Gorbachev apparently missed the clear implication: alternatives to Soviet Socialism were not merely legitimate but might even be preferable. The Party's theoretical monopoly on truth was being undermined.

He soon was aware that Soviet citizens wanted consumer goods and services. Gorbachev's solution was to revive Lenin's NEP (i.e., limited private enterprise). Similar practices already worked in other Communist countries: Hungary, Yugoslavia, and China.[8] Gorbachev seems not to have had the slightest idea of what it meant. He still thought in Party clichés; for example, as late as 1988, he quoted the *Communist Manifesto* when asked about his position on private property.[9] The neo-NEP was unlikely to achieve much because, unlike the countries Gorbachev cited, the Soviet Union had no generation of entrepreneurs left over from a capitalist past. It did have a large black economy which looked like private enterprise, but which worked only because its raw materials and equipment were so often stolen from the state.

Thanks largely to Western radio stations, Soviet citizens were becoming aware that they, like the Poles of the Solidarity movement, had some power of their own. Despite jamming which began in August 1980, enough was known of the successes of Solidarity for some Soviet workers to stage their own strikes in 1980 and in 1981; one Soviet specialist on Western radio said that "Solidarity was a manual for all citizens of the USSR."[10] One irony of the jamming was that although it kept relatively powerless people from hearing Western news, all of those who had a real potential to influence events received the official broadcast transcripts, and thus were well aware of what was being broadcast by the West. According to interviews conducted after the Soviet Union collapsed, by the early 1980s most Soviet citizens no longer believed their own radio stations, and relied, directly or indirectly, on Western stations for their news.[11] The overall effect was that Gorbachev had to take much more radical steps than he might otherwise have considered, simply to get any reaction from his population.

Perestroika could not work instantly; Gorbachev needed a truce in the Cold War.[12] He used an old Soviet ploy, a peace campaign. Gorbachev's spokesmen began to say that by eliminating the Soviet threat they would undermine the U.S. military program. Gorbachev's message was wildly popular in the West, where few were aware that the Soviets had not changed their own policy of massive military production. Gorbachev seemed too good to be true; no one wanted to embarrass the Soviet "man of peace" by questioning his actions or his motives. In January 1986 Gorbachev went Reagan one better by proposing that all nuclear weapons be eliminated by the year 2000.

Gorbachev's need for a truce gave Reagan leverage over internal Soviet affairs. To maintain the détente he needed, Gorbachev had to convince a skeptical Ronald Reagan, who regarded liberalization as a guarantee that this time détente would be neither one-sided nor short-lived. Reagan in effect demanded insurance that the truce was sincere and would endure. Reagan was willing, but he was a skeptical veteran of the failed Nixon-Ford-Carter détente and of Team B.

Gorbachev needed the truce more than ever as he discovered that perestroika had failed. As Khrushchev had learned, any sort of restructuring was an attack on the entrenched Party bureaucracy that ran the country. Neither Gorbachev nor Andropov realized that economic reform meant cutting the Party's power. The petty obstructions in Soviet life and the inefficiencies of the economy were not accidents. They were unavoidable effects of the control the Party exerted over all details of the Soviet system. For that matter, the corruption Gorbachev denounced was really the Party's way of rewarding loyalty and thus of maintaining control. The Party was, moreover, the means by which decisions taken in Moscow were transmitted to the country and then implemented. Without it, Gorbachev could not control very much beyond Soviet troops and border guards. Despite his many years of service to and in the Party, Mikhail Gorbachev seems to have been entirely innocent of these facts.

In the end, perestroika was yet another series of empty slogans. Gorbachev had to do something more radical—more meaningful. He flirted with opening the system to reform from below (glasnost—openness). In 1986 he met with selected editors and writers. Soviet publications already often printed critical articles, but they were not allowed to attack the system in any way. Now Gorbachev told the editors that they could go much further.[13] In theory more open discussion would reveal past problems and help disclose solutions. To the extent that those problems were due to the corruption of the Party, glasnost might help reduce its drag on the country.

To make glasnost work, Gorbachev had to convince citizens that what they said would not be held against them. Stalin had realized that fear was integral to the Soviet system. It was ironic that the KGB's candidate for Soviet leader was now deliberately abandoning it. It is unlikely that Gorbachev entertained any particularly warm feeling towards Soviet dissidents. Probably he thought that the opening would give him a lever to destroy his enemies. It was inconceivable that the editors he had liberated would ever attack him. Like Dubcek almost twenty years earlier, he was sliding towards an open political system without quite comprehending what was happening.

Gorbachev played a classic part in Russian history, the reforming czar who is shocked that people react with something other than total gratitude for the crumbs they are thrown, that they question why he still retains virtually all the power of his autocratic predecessors.

Glasnost had definite limits. On 26 April 1986 one of four reactors at Chernobyl in the Ukraine exploded, sending radioactive fallout over Western Europe. Much more fell in the farming area immediately around Chernobyl. To Gorbachev's intense embarrassment, Soviet citizens learned about the disaster when Westerners discussed the fallout in their countries. Ukrainians found that Moscow did not care enough about them to evacuate them until well after the West publicized what was happening. Given a degree of glasnost, Soviet citizens could suddenly demand information. Gorbachev himself received a lesson in nuclear effects, a subject he had previously blithely ignored. Empty words about arms control suddenly took on some meaning.

Soviet citizens learned about Chernobyl from Western radio stations. Gorbachev's desperate need to maintain the truce with the West precluded jamming them. Yet the disaster exposed much of his program as a lie, as only a more sophisticated version of what had come before. Chernobyl was a particularly embarrassing lie—some said a turning point in Soviet history—because the disaster affected so many Soviet citizens, and because the Soviet government waited so long before it took any action, for example to evacuate those living near the stricken reactor. One important indirect effect was to confirm to many Ukrainians that the central government had no interest in their welfare. That in turn reinforced Ukrainian nationalism, which eventually caused the Ukraine to opt out of the Soviet Union—and which destroyed the Soviet Union in 1991. In this sense Western radio, which had been financed to erode the Soviet Union, may have played a decisive role.[14]

Meanwhile, the Reagan administration continued to combine negotiating offers with strength. A few weeks after Chernobyl, it announced that continued Soviet violations of SALT II freed it from the provisions of that unratified treaty. Reagan and Gorbachev met at Reykjavik, Iceland. Although they could not agree on SDI or on START, they did tentatively agree to eliminate all the INF missiles (cruise, Pershing II, SS-20). Then at Gorbachev's suggestion both sides agreed to scrap all tactical nuclear missiles with ranges beyond six hundred kilometers, the "second zero."

Gorbachev saw such agreements as a way of extending the truce he needed. If the first two zeroes were popular, why not go further? Gorbachev pressed for the "third zero," the elimination of battlefield nuclear weapons. Without Assault Breaker (still not developed), this would have handed dominance in Europe to the big Soviet tank force. Many Europeans fell into this trap, but the NATO foreign ministers knew better; in June 1987 they decided that it would have to await an agreement balancing conventional forces in Europe and also one eliminating chemical weapons (which could offset nuclear ones).[15] The INF treaty was finally signed when Gorbachev visited the United States in December 1987. To many it symbolized real peace, because for the first time an entire category of weapons was destroyed.

Glasnost made it much easier for the citizens of the Soviet republics to express their nationalism. Gorbachev probably had very little idea of just how disunited the Soviet Union was. Instead of loyally thanking him for a bit more freedom, many citizens began to explore the unpleasant past of forced Russification and their hopes for national identity. Arbitrary decisions by the Politburo and the leadership began to cause problems. For example, inside Moslem Azerbaijan lay the Armenian enclave of Nagorno-Karabakh. During the winter of 1987–88 the Armenians in the enclave asked Moscow for union with Armenia. Moscow waffled and the situation deteriorated. Gorbachev found it impossible to suppress a minor but extremely embarrassing war between Armenia and Azerbaijan, both Soviet republics.

By 1987, Gorbachev's economic reforms clearly were not working. He was forced to stretch them out to the year 2000 and also to reorient them towards the service sector and towards agriculture. He began to talk about "democratization," allying himself with the mass of workers against the bureaucrats. The Party would arbitrate among independent groups (i.e., free of the bureaucrats), which would actually run the economy.[16] But democratization turned out to be just another empty slogan.

On 28 May 1987 Mattias Rust, a nineteen-year-old West German, flew a Cessna light aircraft from Helsinki to Red Square, graphically demonstrating that Soviet air defenses were worthless. Gorbachev was visibly shaken. It was particularly poetic that that Rust made his flight on Border Guards' Day.[17] His airplane's radar signature was larger than that of a cruise missile. It was never clear just why Rust made his flight, or whether he received information on the defenses he had to penetrate. Some Soviet officers later said that he had been detected and identified but not shot down, because he was clearly a civilian (i.e., unlike KAL 007). Rust's flight gave Gorbachev the opportunity to fire several senior military officers, including the chief of Soviet air defense. Clearly, very expensive Soviet air defenses had bought little security. Gorbachev could therefore argue that he was achieving more by reducing Western weapons (through the INF treaty) than he would have done by accepting the military's preferred choice, buying more weaponry.

Step by step, Gorbachev was forced to tear down the Party's unique position. To convince workers that he was serious, he had to offer stronger and stronger measures. He had to insure individuals against the consequences of their disloyalty to the Party. He had to reward competence rather than political loyalty. There was no longer much reason for any competent individual to sacrifice for the Party, since competence alone would bring rewards. From the Party's point of view, this was even worse than Khrushchev's bifurcation.

If Gorbachev never realized quite how destructive his program was, others did. By 1987 opposition had solidified around his former assistant, Yegor Ligachev. In March 1988, with Gorbachev out of Moscow, Ligachev orchestrated the publication of an anti-perestroika article in *Sovetskaya Rossiya*, "I Cannot Betray My Principles," a title taken from a recent Gorbachev speech. An obscure chemistry teacher, Nina Andreyeva, wrote the article. In the past, the magazine's publication of such an article would have been the beginning of a classic political upheaval. This time it fizzled. The Party was too used to obeying its chief. It could be obstructive, but it could not yet rouse itself to revolt.

Ligachev's attack probably helped convince Gorbachev that he had to find some way of bypassing the Party. In June 1988 he had the Nineteenth Party Conference formally approve a strong presidency (not easily subject to a Brezhnev-style coup) and open elections to choose a working legislature in 1989. Also at this conference, the Party was forced to give up formal control of the national economy.

At this conference, too, Eduard Shevardnadze, Gorbachev's foreign minister, announced that class war would no longer be the basis of Soviet foreign policy. Ligachev countered that this line would end by destroying the Party and the state. Shevardnadze was toadying to Gorbachev.[18]

Between 1988 and 1990 the national state-party apparatus was ordered dismantled. However, local governments, which were run by the Party, had little interest in dissipating the Party's power. Gorbachev was learning that Brezhnev's social contract—his toleration of the Party's corruption and petty local abuse of power—had not been an accident.

However, Gorbachev had opened the door to non-Party organizations. In 1988 a popular front was formed in each of the Baltic republics. Gorbachev had the first secretaries of the Parties in each republic work with the front there, to co-opt nationalist sentiment. He echoed Stalin's old popular front efforts of the 1940s. This time, however, the nationalists co-opted the Communists. The popular fronts became independence movements.[19] In the past, a few tanks would have solved the problem, but now Gorbachev had to reckon with Western reactions. He hesitated; the independence movements grew. The Baltic popular fronts inspired an Uzhbek equivalent, the Birlik (Unity) Party.[20] Similar organizations developed in the other Moslem republics of Soviet Central Asia.

Having been raised in an atmosphere in which the leader of the Party called the tune, Gorbachev was surprised by the cacophony that even his limited foray into democracy represented. He could not, however, turn back. The 1989 elections, many of them with multiple candidates, produced the first functioning Soviet parliament, a 2,520-member Congress of Deputies empowered to write a new constitution. For the first time local candidates had to build their own power bases. Westerners tended to concentrate on races in which non-Communist candidates won. However, it was probably almost as important that local Party machines chose their own candidates instead of accepting Moscow's writ. They were tasting independent power for the first time.

The Congress of Deputies exposed the Soviet population to more or less free debate on matters that, until then, had been determined in secret by the Party. Parliament was unruly, split between the old Party, a few Party allies, and popularly elected representatives determined to speak their minds. The ongoing war over the economy broke into the open. So did nationalist tensions.

Gorbachev discovered, to his horror, that glasnost could be quite dangerous. A casual call to eliminate the "blank pages" of Soviet history opened up the Party's gross culpability in events such as the Ukrainian famine, the mass terror, and the Polish massacres of 1940. Organizations with names such as "Memory" called up a past the Party had tried to obliterate. The Russian Orthodox Church suddenly emerged as a major independent force. Once people were mobilized, they could not easily be stopped at a point Gorbachev found convenient.

Shevardnadze convinced Gorbachev to reverse the previous standard practice of determining foreign policy and then allocating the necessary resources. If the policy of buying control of Eastern Europe was unaffordable, it had to go.[21] Thus the cost of empire finally affected policy directly. During a debate made public after the Nineteenth Party Conference, a speaker claimed that Eastern Europe had cost the Soviet Union $50 billion in trade losses, due largely to the subsidies Brezhnev had accepted as the price of continuing loyalty.[22] The satellites' debts to the West continued to climb; as Reagan's advisors had realized, only the Soviet Union could provide the hard currency they needed to pay the interest on them. The situation became more critical as Soviet income from oil declined.

All of the satellite governments were chronically desperate for hard currency. Sometimes they demanded that the Soviets pay it in return for their products (preferably without paying the Soviets in hard currency for raw materials and energy). For example, in 1981 the Soviets began development of a new antiship missile, the Kh-35 Uran (NATO SS-N-25). The East German Zeiss plant, the bloc's leading optical producer, was asked to develop an electro-optical seeker for it. The project collapsed because the Soviet customer could not provide enough cash.[23] That is, the Soviets could not command their main satellite regime the way they commanded elements of their own economy. That was a taste of the way the Soviet industrial complex suffered when the Soviet Union later broke up; commands no longer worked. Kh-35 was not a particularly important weapon, but the story shows how the economic ties between the Soviet Union and its satellites were changing.

In 1987 Gorbachev announced that his reforms could be applied in the satellite states. In the Soviet Union, his enemies charged that his liberalization would endanger rule in the East European empire. In this Gorbachev was showing the same blithe ignorance of the structure of power as he was showing at home. He did not realize just how fragile Communist rule was; he thought that it was genuinely popular.

Presumably with Gorbachev's approval, Shevardnadze stopped giving orders to the satellite governments. Gorbachev proclaimed what was eventually called the "Sinatra Doctrine," after the singer's signature tune, "My Way." Now the satellite governments would be allowed to do it "their way." There would not be another Czech invasion, because by definition nothing any of the satellite governments did could be interpreted as a threat to Socialism. Yet Gorbachev could not bring himself to admit that past Soviet invasions had been wrong; he felt compelled to defend the Soviet record. Thus in March 1988 in Yugoslavia he affirmed the right of self-determination, but coyly refused to comment on the events of 1956 and 1968.[24]

The satellite governments still thought something of the political contract remained: Soviet troops would still back them up against their own populations. Thus at a Warsaw Pact meeting in July 1988 the East German and Czech governments opposed Gorbachev's plan for unilateral cuts in Soviet forces in Europe (made to get CSCE talks moving).[25] They did not realize that Gorbachev could not use force at all, for fear of losing détente.

The continuing sore of Afghanistan strengthened the argument against using force in, say, Poland. The Poles had long told the Soviets they would fight if invaded. Shevardnadze could point out just how bad such a fight could be.[26] In 1988 Gorbachev in effect conceded the point, withdrawing his forces from Afghanistan. As the Americans had done in Vietnam, he covered himself by transferring weapons to the Afghan government. Without a powerful army to back them up, the Afghan guerillas took several years to complete their victory.

Having failed to destroy Solidarity, in November 1987 Jaruzelski called a referendum to approve his form of perestroika. He lost; Solidarity lived. It did not help that when he visited in June 1988, Gorbachev refused to give Polish patriots what they demanded, an apology for crimes such as the Katyn Forest massacre. However, he did say, publicly, that the Poles' future was their own business (albeit in oblique language). After Gorbachev left, Jaruzelski sent out feelers to Solidarity.

Gorbachev saw the hard-liners in Eastern Europe as dangers to himself.[27] Just as Dubcek had endangered Brezhnev's Soviet Union by exporting his deviant brand of Socialism, now the conservatives in the satellites (particularly Czechoslovakia and East Germany) were colluding with anti-Gorbachev forces within the Soviet Union. Some Soviet ambassadors and other diplomatic personnel were tacitly encouraging resistance to reforms. To protect himself against defeat at home, Gorbachev would have to destroy the hard-line regimes, particularly those of East Germany and Czechoslovakia. That was ironic. In both countries, the hard line had been adopted out of loyalty to the Soviet Union.

Early in 1989 Oleg Bogomolov's Institute of the Economy of the World Socialist System produced a rationale for what Gorbachev was doing, in the form of a report on the future of the satellites.[28] With a declining economy, the Soviet Union could no longer rule by economism; the Eastern Europeans would inevitably turn West. How much of its position the Soviet Union could maintain would depend on how it managed that change. The institute could not admit (perhaps even to itself) that throughout the bloc Communism itself was deeply hated. Surely people accepted the governments they had had for forty years. The ruling Communist parties could solve their problems by a combination of economic reform and accommodating (and thus neutralizing) legalized opposition. As in Gorbachev's vision of a future Soviet Union, the parties would still be the arbiters controlling each country.

Gorbachev took this advice, but not everyone agreed. The Central Committee International Department, responsible for Party-to-Party relations, knew exactly what legalized opposition could mean. The empire would dissipate. It pointedly reminded Gorbachev that much of the prestige of the Soviet Union derived from the empire (shades of British and French imperialism of the past!). Gorbachev seems not to have understood.

Bogomolov's institute wrote its report as the Polish party resisted Jaruzelski's opening to Solidarity. It warned that if the Party succeeded in blocking political pluralism, by the spring of 1989 there might be another explosion; Poland might turn into an "Afghanistan in Europe."[29] Jaruzelski succeeded; meetings with Solidarity began on 6 February 1989. Solidarity was again legalized in April, and Jaruzelski announced an election in June. The Communist Party and its allies were guaranteed 65 percent of the seats in the main house of parliament, the Sejm. Solidarity won the rest, and all but one of the seats in the reinstated Senate.

As intended, parliament chose Jaruzelski as president. To his surprise, the Communists' nominally non-Communist allies, who had survived as part of the popular front that nominally ran Poland, now deserted to Solidarity. Lech Walesa, the Solidarity leader, refused to form a coalition with the Communists, so Jaruzelski could not form a government. That must have been a terrible surprise not only to Jaruzelski but also to Gorbachev, who had supported him from the start. Gorbachev was certainly aware of just how strategic Poland was, since through it passed the lines of communication to the Soviet troops in East Germany.

These events echoed in Hungary, which had introduced its own version of perestroika in September 1987. Hungary had long been the freest of the satellite states, with a far larger private economy than any of the others had. The contrast with the official planned economy was particularly stark. On the other hand, the Hungarian government was more motivated than others were to buy off its population, so it went deeper into debt. Interest payments eventually sapped growth, so that the standard of living began to decline in 1985. Gorbachev praised the Hungarian reforms, but did not encourage other satellite governments to emulate them.[30]

By 1987 the Hungarians had probably exhausted the potential for growth under their mixed economic system. Inflation reached 17 percent by the spring of 1988. The proffered solution—more austerity—was so unpopular that in May 1988 the Party quietly deposed Janos Kadar, who had come to power after the 1956 revolution. The new first secretary and prime minister, Karoly Grosz, tried to coopt the opposition, in much the manner Gorbachev was then trying to deal with nationalists in popular fronts.[31] He named a commission to investigate—to admit the crimes the Party had committed in—the 1956 uprising, Hungary's equivalent of Katyn.[32] The Communists renamed their party the Hungarian Socialist Party. By early 1989 the Bogomolov Institute had read these signs to indicate that Hungary was evolving towards a "bourgeois republic." Gorbachev apparently did not mind; in February 1989 he rejected Grosz's urgent request for economic help, i.e., for hard currency. He knew he was sending Hungary to the West, the only other source of help.[33]

The institute was right; Hungary was drawing away. In March 1989 its government allowed large-scale demonstrations to commemorate the Hungarian uprising of 1848–49 against Austria—which had been suppressed by Russian troops. Thus the demonstrations were actually anti-Russian, and they soon turned into protests against the Hungarian Communist government. On 16 June the government reburied Imre Nagy, the hero of the 1956 revolution, with full honors.

To the conservative regimes of Eastern Europe, the events in Poland were quite as alarming as Dubcek's changes had been twenty years before. However, Gorbachev was not Brezhnev. At a July 1989 Warsaw Pact meeting in Bucharest he clearly backed the Poles and the Hungarians: Each country was free to choose its own road to socialism. The other four pact members—Bulgaria, Czechoslovakia, East Germany, and Romania—opposed him.[34] In August Ceausescu of Romania (who had opposed the 1968 invasion of Czechoslovakia) demanded that the pact act collectively to put down the "counterrevolutionary" process in Poland.

As if to show their contempt, the Poles made the letter public. Having failed to control Solidarity, Jaruzelski had to resign as Communist Party chairman. As president, he had to name a Solidarity man, Tadeusz Mazowiecki, prime minister. Poland now had a non-Communist government.

Gorbachev feared that the Stalinist East German regime would harbor his Soviet enemies.[35] In 1989 that country was stable mainly because its government had locked in its citizens. In 1989 a poll showed that a third of all East Germans wanted to leave; only Cuba had a higher percentage so determined. Over its lifetime East Germany lost 15 percent of its population by escape.[36] In 1989 East Germany controlled travel even to other Soviet bloc countries. It had treaties under which East Germans illegally in those countries would be sent home to face prison.

Beginning on 2 May 1989 the Hungarians destroyed their part of the Iron Curtain, the barrier that blocked their border to Austria. The act was symbolic; for years most Hungarians had been able to cross the border. Much more importantly, they abrogated the treaty with East Germany. It had been an important part of the barrier preserving East Germany by preventing emigration. Beginning late in July, about sixty-five thousand East Germans entered Hungary, but the Hungarians would not allow onward transit without permission.

The West Germans pressed the Hungarians to allow free transit. The Hungarians knew that once they opened their borders, the East German regime would be doomed. It would be a delicious revenge for 1956.[37] The Hungarians were almost sure that Gorbachev would not intervene, but they wanted to be certain. Shevardnadze reassured them; the affair did not concern the Soviets.[38] On 11 September 1989 the Hungarian government opened its borders completely. Now any German who could reach the Hungarian frontier could get to West Germany. The Hungarians extracted a price from the West Germans, a DM 1 billion loan—which helped replace the funds Gorbachev had refused in February.[39] It was announced in October, a "decent interval" having passed. The East Germans did not understand how far the rot had gone; when they pressed the Soviets to force the Hungarians to close the border, the Soviets cynically blamed the West Germans.

By this time Gorbachev apparently had authorized a coup against the dangerous East German regime, which would be replaced by a more congenial Communist regime. His allies in the Soviet KGB passed the word to the German secret police. For example, they spoke to retired German intelligence chief Markus Wolf when he visited Moscow in the summer of 1989. The Soviets expected that ultimately a liberalized East German regime might join West Germany in a confederation—which would have the effect, finally, of neutralizing that country. That would not have been quite as good as Stalin's hope of seizing all of Germany, but it would have eliminated any NATO force in the heart of Europe.[40]

The East German opposition suddenly became much more vocal; a movement, Neue Forum, was formed at the beginning of September. It may be that the existence of an escape route (via Hungary) suddenly made opposition more viable. It may also be that the German secret police had been told to hold back. Gorbachev certainly told the East Germans that he would not provide the force to prop them up. Visiting for the fortieth anniversary of the Communist German republic on 7 October 1989, he chided its government for its sluggish reforms.

On the sixteenth Neue Forum demonstrated massively in Leipzig. The Soviet ambassador told the Germans not to shoot. Such mass disobedience demonstrated that Erich Honecker, the Stalinist ruler, could no longer control his country. He was ousted in favor of Egon Krenz, who had headed East German security, i.e., who had been close to Gorbachev's allies in the KGB. The winners imagined that they could survive by making limited reforms, negotiating with the opposition as Jaruzelsi was doing.[41] Unimpressed, East Germans continued to flee.

Now the new rulers of East Germany received a devastating economic report: they were on the point of bankruptcy. They secretly approached the West Germans for a big loan. They also went back to Gorbachev, asking him for DM 12 billion. To their surprise, he refused. He probably did not have the money; Reagan's economic strategy had been quite effective.

The East Germans panicked. Before they knew whether the West Germans would provide the big loan, on 9 November they decided to renounce the Party's leading role, to approve free elections, and to allow trips abroad on request. The last was a terrible mistake. The opportunity to go West was too good to miss. Large crowds began to move to the Berlin Wall. To avoid riots, the East Germans simply opened their borders.[42] Soon the opening was made permanent: the wall was torn down. The East Germans had thrown their state away, although probably they did not yet realize that.

Westerners assumed, wrongly, that Gorbachev had been consulted; he basked in Western public adoration after the wall went down. In fact the East Germans had acted alone; the Soviets complained privately that the East Germans had thrown away any chance of survival by going far too quickly. To everyone's surprise, the West German Chancellor, Helmut Kohl, almost immediately saw his opportunity and placed a reunification plan before the Reichstag on 28 November. Soon Kohl maneuvered Gorbachev into accepting not only reunification, but continued German membership in NATO. That took away the one justification Gorbachev might have claimed, that he was finally solving the German problem by neutralizing the country. To the extent that the Cold War had been fought over Germany, Gorbachev had lost.

The Czechs, too, had a hard-line government. Once Honecker was gone, it was likely to be the refuge for Gorbachev's enemies. As in Germany, the Soviet KGB apparently passed the word to the local secret police: the government had to be replaced. There was already a substantial opposition movement, fuelled in part by Gorbachev's obvious adoption of the sort of ideas Dubcek had been quashed for in 1968. The Czech secret police apparently thought that the government would resign in the face of a massive public demonstration, so it covertly organized one.[43] On 17 November 1989 many Czechs demonstrated in central Prague in honor of a student, Jan Opletal, killed half a century before by the Nazis. The demonstration was too peaceful to force a change of government. Clearly it had official backing; only a little more than a year before, police had broken up a demonstration in memory of the August 1968 invasion. This time the secret police spread the rumor that a student had been killed (later it was said that he had been a secret police-man, spirited out of the crowd). The result was more like what was wanted, a larger demonstration the next day. The Charter 77 dissidents met and formed Civic Forum, an opposition group.

As in Germany, the government found that there was no way to stop short of surrender. By this time the Czechs knew the Soviets would not intervene. The government began talks with Civic Forum almost immediately, and Party Secretary Milos Jakes soon resigned. Four days later the Party surrendered its "leading posi-tion" and courses in Marxism-Leninism were no longer mandatory in Czech uni-versities. Early in December the Communist premier resigned. Gustav Husak, who had been installed in power following the 1968 invasion, had to swear in the first Czech cabinet since 1948 without a Communist majority. He then resigned.

The Communist positions in Poland and Hungary collapsed completely at about this time. In October 1989 the Hungarians announced constitutional changes which eliminated the "leading role" of the Communist Party and removed the world "People's" from the country's name. In Poland Jaruzelski resigned as president the following month; the next year Walesa won the country's first pres-idential election by a landslide. The Hungarians held their own free elections in March 1990. By this time the Bulgarian government had also collapsed; its long-time head, Todor Zhivkov, resigned on 10 November.

In Romania, Ceausescu held out, depending on his own power base. On 24 November he had himself unanimously reelected as Party secretary. In theory he should have been more immune than any of the other candidates to Soviet pres-sure. However, by this time it was clear that the West could offer a great deal, and that the Soviets would no longer punish any bloc government that went in their direction. Ceausescu's own secret police overthrew him, executing him (as one of the very few victims of a seismic shift) on 25 December 1989. It is not clear whether the KGB was involved (Ceausescu had opposed perestroika). Albania's iso-lationist Communist regime held onto its power for a few more years.

Gorbachev seems to have blundered into these changes. Without quite understanding how, he lost an immense empire in Eastern Europe. At the beginning of 1989 it had seemed entirely stable. At the end of the year the empire was in shambles, and it was clearly moving out of Soviet control. Everywhere, Communist governments were abandoning power. Yet nowhere, except perhaps in Romania, had shots been fired. An empire held by force for over forty years had been allowed to collapse.

With the end of Soviet rule, the Warsaw Pact collapsed. Many in the West would date the end of the Cold War to the collapse of the Berlin Wall and of the Communist regimes in Central Europe. Some saw Gorbachev's hand in these events, speeding them along. To many Russians, the withdrawal from Eastern Europe smelled more of defeat than of careful policy. The empire had been the tangible symbol of the Soviets' very expensive World War II victory, which for more than four decades had been a unifying force in an extremely diverse Soviet Union. Now it was being thrown away.

This was not quite the end of the Cold War. As Eisenhower had pointed out, once the Soviets had massive numbers of nuclear weapons, whether or not they ruled Eastern Europe had little military significance. The loss of Eastern Europe did drastically reduce the KGB's ability to mount and support terrorism (much of its support had come from East Germany and Czechoslovakia), but the core of Soviet military power remained. For the moment, Gorbachev was friendly, but he could change, or he could be deposed. Moreover, none of his tinkering with the Soviet economy had had much impact on military production.

For years, Soviet dissidents had been sentenced to prison with the homily that they had to be insane to imagine fighting something as permanent as Soviet power. Now Soviet power was clearly sinking. Dissidence was no longer at all irrational. To an ambitious man in the Soviet Union, the Party no longer offered much of a future. It might be far better to ride anti-Party sentiment.

By this time Reagan had been succeeded by his vice president, George Bush. Bush was a veteran Soviet-watcher, having been director of central intelligence during the Team B episode. He understood just how delicate the situation was. Gorbachev could still kill reform, accepting Western discomfort or even enmity as his price. Reforming czars had often turned into despots. Gorbachev kept vacillating; he could not seem to follow any consistent pattern. Bush had to convince him that the West was friendly and would remain so. That might help convince Gorbachev that he had something vital to lose if he turned back towards classic Soviet methods of repression.

President Bush understood that Gorbachev had no real idea of where he was heading. He certainly did not realize that his path towards constitutional government entailed a real possibility that he could be voted out of office. Thus Bush and his associates continued to assure Gorbachev that everything depended on him, even after his great rival, Boris Yeltsin, became a serious contender for power. The Western press roundly criticized the Bush administration for what looked like sycophancy. In retrospect, the alternative was to show Gorbachev exactly where he was heading, by treating his rival as a likely replacement. Surely Gorbachev would then have derailed reform.

Elections to the 1989 Soviet Congress were held in March 1989. Deputies from the three Baltic states demanded a commission to reveal the secret protocols to the 1939 Hitler-Stalin Pact, under which the Germans had given their countries to Stalin. The official line was still that their countries had voluntarily joined the union. The members of the commission thought that an admission that the protocols existed would relieve growing tension in the Baltic republics. Gorbachev vacillated, but the protocols were revealed anyway in the Congress of Deputies.[44] Gorbachev was learning anew that he could not control the elected Congress.

On 11 January 1990, Gorbachev arrived in Vilnius to find a crowd of three hundred thousand, holding placards demanding that the Soviets leave. When he refused to end the fifty-year marriage between Lithuania and the rest of the Soviet Union, a Lithuanian quipped that "We were never married, we were raped." On 11 March 1990 the Lithuanians' Supreme Council (ex–Supreme Soviet) voted unanimously to declare independence. Estonia had already declared popular sovereignty on 16 November 1988 and independence on 2 February 1990. Latvia declared sovereignty on 28 July 1989 and independence on 4 May 1990.

Gorbachev may well have seen his democratic concessions as little more than a tactic to outflank his political opponents within the Communist Party, first the conservatives and then the liberals led by Boris Yeltsin. The concessions could be withdrawn later.[45] Gorbachev established the post of president outside the Party apparatus. In December 1990, as conditions worsened, he extracted emergency powers from the Congress of People's Deputies; they were immediately put to use. Joint military-police patrols of cities began, and the police and the KGB were formally given the right to search offices without warrant and to confiscate documents as they liked. On this basis troops moved into the Baltic republics in January 1991. Gorbachev's foreign minister, Eduard Shevardnadze, resigned, charging that Gorbachev was preparing to become dictator. To the extent that, paradoxically, the Communist Party acted as a brake on Gorbachev (and the Congress was largely powerless), Shevardnadze may have been right. Events certainly soon showed that Gorbachev had little willingness to tolerate real opposition. He was particularly hostile to Boris Yeltsin, then president of the Russian Republic, whom he had previously banished from the Moscow government—and who had been popularly elected. In Minsk in March 1991 Gorbachev revived the old Communist tactic of charging that his opponents, such as Yeltsin, were tools of foreign governments.

The 1990 congressional delegation from the three Baltic republics refused to recognize the legitimacy of the Soviet government itself.[46] Its members would sit as observers, but they refused to vote. As was his custom, Gorbachev tried to have it both ways, sending in the KGB while claiming that he had been asleep when the decision was taken.[47] He blockaded Lithuania, and in January 1991 his troops took the Vilnius television station, killing fourteen people. However, he could not get the Lithuanians to surrender. Gorbachev faced similar problems in Estonia and Latvia. He began to realize that he had to surrender some sovereignty to them.

Gorbachev had himself declared president of the Soviet Union in 1990. He had the Soviet constitution amended to remove the Party's monopoly on political power. As speech became freer, Gorbachev discovered that many Soviet citizens had no real use for the Soviet Union. Nationalist pressure was clearly not limited to the Baltic states. Ukrainian nationalism grew enormously after what was seen as a betrayal at Chernobyl. The Party's great historical crime against the Ukraine was the horrific famine Stalin had imposed as part of collectivization.

Despite Gorbachev's discomfort, he could not lightly squelch openness. Not only did it offer Gorbachev the possibility of some kind of economic revival, but it had also come to be the West's only guarantee that Gorbachev's claims of détente were worth believing. Gorbachev wavered. This was not what he had expected when he bravely opened up his system. It seemed that no one in the Baltic republics was at all grateful for what had been granted; all wanted much more, too much more. Gorbachev called in KGB troops. They could not do nearly enough in the glare of Western publicity, which was inescapable under glasnost. Western support was now too important to sacrifice lightly. Gorbachev seems not to have had the stomach for the sort of gross repressive measures a Stalin might have chosen. Nothing less would have stopped the Baltic independence movement. Gorbachev had to let the Baltic states go.

However, to Gorbachev's surprise, even old-line Communist bosses in the republics wanted more independence. They suddenly scented an opportunity to break away from the power which in the past Moscow had always wielded. In some cases, particularly in Central Asia, the most important attraction of greater freedom of action may have been a guarantee that traditional corruption and nepotism could now flourish unpunished by any reformist regime in Moscow.

Gorbachev found a formula to combine independence with some degree of coordination, particularly in defense: The republics would form a new Union of Sovereign States. The rump of the Party could accept neither the treaty with the republics nor any of the other trappings of openness that Gorbachev had provided. Gorbachev's opponents had taken a very long time to realize just how dangerous he was. His opponents had been unhappy for a long time, but they could say that Gorbachev's reforms were more form than substance. The armed forces had not been badly hurt, and the military industry was still functioning. It seemed that nothing permanent had been done which a successor better attuned to past Soviet themes could not undo.

The treaty with the republics (essentially, freeing them from central control) was the last straw because it would have undermined the Soviet military-industrial base. When Stalin had first created it, he had deliberately spread plants all over the

Soviet Union, each dependent on others in different republics. Without an integrated Soviet economy, almost no sophisticated weaponry at all could be made. Existing weapons could not be maintained for very long. Soviet military power would collapse in short order. It is not clear that Gorbachev realized just how drastic a move he was planning.

A coup was prepared. It should have worked roughly the way the anti-Khrushchev coup worked; the Party chairman would gracefully accept removal by the senior members of the Party. On 19 August, with Gorbachev away in the Crimea, the plotters announced a state of emergency. He had been just about to return to sign the treaty with the republics. The plotters did not realize how far Gorbachev's revolution had gone, probably against his own intentions. Glasnost had worked. Ordinary citizens had learned to love their freedom too much. Many of them rallied to the elected Russian Republic president, Boris Yeltsin. Soviet army units refused to storm his headquarters, the White House. The coup collapsed within a week.

Yeltsin had clearly demonstrated his own political power. There was an implication that Gorbachev had seen, and perhaps even helped engender, the coup as a way of stopping reforms that were getting out of hand, without having the West blame him. Yeltsin demanded that the Communist Party, which had fomented the coup, be outlawed. Gorbachev, who had been elected only by the Soviet Congress—itself chosen in a largely rigged election—lamely said that he could not abandon his faith, Communism. He had clearly lost most of his power. On 6 November Yeltsin abolished the Communist Party in Russia, confiscating its property. Eventually he put it on trial for its role in the coup.

In the aftermath of the failed coup, on 6 September 1991, the new State Council of the USSR voted unanimously to recognize the independence of the three Baltic republics. Then the others began to declare independence, beginning with Ukraine on 24 August (subject to a 1 December referendum). Most of the republics agreed to negotiate a new union (later confederation) treaty with Gorbachev, but late in November negotiations broke down completely. The deathblow was the Ukrainian decision for independence after the December referendum.[48] Gorbachev himself was swept away, because he was now president of a nonexistent country.

The Cold War was over because the Soviet system, with its inherent hostility, was dead. Gorbachev's opponents had been right. As long as the state survived, he could be dismissed as a transient phenomenon. For all of their worship of Gorbachev, the Western powers should have known that it was always possible that he would vanish from the scene, to be replaced by someone more like Brezhnev, or even more like Stalin. When Gorbachev left, Russia began slow and uncertain progress towards a system in which individuals would feel themselves bound by laws, not simply by the will of the monolithic Party.

Once the Soviet Union had broken up, its military industries, the backbone of its physical power, began to shrivel. In the past, they had survived by command:

the necessary materials and subcomponents had all been supplied from the different republics. Now the republics were separate sovereign countries, and the manufacturers had to survive economically. They had to demand cash for the components other plants needed. With the Soviet cash economy largely dead, that proved extremely difficult. Plants had built up large stocks of components, so the impact of dissolution was delayed. Even so, it was inevitable. The system that had demanded frequent overhauls and modernization could do neither. None of the successor countries could spend the sort of economic effort on defense that the Soviet Union had, because none of the governments could command resources to a similar extent.

Mikhail Gorbachev seems to have been squarely responsible for the collapse. He never understood that his state was built on terror, not on any kind of popular support. Few if any Russians saw the Party as anything but a self-promoting, utterly selfish parasite. They might later regret the loss of order, and the loss of what seemed to be a reasonable degree of economic security; but they were also uncomfortably aware of just how much the "bosses" had stolen. When the crisis came, few rushed to defend the Party.

In the wake of collapse, the remnants of the Party still retained considerable control over the economy, and they managed to steal whatever they could, allying themselves with criminals to form what Russians called the mafia. The military industrialists survived, as did the vast stock of weapons built up to fight World War III (though it could not be maintained). What died was the Party's ingrained need to expand beyond Soviet borders, to eliminate the rival political and social system of the West. Many Russians blamed the West for their misfortunes, and many nostalgically remembered the time when Russian whispers would make the West tremble, but they lacked the ideological dimension that had made the Soviet assault on the West so effective.

The disaster recalled the collapse of the czarist state, whose rulers also did not understand just how much their system depended on military/police prestige (i.e., largely terror) and how little on popular support.

There is also an eerie parallel to the end of World War I. In October 1918 Marshal Erich Ludendorff, the military dictator of Germany, suffered what amounted to a nervous breakdown. His last great offensive had failed; the Allies were counterattacking successfully. He told the kaiser that the game was up, that Germany might as well surrender. The word spread. Germans who had borne terrible sacrifices in hopes of victory suddenly saw that it had all been a waste. Within a few days, however, Ludendorff realized that all was not lost. The German army could retreat into defensive positions, and could probably last at least through 1919. The longer the army lasted, the better the terms on which the war could be concluded. Unfortunately, by the time Ludendorff went to give the kaiser the good news, the damage had been done. Too many Germans had learned that they had lost.

The Soviet military leadership played Ludendorff's role by telling its master,

Gorbachev, that the game was over unless he managed drastic modernization. To do that, he found himself taking worse and worse risks, which ultimately proved fatal. Like Ludendorff, the military leadership came to realize that the situation was not quite so bad as it had seemed. "Star Wars" still lay well in the future, so the Soviet nuclear deterrent retained all or most of its value. That made the Western edge in "brilliant" weapons far less important. Meanwhile the results of Gorbachev's risk-taking (i.e., of accepting the military's initial advice) seemed worse and worse. His drastic remedies included telling too many people—including, because of glasnost, Soviet citizens—that the Cold War was over, that it had all been a dreadful mistake.

The collapse surprised the West, just as victory in 1918 had. Would firmer policies have caused it much earlier and thus cut our own costs and our agony? Ronald Reagan appeared at a particularly propitious time, when a maturing Western technology offered advantages out of proportion to the investment needed. A few years earlier a comparable investment would have bought only a better defense, probably not even up to the threat the Soviets presented. A decade later, the Soviets might have been able to buy the new technology from a demoralized West and thus avoid any need to reform their society to meet the challenge. After all, the reform that destroyed the Soviet system was unavoidable only because Soviet military industry could not match the new revolution in military affairs, not because the system was failing to maintain the Soviet standard of living. That failure in turn can probably be traced to Brezhnev's decision, a quarter century before, to allow Soviet military industrialists to get completely out of hand. Perhaps the Soviet Union lost the Cold War when its self-serving Party hacks disposed of Nikita Khrushchev in 1964.

Growing Western strength and confidence made it difficult for Gorbachev to choose alternatives that might have helped him protect the Party's power. That no one in the West realized just how decisive the offensive of the 1980s was likely to be was merely one more of the many ironies of the Cold War. Wars are messy, murky affairs. The winner is usually the side that makes fewer mistakes, not the side which perfectly executes a masterly strategy.

A case can be made that had the West *not* counterattacked in the 1980s, the correlation of forces might have tipped irretrievably in the Soviets' direction. That attack and counterattack generally occurred in very slow motion did not make them any less real.

The West won the Cold War. The Soviets did not merely lose interest in the competition. They lost the war, and they paid the usual price of defeat.

For the West, victory seemed strangely tasteless. Its main fruit, the end of direct Soviet threats to invade Western Europe and to atomize North America, brought little jubilation. These threats had persisted for so long that most people no longer thought about them. The same people were surprised that the world had become so much more unruly. If this was peace, what had war been? For the United States, the consequences of the way the Cold War ended are still being felt, and indeed are likely to continue to unroll for decades. Perhaps because the war was fought in very slow motion, the postwar period will be protracted.

Those most interested in the lessons of the end of the Cold War are the surviving Communist governments, in China, Cuba, North Korea, and Vietnam. Before the Soviet crash, both the Chinese and the Vietnamese apparently drew the lesson from the Soviet case that it is impossible to command an economy to produce military strength. Unfortunately, industries which seem vital to the military one year may be almost irrelevant a decade hence. Deng Xiaoping therefore decided to concentrate on building up the Chinese economy, with defense a secondary priority. That made particularly good sense as long as he held the "American card." He hoped to build up a strong economy by drastically relaxing state intervention. However, he could not (or would not) break the Party's hold on most Chinese industry. The patronage and corruption endemic to state industry in the Soviet Union are quite evident in China, and attempts to develop modern weaponry have been relatively unsuccessful. Deng's successors have talked reform, meaning attempts to make the Party-run industries truly efficient. They have drawn back because of the political consequences: firing loyal Party servants and, perhaps worse, creating a larger army of the unemployed.

China thus has the sort of mixed economy Gorbachev might have envisaged. It seems unlikely to be stable. In a way, it is a national equivalent of the sort of mixed system that proved unstable in Eastern Europe. Many Chinese citizens want Western goods; the supply of those goods keeps them more or less content. Some can earn the necessary hard currency via the reasonably efficient emerging Chinese private sector, which produces exportable goods. However, many more of those same citizens work for the government, and produce nothing really saleable. To pay them in usable currency, the central government has to tax the emerging sector.

This is goulash Communism on a vast scale, with about 15 percent of the Chinese economy paying the bills—just as the Soviet oil industry ultimately had to pay goulash Communism's bills. Perhaps the downturn in world, particularly Asian, markets will be for China what the crash in world oil prices was for the Soviets.

The serious problem is the Chinese Communist Party. As in the old Soviet Union, the Party attracts adherents because it offers patronage. When China was poor, it was enough that the Party had a monopoly on scarce luxuries. Now in effect it offers a license to steal. The Party is the law; it can squeeze any enterprise that wants to stay in business. That is in effect a tax, but it is not paid to the central government.

Certainly democracy was never on Deng's agenda, just as it was not really on Mikhail Gorbachev's. However, as Reagan realized, a free economy almost inevitably opens up politics. Although the Chinese tried to squelch their democrats at Tienanmen Square in 1989, they could not abandon the open economy, and presumably at some point they will have to face the consequences. The Party just cannot control a situation in which there is an alternative road to prosperity. For Deng, a mortal Soviet threat justified risking such a loss of power. Now that the Soviet Union is gone, national military efficiency may not be nearly as important as maintaining the Party's power. In that case, the free market may emerge as the Party's enemy. Perhaps the Party will soon conclude that it is time to send the entrepreneurs to a Chinese gulag.

In its search for legitimacy, the Chinese Communist Party now advertises itself as the guardian of Chinese sovereignty, ready to wipe out the humiliations of the past. If it is serious, it needs the sort of modern economy that can modernize a large but outdated military machine. The Chinese adventure in Vietnam in 1979 suggests an alternative. The Chinese, like Stalin, may delude themselves into imagining that they actually have an efficient modern military machine, without making the political sacrifices it entails. They may try to bluff their way, as they did when they fired a few rockets at Taiwan in 1996.

Something more than twenty years before the Soviet Union disintegrated, Mao commented that Khrushchev would never have fallen, had he had the sense to create a Stalin-like "cult of personality" around himself. Two decades later, Mao's successors may have wondered whether Gorbachev lost everything because he had not had the courage (or the sense) to use nationalism to hold his country together when Communism itself clearly no longer appealed. Gorbachev might well have retorted that he could not have afforded to play the nationalist card, because the Soviet Union was always so clearly a multinational state. Russians might well (and in fact did) react to a Russian nationalist message, but what of the Ukrainians or the Uzhbeks? The Soviets never did work out a way of satisfying the nationalism of the constituent nations, who, despite claims to the contrary, rightly considered themselves part of an empire run mainly by ethnic Russians. In the end, nationalism tore the country apart, because it helped propel the non-Russian republics right out of the Soviet Union. China, too, is a multinational empire, but it is a unitary state, the fiction being that all its regions are part of the same nation. Thus the nationalism evident in Tibet or Sinkiang is dismissed as subversion; the Chinese leadership is free to choose nationalism as an alternative to Communist ideology, where Gorbachev had no such choice. Now that the Soviet Union has broken apart, Russian politicians are of course free to appeal to a classic chauvinistic Russian nationalism.

In this sense Yugoslavia offers an interesting analogy to the Cold War Soviet state. Like the old Soviet Union, Tito's Yugoslavia was a multi-ethnic (multinational) state ruled largely by one of its ethnic constituents, the Serbs. Like the Soviet Union, Yugoslavia was a formally multinational state, each main ethnic (national) group having its own quasi-autonomous republic. Tito kept his country together partly by forbidding any appeal to nationalism within it. With Tito dead and his Communist ideology clearly discredited, appeals to nationalism became politicians' routes to power—and the recipe that tore Yugoslavia apart.

Nationalism would be a very threatening sort of salvation for the Chinese Communist Party. Serbia under Slobodan Milosevic may offer a frightening glimpse into just that sort of future. President Milosevic was a long-time *apparatchik* in the Yugoslav Communist government. In 1987 he realized that the Party's future was likely to be limited. By adopting a rabidly nationalist platform, he was able to gain supreme power in Serbia. As under Communism, he saw raw power as the only worthwhile goal. Social policies were only window dressing, and with the downfall of Communism they could easily be dropped. This concentration on simply retaining political power made it particularly difficult for other governments to deal with Milosevic. He was impervious to threats to damage those who supported him. Indeed, he apparently calculated that Western attacks on Serbians (first in Bosnia, then in Kosovo) would merely make him more popular. Presumably there are many former *apparatchiki* in the old Soviet Union who are watching Milosevic—and who plan to exploit much the same nationalist impulses.

The Vietnamese followed the Chinese semi-capitalist example in the late 1980s, probably because they wanted to defend themselves against China. It seems noteworthy that they pulled back from political and economic reform in the 1990s, probably precisely because their ruling Communist Party saw no point in giving up any of its power.

Cuba is an interesting case. When the Russians withdrew their aid, Fidel Castro announced a combination of austerity measures and a program to attract foreign capital, for example for tourism. Within a few years some of his economists were urging the virtues of a free market. By the fall of 1997 he had made his decision: Communism (i.e., continued Party rule) was more important than prosperity. Cubans would continue to experience revolutionary austerity. Since the United States obviously has no interest in invading, Cuba can make do without the imports needed to maintain serious defenses. Castro has seen too many newsreels of jubilant East European and Russian crowds pulling down Communist monuments.

The North Korean Communists chose Mao's path, relying on a nuclear bomb to hold off potential enemies. In 1999 they are holding onto power despite several years of serious famine, only reluctantly accepting food aid and making it quite clear that they will never open up their economy (apart from a small free trade zone in the north, on the Russian border). The situation is clearly unstable. Some Koreans are undoubtedly aware that the sudden fall of the Ceausescu regime in Romania opened the country to Western aid even though many Communists were able to retain power.

All four Communist countries must feel the shadow of Gorbachev's disaster and the West's victory.

NOTES

Abbreviations Used in the Notes

CIA   CIA Cold War Records.

CWIHP   Cold War International History Project of the Woodrow Wilson Center.

FRUS   Foreign Relations of the United States, an official series published by the State Department but including other papers, such as those of the National Security Council.

IDA   Institute for Defense Analysis.

JCS   The History of the Joint Chiefs of Staff.

NIEs   National Intelligence Estimates, coordinated by the CIA but including the views of the other intelligence agencies.

NSAM   National Security Action Memorandum.

NWD   Nuclear Weapons Databook.

PRO   British Public Record Office.

Chapter 1. War and Communism

1. See, e.g., Sarin and Dvoretsky, *Alien Wars,* 6, 19. Their most telling evidence is an account of a late-1937 Politburo meeting at which a directive to the Spanish government was drafted; the tone was that of a Party order to a district committee or a Soviet ministry, rather than to an allied government. Costello and Tsarev, *Dangerous Illusions,* make much the same point. Unfortunately, no account of Stalin's decision to try to make Spain into a satellite seems to have appeared.

2. Gaddis, *We Now Know,* 13.

3. See, e.g., P. Sudoplatov et al., *Special Tasks,* 102.

4. Raack, *Stalin's Road to the West,* particularly 21.

5. Pipes, *Russia under the Bolshevik Regime,* 155.

6. Ibid., 163.

7. R. J. Popplewell, "The KGB and the Control of the Soviet Bloc: The Case of East Germany," in *Knowing Your Friends,* ed. Alexander, 258.

8. Volkogonov, *Autopsy for an Empire,* 185.

9. Berezhkov, *At Stalin's Side,* 29.

10. Conquest, *Stalin: Breaker of Nations,* 173; Tucker, *Stalin in Power,* 230.

11. Conquest, *Stalin: Breaker of Nations,* 175.

12. Raack, *Stalin's Road to the West,* 17–18. Stalin initiated contacts with the Germans in October 1933 (Conquest, *Stalin: Breaker of Nations,* 217). Hitler made his own overtures beginning in March 1933, declaring his battle against Communists internal only (Tucker, *Stalin in Power,* 234).

13. Mastny, *The Cold War and Soviet Insecurity,* 14; Antonov-Ovseyenko, *The Time of Stalin,* 113.

14. Berezhkov, *At Stalin's Side,* 9–10, quoting Mikoyan.

15. See, for example, Antonov-Ovseyenko, *The Time of Stalin,* 84–104. He had access to the Khrushchev-era investigation of Stalin's crimes. According to Antonov-Ovseyenko (143), Khrushchev reported in 1956 that ninety-eight of the 139 members of the 1934 Central Committee were killed in 1936–38; some Soviet historians put the number at 110. One hundred eleven of the 138 members of the 1930 Congress were killed. See also Volkogonov, *Stalin: Triumph and Tragedy,* 207–9. P. Sudoplatov et al., *Special Tasks,* 50–56, argue, partly from the personal knowledge of their friends and relatives (members of the KGB and its predecessors), that Kirov's murder was an act of personal vengeance by a jealous husband (Kirov was a notorious womanizer), which Stalin exploited. The Party, which ironically demanded a very bourgeois kind of morality, could not admit to Kirov's behavior. No documents were ever found connecting Stalin to the murder. Stalin may still have been responsible; he could easily have arranged for the woman to seduce Kirov. Whether or not the husband shot Kirov, the scandal would have been a means to control Kirov. The woman involved was executed a few months after the murder.

16. Volkogonov, *Sem' vozhdei,* 275–340. Antonov-Ovseyenko, *The Time of Stalin,* 297–99, gives the flavor of the purge. His father having been shot, he lived in an apartment house reserved for children of "enemies of the people." Sometime in 1943 Beria observed that Stalin passed it every day en route to the Kremlin; what if one of the children living there decided to exact revenge? A trial was arranged. The children were all drilled in their parts in an imaginary plot against Stalin. Then it emerged that the woman who was to have thrown the bomb at Stalin's car did not have a window overlooking the street Stalin used. Everyone's part had to be changed. The trial proceeded, and everyone went into exile.

17. Not until ten years after Stalin's death was it permissible to publish documents about Ivan's terror (Antonov-Ovseyenko, *The Time of Stalin,* 159).

18. Ibid., 210–14.

19. Tucker, *Stalin in Power,* 527–28, gives some examples. Sergei Gorshkov became a rear admiral at thirty-one. Dmitri F. Ustinov was director of a Leningrad arms plant in 1937 and in 1941, aged thirty-three, became commissar for armaments. Leonid Brezhnev joined the Party in 1931; in 1939 he was head of the Dnepropetrovsk City Committee. His friend Konstantin U. Chernenko joined the same year, and in 1941, aged thirty, was head of the Krasnoyarsk Regional Party Committee. Yuri Andropov joined in 1939, and in 1940 (at twenty-six) was secretary to the *komsomol* of the Karelo-Finnish Republic.

20. Howson, *Arms for Spain,* 121–22, 146–52.

21. Ibid., 123.

22. Ibid., 239–45.

23. Raack, *Stalin's Road to the West,* 19.

24. Ibid., 24–27.

25. McDermott and Agnew, *The Comintern,* 192–203.

26. Raack,*Stalin's Road to the West,* 35.

27. Ibid., 31.

28. Bullock, *Hitler and Stalin: Parallel Lives,* 906.

29. G. Warner, "From 'Ally' to Enemy: Britain's Relations with the Soviet Union, 1941–1948," in *The Soviet Union and Europe,* ed. Gori and Pons, 296–97. See also Hyland, *The Cold War,* 37.

30. Raack, *Stalin's Road to the West,* 45.

31. Bullock, *Hitler and Stalin: Parallel Lives,* 749.

32. Berezhkov, *At Stalin's Side,* 46–47.

33. A. M. Filitov, "Problems of Post-War Construction in Soviet Foreign Policy Conceptions During World War II," in *The Soviet Union and Europe,* ed. Gori and Pons. The Maisky memorandum is also summarized by Zubok and Pleshakov, *Inside the Kremlin's Cold War,* 28–29.

34. E. Aga-Rossi and V. Zaslavsky, "The Soviet Union and the Italian Communist Party, 1944–1948," in *The Soviet Union and Europe,* ed. Gori and Pons, 162–63.

35. Ibid., 163.

36. Gaddis, *We Now Know,* 42; Zubok and Pleshakov, *Inside the Kremlin's Cold War,* 29.

37. Djilas, *Conversations with Stalin,* 113.

38. Kennedy-Pipe, *Stalin's Cold War,* 23–26.

39. Ibid., 53.

40. The secret protocol is in Hugh Thomas, *Armed Truce,* 560–61.

41. Bullock, *Hitler and Stalin: Parallel Lives,* 996.

42. Zubok and Pleshakov, *Inside the Kremlin's Cold War,* 53, citing Molotov's account of one of Stalin's sayings.

43. Djilas, *Conversations with Stalin,* 114–15.

Chapter 2. Stalin's Soviet Union

1. Pipes, *Russia under the Bolshevik Regime,* 452.

2. For Kennan's "long telegram" (February 1946) presenting this analysis, see FRUS (1946) 6:696–709. For his background, see Isaacson and Thomas, *The Wise Men,* particularly 140–78.

3. Zubok and Pleshakov, *Inside the Kremlin's Cold War,* 37, mention a 27 January 1946 secret police report that Soviet veterans were making anti-Soviet (i.e., anti-Stalin) remarks, clashing with local authorities, and even distributing anti-Soviet leaflets.

4. FRUS (1952–54) 8:962.

5. Volkogonov, *Autopsy for an Empire,* 67–71.

6. Of 750,000 *nomenklatura* positions in 1984, about three hundred thousand were controlled by the Party's Central Committee (Pryce-Jones, *The War That Never Was,* 47).

7. Pipes, *Russia under the Bolshevik Regime,* 403.

8. Recently obtained data in M. Lewin, "Stalin in the Mirror of the Other," in *Stalinism*

and Nazism, ed. Kershaw and Lewin, show the results. In early 1937, before the great purge, only 17.7 percent of regional Party secretaries had higher education, and 70.4 percent had only elementary education.

9. Volkogonov, *Stalin: Triumph and Tragedy,* 316–29.

10. Bellamy, *The Evolution of Modern Land Warfare,* 86–91.

11. See, e.g., B. Bonwetsch, "Stalin, the Red Army, and the 'Great Patriotic War,'" in *Stalinism and Nazism,* ed. Kernshaw and Lewin.

12. In Hungary, the worst case, 2,000 were executed, 150,000 imprisoned, and 350,000 expelled from the Party. In Czechoslovakia a total of 136,000 were imprisoned or executed (Dunbabin, *The Cold War,* 419).

13. Bullock, *Hitler and Stalin: Parallel Lives,* 1,053; P. Sudoplatov et al., *Special Tasks,* 298–307. According to the authors of *Special Tasks,* the anti-Semitic campaign was preliminary to a new purge in which Stalin, allied with Malenkov and Khrushchev, would have destroyed Beria and the old guard (Molotov, Voroshilov, and Mikoyan).

14. Radzinsky, *Stalin,* 560–62.

15. P. Sudoplatov et al., *Special Tasks,* 48.

16. For example, Murphy, Kondrashev, and Bailey, *Battleground Berlin,* 62–70, describe distorted reports on the evolving Berlin blockade crisis. The supposed British Foreign Office telegram on page 65 appears to be a fabrication or at least a distortion.

17. Bullock, *Hitler and Stalin: Parallel Lives,* 792, describes Stalin's refusal to credit Sorge's reports.

18. The hunt, described by Mangold, *Cold Warrior,* was led by James Jesus Angleton—whom Philby had thoroughly fooled when the latter was British intelligence liaison with the U.S. in 1949–51. Mangold argues that the experience with Philby inspired Angleton's almost paranoid attempt to catch supposed CIA moles (69). After Angleton's departure the CIA nearly destroyed any ability for self-investigation, and thus opened the way to spies such as Aldrich Ames

19. Gaddy, *The Price of the Past,* 34–37.

20. Pryce-Jones, *The War That Never Was,* 50–54.

21. Laqueur, *Europe in Our Time,* 220.

22. Ibid., 223.

23. FRUS (1955–57) 4:225.

24. Holmes, *The End of Communist Power,* 101–2.

25. Volkogonov, *Stalin: Triumph and Tragedy,* 166, estimated 8.5 to nine million affected, some of whom were exiled rather than killed immediately. Based on Ukrainian census figures for 1928 and 1939, Antonov-Ovseyenko, *The Time of Stalin,* 65, estimates a net population loss of about twelve million, but this includes people who would have been born had their parents not died when they did. The 1939 census was faked to conceal the effects of Stalin's purges, so Antonov-Ovseyenko's figures may be low.

26. Heller and Nekrich, *Utopia in Power,* 473.

Chapter 3. The West in 1945

1. Gaddis, *Strategies of Containment.*

2. See, for example, the rationale for resistance in the conclusions of the Clifford-Elsey report (24 September 1946) for President Truman in *Containment,* ed. Etzold and Gaddis,

65. See also JCS 1769/1 dated 29 April 1947, "United States Assistance to Other Countries from the Standpoint of National Security" (71–83).

3. Gaddis, *We Now Know*, 12.

4. Walker, *The Cold War*, 28–30.

5. Brands, *Inside the Cold War*, 66.

6. Powers, *Not Without Honor*, 183.

7. Hugh Thomas, *Armed Truce*, 195.

8. Kunz, *Butter and Guns*, 20–21.

9. Ibid., 8–10.

10. Hugh Thomas, *Armed Truce*, 71; for White's identification as an agent, see Venona material in Benson and Warner, *Venona*.

11. Gaddis, *We Now Know*, 193.

12. Kunz, *Butter and Guns*, 19–22, 27.

13. Ibid., 97–99, 113.

14. Ibid., 112.

15. Ibid., 192.

16. Kennedy-Pipe, *Stalin's Cold War*, 53–54.

17. Hugh Thomas, *Armed Truce*, 357–63.

18. Ibid., 422.

19. Ibid., 214.

20. Kunz, *Butter and Guns*, 72.

Chapter 4. The Nuclear Revolution in Warfare

1. See, e.g., NWD 1, 28 n. 5.

2. Lewis, *Changing Direction*, 234; Laming, *V-Bombers*, 17. The Joint Technical Warfare Committee created in November 1943 made these estimates; its study of the future of warfare was led by Sir Henry Tizard, a very senior scientist who had been deeply involved in prewar and wartime work on air defense. Lewis gives a map and a list of groups of Soviet cities which would have to be attacked (frontispiece, 357–58). He also gives the corresponding list of British targets (231, 358).

3. See, e.g., Dinerstein, *War and the Soviet Union*, which was based on contemporary RAND studies.

4. P. Sudoplatov et al., *Special Tasks*, 209–10.

5. Rosenberg, "Toward Armageddon," 119–20.

6. Walker, *The Cold War*, 361.

7. Gaddis, *We Now Know*, 90.

8. Botti, *The Long Wait*, 28–29.

9. FRUS (1949) 1:419–22.

10. Botti, *The Long Wait*, 75–77.

11. Ibid., 74.

12. IDA, 9.

Chapter 5. Initial Probes

1. Hoopes and Brinkley, *Driven Patriot*, 261.

2. Hugh Thomas, *Armed Truce*, 121.

3. Rogow, *James Forrestal*, 331.

4. Hugh Thomas, *Armed Truce*, 131–36.

5. Embarrassingly, it proved difficult to locate the U.S. copies.

6. Walker, *The Cold War*, 30.

7. Kent, *British Imperial Strategy*, 19–20.

8. J. Kent and J. W. Young, "The 'Western Union' Concept and British Defence Policy, 1947–1948," in *British Intelligence and the Cold War*, ed. Aldrich.

9. A. Gorst, "'We Must Cut Our Coat According to Our Cloth': The Making of British Defence Policy, 1945–1948," in *British Intelligence and the Cold War*, ed. Aldrich.

10. Hugh Thomas, *Armed Truce*, 187; the joint declaration is on 558–59.

11. Kuhns, *Assessing the Soviet Threat*, 89–90, is an excerpt from the 8 November 1946 Weekly Summary prepared by the CIA: "The Communist electoral pattern, so successfully delineated in Yugoslavia and Bulgaria, will be repeated with only minor variations on 17 November when the Rumanian [*sic*] people vote in their first post-war election. The Groza [Communist] government, although faced with an opposition conservatively estimated at 75 percent of the electorate, is determined to win an 85 percent victory. It has accordingly conducted a campaign of violence and terrorism."

12. S. Fischer-Galati, "The Communist Takeover of Rumania: A Function of Soviet Power," in *Communist Takeovers*, ed. Hammond; JCS 1:28–29.

13. N. Oren, "A Revolution Administered: The Sovietization of Bulgaria," in *Communist Takeovers*, ed. Hammond.

14. Walker, *The Cold War*, 35.

15. Zubok and Pleshakov, *Inside the Kremlin's Cold War*, 48, quoting Stalin at a 4 June 1945 meeting of Comintern veterans being sent to set up the government of East Germany.

16. Hugh Thomas, *Armed Truce*, 304.

17. Ibid., 299.

18. Ibid., 305.

19. D. G. Kousalas, "The Greek Communists Tried Three Times—and Failed," in *Communist Takeovers*, ed. Hammond.

20. Hugh Thomas, *Armed Truce*, 303.

21. JCS 1: 41–52.

22. S. S. Lotarski, "The Communist Takeover in Poland," in *Communist Takeovers*, ed. Hammond; U.S. reaction is in JCS 1: 31–33. Kuhns, *Assessing the Soviet Threat*, 95, is a 3 January 1947 excerpt from the CIA's Weekly Summary, describing the run-up to the first post-war Polish election, scheduled for 19 January. It would be little different from elections that had swept left-wing regimes to victory in Bulgaria and Romania: "The Polish Government has flagrantly disregarded the Potsdam agreement." According to the CIA, Vice Premier Mikolajczyk's Peasant Party was backed by 70 percent of the electorate—but would be allowed no more than 25 percent of the vote. Communist tactics had included mass arrests of opposition leaders and candidates, restriction of public speech and assembly, intimidation, and simple election rigging. These were the data President Truman received.

23. Hugh Thomas, *Armed Truce*, 155.

24. Woods and Jones, *Dawning of the Cold War*, 33–34.

25. Converse, "U.S. Plans," 154.

26. Martel, *Lend-Lease*, 169.

27. Ibid., 170.
28. Ibid., 181.
29. Ibid., 177.
30. Ibid., 179.
31. Ibid., 180.
32. Ibid., 195.
33. Walker, *The Cold War,* 21.
34. Hugh Thomas, *Armed Truce,* 183–86.
35. Walker, *The Cold War,* 46.
36. Martel, *Lend-Lease,* 215.
37. JCS 1: 82–85, 96–99.
38. Converse, "U.S. Plans," 174.
39. S. G. Holtsmark, "The Limits to Soviet Influence: Soviet Diplomats and the Pursuit of Strategic Interests in Norway and Denmark, 1944–1947," in *The Soviet Union and Europe,* ed. Gori and Pons.
40. Hugh Thomas, *Armed Truce,* 133–35.
41. Ibid., 67.
42. G.-H. Soutou, "France," in *The Origins of the Cold War in Europe,* ed. Reynolds, 99.
43. Ibid., 100–101.
44. Hugh Thomas, *Armed Truce,* 364.
45. Ibid., 370.
46. Soutou, "France," 100.
47. Ibid., 101.
48. Ibid., 102.
49. JCS 1:108–20.
50. The U.S. services were not yet unified, but the wartime organization of the service chiefs, the Joint Chiefs, was responsible for war planning.
51. Hugh Thomas, *Armed Truce,* 199. He compared Stalin's policies to Hitler's. See also Warner, "From 'Ally' to Enemy."
52. Warner, "From 'Ally' to Enemy," 301.
53. Hugh Thomas, *Armed Truce,* 163, 211; Gaddis, *The United States,* 88–89. The most striking case of reluctance to spy on the Soviets was the Roosevelt administration's insistence in December 1944 that the OSS turn over to the Soviets code and cipher material obtained from the Finns (Benson and Warner, *Venona,* xviii).
54. See, e.g., Hugh Thomas, *Armed Truce,* 71, 127.
55. Document 13 in Benson and Warner, *Venona.*
56. Hugh Thomas, *Armed Truce,* 96.
57. Klehr and Radosh, *The Amerasia Spy Case.* Prosecution was difficult because the FBI's evidence was derived from illegal break-ins and wiretaps. The FBI counted on confessions, but they were not forthcoming.
58. Powers, *Not Without Honor,* 195.
59. Moynihan, *Secrecy,* 70–72.
60. West and Tsarev, *The Crown Jewels,* 181–82; Weinstein and Vassiliev, *The Haunted Wood,* 286.
61. Moynihan, *Secrecy,* 74.
62. Weinstein and Vassiliev, *The Haunted Wood,* 285.

Chapter 6. Open War

1. Hugh Thomas, *Armed Truce,* 7–13.
2. Ibid., 97.
3. The "long telegram" of 22 February 1946 is in FRUS (1946) 6:696–709.
4. Chuev, *Conversations with Stalin,* 63–64, reporting a 14 January 1975 conversation.
5. Ibid., 20, reporting a 7 July 1976 conversation.
6. Ibid., 59, reporting a 28 November 1974 conversation.
7. Ibid., 65, reporting a 4 November 1978 conversation.
8. Ibid., 71, reporting a 1 May 1981 conversation.
9. Powers, *Not Without Honor,* 209.
10. Ibid., 211.
11. According to ibid., 328, in the *New York Times* for 27 April 1966.
12. Clifford and Holbrooke, *Counsel to the President,* 99–108. By December 1946 Churchill's points had been so well accepted that he wrote that "if I made the Fulton speech today it would be criticized as consisting of platitudes."
13. G.-H. Soutou, "General de Gaulle and the Soviet Union, 1943–1945: Ideology or European Equilibrium," in *The Soviet Union and Europe,* ed. Gori and Pons, 301.
14. Warner's 2 April 1946 memorandum is reproduced in Lewis, *Changing Direction,* 359–63.
15. Warner, "From 'Ally' to Enemy," 304.
16. JCS 1:161; the JCS memo was submitted to Clark Clifford to feed into the Clifford-Elsey report.
17. When the previous draft was voted in 1940, the United States was still at peace but Europe was at war.
18. Tsouras, *Changing Orders,* 15.
19. For the origin of this idea, see Pisani, *The CIA and the Marshall Plan,* 74.
20. Converse, "U.S. Plans," 204.
21. Leffler, *A Preponderance of Power,* 112–13. See also A. Danchev, "In the Back Room: Anglo-American Defence Cooperation, 1945–1951," in *British Intelligence and the Cold War,* ed. Aldrich.
22. Baylis, *Anglo-American Defense Relations,* 69.
23. Converse, "U.S. Plans," 217.
24. Botti, *The Long Wait,* 25.
25. JCS 1:149–71.
26. For the navy's strategic concepts, see Palmer, *Origins of the Maritime Strategy.*
27. Rhodes, *Dark Sun,* 283–84.
28. Nitze, *From Hiroshima to Glasnost,* 56–57.
29. A. A. Ulunian, "The Soviet Union and the 'Greek Question,'" in *The Soviet Union and Europe,* ed. Gori and Pons.
30. The deal was approved while Bevin, the foreign secretary, was absent in Moscow (Hugh Thomas, *Armed Truce,* 200–201). Probably the key was that Sir Stafford Cripps, a very left-leaning Labourite, was president of the Board of Trade. He had been expelled from the Labour Party in 1939 for advocating a popular front and had served as wartime ambassador to Moscow. According to the cabinet office file in the PRO (PREM 8/345), an ad hoc

Ministerial Committee (the under secretaries of state for the Foreign Office, Air Ministry, and Ministry of Supply) opposed the sale. U.S. Secretary of State Byrnes personally opposed it (as well as a sale of obsolescent military aircraft—Mosquitoes and Spitfires—to Czechoslovakia), and Prime Minister Attlee was "anxious not to get completely out of step with the Americans on this matter." By this time the engines were three years old, and production licenses had been sold or were on offer to France, Switzerland, and Turkey, of which France and Turkey were considered security risks. The British considered the key technology to be the method of producing the Nimonic turbine blade alloy, which insured long operating life (which could be obtained only by disclosure, not by examination of a complete engine). The Soviets were apparently more interested in the configuration, which they could get simply by copying an engine; short engine life was quite acceptable. The chiefs of staff opposed a manufacturing license rather than export of the engines alone. Cripps argued that, since the engines were already being exported, it was futile to put them on the secret list. Attlee therefore approved the sale. Cripps met with Attlee before cabinet on 26 September 1946. Remarkably, British cabinet papers for 1946 show no entry for the sale.

31. Cornish, *British Military Planning,* 98–99.

32. Warner, "From 'Ally' to Enemy," 301.

33. Bevin had sought an alliance with France since entering office (Bullock, *Ernest Bevin,* 357).

34. Ambassador Walter Bedell Smith's account of the interview is in FRUS (1946) 6:763.

35. Zubok and Pleshakov, *Inside the Kremlin's Cold War,* 37–38.

36. Clifford and Holbrooke, *Counsel to the President,* 109–13, 123–29; the paper is in Krock, *Memoirs,* 421–82.

37. Henry Wallace must be the great might-have-been of the Cold War. Had Roosevelt renominated him in 1944, the president's death in April 1945 would have left a strongly pro-Soviet U.S. president in office. Although events probably would have led to some sort of Cold War, Wallace most likely would not have pursued Truman's bold initiatives, such as the Marshall Plan. Without them, Western Europe would have fared much worse in 1947–48. The Communists probably would have come to power in France and in Italy. As it was, in 1944 key Democratic Party bosses, with Roosevelt's tacit support, dropped Wallace from the 1944 ticket, not because of his Communist sympathies, but because he was considered a political liability due to his personal religious views. Soon after he had chosen Wallace as vice president in 1940, Roosevelt learned of his embarrassing, wooly-headed fascination with exotic religious cults. The Republicans planned to use letters Wallace had written to his "guru" as ammunition in the 1940 campaign; they were headed off only when the Democrats threatened to expose an ongoing adulterous affair on the part of their own candidate, Wendell Wilkie. Roosevelt apparently concluded that his choice had been a mistake, but he could not afford to withdraw Wallace's name after the Democratic convention. As another example of Wallace's wholehearted support for Stalin, in April 1947 he said that "it would be unfortunate for world peace if anything happens inside Russia to upset its system of government at the present time." During the 1948 presidential campaign, Wallace said that, if elected, he would choose Harry Dexter White as his secretary of the treasury (Haynes and Klehr, *Venona,* 139). One of his close foreign policy advisors was Lawrence Duggan (Haynes and Klehr, *Venona,* 202). By 1948 both men were under suspicion of being Soviet agents (a contemporary news account described Wallace's April 1948 choice of White as "startling").

Both Wallace and White were strongly defended at the time, but Venona intercepts show that both men not only were secret Communists but also Soviet spies (see Haynes and Klehr, *Venona,* 138–45, 201–4). For details of Wallace's career, see Arnold Beichman, "In a Smoke-Filled Room . . . Stalin's Defeat in 1944: A Look back at Henry Wallace's Ouster as Vice-President," Working Paper I-94-10 in International Studies of the Hoover Institution, Stanford University (August 1994). This paper also appeared in reduced form in the *National Review* for 1 August 1994. Beichman was a newspaperman in 1944, well connected with senior Democratic politicians, and also with figures in the Communist Party of the United States. After Truman fired him, Wallace decided to run for president in 1948. It is clear from a 10 April 1947 memorandum (an analysis of the current political situation by Morris Childs, a member of the politburo of the American party) reproduced in this book (265–69) that the third party was a Communist initiative, and that Wallace had to be persuaded to join it. The Soviet reply to Childs, also reproduced, was that the Party itself could not hope to challenge the major parties, that success would depend upon unifying the "progressive" movement—i.e., on something like a popular front. Note that the Communists fielded no candidate of their own in 1948, since they were supporting Wallace. For the Communist role in the 1948 Progressive Party campaign, see Klehr, Haynes, and Anderson, *The Soviet World of American Communism,* 258, 266. In fact Wallace gained only 2.3 percent of the national vote. Truman found the "Dixiecrats"—Democrats who defected to protest his support for civil rights—a far more serious challenge. Perhaps disillusioned by Communist interference in the 1948 campaign, Wallace turned against the Party; in 1950 he supported American participation in the Korean War and blamed Stalin for the Cold War. By that time he was no longer an important public figure.

38. Warner, "From 'Ally' to Enemy," 302.
39. Ibid., 305.
40. L. Ia. Gibianskii, "The Soviet-Yugoslav Conflict and the Soviet Bloc," in *The Soviet Union and Europe,* ed. Gori and Pons, particularly 229–30.
41. JCS 1:111.
42. Ibid., 120–23.
43. Warner, "From 'Ally' to Enemy," 304.
44. This analogy is drawn in JCS 1:133.
45. Soutou, "France," 103.
46. Ibid., 104.

Chapter 7. The Marshall Plan and NATO

1. Kunz, *Butter and Guns,* 31–36; for the struggle to convince Congress, see 37–46.
2. P. Sudoplatov et al., *Special Tasks,* 285–94.
3. Ibid., 293, dates Stalin's disenchantment with Jewish alliances abroad to the second half of 1946. In the authors' view, Stalin was interested in anti-Semitism only for the political leverage it could provide.
4. Mastny, *The Cold War and Soviet Insecurity,* 28.
5. Ibid., 28.
6. Gaddis, *We Now Know.*
7. Ibid., 42.

8. S. Pons, "A Challenge Let Drop: Soviet Foreign Policy, the Cominform, and the Italian Communist Party, 1947–1948," in *The Soviet Union and Europe,* ed. Gori and Pons.

9. Mastny, *The Cold War and Soviet Insecurity,* 29.

10. P. Ignotus, "The First Two Communist Takeovers in Hungary: 1919 and 1948," in *Communist Takeovers,* ed. Hammond.

11. J. Baylis, "Britain and the Formation of NATO," in *The Origins of NATO,* ed. Joseph Smith, 10.

12. Bullock, *Ernest Bevin,* 517, gives extracts from the cabinet paper on which the speech was based.

13. M. H. Folly, "The British Military and the Making of the North Atlantic Treaty," in *The Origins of NATO,* ed. Joseph Smith, 34; Cornish, *British Military Planning,* 115, 118.

14. P. Sudoplatov et al., *Special Tasks,* 233–35.

15. Zubok and Pleshakov, *Inside the Kremlin's Cold War,* 118, quote Molotov: Finland would have been "an open wound." K. Devlin, "Finland in 1948: The Lessons of a Crisis," in *Communist Takeovers,* ed. Hammond, suggests that the Soviets were simply frightened off. J. Nevakivi, "The Soviet Union and Finland after the War, 1944–1953," in *The Soviet Union and Europe,* ed. Gori and Pons, based on Zhdanov's papers, explains why Finland was not occupied in 1944–45 and points out that an invasion would have come just after the Czech coup, which had already alarmed the West. Hanhimaki, *Containing Coexistence,* 43, points out that the success of the Prague coup in February 1948 encouraged Finnish Communists to call in March for a similar coup—which mobilized forces against them and thus made a coup much more difficult to execute. In the July 1948 election the Communists were soundly defeated. In May Stalin had ordered the Finnish Communists to abandon strikes intended to destabilize the state (44). Hanhimaki argues that after the Prague coup the Soviets feared that a similar coup in Finland would have drawn a drastic Western reaction and might have propelled Sweden out of her neutrality (45). In 1948 NATO was a possibility rather than a reality. It was enough to neutralize Finland sufficiently that it could not be used as a base to attack the Soviet Union.

16. Popplewell, "The KGB and the Control of the Soviet Bloc," 255.

17. Kunz, *Butter and Guns,* 47.

18. JCS 4:145–46.

19. For example, although the air force did not receive any B-36 heavy bombers until well after the end of the war, the first ninety-five were bought with FY44 money (after which no more were bought until FY49). Wartime funds also paid for first-generation jet fighters.

20. Air force bomber procurement amounted to seventy-three B-36D/F bombers (and earlier versions upgraded to this standard); the first fifteen production B-47 jet bombers; the last 132 (of 222) B-50Ds (B-29 successors); and the two prototype B-52s. Other purchases included 561 F-80Cs; 410 F-84Es and the F-84F prototype; 233 F-86 Saberjets (up from 188 in FY48); the first forty-eight production F-89 Scorpion jet night fighters; and all 110 F-94A night fighters.

21. FRUS (1949) 1:259–67, an 18 August 1948 report by the SANACC (State-Army-Navy Coordinating Committee) Subcommittee for Rearmament.

22. Futrell, *Ideas, Concepts, Doctrine,* 204. For the work of the Finletter Commission (President's Air Policy Commission), which reported on 30 December 1947, see 224–30.

23. The careers of these aircraft overlapped. The F-84 became a fighter-bomber when

the F-86 replaced it as an interceptor, and the F-86 was similarly downgraded when the F-100 appeared.

24. Feis, *From Trust to Terror,* 296.

25. Jean Edward Smith, *Lucius D. Clay,* 467–68.

26. FRUS (1949) 1: 275.

27. Zubok and Pleshakov, *Inside the Kremlin's Cold War,* 51.

28. JCS 2:283–303.

29. Cornish, *British Military Planning,* 17–19.

30. Ibid., 25.

31. Kent and Young, "The 'Western Union' Concept."

32. Soutou, "France," 105.

33. Baylis, "Britain and the Formation of NATO."

34. JCS 2:132–33, 139.

35. E. M. Grove, "The Myth of the Postwar 'Ten Year Plan,'" *Journal of the Royal United Services Institute* (December 1994); Cornish, *British Military Planning,* 71–85. See also Lewis, *Changing Direction,* which makes it clear that British defense thinking in 1946–47 focussed on a medium-term five-year plan (1947–51) and a longer-term plan (1952–57). According to Lewis, 281, in November 1946 the British estimated that the Russians might have no more than 5 atomic bombs by the end of 1951 (25 was the worst case), and 40–60 by 1956; since it was assumed that it would take 30–120 bombs, accurately delivered, to knock out the United Kingdom, in a 1956 war the Soviets probably would supplement them with nerve gas and biological weapons (anthrax). By December 1946 (283, 289) attention was being focussed on 1956, partly on the theory that "the [Soviet] temptation to aggression would probably not be completely formed" by 1951. A March 1947 report by the British Future Planning Section projected the size and shape of British armed forces required for a war breaking out in 1956. According to Lewis, 299, in the spring of 1947 the British planners estimated that as few as twenty atomic bombs, accurately delivered, might cause the collapse of the United Kingdom, whereas it would take 200–250 to cause the Soviet Union to collapse. Thus by 1956 the Soviets would have enough bombs to deal with the UK. The British did not expect to have the requisite capacity by 1957; but they did estimate that by 1953 the Americans would be able to destroy much of the Soviet Union. Due to recent known leaks of classified information (which Lewis ascribes to Dr. Alan Nunn May, a British nuclear physicist), they assumed the Soviet leaders knew. They expected that by 1956–57 the Americans would have the 400–500 bombs needed to cause a Soviet collapse. By 1963 all three countries would have enough bombs to destroy each other (309). Lewis, 370–87, includes the British Chiefs f Staff May 1947 report on "Future Defence Policy." It mentions 1956 as the critical period (375, 378). Clark and Wheeler, *The British Origins of Nuclear Strategy,* 57–58, 64.

36. Evidence is indirect. When Stalin exploded his bomb three years earlier than expected, NSC 68 set 1954, three years earlier than 1957, as the "year of maximum danger."

37. Bullock, *Ernest Bevin,* 401. The CIA report was "The Current Situation in Italy" (16 February 1948), reproduced in CIA, *The CIA Under Harry Truman,* 181–89. Declassified Soviet archives show that the Italian Communist leader, Togliatti, proposed armed action in the event he lost the election (his excuse was that if his group won, the Christian Democrats would create their own disorders as a pretext for canceling the election results). Molotov vetoed the plan. See E. Aga-Rossi and V. Zaslavsky, "The Soviet Union and the Italian Com-

munist Party," in *The Soviet Union and Europe,* ed. Gori and Pons. These judgements echo those in a 12 September 1947 CIA Weekly Summary, the material provided to President Truman (Kuhns, *Assessing the Soviet Threat,* 134–36). The Communists were credited with the ability to overthrow the Italian government once Allied occupation troops were withdrawn. Although their 50,000 guerillas would be opposed by 200,000 Italian troops and carabinieri, some Italian troops would have to be deployed to the Yugoslav frontier, and Communist numbers could be swollen by partially armed and trained Italian and Yugoslav Communists and fellow travellers. It also appeared that the Italian Communist Party was moving towards a more military approach; the CIA saw a split between Togliatti's faction, which favored political action, and a pro-revolutionary group headed by Luigi Longo, who had fought in the Spanish civil war. Eight members of the latter group had just left for Moscow, suggesting some sort of coordination with the Soviets, and Togliatti himself had just made a speech amounting to a call to arms; to the CIA, that meant that he had possibly joined the revolutionary group. The CIA discounted these indications on the ground that Stalin would fear that violence in Italy might lead to war with the United States. He might also hope that continued economic disaster (due, e.g., to U.S. failure to deliver needed cash aid or emergency wheat, or the failure of the embryonic Marshall Plan) would deliver Italy into his hands without any such action. The 9 April 1948 Weekly Summary (189–91) described declining Communist prospects; it was no longer likely that they would win the 18 April election, and "the Party's capabilities for large-scale insurrection, without active military assistance from Yugoslavia, have been considerably reduced" due in part to improvements in the Italian armed forces and also to government successes in seizing Communist arms dumps (and in stopping shipments from abroad). Nor was there now evidence of Yugoslav readiness to intervene in Italy. This was despite an increase in the estimated number of Communist troops: 100,000 trained ex-partisans and another 100,000 in training. Against them the government could muster 336,000 military plus security forces: 75,000 carabinieri, a special mobile reserve of 16,000 police (plus 80,000 regular police), 36,357 finance guards, and 5,000 railway police. The 23 April 1948 Weekly Summary (193–96) gives the CIA's estimate of overall Communist strategy following defeat in the election.

38. M. M. Narinskii, "The Soviet Union and the Berlin Crisis," in *The Soviet Union and Europe,* ed. Gori and Pons, 62.

39. Mastny, *The Cold War and Soviet Insecurity,* 57.

40. J. Edwards, "Incorporating Spain in Western Defence," in *Securing Peace in Europe,* ed. Heuser and O'Neill.

41. Ibid., 165.

42. Ibid., 168–69.

43. E. Calandri, "The Neglected Flank? NATO in the Mediterranean, 1949–1956," in *Securing Peace in Europe,* ed. Heuser and O'Neill.

44. Ibid., 177.

45. Ibid., 181.

46. Ibid, 186–87.

47. FRUS (1949) 1:381–84.

48. JCS 2: 215–27.

49. From an analysis written for Secretary of State Dean Acheson on 17 February 1950. Kennan was then counselor of the department, the secretary's senior advisor on policy formulation. FRUS (1950) 1:160–67.

50. M. H. Folly, "The British Military and the Making of NATO," in *The Origins of Nato,* ed. Joseph Smith.

51. B. Heuser, "Covert Action Within British and American Concepts of Containment, 1948–1951," in *British Intelligence and the Cold War,* ed. Aldrich, 65.

52. The Albanian army reportedly mutinied in October, after the first agents landed, and two hundred of its officers were purged early in 1950, perhaps to avert further trouble (Mastny, *The Cold War and Soviet Insecurity,* 81).

53. Heuser, "Covert Action," 73.

54. Ibid., 71.

55. Nelson, *War of the Black Heavens,* 15–19 (Voice of America), 39–45 (Radio Free Europe, a covert CIA operation).

56. Ibid., 21–22. Jamming increased drastically in April 1949 during discussions of the lifting of the Berlin blockade. At that time the Soviets had at least 100 long-range and 250 short-range jammers, the latter increasing to 500 by 1950. In 1952 the U.S. government esti-mated that only 5 percent of Russian-language Voice of America programs could be heard in Moscow. The BBC thought that about a third of its Russian-language programming could be heard. Nelson contrasts Soviet jamming, which aimed to obliterate the offending signal, with wartime German jamming, which distorted the signal and made it difficult to hear. By 1958 (91) more Soviet resources were going into jamming than into their own radio stations: against 50 to 60 Western radio transmitters the Soviets operated 1,660 long-range jammers. Because the jammer had to be about the same distance from the target area as the offending radio, jammers covering Eastern Europe had to be located in the Soviet Union; they are included in the Soviet figure. Despite all of this effort, in 1958 the Soviets reported that, apart from the centers of Moscow, Leningrad, Kiev, and Riga, Western broad-casts generally could be received throughout the Soviet Union. One delicious irony was that the Soviets mass-produced exactly the short-wave receivers their citizens needed to listen to Western broadcasts, despite official decisions to abandon production. In 1958, 85 percent of all Soviet-made short-wave receivers were located in the Western part of the country, where Soviet short-wave broadcasts could not even be heard. Ironically, few Westerners were buy-ing short-wave sets capable of receiving Soviet broadcasts. In 1958 the Soviets finally did stop the sale of receivers capable of picking up the most useful short-wave bands, but ingen-ious citizens were able to adapt the sets they could buy (92–93).

57. Heuser, "Covert Action," 69.

58. See Document 89 in Benson and Warner, *Venona,* a cable sent on 30 March 1945 and not decoded until 1969. Hiss had been working for the GRU since 1935, and recently he had become a group leader for GRU agents. Hiss had seemed vindicated when Dmitri Volkogo-nov announced that he had been unable to find any reference to him in Soviet KGB files (Hiss was working for the rival GRU). The decoded KGB cables also exposed the Rosenbergs, among many others. For details of Hiss's career as a Soviet agent, and of the extent of Venona evidence about him, see Haynes and Klehr, *Venona,* 167–73.

59. Powers, *Not Without Honor,* 216; Hoover testified on 26 March 1947.

60. According to ibid., 219, Ronald Reagan first became aware of Communist efforts of this type when he was appointed to the board of the Hollywood Independent Citizens Committee of the Arts, Sciences, and Professions in 1947, to discover that it was dominated by a group of secretly Communist actors and screenwriters. When he became openly anti-Communist, board members clearly showed their distaste for him. He resigned after the FBI

warned him that the Communist directors were plotting against him. Later, as president of the Screen Actors Guild, he was warned that he was in physical danger from the Communists that he was trying to purge from that union; he began to carry a gun.

61. The blacklist began with the Hollywood Ten, a group of Communists who took the Fifth Amendment rather than answer the committee's questions (ibid., 218).

62. Ibid., 257, argues that the facile psychological explanations blinded liberals to the fact that the public's anti-Communism, which McCarthy exploited, was based just as much on real knowledge of Communism as was their own rather differently directed opposition to Stalin. McCarthy was a typical extremist countersubversive, a perverted version of a legitimate form of anti-Communism—which he thoroughly discredited.

63. The attack on the army seems to have been precipitated by a failed attempt to curry favor for G. David Schine, a recently drafted friend of Roy Cohn, McCarthy's chief counsel.

Chapter 8. Tito and Mao

1. So did Stalin's man, Dimitrov; in January 1949 he was flown to Moscow, where he died in July 1950, probably having been murdered (Mastny, *The Cold War and Soviet Insecurity,* 69).

2. R. Craig-Nation, "A Balkan Union?" in *The Soviet Union and Europe,* ed. Gori and Pons.

3. Mastny, *The Cold War and Soviet Insecurity,* 53.

4. Ulunian, "The Soviet Union and the 'Greek Question.'"

5. Partos, *The World That Came in from the Cold,* 21–22; Stuek, *The Korean War,* 352, quoting Hungarian Maj. Gen. Bela Kiraly, commander of Hungarian infantry forces in 1950.

6. Volkogonov, *Sem' vozhdei* (Seven rulers), 247. Some of the ideas, such as presenting Tito with a boxed diamond ring concealing poison gas, recall the more ludicrous U.S. plots against Castro.

7. NIE 29, "Probability of an Invasion of Yugoslavia in 1951," 20 March 1951, in CIA 2:117–27. This assessment justified military aid extended in 1951. According to a 1952 follow-on NIE (4 January 1952), attack was now unlikely. FRUS (1952–1954) 8:1, 264–66.

8. The Pact was still in force in 1968, when the Yugoslavs became nervous following the Soviet invasion of Czechoslovakia. NATO had never taken official cognizance of it. FRUS (1964–1968) 17:97.

9. Hammond, ed., *Communist Takeovers.*

10. Hugh Thomas, *Armed Truce,* 411.

11. Ibid., 414–16.

12. Hooton, *The Greatest Tumult,* 34–35. There really was some treason, as the Venona decrypts later showed. According to Haynes and Klehr, *Venona,* 142–43, a Soviet spy, Harry Dexter White (then assistant secretary of the treasury), was able to sabotage wartime U.S. plans to lend the Chinese $200 million to stabilize their currency. White and other Communists in the Treasury Department stalled the loan with the argument that it would do little good due to pervasive corruption and a need for financial reform. Without the gold, the Chinese experienced inflation of over 1,000 percent a year, which cannot have helped the Nationalist cause. In addition to this direct action, in 1941 White had managed to place a U.S.-educated Communist, Chi Chao-ting, in a senior position in the Chinese Ministry of Finance, where he could help fuel wartime inflation which helped to destabilize the Nation-

alist regime (140). White also was able to stymie a number of security investigations of other Soviet spies in the wartime U.S. government.

13. Medvedev, *China and the Superpowers*, 19–20. In 1948 Stalin said that he had told Mao to limit himself to north China.

14. Gaddis, *We Now Know*, 65.

15. Hooton, *The Greatest Tumult*, 150, 153.

16. R. Medvedev and J. Domes, "The Model for Revolutionary People's War: The Communist Takeover of China," in *Communist Takeovers*, ed. Hammond.

17. In early 1950 the Soviets provided Mao with a detachment of one hundred aircraft, including MiG-15s, to protect Shanghai against Nationalist aircraft operating out of the Tinghai Islands off Hangchow Bay. After several Nationalist aircraft had been shot down in April (one by a MiG), the islands were evacuated. This was the first combat use of a MiG-15 (the victim was a Nationalist B-24) (Hooton, *The Greatest Tumult*, 170–71, confirmed by Russian accounts).

18. Leffler, *A Preponderance of Power*, 293–98; Gaddis, *We Now Know*, 61.

19. Goncharov, Lewis, and Xue, *Uncertain Partners*, 98.

20. Ibid., 106–8.

21. JCS 2: 479–80; Hooton, *The Greatest Tumult*, 57–59.

22. Goncharov, Lewis, and Xue, *Uncertain Partners*, 46.

23. Zubok and Pleshakov, *Inside the Kremlin's Cold War*, 56.

24. Goncharov, Lewis, and Xue, *Uncertain Partners*, 105.

25. See Shu Zhang, "Threat Perceptions and Chinese Communist Foreign Policy," in *Origins of the Cold War*, ed. Leffler and Painter.

26. Zubok and Pleshakov, *Inside the Kremlin's Cold War*, 213. Mao announced his preference for the Soviets ("leaning to the left") in a 30 June 1949 article, "On the People's Democratic Dictatorship" (Goncharov, Lewis, and Xue, *Uncertain Partners*, 44).

27. Volkogonov, *Sem' vozhdei* (Seven rulers), 251.

28. Medvedev, *China and the Superpowers*, 22–23. The entire loan was probably used to buy weapons, since Soviet military deliveries to China between 1950 and 1955 were priced at exactly $300 million (1,200 million rubles) (Goncharov, Lewis, and Xue, *Uncertain Partners*, 99–100).

29. Zubok and Pleshakov, *Inside the Kremlin's Cold War*, 58; Goncharov, Lewis, and Xue, *Uncertain Partners*, 122, 125–26.

30. Goncharov, Lewis, and Xue, *Uncertain Partners*, 69.

31. Ibid., 119.

32. Mastny, *The Cold War and Soviet Insecurity*, 93; Zubok and Pleshakov, *Inside the Kremlin's Cold War*, 59.

33. Goncharov, Lewis, and Xue, *Uncertain Partners*, 68.

34. Ibid., 98. For the text of NSC 48/2 see *Containment*, ed. Etzold and Gaddis, 269–76, especially 274–75.

35. Goncharov, Lewis, and Xue, *Uncertain Partners*, 98–99.

36. Ibid., 100.

37. Mastny, *The Cold War and Soviet Insecurity*, 91.

38. Dulles had been deeply involved in U.S. foreign policy for many years, and had served several times as a member of State Department delegations. He was the Republican Party's foreign policy expert.

Chapter 9. Rising Nationalism

1. Louis, *Imperialism at Bay.*
2. Zubok and Pleshakov, *Inside the Kremlin's Cold War,* 57.
3. Mastny, *The Cold War and Soviet Insecurity,* 55.
4. Ibid.
5. Marshall, *To Have and Have Not.*
6. The Japanese occupied British Burma, Malaya, and Hong Kong, the Dutch East Indies (now Indonesia), French Indochina, and the U.S. Philippines.
7. See the British Cabinet Minute (24 October 1946) in PRO file CAB 128/6 on continuing the draft. However, even India could not provide enough troops to garrison Germany and Austria, or to provide a viable army on the Continent. See Scott, *Conscription and the Attlee Governments,* 16.
8. JCS 4:333.
9. A British attempt to negotiate a replacement treaty failed when the Iraqi regent refused to ratify it after signature at Portsmouth on 15 January 1948. Louis, *Imperialism at Bay,* 331–44.
10. McGhee, *On the Frontline in the Cold War,* 100–104; the November 1950 fifty-fifty announcement was called the "McGhee bombshell."
11. Yergin, *The Prize,* 453.
12. Ibid., 452–54.
13. JCS 4: 354.
14. Yergin, *The Prize,* 465, 467.
15. JCS 4:355, 357.
16. Ibid., 359.
17. Ibid., 338.
18. Oren, *The Origins of the Second Arab-Israeli War,* 61.
19. W. R. Louis, "The Anglo-Egyptian Settlement of 1954," *Suez 1956,* ed. Louis and Owen, 53–54.
20. JCS 4:343–44. The U.S. ambassador reported that only Farouk's intervention had precluded a Communist coup.
21. Ibid., 349; Louis, "The Anglo-Egyptian Settlement," 51.
22. Ibid., 371–72, 374.
23. Ibid., 363, 365.
24. Ibid., 362.
25. Ibid., 366.
26. Bill, *The Eagle and the Lion,* 85.
27. Ambrose, *Eisenhower: The President,* 112; Yergin, *The Prize,* 468.
28. Bill, *The Eagle and the Lion,* 85–94; Yergin, *The Prize,* 467–70.
29. Ovendale, *Britain, the United States and the Transfer of Power,* 73–74.
30. Louis, *Imperialism at Bay,* 27.
31. See, e.g., Martin Thomas, *The French Empire at War,* 197.
32. Louis, *The British Empire,* 124, 147–51.
33. JCS, *The Joint Chiefs of Staff and the War in Vietnam,* 1: 64–65. See also Marr, *Vietnam 1945,* 116.

34. JCS, *The Joint Chiefs of Staff and the War in Vietnam*, 1: 42, 46. See also Marr, *Vietnam 1945*, 438–53.

35. Martin Thomas, *The French Empire at War*, 428.

36. JCS, *The Joint Chiefs of Staff and the War in Vietnam*, 1: 50, 74–75.

37. Ibid., 79–85.

38. Ibid., 45. Dunn, *The First Indochina War,*, 367, argues that this was the crucial decision. The British, who occupied the south of the country and disarmed the Japanese, made it possible for the French to take back control, and thus indirectly created South Vietnam. The Chinese, who hindered the French, in his view made it possible for Ho Chi Minh's Viet Minh to take control, and thus give them the power base they needed. Since it was U.S. pressure that gave the Chinese the north to occupy, in effect the U.S. government provided Ho with the initial boost he needed. The French had wanted the British, in the form of South-East Asia Command (SEAC) to take over the whole of French Indochina at the end of the war; Dunn argues that, had a British force gone to Hanoi, it would have exposed "the hollowness of the Viet Minh claim to speak and act for the whole of the Vietnamese people" (368).

39. JCS, *The Joint Chiefs of Staff and the War in Vietnam,*1: 91–100.

40. Ibid., 103.

41. Ibid., 105–6.

42. Ibid., 121–31.

43. "The Break-Up of the Colonial Empires and Its Implications for U.S. Security," a 3 September 1948 CIA report, ORE 25-48, in CIA 1:219–34.

44. Kuhns, *Assessing the Soviet Threat*, 97, an excerpt from the CIA Weekly Summary of 10 January 1947 (which went to President Truman).

45. Ibid., 145–46 (the CIA weekly summary of 24 October 1947).

46. Ibid., 316–17 (Weekly Summary, 10 June 1949). The French had just signed an agreement with Bao Dai, and they claimed that some substantial success against the Viet Minh was necessary if he was to have any chance of political success. Given U.S. insistence on Vietnamese independence, this argument was probably made to convince the U.S. government to provide the needed support.

47. Mastny, *The Cold War and Soviet Insecurity*, 85.

48. Kuhns, *Assessing the Soviet Threat*, 355–56 (Weekly Summary, 10 February 1950).

49. Kuhns, *Assessing the Soviet Threat*, 350 (Weekly Summary, 1 February 1950, on implications of Soviet recognition of the Ho Chi Minh regime).

50. JCS, *The Joint Chiefs of Staff and the War in Vietnam,*1: 134–35, Terrence J. Gough, introduction.

51. C. Wiebes, "The National Security Policy of the Netherlands, 1940–1949," in *The Origins of NATO*, ed. Joseph Smith. Cribb and Brown, *Modern Indonesia*, describe the struggle for Indonesian independence.

Chapter 10. Stalin's Military Buildup

1. May, Steinbruner, and Wolfe, *History of the Strategic Arms Competition*, 81.

2. Glantz, *Soviet Military Deception*.

3. For manpower losses, see Glantz and House, *When Titans Clashed*, 156–57. See 180–81, 288–89 for the more lavish scale of equipment adopted.

4. As yet only the naval part of the Ten Year Plan has been published. See Pavlov, *Warships of the Soviet Union,* data for which is taken from a variety of recently published Russian articles.

5. British administrative records and some of the program's reports are now available in the British Public Records Office (classes DEFE 41 and 44). Repatriation of the German engineers began in 1951. According to Laquer, *The Uses and Limits of Intelligence,* 143, early Western knowledge of the Soviet rocket program came from Lt. Col. G. A. Tokaty-Tokaev, who defected to British intelligence in 1948, and provided information about the establishment of the Soviet program in 1947; he claimed that he had had personal contact with Stalin.

6. Lyelchuka and Pivovara, *SSR i Kholodnaya Voenia* (USSR and Cold War), 165.

7. Ibid., 172.

8. Ibid., 176.

9. Figures from Simonov, *Voenno-promyshlenniy kompleks SSSR* (Military-industrial complex of the USSR). The defense budget was divided into (i) personnel costs, (ii) weapons and other expendables including vehicles, and (iii) capital costs. Normally (ii) accounted for a third of the costs, but in 1953–55 it rose to half the budget. A decreed cut in wholesale costs in 1954–55 makes it difficult to compare figures.

10. Pryce-Jones, *The War That Never Was,* 98.

11. Gaddy, *The Price of the Past,* 42.

12. For example, Michael Taylor, ed., *Brassey's World Aircraft and Systems Directory, 1996–1997,* 178, shows an Ilyushin "Maxdome" strategic command and control aircraft in Aeroflot colors. All four aircraft of this type have civilian registrations (which are listed on p. 178). Page 177 shows an Il-76 communications relay aircraft; page 180 shows a Tu-135 military transport and communications version of the Tu-134 airliner. Both are in Aeroflot markings. The Il-76 and -86 versions (in Aeroflot markings) are also shown on pages 211–12 of David Donald and Jon Lake, eds., *Encyclopedia of World Military Aircraft,* vol. 1 (London: Aerospace Publishing, 1994).

13. See, for example, V. Shlykov, "Fatal Mistakes of the U.S. and Soviet Intelligence: Part One," *International Affairs* 42, no.5/6 (1996): 159–78, particularly the GRU's claim that the United States could mobilize to produce fifty thousand tanks a year (171–78).

14. Gaddy, *The Price of the Past,* 130–47.

15. Ibid., 12–13.

16. Ibid., 10, referring to the early 1970s.

17. Ibid., 14.

18. Ibid., 45–46.

Chapter 11. Countering Stalin's Hordes

1. Clifford and Holbrooke, *Counsel to the President,* 148–58, credit Truman (who probably was responding to Marshall) with the idea of unifying the services.

2. JCS 2:165–84.

3. Ibid., 184.

4. Ibid., 185.

5. Kunz, *Butter and Guns,* 54; unemployment rose more slowly than had been expected, from 3.8 percent in 1948 to 5.9 percent in 1949.

6. IDA, 15–16.

7. May, Steinbruner, and Wolfe, *History of the Strategic Arms Competition,* 81.

8. IDA, 71–72.

9. Rosenberg, "Toward Armageddon," 108.

10. JCS 1:158–60.

11. JCS 2: 229–55.

12. JCS 4: 144–45; May, Steinbruner, and Wolfe, *History of the Strategic Arms Competition,* 60; and FRUS (1949)1:560–62.

13. JCS 2: 299.

14. Cornish, *British Military Planning,* 141, 148.

15. Rosenberg, "Toward Armageddon," 121. Rhodes, *Dark Sun,* 188–89, explains levitation, which was conceived at the end of World War II.

16. Mk 5 (3,175 pounds, 43.75 inches in diameter) was the first U.S. bomb small enough to be carried by the air force's B-45 light bomber, which had not been designed with nuclear attack in mind (it could not carry a 10,000-pound bomb). In the fall of 1949 a committee headed by Lt. Gen. John E. Hull, USA, recommended that Mk 5 arm four missiles already under development: the navy's Regulus cruise missile, the army's Hermes A-3 (later abandoned in favor of Corporal), and the air force's Rascal and Snark. In fact Mk 5 armed only Regulus. It was too heavy for Corporal, and the air force missiles were so delayed that they got the later thermonuclear warheads.

17. Hansen, *U.S. Nuclear Weapons,* 25–27.

18. IDA, 33–34.

19. Hansen, *U.S. Nuclear Weapons,* 38; NWD 2: 46–51.

20. With a 3,000-foot CEP; half of all bombs dropped would fall within a 3,000-foot circle drawn around the target.

21. Barlow, *Revolt of the Admirals,* 108–14.

22. JCS 2:351–53; IDA, 20–22.

23. From 30 September 1949 report by the chairman (Edwin G. Nourse) of the Council of Economic Advisors in FRUS (1949) 1:394–96.

Chapter 12. Living With Stalin's Bomb

1. See, e.g., ORE 32–50, "The Effect of the Soviet Possession of Atomic Bombs on the Security of the United States," a report by a Joint Ad Hoc Committee dated 9 June 1950, in CIA 1:327–33.

2. The 200-bomb figure (to insure delivery of 100 with reasonable certainty) seems to have surfaced in 1946 as a U.S. goal (Botti, *Ace in the Hole,* 5) to attack seventeen Soviet cities with a total of 98 bombs. Botti, 21, cites a February 1950 CIA statement that the Soviets would have to deliver 100 bombs to knock out the United States. There is no evidence of much analysis to back this figure up. Some JCS studies suggested that much smaller numbers could cripple U.S. industry.

3. Rhodes, *Dark Sun,* 196–97.

4. JCS 2:525.

5. FRUS (1949) 1: 339–45. According to a 20 September 1949 CIA memo, issued on 20 September 1949 (*after* the Soviet test had been detected but before it had been made pub-

lic), the Joint Nuclear Energy Intelligence Committee predicted that the Soviets might have a bomb by mid-1950 but more likely would have one in mid-1953 (CIA 1:319–20).

6. P. Sudoplatov et al., *Special Tasks,* 199.

7. Ziegler and Jacobsen, *Spying Without Spies,* describe alternative techniques.

8. Ibid., 203–10.

9. A. Il'in, "The First Testing of Russian Nuclear Weapons: From the Annals of the Arms Race," *International Affairs* 43, no. 2 (1997): 203–24.

10. FRUS (1949) 1:466.

11. JCS 2: 257–81.

12. FRUS (1950) 1:142–43.

13. FRUS (1949) 1: 414

14. Ibid.

15. FRUS (1950) 1:179.

16. For the text of NSC 68, see ibid., 235–92. For the more detailed Annex VIII, NSC 68/1, "The Strategy of Freedom" (10 November 1950) see 404–7.

17. Ibid., 317 (29 May 1950 report).

18. JCS 2: 420–22.

19. Ibid., 436.

20. J. S. Duffield, "The Soviet Military Threat to Western Europe: U.S. Estimates in the 1950s and 1960s," in *Journal of Strategic Studies* 15 (1992): 217.

21. JCS 4: 25–35.

22. Duffield, "The Soviet Military Threat," 49.

23. Cornish, *British Military Planning,* 24–25, 47–49, 126–27.

24. Duffield, "The Soviet Military Threat," 74–75.

25. NWD 5:183.

26. Ibid., 184–85.

27. Botti, *The Long Wait,* 74.

28. T. D. Biddle, "Handling the Soviet Threat: 'Project Control' and the Debate on American Strategy in the Early Cold War Years," in *Journal of Strategic Studies* 12 (1989): 273–302.

29. IDA, 22, credits the categories to SAC.

30. Rosenberg, "Toward Armageddon," 162.

31. JCS 4:165–66.

32. Ibid., 169–70.

33. May, Steinbruner, and Wolfe, *History of the Strategic Arms Competition,* 141–42.

34. Rosenberg, "Toward Armageddon," 167.

Chapter 13. The "Super"

1. Zubok and Pleshakov, *Inside the Kremlin's Cold War,* 151.

2. FRUS (1949) 1:570–71.

3. Ibid., 598.

4. The 9 November 1949 AEC report is in ibid., 577–85.

5. Ibid., 590–91.

6. Ibid., 595–96.

7. Ibid., 611.

8. The question of whether the H-bomb secret was indeed secure was raised publicly when Howard Morland described an H-bomb in the November and December 1979 issues of *The Progressive* magazine. See Morland, *The Secret That Exploded;* and Hansen, *U.S. Nuclear Weapons,* 5, 28–29.

9. Hansen, *U.S. Nuclear Weapons,* 54–60.

10. Ibid., 61–68.

11. Wynn, *RAF Nuclear Deterrent Forces,* 239.

12. See, e.g., Nash, *The Other Missiles of October,* 8–9.

13. Laming, *V-Bombers,* 95–96.

14. Ibid., 107.

15. NWD 5:48–49.

16. Wynn, *RAF Nuclear Deterrent Forces,* 263.

Chapter 14. Crisis in the East

1. Shu, *Mao's Military Romanticism,* 44.

2. Suh, *Kim Il Sung;* Goncharov, Lewis, and Xue, *Uncertain Partners,* 131.

3. CWIHP 3:15–17, a 1966 Soviet Foreign Ministry report on events leading up to the Korean War, prepared for Brezhnev and Kosygin.

4. Suh, *Kim Il Sung,* 112–21.

5. Ibid., 121.

6. Goncharov, Lewis, and Xue, *Uncertain Partners,* 135; Volkogonov, *Sem' vozhdei* (Seven rulers), 284–85. Shu, *Mao's Military Romanticism,* 45, reports claims of a South Korean historian, Pak Toufo, concerning the 1948–49 meetings. Chinese historians have neither confirmed nor disproved these statements.

7. Goncharov, Lewis, and Xue, *Uncertain Partners,* 135–36. The guerilla concept was important to Kim, who revived it in later years.

8. "Consequences of U.S. Troop Withdrawal From Korea in Spring, 1949" (ORE 3-49), 28 February 1949, in CIA 1:265–74.

9. Whelan, *Drawing the Line,* 90–91.

10. Kuhns, *Assessing the Soviet Threat,* 349 (Weekly Summary, 13 January 1950). This was also the contemporary U.S. Army view (17).

11. Ibid., 390, an excerpt from an NIE (ORE 18-50).

12. Goncharov, Lewis, and Xue, *Uncertain Partners,* 135.

13. Volkogonov, *Sem' vozhdei* (Seven rulers), 285; the date was 27 October 1949.

14. Goncharov, Lewis, and Xue, *Uncertain Partners,* 140.

15. According to ibid., 147, in June 1950 the Soviets considered that the North had decisive advantages in tanks, personnel, artillery and mortars, and aircraft.

16. Whelan, *Drawing the Line,* 101. One reason U.S. units crumbled in the face of the tank attack was that their bazookas, the same as those supplied to the South Koreans, also were ineffective. The cure was a new "super bazooka" with a heavier warhead.

17. Mastny, *The Cold War and Soviet Insecurity,* 91.

18. According to Zubok and Pleshakov, *Inside the Kremlin's Cold War,* 63, Stalin had to agree because Kim would have gone ahead in any case. Better to achieve a quick victory than to start a long guerilla war that would invite U.S. intervention, as in Greece. But Goncharov, Lewis, and Xue, *Uncertain Partners,* emphasize Stalin's interest in levering Mao into a war.

19. Goncharov, Lewis, and Xue, *Uncertain Partners,* 148, 152.

20. Ibid., 146, citing a 1955 recollection by Marshal Peng Dehuai and a later recollection by a senior Soviet diplomat.

21. Ibid., 153–54.

22. Ibid.

23. Ibid., 143.

24. Volkogonov, *Sem' vozhdei* (Seven rulers), 287.

25. Mastny, *The Cold War and Soviet Insecurity,* 91.

26. Ibid., 100.

27. Goncharov, Lewis, and Xue, *Uncertain Partners,* 143.

28. Ibid., 137.

29. Ibid., 155, quoting retired North Korean Gen. Yoo Soong Chul. Another North Korean general, Chung Sang Chin, said that Kim assumed that the South would surrender when Seoul fell. There were no detailed plans for what to do in the event resistance continued after that.

30. Volkogonov, *Sem' vozhdei* (Seven rulers), 289. In earlier messages he had used the cover name "Filippov."

31. Mastny, *The Cold War and Soviet Insecurity,* 96, argues that, as Nitze surmised, Stalin backed Kim to prove to Mao that he was still sufficiently militant.

32. Volkogonov, *Sem' vozhdei* (Seven rulers), 291.

33. In October 1949 North Korea sent a letter to the UN secretary general claiming the right to unify the country by force (JCS vol. 3, pt. 1, 49). When James F. Schnabel, then a historian for the U.S. Far East Command and later a JCS historian, arrived in Tokyo in November 1949, it was generally accepted that the North Koreans would invade and conquer the South the following summer (Whelan, *Drawing the Line,* 90). In 1950 "Americans in Korea generally believed that a North Korean attack was certain" (JCS vol. 3, pt. 1, 48). In April 1950 U.S. intelligence apparently decoded a message from the Soviet ambassador in Pyongyang reporting that Kim had told him that he planned to invade in June (Mastny, *The Cold War and Soviet Insecurity,* 95). On 10 May 1950 the South Korean minister of defense told a Seoul press conference that the North Koreans had 173 tanks and 185,000 men concentrated at the 38th Parallel for an invasion; he badly wanted U.S. arms to resist (Whelan, *Drawing the Line,* 106). U.S. intelligence failed to interpret the evacuation of civilians along the 38th Parallel as a war warning.

34. Mastny, *The Cold War and Soviet Insecurity,* 101.

35. Conclusions of an NSC consultants' meeting, 29 June 1950; FRUS (1950) 1:324–26.

36. Average strength was thirteen thousand, compared to an authorized war strength of 18,900 (JCS vol. 3, pt. 1, 44).

37. The British sent an infantry brigade (adding a second, smaller, one later). Canada sent another brigade, and Australia and New Zealand contributed battalions. Turkey, Thailand, and the Philippines each offered a regimental combat team, equivalent to a brigade. Although the Thai team was weakly equipped, the JCS welcomed it for the political and propaganda value of having Asian troops fight in Korea. France, Belgium, the Netherlands, Greece, Ethiopia, and Colombia each sent a battalion; Luxembourg sent a company (JCS VOL. 3, PT. 1, 161–75). Other countries, such as Greece and South Africa, provided ships and aircraft.

38. Zubok and Pleshakov, *Inside the Kremlin's Cold War,* 64.

39. Shu, *Mao's Military Romanticism,* 55–56.

40. Ibid., 56–58.

41. The vulnerability of Japan became an issue late in 1950 when the British reported that Stalin had moved twelve divisions from Siberia to Sakhalin, possibly for an invasion of the northern Japanese island, Hokkaido. Two U.S. divisions (called-up national guards) arrived in Japan in April 1951.

42. JCS vol. 3, pt. 1, 188.

43. JCS 4:94–101.

44. Memorandum by Nitze to the secretary of state, 31 July 1951, in FRUS (1951) 1:110–12.

45. In billions of 1947 dollars, GNP rose from $264.7 in 1950 to $293.7 in 1952 and $305.3 in 1953, falling to $300.8 in 1954 but then rising to $322.4 in 1955. Figures are from the 1957 edition of *Statistical Abstract of the United States,* 296. On a scale in which the 1947–49 dollar was worth one hundred cents, in terms of consumer prices the 1950 dollar was worth 97.3 cents. In 1951 that fell to 90.1 cents, an inflation rate of about 7 percent. In 1952, with prices largely stabilized, it was worth 88.1 cents, falling to 87.4 cents in 1953 and to 87.3 cents in 1955. Figures are from the 1960 edition of *Statistical Abstract of the United States,* 331.

46. FRUS (1951) 1:245–54.

47. FRUS (1950) l: 428–31.

48. JCS vol. 3, pt. 1, 108–9, 116, 118–19, 179, 183, 185.

49. Ibid., 1, 103–5.

50. Ibid., 1, 191.

51. NSC consultants' meeting, 29 June 1950, and NSC report on possible U.S. actions, 25 August 1950, are in FRUS (1950) 1:327–28, 376–91.

52. JCS 4:397.

53. JCS vol. 3, pt. 1, 196–201. From outside the Far East MacArthur received, in 1950, three full divisions (one marine) and two regimental combat teams, to supplement his pre-invasion force of four divisions and one regiment (from Okinawa). UN units added up to the equivalent of another division. MacArthur thus had more than the eight divisions he asked for.

54. Volkogonov, *Sem' vozhdei* (Seven rulers), 293.

55. Shu, *Mao's Military Romanticism,* 63. At a 4 August Chinese politburo meeting, Mao said that China would have to intervene with volunteer troops to insure a North Korean victory.

56. Mastny, *The Cold War and Soviet Insecurity,* 100.

57. Ibid.

58. Ibid., 101.

59. Goncharev, Lewis, and Xue, *Uncertain Partners,* 107. Mao feared that the French would support these troops.

60. Shu, *Mao's Military Romanticism,* 69–70.

61. JCS vol. 3, pt. 1, 203; Shu, *Mao's Military Romanticism,* 72 (for intelligence). It is not yet clear whether Stalin's spies warned him about Inchon.

62. Shu, *Mao's Military Romanticism,* 74. Chou personally addressed the officers on 17 September, before they left for Korea.

63. JCS vol. 3, pt. 1, 223.

64. Ibid., 224–25.

65. Ibid., 227.

66. Ibid., 231.

67. Ibid., 236–37. The JCS questioned whether higher authority should approve the contemplated advance beyond the 38th Parallel.

68. Mastny, *The Cold War and Soviet Insecurity,* 103; Shu, *Mao's Military Romanticism,* 77–79.

69. Shu, *Mao's Military Romanticism,* 75–77, 80; Gaddis, *We Now Know,* 81.

70. Shu, *Mao's Military Romanticism,* 80–81. In 10–11 and 12–30, Shu describes Mao's belief in human superiority over technology.

71. Volkogonov, *Stalin: Triumph and Tragedy,* 296.

72. Mastny, *The Cold War and Soviet Insecurity,* 107.

73. Chen, *China's Road to the Korean War,* 24–26; Goncharov, Lewis, and Xue, *Uncertain Partners,* 181.

74. Mastny, *The Cold War and Soviet Insecurity,* 107; Chen, *China's Road to the Korean War,* 197.

75. Chen, *China's Road to the Korean War,* 196–99.

76. Ibid., 200–203.

77. Mastny, *The Cold War and Soviet Insecurity,* 106.

78. JCS vol. 3, pt. 1, 244; it passed forty-seven to five, with seven abstentions.

79. Top Secret Memo dated 12 October 1950 in CIA 1:349–72.

80. JCS vol. 3, pt. 1, 264–69.

81. Ibid., 275.

82. Ibid., 290–94.

83. Ibid., 319. This plan had been proposed before Inchon.

84. Ibid., 261, 301.

85. Ibid., 307.

86. Ibid., 326–31.

87. Shu, *Mao's Military Romanticism,* 118, argues that this initial victory made the Chinese overconfident; they imagined that they had won through superior strategy and tactics, rather than through good luck.

88. JCS vol. 3, pt. 1, 339.

89. JCS 4:67; Whelan, *Drawing the Line,* 261, 262.

90. Botti, *The Long Wait,* 80–81.

91. Shu, *Mao's Military Romanticism,* 121, 123, 131; JCS vol. 3, pt. 1, 394.

92. JCS vol. 3, pt. 1, 524.

93. Mastny, *The Cold War and Soviet Insecurity,* 111.

94. JCS vol. 3, pt. 1, 359.

95. Ibid., 399–401.

96. National Intelligence Estimate, "Consequences of the Early Employment of Chinese Nationalist Forces in Korea" (NIE-12), 27 December 1950, in CIA 1: 373–81.

97. For CIA Korean War programs see N. B. Tucker and H. Ford, "CIA and the Cold War in Asia," in CIA Conference Report, 102. JCS vol. 3, pt. 1, 487, 492; Whelan, *Drawing the Line,* 296 (for the Soviet attack rumor).

98. Shu, *Mao's Military Romanticism,* 145, 154.

99. Whelan, *Drawing the Line,* 267–68. According to Whelan, 289, in March 1951 a Gal-

lup poll showed that two-thirds of Americans wanted withdrawal from Korea unless Chinese territory could be attacked.

100. JCS vol. 3, pt. 1, 527.

101. Ibid., 529–30; Whelan, *Drawing the Line,* 295–99.

102. Mastny, *The Cold War and Soviet Insecurity,* 123.

103. Ibid., 124.

104. JCS vol. 3, pt. 1, 363–64.

105. FRUS (1951) 1:240–44.

106. Mastny, *The Cold War and Soviet Insecurity,* 148.

107. JCS 3:843–48.

108. Donaldson, *America at War Since 1945,* 51–52.

109. Zubok and Pleshakov, *Inside the Kremlin's Cold War,* 155.

110. According to Shu, *Mao's Military Romanticism,* 247, in Korea the Chinese deployed twenty-five infantry armies (73 percent of the PLA total), sixteen artillery (67 percent), ten armored (100 percent), twelve air force (52 percent), and six guard divisions. The Chinese lost 390,000 men (148,400 dead, twenty-one thousand captured, four thousand missing in action, the rest wounded). Other losses included 399 aircraft and 12,916 vehicles.

111. Ibid., 247–48. Peng Dehuai claimed that the Chinese had inflicted 390,000 casualties on UN forces and seven hundred thousand on South Korean forces. Shu points out that this was the first time in its history that China had successfully stood up to Western powers.

112. Ibid., 251–52. According to Shu, a PLA command meeting held between 7 December 1953 and 26 January 1954 to summarize lessons of the war considered the most important that political will could trump modern weaponry.

113. Ibid., 250.

114. Ibid., 249.

115. Stueck, *The Korean War,* 367–68.

116. According to E. Grove, "Japan," in *Spheres of Influence,* ed. Gardner, 220, two Japanese sweepers were lost. Operations between 2 October 1950 and 15 December 1950 involved forty-six sweepers and a mine destructor ship. The experienced Japanese were considered the best mine countermeasures force in the Far East at the time.

Chapter 15. Defending Europe

1. OSD 2:326–32.

2. Ibid., 319, 340.

3. Duffield, "The Evolution," 219–20.

4. JCS 4: 208.

5. Ibid., 241.

6. Ibid.

7. M. Dockrill, "The Changing Shape of Britain's Defence during the 1950s," in *The Origins of NATO,* ed. Joseph Smith, 53.

8. Apparently the East Germans took Stalin at his word; they thought he would soon lead them to power over all of Germany. According to Trachtenberg, *History and Strategy,* 151, late in 1950 their premier, Grotowohl, threatened to attack West Germany as North Korea had attacked the South. Party Leader Ulbricht said that he had rejected plans to build a new seaport, because soon the "democratic Germany" would have Hamburg and Lübeck.

By early 1952, presumably because the war in Korea had gone so badly (and because the West clearly was rearming), the East Germans were talking more about defense, and were warning of the danger of a "fratricidal" war—which was part of Stalin's argument for general withdrawal from Germany.

9. JCS 4:249–50.

10. Ibid., 253.

11. Duffield, "The Evolution," 127–28.

12. Mastny, *The Cold War and Soviet Insecurity,* 114. See also Heller and Nekrich, *Utopia in Power,* 504–6; the 1951 Stalin speech was found in the archives of the Czech Communist Party and published by a Czech historian, Karel Kaplan, in 1973. Holloway, *Stalin and the Bomb,* 286–87, describes the meeting in greater detail, citing a former Polish Central Committee secretary, Edward Ochab. Holloway speculates that Stalin expected both his remarks to Togliatti and the results of the 1951 conference to filter out to the West, and hence to deter any Western attempt to expand the war in Asia by striking in Europe.

13. Mastny, *The Cold War and Soviet Insecurity,* 113.

14. Ibid., 115.

15. FRUS (1950) 1:414–16; staff discussions on the shift to 1952 are in JCS 4:80–81 and in FRUS (1951) 1:112–14, 127–57.

16. Wags said that the purpose of NATO was to keep the Russians out, the Americans in, and the Germans down.

17. On 1 January 1945 the Red Army had 634 line divisions, but many were no stronger than a U.S. regiment.

18. May, Steinbruner, and Wolfe, *History of the Strategic Arms Competition,* 57 (citing an interview with Ray Cline), 81.

19. For example, in 1952 it was estimated that a U.S. division had about 50 percent more firepower than a fully manned Soviet equivalent. Moreover, early in 1953 it was estimated that in peacetime a Soviet division was at only 60 to 80 percent of its wartime strength. The U.S. division also had far more combat support, which could be estimated by dividing total manpower by the number of divisions: 14,300 for the Soviets, 59,000 for the U.S. division in 1951, at least 76,000 through mid-1952. In 1952 the Soviets had only about 50 percent more men in East Germany than the United States had in six division-equivalents in West Germany. Other NATO units in Germany improved the odds. Duffield, "The Soviet Military Threat," 214.

20. Tsouras, *Changing Orders,* 20.

21. Radzinsky, *Stalin,* 560–62.

22. FRUS (1952–54) 8: 971–77.

23. Tsouras, *Changing Orders,* 26.

24. According to NSC 114/2 of 12 October 1951 (FRUS [1951] 1:182–92, esp. 186), "taking account of terrain factors, Soviet logistical problems, and atomic developments . . . areas of major strategic importance in continental Europe can be held by mid-1953." Previous NSC 114 series papers had predicted that the Soviets could overrun Europe at will.

25. Ibid., 190–93.

26. Bluth, *Britain, Germany, and Western Nuclear Strategy,* 33–34. Carte Blanche was conducted in June 1955. In the initial attack, twenty-five nuclear weapons "destroyed" six air bases. The initial counterattack involved twenty-four strikes on enemy targets; in all, 355 simulated nuclear weapons were used.

27. Duffield, "The Evolution," 185.

28. Tsouras, *Changing Orders,* 109–10.

Chapter 16. Crisis

1. Tsouras, *Changing Orders,* 64–65.

2. See, e.g., FRUS (1951) 1: 44–48, and the CIA's 24 September 1951 Special Estimate (SE-13), "Probable Development of the World Situation Through Mid-1953," 193–207. The *New York Times* summary of the "Pentagon Papers" includes an NSC document dated "early 1952" (28–33, document no. 2, c.1), "United States Objectives and Courses of Action With Respect to Southeast Asia." The mid-1953 version of the Eisenhower administration's NSC document on Basic National Security Policy (FRUS [1952–54] 2:578–97) stated (584) that "certain other countries, such as Indo-China or Formosa, are of such strategic importance to the United States that an attack on them would probably compel the United States to react with military force either locally at the point of attack or generally against the military power of the aggressor."

3. James R. Arnold, *The First Domino,* 114.

4. A. Zervoudakis, "*Nihil mirare, nihil contemptare, omnia intelligere:* Franco-Vietnamese Intelligence in Indochina, 1950–1954," in *Knowing Your Friends,* ed. Alexander, 214–15.

5. Ibid., 217.

6. James R. Arnold, *The First Domino,* 131.

7. Ibid., 132.

8. Zervoudakis, "*Nihil mirare, nihil contemptare,* " 216.

9. James R. Arnold, *The First Domino,* 130–31.

10. Zervoudakis, "*Nihil mirare, nihil contemptare,* " 216.

11. Davidson, *Vietnam at War,* 262–69; Botti, *Ace in the Hole,* 57.

12. FRUS (1952–54) 2:835.

13. Anthony Clayton, *The Wars of French Decolonization,* 72.

14. Bissell, *Reflections of a Cold Warrior,* 78–79.

15. D. Artaud, "The United States, France, and Southeast Asia as a Threat to the Cohesion of the Atlantic Alliance, 1954–1955," in *The Origins of NATO,* ed. Joseph Smith.

16. To aid in U.S. decisionmaking, a Special NIE (SNIE) was ordered. SNIE 10-4-54, "Communist Reactions to Certain U.S. Courses of Action With Respect to Indochina," 15 June 1954, examined Soviet and Chinese reactions in the event U.S. forces intervened after the newly independent Associated States asked for direct military assistance by SEATO.

17. Lansdale, *In the Midst of Wars,* 345–47; on 11 April 1956 representatives of the governments who had sponsored the 1954 accords agreed that the plebiscite was "unfeasible" under conditions then prevailing.

18. Tsouras, *Changing Orders,* 29–30.

19. Ibid., 30.

Chapter 17. Enter Khrushchev

1. SE-39, "Probable Consequences of the Death of Stalin and of the Elevation of Malenkov to Leadership in the USSR," 12 March 1953, in CIA 2:3–9.

2. Beria's reform program is detailed in Knight, *Beria: Stalin's First Lieutenant,* 183–86.

3. Mehl and Schaefer, *Die andere deutsche Marine,* 17–19.

4. According to Knight, *Beria: Stalin's First Lieutenant,* 196, there were two MVD (Ministry of Internal Affairs, under Beria) divisions in Moscow, and the MVD guarded the Kremlin. The officers who arrested Beria had to be smuggled in. Mastny, *The Cold War and Soviet Insecurity,* 185–89, doubts that Beria had any plans at all for a coup; the only coup was that hatched against him.

5. Zubok and Pleshakov, *Inside the Kremlin's Cold War,* 167, 188.

6. Ibid., 142; their ideology "derived not from Marxism-Leninism but from the 'plan.'"

7. Ibid., 166; the speech was to Soviet electors, on 12 March 1954. Malenkov had previously announced, on 8 August 1953, that "there are no objective grounds for a collision between the United States and the USSR" (164).

8. FRUS (1952–54) 8:1, 210–12.

9. A review of relations with Yugoslavia began immediately after Stalin died. Beria concluded that they should be normalized, but Molotov's veto won the Presidium vote in mid-1953 (Zubok and Pleshakov, *Inside the Kremlin's Cold War,* 158).

10. Ibid., 158 and 171; the treaty was concluded after secret talks with the Austrian chancellor, begun early in 1955.

11. Volkogonov, *Sem' vozhdei (Seven rulers),* 406.

12. Ibid., 369.

13. Zubok and Pleshakov, *Inside the Kremlin's Cold War,* 186.

14. Ibid, 184. While he was preparing to intervene, Khrushchev told Tito that many in the Soviet Union blamed Hungary on his de-Stalinization; when Stalin was in charge, there were no such setbacks.

Chapter 18. The "New Look"

1. FRUS (1952–54) 2:534–49.

2. Ambrose, *Eisenhower: The President,* 123.

3. FRUS (1952–54) 2:672–75.

4. S. Twigge and A. Macmillan, "Britain, the United States, and the development of NATO Strategy, 1950–1964," in *Journal of Strategic Studies* 19, no. 2 (June 1996): 260–81, esp. 261–62 on the origins and implications of the Global Strategy paper.

5. FRUS (1952–54) 2: 276.

6. Ibid. 443–55.

7. Ibid., 323–26, established the study. Notes on the plenary sessions, 26 June 1953, are in pages 388–93, and the discussion by the NSC plus the written reports is in pages 394–434.

8. FRUS (1955–57) 19:126–30, 188–91.

9. FRUS (1952–54) 2:686–98 (NSC meeting 24 June 1954), 716–31.

10. Ibid., 457–60, in a memorandum seen and commented upon by President Eisenhower.

11. For the onset of the European problem, see NIE-99, "Estimate of the World Situation Through 1955" (issued 23 October 1953), in ibid., 551–62.

12. Bacevich, *The Pentomic Era.*

13. Between FY53 and FY55 the army budget was halved; the army was the smallest of the services through the Eisenhower administration.

14. Bacevich, *The Pentomic Era,* 46.

15. See, e.g., an 11 October 1954 NSC working paper, FRUS (1952–54) 2:740–59, 833.

16. The Net Evaluation Subcommittee established on 14 February 1955 (FRUS [1955–57] 19:56) reported its first annual assessment of a strategic war on 27 October 1955. The forces used were those expected to be in service three years hence. The 1956 study (1959 war) is in FRUS (1955–57) 19:379–81; the 1957 study is in ibid., 672–76; for the 1958 study see FRUS (1958–60) 3:147–52, 183; for the 1959 study (discussed in April 1960) see ibid., 397–404. Studies continued at least through 1961 (for a 1964 war).

17. FRUS (1952–54) 2:332–49, 367–70.

18. Ibid., 339, gives the 1953 figures.

19. IDA, 205–7.

20. Duffy and Kandalov, *Tupolev,* 220.

21. For the 1948 project, see A. Shirokorad, "Tank Landings at the Pole," in *Tekhnika molodezhi,* no. 42 (1996): 9. A photograph of a model of the 1974 nuclear-powered transport submarine design (Project 717) appears on p. 306 of A. M. Vasil'ev, S. I. Logachev, O. P. Maidanov, B. Yu. Marinin, et al., *Istoria otechestvennogo sudostroyeniya (History of shipbuilding),* vol. 5 (1946–91)(St. Petersburg: "Sudostroyeniye," 1996).

22. In July 1953 the U.S. Air Attaché submitted a fuzzy photograph which later proved to show a Bison. The first Bison flew on 20 January 1953, the first Bear on 12 November 1952, and the first Badger on 27 April 1952 (Gunston, *The Encyclopedia of Russian Aircraft,* 258, 421, 425).

23. FRUS (1955–57) 19:148–49.

24. Ibid., 148. We now know that in November 1953 the Central Committee Presidium (ex-Politburo) decided that in two years the Ministry of Medium Machine Building should build and test Sakharov's H-bomb. At the same meeting, according to Holloway, *Stalin and the Bomb,* the Presidium decided that the R-7 ICBM should be developed specifically to carry the new weapon.

25. NIE 11-8-59, "Soviet Capabilities for Strategic Attack through Mid-1964," 9 February 1960, in CIA 4: 71–107, seems to have been the first report to point out that not all Badgers were strategic bombers; 290 were assigned to Soviet Naval Aviation and 120 to Frontal (tactical) aviation.

26. Ibid. These data were quite good. The report gave the total number of operational Badgers as 1,460. According to Tupolev figures in Duffy and Kandalov, *Tupolev,* 222, a total of 1,511 were actually built.

27. Rosenberg, "Toward Armageddon," 205.

28. A. E. Rosenberg, "A smoking, radiating ruin at the end of two hours," *International Security* 6, no. 3 (1981).

29. Probably the most complete account of pre–U-2 air force flights is R. C. Hall, "The Truth about Overflights," in *MHQ9,* no. 3 (spring 1997): 24. Hall is an air force official historian.

30. The 1955 figures are from a 15 July 1955 speech by the SAC commander, Gen. Curtis LeMay (IDA, 257). The 1957 figures are from Roman, *Eisenhower and the Missile Gap,* 52; the failure was discovered in September 1957 by Robert Sprague (53–54). See also Rhodes, *Dark Sun,* 568.

31. IDA, 157.

32. For example, a September 1953 report on continental air defense (FRUS [1952–54] 2:

475–89) included submarine-launched missiles as a near-term threat, despite the admitted lack of hard evidence. See also IDA, 87; NIE 11-56 of 6 March 1956, "Soviet Gross Capabilities for Attack on the U.S. and Key Overseas Installations and Forces Through Mid-1959" (in CIA 4: 9–37); and NIE 11-4-57 of 12 November 1957, "Main Trends in Soviet Capabilities and Policies," in FRUS (1955–57) 19:665–72. In fact in September 1955 the Soviets tested a short-range (166-kilometer) submarine-launched ballistic missile (R-11FM, an adapted Scud). The system was accepted into service on 28 January 1958. The Soviets also developed a transonic cruise missile, P-5 (NATO SS-N-3 Shaddock, comparable to the U.S. Regulus). The first operational Soviet cruise missile submarines were ready in 1960.

33. Rosenberg, "Toward Armageddon," 205.

34. FRUS (1958–60) 3: 492. According to Rosenberg, "Toward Armageddon," 297, Kistiakowsky told Eisenhower that SAC's computer procedures were often "sheer bull."

35. Rosenberg, "Toward Armageddon," 240.

36. A. D. Rosenberg, "The Origins of Overkill," *International Security* (spring 1971): 3–71.

37. May, Steinbruner, and Wolfe, *History of the Strategic Arms Competition*, 459–60.

38. FRUS (1958–60) 3:147–52, 183.

39. Ibid., 1–3, 49–51, and 65–68.

40. For the relevant documents, see ibid., 382–85, 407–8, 420–21, and 442–51; May, Steinbruner, and Wolfe, *History of the Strategic Arms Competition*, 466.

41. Roman, *Eisenhower and the Missile Gap*, 85.

42. FRUS (1958–60) 3: 483 n. 2, 492. According to Rosenberg, "Toward Armageddon," 293–95, SIOP-62 was designed to attack about 1,050 designated ground zeroes (DGZs) out of 2,600 desired ones, which had been chosen from the roughly 4,100 in the national strategic target list (NSTL). The targeters rigged the plan by demanding a very high probability of destroying the top six hundred targets (well above JCS standards), so several weapons had to be assigned to each target. The navy charged that the targeters were demanding 300–500 kilotons to do the damage which 13 kilotons had inflicted at Hiroshima. Even the alert force would cause too much fallout in Helsinki, Berlin, Budapest, northern Japan, and Seoul.

43. May, Steinbruner, and Wolfe, *History of the Strategic Arms Competition*, 593. See also Pedlow and Welzenbach, *The CIA and the U-2 Program*, the CIA's official (now declassified) report on the program.

44. Bissell, *Reflections of a Cold Warrior*, 92–93. For details of the program, see Peebles, *The Corona Project*, and CIA, vol. 5. CIA, vol. 5 includes one of the first NIEs based on Corona photographs, NIE 11-8/1-61, "Strength and Deployment of Soviet Long-Range Ballistic Missile Forces," 21 September 1961.

45. FRUS (1958–60) 3: 409.

46. The prominence accorded Col. Oleg Penkovskiy in 1961–62 suggests just how little inside information was then available on Soviet programs. As a GRU scientific intelligence officer, Penkovskiy offered insight into the structure of the Soviet military bureaucracy as well as copies of numerous reports and articles from the Secret and Top Secret versions of the journal *Voyennaya Mysl'* (Military thought). Both the articles and sanitized versions of his debriefings are available in the "Soviet Estimate" collection at the National Security Archive.

47. IDA, 218.

48. Ibid., 158.

49. This horrific possibility was the basis for the movie *Dr. Strangelove* and for a novel, *Failsafe.*

50. IDA, 329

51. NIE 11-3-61, "Sino-Soviet Air Defense Capabilities Through Mid-1966" (11 July 1961).

52. See Knaack, *Size, Post–World War II Bombers,* 137–42 (for the B-47), and 386, 389 (for the B-58); for the British Valiant bomber, see Wynn, *RAF Nuclear Deterrent Forces,* 464–65.

53. Roman, *Eisenhower and the Missile Gap,* 161–63.

54. Bissell, *Reflections of a Cold Warrior,* 92–99.

55. Evan Thomas, *The Very Best Men,* 157–60; Prados, *Presidents' Secret Wars,* 130–44.

56. Prados, *Presidents' Secret Wars,* 150–70. A very recent account, based on declassified official U.S. sources, is Knaus, *Orphans of the Cold War.*

Chapter 19. Khrushchev's "New Look"

1. According to Soviet statistics quoted by Antonov-Ovseyenko, *The Time of Stalin,* 212, the birthrate per thousand fell from 44.3 in 1928 to 32.6 in 1931, the year the terrible Ukrainian famine began. It fell to 31.6 in 1934, and then slowly rose before falling again in 1939–40 to reflect the imprisonment of millions of people.

2. NIE 11-4-65, "Main Trends in Soviet Military Policy," 14 April 1965, in CIA 3:191–214.

3. Tsouras, *Changing Orders,* 121.

4. Duffield, "The Evolution," 254.

5. Lyelchuka and Pivovara, *SSR I Kholodnaya Voenia* (USSR and Cold War), 183.

6. The Soviets called bombers equipped with standoff weapons "missile carriers." Under a 1954 decree, missiles were developed for both the new intercontinental bombers, the 3M (Bison) and the Tu-95 (Bear). Only the latter, Kh-20 (NATO AS-3), was successful. Tactical bombers probably avoided a similar fate because no suitable standoff nuclear missile was developed (warheads were probably too large). The only missile developed for the new-generation tactical bomber, the Yak-28, was the Kh-28 defense-suppression (ARM) weapon, intended for a special but abortive Yak-28N version (1964–65). Gunston and Gordon, *Yakovlev Aircraft,* 144–45, 149–50, 157–169. Yak-28 production may have been limited because the Soviet army began to receive medium-range missiles, both ballistic (Scud) and cruise (SSC-1, a land-based equivalent to the naval P-6 [SSN-3 Shaddock]).

7. Fursenko and Naftali, *"One Hell of a Gamble,"* 70.

8. See, for example, ibid., 58–59 (Castro's revolutionary 1960 Declaration of Havana).

9. According to Nelson, *War of the Black Heavens,* 70, three Radio Free Europe (RFE) news stories helped ignite the 1956 uprisings: a series of taped interviews with Col. Josef Swiatlo of the Polish secret police, who defected on 5 December 1953 (and who revealed the depth of corruption of the Polish Communist leadership); the May 1955 agreement between Tito and Bulganin that there could be different roads to Socialism; and Khrushchev's secret speech. The State Department considered the Swiatlo disclosures the most effective political warfare attack since 1945. When the Polish workers at Poznan rioted in June 1956, Radio Free Europe published the two themes of their banners, which were soon

censored out of photographs: "Bread and Freedom" and "Russians Go Home." According to Nelson, 70, RFE discouraged the riots on the ground that they would only encourage further repression; a Polish Communist official told an RFE reporter in Stockholm that RFE's calls for calm had likely been decisive. In the case of Hungary, RFE did commit the error of misreading a Radio Budapest broadcast and thus charging Premier Imre Nagy of calling in the Soviet troops (72). It appears that the Hungarian-language service was insufficiently supervised, and that its programs were grossly overexcited (73–81). Some of them offered military advice to the rebels, and a 27 October 1956 program (which had been misrepresented to those in charge) implied that foreign assistance would be forthcoming if the revolutionaries were able to set up a central military command. A few other programs also clearly violated standing instructions not to incite the East Europeans to revolt. The most notorious was a 4 November "short world press review" which quoted the British *Observer* newspaper as saying that "if . . . the Hungarians hold out for three or four days, then the pressure upon the government of the United States to send military help . . . will become irresistible." Bela Kovacs, former secretary of the Smallholders' Party (the largest pre-Communist party in Hungary) sheltered in the American Legation on 4 November; the legation reported that he "left little doubt that in his opinion the U.S., for the attainment of its selfish goals, had cynically and cold-bloodedly maneuvered the Hungarian people into action against the USSR." In a poll of Hungarian refugees early in December 1956, the U.S. Information Agency found that 96 percent had expected Western aid, and 77 percent had expected Western military aid. Of those who expected aid, 8 percent did so on the basis of RFE broadcasts.

10. Zubok and Pleshakov, *Inside the Kremlin's Cold War,* 187.

11. May, Steinbruner, and Wolfe, *History of the Strategic Arms Competition.* 354–55.

12. Allen Dulles's comments at a 21 January 1960 NSC meeting in FRUS (1958–60) 3:366–69.

13. From a memo by Maxwell Taylor to the president, 25 May 1962, in FRUS (1961–63) 8: 299–300. Presumably the account was from a document provided by Colonel Penkovskiy. Taylor may well have been referring to "New Developments in Operational Art and Tactics," by Lt. Gen. V. Baskakov, a CIA translation of which was distributed to cleared American readers on 31 January 1962; it referred to a 1959 exercise. The article had appeared in the first issue of the "Special Collection," and the special series of "Military Thought" was described by the CIA as a Top Secret publication distributed only within the Ministry of Defence, and down only to the level of army commanders. The U.S. version of this article (and of others of the "Special Collection," presumably provided by Penkovskiy) was declassified on 30 June 1992. Copies are in the U.S. National Archives and in the private National Security Archives, the latter in the collection titled "The Soviet Estimate."

Chapter 20. Disaster in the Middle East

1. See, for example, S. Dockrill, "Retreat From the Continent? Britain's Motives for Troop Reductions in West Germany, 1955–1958," in *Journal of Strategic Studies* 20, no. 3 (September 1997).

2. William R. Louis, "The Anglo-Egyptian Settlement of 1954," in *Suez 1956,* ed. Louis and Owen, 62.

3. JCS 4:353; Oren, *The Origins of the Second Arab-Israeli War,* 67.

4. Oren, *The Origins of the Second Arab-Israeli War,* 66.

5. William R. Louis, "The Anglo-Egyptian Settlement of 1954," in *Suez 1956,* ed. Louis and Owen, 50–51.

6. Kunz, *Butter and Guns,* 71. For details of the various attempted settlements (1952–56) see S. Shamir, "The Collapse of Project Alpha," in *Suez 1956,* ed. Louis and Owen.

7. Kunz, *Butter and Guns,* 72–76.

8. R. R. Bowie, "Eisenhower, Dulles, and the Suez Crisis," in *Suez 1956,* ed. Louis and Owen.

9. Oren, *The Origins of the Second Arab-Israeli War,* 70, and H. F. Eilts, "Reflections on Suez: Middle East Security," in *Suez 1956,* ed. Louis and Owen.

10. Eilts, "Reflections on Suez," 352.

11. Shamir, "The Collapse of Project Alpha," 90.

12. Oren, *The Origins of the Second Arab-Israeli War,* 73–74.

13. The wooing is described in Copeland, *The Game of Nations.* See also Copeland, *The Game Player,* 158–71.

14. R. R. Bowie, "Eisenhower, Dulles, and the Suez Crisis," in *Suez 1956,* ed. Louis and Owen,

15. Rodman, *More Precious than Peace,* 75–76.

16. K. Kyle, "Britain and the Crisis, 1955–1956," in *Suez 1956,* ed. Louis and Owen, 109.

17. Bowie, "Eisenhower, Dulles, and the Suez Crisis," 192.

18. Rodman, *More Precious than Peace,* 77.

19. Oren, *The Origins of the Second Arab-Israeli War,* 91–92.

20. Ibid., 137.

21. Copeland, *The Game of Nations,* 202.

22. A. Watson, "The Aftermath of Suez: Consequences for French Decolonization," in *Suez 1956,* ed. Louis and Owen, 341.

23. Oren, *The Origins of the Second Arab-Israeli War,* 138.

24. Ibid., 139.

25. Kyle, "Britain and the Crisis," 266–71; M. Bar-On, "David Ben-Gurion and the Sevres Collusion," in *Suez 1956,* ed. Louis and Owen, 147.

26. Rodman, *More Precious than Peace,* 79.

27. Grove, *Vanguard to Trident,* 184.

28. Kunz, *Butter and Guns,* 85–86.

29. Rodman, *More Precious than Peace,* 84–85. British Foreign Secretary Selwyn Lloyd said that when he visited Dulles in hospital in mid-November Dulles "said at once with a kind of twinkle in his eye, 'Selwyn, why did you stop? Why didn't you go through with it and get Nasser down.'" On the morning of 3 November, with Anglo-French forces off the Egyptian coast but not yet in combat, the CIA deputy director called the station chief in London: "Tell your friends to comply with the goddamn cease-fire [ordered by the UN] or go ahead with the goddamn invasion. Either way, we'll back 'em up if they do it fast. What we can't stand is their goddamn hesitation waltz while Hungary is burning."

30. M. Vaisse, "Post-Suez France," in *Suez 1956,* ed. Louis and Owen.

31. Ibid., 339.

32. Ibid., 340.

33. FRUS (1955–57) 27:736–38, describes the conversation at the Mid-Ocean Club in Bermuda on 22 March 1957.

34. Duffield, "The Evolution," 263–64.

35. Ibid., 287–88; Navias, *Nuclear Weapons and British Strategic Planning,* 134–87. Prime Minister Macmillan announced the outline of the new strategy to President Eisenhower and his aides during the Bermuda conference on 22 March 1957 (FRUS [1955–57] 27: 749).

36. Horne, *Harold Macmillan,* 195–98.

37. A few years later Secretary of Defense McNamara used this figure for relative strengths.

38. FRUS (1955–57) 27: 78–79, 148–49.

39. Anthony Clayton, *The Wars of French Decolonization,* 135–41, 160.

40. Ibid., 144–50.

41. C. Buffet, "The Berlin Crises, France, and the Atlantic Alliance, 1947–1962: From Integration to Disintegration," in *Securing Peace in Europe,* ed. Heuser and O'Neill, 91.

42. Anthony Clayton, *The Wars of French Decolonization,* 132, 134–35.

43. R. Khalidi, "Consequences of Suez in the Arab World," in *Suez 1956,* ed. Louis and Owen; Gerges, *The Superpowers and the Middle East,* 101.

44. Gerges, *The Superpowers and the Middle East,* 112–14.

45. Ibid., 80.

46. Ambrose, *Eisenhower: The President,* 463–66, 471–75; A. Rathmell, "Brotherly Enemies: The Rise and Fall of the Syrian-Egyptian Intelligence Axis, 1954–1967," in *Knowing Your Friends,* ed. Alexander, especially pp. 236–39. Eisenhower seems to have framed his doctrine with Lebanon in mind.

47. Gerges, *The Superpowers and the Middle East,* 129–30. 47. See also Ashton, *Eisenhower, Macmillan, and the Problem of Nasser,* 194–95.

48. Gerges, *The Superpowers and the Middle East,* 126.

49. Ibid., 132–33.

50. Ibid., 148–49.

51. Ibid., 151.

52. Ibid., 156–57.

53. Ibid., 159.

54. Ibid., 161.

55. Ibid., 162–63.

56. Ibid., 164.

Chapter 21. The Missile Race

1. FRUS (1955–1957) 19:401–9; Neufeld, *Ballistic Missiles in the United States Air Force,* 147, attributes the equal priority given IRBM and ICBM programs to this report.

2. According to Laquer, *The Uses and Limits of Intelligence,* 143–44, the Kapustin Yar IRBM range was discovered by Western intelligence in 1954 through monitoring of Soviet domestic (military and civilian) communications. An FPS-17 radar became operational in the summer of 1955 at Samsun, Turkey, to monitor it; it was supplemented by installation in the Elburz Mountains of Turkey, at Meshed in Iran, and at Peshawar in Pakistan. ICBMs were fired from a new launch complex at Tyuratam. Radar revealed the existence of the Tyuratam range in 1956, and early in the summer of 1957 a U-2 photographed an ICBM on its launcher there. This photograph led the CIA to predict imminent tests. However, the FPS-17 radar built specifically to monitor Tyuratam, near Diyarbakir in southeast Turkey, seems not to have become operational until the fall of 1957. According to Buderi, *The Invention that*

Changed the World, 436, it covered the Sputnik launching (which was, by implication, one of the first on which it was used). In a 14 April 1958 NSC briefing CIA Director Allen Dulles mentioned the recent completion of a U.S. detection system, probably an FPS-17 (FRUS [1958–60] 3:69). The lack of concrete data is evident in NIE 11-5-57, "Soviet Capabilities and Probable Programs in the Guided Missile Field" (12 March 1957) in CIA 2:59–62.

3. Zaloga (forthcoming).

4. Robinson, *The End of the American Century,* 211.

5. Neufeld, *Ballistic Missiles in the United States Air Force,* 160; OSD 4:512.

6. Nash, *The Other Missiles of October,* 14.

7. Ibid., 22–26.

8. On 4 June 1959 CIA Director Allen Dulles reported to the NSC that a 30 May 1959 flight from Tyuratam had apparently been the first Soviet test firing to a range beyond 3,500 nautical miles (FRUS [1958–60] 3:215). According to Volkov et al., *Mezhkontinentalniye ballisticheskiye raketi SSSR* (Intercontinental Ballistic Missiles of the USSR), 316, the original R-7, which was designed for a range of 8,000 kilometers (about 4,400 nautical miles), made its first full proof flight on 30 July 1959. It was formally accepted into service on 20 January 1960.

9. FRUS (1955–57) 19:638–61.

10. Aerojet ex-employees, c. 4, p.83.

11. For example, Kalugin, *The First Directorate,* 2–4, recalls how valuable it was to gain access to a U.S. rocket fuel chemist in 1959.

12. FRUS (1955–57) 19:620–24.

13. FRUS (1958–60) 3:135–36.

14. Ibid., 184–87.

15. Ibid., 153–68.

16. FRUS (1955–57) 19:621.

17. FRUS (1961–63) 8:87–88.

18. In contrast to SAC, the RSVN was created primarily out of the rocket arm of the artillery branch, although three of its first nine divisions (raised in July 1960) came from the staffs of air force bomber units.

19. FRUS (1958–60) 3:325–30.

20. Roman, *Eisenhower and the Missile Gap,* 129–30.

21. FRUS (1958–60) 3:375–80 (NIE of 3 November 1959).

22. Roman, *Eisenhower and the Missile Gap,* 140.

23. Ibid., 131.

24. Bundy, *Danger and Survival,* 345–46.

25. May, Steinbruner, and Wolfe, *History of the Strategic Arms Competition,* 375–76.

26. R-7s were deployed only at two pads at Baikonur (Tyuratam) and four at Plesetsk, which was completed in 1959 (Harford, *Korolev,* 112).

27. Reeves, *President Kennedy: Profile of Power,* 37, 58.

28. Roman, *Eisenhower and the Missile Gap,* 145.

29. Shapley, *Promise and Power,* 97; Reeves, *President Kennedy: Profile of Power,* 58–59.

30. FRUS (1961–63) 8:46 (20 February 1961); Shapley, *Promise and Power,* 99. McNamara's paper showed that the United States had test-fired ninety-six ICBMs, compared to thirty-three for the Soviets.

31. Gibson, *Nuclear Weapons of the United States,* 194–95.

32. Test shots at the Sary Shagan range included interception of an R-12 (SS-4) IRBM by an experimental V-1000 missile. Production and installation of an A-35 system (NATO ABM-1 Galosh) around Moscow was authorized on 8 April 1958.

33. The "Leningrad missile" was actually an antiaircraft system, Semyon P. Lavochkin's Dal (distance). Although the first three launcher sites were begun, Dal was cancelled in favor of a new long-range system, S-200 Angara (NATO SA-5 Gammon). In 1963, with Dal quite dead, Khrushchev had its missile paraded through Moscow as an antiballistic missile weapon, resulting in the speculation about the "Leningrad system." In the 1970s, after the Soviets had signed a treaty limiting ABMs, those opposing such treaties often treated continued SA-5 deployment as cheating (S. J. Zaloga, "Defending the Capitals: The First Generation of Soviet Strategic Air Defense Systems, 1950–1960," in *Journal of Slavic Military Studies* 10, no. 4 [December 1997]: 30–44).

34. IDA, 243, 281.

35. Ambrose, *Eisenhower: The President,* 612–13.

Chapter 22. Crisis Time

1. The first proof was China's ability to call a conference of "nonaligned" countries at Bandung, Indonesia, in 1955. The Soviets were not invited to this "anti-imperialist" conference.

2. Medvedev, *China and the Superpowers,* 29–30.

3. Ibid., 42.

4. Zubok and Pleshakov, *Inside the Kremlin's Cold War,* 216.

5. Medvedev, *China and the Superpowers,* 29.

6. Zubok and Pleshakov, *Inside the Kremlin's Cold War,* 170; Medvedev, *China and the Superpowers,* 26.

7. Stueck, *The Korean War,* 363; the Chinese never forgave the Soviets for failing to renounce the debt. Zubok and Pleshakov, *Inside the Kremlin's Cold War,* 170, describe Khrushchev's concessions.

8. For example, Maj. J. E. Thach Jr., USAR, "Modernization and Conflict: Soviet Assistance to the PRC, 1950–1960," *Military Review* 58 (January 1978): 72–89, cites a 1957 official Chinese statement that it would take at least ten more years to pay off the costs of the Korean War, if they could be paid at all. Interest was being charged on these loans. At this time the Chinese stated that their debt to the Soviets was $2.4 billion, 80 percent of which was reportedly for military aid.

9. Stueck, *The Korean War,* 364.

10. Duiker, *The Communist Road to Power,* 194.

11. Medvedev, *China and the Superpowers,* 31–32.

12. Stone, *Satellites and Commissars,* 33.

13. Ibid., 30–31.

14. Zubok and Pleshakov, *Inside the Kremlin's Cold War,* 219.

15. Becker, *Hungry Ghosts: China's Secret Famine,* 270–74. An internal Chinese government document said that Mao was responsible for eighty million deaths, most of them during the great famine (275).

16. Medvedev, *China and the Superpowers,* 33.

17. Zubok and Pleshakov, *Inside the Kremlin's Cold War,* 219.

18. FRUS (1958–60) 19:52–53.

19. Ambrose, *Eisenhower: The President,* 484.

20. Khrushchev's 7 September 1958 warning letter is in FRUS (1958–60) 19:145–53.

21. Lewis and Xue, *China Builds the Bomb,* 64, 71–72.

22. Zubok and Pleshakov, *Inside the Kremlin's Cold War,* 212.

23. Ibid., 197–98.

24. FRUS (1958–60) 3:79–97.

25. Medvedev, *China and the Superpowers,* 33.

26. Zubok and Pleshakov, *Inside the Kremlin's Cold War,* 201, 230–31.

27. Duiker, *The Communist Road to Power,* 195–96.

28. Karnow, *Vietnam: A History,* 240–41; Davidson, *Vietnam at War,* 286–87.

29. Duiker, *The Communist Road to Power,* 200–201.

30. Neil Sheehan, *The Pentagon Papers,* 78, 81.

31. Medvedev, *China and the Superpowers,* 34–35.

32. Thompson, *The Communist Movement Since 1945,* 71.

33. See, e.g., FRUS (1958–60) 3:54–55.

34. 18 August 1959 memo in FRUS (1958–60) 3:317–18.

35. FRUS (1958–60) 3:422–33.

36. Dunbabin, *The Cold War,* 235.

37. Evan Thomas, *The Very Best Men,* 221–22.

38. McClintock, *Instruments of Statecraft,* 150; Evan Thomas, *The Very Best Men,* 222.

39. Evan Thomas, *The Very Best Men,* 225.

40. Edmund A. Gullion (ambassador to the Congo in the early 1960s), interview, in *National Security Decisions,* ed. Pfaltzgraff and Davis, 345–46.

41. Guy Arnold, *Wars in the Third World,* 411–16.

42. Ambrose, *Eisenhower: The President,* 556–57, 584.

43. FRUS (1958–60) 3:432 (NSC meeting 25 July 1960).

44. FRUS (1958–60) 15:1, 118–19, a report by the Operations Coordinating Board of the NSC.

45. Bissell, *Reflections of a Cold Warrior,* 145–49.

46. Reeves, *President Kennedy: Profile of Power,* 30–32. See also Bissell, *Reflections of a Cold Warrior,* 145–49.

47. Roman, *More Precious than Peace,* 94–95; Reeves, *President Kennedy: Profile of Power,* 40–41; and Beschloss, *The Crisis Years,* 60. Delivered behind closed doors on 6 January, the speech was published in the Soviet press on the eighteenth. Much of what Khrushchev said in January he had already said in the December 1960 meeting of eighty-one world Communist parties.

Chapter 23. Kennedy and "Wars of National Liberation"

1. A. Schlesinger Jr., "On JFK: An Interview with Isaiah Berlin," *New York Review of Books,* 22 October 1998; this is an edited version of a 12 April 1965 interview in which Berlin recounts his impressions at a 1962 dinner. Berlin's comments on Kennedy the politician are comparisons with Roosevelt, whom he knew well, and whom he considered a far better politician.

2. Ibid. Berlin was much impressed by Kennedy's intense style of questioning (which he compares to Lenin's); but he also noted, in effect, that nothing seemed to penetrate.

3. Reeves, *President Kennedy: Profile of Power,* 52–53.

4. McMaster, *Dereliction of Duty,* 4.

5. Beschloss, *The Crisis Years,* 62–63.

6. Zubok and Pleshakov, *Inside the Kremlin's Cold War,* 238–40.

7. Reeves, *President Kennedy: Profile of Power,* 69–70.

8. Ibid., 91.

9. Ibid., 91, 95.

10. Ibid., 102–3.

11. Bissell, *Reflections of a Cold Warrior,* 191.

12. Ibid., 197.

13. McMaster, *Dereliction of Duty,* 6.

14. Reeves, *President Kennedy: Profile of Power,* 105. Early in May 1961 Kennedy approved a "Record of Action" stating that U.S. policy toward Cuba should aim at the overthrow of Castro.

15. Bissell, *Reflections of a Cold Warrior,* 162–92.

16. Reeves, *President Kennedy: Profile of Power,* 105.

17. Zubok and Pleshakov, *Inside the Kremlin's Cold War,* 242.

18. Kunz, *Butter and Guns,* 125–32.

19. FRUS (1961–63) 12:99, 101.

20. Ibid., 14.

21. Ibid., 88.

22. Ibid., 103.

23. Ibid., 11–12 ("Report to the President on Latin American Mission, Feb. 12–March 3, 1961").

24. Ibid., 79–85, RAR-12 of 17 January 1962, a report on "Latin American Political Stability and the Alliance for Progress" prepared by the State Department Bureau of Intelligence and Research.

25. Ibid., 116–17, gives specific achievements as of November 1962: improved tax administration, expanded educational programs, and agrarian reform.

26. Kunz, *Butter and Guns,* 123, 132–33.

27. Evan Thomas, *The Very Best Men,* 221.

28. Blasier, *The Hovering Giant,* 251.

29. Donghi, *The Contemporary History of Latin America,* 296.

30. Weis, *Cold Warriors and Coups d'Etat,* 165.

31. FRUS (1961–63) 12:152.

32. Quirk, *Fidel Castro,* 397.

33. Rouquie, *The Military and the State,* 136–37.

34. Moss, *Chile's Marxist Experiment,* 155–56.

35. Weis, *Cold Warriors and Coups d'Etat,* 149.

36. FRUS (1961–63) 12:445.

37. Ibid., 452; see also Special National Intelligence Estimate (SNIE) 93-2-61 (7 December 1961), 453–54.

38. Weis, *Cold Warriors and Coups d' Etat,* 156.

39. Ibid., 157.

40. FRUS (1961–63) 12:490–93 (Special National Intelligence Estimate 93-63, 27 February 1963).

41. Weis, *Cold Warriors and Coups d' Etat,* 157.

42. Kunz, *Butter and Guns,* 145; Weis, *Cold Warriors and Coups d' Etat,* 165.

43. Rouquie, *The Military and the State,* 283–84.

44. Donghi, *The Contemporary History of Latin America,* 309.

45. Sigmund, *The Overthrow of Allende,* 103.

46. Ibid., 40–42.

47. NSAM 124 (18 January 1962) created a Special Group (Counter-Insurgency) which initially concentrated on Laos, South Vietnam, and Thailand (FRUS [1961–63] 8:236–38). In October 1961, when Kennedy visited Fort Bragg to see the Special Forces in action, two of their three groups were operating in Southeast Asia. In December a third was activated; three more followed in 1963. Nine reserve groups were set up in 1961. Each of the original three groups was quadrupled to fifteen hundred men.

48. Tolson, *Airmobility,* 4.

49. Kevin Patrick Sheehan, "Preparing for an Imaginary War?" 294.

50. Neil Sheehan, *The Pentagon Papers,* 92–93.

51. Reeves, *President Kennedy: Profile of Power,* 111–12; McMaster, *Dereliction of Duty,* 7.

52. Beschloss, *The Crisis Years,* 395–96.

53. Ibid., 397.

54. Reeves, *President Kennedy: Profile of Power,* 255. The United States had Special Forces Groups (CIDGs) and hamlet militia (Tsouras, *Changing Orders,* 91).

55. Reeves, *President Kennedy: Profile of Power,* 240–41.

56. Neil Sheehan, *The Pentagon Papers,* 146–48, 153–55.

57. Bissell, *Reflections of a Cold Warrior,* 148, 151.

58. Reeves, *President Kennedy: Profile of Power,* 241.

59. In 1995 the North Vietnamese claimed that they had lost 1.1 million dead and 300,000 missing, compared to a 1965 population of 16 million (plus 4 million in Communist-controlled areas of South Vietnam) (Record, *The Wrong War,* 36). This cost, something more than 5 percent of the Communist Vietnamese population, compares with about 27 million out of perhaps 200 million Soviet citizens in World War II (i.e., about 13.5 percent), inflicted over a much shorter period.

60. Karnow, *Vietnam: A History,* 240–41; Davidson, *Vietnam at War,* 286–87.

61. L. Binyan and P. Link, "A Great Leap Backward?" in *New York Review of Books,* 8 October 1998; this is a synopsis of *Zhongguo de xianjing* (China's pitfall), a book recently published in Hong Kong.

62. M. Falcoff, "Latin America: Was There a 'Kirkpatrick Doctrine'?" in *President Reagan and the World,* ed. Schmertz, Datlof, and Ugrinsky, 394.

63. L. Berman, "NSAM 263 and NSAM 273: Manipulating History," in *Vietnam: The Early Decisions,* ed. Gardner and Gittinger, 186.

64. Reeves, *President Kennedy: Profile of Power,* 610.

65. Ibid., 563.

66. Ibid., 567.

67. Ibid., 566.

68. Ibid., 577.

69. Ibid., 595.

70. FRUS (1961–63) 4:328–30, 336–46.

71. Ibid., 393.

72. Ibid., 395–96, 371–79 (an associated telegram to Lodge in Saigon). This was NSAM 263, Kennedy's last policy statement on Vietnam, on 11 October 1963. The controversy over Kennedy's intentions was reignited when the Assassination Documents Review Commission released a copy of NSAM 263 in 1997.

73. Talking Points prepared on 29 October 1963 by Roger Hilsman, assistant secretary of state for Far Eastern Affairs, is in FRUS 1961–63, vol. 4.

74. Reeves, *President Kennedy: Profile of Power,* 616–18, 650.

75. Berman, "NSAM 263 and NSAM 273," 190–92.

76. NSAM 273 (26 November 1963).

77. John M. Newman, "The Kennedy-Johnson Transition: The Case for Policy Reversal," in *Vietnam: The Early Decisions,* ed. Gardner and Gittinger.

78. See, e.g., a 21 December 1963 memorandum for the record by Robert S. McNamara, cited in Reeves, *President Kennedy: Profile of Power,* 610–11.

Chapter 24. Crises in Europe and Cuba

1. Reeves, *President Kennedy: Profile of Power,* 187.

2. Zubok and Pleshakov, *Inside the Kremlin's Cold War,* 249.

3. Ibid.

4. Duffield, "The Evolution," 344.

5. Zubok and Pleshakov, *Inside the Kremlin's Cold War,* 243–47, based on Khrushchev's account to his advisors.

6. Reeves, *President Kennedy: Profile of Power,* 159–71, 177.

7. FRUS (1961–63) 8:156–58.

8. Reeves, *President Kennedy: Profile of Power,* 176.

9. Ibid., 183–84.

10. May, Steinbruner, and Wolfe, *History of the Strategic Arms Competition,* 681–82; Gelb, *The Berlin Wall,* 141.

11. Zubok and Pleshakov, *Inside the Kremlin's Cold War,* 250–51.

12. Reeves, *President Kennedy: Profile of Power,* 187.

13. Gelb, *The Berlin Wall,* 115.

14. Walker, *The Cold War,* 157.

15. From a heavily censored 19 September 1961 memo by General Taylor, quoting a memo by Carl Kaysen, in FRUS (1961–63) 8:126–29. Botti, *Ace in the Hole,* 158, describes the underlying study.

16. The Gagra conference is described in the memoirs of Khrushchev's son, quoted in Zaloga (forthcoming).

17. The new missiles were R-9 (NATO SS-8) and R-16 (NATO SS-7).

18. As reflected in contemporary NIEs.

19. Beschloss, *The Crisis Years,* 378–79.

20. Volkogonov, *Sem' vozhdei* (Seven rulers), 420–21.

21. Ibid., 419.

22. Ibid., 423–24.

23. Gaddis, *We Now Know,* 266.

24. Ibid., 264.

25. Nash, *The Other Missiles of October,* 151.

26. Ibid., 154.

27. Ibid., 159.

28. Wynn, *RAF Nuclear Deterrent Forces,* 359.

29. Quirk, *Fidel Castro.* 449.

30. CWIHP 5, 111.

31. IDA, 311.

32. Quirk, *Fidel Castro,* 477; Bethell, *Latin America: Economy and Society,* 112–13.

33. Quirk, *Fidel Castro,* 226.

34. Ibid., 477–78.

35. Bethell, *Latin America: Economy and Society,* 112.

36. Quirk, *Fidel Castro,* 554–55; the thesis was most prominently publicized in Régis Debray's *Revolution in the Revolution? Armed Struggle and Political Struggle in Latin America,* trans. Bobbye Ortiz (New York: MR Press, 1967).

37. Donghi, *The Contemporary History of Latin America,* 295.

38. W. Tapley Bennett Jr., interview, in *National Security Decisions,* ed. Pfaltzgraff and Davis, 318.

39. Blasier, *The Hovering Giant,* 246–47; Dallek, *Flawed Giant,* 262–67.

40. Guy Arnold, *Wars in the Third World,* 520.

41. Quirk, *Fidel Castro,* 568–69.

42. Ibid., 572.

43. May, Steinbruner, and Wolfe, *History of the Strategic Arms Competition,* 369–70, 486; the Arctic identification is from open Soviet writings, the description in the official publication having been excised.

44. Zubok and Pleshakov, *Inside the Kremlin's Cold War;* CWIHP (1996–97) 10.

Chapter 25. The McNamara Broom

1. Kunz, *Butter and Guns,* 65–66.

2. For an example, see Shapley, *Promise and Power,* 128.

3. For an example, see the description of the F-111 decision in ibid., 205–11.

4. Ibid., 127.

5. Ibid.; McMaster, *Dereliction of Duty,* 18.

6. McMaster, *Dereliction of Duty,* 5.

7. Roman, *Eisenhower and the Missile Gap,* 139.

8. John Taylor, *General Maxwell Taylor,* 227.

9. Ibid., 226.

10. Bundy, *Danger and Survival,* 352.

11. FRUS (1961–63) 8:275–81.

12. Reeves, *President Kennedy: Profile of Power,* 306; having read the book, Kennedy told his secretary of the army to make sure every officer read it.

13. Hansen, *U.S. Nuclear Weapons*, briefly describes some of the PALs.

14. Walker, *The Cold War*, 145.

15. Brinkley, *Dean Acheson*, 123. The policy direction portion of NSAM 40 is in FRUS (1961–63) 8:285–91.

16. Bundy, *Danger and Survival*, 488.

17. John Taylor, *General Maxwell Taylor*, 234–35.

18. McMaster, *Dereliction of Duty*, 11.

19. Shapley, *Promise and Power*, 139; FRUS (1961–63) 8:35–48.

20. McMaster, *Dereliction of Duty*, 22–23.

21. Brinkley, *Dean Acheson*, 118–23.

22. FRUS (1961–63) 8:565–87; NIE 11-14-62, "Capabilities of the Soviet Theater Forces," dated 5 December 1962 (FRUS [1961–63] 8: 431–35); and McNamara FY65–69 Draft Presidential Memorandum on general purpose forces, 19 December 1963 (FRUS [1961–63] 8:565–87).

23. Reeves, *President Kennedy: Profile of Power*, 179.

24. Bundy, *Danger and Survival*, 348.

25. See McNamara's 3 December 1962 draft presidential memorandum on FY64–68 general purpose forces; the proposed $3.3 billion was more than twice the average for FY57–61. Money was provided for modern equipment for the sixteen active divisions plus six priority reserve divisions (FRUS [1961–63] 8:423).

26. FRUS (1961–63) 8:426–27.

27. Duffield, "The Evolution," 352.

28. Ibid., 375.

29. Kunz, *Butter and Guns*, 99–100.

30. Shapley, *Promise and Power*, 90; OSD 2:274.

31. For the flavor of McNamara's analysis, see Einthoven and Smith, *How Much Is Enough?* McNamara summarized his views in Draft Presidential Memoranda (DPMs) on various programs. Declassified versions of many of the early ones are included in FRUS (1961–63) volumes.

32. FRUS (1961–63) 8:382–83.

33. Shapley, *Promise and Power*, 188.

34. FRUS (1961–63), 8:143, 145.

35. See McNamara's 21 November 1962 Draft Presidential Memorandum in FRUS (1961–63) 8:398–415 and his 8 December 1963 Draft Memorandum in FRUS (1961–63) 8:545–64.

36. FRUS (1961–63) 8:195–97.

37. E. Diamond, "The Ancient History of the Internet," in *American Heritage* 46, no. 6 (October 1995).

38. Bundy, *Danger and Survival*, 352–53.

39. FRUS (1961–63) 8:392–97; May, Steinbruner, and Wolfe, *History of the Strategic Arms Competition*, 548–50.

40. Zaloga (forthcoming).

41. May, Steinbruner, and Wolfe, *History of the Strategic Arms Competition*, 569.

42. Ibid. 569–70.

43. Ibid., 570.

44. The first U.S. decoys went onto Atlas F missiles in mid-1963. Ibid., 577–78; FRUS (1961–63) 8:373–74.

45. May, Steinbruner, and Wolfe, *History of the Strategic Arms Competition,* 585–86.

Chapter 26. De Gaulle vs. NATO

1. Brinkley, *Dean Acheson,* 119–20.
2. FRUS (1961–63) 13:641.
3. Duffield, "The Evolution," 338.
4. FRUS (1961–63) 13:743.
5. Horne, *A Savage War of Peace,* 436–60.
6. A. Kolodziej, "France," in *The Structure of the Defense Industry,* ed. Ball and Leitenberg, 86–89.
7. Kolodziej, "France," 91–100.
8. Duffield, "The Evolution," 339.
9. Ibid., 369.
10. Ibid., 389.
11. Ibid., 386.
12. Haftendorn, *NATO and the Nuclear Revolution,* 224.
13. Duffield, "The Evolution," 391.
14. François De Rose, interview, in *National Security Decisions,* ed. Pfaltzgraff and Davis, 102.
15. Ibid., 103.
16. Lawrence Eagleburger, interview, in *National Security Decisions,* ed. Pfaltzgraff and Davis, 100.

Chapter 27. The Brezhnev Coup

1. Tsouras, *Changing Orders,* 256–58.
2. Heller and Nekrich, *Utopia in Power,* 618.
3. For Brezhnev's military-industrial connection, see e.g. Volkogonov, *Stalin: Triumph and Tragedy,* 31.
4. Stone, *Satellites and Commissars,* 39–40.
5. Volkogonov, *Stalin: Triumph and Tragedy,* 26.
6. Beschloss, *The Crisis Years,* 697.
7. Arbatov, *The System,* 119–20.
8. Ibid., 121, describes Kosygin as more experienced (as an executive) than Brezhnev, and a seasoned technocrat, open to new economic ideas despite his Stalinist politics. Kosygin's power was inherently limited because he was not first secretary of the Party; he did not control the Party bureaucracy (*apparat*).
9. Of the two others who might have sought to unseat Brezhnev after the October 1964 coup against Khrushchev, Arbatov (ibid., 122) claims that Suslov refused to accept any position involving open personal responsibility of any kind. He preferred to operate behind the scenes. Arbatov describes Nikolai Podgorny simply as a very sinister and conservative figure, without clear ambitions. However, he points out (247) that Podgorny did make a move

towards power, by trying to establish for himself the formal position of second secretary of the Central Committee. In the past, this office had not been an official one, but it had become extremely powerful because the Central Committee Secretariat itself was so powerful; a great deal had to be delegated to it. The second secretary was responsible for the Secretariat itself and for Central Committee members' affairs, as well as for regional Party secretaries; it dealt with all day-to-day issues. This was essentially Stalin's role before he gained power. To eliminate the political threat posed by a permanent second secretary, Khrushchev had made the job a rotating one. Podgorny's proposal was thus a direct threat to Brezhnev, who dealt with it by relegating Podgorny to the ceremonial post of president of the Supreme Soviet. Brezhnev generally had two men running the Secretariat, each competing with the other for power and thus unable to spend his time competing with Brezhnev. They were Kirilenko and Suslov; when Kirilenko fell ill, Chernenko took his place. When Suslov died, Andropov immediately was appointed to his position.

10. Brezhnev very skillfully and subtly dealt with potential rivals Shelepin, Polyansky, Voronov, Podgorny, and Shelest, elbowing them out of the leadership, hence out of positions from which they could threaten him. Political supporters of Shelepin, his most serious rival, suddenly were transferred to jobs without influence, with no explanation. The final blow was the surprise replacement of Shelepin's patron, then-KGB chairman Semichastny, by Yuri Andropov in May 1967. Unlike Khrushchev, Brezhnev never verbally assaulted his victims; he merely shifted them (without warning) to minor jobs (ibid., 133).

11. The ideological crackdown was first openly announced at the Moscow City Party Committee plenum in February or March 1968, perhaps under the influence of events in Czechoslovakia; but it is clear from earlier statements that Brezhnev and his associates had been moving the country away from Khrushchev's ideas since Brezhnev's accession in 1964. Arbatov presents himself as one of the liberals, still hopeful in 1967 that the county could develop along less constricting lines (ibid., 136).

12. Ibid., 143. Arbatov also dates from late 1968 the systematic use of anti-Semitism as a buttress for the regime, including support for Pamyat, the xenophobic Russian nationalist group.

13. According to ibid., 149, there was even a massive attept to pretend that the Twentieth Party Congress, including Khrushchev's secret speech, had never occurred. Party histories written during the 1970s carried only the most limited references to the Congress and to the attack on the "cult of personality."

14. Whitefield, *Industrial Power and the Soviet State,* 19.

15. The CIA emphasized the general staff's newly independent position in its 1965 evaluation of main Soviet military trends, NIE 11-4-65; see particularly CIA 3:202–3.

16. Israelyan, *Inside the Kremlin,* 27, 192–93.

17. See, e.g., Heller and Nekrich, *Utopia in Power,* 658; Volkogonov, *Autopsy for an Empire,* 263–64.

18. Heller and Nekrich, *Utopia in Power,* 612–20.

19. Simons, *The End of the Cold War?* 14.

20. Volkogonov, *Autopsy for an Empire,* 278–79.

21. Nelson, *War of the Black Heavens,* 122–26.

22. Medvedev, *China and the Superpowers,* 43.

Chapter 28. Vietnam

1. Duiker, *The Communist Road to Power*, 242–43.

2. Ibid., 244.

3. Gaiduk, *The Soviet Union*, 16.

4. Moise, *Tonkin Gulf*, 49.

5. Gaiduk, *The Soviet Union*, 16–17.

6. Brackman, *The Communist Collapse in Indonesia*, 199.

7. R. E. Ford, "Tet Revisited: The Strategy of the Communist Vietnamese," in *Journal of Intelligence and National Security* (April 1994) 9:255, based on a Vietnamese White Paper released after the 1979 Chinese invasion.

8. Neil Sheehan, *The Pentagon Papers*, 249.

9. Herring, *LBJ and Vietnam*, 37–38, 40.

10. In 1965 Col. Bui Tin of the North Vietnamese army saw in Herman Kahn's newly published *On Escalation: Metaphors and Scenarios* (New York: Praeger, 1965) the American way of fighting a war in which the issue was not of fundamental importance (Moise, *Tonkin Gulf*, 34–35).

11. Neil Sheehan, *The Pentagon Papers*, 261.

12. Ibid., 442.

13. According to Suh, *Kim Il Sung*, the Korean deployment—the first foreign deployment in Korean history—was quite popular, because it was seen as an extension of the country's fight against the North Koreans and the Chinese.

14. Neil Sheehan, *The Pentagon Papers*, 245–46.

15. Moise, *Tonkin Gulf*, 5.

16. Neil Sheehan, *The Pentagon Papers*, 248–49, 282–85.

17. Ibid., 253.

18. Ibid., 251, 255, 291–93.

19. Duiker, *The Communist Road to Power*, 239.

20. Ibid., 249.

21. Karnow, *Vietnam: A History*, 373.

22. Schulzinger, *A Time for War*, 145–50.

23. Davidson, *Vietnam at War*, 314–15.

24. Moise, *Tonkin Gulf*, 50–55.

25. Ibid., 59–61.

26. Ibid., 69.

27. Ibid., 60–61.

28. The "paper tiger" thesis was apparently first raised in 1964. Davidson, *Vietnam at War*, 315–22.

29. Moise, *Tonkin Gulf*, 112–13. He believes the message was misinterpreted, that it ordered an attack on an OPLAN 34A raid.

30. Ibid., 208–10.

31. Ibid., 209.

32. Ibid., 226–27.

33. Davidson, *Vietnam at War*, 326–27.

34. Duiker, *The Communist Road to Power*, 251.

35. Davidson, *Vietnam at War*, 324.

36. Gaiduk, *The Soviet Union,* 16.

37. Ibid., 59.

38. Ibid., 72.

39. Ibid., 64.

40. Duiker, *The Communist Road to Power,* 251.

41. Gaiduk, *The Soviet Union,* 19.

42. Duiker, *The Communist Road to Power,* 246.

43. Schulzinger, *A Time for War,* 165–66.

44. A. S. Cochran Jr., "Eight Decisions for War, January 1965–February 1966," in *Second Indochina War Symposium,* ed. Schlight.

45. Gaiduk, *The Soviet Union,* 18.

46. Brackman, *The Communist Collapse in Indonesia,* 11.

47. Ibid., 18–19.

48. Guy Arnold, *Wars in the Third World,* 260.

49. Brackman, *The Communist Collapse in Indonesia,* 200.

50. Ibid., 26–27.

51. Ibid., 195–96.

52. Ibid., 47–48.

53. Ibid., 55.

54. Ibid., 56.

55. Ibid., 74–84.

56. Ibid., 88–89.

57. Ibid., 114–15. To some extent the destruction of the PKI became an excuse for Indonesians to settle scores with ethnic Chinese; both the People's Republic and Taiwan claimed that the dead were predominantly Chinese. Estimates of the number killed range from fewer than one hundred thousand to two million (Brackman thinks all these figures err on the high side, and in other connections mentions an Indonesian tendency to exaggerate figures).

58. Duiker, *The Communist Road to Power,* 256.

59. Gaiduk, *The Soviet Union,* 24, 36; D. Pike, "North Vietnamese Air Defenses During the Vietnam War," in *Looking Back on the Vietnam War,* ed. Head and Grinter.

60. Gaiduk, *The Soviet Union,* 61, 71.

61. Ibid., 37. Copies included the SA-7 and improved versions of the SA-2 surface-to-air missiles.

62. Herring, *LBJ and Vietnam,* 4–5; Davidson, *Vietnam at War,* 339.

63. Davidson, *Vietnam at War,* 339.

64. Herring, *LBJ and Vietnam,* 42.

65. Davidson, *Vietnam at War,* 391.

66. Record, *The Wrong War,* 46.

67. Davidson, *Vietnam at War,* 342–43.

68. Ibid., 344–45.

69. Neil Sheehan, *The Pentagon Papers,* 394–95.

70. Davidson, *Vietnam at War,* 348–49.

71. Neil Sheehan, *The Pentagon Papers,* 412–13, 417–18.

72. Ibid., 420.

73. Brinkley, *Dean Acheson,* 244–47; Schulzinger, *A Time for War,* 176–79.

74. J. W. Garver, "China and the Revisionist Thesis," in *Looking Back on the Vietnam War,* ed. Head and Grinter.

75. Duiker, *The Communist Road to Power,* 266.

76. Garver, "China and the Revisionist Thesis."

77. Ibid., 110.

78. Davidson, *Vietnam at War,* 364–65.

79. Duiker, *The Communist Road to Power,* 265–66.

80. Record, *The Wrong War,* 14.

81. Gaiduk, *The Soviet Union,* 65.

82. W. LaFeber, "Commentary," in *Second Indochina War Symposium,* ed. Schlight.

83. Herring, *LBJ and Vietnam,* 121–50.

84. Kunz, *Butter and Guns,* 109.

85. Record, *The Wrong War,* 98, argues that Westmoreland thought the war would be short, and wanted to give combat experience to as many officers as possible in view of the likely needs of a future major war.

86. Ibid., 99.

87. Ibid., 87–89.

88. McMaster, *Dereliction of Duty,* 312.

89. Ibid., 310.

90. Record, *The Wrong War,* 148.

91. Herring, *LBJ and Vietnam,* 6.

92. *Second Indochina War Symposium,* ed. Schlight, 73–74.

93. Neil Sheehan, *The Pentagon Papers,* 474.

94. Scales, *Firepower in Limited War,* 63–73.

95. Davidson, *Vietnam at War,* 365.

96. Duiker, *The Communist Road to Power,* 282.

97. Ibid., 282–83.

98. Davidson, *Vietnam at War,* 428–29.

99. Record, *The Wrong War,* 88–91.

100. Davidson, *Vietnam at War,* 392.

101. Gaiduk, *The Soviet Union,* 77; Haftendorn, *NATO and the Nuclear Revolution,* 8.

102. Haftendorn, *NATO and the Nuclear Revolution,* 8.

103. Gaiduk, *The Soviet Union,* 87.

104. Sevel'yev and Detinov, *The Big Five,* 8–9. These approaches are not mentioned in the official U.S. history (May, Steinbruner, and Wolfe, *History of the Strategic Arms Competition*).

105. Haftendorn, *NATO and the Nuclear Revolution,* 8, cites as evidence that a Thanksgiving 1966 meeting between Johnson and his close advisors, which had been called to discuss urgent NATO issues, was dominated instead by Vietnam.

106. Ibid., 321.

107. Laquer, *Europe in Our Time,* 329.

108. Haftendorn, *NATO and the Nuclear Revolution,* 389.

109. Ibid., 374.

110. Gerges, *The Superpowers and the Middle East,* 205. Egyptian domestic debt was $1.5 billion; foreign debt was $2.5 billion; and the war in Yemen was costing more than $60 million per year. When West Germany sold weapons to Israel, Nasser felt compelled to sever

relations (as the leader of an Arab bloc doing so), and thus jeopardized a planned $290 million credit.

111. Ibid., 196–97.

112. Bregman and El-Tahri, *The Fifty Years War,* 65.

113. Andrew and Gordievsky, *KGB: The Inside Story,* 414.

114. Parker, *The Politics of Miscalculation,* 29, citing a Soviet source.

115. Gerges, *The Superpowers and the Middle East,* 217; Parker, *The Politics of Miscalculation,* 8. The latter recounts a conversation between Minister of War Shams Badran and Kosygin.

116. Gerges, *The Superpowers and the Middle East,* 215.

117. Ibid., 217.

118. Ibid., 224.

119. Part of the Israeli air strike had been directed at the U.S. electronic surveillance ship *Liberty,* operating in the Mediterranean. The Israelis maintained that the strike was a tragic accident. However, it appears to have been a security measure taken for fear that Arab sympathizers in the U.S. government might be willing to pass them information.

120. Allin, *Cold War Illusions,* 46.

121. David Newsom (U.S. ambassador to Libya in the late 1960s), interview, in *National Security Decisions,* ed. Pfaltzgraff and Davis, 269–72.

Chapter 29. Disaster

1. Col. Bui Tin, speaking at the Robert R. McCormick Tribune Fund "Vietnam 1954–1965" conference, 6–7 March 1996, at Cantigny, Ill. (reported in *Naval History* [March/April 1996]).

2. Davidson, *Vietnam at War,* 352.

3. Neil Sheehan, *The Pentagon Papers,* 476–78.

4. Ibid., 492–93.

5. Davidson, *Vietnam at War,* 515.

6. Record, *The Wrong War,* 165.

7. Davidson, *Vietnam at War,* 435.

8. Brinkley, *Dean Acheson,* 255.

9. Record, *The Wrong War,* 81–82.

10. Gaiduk, *The Soviet Union,* 79, citing Soviet diplomatic reports (1966–67).

11. R. E. Ford, "Intelligence and the Significance of Khe Sanh," in *Intelligence and National Security* 10, no. 1 (January 1995).

12. Gaiduk, *The Soviet Union,* 108.

13. Ibid., 109.

14. The Party resolution, dated 25 October 1967, was named after Emperor Quang Trung, who led the most famous Tet attack in Vietnamese history (1789), against unsuspecting Chinese occupiers, who then withdrew. U.S. intelligence became aware of the name of the resolution but did not understand its significance.

15. Gaiduk, *The Soviet Union,* 79.

16. Karnow, *Vietnam: A History,* 556, reports Westmoreland's 20 December 1967 warning—but Westmoreland expected a major attack in the northern highlands.

17. Duiker, *The Communist Road to Power,* 295.

18. Davidson, *Vietnam at War,* 447.

19. Ibid., 541.

20. Ibid., 438, quoting a former NLF leader speaking in 1982.

21. Ford, "Intelligence." Davidson, *Vietnam at War,* 551–71, gives the more conventional view accepted by U.S. intelligence at the time.

22. Davidson, *Vietnam at War,* 543.

23. Ibid., 357.

24. Ibid., 497; Record, *The Wrong War,* 166.

25. Davidson, *Vietnam at War,* 502–6.

26. Schulzinger, *A Time for War,* 265; Davidson, *Vietnam at War,* 510–21.

27. Davidson, *Vietnam at War,* 524–25.

28. Ibid., 615–19, 631, 661–62.

29. Walker, *The Cold War,* 207–9.

30. Tsouras, *Changing Orders,* 154, 214–15.

31. Suh, *Kim Il Sung,* 228.

32. Agulhon, *The French Republic,* 421–29.

33. Ginsbourg, *A History of Contemporary Italy,* 298.

34. Ibid., 360.

35. Wolf, *Memoirs of a Spymaster,* 271–72, 277–79. East German terrorist contacts included the IRA and Carlos, "the Jackal." Wolf, who was responsible for foreign intelligence, takes pains to deny direct involvement with terrorists, which was the responsibility of another part of the East German security service.

Chapter 30. Repression

1. Laquer, *Europe in Our Time,* 510, quoting figures developed during glasnost. According to Arbatov, *The System,* 212, the turning point towards economic decline was 1972, during the 1971–76 plan period.

2. R. E. Ericson, "The Soviet Statistical Debate: Khanin versus TsSU," in *The Impoverished Superpower,* ed. Rowen and Wolf.

3. Ibid, 74.

4. Laquer, *The Long Road to Freedom,* 26–28. Laquer periodically visited the Soviet Union at that time, and had relatives there. He quotes an anonymous Soviet writer: "There was no reason to fear an attack from the outside. What enemy would take the risk of an attack if he could be reasonably sure that in another decade or two, half the country would be in an alcoholic stupor and unable to defend themselves?"

5. Volkogonov, *Autopsy for an Empire,* 321.

6. Kaiser, *Why Gorbachev Happened,* 54–55; Laquer, *The Long Road to Freedom,* 30; Gates, *From the Shadows,* 185–86.

7. M. Kramer, ed., "Ukraine and the Sov-Czech Crisis of 1968 (Part 1): New Evidence from the Diary of Petro Shelest," in CWIHP 10 (1997/98).

8. Volkogonov, *Autopsy for an Empire,* 285.

9. M. Kramer, CWIHP 3.

10. Kramer, "Ukraine and the Sov-Czech Crisis."

11. Ibid.

12. M. Kramer, CWIHP 3, 12.

13. Heller and Nekrich, *Utopia in Power,* 629.

14. H. E. Meyer, interview, in *President Reagan and the World,* ed. Schmertz, Datlof, and Ugrinsky, 125.

15. Arbatov, *The System,* 137.

16. Ibid., 138.

17. Quirk, *Fidel Castro,* 587.

18. Crampton, *East Europe,* 347.

19. Ibid., 345–46.

20. Stone, *Satellites and Commissars,* 41; Crampton, *East Europe,* 363.

21. Stone, *Satellites and Commissars,* 116.

22. Ibid., 36.

23. Ibid., 43.

24. In April 1968 the deputy under secretary of state for political affairs, Charles E. Bohlen, asked for analyses of two possible contingencies, Soviet intervention and Soviet economic sanctions (FRUS [1964–68] 17:72–75). In a 28 April 1968 memo to the under secretary of state, he suggested that the U.S. consult with the Germans regarding the possibility of Soviet intervention in Czechoslovakia. Eastern Europe was "in the highest state of flux"—in terms of domestic change and the weakening of Soviet authority—since the events of 1956.

25. M. Kramer, CWIHP 3, 8.

26. Warheads were guarded by KGB troops, backed up by the local army—where possible, by Soviet army troops. In countries without Soviet forces (e.g., pre-invasion Czechoslovakia), the local Warsaw Pact army backed the KGB detachments. Once the Prague Spring had begun, the Soviets could no longer rely on the Czech army.

27. Duffield, "The Evolution," 430.

28. Medvedev, *China and the Superpowers,* 46.

29. Quirk, *Fidel Castro,* 587.

30. Meisner, *Mao's China and After,* 354.

31. Ibid., 357.

32. Ibid., 371. A widely accepted figure, first reported in 1979, is 400,000. The number cited at the 1980 trial of the "Gang of Four" blamed for the Cultural Revolution was 34,000 innocent people, during 1966–76, but the indictment claimed 14,000 deaths in Yunnan alone and more than 16,000 in Inner Mongolia. According to Courtois et al., *Le livre noire,,* 60 percent of the members of the Chinese Central Committee were expelled (most being arrested), together with three-quarters of provincial Communist Party secretaries (573). In all, 3 to 4 million cadres (Party workers) were imprisoned (out of a total of 6 to 8 million), as well as 400,000 military personnel. The repression that ended the revolution was savage, including artillery and napalm attacks on Wuzhou. An army of 30,000 reconquered Gueilin after a siege. Terror was widespread; perhaps 100,000 were killed in Guangxi, 40,000 in Guangdong, 30,000 in Yunnan (584–85). Hua Guofeng, eventually president of the Republic, was called the "Butcher of Hunan" for the excesses of his security forces (585). After Mao died, 12 to 20 million young Chinese, who were considered Red Guard sympathizers, were forcibly moved out of the cities; they included a million from Shanghai, the most radical Chinese city. This loss of population, amounting to 18 percent, was a record. About three million cadres were placed in semi-prison camps.

33. Nancy B. Tucker, "China Under Siege: Escaping the Dangers of 1968," in *1968: The World Transformed,* ed. Fink, Gassert and Junker.

34. The defection of a Chinese diplomat two days before the scheduled talks (February 1969) temporarily stopped this initiative.

35. Tsouras, *Changing Orders,* 213.

Chapter 31. Peace without Victory

1. Kunz, *Butter and Guns,* 181.

2. Nixon, *RN,* 347.

3. Davidson, *Vietnam at War,* 587–88; the concept was published in the January 1969 issue of *Foreign Affairs* by Nixon's foreign policy advisor, Dr. Henry Kissinger.

4. Nixon, *RN,* 298.

5. Davidson, *Vietnam at War,* 590–91, quotes the Communist attack directive (31 January 1969).

6. Ibid., 595.

7. Ibid., 592–93; he interviewed the defector, who said he had recently been in the COSVN headquarters area.

8. Ibid., 594.

9. Nixon, *RN,* 391.

10. Ibid., 392; Davidson, *Vietnam at War,* 602.

11. Nixon, *RN,* 394–95.

12. Ibid., 393.

13. Ibid., 396; Bundy, *Danger and Survival,* 539.

14. Kimball, *Nixon's Vietnam War,* 158–65.

15. Nixon, *RN,* 400.

16. Ibid., 399.

17. Ibid., 401–3, quotes a 14 October 1969 radio message from North Vietnamese Premier Pham Van Dong (he had just succeeded Ho, who had died) congratulating the U.S. antiwar movement and wishing its "fall offensive" success.

18. Davidson, *Vietnam at War,* 600–601.

19. Nixon, *RN,* 404–5, 413.

20. Gaiduk, *The Soviet Union,* 203.

21. Ibid., 218.

22. Ibid., 215.

23. Ibid., 216.

24. Dunbabin, *The Cold War,* 286.

25. Medvedev, *China and the Superpowers,* 50.

26. "Soviet Nuclear Doctrine: Concepts of Intercontinental and Theater War," a declassified (formerly Top Secret) June 1973 CIA Research Paper, in the Soviet Estimate collection at the National Security Archives.

27. Medvedev, *China and the Superpowers,* 50–51.

28. Gaiduk, *The Soviet Union,* 226.

29. NIE 11-4-72, "Issues and Options In Soviet Military Policy" (copy in the Soviet Estimate collection at the National Security Archives).

30. Medvedev, *China and the Superpowers,* 58.

31. Gaiduk, *The Soviet Union,* 216.

32. Medvedev, *China and the Superpowers,* 95–96.

33. Ibid., 56, 99–100.

34. By 1971 the Viet Cong were largely confined to ten provinces, where only a quarter of the population lived; even there most villages were rated as secure.

35. Davidson, *Vietnam at War,* 624–29.

36. Ibid., 637–64.

37. Gaiduk, *The Soviet Union,* 231.

38. Ibid., 232.

39. Ibid., 231, 232.

40. Tsouras, *Changing Orders,* 209–10; Davidson, *Vietnam at War,* 673–711.

41. Gaiduk, *The Soviet Union,* 240.

42. Ibid., 236.

43. Ibid., 234; Davidson, *Vietnam at War,* 706.

44. Gaiduk, *The Soviet Union,* 242–43, quoting the Soviet version of the transcript of the last meeting between Le Duc Tho and Kissinger.

45. There were 729 B-52 sorties and about 640 other attack sorties plus more than 1,384 support sorties (including SAM suppression). Losses totaled fifteen B-52s and eight other aircraft. See John T. Smith, *The Linebacker Raids,* 116–38.

46. Karnow, *Vietnam: A History,* 668.

47. For Nixon's promise, see Davidson, *Vietnam at War,* 723.

48. Ibid., 718.

49. Note that the Communist members of the International Commission were Soviet, not Chinese, satellites.

50. Rodman, *More Precious than Peace,* 148–49.

51. Gaiduk, *The Soviet Union,* 250; Rodman, *More Precious than Peace,* 148–50.

52. See, for example, the list of measures to combat the Pershing/Cruise deployment, discussed at a 9 December 1983 meeting of Central Committee secretaries of the Socialist countries (Volkogonov, *Autopsy for an Empire,* 378–79); they were told to intensify their efforts in the antiwar movement and to use events such as the coming extraordinary meeting of the World Peace Council (January 1984).

53. Sigmund, *The Overthrow of Allende,* 113.

54. Ibid., 103.

55. Collier and Sater, *A History of Chile,* 332.

56. Horne, *A Small Earthquake in Chile,* 32. Horne argues that the central thesis of the Alliance, that a reformist middle class could be created, was mistaken; in Latin America members of the rising middle class wanted simply to join the ruling oligarchy, and thus refused to press for any real reform. Too, Kennedy himself had caught the imagination of Latin Americans in a way his successors could not; he was Catholic (like most of them), young, and macho. Horne met many Latin Americans who said that Kennedy had been the only American leader to understand them.

57. Ibid., 25.

58. Ibid., 26.

59. For an application to agriculture, see Collier and Sater, *A History of Chile,* 341–42.

60. Horne, *A Small Earthquake in Chile,* 131–32.

61. Collier and Sater, *A History of Chile,* 342.

62. Ibid., 331.

63. Ibid., 338–40.

64. Moss, *Chile's Marxist Experiment*, 92.

65. Collier and Sater, *A History of Chile*, 335–36.

66. Moss, *Chile's Marxist Experiment*, 132. Debray had become famous by joining Che Guevara in Bolivia in 1967. Arrested by the Bolivians, he was sentenced to thirty years' imprisonment, then amnestied and expelled to Chile. There he interviewed Allende at length. A believer in the Castro-Guevara school of revolution, he rejected Allende's legalism and got him to admit in these interviews that sooner or later he would have to resort to "unconstitutional" revolutionary methods. To Horne, in *A Small Earthquake in Chile*, 135, the interviews encapsulated the problem in Chile: the situation was no more than a temporary truce between the old Establishment and the "popular forces," and the latter would have to decide whether to allow their enemies to steal back the state, or whether to settle accounts once and for all. To Debray, Allende had not yet had the courage to take the necessary steps, and unless he did so the UP was doomed. In reply, Allende pointed out that there was already a law on the books (strengthened by his predecessor, President Frei) allowing him to call a referendum (*plebescito*) in the event Congress rejected his proposals. In this way he could form a single-house "people's assembly" and he could even postpone the next presidential election—assuming he could win the necessary referenda. In 1971 it was generally assumed that the UP planned to form the single-chamber Congress. However, because it failed to gain 50 percent of the votes in the 1971 congressional elections, it held back, for fear of a defeat in the necessary referendum. The Chilean constitution provided for two houses of Congress, their members elected for four and eight years (in no year were legislators from both chambers elected). Presumably electors dissatisfied with the results of one chamber's election could cancel the result by voting in the opposition party in the other chamber. Allende apparently expected the UP to be able to win the election to a single chamber, and thus to preclude any balance provided by the two-chamber system.

67. Moss, *Chile's Marxist Experiment*, 134.

68. Ibid., 22.

69. Collier and Sater, *A History of Chile*, 331, 333.

70. Moss, *Chile's Marxist Experiment*, 107.

71. Horne, *A Small Earthquake in Chile*, 140.

72. Collier and Sater, *A History of Chile*, 343–44.

73. Horne, *A Small Earthquake in Chile*, 148.

74. Debray's dialogues with Allende, which had not yet been published, support this view. Debray's conversations with Allende are given in *Conversations with Allende: Socialism in Chile*, trans. Peter Beglen (London: NLB, 1971). Debray noted that both sides were arming for a possible confrontation; Allende answered that "we shall wait for them [the Right] to start . . . we shall meet reactionary violence with revolutionary violence because we know that they are going to break the rules" (Horne, *A Small Earthquake in Chile*, 149).

75. Moss, *Chile's Marxist Experiment*, 99.

76. Horne, *A Small Earthquake in Chile*, 349, gives an example. In March 1972 Allende received thirteen heavy crates from Havana. Asked about their contents, Allende claimed that they contained mango-flavored ice cream intended as a tribute from Cuba. After the coup, the papers of the former secret police chief revealed a detailed list of contents: Czech-made automatic weapons, pistols, grenades, and ammunition, for Allende's private arsenal.

77. Moss, *Chile's Marxist Experiment*, 119.

78. Quirk, *Fidel Castro,* 664.

79. Moss, *Chile's Marxist Experiment,* 202.

80. Collier and Sater, *A History of Chile,* 345, claim $350 million, probably based on a statement by Allende's foreign minister; Moss, *Chile's Marxist Experiment,* mentions none.

81. Horne, *A Small Earthquake in Chile,* 347.

82. Collier and Sater, *A History of Chile,* 360, cite a Soviet report that seven hundred thousand had died during the two-day coup.

83. According to the Church Committee investigation of CIA involvement (1975), the agency spent a total of $6 million on all recipients during Allende's rule. The committee estimated that the Soviets had spent $20 million to support Allende's 1970 campaign. Nor did the Chilean plotters inform the U.S. government in any detail about their plans. These data are given by Horne, *A Small Earthquake in Chile,* 354–55.

84. Collier and Sater, *A History of Chile,* 355.

85. According to a March 1996 Amnesty International report on Chile (AMR 22/01/96), investigators have identified 1,102 people who were "disappeared" (and killed) and another 2,095 who were executed or died under torture. Some victims of the Chilean police state probably have not yet been found. By way of comparison, a typical figure previously given for killings during the "dirty war" is twenty thousand (Brogan, *World Conflicts,* 624).

86. Rouquie, *The Military and the State,* 312–13.

87. Ibid., 249–57.

88. Ibid., 325–27.

Chapter 32. Brezhnev's Buildups

1. Thus May, Steinbruner, and Wolfe, *History of the Strategic Arms Competition,* 552: "Since Soviet strategic forces were being maintained during this period [1964] at a rather low rate of readiness and since U.S. forces were reasonably alert most of the time, the preponderant probability was that the United States attack would develop far more rapidly regardless of which side first made the decision to initiate war. This could not be publicly acknowledged, but it did affect the balance of judgement within the Government."

2. See, e.g., A. Dollin, "Communications in the RSVN Are More Than Just Communications," a Foreign Broadcast Information Service translation of an article in the 30 January 1997 issue of *Krasnaya zvezda* (translation SOV-97-021, 30 January 1997).

3. Signal was accepted into service in 1969 and was upgraded in 1972. It was associated with the new SS-9 and SS-11 ICBMs and with a ballistic missile warning radar, Dnepr, work on which began in 1957 (it was deployed about 1967).

4. IDA, 380.

5. Savel'yev and Detinkov, *The Big Five,* 2.

6. Ibid., 7.

7. Ibid., 4.

8. Ibid.

9. Ibid., 22, describing a key meeting chaired by Ustinov.

10. May, Steinbruner, and Wolfe, *History of the Strategic Arms Competition,* 735.

11. Sevel'yev and Detinov, *The Big Five,* make the fiscal argument. May, Steinbruner, and Wolfe, *History of the Strategic Arms Competition,* does not mention the January 1969 initiative.

12. Sevel'yev and Detinov, *The Big Five,* 9–10.

13. Ibid., 26.

14. "Basic Principles of Relations Between the United States of America and the Union of Soviet Socialist Republics," signed in Moscow, 29 May 1972.

15. Sevel'yev and Detinov, *The Big Five,* 35.

16. Israelyan, *Inside the Kremlin,* 3738.

17. Zaloga (forthcoming).

18. NIE 11-4-65, "Main Trends in Soviet Military Policy," 14 April 1965, in CIA 3:191–214.

19. Tsouras, *Changing Orders,* 175, 256.

20. Ibid., 173–75.

21. Ibid., 175–76.

Chapter 33. Détente and Discontent

1. Dunbabin, *The Cold War,* 278. Soviet interest in an all-European security conference goes back to a 1954 proposal by then–foreign minister Vyacheslav Molotov; the idea was revived in a July 1966 declaration by the Warsaw Pact states "on strengthening peace and security in Europe" (Kissinger, *Years of Renewal,* 636).

2. Kissinger, *Years of Renewal,* 635–36.

3. Ibid., 637, sees these actions as an attempt both to defuse a continuing uproar over Czechoslovakia and to limit the newly elected Nixon's freedom of action.

4. Allin, *Cold War Illusions,,* 38; Dunbabin, *The Cold War,* 276.

5. Allin, *Cold War Illusions,*39.

6. Kissinger, *Years of Renewal,* 638.

7. Allin, *Cold War Illusions,* 41–42; Kunz, *Butter and Guns,* 192–211.

8. Allin, *Cold War Illusions,* 40; the West German was Egon Bahr.

9. Zumwalt, *On Watch,* 319–21. See also Allin, *Cold War Illusions,* 29–30.

10. Hoff, *Nixon Reconsidered,* 180.

11. Ibid., 269–74.

12. Kunz, *Butter and Guns,* 186; Allin, *Cold War Illusions,* 43.

13. Hoff, *Nixon Reconsidered,* 182.

14. SNIE 11-4-73, "Soviet Strategic Arms Programs and Détente: What Are They Up To," in CIA 4:297–308.

15. Israelyan, *Inside the Kremlin,* 9.

16. Allin, *Cold War Illusions,* 46.

17. Isaacson, *Kissinger: A Biography,* 311.

18. Israelyan, *Inside the Kremlin,* 148–49, 177–78.

19. Ibid., 215.

20. Nixon had ordered the firing of Archibald Cox, the special prosecutor investigating Watergate. He fired Attorney General Elliot Richardson when the latter refused to fire Cox. Finally, Robert Bork fired the prosecutor. The "massacre" led to the current law under which a special prosecutor investigating the executive branch cannot be fired by that branch.

21. Israelyan, *Inside the Kremlin,* 16–17.

22. Van Creveld, *The Sword and the Olive,* 220.

23. Israelyan, *Inside the Kremlin,* 3.

24. Ibid., 33.

25. Ibid., 14.

26. Ibid., 9–10.

27. Ibid., 5.

28. Allin, *Cold War Illusions,* 48.

29. Van Creveld, *The Sword and the Olive,* 219–20.

30. Herzog, *The Arab-Israeli Wars,* 234.

31. Ibid., 234.

32. Gen. Johann Adolf Graf von Kielmansegg, interview, in *National Security Decisions,* ed. Pfaltzgraff and Davis, 285–86.

33. Herzog, *The Arab-Israeli Wars,* 227–28.

34. Van Creveld, *The Sword and the Olive,* 223.

35. Ibid., 224.

36. Israelyan, *Inside the Kremlin,* 21–22.

37. Van Creveld, *The Sword and the Olive,* 225.

38. Israelyan, *Inside the Kremlin,* 31–32.

39. Wald, *The Wald Report,* 104–10.

40. Van Creveld, *The Sword and the Olive,* 232.

41. Israelyan, *Inside the Kremlin,* 53–56.

42. Brent Scowcroft, interview, in *National Security Decisions,* ed. Pfaltzgraff and Davis, 287–88.

43. Allin, *Cold War Illusions,* 43–44.

44. Israelyan, *Inside the Kremlin,* 105, 107.

45. Ibid., 121–22.

46. Adm. Thomas Moorer, interview, in *National Security Decisions,* ed. Pfaltzgraff and Davis, 286.

47. Israelyan, *Inside the Kremlin,* 143–45.

48. Ibid., 167–70.

49. Isaacson, *Kissinger: A Biography,* 530–31.

50. Israelyan, *Inside the Kremlin,* and private communication with author.

51. Isaacson, *Kissinger: A Biography,* 529.

52. Allin, *Cold War Illusions,* 47.

53. Ibid., 49.

54. Scowcroft, interview, 289.

55. Bellamy, *The Evolution of Modern Land Warfare,* 121.

Chapter 34. The West at Bay

1. Davidson, *Vietnam at War,* 738.

2. Karnow, *Vietnam: A History,* 672.

3. Davidson, *Vietnam at War,* 741.

4. Ibid., 748.

5. Ibid., 750; Duiker, *The Communist Road to Power,* 334.

6. Karnow, *Vietnam: A History,* 675.

7. Davidson, *Vietnam at War,* 750.

8. Ibid., 753.

9. Gen. Van Tien Dung, who commanded the 1975 invasion, quoted in J. Record, "Vietnam in Retrospect: Could We Have Won?" in *Parameters* 26, no. 4 (winter 1996/97).

10. Karnow, *Vietnam: A History,* 676–79; Davidson, *Vietnam at War,* 758–63, based on Tra's 1982 memoirs. Lieutenant General Tra commanded the B-2 or "Bulwark" Front comprising the southern half of South Vietnam.

11. Karnow, *Vietnam: A History,* 53.

12. Ibid., 679.

13. Ibid., 681.

14. Ibid., 679–83; Davidson, *Vietnam at War,* 767–91.

15. Karnow, *Vietnam: A History,* 43.

16. O. A. Westad, "Moscow and the Angolan Crisis, 1974–1976: A New Pattern of Intervention," in CWIHP 5 (winter 1995/96).

17. Nixon, *The Real War,* 23, quoting Somalian President Siad Barre, to whom Brezhnev had spoken when still an ally; he said that he planned to get both the mineral treasure house of central and southern Africa and the energy treasure house of the Persian Gulf, in order to deny them to the West.

18. P. Gleijeses, "Havana's Policy in Africa, 1959–1976: New Evidence from Cuban Archives," in CWIHP 5 (winter 1996/97).

19. Westad, "Moscow and the Angolan Crisis."

20. Kissinger, *Years of Renewal,* 629–30, quoting then-Ambassador to Portugal Frank Carlucci. Kissinger describes Gonçalves as "if not an outright Communist, only refrained from membership in order to save paying his dues." At the 1975 Helsinki summit he told President Ford that the democratic parties were not really democratic because each represented only a segment of the population; he represented politics above party, a view Kissinger recognized as Lenin's excuse for eliminating all opposition parties.

21. Ibid., 630–31.

22. Allin, *Cold War Illusions,* 117.

23. Rodman, *More Precious than Peace,* 166.

24. Ibid., 166.

25. Ibid., 168.

26. According to Kissinger, *Years of Renewal,* 791, this U.S. policy was taken after President Kenneth Kaunda of Zambia personally convinced President Ford and Kissinger of the seriousness of the problem during a state visit on 19 April 1975.

27. Rodman, *More Precious than Peace* 167–68.

28. Ibid., 172–75. Kissinger, *Years of Renewal,* 792, ascribes hostility to intervention to a combination of causes: liberals' unrealistic desire to insulate Africa from the Cold War and conservatives' unwillingness to support what they saw as a soft Ford administration merely to keep the Soviets out of a secondary theater of Cold War. Moreover, Congress was clearly hostile to any foreign adventures.

29. Ibid., 156.

30. Dunbabin, *The Cold War,* 324–25; Guy Arnold, *Wars in the Third World,* 222–25.

31. Rodman, *More Precious than Peace,* 171, quoting Georgii Arbatov.

32. Guy Arnold, *Wars in the Third World,* 364–77.

33. Rodman, *More Precious than Peace,* 181–82.

34. Safran, *Saudi Arabia,* 123.

35. Ibid., 128.

36. Ibid., 130.

37. Ibid., 282–83.

38. Ibid., 286. The Saudis finally agreed to establish diplomatic relations with South Yemen on 10 March 1976; reportedly the Yemenis expected about $400 million in aid over five years, about twice the total the South Yemenis had expected to invest over that period. Relations soured after a year and a half, about $50 million actually having been provided. However, Soviet aid reportedly increased considerably, which suggests that Rubaya had succeeded by playing off the Saudis against the Soviets.

39. Yapp, *The Near East*, 365. In the 1980s, the refinery accounted for 80 percent of industrial output. The refinery, owned by British Petroleum, was the only foreign company not to be nationalized in 1969; it was taken over in 1977. The 100,000 South Yemenis working abroad amounted to 15 percent of the country's work force. In 1984, half the country's GNP came from remittances from these workers. According to Brogan, *World Conflicts*, 370, dependence on remittances softened South Yemeni Marxism, because the workers abroad demanded that their money go to their families rather than to the state. The PDRY was the only Communist country in the world with a state religion, Islam, because the government in Aden had to deal with the deeply conservative tribesmen in the countryside.

40. E. Abebe, "The Horn, the Cold War, and Documents from the Former East Bloc: An Ethiopian View," in CWIHP 5 (winter 1996–97).

41. Dunbabin, *The Cold War*, 325.

42. See documents in CWIHP 5 (winter 1996–97).

43. Safran, *Saudi Arabia*, 289. One factor in the break with the Saudis was the assassination of the *North* Yemeni leader, Col. Ibrahim al-Hamdi, on 11 October 1977. Hamdi had been following a conciliatory policy toward South Yemen. It was widely believed that the Saudis had ordered the killing because Hamdi had been too independent. Rubaya's policy of conciliation towards the Saudis was discredited. He lost some of his power; this was probably the beginning of the slide that led to Rubaya's death a few months later.

44. Ginsbourg, *A History of Contemporary Italy*, 374.

45. Ibid., 351–52.

46. Ibid., 363.

47. Ibid., 355.

48. Ibid., 374.

49. Allin, *Cold War Illusions*, 130.

50. Allin, *Cold War Illusions*, 126.

51. Ibid., 131.

52. Clogg, *A Concise History of Greece*, 178.

53. Ibid., 190.

54. Kissinger, *Years of Renewal*, 639.

55. Revel, *How Democracies Perish*, 130–32.

56. Gates, *From the Shadows*, 88–89, quotes an 18 February 1977 CIA report to the effect that the Soviets were already quite unhappy about the U.S. human rights campaign because it compounded an already serious problem. "The emergence of dissident activity throughout Eastern Europe since the beginning of 1976 has added a new dimension to the problems of East Germany and Poland. It is linked in the Soviet view with the behavior of dissidents in the USSR as a single challenge which the West is encouraging against the existing order in

the East." This was a report to President Carter, who was deeply interested in human rights and was therefore likely to want to hear that his concerns mattered. Moreover, the Soviets always showed extreme sensitivity to any threat to their control, no matter how little potential it might have. The CIA did report unrest in both Poland and East Germany in 1976, following the Helsinki accords.

57. Dunbabin, *The Cold War,* 314–15, 450–51.

58. Kissinger, *Years of Renewal,* 861–67. Defending himself against the charge of softness on the Soviets, Kissinger claimed that the Ford administration had clearly proven its mettle in its failed attempt to fight in Indochina, in its attempts to resist in Angola, in its threats to use force to prevent an oil embargo, in its resistance to Eurocommunism, and in its support for the Helsinki human rights "basket," which at least in theory challenged Soviet control of Eastern Europe. Kissinger denied that the "Sonnenfeldt doctrine" had ever really existed; Sonnenfeldt's remarks had been an unfortunate formulation of quite orthodox U.S. policy. There was an ironic result. The "doctrine" became a staple of the 1976 presidential campaign, and President Gerald Ford was briefed extensively to deny that it existed. During the 6 October debate he unfortunately went far beyond his briefing to deny that the Soviets actually dominated Poland (it was U.S. policy to treat Poland as relatively independent, in hopes that it would become more so). His gaffe seemed to prove that Ford was, as had widely been rumored, incompetent, and thus helped defeat him.

59. May, Steinbruner, and Wolfe, *History of the Strategic Arms Competition,* 717–18.

60. The CIA's estimate was NIE 11-3/8-76, "Soviet Forces for Intercontinental Conflict Through the Mid-1980s," dated 21 December 1976, in CIA 2:225–312. The Team B report is in CIA 2:313–75.

61. NIE 11-4-77 of 18 January 1977, in CIA 4:391–95.

Chapter 35. Nadir

1. Taken from President Carter's Notre Dame commencement speech, 22 May 1977.

2. Famously, Brzezinski is said to have asked only one question after his briefing on the U.S. strategic attack plan (SIOP): "How may Russians will be killed?" The plan had always been framed to destroy Soviet military and industrial capacity, not Soviet citizens; supposedly Brzezinski was particularly upset to find that, in a nuclear war, more Americans than Russians probably would die (because the U.S. population was more concentrated, particularly around places likely to be hit). Gates, *From the Shadows,* 70, describes Brzezinski as "by far the most realistic, experienced, and balanced of Carter's foreign policy team."

3. Gates, *From the Shadows,* gives several examples of President Carter's approval of covert operations which afterwards were not pursued due to bureaucratic foot-dragging. In March 1977 Carter formally approved Brzezinski's proposals for covert propaganda within the Soviet Union (91), based partly on a CIA report that, according to a Hungarian leader, the Soviet leadership was "worried to death about what it perceives as a genuine threat or challenge to its power . . . and, incredible as it may seem, believing that the U.S. stand on human rights is a deliberate strategy designed to overthrow the Soviet regime." One of Brzezinski's ideas was to use the very serious internal Soviet nationality problems as leverage to weaken the Soviet state. Both the State Department and the CIA refused to do very much about his ideas (ibid., 92–94, describes the stalling tactics). Probably the only real consequence of the March 1977 decisions was the enlargement of the U.S.-sponsored radio sta-

tions, Radio Free Europe and Radio Liberty, which broadcast into Eastern Europe. Because they carried news of dissidents back into the Soviet bloc, they helped those dissidents realize that they were not alone. That enormously affected morale—which came to matter as other strains affected the Soviet system. As another case in point (74), on 1 June 1978 Admiral Turner, the director of central intelligence, along with several of his officers, briefed the president on increasing Soviet aggressiveness in the Third World, an aggressiveness backed by their increasing military superiority. Carter in turn signed a pair of Presidential Review Memoranda (PDMs), calling for a new strategy of global nonmilitary competition and for increased U.S. global presence. Both efforts were stalled. Gates, a career CIA officer, was on Carter's NSC staff, and thus was well aware of Brzezinski's thinking. He argues (76) that the bureaucracy's "nerves were shot." However, it is difficult to avoid the view that the State Depatment was following Vance's well-known preference not to upset détente, and that the CIA had been paralyzed by the turmoil attendant on Stansfield Turner's accession to power and his purge of veteran CIA staffers.

4. NIE 11-3/8-79, "Soviet Capabilities for Strategic Nuclear Conflict Through the 1980s," issued March 1980, in CIA 4:407–27.

5. NIE 11-3/8-80, "Soviet Capabilities for Strategic Nuclear Conflict Through the Late 1980s," issued in December 1980, in CIA 4:429–65.

6. Carter adopted RAND's November 1976 study, "Alliance Defense in the Eighties" (AD-80), which revived an earlier AD-70 (1970) proposal.

7. Gates, *From the Shadows,* 110, claims that the Soviet campaign against the neutron bomb, "one of the most aggressive covert operations ever mounted in Europe by the Soviets," was conducted in July and August 1977. Apparently the CIA reported the campaign in September 1977 (142) and was authorized to counter it with a campaign publicizing the fact that the Soviets already had a neutron bomb of their own. That campaign was entirely unsuccessful. It seems noteworthy that President Carter's decision not to develop or deploy neutron bombs was unaffected by the CIA's revelation that the Soviets had largely fabricated the European sentiment to which he was reacting.

8. See interviews (Bennett, then ambassador to NATO, 109, and Lord Mulley, then British defense secretary, 111), in *National Security Decisions,* ed. Pfaltzgraff and Davis.

9. See especially Gen. Pierre Galois, interview, in *National Security Decisions,* ed. Pfaltzgraff and Davis, 149–50. He may have exaggerated the problem to explain why France would not buy the neutron bomb (which was quite expensive).

10. B. Heuser, "Warsaw Pact Military Doctrine in the 1970s and 1980s: Findings in the East German Archives," *Comparative Strategy* 12 (1993): 437–57. The official German report is in CWIHP no. 2 (fall 1992). Some details are from L. Ruhl, "Offensive Defence in the Warsaw Pact," *Survival* 33 (Sept/Oct. 1991): 442–50.

11. F. Tusa, "Soviets Feared Battle for Berlin Might Have Pushed Allies Toward Minsk," *Armed Forces Journal International* (Feb.1992): 21.

12. In a book of arms control treaties by C. D. Blacker and G. Duffy, *International Arms Control: Issues and Agreements* (Stanford: Stanford University Press, 1984), SALT I and its associated "understandings" take up eleven pages, many of them concerned with ABMs. The corresponding SALT II material occupies thirty-one pages of somewhat smaller type.

13. Sevel'yev and Detinov, *The Big Five,* 51.

14. Simons, *The End of the Cold War?* 25.

15. Ibid., 23.

16. Allin, *Cold War Illusions,* 87.

17. The policy was agreed at a summit attended by Schmidt, Carter, and French President Giscard d'Estaing at Guadeloupe, 5–6 January 1979. Because only 108 Pershing II and 464 ground-launched cruise missiles, each with a single warhead, were involved, this was a net reduction in the number of NATO nuclear warheads.

18. Allin, *Cold War Illusions,* 89.

19. Medvedev, *China and the Superpowers,* 58.

20. According to Gates, *From the Shadows,* 82, on 3 April 1977 the CIA learned that, during a cross-country rail trip with Defense Minister Ustinov, Brezhnev had told the chiefs of the Trans-Baikal Military District that China was now "the primary enemy." It is not clear to what extent he was simply posturing to encourage those who faced Chinese, rather than NATO, forces.

21. Rodman, *More Precious than Peace,* 226; Keep, *Last of the Empires,* 201.

22. The U.S. government obtained a document outlining Sandinista policy, as described at a three-day assembly held by the Sandinista National Directorate from 21 to 23 September 1979. According to Gates, *From the Shadows,* 126, from late June on the U.S. covert action group, the Special Coordinating Committee (SCC), met regularly to discuss Cuban penetration of Nicaragua. With the Sandinistas not yet in power, Brzezinski went so far as to propose sending U.S. fighter aircraft to Panama as a signal to the Cubans and the Sandinistas, but he was fought down. Early in August 1979 (127) the CIA predicted that the Cubans would soon use the Nicaraguans, whose military they were building up, to spread revolution into the northern tier of Central America, which meant at least El Salvador. Late in July (151), President Carter authorized covert action in Nicaragua, amounting mainly to a propaganda campaign to expose Cuban backing for the Sandinistas.

23. Rodman, *More Precious than Peace,* 226. According to Gates, *From the Shadows,* 150–51, in late July 1979 Carter did approve covert action to support the government of El Salvador, apparently by providing anti-insurgency advice and equipment.

24. According to Gates, *From the Shadows,* 125, the State Department initially maintained that Bishop was still open to U.S. influence. On 14 April the Cubans delivered a shipload of ammunition, to be overseen by fifty advisors, and by September 400 Cuban troops were training a special 3,000-man Grenadian force; beginning in December the Cubans began building a big airport suitable for jets. Carter formally expressed his concern over the situation in Grenada in a memo to the CIA (8 May 1979). On 3 July 1979 (143) Carter approved covert action in Grenada, both to resist Marxism and to promote democracy. However, the Senate Intelligence Committee strongly opposed the action, and the CIA backed off—even though the committee had no legal authority to stop the operation. Gates attributes the CIA's action to its fear of further congressional investigation.

25. Gates, *From the Shadows,* 78, quoting a CIA evaluation. According to Gates, the Cubans may have received additional arms as rewards for their efforts in Angola and in Ethiopia. The new relationship was apparently symbolized by the establishment, in Lourdes, Cuba, of a large Soviet signals intelligence (SIGINT) station, which Americans credited with the ability to tap into U.S. telephone conversations. The latter are carried by microwave relays, and presumably ducting (an electronic propagation phenomenon) over the Caribbean carried some of these signals to Cuba. It seems more likely that Lourdes was the downlink station for a new Soviet signals intelligence satellite, which picked up signals leaking up

from the microwave relays over the United States. Lourdes was also credited with the ability to pick up important missile telemetry from shots from Cape Kennedy.

26. Gates, *From the Shadows,* 124–25.

27. As late as 1978 a State Department representative assured the author that Iran was particularly stable because the shah was so popular, due in part to the "white revolution" he had carried out. Saudi Arabia, by way of contrast, was inherently unstable.

28. Allin, *Cold War Illusions,* 142.

29. According to Gates, *From the Shadows,* 130, the Soviet forces would have come as far south as Esfahan in central Iran. However, in the August 1980 exercise, a two-front attack (12 divisions from the Transcaucasus Military District, 3 or 4 from Turkestan, and part of the Fortieth Army, then fighting in Afghanistan) would have seized all of Iran. These data are from a CIA estimate (presumably an NIE) produced in August 1980.

30. Volkogonov, *Stalin: Triumph and Tragedy,* 54.

31. Arbatov, *The System,* 198.

32. Gates, *From the Shadows,* 131.

33. Gates, *From the Shadows,* 143.

34. Walker, *The Cold War,* 252.

35. Volkogonov, *Stalin: Triumph and Tragedy,* 56.

36. Walker, *The Cold War,* 253.

37. On 20 August (Gates, *From the Shadows,* 132) the CIA warned that Soviet involvement in Afghanistan was so extensive that the Soviets might believe they had the wherewithal to stage a coup against the Taraki regime—but the agency doubted that would happen. On 14 September the CIA sent President Carter an "alert" memorandum warning that the Soviets might be about to commit their own forces to prevent the collapse of the Afghan regime (but then softened the warning by arguing that the Soviets would prefer not to take that risk). As a result of this memo, on 20 September there was an interagency meeting to decide what steps to take in the event that the Soviets intervened militarily in Afghanistan, looking mainly at possible diplomatic, political, and propaganda actions. On 19 December a CIA "alert" memo warned of a substantial Soviet buildup on the Afghan border, for what turned out to be the 25 December invasion.

38. Volkogonov, *Stalin: Triumph and Tragedy,* 58.

39. Walker, *The Cold War,* 254.

40. According to Arbatov, *The System,* 198–200, the decision was taken by Ustinov, Gromyko, and Andropov, and rubber-stamped by an ailing Brezhnev. Ustinov was apparently a strong supporter, although when intervention was actually ordered, Soviet generals were unenthusiastic (197). Arbatov presents Gromyko as frightened of Ustinov, unwilling to defy him. As for Andropov, until the fall of 1979 he apparently rejected intervention. He seems to have switched partly because he deeply distrusted Hafizullah Amin (there were rumors that Amin had been recruited by the CIA when he was in the United States) while he believed that Amin's vicious domestic policies were alienating the population. Arbatov speculates that Andropov imagined in Babrak Kamal, the ruler the Soviets installed in 1979, a resemblance to Janos Kadar, the very successful and conciliatory Hungarian ruler the Soviets installed after the 1956 revolt. In the fall of 1989 Arbatov was chairman of the Supreme Soviet Subcommittee on Political Issues and Negotiations, responsible for a report on the decision to commit troops to Afghanistan.

41. Volkogonov, *Stalin: Triumph and Tragedy,* 58.

42. Ibid., 60. He set up and ran the psychological warfare operation in Kabul.

43. Gates, *From the Shadows,* 147.

44. Safran, *Saudi Arabia,* 290, claims that the bombing was a frame-up.

45. According to Yapp, *Near East,* 369, Ismail, a northern Yemeni, had his main strength in the Party and the internal security organizations and among fellow northern Yemenis. His rival, Ali Nasser al-Hassani (also given as Muhammad), enjoyed army support and had a regional and tribal following. When al-Hassani won his 1980 coup, he became president, prime minister, and general secretary of the Party.

46. Gates, *From the Shadows,* 149.

47. Safran, *Saudi Arabia,* 236. Abd al-Fattah Ismail returned in 1985 and a new triumvirate was formed; but Ali Nasser al-Hassani had his colleagues (including Ismail) killed at a 13 January 1986 politburo meeting (which he did not attend). However, opponents rallied and overthrew al-Hassani. This time the Soviets were apparently taken completely by surprise; their diplomats and military advisors took refuge on board a Soviet freighter in the harbor. In the fight that followed, 4,230 members of the ruling party were killed; total deaths were probably about 13,000, and about 60,000 fled to North Yemen. Soviet aid, until 1986 the sole prop of the PDRY, was cut back

48. According to Gates, *From the Shadows,* 148, in February 1980 Brzezinski discussed an expanded aid program with Pakistani President Mohammed Zia, then went on to Saudi Arabia where he obtained an agreement that the Saudis would match U.S. aid to the Afghan rebels.

49. Carter's announcement was a major defeat for Cyrus Vance and the State Department, which tried to delete the crucial sentence from his address; Brzezinski saved it (Gates, *From the Shadows,* 113).

50. Allin, *Cold War Illusions,* 146.

51. Ibid., 144.

52. Ibid., 146.

53. Rodman, *More Precious than Peace,* 189 and Karnow, *Vietnam: A History,* 53.

54. Rodman, *More Precious than Peace,* 190.

55. Karnow, *Vietnam: A History,* 56.

56. Rodman, *More Precious than Peace,* 191.

57. According to Gates, *From the Shadows,* 120–21, when Deng Xiaoping met President Carter, Vance, and Brzezinski on 30 January 1979 he announced that China would invade Vietnam "to give them an appropriate limited lesson." The next day Carter outlined likely consequences, but did not try to dissuade Deng; he did not threaten, for example, to cut off normalization or military or economic cooperation. Gates, who was not present, suspects that Brzezinski and others were positively encouraging.

58. Remarks to the author by Chinese officials in Sinkiang and in Harbin, November 1980.

59. According to members of the Chinese National War College visiting the Hudson Institute in the spring of 1980.

60. Brzezinski, *Power and Principle,* 424.

61. As described to the author by Chinese Foreign Ministry officials in Harbin in November 1980.

62. Crampton, *East Europe*, 365.

63. Volkogonov, *Stalin: Triumph and Tragedy*, 64–65.

64. Volkogonov, *Stalin: Triumph and Tragedy*, 65.

65. From notes of a conference held by the Poles and Russians in Warsaw in November 1997 to discuss the crises of 1980–81 (J. Perlez, "Old Cold War Enemies Exhume One Battlefield," *New York Times*, 11 November 1997, sec. A, p. 4).

Chapter 36. The Computer Bomb

1. Analog devices are physical models of situations, generally using electrical circuits to mimic mechanical situations or mathematical equations. An analog computer, for example, has to be rewired to represent a changed situation or equation. By way of contrast, a digital computer handles abstract numbers according to a program in its memory. To change what it does, only the program (software) need be changed. That is why digital computers are so flexible.

2. Buderi, *The Invention that Changed the World*, 363; Gough, *Watching the Skies*, 37–39, 71–74 (describing the British CDS system, the first to offer automatic data handling). For a manual vs. automatic tracking, see Gough, *Watching the Skies*, appendix C.

3. Buderi, *The Invention that Changed the World*, 365–68, 385–88; Schaffel, *The Emerging Shield*, 198, 200–202.

4. Schaffel, *The Emerging Shield*, 201; IDA 209–12.

5. Schaffel, *The Emerging Shield*, 264. It would have been the basis for second-generation SAGE centers.

6. For NADGE, see Gough, *Watching the Skies*, 230–37. For the British UKADGE project, see 301–10. Gough does not mention the connection with SAGE.

7. Friedman, *U.S. Naval Weapons*, 143–45.

8. See, for example, the book *Idea, Algorithm, Decision*, as described in Hemsley, *Soviet Troop Control*. The book was translated and published by the U.S. Air Force in its series of Soviet professional handbooks.

9. Igloo White is described in James William Gibson, *The Perfect War*, 397–98. See also Prados, *Blood Road*, 267–68.

10. James William Gibson, *The Perfect War*, 399–400. See also Prados, *Blood Road*, 269.

11. Col. T. P. Kehoe, USA, "BETA . . . An Idea Whose Time Had Come," *Signal* (October 1981), 11–13.

12. See M. C. Fitzgerald, "Marshal Ogarkov on Modern War: 1977–1985," Professional Paper 443.10 of the Center for Naval Analyses (November 1986). An associate of Andropov's, Ogarkov was removed in 1984 for "unpartylike behavior," presumably when Chernenko succeeded Andropov. Most likely he had been criticizing the Party for failing to produce the computer-based systems he wanted.

13. Arbatov, *The System*, 160. Arbatov was then running the Institute for the Study of the USA and Canada (IMEMO). He makes no mention of the profound military consequences of this industrial revolution, which actually meant computers.

14. Ibid., 160–61. Arbatov was one of the two authors. In his book, Arbatov compares the ideas he espoused in 1973 with Gorbachev's, but probably the most important issue from a Cold War perspective was whether to create a new large-scale computer industry at

the expense of existing ones. The report was unacceptable because it demanded fundamental change, whereas the authorities, according to Arbatov, wanted something envisaging little more than administrative improvements.

Chapter 37. Counterattack

1. D. Oberdorfer, interview, in *President Reagan and the World,* ed. Schmertz, Datlof and Ugrinsky, 129–30.

2. K. L. Adelman, "United States and Soviet Relations: Reagan's Real Role in Winning the Cold War," in *President Reagan and the World,* ed. Schmertz, Datlof and Ugrinsky, particularly 82–84.

3. H. E. Meyer, interview, 126.

4. Paul Nitze, interview, in *President Reagan and the World,* ed. Schmertz, Datlof and Ugrinsky, 249.

5. Simons, *The End of the Cold War?* 45.

6. Schweizer, *Victory,* 6. The formal economic warfare policy, approved in November 1982, was NSDD 66 (Simpson, *National Security Directives,* 80–81).

7. Simpson, *National Security Directives,* 62–63. According to Gates, *From the Shadows,* 188, on 3 August 1982 Casey sent President Reagan a report on the atmosphere in Moscow. There was a pervasive malaise due to corruption, violent crime, and hardship. By this time corruption was extremely widespread, and it had almost completely sapped morale; it was obvious that everyone in the Communist Party was simply stealing whatever was available. Six fur hats had even been stolen from the hat rack outside Andropov's office in the Lubyanka, the KGB headquarters. There had been serious strikes in 1981 in Gork'iy and in Togliatti. Internal criticism of Soviet institutions was growing. The CIA concluded that "to embark on reform in any circumstances would be to court disaster. In East Europe, some experimentation can be tolerated because if the situation gets out of hand there, Soviet troops are on hand to reassert control; if things go wrong in the Soviet Union itself, however, no one will protect the Party."

8. J. F. Matlock Jr., interview, in *President Reagan and the World,* ed. Schmertz, Datlof and Ugrinsky, 123–24.

9. Simpson, *National Security Directives,* 18.

10. National Security Decision Document 17, decided 16 November 1981 and distributed 4 January 1982.

11. Falcoff, "Latin America," particularly 396–97.

12. G. A. Trofimenko, interview, in *President Reagan and the World,* ed. Schmertz, Datlof and Ugrinsky, 135.

13. The book was Richard Pipes's *Russia under the Old Regime.*

14. The first batch of intact missiles arrived in Moscow in the fall of 1986 (Dobbs, *Down with Big Brother,* 169, 171).

15. Schweizer, *Victory,* 118–19.

16. Volkogonov, *Stalin: Triumph and Tragedy,* 61.

17. Schweizer, *Victory,* 32.

18. Ibid., 75. According to Gates, *From the Shadows,* 237, the administration began serious discussion of covert action on Poland only after martial law had been declared. The

CIA in particular emphasized deniability in its support of the Solidarity union, working only through intermediaries. Its effort began in earnest in the fall of 1982.

19. Andrew and Gordievsky, *KGB: The Inside Story,* 537. According to Gates, *From the Shadows,* 354–56, during the winter of 1984–85 the CIA secretly received information on the Bulgarian and Soviet roles in the assassination. A draft CIA paper on the subject was widely criticized within the agency, and Gates considers the question of whether the Soviets ordered the attack or knew about it in advance still unanswered.

20. Schweizer, *Victory,* 8, with special reference to some insights of Herman Kahn's. One of Reagan's advisors, Dr. William Schneider, had been a senior Hudson Institute staff member and had had extensive experience with Kahn's strategic concepts.

21. The anti-Reagan propaganda of this period is exemplified by Michio Kaku and David Axelrod's *To Win a Nuclear War: The Pentagon's Secret War Plans* (Boston: South End Press, 1987). This is not to imply that the Kaku/Axelrod book was Soviet-financed. The book posits that the United States is now in a prewar stance, developing systems specifically to execute a first strike against a defensively minded Soviet Union. See Schweizer, *Victory,* 172–73, for Soviet "active measures" to try to defeat Reagan in 1984.

22. Andrew and Gordievsky, *KGB: The Inside Story,* 488–89.

23. John F. Lehman Jr., private communication with the author. Lehman had worked on Seaplan 2000, a Carter-era navy study which argued, among other things, that emerging technology (e.g., Aegis, the F-14/Phoenix combination, towed arrays, and the Mk 48 ADCAP torpedo) could overcome growing Soviet numbers at sea.

24. D. S. Zakheim, "The Military Buildup," in *President Reagan and the World,* ed. Schmertz, Datlof and Ugrinsky, 206–7.

25. Schweizer, *Victory,* 81, quoting the 1982 Defense Guidance.

26. Ibid., 187.

27. Ibid., 188.

28. Ibid., 47.

29. Dobbs, *Down with Big Brother,* 129–30.

30. Schweizer, *Victory,* 59.

31. Ibid., 83.

32. Ibid., 31; Dobbs, *Down with Big Brother,* 137.

33. Schweizer, *Victory,* 133.

34. The Strategic Defense Initiative was ordered by NSDD 85 (25 March 1983); see Simpson, *National Security Directives,* 233.

35. H. E. Meyer, interview, 127.

36. Lehman asked his staff to explain just what the navy would do in wartime. He was asking Congress for a much larger fleet, and had to explain what it was designed to do.

37. Dov Zakheim, interview, in *President Reagan and the World,* ed. Schmertz, Datlof, and Ugrinsky, 209.

38. Volkogonov, *Autopsy for an Empire,* 324. Brezhnev had been quite ill for years. According to Arbatov, *The System,* 191, Brezhnev fell ill in December 1974, while visiting the air base near Vladivostok, having seen off President Ford after a summit meeting; his illness became a major state secret. He never fully recovered, and his problems were aggravated by his excessive use of sleeping pills.

39. Ibid., 322–23.

40. Ibid., 344.

41. Solovyov and Klepikova, *Inside the Kremlin,* 31–33.

42. Simons, *The End of the Cold War?* 49–53.

43. Allin, *Cold War Illusions,* 91.

44. U.S. intelligence assessments of SS-N-21 deployment can be traced from statements in the annual issues of Soviet Military Power, which was published by the Defense Department. In March 1983 it was under development, soon to enter service; in March 1984 would "probably become operational this year." The same statement was repeated in the April 1985 edition, but in March 1986 its status was downgraded to the advanced test stage. According to Karpenko, *Rossiskoye raketnoye oruzhiye,* 54, SS-N-21 was accepted into service only in 1987.

45. Pry, *War Scare.* See also Gates, *From the Shadows,* 270–73.

46. Simons, *The End of the Cold War?* 59.

47. Volkogonov, *Autopsy for an Empire,* 384. According to Arbatov, *The System,* 287, Andropov actually named Gorbachev as his successor, but the troika of Chernenko, Tikhonov, and Ustinov deleted the paragraph in the crucial memo. Nikolai A. Tikhonov, one of Brezhnev's cronies, was prime minister (chairman of the Council of Ministers). The day the Politburo met after Andropov died, Ustinov told Tikhonov that "Kostya [Chernenko] will be easier to get along with than the other one [Gorbachev]." As the most powerful man in the Politburo, he easily carried the day. A year earlier Yevgeni Chazov, who headed the Ministry of Health arm responsible for members of the Politburo, had warned that Chernenko was so ill that he could not work; he would soon die. That apparently meant little to the ailing Ustinov, who had only six months to live.

48. Ibid., 403.

49. Ibid., 423.

50. A remark made to Volkogonov and mentioned in ibid.

Chapter 38. Unexpected Victory

1. Volkogonov, *Autopsy for an Empire,* 435.

2. Bush and Scowcroft, *A World Transformed,* 4.

3. Pryce-Jones, *The War That Never Was,* 100; Henry Trofimenko, interview, in *President Reagan and the World,* ed. Schmertz, Datlof, and Ugrinsky, 137.

4. Dobbs, *Down with Big Brother,* 131.

5. Ibid., 350.

6. Pryce-Jones, *The War That Never Was,* 76.

7. Gates, *From the Shadows,* 336–37. Gates is skeptical of later claims that it was in 1985 that Gorbachev decided to end the war in Afghanistan or to withdraw from other Third World wars.

8. Pryce-Jones, *The War That Never Was,* 39–40.

9. Ibid., 101.

10. Nelson, *War of the Black Heavens,* 160–61, quoting Georgui Vatchnadze. He thought that there would have been no perestroika had it not been for Western radio.

11. Ibid., 163. A 1984 RFE survey estimated that on average the Voice of America reached 14 to 18 percent of the Soviet population, compared to 8 to12 percent for Radio Liberty (RFE), 7 to 10 percent for the BBC, and 3 to 6 percent for the German station Deutsche

Welle. In each case the impact was probably far greater, because each listener would tell others about the programs.

12. Trofimenko, interview, 138.

13. Pryce-Jones, *The War That Never Was,* 79.

14. Nelson, *War of the Black Heavens,* 164, makes this point.

15. Simons, *The End of the Cold War?* 153–54.

16. Levesque, *The Enigma of 1989,* 21.

17. Dobbs, *Down with Big Brother,* 179; Volkogonov, *Autopsy for an Empire,* 521.

18. Pryce-Jones, *The War That Never Was,* 108–9.

19. Ibid., 96–97, 147–48.

20. Ibid., 139.

21. Ibid., 112–13, quoting Shevardnadze's deputy, Sergei Tarasenko.

22. Levesque, *The Enigma of 1989,* 87–88.

23. *Soldat und Technik* (July 1991), 442.

24. Levesque, *The Enigma of 1989,* 47.

25. Ibid., 77–79.

26. Pryce-Jones, *The War That Never Was,* 115.

27. Levesque, *The Enigma of 1989,* 98–99.

28. It was prepared for Aleksandr Yakovlev, Gorbachev's close associate, who was then president of the Central Committee's new International Affairs Committee. This report is described in detail in ibid.

29. Ibid., 95.

30. Ibid., 53.

31. Ibid., 96.

32. Pryce-Jones, *The War That Never Was,* 221–22.

33. Levesque, *The Enigma of 1989,* 86.

34. Ibid., 119.

35. Ibid., 150–51.

36. Pryce-Jones, *The War That Never Was,* 234.

37. Ibid., 223.

38. Levesque, *The Enigma of 1989,* 153.

39. Ibid., 153.

40. Ibid., 150–52.

41. Pryce-Jones, *The War That Never Was,* e.g. 265.

42. Levesque, *The Enigma of 1989,* 159.

43. Dunbabin, *The Cold War,* 464.

44. Pryce-Jones, *The War That Never Was,* 94–95. The original had been locked up, but a copy made in 1946 came to light.

45. Arbatov, *The System,* 332, cites Gorbachev's spring 1990 "Open Letter of the Central Committee to the Country's Communists," which he saw as the beginning of a campaign against Party dissidents and liberals. Arbatov says that as a Central Committee member he strongly protested.

46. Pryce-Jones, *The War That Never Was,* 149.

47. Arbatov, *The System,* 334, observes that "committees of national salvation" had been established in all three republics to provide Gorbachev's government with a pretext to send in troops and to overthrow the local governments (which were pro-independence). This was

much the same tactic that had been used in Czechoslovakia in 1968. Lt. Col. Viktor Alksnis, who had been involved in this operation, later charged that Gorbachev had initially sanctioned the operation, then had pulled back in the face of public protests (and political action by Boris Yeltsin, who, as president of the Russian republic, met with the Baltic governments and signed treaties with them). Another evidence of Gorbachev's direct involvement in the attacks in the Baltics was the use of the KGB's Alpha Group in the attack in Vilnius. This organization reported directly to the head of the KGB and thence to the president of the Soviet Union, Gorbachev.

48. Matlock, *Autopsy on an Empire,* 607–8, 612, 622–29.

BIBLIOGRAPHY

Aerojet ex-employees (Bernie Dornan, Shorty Feldbush, Bob Gordon, Myra Grenier, Carson Hawk, Myron Lipow, Jack Orr, Joe Peterson, Mike Pompa, Ken Price, Phil Umholtz, and Howard Williams). *Aerojet: The Creative Company.* San Dimas, Calif.: Aerojet History Group, 1995.

Aldous, Richard, and Sabine Lee. *Harold Macmillan and Britain's World Role.* Basingstoke, England: Macmillan, 1996.

Aldrich, Richard J., ed. *British Intelligence and the Cold War, 1943–1951.* London: Routledge, 1992.

Alexander, Martin S., ed. *Knowing Your Friends: Intelligence Inside Alliances and Coalitions from 1914 to the Cold War.* London: Frank Cass, 1998.

Allin, Dana H. *Cold War Illusions: America, Europe, and Soviet Power, 1969–1989.* New York: St. Martin's Press, 1994.

Ambrose, Stephen E. *Eisenhower: The President.* New York: Simon & Schuster, 1984.

———. *Ike's Spies: Eisenhower and the Espionage Establishment.* Garden City, N.J.: Doubleday, 1981.

Andrew, Christopher, and Oleg Gordievsky. *KGB: The Inside Story.* London: Hodder & Stoughton, 1990.

Antonov-Ovseyenko, Anton. *The Time of Stalin: Portrait of a Tyranny.* New York: Harper & Row, 1981.

Arbatov, Georgi. *The System: An Insider's Life in Soviet Politics.* New York: Times Books, 1992.

Arnold, Guy. *Wars in the Third World since 1945.* London: Cassell, 1991.

Arnold, James R. *The First Domino: Eisenhower, the Military, and America's Intervention in Vietnam.* New York: William Morrow, 1991.

Ashton, Nigel John. *Eisenhower, Macmillan, and the Problem of Nasser: Anglo-American Relations and Arab Nationalism, 1955–1959.* London: Macmillan, 1996.

Bacevich, A. J. *The Pentomic Era.* Washington, D.C.: National Defense University, 1986.

Ball, Nicole, and Milton Leitenberg, eds. *The Structure of the Defense Industry: An International Survey.* New York: St. Martin's, 1983.

Ball, S. J. *The Cold War: An International History, 1947–1991.* London: Arnold, 1998.

Barlow, Jeffrey G. *Revolt of the Admirals: The Fight for Naval Aviation, 1945–1950.* Washington, D.C.: Naval Historical Center, 1994.

Barron, John. *Operation Solo: The FBI's Man in the Kremlin.* Washington, D.C.: Regnery, 1996.

Baylis, John. *Ambiguity and Deterrence: British Nuclear Strategy, 1945–1964.* Oxford: Clarendon Press, 1995.

———. *Anglo-American Defense Relations, 1939–1984.* London: Macmillan, 1984.

Becker, Jasper. *Hungry Ghosts: China's Secret Famine.* London: John Murray, 1997.

Bellamy, Christopher. *The Evolution of Modern Land Warfare: Theory and Practice.* London: Routledge, 1990.

Benson, Robert Louis, and Michael Warner, eds. *Venona: Soviet Espionage and the American Response, 1939–1957.* Washington, D.C.: NSA and CIA, 1996. "Venona" was the code name for decryption of a series of wartime and early postwar KGB messages, code names in which revealed numerous Soviet spies, such as the Rosenbergs and Alger Hiss. This volume includes some summaries of contemporary U.S. data on Soviet espionage activities.

Berdal, Mats R. *The United States, Norway, and the Cold War, 1954–1960.* London: MacMillan/St. Anthony's, 1997.

Berezhkov, Valentin M. *At Stalin's Side: His Interpreter's Memoirs, from the October Revolution to the Fall of the Dictator's Empire.* New York: Birch Lane Press, 1994.

Beschloss, Michael R. *The Crisis Years: Kennedy and Khrushchev, 1960–1963.* New York: HarperCollins, 1991.

———, ed. *Taking Charge: The Johnson White House Tapes, 1963–1964.* New York: Simon & Schuster, 1997.

Bethell, Leslie, ed. *Latin America: Economy and Society Since 1930.* Cambridge, England: Cambridge University Press, 1998.

———. *Latin America: Politics and Society Since 1930.* Cambridge, England: Cambridge University Press, 1998.

Bill, James A. *The Eagle and the Lion: The Tragedy of American-Iranian Relations.* New Haven: Yale University Press, 1988.

Bill, James A., and William Roger Louis, eds. *Musaddiq, Iranian Nationalism, and Oil.* London: I. B. Taurus, 1988.

Bissell, Richard M., Jr. *Reflections of a Cold Warrior.* New Haven: Yale University Press, 1996.

Blacker, Coit D. *Hostage to Revolution: Gorbachev and Soviet Security Policy, 1985–1991.* New York: Council on Foreign Relations, 1993.

Blasier, Cole. *The Hovering Giant: U.S. Response to Revolutionary Change in Latin America, 1910–1985.* Pittsburgh: University of Pittsburgh Press, 1985.

Bloodworth, Dennis. *The Messiah and the Mandarins: Mao Tse-Tung and the Ironies of Power.* New York: Atheneum, 1982.

Bluth, Christoph. *Britain, Germany, and Western Nuclear Strategy.* Oxford: Clarendon Press, 1995.

Botti, Timothy J. *Ace in the Hole: Why the United States Did Not Use Nuclear Weapons in the Cold War, 1945 to 1965.* New York: Greenwood, 1996.

———. *The Long Wait: The Forging of the Anglo-American Nuclear Alliance, 1945–1958.* New York: Greenwood, 1987.

Bowie, Robert R., and Richard H. Immerman. *Waging Peace: How Eisenhower Shaped an Enduring Cold War Strategy.* New York: Oxford University Press, 1998.

Brackman, Arnold C. *The Communist Collapse in Indonesia.* New York: W. W. Norton, 1969.

Brands, H. W. *Inside the Cold War: Loy Henderson and the Rise of the American Empire, 1918–1961.* New York: Oxford University Press, 1991.

Bregman, Ahron, and Jihan El-Tahri. *The Fifty Years War: Israel and the Arabs.* London: BBC/Penguin Books, 1998.

Brinkley, Douglas. *Dean Acheson: The Cold War Years, 1953–1971.* New Haven: Yale University Press, 1992.

Brogan, Patrick. *World Conflicts: Why and Where They are Happening.* Rev. ed. London: Bloomsbury, 1992.

Bruce-Briggs, B. *Shield of Faith: The Hidden Struggle for Strategic Defense.* New York: Simon & Schuster, 1988.

Brzezinski, Zbigniew. *Power and Principle: Memoirs of the National Security Advisor, 1977–1981.* Rev. ed. New York: Farrar Straus Giroux, 1985.

Buderi, Robert. *The Invention That Changed the World: How a Small Group of Radar Pioneers Won the Second World War and Launched a Technological Revolution.* New York: Simon & Schuster, 1996.

Bullock, Alan. *Ernest Bevin, Foreign Secretary.* Oxford: Oxford University Press, 1985.
———. *Hitler and Stalin: Parallel Lives.* London: HarperCollins, 1991.

Bundy, McGeorge. *Danger and Survival: Choices about the Bomb in the First Fifty Years.* New York: Random House, 1988.

Bush, George, and Brent Scowcroft. *A World Transformed.* New York: Alfred A. Knopf, 1998.

Chuev, Felix. *Molotov Remembers: Inside Kremlin Politics.* Chicago: Ivan R. Dee, 1993.

CIA Center for the Study of Intelligence. *The Origin and Development of the CIA in the Administration of Harry S. Truman: A Conference Report.* CSI 95-001. March 1995. (Referred to in text as "CIA Conference Report.")

Clark, Ian. *Nuclear Diplomacy and the Special Relationship: Britain's Deterrent and America, 1947–1962.* Oxford: Clarendon Press, 1994.

Clark, Ian, and Nicholas J. Wheeler. *The British Origins of Nuclear Strategy, 1945–1955.* Oxford: Clarendon Press, 1989.

Clayton, Anthony. The Wars of French Decolonization. London: Longman, 1994.

Clayton, David. *Imperialism Revisited: Political and Economic Relations Between Britain and China, 1950–1954.* London: Macmillan, 1997.

Clifford, Clark, and Richard Holbrooke. *Counsel to the President.* New York: Random House, 1991.

Clogg, Richard. *A Concise History of Greece.* Cambridge, England: Cambridge University Press, 1992.

Cochran, T. B., W. M. Arkin, and M. M. Hoenig. *U.S. Nuclear Weapons.* Vol. 1 of *Nuclear Weapons Databook.* Cambridge: Ballinger, 1984.

Cochran, T. B., W. M. Arkin, R. S. Norris, and M. M. Hoenig. *U.S. Nuclear Warhead Production.* Vol. 2 of *Nuclear Weapons Databook.* Cambridge: Ballinger, 1987.

Cochran, T. B., W. M. Arkin, R. S. Norris, and J. I. Sands. *Soviet Nuclear Weapons.* Vol. 4 of *Nuclear Weapons Databook.* New York: Harper & Row, 1989.

Cohen, M. J. *Fighting World War Three from the Middle East: Allied Contingency Plans, 1945–1954.* London: Frank Cass, 1997.

Collier, Simon, and William F. Sater. *A History of Chile, 1808–1994.* Cambridge Latin American Studies Series, vol. 82. Cambridge, 1996.

Condit, D. M. *See* U.S. Office of the Secretary of Defense.

Condit, K. W. *See* U.S. Joint Chiefs of Staff.

Conquest, Robert. *Stalin and the Kirov Murder.* Oxford: Oxford University Press, 1989.

————. *Stalin, Breaker of Nations.* London: Weidenfeld & Nicholson, 1991.

Converse, E. V., III. "U.S. Plans For A Postwar Overseas Military Base System, 1942–1948." Ph.D. diss., Princeton University, 1984.

Copeland, Miles. *The Game of Nations: The Amorality of Power Politics.* New York: Simon & Schuster, 1969.

————. *The Game Player: Confessions of the CIA's Original Political Operative.* London: Aurum Press, 1989.

Cornish, Paul. *British Military Planning for the Defence of Germany, 1945–1950.* London: Macmillan, 1996.

Costello, John, and Oleg Tsarev. *Dangerous Illusions.* New York: Crown, 1993.

Courtois, Stephane, Nicolas Werth, and Jean-Louis Panne et al. *Le livre noire du communisme: Crimes, terreur, répression* (The black book of communism: Crimes, terror, and repression). Paris: Robert Laffont, 1997.

Cowell, Alan. *Killing the Wizards: Wars of Power and Freedom from Zaire to South Africa.* New York: Simon & Schuster, 1992.

Crampton, R. J. *East Europe in the Twentieth Century—-and After.* 2d ed. London: Routledge, 1997.

Cribb, Robert, and Colin Brown. *Modern Indonesia: A History Since 1945.* London: Longman, 1995.

Cronin, James E. *The World the Cold War Made: Order, Chaos, and the Return of History.* London: Routledge, 1996.

Dallek, Robert. *Flawed Giant: Lyndon Johnson and His Times, 1961–1973.* Oxford: Oxford University Press, 1998.

Darwin, John. *Britain and Decolonisation: The Retreat from Empire in the Post-War World.* London: Macmillan, 1988.

Davidson, Phillip B. *Vietnam At War: The History, 1946–1975.* New York: Oxford University Press, 1988. Lieutenant General Davidson was chief intelligence officer in Vietnam in 1968–69.

Deighton, Anne. *The Impossible Peace: Britain, the Division of Germany, and the Origins of the Cold War.* Oxford: Clarendon Press, 1993.

Destler, I. M., Leslie H. Gelb, and Anthony Lake. *Our Own Worst Enemy: The Unmaking of American Foreign Policy.* New York: Simon & Schuster, 1984. Lake was President Bill Clinton's first national security advisor.

Devereux, David R. *The Formulation of British Defence Policy towards the Middle East, 1948–1956. London: Macmillan, 1990.*

Dinerstein, H. S. *War and the Soviet Union.* Rev. ed. New York: Praeger, 1962.

Djilas, Milovan. *Conversations With Stalin.* New York: Harcourt, Brace & World, 1962.

————. *Fall of the New Class: A History of Communism's Self-Destruction.* New York: Alfred A. Knopf, 1998.

Dobbs, Michael. *Down with Big Brother: The Fall of the Soviet Empire.* New York: Alfred A. Knopf, 1996.

Donaldson, Gary A. *America at War since 1945: Politics and Diplomacy in Korea, Vietnam, and the Gulf War.* Westport, Conn.: Praeger, 1996.

Donghi, Tuilio Halperin. *The Contemporary History of Latin America.* Durham, N.C.: Duke University Press, 1993.

Duffield, John Stuart. "The Evolution of NATO's Conventional Force Posture." Ph.D. diss., Princeton University, 1989.

———. *Power Rules: The Evolution of NATO's Conventional Force Posture.* Stanford, Calif.: Stanford University Press, 1995. This revised version of Duffield's Ph.D. dissertation includes new tables showing NATO forces at various times.

Duffy, Paul, and Andrei Kandalov. *Tupolev: The Man and His Aircraft.* Shrewsbury, England: Airlife, 1996.

Duiker, William J. *The Communist Road to Power in Vietnam.* Rev. ed. Boulder, Colo.: Westview, 1996.

Dunbabin, J. P. D. *The Cold War: The Great Powers and Their Allies.* London: Longman, 1994.

Dunlop, John B. *The Rise of Russia and the Fall of the Soviet Union.* Princeton: Princeton University Press, 1993.

Dunn, Peter M. *The First Vietnam War.* New York: St. Martin's Press, 1985.

Einthoven, Alain C., and Wayne K. Smith. *How Much Is Enough? Shaping the Defense Program, 1961–1969.* New York: Harper & Row, 1971.

Erickson, John. *The Road to Stalingrad.* London: Weidenfeld & Nicholson, 1975.

Erickson, John, Lynn Hansen, and William Schneider. *Soviet Ground Forces: An Operational Assessment.* Boulder, Colo.: Westview; London: Croom Helm, 1986.

Etzold, Thomas H., and John Lewis Gaddis, eds. *Containment: Documents on American Policy and Strategy.* New York: Columbia University Press, 1978.

Fairbank, John K. *China's Revolution: From 1800 to 1985.* New York: Harper & Row, 1986.

Faringdon, Hugh. *Strategic Geography: NATO, the Warsaw Pact, and the Superpowers.* 2d ed. London: Routledge, 1989.

Feis, Herbert. *From Trust to Terror: The Onset of the Cold War, 1945–1950.* New York: Norton, 1970.

Fink, Carole, Philipp Gassert, and Detlef Junker, eds. *1968: The World Transformed.* Cambridge, England: Cambridge University Press; Washington, D.C.: The German Historical Institute, 1998.

Ford, Ronnie F. *Tet 1968: Understanding the Surprise.* London: Frank Cass, 1995.

Friedman, Norman. *U.S. Naval Weapons: Every Gun, Missile, Mine and Torpedo Used by the U.S. Navy from 1883 to the Present Day.* Annapolis, Md.: Naval Institute Press, 1983.

Fursenko, Aleksandr, and Timothy Naftali. *"One Hell of a Gamble": The Secret History of the Cuban Missile Crisis.* New York: Norton, 1997.

Futrell, Robert Frank. *Ideas, Concepts, Doctrine: Basic Thinking in the United States Air Force.* 2 vols. Maxwell, Ala.: Air University Press, 1989.

Gaddis, John Lewis. *Strategies of Containment: A Critical Appraisal of Postwar American National Security Policy.* Oxford: Oxford University Press, 1982.

———. *The United States and the End of the Cold War: Implications, Reconsiderations, Provocations.* New York: Oxford, 1992.

———. *We Now Know: Rethinking Cold War History.* Oxford: Clarendon Press, 1997.

Gaddy, Clifford G. *The Price of the Past: Russia's Struggle with the Legacy of a Militarized Economy.* Washington, D.C.: Brookings Institution Press, 1996.

Gaiduk, Ilya V. *The Soviet Union and the Vietnam War.* Chicago: Ivan R. Dee, 1996.

Gardiner, Robert, ed. *Conway's All the World's Fighting Ships, 1947–1995.* London: Conway Maritime Press, 1995.

Gardner, Lloyd C., ed. *Spheres of Influence: The Great Powers Partition Europe, from Munich to Yalta.* Chicago: Ivan R. Dee, 1993.

Gardner, Lloyd C., and Ted Gittinger. *Vietnam: The Early Decisions.* Austin: University of Texas Press, 1997.

Gates, Robert M. *From the Shadows: The Ultimate Insider's Story of Five Presidents and How They Won the Cold War.* New York: Simon & Schuster, 1996. Gates is a former CIA director.

Gelb, Norman. *The Berlin Wall: Kennedy, Khrushchev, and a Showdown in the Heart of Europe.* New York: Times Books, 1987.

Gerges, Fawaz A. *The Superpowers and the Middle East: Regional and International Politics, 1955–1967.* Boulder, Colo.: Westview, 1994.

Getting, Ivan A. *All in a Lifetime: Science in the Defense of Democracy.* New York: Vantage, 1989. Getting was a key defense scientist and president of the Aerospace Corp. at its founding in 1960.

Gibson, James N. *Nuclear Weapons of the United States.* Atglen, Pa.: Schiffer, 1996.

Gibson, James William. *The Perfect War: Technowar in Vietnam.* Boston: Atlantic Monthly Press, 1986.

Ginsbourg, Paul. *A History of Contemporary Italy: Society and Politics, 1943–1988.* London: Penguin Books, 1990.

Glantz, David. *Soviet Military Deception in the Second World War.* London: Frank Cass, 1989.

Glantz, David M., ed. *The Initial Period of War on the Eastern Front, 22 June–August 1941.* London: Frank Cass, 1993. Proceedings of the Fourth Art of War Symposium, Garmisch, Germany (Bavaria), October 1987.

———. *The Military Strategy of the Soviet Union: A History.* London: Frank Cass, 1992.

Glantz, David, and Jonathan House. *When Titans Clashed: How the Red Army Stopped Hitler.* Lawrence: University Press of Kansas, 1995.

Godement, François. *La renaissance de l'Asie* (The new Asian renaissance: From colonialism to the post Cold War). Trans. Elisabeth J. Parcell. London: Routledge, 1997.

Goncharov, Sergei N., John W. Lewis, and Xue Litai. *Uncertain Partners: Stalin, Mao, and the Korean War.* Stanford, Calif.: Stanford University Press, 1995.

Gordon, Yefim, and Vladimir Rigmant. *Tupolev Tu-95/-142 "Bear": Russia's Intercontinental-Range Heavy Bomber.* "Aerofax" Series. Earl Shilton, England: Midlands Publishing, 1997.

Gori, Francesca, and Silvio Pons. *The Soviet Union and Europe in the Cold War, 1943–1953.* London: Macmillan, 1996; sponsored by the Fondazione Giangiacomo Feltrinelli and Fondazione Istituto Gramsci; papers from a conference held in collaboration with the Institute of World History of the Academy of Sciences, Moscow, with the support of the Italian National Research Council and the Italian Ministry of Foreign Affairs, Cortona, Italy, 23–24 September 1994.

Gough, Jack. *Watching the Skies: The History of Ground Radar in the Air Defence of the United Kingdom.* London: HMSO, 1993.

Grove, Eric J. *Vanguard to Trident: British Naval Policy since World War II.* London: The Bodley Head, 1987.

Gunston, Bill. *The Encyclopedia of Russian Aircraft, 1875–1995.* London: Osprey, 1995.

Gunston, Bill, and Yefim Gordon. *Yakovlev Aircraft since 1924.* London: Putnam, 1997.

Haftendorn, Helga. *NATO and the Nuclear Revolution: A Crisis of Credibility, 1966–1967.* Oxford: Clarendon Press, 1996.

Hail, J. A. *Britain's Foreign Policy in Egypt and Sudan, 1947–1956.* Reading, England: Ithaca Press, 1996.

Halle, Louis J. *The Cold War as History.* London: Chatto & Windus, 1967.

Hammond, Thomas T., ed. *Communist Takeovers.* Baltimore: Johns Hopkins University, 1975.

Hanhimaki, Jussi M. *Containing Coexistence: America, Russia, and the "Finnish Solution," 1945–1956.* Kent, Ohio: Kent State University Press, 1997.

Hansen, Chuck. *U.S. Nuclear Weapons: The Secret History.* Arlington, Tex.: Aerofax; New York: Orion, 1988.

Harford, James. *Korolev: How One Man Masterminded the Soviet Drive to Beat America to the Moon.* New York: James Wiley & Sons, 1997.

Haynes, John Earl, and Harvey Klehr. *Venona: Soviet Espionage in America.* New Haven: Yale University Press, 1999.

Head, William, and Lawrence E. Grinter, eds. *Looking Back on the Vietnam War: A 1990s Perspective on the Decisions, Combat, and Legacies.* Westport, Conn.: Praeger, 1993.

Heller, Francis H., and John R. Gillingham. *NATO: The Founding of the Atlantic Alliance and the Integration of Europe.* Basingstoke: Macmillan, 1992. Papers from a conference at the Harry S. Truman Presidential Library, Independence, Mo., September 1989.

Heller, Michel (Mikhail) and Aleksandr Nekrich. *Utopia in Power: A History of the USSR from 1917 to the Present.* London: Hutchinson, 1986.

Hemsley, John. *Soviet Troop Control: The Role of Command Technology in the Soviet Military System.* London: Brassey's, 1982.

Herring, George C. *LBJ and Vietnam: A Different Kind of War.* Austin: University of Texas Press, 1995.

Herzog, Chaim. *The Arab-Israeli Wars: War and Peace in the Middle East, from the War of Independence through Lebanon.* New York: Random House, 1982.

Heuser, Beatrice, and Robert O'Neill, eds. *Securing Peace in Europe, 1945–1962: Thoughts for the Post–Cold War Era.* New York: St. Martin's Press, 1992.

Hixson, Walter L. *Parting the Curtain: Propaganda, Culture, and the Cold War, 1945–1961.* London: Macmillan Press, 1998.

Hoff, Joan. *Nixon Reconsidered.* New York: Basic Books, 1994.

Hogan, Michael J. *A Cross of Iron: Harry S. Truman and the Origins of the National Security State, 1945–1954.* Cambridge, England: Cambridge University Press, 1998.

Holloway, David. *Stalin and the Bomb: The Soviet Union and Atomic Energy, 1939–1956.* New Haven: Yale University Press, 1994.

Holmes, Leslie. *The End of Communist Power: Anti-Corruption Campaigns and Legitimation Crisis.* New York: Oxford University Press, 1993.

Hoopes, Townsend, and Douglas Brinkley. *Driven Patriot: The Life and Times of James Forrestal.* New York: Vintage, 1992.

Hooton, E. R. *The Greatest Tumult: The Chinese Civil War, 1936–1949.* London: Brassey's, 1991.

Horne, Alistair. *Harold Macmillan, 1957–1986.* Vol. 2. New York: Viking, 1989.

———. *A Savage War of Peace: Algeria, 1954–1962.* Rev. ed. London: Papermac, 1996.

————. *A Small Earthquake in Chile.* 2d ed. London: Macmillan, 1990.

Howson, Gerald. *Arms for Spain: The Untold Story of the Spanish Civil War.* London: John Murray, 1998.

Hunt, Michael H. *The Genesis of Chinese Communist Foreign Policy.* New York: Columbia University Press, 1996.

Hyland, William G. *The Cold War.* New York: Random House, 1991.

Ilan, Amitzur. *The Origin of the Arab-Israeli Arms Race: Arms, Embargo, Military Power, and Decision in the 1948 Palestine War.* St. Anthony's Series. London: Macmillan, 1996.

Institute for Defense Analysis. *The Evolution of U.S. Strategic Command and Control and Warning.* Study S-467, June 1975. Project leader L. Wainstein, with C. D. Cremeans, J. K. Moriarty, and J. Ponturo (declassified 1991).

Isaacson, Walter. *Kissinger: A Biography.* New York: Simon & Schuster, 1992.

Isaacson, Walter, and Evan Thomas. *The Wise Men: Six Friends and the World They Made.* New York: Simon & Schuster, 1986.

Isby, David C. *Weapons and Tactics of the Soviet Army.* Rev. ed. London: Jane's, 1988.

Israelyan, Viktor L. *Inside the Kremlin during the Yom Kippur War.* University Park: Pennsylvania State University Press, 1995.

Jiang, Chen. *China's Road to the Korean War: The Making of the Sino-American Confrontation.* New York: Columbia University Press, 1994.

The Joint Chiefs of Staff and the War in Vietnam. Vol. 1. *1940–1954.* Wilmington, Del.: Michael Glazier, 1982.

Kaiser, Robert G. *Why Gorbachev Happened.* New York: Simon & Schuster, 1991.

Kalugin, Oleg. *The First Directorate: My Thirty-two Years in Intelligence and Espionage against the West.* New York: St. Martin's, 1994. Kalugin was a KGB major general, former head of Soviet counterintelligence.

Karnow, Stanley. *Vietnam: A History.* 2d ed. New York: Penguin Books, 1997.

Karpenko, A. V. *Rossiskoye raketnoye oruzhiye, 1943–1995: Spravochnik* (Russian rocket weapons, 1943–1995: Handbook). St. Petersburg: "PIKA," 1993.

Kasatonova, I. V. *Tri veka Rossiyskogo flota* (Three centuries of the Russian fleet). Vol. 3. St. Petersburg: "LOGOS," 1996.

Keegan, John. *World Armies.* 2d ed. Detroit: Gale Research Company, 1983.

Keep, John. *Last of the Empires: A History of the Soviet Union, 1945–1991.* New York: Oxford, 1995.

Kennedy-Pipe, Caroline. *Stalin's Cold War: Soviet Strategies in Europe, 1943 to 1956.* Manchester: Manchester University Press, 1995.

Kent, John. *British Imperial Strategy and the Origins of the Cold War, 1944–1949.* London: Leicester University Press, 1993.

Kershaw, Ian, and Moshe Lewin, eds. *Stalinism and Nazism: Dictatorships in Comparison.* Cambridge, England: Cambridge University Press, 1997.

Kimball, Jeffrey. *Nixon's Vietnam War.* Lawrence: University Press of Kansas, 1998.

Kissinger, Henry, *Years of Renewal: The Concluding Volume of His Memoirs.* New York: Simon & Schuster, 1999.

Klehr, Harvey, John Earl Haynes, and Kyrill M. Anderson. *The Soviet World of American Communism.* New Haven: Yale University Press, 1998.

Klehr, Harvey, John Earl Haynes, and Fridrikh Igorevich Firsov. *The Secret World of American Communism.* New Haven: Yale University Press, 1995.

Klehr, Harvey, and Ronald Radosh. *The Amerasia Spy Case: Prelude to McCarthyism.* Chapel Hill: University of North Carolina Press, 1996.

Klinghoffer, Judith A. *Vietnam, Jews, and the Middle East: Unintended Consequences.* London: Macmillan Press, 1999.

Knaack, Marcelle. *Size, Post–World War II Bombers.* Washington, D.C.: Office of Air Force History, 1988.

Knaus, John Kenneth. *Orphans of the Cold War: America and the Tibetan Struggle for Survival.* New York: Public Affairs, 1999.

Knight, Amy. *Beria: Stalin's First Lieutenant.* Princeton, N.J.: Princeton University Press, 1993.

Koch, S. A. *See* U.S. Central Intelligence Agency, History Staff.

Kolodziej, Edward A. *Making and Marketing Arms: The French Experience and Its Implications for the International System.* Princeton, N.J.: Princeton University Press, 1987.

Krock, Arthur. *Memoirs: Fifty Years on the Firing Line.* New York: Funk & Wagnalls, 1968.

Kuhns, Woodrow J., ed. *Assessing the Soviet Threat: The Early Cold War Years.* Washington, D.C.: Central Intelligence Agency, 1997. In contrast to other CIA volumes, which are collections of National Intelligence Estimates (NIEs), this one presents daily and weekly intelligence digests prepared specifically for President Truman. The introduction notes that this material, dated 1946–50, did *not* include signals intelligence, which was used in summaries from 1951 on.

Kuniholm, Bruce R. *The Origins of the Cold War in the Near East: Great Power Conflict and Diplomacy in Iran, Turkey, and Greece.* Rev. ed. Princeton, N.J.: Princeton University Press, 1994.

Kunz, Diane B. *Butter and Guns: America's Cold War Economic Diplomacy.* New York: The Free Press, 1997.

———, ed. *The Diplomacy of the Crucial Decade: American Foreign Relations during the 1960s.* New York: Columbia University Press, 1994.

Kyle, Keith. *Suez.* London: Weidenfeld & Nicholson, 1991.

Laming, Tim. *V-Bombers: Vulcan, Victor, and Valiant—Britain's Airborne Nuclear Deterrent.* Sparkford, England: Patrick Stephens Ltd., 1997.

Lane, Ann, and Howard Temperley, eds. *The Rise and Fall of the Grand Alliance, 1941–1945.* London: Macmillan, 1995.

Lansdale, Edward Geary. *In the Midst of Wars: An American's Mission to Southeast Asia.* Reprint, with a foreword by William E. Colby. New York: Fordham University Press, 1991.

Laquer, Walter. *Europe in Our Time: A History, 1945–1992.* New York: Viking, 1992.

———. *The Long Road to Freedom.* New York: Charles Scribner's Sons, 1989.

———. *The Uses and Limits of Intelligence.* Rev. ed. New Brunswick, N.J.: Transaction Publishers, 1993.

Lashmar, Paul. *Spy Flights of the Cold War.* Annapolis, Md.: Naval Institute Press, 1996.

Lee, Steven Hugh. *Outposts of Empire: Korea, Vietnam, and the Origins of the Cold War in Asia, 1949–1954.* Montreal: McGill-Queen's University Press, 1995.

Lees, Lorraine M. *Keeping Tito Afloat: The United States, Yugoslavia, and the Cold War.* University Park: Pennsylvania State University Press, 1997.

Leffler, Melvyn P. *A Preponderance of Power: National Security, the Truman Administration, and the Cold War.* Stanford, Calif.: Stanford University Press, 1992.

Leffler, M. P., and D. S. Painter, eds. *Origins of the Cold War: An Infiltration, Israeli Retaliation, and the Countdown to the Suez War.* Oxford: Clarendon Press, 1993.

Moss, Robert. *Chile's Marxist Experiment.* New York: John Wiley & Sons, 1973.

Moynihan, Daniel Patrick. *Secrecy.* New Haven: Yale University Press, 1998.

Murphy, David E., Sergei A Kondrashev, and George Bailey. *Battleground Berlin: CIA vs. KGB in the Cold War.* New Haven: Yale University Press, 1997.

Nash, Philip. *The Other Missiles of October: Eisenhower, Kennedy, and the Jupiters, 1957–1963.* Chapel Hill: University of North Carolina Press, 1997.

Navias, Martin S. *Nuclear Weapons and British Strategic Planning, 1955–1958.* Oxford: Oxford University Press, 1991.

Nelson, Michael. *War of the Black Heavens: The Battles of Western Broadcasting in the Cold War.* London: Brassey's, 1997.

Neufeld, Jacob. *Ballistic Missiles in the United States Air Force, 1945–1960.* Washington, D.C.: Office of Air Force History, 1990.

Nitze, Paul H. *From Hiroshima to Glasnost: At the Center of Decision—A Memoir.* New York: Grove Weidenfeld, 1989.

Nixon, Richard M. *RN: The Memoirs of Richard Nixon.* Richard Nixon Library ed. New York: Touchstone, 1990.

———. *The Real War.* New York: Warner Books, 1980.

Norris, R. S., A. S. Burrows, and R. W. Fieldhouse. *British, French, and Chinese Nuclear Weapons.* Vol. 5 of *Nuclear Weapons Databook.* Boulder, Colo.: Westview, 1994.

Nove, Alec. *An Economic History of the USSR, 1917–1991.* London: Penguin Books, 1992.

Odom, William E. *The Collapse of the Soviet Military.* New Haven: Yale University Press, 1998.

Oren, Michael B. *The Origins of the Second Arab-Israeli War: Egypt, Israel, and the Great Powers, 1952–1956.* London: Frank Cass, 1992.

Ovendale, Ritchie. *Britain, the United States, and the Transfer of Power in the Middle East, 1945–1962.* London: Leicester University Press, 1996.

Pach, Chester J., Jr. *Arming the Free World: The Origins of the United States Military Assistance Program, 1945–1950.* Chapel Hill: University of North Carolina Press, 1991.

Page, Caroline. *U.S. Official Propaganda during the Vietnam War, 1965–1973: The Limits of Persuasion.* London: Leicester University Press, 1996.

Palmer, Michael A. *Origins of the Maritime Strategy: American Naval Strategy in the First Postwar Decade.* Washington, D.C.: Naval Historical Center, 1988.

Parker, Richard B. *The Politics of Miscalculation in the Middle East.* Bloomington: Indiana University Press, 1993.

Partos, Gabriel. *The World That Came in from the Cold.* London: Royal Institute of International Affairs and BBC, 1993.

Pavlov, A. S. *Warships of the Soviet Union, 1945–1991.* Annapolis, Md.: Naval Institute Press, 1997.

Pedlow, Gregory W., and, Donald E. Welzenbach. *The CIA and the U-2 Program, 1954–1974.* Washington, D.C.: Central Intelligence Agency, 1998.

Peebles, Curtis. *The Corona Project: America's First Spy Satellites.* Annapolis, Md.: Naval Institute Press, 1997.

Pfaltzgraff, Robert L., Jr., and Jacqueline K. Davis. *National Security Decisions: The Participants Speak.* Lexington, Mass.: Lexington Books, 1990.

Pipes, Richard. *Russia under the Bolshevik Regime: Lenin and the Birth of the Totalitarian State.* New York: Alfred A. Knopf, 1994.

———. *Russia under the Old Regime.* London: Weidenfeld & Nicholson, 1974.

Pisani, Sallie. *The CIA and the Marshall Plan.* Lawrence: University of Kansas Press, 1991.

Poole, W. S. *See* U.S. Joint Chiefs of Staff.

Powers, Richard Gid. *Not Without Honor: The History of American Anticommunism.* New York: The Free Press, 1995.

Prados, John. *The Blood Road: The Ho Chi Minh Trail and the Vietnam War.* New York: John Wiley & Sons, 1999.

———. *Presidents' Secret Wars: CIA and Pentagon Covert Operations from World War II through the Persian Gulf.* Chicago: Ivan R. Dee, 1996.

———. *The Soviet Estimate: U.S. Intelligence Analysis and Russian Military Strength.* New York: Dial Press, 1982.

Pry, Peter V. *War Scare: Nuclear Countdown after the Soviet Fall.* Atlanta: Turner, 1997.

Pryce-Jones, D. *The War That Never Was: The Fall of the Soviet Empire, 1985–1991.* London: Weidenfeld & Nicholson, 1995.

Quirk, Robert E. *Fidel Castro.* New York: Norton, 1993.

Raack, R. C. *Stalin's Road to the West, 1938–1945.* Stanford, Calif.: Stanford University Press, 1995.

Radzinsky, Edvard. *Stalin: The First In-Depth Biography Based on Explosive New Documents from Russia's Secret Archives.* New York: Doubleday, 1996.

Record, Jeffrey. *The Wrong War: Why We Lost in Vietnam.* Annapolis, Md.: Naval Institute Press, 1998.

Reeves, Richard. *President Kennedy: Profile of Power.* New York: Simon & Schuster, 1993.

Revel, Jean-François. *How Democracies Perish.* New York: Doubleday, 1984.

Reynolds, David. *The Origins of the Cold War in Europe: International Perspectives.* New Haven: Yale University Press, 1994.

Rhodes, Richard. *Dark Sun: The Making of the Hydrogen Bomb.* New York: Simon & Schuster, 1995.

———. *The Making of the Atomic Bomb.* New York: Simon & Schuster, 1986.

Robinson, Jeffrey. *The End of the American Century: Hidden Agendas of the Cold War.* New York: Simon & Schuster, 1997. Despite its title, this is a history of Sputnik and the U.S. reaction to it.

Rodman, Peter W. *More Precious than Peace: The Cold War and the Struggle for the Third World.* New York: Scribner's, 1994.

Rogow, A. *James Forrestal: A Study of Personality, Politics, and Policy.* New York: Macmillan, 1963.

Roman, Peter J. *Eisenhower and the Missile Gap.* Ithaca: Cornell University Press, 1995.

Rosenberg, Alan David. "Toward Armageddon: The Foundations of U.S. Nuclear Strategy, 1945–1961." Ph.D. diss., University of Chicago, 1983.

Ross, Steven T. *American War Plans, 1945–1950.* London: Frank Cass, 1996.

Rouquie, Alain. *The Military and the State in Latin America.* Reprint, Berkeley: University of California Press, 1989.

Rowen, Henry S., and Charles Wolf, Jr., eds. *The Impoverished Superpower:* Perestroika *and the Soviet Military Burden.* San Francisco: Institute for Contemporary Studies, 1990. This book was developed from proceedings of a 23–24 March 1988 conference at the Hoover Institution, Stanford University.

Ruffner, K. C., ed. *See* U.S. Central Intelligence Agency, History Staff.

Safran, Nadav. *Saudi Arabia: The Ceaseless Quest for Security* Ithaca: Cornell University Press, 1985.

Sarin, Gen. Oleg, and Col. Lev Dvoretsky. *Alien Wars: The Soviet Union's Aggressions against the World, 1919 to 1989.* Novato, Calif.: Presidio, 1996.

Savel'yev, Aleksandr G., and Nikolay N. Detinov. *The Big Five: Arms Control Decision-Making in the Soviet Union.* Westport, Conn.: Praeger, 1995.

Sayigh, Yazid, and Avi Shlaim. *The Cold War and the Middle East.* Oxford: The Clarendon Press, 1997.

Scales, Robert H., Jr. *Firepower in Limited War.* Novato, Calif.: Presidio, 1995.

Schaffel, Kenneth. *The Emerging Shield: The Air Force and the Evolution of Continental Air Defense, 1945–1960.* Washington, D.C.: Office of Air Force History, 1991.

Schlight, John, ed. *Second Indochina War Symposium.* Washington, D.C.: Center for Military History, 1986. Proceedings of a 7–9 November 1984 symposium at Airlie, Virginia.

Schmertz, Eric J., Natalie Datlof, and Alexej Ugrinsky, eds. *President Reagan and the World.* Westport, Conn.: Greenwood Press, 1997.

Schnabel, J. F. *See* U.S. Joint Chiefs of Staff.

Schnabel, J. F., and R. J. Watson. *See* U.S. Joint Chiefs of Staff.

Schulzinger, Robert D. *A Time for War: The United States and Vietnam, 1941–1975.* New York: Oxford University Press, 1997.

Schweizer, Peter. *Victory: The Reagan Administration's Secret Strategy That Hastened the Collapse of the Soviet Union.* New York: Atlantic Monthly Press, 1994.

Scott, L. V. *Conscription and the Attlee Governments: The Politics and Policy of National Service, 1945–1951.* Oxford: Clarendon Press, 1993.

Shapley, Deborah. *Promise and Power: The Life and Times of Robert McNamara.* Boston: Little, Brown, 1993.

Sheehan, Kevin Patrick. "Preparing For an Imaginary War? Examining Peacetime Functions and Changes of Army Doctrine." Ph.D. diss., Harvard, 1988.

Sheehan, Neil. *The Pentagon Papers: The Secret History of the Vietnam War.* New York: Quadrangle Books, 1971. The *New York Times*'s summary of the secret Defense Department report on the war in Vietnam, with annexed documents. This is not a reproduction of the report itself. It embodies investigative reporting by Neil Sheehan and was written by E. W. Kenworthy, Fox Butterfield, Hedrick Smith, and Neil Sheehan.

Shirokorad, A. B. *Sovetskiye podvodniye lodki: Poslevoennoiye postroiykiy* (Soviet submarines: Postwar classes). Moscow: Arsenal, 1997.

Shuckburgh, Evelyn. *Descent to Suez: Foreign Office Diaries, 1951–1956.* New York: Norton, 1987.

Shu Gang Zhang. *Mao's Military Romanticism: China and the Korean War, 1950–1953.* Lawrence: University Press of Kansas, 1995. Despite its title, this is a history of the Chinese armed forces in Korea, from Chinese sources.

Sigmund, Paul E. *The Overthrow of Allende and the Politics of Chile, 1964–1976.* Pittsburgh: University of Pittsburgh Press, 1977.

Simonov, N. *Voenno-promyshlenniy kompleks SSSR v 1920–1950-e gody* (Military industrial complex of the USSR from 1920 to the 1950s). Moscow: Rosspen, 1996.

Simons, Thomas W., Jr. *Eastern Europe in the Postwar Period.* 2d. ed. New York: St. Martin's Press, 1993.

———. *The End of the Cold War?* New York: St. Martin's Press, 1990.

Simpson, Christopher. *National Security Directives of the Reagan and Bush Administrations: The Declassified History of U.S. Political and Military Policy, 1981–1991.* Boulder, Colo.: Westview, 1995.

Sluggett, Peter, and Marion Farouk-Sluggett. *The Times Guide to the Middle East: The Arab World and its Neighbours.* London: Times Books, 1991.

Smith, Jean Edward. *Lucius D. Clay: An American Life.* New York: Henry Holt & Co., 1990.

Smith, John T. *The Linebacker Raids: The Bombing of North Vietnam, 1972.* London: Arms & Armour, 1998.

Smith, Joseph, ed. *The Origins of NATO.* Exeter Studies in History, no. 28, University of Exeter Press, 1990.

Smith, R. B. *An International History of the Vietnam War.* 2 vols. London: Macmillan, 1983–87.

Solovyov, Vladimir, and Elena Klepikova. *Inside the Kremlin: A Penetrating Portrait of the Inner Circles of Soviet Power and Premier Mikhail Gorbachev by the Best Informed Russian Journalists in the West.* London: W. H. Allen, 1987.

Spence, Jonathan D. *The Search for Modern China.* New York: Norton, 1990. Steury, D. S., ed. See U.S. Central Intelligence Agency, History Staff.

Stone, Randall W. *Satellites and Commissars: Strategy and Conflict in the Politics of Soviet-Bloc Trade.* Princeton, N.J.: Princeton University Press, 1996.

Stueck, William. *The Korean War: An International History.* Princeton, N.J.: Princeton University Press, 1995.

Sudoplatov, Pavel, Anatoli Sudoplatov, Jerrold L. Schecter, and Leona P. Schecter. *Special Tasks: The Memoirs of an Unwanted Witness—A Soviet Spymaster.* New York: Little, Brown, 1994.

Suh, Dae-Sook. *Kim Il Sung, The North Korean Leader.* New York: Columbia University, 1988.

Tarling, Nicholas. *Britain, Southeast Asia, and the Onset of the Cold War, 1945–1950.* Cambridge, England: Cambridge University Press, 1998.

Taylor, John M. *General Maxwell Taylor: The Sword and the Pen.* New York: Doubleday, 1989.

Taylor, Michael, ed. *Brassey's World Aircraft and Systems Directory 1996/97.* McLean, Va.: Brassey's Inc., 1996.

Thomas, Evan. *The Very Best Men: Four Who Dared: The Early Years of the CIA.* New York: Simon & Schuster, 1995.

Thomas, Hugh. *Armed Truce: The Beginnings of the Cold War, 1945–1946.* London: Hamish Hamilton, 1986.

Thomas, Martin. *The French Empire At War, 1940–1945.* Manchester: Manchester University Press, 1998.

Thompson, Willie. *The Communist Movement Since 1945.* Oxford: Blackwell, 1998.

Tolson, Lt. Gen. John J. *Airmobility, 1961–1971.* Vietnam Studies Series. Washington, D.C.: Department of the Army, 1973.

Tompson, William J. *Khrushchev: A Political Life.* 1995. Reprint, New York: St. Martin's Griffin, 1997.

Trachtenberg, Marc. *History and Strategy.* Princeton, N.J.: Princeton University Press, 1991.

Tsouras, Peter G. *Changing Orders: The Evolution of the World's Armies, 1945 to the Present.* New York: Facts on File, 1994.

Tucker, Robert C. *Stalin in Power: The Revolution from Above, 1928–1941.* New York: Norton, 1990.

Ulam, Adam B. *The Communists: The Story of Power and Lost Illusions, 1948–1991.* New York: Scribner's, 1992.

U.S. Central Intelligence Agency, History Staff. *CIA Cold War Records.* Vol. 1. *The CIA under Harry Truman.* Edited by M. Warner. Washington, D.C.: U.S. Central Intelligence Agency, 1994.

———. *CIA Cold War Records.* Vol. 2. *Selected Estimates on the Soviet Union, 1950–1959.* Edited by S. A. Koch. Washington, D.C.: U.S. Central Intelligence Agency, 1993.

———. *CIA Cold War Records.* Vol. 3. *Estimates on Soviet Military Power, 1954 to 1984: A Selection.* Washington, D.C.: U.S. Central Intelligence Agency, 1994.

———. *CIA Cold War Records.* Vol. 4. *Intentions and Capabilities: Estimates on Soviet Strategic Forces, 1950–1983.* Edited by D.S. Steury. Washington, D.C.: U.S. Central Intelligence Agency, 1996.

———. *CIA Cold War Records.* Vol. 5. *CORONA: America's First Satellite Program.* Edited by K. C. Ruffner. Washington, D.C.: U.S. Central Intelligence Agency, 1995.

U.S. Joint Chiefs of Staff. *The History of the Joint Chiefs of Staff.* Vol. 1. *The Joint Chiefs of Staff and National Policy, 1947–1949,* by J. F. Schnabel. Wilmington, Del.: Michael Glazier, 1979.

———. *The History of the Joint Chiefs of Staff.* Vol. 2. *The Joint Chiefs of Staff and National Policy, 1947–1949,* by K. W. Condit. Wilmington, Del.: Michael Glazier, 1979.

———. *The History of the Joint Chiefs of Staff.* Vol 3. *The Joint Chiefs of Staff and National Policy: The Korean War,* by J. F. Schnabel and R. J. Watson. 2 parts. Wilmington, Del.: Michael Glazier, 1979.

———. *The History of the Joint Chiefs of Staff.* Vol. 4. *The Joint Chiefs of Staff and National Policy, 1950–1952,* by W. S. Poole. Wilmington, Del.: Michael Glazier, 1980.

———. *The History of the Joint Chiefs of Staff.* Vol. 5. *The Joint Chiefs of Staff and National Policy, 1953–1954,* by R. J. Watson. Washington, D.C.: Historical Division, JCS, 1986.

———. *The History of the Joint Chiefs of Staff.* Vol. 6. *The Joint Chiefs of Staff and National Policy, 1955–1956,* by K. W. Condit. Washington, D.C.: Historical Division, JCS, 1992.

U.S. Congress Joint Economic Committee. *Soviet Economy in the 1980s: Problems and Prospects.* 2 vols. Washington, D.C., 31 December 1982.

U.S. Office of the Secretary of Defense. *The Test of War: 1950–1953.* Vol. 2, by D. M. Condit. Washington, D.C.: Historical Office of OSD, 1988.

———. *Into the Missile Age, 1956–1960.* Vol. 4, by Robert J. Watson. Washington, D.C.: Historical Office of OSD, 1998.

U.S. Special Operations Research Office (SORO) at The American University. *Casebook on Insurgency and Revolutionary Warfare: Twenty-three Summary Accounts.* Washington, D.C.: SORO, December 1962. Researched by Norman A. La Charite, Bert H. Cooper, Paul A. Jureidini, and William A. Lybrand.

Van Creveld, Martin. *The Sword and the Olive: A Critical History of the Israeli Defense Force.* New York: Public Affairs, 1998.

Vasiliev, Alexei. *Russian Policy in the Middle East: From Messianism to Pragmatism.* Reading, England: Ithaca Press, 1993.

Volkogonov, Dmitriy T. *Autopsy for an Empire: The Seven Leaders Who Built the Soviet Regime.* Trans., 1996. Revised, with a new translation, New York: Free Press, 1998.

———. *Sem' vozhdei* (Seven rulers). Moscow: Novosti, 1996. General Volkogonov was a senior Soviet military historian, and had considerable access to the private papers of the rulers of the Soviet era.

———. *Stalin: Triumf i tragediia* (Stalin: Triumph and tragedy). Trans. Harold Shukman. Rocklin, Calif.: Prima, 1996.

Volkov, Ye. B., Filimonov, A. A., Bob'rev, V. N., and Kobyakov, V. A. *Mezhkontinentalniye Ballisticheskiye Raketi SSSR (RF) i CShA: Istoria Sozdaniya, Razbitiya i Sokrashcheniya.* Privately printed by Ye. B. Volkov, 1996. This is an RVSN report; Volkov worked for the service's study arm.

Wald, Emanuel. *The Wald Report: The Decline of Israeli National Security since 1967.* Trans. Boulder, Colo.: Westview, 1992. Colonel Wald wrote this official report in 1982 for Israeli Chief of Staff Moshe Levi.

Walker, Martin. *The Cold War.* London: Fourth Estate, 1993.

Warner, M., ed. *See* U.S. Central Intelligence Agency, History Staff.

Statistical Abstract of the United States. Washington, D.C.: Treasury Dept. (Bureau of Statistics), 1967.

Watson, R. J. *See* U.S. Joint Chiefs of Staff.

Watson, Robert J. *See* U.S. Office of the Secretary of Defense.

Wehling, Fred. *Irresolute Princes: Kremlin Decision Making In Middle East Crises, 1967–1973.* New York: St. Martin's Press, 1967.

Weinstein, Allen, and Alexander Vassiliev. *The Haunted Wood: Soviet Espionage in America— The Stalin Era.* New York: Random House, 1999.

Weis, W. Michael. *Cold Warriors and Coups d'Etat: Brazilian-American Relations, 1945–1964.* Albuquerque: University of New Mexico Press, 1993.

West, Nigel. *Venona: The Greatest Secret of the Cold War.* London: HarperCollins, 1999.

West, Nigel, and Oleg Tsarev. *The Crown Jewels: The British Secrets at the Heart of the KGB Archive.* London: HarperCollins, 1998.

Westad, Odd Arne. *Brothers in Arms: The Rise and Fall of the Sino-Soviet Alliance, 1945– 1963.* Washington, D.C.: Woodrow Wilson Center Press; Stanford, Calif.: Stanford University Press, 1998.

Westad, Odd Arne, Sven Holtsmark, and Iver B. Neumann. *The Soviet Union in Eastern Europe, 1945–1989.* London: St. Martin's Press, 1994.

Whelan, Richard. *Drawing the Line: The Korean War, 1950–1953. London: Faber & Faber, 1990.*

Whitefield, Stephen. *Industrial Power and the Soviet State.* Oxford: Clarendon Press, 1993.

Winter, F. X. *The Year of the Hare: America in Vietnam, January 25, 1963–February 15, 1964.* Athens: University of Georgia Press, 1997.

Wolf, Markus, and Anne McElvoy. *Memoirs of a Spymaster: The Man Who Waged a Secret War against the West.* London: Pimlico, 1998. Paperback edition of a book published in 1997 as *Man without a Face: The Memoirs of a Spymaster.*

Wood, Derek. *Project Cancelled: The Disaster of Britain's Abandoned Aircraft Projects.* Rev. ed. London: Jane's, 1986.

Woods, Randall B., and Howard Jones. *Dawning of the Cold War: The United States' Quest for Order.* Athens: University of Georgia, 1991; Chicago: Ivan R. Dee, 1994.

Wynn, Humphrey. *RAF Nuclear Deterrent Forces.* London: HMSO, 1994.

Yapp, M. E. *The Near East since the First World War: A History to 1995.* 2d ed. London: Long-man, 1996.

Yergin, Daniel. *The Prize: The Epic Quest for Oil, Money, and Power.* New York: Simon & Schuster, 1991.

Zaloga, Steven J. *Soviet Strategic Weapons.* Forthcoming.

———. *Target USA.* Novato, Calif.: Presidio, 1993.

Ziegler, Charles A., and David Jacobson. *Spying without Spies: Origins of America's Secret Nuclear Surveillance System.* Westport, Conn.: Praeger, 1995.

Zubok, Vladislav, and Constantine Pleshakov. *Inside the Kremlin's Cold War: From Stalin to Khrushchev.* Cambridge: Harvard University Press, 1996.

Zumwalt, Elmo M., Jr. *On Watch.* New York: Quadrangle, 1976.

INDEX

Aaron, David, 434

Abd al-Fattah Ismail, 405, 437

Abrams, Creighton, 356, 360

Acheson, Dean, 333; Albanian resistance and, 84; on Berlin crisis, 272; on British/French rearmament, 140; on Chiang's Nationalist government, 95–96; JFK and, 254; Kennedy's European "Grand Design" policy and, 295; on Korea's defense, 154; on Korea's importance, 149; on nonnuclear defense, 287; Taylor and, 284

Aden. *See* South Yemen

Adenauer, Konrad, 189, 326

Afghanistan: map of, 300; Reagan's strategy for, 454; Soviet Union and, 210, 433–35, 469, 476

Africa: Angolan guerilla wars, 399, 401–2, 403–4; Communism near Suez Canal, 404–5; French colonies in, 296; Mozambique guerilla wars, 399, 404; North, nationalism in, 109; Portuguese colonies of, 399–400; S. Yemen, Communism in, 404, 405–6; as Western raw materials source, 399

African-Americans, 169, 322

African National Congress (ANC), 403

Air Battle Management System, 449

aircraft: British offensive and, 62–63; industry, U.S. rearmament and, 74–75; for nuclear arms delivery, 36–37; Soviet use of U.S./British technology for, 116–17

air defense: Soviet, Rust flight and, 473; U.S. computer analysis of, 445–46

Air Force, U.S.: Atlas long-range missile, 232; on bomber gap, 198, 202, 206; bombers for during

Berlin Blockade, 79; budget cuts and atomic air offensive, 127; on Cold War readiness, 123; command structure in, 124; Congress forces spending for, 292; East Anglia bases for, 63; Korean conflict growth in, 156–57; Libya and, 331; and McNamara's command structure, 289; McNamara's system analysis and, 289–90; Minuteman rockets, 236; MIRVs for, 294; nuclear arms monopoly hopes of, 39–40; nuclear bomber costs for, 125; nuclear monitoring program of, 136; post-WWII demobilization of, 61; on Soviet bomber count, 200–201; on Soviet buildup (1976), 419; Tactical Air Command (TAC) in Europe, 177. *See also* Strategic Air Command (SAC)

Air Force Intelligence (U.S.), 142

AirLand battle: German idea for, 178; NATO and, 463; U.S. Army, 462–63

Akromeeyev, Sergei F., 435–36

Albania, 46, 84, 247, 480

Algeria, 109, 221, 222, 224–25, 296

Allen, Richard, 458

Allende, Salvador, 256, 260, 365; military and, 367, 368–69; MIR guerillas and, 368–69; nationalization power of, 366; Unidad Popular and, 365, 367

Alliance for Progress, 256–58; Brazil and, 258–59

Ambler, Eric, 249

American Communists, 57, 87, 89

American Federation of Labor, 27

American ideology, demise of, 90

Amin, Hafizulah, 434, 435, 436

Anderson, Orvil, 141

de Lattre de Tassigny, Jean, 180–81
democracy: in East Asia, problems of, 266;
    guerilla movements and, 267; in U.S., virtues
    of, 26–28. *See also* free societies
Democratic Republic of Vietnam, 110; enforce-
    ment system in, 265; Sino-Soviet split and,
    246–47; U.S. understanding of, 263–64,
    266–67. *See also* North Vietnam
Denfeld, Louis, 127, 129
Deng Xiaoping, 487–88
Dewey, Thomas E., 158
dictatorships: aggressive/illegitimate nature of,
    26–28. *See also* authoritarian government(s);
    totalitarian government(s)
Diem. *See* Ngo Dinh Diem
Dien Bien Phu: French focus on, 181–82; Viet
    Minh attack, 182–83
Dillon, Douglas, 333
Djilas, Milvan, 95
Dobrynin, Anatoly F., 383
Dominican Republic, 279–80
domino theory, 310; Indonesia and, 316
draft, Soviet military, 426–27
draft, U.S. military, 61; deferment problems for,
    322; Vietnam War opposition and, 364–65
Dragon Returns/Wringer, 116
Dubcek, Aleksandr, 345
Duclos, Jacques, 57
Dulles, Allen, 108, 248, 255
Dulles, John Foster, 100, 158; Anglo-French
    attack on Suez and, 221, 222; Baghdad Pact
    and, 219; on Berlin defense, 246; Bevin and,
    54; on brinkmanship, 195; on Egyptian-Israeli
    peace plan, 218; on Egyptian-Israeli war, 220;
    on Indochina importance (1954), 182; on
    Indonesian coup failure, 209; Iranian coup
    and, 108; on SEATO, 183–84
Dutch South East Asian colonies, 113–14
Dutton, Fred, 272

Eaker, Ira C., 74
Earle, George, 43
Eastern Europe: Brezhnev's Comprehensive
    Program for Socialist Economic Integration
    and, 349–50; economic stagnation in, 345–50;
    on Khrushchev's Secret Speech, 191–92; Stalin
    invasion of Western Europe by, 173; unrest in,
    343; U.S. economic warfare against, 460. *See
    also* Soviet satellites

East Germany: bankruptcy for, 479; Brandt and,
    383; Chile and, 369; Gorbachev's coup for,
    478–79; Khrushchev's plans for, 245; on
    Prague Spring, 346
economism policy: Brezhnev's use of, 349–50;
    Khrushchev's, 243; Soviet disintegration and,
    476
Eden, Anthony, 106, 218, 220, 221, 222–23
Egypt: Aswan Dam in, 218–19; Baghdad Pact
    and, 219; British mandates with, 103; hostility
    toward Britain by, 104–5; Nasser and, 227;
    nationalism in, 106–7; Six Day War (1967),
    329; Soviet arms for, 213, 218, 327–29; UAR
    and, 225, 226–27; U.S. and, 226; war with
    Israel, 219–20; Yom Kippur (October) War
    (1973) and, 387–90
Eisenhower, Dwight D., 63; Anglo-French
    attack on Suez and, 221; on Berlin defense,
    246; Britain and, 147, 223; on carrier forces,
    128; on Castro, 249; China and, 241–42, 244;
    Egypt and, 107; Egyptian-Israeli war and,
    220; farewell address of, 240; on French sup-
    port in Indochina, 182; Korean conflict and,
    169; on Laotian turmoil, 251; McCarthy and,
    88; military strategy study, 194–95; on mis-
    sile gap, 240; missile race and, 232, 237,
    238–39; NATO and, 146–47, 171, 224; on
    nuclear arms management/storage, 148;
    nuclear poker politics of, 201–2; SAC and,
    203–4; on SEATO, 183–84; Soviet rejection of
    Baruch Plan and, 38; spending controls by,
    193–94, 201; *Sputnik* and, 234; Thailand and,
    184; Truman and, 127–28; on Vietnam tur-
    moil, 250–51. *See also* "New Look" national
    strategy
Eisenhower Doctrine, Middle East policy and,
    226
El Salvador, 431, 454
Elsey, George, 66–67
Enhanced Radiation Weapons (ERWs), 131
Estonia, 4, 482–83, 484
Ethiopia, 407
Europe. *See* Eastern Europe; Western Europe
European Defense Community (EDC), 171, 172,
    176; NATO approval of, 175
European Economic Community, 222, 295
European Recovery Program (ERP), 70, 73, 138
European Union, ERP and, 76
Export-Import Bank, 49

Namibia, 455

Nasser, Gamal Abdel, 218, 225, 226–27; Soviets and, 327–29; "war of attrition," 330

Nasution, Abdul Haris, 316

National Command Authority, U.S., 278

National Intelligence Estimate (NIE). *See* Central Intelligence Agency (U.S. CIA)

nationalism, 102–14; in British Far East colonies, 108; in British Middle Eastern colonies, 103–8; colonial significance to world powers, 102–3; in Dutch Southeast Asian colonies, 113–14; in French N. African colonies, 108–9; in French Southeast Asian colonies, 109–13; JFK and, 256–57; movements of, workers and, 3; in Soviet constituent nations, 488; in U.S. Philippines, 114

Nationalist Chinese government, 92

National Security Act (1947), 124

National Security Council (U.S. NSC), 124; on Indochina as U.S. security interest, 112–13; JFK and, 253; SAGE centers of, 446; on Stalin's year of maximum danger, 174

National Training Center, U.S., 463

NATO: Brezhnev's buildup and, 379–81; budget cuts in, 223–24; Communist leadership in, 400–401; Czech invasion and, 350–51; defense budgets *versus* living standard for, 138; de Gaulle's return to power and, 225; détente and military security goals for, 326–27; German participation in, 171, 172; Greece and, 411; IRBMs for, 235; Korean conflict and, 176; Medium Term Defense Plan (1950), 139; Military Assistance Plan (1949), 138–39; military capability of (1961), 273; Mitterand and, 410; Multi-Lateral Force (MLF) and, 285; nuclear capacity of, 177–78; rising cost of, 288–89; signing of, 81; Soviet military strength estimates and, 175; U.S. military presence in Europe for, 171–72; on U.S. neutron bomb, 423; Warsaw Pact and, 178; Western European economies and, 172–73; Yom Kippur War and, 390, 392; Yugoslavia and, 92

Navarre, Henri, 181, 182

Navy, Soviet: and African coastal states, 408; under Brezhnev, 304, 380–81; expansion of, 398–99, 427; Stalin's ambitions for, 13–14; on U.S. Maritime Strategy, 462

Navy, U.S.: Air Force Intelligence and, 142; carrier strike forces of, 64, 128–29; Cold War readiness viewpoint of, 123; command structure in, 123–24; Korean conflict growth in, 157; Maritime Strategy of, 461–62; and McNamara's command structure, 289; MIRVs for, 294; NTDS (naval tactical data system) for, 446; nuclear-armed, 197; nuclear arms development and, 34, 40; post-WWII demobilization of, 61; post-WWII plan for, 30–31; Revolt of the Admirals, 128–29; sea control *versus* naval operations for, 126–27; on Soviet buildup (1976), 419; strategic function of, 124; supercarrier for, 124–25; Vietnam War effect on, 398; war concept of, 63–64

Nazi Party, and Soviet Communist Party, 6–7

Near East Coordinating Committee (NEACC), 107

Nedelin, M. I., 117

Nehru, Jawaharlal, 190, 246

Nepal, 210

Netherlands: nationalism in colonies of, 102–3, 113–14

Netherlands East Indies, 113

Neto, Agostinho, 400, 401–2

neutron bomb(s), 131, 423–24

"New Look" national strategy, 194–95; bomber gap and, 198, 202, 206; CIA and, 208–10; critics of, 196–97; Eisenhower budget cutting and, 196, 201; missile warning systems and, 206–7; revolt of the colonels and, 197–98; SAC Basic War Plans and, 202–4; SAC's Single Integrated Operational Plan and, 204–5; satellite overflights and, 205; Skybolt for, 208; Soviet defense against, 207–8; strategic advantage and, 198–200; U-2 overflights and, 205

Newsom, David, 434

Ngo Dinh Diem, 109, 247, 250; coup/death of, 267, 269; deception by, 270; JFK and, 255, 263; Lansdale and, 261; SEATO troops for, 262–63; U.S. officials and, 268

Ngo Dinh Nhu, 269

Nguyen Chi Thanh, 314, 323–24, 334

Nguyen Van Thieu, 361, 395–96, 397

Nicaragua, 430–31, 454, 455, 469

Nigeria, 223

Nimitz, Chester W., 63

Nitze, Paul H.: on deterrence *versus* conventional forces, 158; on hydrogen bomb, 145; JFK and, 254; on Korean conflict defense

Panama, 371–72, 430

Papandreaou, Andreas, 410–11

Pash, Glubb, 219

Pathet Lao, 262

peace movements: European, on neutron bomb, 423; on NATO missile deployments, 464–65; Soviet support for, 364; U.S. Vietnam War withdrawal and, 384, 397. *See also* student discontent

Peng Dhuai, 168

Penkovskiy, Oleg, 215

People's Republic of China: Afghan rebels and, 434; after end of Cold War, 487–88; on armed revolution, 242; atomic bomb test by, 306; Central Committee of, Moscow and, 97; CIA and, 209–10; friendship treaty with Moscow of, 98–99; Khmer Rouge and, 439–40; and Korean conflict, 163; Mao creates, 95; military modernization, Korean conflict and, 170; modernization of, U.S. and, 440–41; as multinational empire, 488; N. Vietnam troop support by, 314; New Defense Technical Accord with Soviet Union, 243; recognition of, 96; Red Guards and repression in, 352–53; Soviet missiles and, 275; split with Soviet Union, 241–45, 246, 281; U.S. diplomatic relations with, 430; and U.S. during Vietnam War, 319–20; Vietnam War peace negotiations and, 334. *See also* Chou En-lai; Mao Tse-Tung

perestroika, 469, 470–71, 476–77

permissive action links (PALs), 285

Persian Gulf, Carter Doctrine and, 438

Philbrick, Herbert, 87

Philby, Kim, 56, 136

Philippines, 114

Philosophy of the Revolution, The (Nasser), 218

Pieck, Wilhelm, 77

PINCHER, 63

Pinochet, Augusto, 370, 371

Pipes, Richard, 416–17, 454

planning system; Soviet, 22–24

Pleven, René, 173

Podgorny, Nikolai, 304, 305

Poland: anti-Communist riots in, 191–92; Communism collapses in, 480; on Czech invasion, 346; Home Army of, 11–12; Marshall Plan invitation and, 71; martial law in, 441–42; Reagan's strategy for, 455–56; secret police, KGB and, 73; Solidarity movement in,

441, 470, 476; Soviet takeover of, 45, 47; unrest in, 348, 349; U.S. and resistance movements in, 84; U.S. economic warfare against, 460; U.S. postwar loan rejection to, 50

Polish Communist Party, 476–77

Pompidou, Georges, 340

popular fronts, 12; in Baltic States, 474; European Communists join, 7; French, Italian abandonment of, 67; Spain, 9; Stalin abandons, 68; in Uzhbeck Republic, 474; Western perception of, 45

Portugal, 399–400, 401. *See also* Angola; Mozambique

Post-Hostilities Planning Staff, British, 44

Potsdam conference (1945), 47

Powers, Gary, 210, 239

Prats, Carlos, 366, 370

preventive war: SAC's Basic War Plan for, 202–3; U.S. on, 141, 194

Programming, Planning, and Budgeting System (PPBS), McNamara's, 290

public, U.S., 423; on containment policy of, 85; Tet offensive reaction in, 336–37. *See also* peace movements; student discontent

Pueblo incident, 339

purges, Soviet: of Bolsheviks, 8; of industry specialists, 18–19; of Polish army officers, 10–11; of Soviet military, 19; Stalin's, 19–20. *See also* terrorism

Pyrin, Evgeny, 328

Qaddafi, Muammar, 296, 331

Quadros, Janios, 259

Quebec Agreement (1943), 37

Quemoy Island, Mao attacks, 244

Quirino, Elpidio, 114

Radford, Arthur W., 129

radio, Western, 84, 268, 470, 472

Radio Free Europe, 84

Rakosi, Matyas, 71

Ramadier, Paul, 67, 69

Rapid Deployment Force, U.S., 438

Reagan, Ronald: aggressiveness toward Soviet Union by, 456; arms control negotiations and, 463; deception operations of, 458–59; on economic sanctions for Poland, 442; Falkland Islands War and, 457; Gorbachev and, 469, 470, 472; Grenada invasion and, 457; Iran-

Westmoreland, William, 319, 323, 332, 337
Wheeler, Earle, 239, 309, 318, 333, 337
White, Harry Dexter, 29, 48, 55, 65
"Wise Old Men," 319, 333, 338
Wisner, Frank, 59
Wohlstetter, Albert, 239
Wohlstetter, Robert, 198
Wojtyla, Karol, 441
Wolf, Markus, 478–79
World Bank, 28–29
World Peace Council (Soviet), 174

Yeltsin, Boris, 481–82, 484
Yemen, 219, 225, 227, 437. *See also* North Yemen;
    South Yemen
Yom Kippur (October) War (1973), 386–91;
    cease-fire resolution and, 389–90; Egypt and,
386–90; NATO and, 393; nuclear weapons and,
393; Soviet Union and, 386–87, 389, 392–93;
Syria and, 387–89; U.S. and, 389–90, 392, 393
Young, Andrew, 424
Yugoslavia: Chinese relations with, 353; expelled
    from Cominform, 91; nationalism within
    multinationalism of, 488–89; self-determina-
    tion in, 475; Soviet war game in (1951), 92;
    Tito control in, 46

Zaire, 400
Zeldovich, E. B., 146
Zhang Zhizhong, 97
Zhdanov, Andrei A., 68, 73
Zhukov, Georgy K., 20, 186, 189, 192, 215

ABOUT THE AUTHOR

Norman Friedman is a strategist particularly concerned with the interaction of policy and technology. During the Cold War he worked for eleven years at Herman Kahn's Hudson Institute, a major think tank, ultimately as its deputy director of national security studies. Since then, he has been a consultant to the U.S. Navy and to a variety of government and private defense organizations. He has written books on the U.S. Navy's maritime strategy of the Cold War and also on the 1990–91 campaign against Iraq. An internationally known specialist in the fields of weapons design and development, Dr. Friedman has written highly respected design histories of U.S. Navy carriers, battleships, cruisers, destroyers, and small attack craft, in each case integrating an account of technical change with the accompanying strategy which often drove it. He has also published studies of the Cold War revolution in naval warfare, of carrier aviation in the Royal Navy, of naval radars, and of U.S. naval weapons, as well as a comprehensive series of books on world naval weapons systems. Dr. Friedman's articles have appeared in a number of journals and newspapers, and he contributes a monthly column on world naval developments to the U.S. Naval Institute *Proceedings*. He is frequently seen on television as a commentator on defense affairs and on military history.